China in Crisis VOLUME 1

China in Crisis VOLUME 1

China's Heritage and the Communist Political System

Book One

Edited by Ping-ti Ho and Tang Tsou
With a Foreword by Charles U. Daly

SBN: 226-34518-1 (clothbound) ; 226-34521-1 (paperbound)
Library of Congress Catalog Card Number 68-20981

The University of Chicago Press, Chicago 60637
The University of Chicago Press, Ltd., London

Foreword

China, as perhaps no other country, offers an opportunity to examine the dynamics of revolution in a way that may shed light on important issues affecting nations today. The problems of modernity, of continuity and change at work in political and social institutions, are immense. Clearly, there has arisen a need to place within perspective the rise of the Chinese Communist movement and such subsequent developments as the Great Leap Forward and the Great Proletarian Cultural Revolution. Never has it been more important to obtain a clear understanding of these events and their relevance to international affairs.

These were among the compelling reasons for The University of Chicago's new Center for Policy Study to undertake as its inaugural project a year-long examination of China. The China project began in March, 1966, with a series of seminars, public lectures, and less formal meetings held on the average of once a month with the support of the New World Foundation. The series culminated in February, 1967, with two five-day conferences supported by the University. The first was devoted to "China's Heritage and the Communist Political System" and the second to "China, the United States, and Asia." These conferences assembled seventy scholars and non-academic experts from Asia, Europe, the Middle East, and the Americas.

The first conference brought together the leading historians specializing in pre-1949 China with other selected experts whose fields involved Communist China and the Chinese Communist movement. They examined the process of changes leading to the establishment of the Communist regime and the major aspects of the political system of Communist China in light of Chinese political tradition. Even before the first paper was submitted the Cultural Revolution had pushed the participants to new attempts at understanding the patterns of movement and change.

Ping-ti Ho, the James Westfall Thompson Professor of History, and Tang Tsou, Professor of Political Science, were vital in planning the Center's China project and seeing it through to fruition. Professor Ho assumed responsibility for the first three chapters in this volume, while Professor Tsou edited chapters four through thirteen. Both men are fellows of the Center.

Participation of the Center's twenty-seven other faculty fellows and faculty from nearly every discipline at The University of Chicago was invaluable to this interdisciplinary project.

This volume contains papers presented at the first conference and some of the commentaries on them, together with several others which the editors selected from the second conference as being more appropriate to the discussion of continuity and change in political development than to that of the foreign policy of Communist China.

The volume opens with a sweeping summary by Professor Ho of aspects of China's heritage salient to the study. K. C. Liu, in a study of nineteenth-century institutions and intellectual history, stresses the discontinuity with the past as China entered the twentieth century. In his paper, C. Martin Wilbur next examines the role of the military in the early twentieth century. The pivotal paper by Tang Tsou suggests basic categories for the analysis of the problems of continuity and change in history. He offers interpretations of the early success of the Chinese Communist Party (CCP) and current turmoils in terms of the relationship between the thought of Mao Tse-tung and socio-political reality. He examines the interrelationship among the ideology, the leader, and the organization. Benjamin Schwartz examines the origins of the thought of Mao Tse-tung in the revolutionary tradition of the West and in the Chinese heritage. Chalmers Johnson deals with the mass line, the most interesting method of leadership developed by the CCP. John W. Lewis traces the conflict between Mao Tse-tung and Liu Shao-ch'i to the different conceptions of the political system espoused by the two men. C. K. Yang develops an interpretation of the Cultural Revolution in terms of goal instability and its concomitant violent conflicts which characterize the process of a major revolution. Franz Schurmann broadens this examination to include lower echelons and touches on external as well as internal influences. Francis Hsu adds a significant note on kinship and its relationship to the revolution, the change and the continuity in social relationships of the Chinese people. T. C. Liu analyzes the economic development of the mainland. Alexander Eckstein examines the economic fluctuations in China since 1949 in terms of the impact of the thought of Mao Tse-tung on the regime's economic policy. The theme of continuity and change is developed in theoretical and comparative terms in the concluding paper by S. N. Eisenstadt.

In addition to thanking all of the participants in these studies, on behalf of the fellows of the Center I extend particular appreciation to Jonathan Kleinbard, my assistant, and to Chung-chi Wen, Peter Sharfman, and David Adams, graduate students at the University during the China study, for their aid during the conferences and help in preparing the material for the books.

Charles U. Daly
Director, Center for Policy Study
Vice-President
The University of Chicago

Contents

IX

Tables and Figures

Tables

Figures

Ping-ti Ho

Salient Aspects of China's Heritage

It is fairly safe for students of Chinese history to say that the current revolution that has been going on in mainland China since 1949 will overshadow in nature and scope the one which from the late third century B.C. onward swept away the remnants of feudalism and ushered China into two thousand years of imperial rule. For many students of world history, the present Chinese revolution deserves to be ranked with the French and Russian revolutions as one of the most momentous events in recent centuries. In spite of various domestic difficulties and international setbacks within a short span of seventeen years, the Chinese Communists have profoundly altered the form and substance of the Chinese society, including the destruction of the pre-1949 power elite—an aspect which is regarded by two leading experts of Communist China to be the mark of a true revolution.[1] It is with a full awareness of the profundity of the many-sided changes, therefore, that I undertake the task of analyzing certain salient aspects of China's heritage in the hope that they may help to sharpen our perception of the present. While in this paper China's heritage is approached fairly comprehensively from the geographic-ethnic, demographic, political, social-educational, and economic points of view, I purposely eschew the legacy of the traditional tributary system and its likely influence on present-day China's international policy and behavior. This is partly because the focus of this first Conference is on historical background and Communist China's internal policies and partly because, of all aspects of Chinese history, China's international relations are the most studied and best understood in the West.

[1] Franz Schurmann, *Ideology and Organization in Communist China* (Berkeley: University of California Press, 1966), p. 2; Chalmers Johnson, *Revolution and the Social System* (Stanford, Calif.: Stanford University Press, 1964), p. 8.

I

However much China experts may differ in their appraisals of the strengths and weaknesses of mainland China as a major power, they are unanimous in recognizing the basic fact that much of its impact on the outside world is due to its sheer physical size and the location of its frontiers. It seems pertinent therefore to begin a survey of China's heritage with a brief review of the growth of modern China as a geographic and ethnic entity.

Even after the legal secession of Outer Mongolia, the People's Republic of China still embraces an area of 3,657,765 square miles, which makes it the second largest country in the world. The consolidated land mass of China, which stretches longitudinally from the Pamir and the "roof of the world" to the Pacific Ocean and latitudinally from the cool northern Eurasian steppe to the tropics of southern Asia, gives it a commanding position in the continent of Asia. To use some erstwhile interesting geopolitical expressions, China and the Soviet Union share the "heartland" of the Eurasian land mass but China alone possesses the important warm-water east Eurasian "rimland." China's deep concern with and potent influence on Korea and Vietnam—two areas which may be regarded as its additional and strategically vital "rimlands"—make it the chief target of the United States' long-range world policy. While the revolutionary development in military technology during and after World War II has considerably invalidated certain fundamental assumptions of geopolitics, the very fact that China, notwithstanding its relative military and industrial weakness, has almost replaced the Soviet Union as the most urgent concern of the United States must be partially accounted for by its physical size and strategic geographic location.

One striking fact which is not too clearly known to students of world affairs is that throughout much of its long history China was actually a far smaller country than it is today. Historically, the area under abiding effective Chinese jurisdiction lies south of the Great Wall, which in modern times is called China Proper. China Proper, with an area of about 1,532,800 square miles, amounts to only one-half of that of the United States. It is true that at the peak of the Han (B.C. 206–220 A.D.) and T'ang (618–907) empires the Chinese reached as far west as present Russian Turkestan and that the Mongol empire is the largest in the annals of man. But the westward expansions of Han and T'ang were ephemeral at best and the Mongol empire was too loosely organized to leave any permanent imprint. It was during the last dynasty of Ch'ing (1644–1912) that China was geographically transformed from China Proper to what from the historian's point of view may be called "Greater China."[2]

The first important contribution that the Manchus made to the growth of China as a geographic and ethnic entity was the addition of Inner Mongolia and Manchuria to China Proper. Thanks to their geographic propinquity to the Mongols and especially to their farsightedness, the early Manchu rulers had worked out, even before the conquest of China in 1644, a long-range policy toward the Mongols of Inner Mongolia, which was continued and amplified down to the very end of the dynasty in 1912. The policy consisted of perennial intermarriage between the Manchu imperial clan and Mongol princedoms, periodic conferring of noble ranks on the various strata of the Mongol ruling class, the endorsement of Lamaism as the official religion for the Mongols, and the setting up of administrative machinery from *aimaks* ("principalities"), *chigolgans* ("leagues"), down to *hoshigo* ("banners"), a system which not only suited Mongol customs but also allowed the Manchus to play a policy of divide and rule. In addition, a significant number of Mongols were incorporated into the Eight Banner system and into central and provincial administration. Although early Ch'ing statutes prohibited the Chinese from entering the domains reserved for Mongol nomads, the imperial government from the late seventeenth century onward connived at Chinese immigration to Inner Mongolia, especially at times of famine. Chinese immigration at first received also the tacit blessing of Mongol nobles who found their new role as *rentiers* profitable. Wherever sizable Chinese agricultural colonies were established, the imperial government set up regular local administrations, that is, counties and prefectures. By late Ch'ing times Chinese migrations to the northern steppe had reached much larger scales, and Inner Mongolia had become increasingly Sinicized. Similar Chinese migrations to Manchuria, where the Manchus originated, have made Manchuria thoroughly Chinese, despite the onslaughts of Czarist Russia and Japan.

The need in the late seventeenth and early eighteenth centuries to defend Khalkha or Outer Mongolia from the warlike Zunghars of northern Chinese Turkestan led the Manchus to a long series of wars which resulted in the establishment of Chinese suzerainty over Outer Mongolia and Tibet and the conquest of Kokonor and Chinese Tur-

[2] Much of this section is taken from my article, "The Significance of the Ch'ing Period in Chinese History," *Journal of Asian Studies*, 26, no. 2 (1967).

kestan. All these vast outlying areas, together with Inner Mongolia, were supervised from Peking by *Li-fan yüan*, or Court of Colonial Affairs.[3] The effectiveness of Manchu control of these far-flung areas varied in inverse proportion to the magnitude of such difficulties as distance, terrain, transportation of men and supplies, and financial resources. An indication that the complex Ch'ing system of control was by and large viable may be seen from the following facts: Chinese Turkestan and Kokonor were made into new provinces of Sinkiang and Chinghai, respectively, in 1884 and 1928; the imperial resident and garrisons in Lhasa were not withdrawn until after the fall of the dynasty in 1912; and Outer Mongolia did not legally secede from China until after the end of World War II.

From 1840 onward the Manchu empire was greatly weakened by successive international wars and domestic rebellions. Various imperialist powers began to launch their onslaughts on the peripheries of the Manchu empire. Step by step, Russia, Britain, France, and Japan reduced the question of the legal statuses of China's outlying territories and dependent states to an almost purely academic one. For every party had learned from *Realpolitik* that the true status of any of these disputed areas depended on China's ability to exert effective control. It is this rude historical lesson that prompted the People's Republic of China to seize the first opportunities to rush its army into Sinkiang and Tibet. Because of the secession of Outer Mongolia, the area of the People's Republic of China is approximately 606,000 square miles smaller than that of the late Manchu empire, which in turn had shrunken considerably from its fullest extent attained before 1800.

Any review of the evolution of China as a geographic and ethnic entity would be misleading without pointing out that the extension of China's internal frontiers, if less spectacular than empire building, is historically equally important. Although the history of the extension of China's internal frontiers is practically as old as Chinese history itself, it was from the 1720's onward that a more energetic policy of Sinicization was directed against various non-Chinese ethnic groups who constituted a majority in a number of mountainous enclaves in the southwestern provinces of Yunnan, Kweichow, Szechwan, and Kwangsi, and in the central Yangtze provinces of Hunan and Hupei. The core of this policy was to replace the native tribal system with

---

[3] The predecessor of *Li-fan yüan* was the *Meng-ku ya-men* (Office for Mongolian Affairs), which came into being in 1634 at the latest. See *Ch'ing T'ai-tsung shih-lu*, chap. 18, p. 32b. In 1638 the name of this office was changed to *Li-fan yüan*.

Chinese local administration. To a more limited extent, it was applied also to parts of Kansu, Kokonor, Chinese Turkestan, and eastern Tibet, the latter becoming Sikang province during the Nationalist period. Even the last few years of Manchu dynasty witnessed a recrudescence of this policy in Sikang, in response to Britain's growing influence in Tibet. In its broader aspects, this Ch'ing policy of Sinicization of non-Chinese ethnic groups considered the feasibility of carrying out limited economic and social reforms and included such measures as the setting-up of county and prefectural schools and of local quotas for degree-holders as a means of gradual cultural assimilation. Needless to say, the late Ch'ing, the early Republican, and the Nationalist governments were so beset by domestic difficulties and international crises that they fell far short of the long-range goals set by statesmen of the 1720's.

There is every indication that the historical movement of consolidating China's internal frontiers, which up to the end of the imperial age was confined to China Proper, Inner Mongolia, and Manchuria, has since the founding of the People's Republic of China in 1949 been extended to the vast outlying regions of Sinkiang, Chinghai, Sikang, and Tibet. Superficially, the policy of the present Peking regime toward the fifty or so national minorities seems to be a reversal of the traditional policy of suppression and forced Sinicization, for it has conferred on them constitutional rights of self-rule and regional administrative and cultural autonomy. These constitutional rights, together with some genuine efforts on the part of Peking to help them in agriculture, stock-raising, industry, education, public health, and social reform, have led some Western observers to believe that there has been a complete reorientation of policy.[4]

Yet it may be argued that the basic reason the Peking government has adopted a more enlightened approach to the problem of national minorities is its exuberant confidence in its ability to exert potent control over all minority areas, and in the strength of Chinese culture gradually to assimilate all the non-Han ethnic groups, which—after all —constitute only 6 per cent of the total national population.[5] Whereas

[4] Josef Kolmas, "The Minority Nationalities," *Bulletin of the Atomic Scientists*, "China Today," June, 1966, pp. 71–75.

[5] The 1953 census gave the total minority population as 35,320,360. Numerically the more important groups are the Chuang (6,611,455), Uighur (3,640,125), Hui (Moslems, 3,559,350), Yi (3,254,269), Tibetan (2,775,622), Miao (2,511,339), Manchu (2,418,931), Mongolian (1,462,956).

the Manchu empire was severely handicapped by difficulties of distance, terrain, and communication, the People's Republic of China has at its disposal more varied and effective instruments of control. We need mention only such factors as, for example, the presence of significant numbers of the People's Liberation Army (PLA) in all outlying areas of national minorities including Tibet; the impending completion of the Peking-Lanchow-Sinkiang Railway, which already has reached Urumchi, capital of Sinkiang; the completion of three trunk roads which link Sinkiang, Chinghai, Sikang, and Tibet with the rest of China; the establishment of colleges and universities in Sinkiang and Inner Mongolia and of nationality institutes in Peking, Lanchow, Hsining (capital of Chinghai), Wuhan, Chengtu, Nanning and Kunming, which have attracted thousands of non-Han students; the migration of significant numbers of Chinese technological personnel to the northwest where they serve as additional catalysts to inter-ethnic acculturation; and the increasing use of various mass media and of party cadres and native activists to transform the national minorities socially, ideologically, and organizationally. Peking can afford to grant the various non-Han ethnic groups regional administrative and cultural autonomy because of its unprecedented position of strength vis-à-vis them.

In spite of the constitutional rights granted to the national minorities, we find a remarkable continuity between traditional and present policies. Historically, the extension of internal frontiers often contained an element of coercion and was not infrequently accompanied by bloodshed. Even Peking's seemingly enlightened policy toward the national minorities has on occasions required the use of military force. The pacification of the unrest of the Uighurs and Kazaks in Sinkiang in recent years and the suppression of the armed revolt of the Tibetans in 1959 are outstanding examples. The cynic could say that Peking respects the constitutional rights of national minorities only to the extent that they do not resist its imposition of far-reaching social reform. It should be pointed out, however, that, for all its high-handed measures and its technical violation of some non-Han groups' constitutional rights, Peking is not unconcerned with the welfare of the downtrodden within various national minorities. For example, the 1959 revolt was engineered by the old Tibetan ecclesiastical and temporal vested interests because Peking was determined to emancipate Tibetan commoners from the *ula* (feudal *corvée*) and other economic and social abuses. In fact, even in the late imperial age some far-sighted provincial and local officials in the southwest realized that the fundamental solution for the problem of national minorities was for Chinese authorities to eliminate, by force if necessary, the inherent injustice in the non-Han tribal system, although the high price for implementing such a policy made the imperial government reluctant to sanction anything more drastic than palliatives. Put in a proper historical perspective, therefore, the present Peking government's policy toward national minorities is an amplification rather than a reversal of the traditional.

In view of Peking's vastly improved means of control, it is not unlikely that the historical movement of consolidating China's internal frontiers will be reasonably successfully extended, for the first time in Chinese history, from China Proper to "Greater China."

II

Another important inheritance which China has received from the past is its large population. Prior to the Ch'ing, the peak officially registered population was 60,000,000, although there is strong reason to believe that during certain earlier periods, such as the latter halves of Sung (960–1279) and Ming (1368–1644), the population may well have exceeded 100,000,000. In spite of the wars and turmoil of the twelfth and mid-fourteenth centuries which exacted heavy tolls of human lives, the general demographic trend during the past millennium was toward growth, mainly because of two long-range revolutions in land utilization and food production. The first was brought about by an ever-increasing number of varieties of early-ripening and relatively drought-resistant rice, consequent upon the introduction of the Champa rice from central coastal Indochina at the beginning of the eleventh century. Throughout subsequent centuries the early-ripening rice was responsible for the conquest of hilly regions where the topsoil was sufficiently heavy and rainfall or spring water was adequate and made feasible the double-cropping system for which China's rice area is famous.[6] The second revolution in land utilization began with the introduction in the sixteenth century of such American food crops as maize, the sweet potato and the peanut, which, along with a much later arrival, the Irish potato, enabled the Chinese—hitherto mainly a plain and valley folk—systematically to tackle dry hills, mountains, and sandy loams.[7] As a result of centuries of gradual dissemination of

[6] Ping-ti Ho, "Early-Ripening Rice in Chinese History," *Economic History Review,* new series, 9, no. 2 (1956).

[7] Ping-ti Ho, "The Introduction of American Food Plants into China," *The American Anthropologist,* 57, no. 2, pt. 1 (1955); and "American Food Plants

these new crops, large areas of new land were opened up and China's food supply became much more abundant than during pre-Sung times.

Yet, like other pre-industrial populations, China's population could not grow at a sustained high rate over a long period unless institutional and economic factors other than agricultural production were also favorable. As has been discussed in detail in my *Studies on the Population of China, 1368–1953*,[8] such a combination of unusually favorable economic and institutional factors did exist in the century from the dawn of domestic peace and prosperity in 1683 to the late eighteenth century. Consequently, China's population shot up to 300,-000,000 by 1800 and even an increasingly unfavorable population-land ratio could not prevent the population from reaching 430,000,000 by 1850. It was precisely at this juncture where a vastly increasing population was straining at resources and a large part of it living near the margin of subsistence, that the Taiping, Nien, and Moslem rebellions broke out in succession.

The decimation of the population of central and lower Yangtze provinces, the Huai River area and the northwest brought about by the rebellions of the third quarter of the nineteenth century at best conferred upon the nation a brief breathing spell and failed to redress the old population-land ratio. The absence of major technological revolution has made it impossible for China to broaden the scope of her land economy to any appreciable extent. But though the economy failed to make a breakthrough, the ideal of benevolent despotism of the late seventeenth and early eighteenth centuries was dead once and forever. After the downfall of the Manchu dynasty, an era of warlordism was ushered in at a time when the nation had so little economic reserve that natural calamities exacted disproportionately heavy tolls of human lives. Even during twenty-two years of Nationalist rule, the nation hardly enjoyed a year without war, civil or international. Small wonder, then, that the 1953 census yielded a total of 583 millions, which gives a total gain of a mere 35.5 per cent in 103 years and an average annual rate of growth of only 0.3 per cent.

After the Communist takeover in 1949, however, population growth is reported to have been rapid. The return of peace and order, the beginnings of large-scale industrialization, and especially the nation-wide health campaign apparently have stimulated population growth.

---

in China," *Plant Science Bulletin* (The Botanical Society of America), 2, no. 1 (1956).

[8] Cambridge, Mass.: Harvard University Press, 1959.

During the past six centuries the Chinese population has responded quickly to favorable economic and political conditions but has failed to show the same alacrity in adjusting itself to hard times. The result has been an almost progressive deterioration in the national standards of living since the late eighteenth century. Whether history will repeat itself or whether the new China can achieve a rate of economic growth greater than her current rate of population growth remains to be seen. But the existence of so large a population, currently estimated to be in the neighborhood of 700,000,000 (more than 40 per cent under seventeen years of age), is a major factor to be reckoned with in world politics.

III

To understand the true character of the traditional Chinese state, it is necessary first to study the ideology on which the traditional Chinese state was based. While it is not entirely unjustified to label the Chinese state during the two thousand years of the imperial age as Confucian, the nature of the traditional Chinese state actually was far more complex than such an appellation would indicate. This apparent over-simplification has resulted from these—among other—reasons: Since the Western Han Emperor Wu (140–87 B.C.), the traditional state itself during greater parts of the imperial age declared Confucianism as the orthodox ideology;[9] there was the progressive deification of Confucius, which, though not without interruptions, reached a peak in the last dynasty of Ch'ing;[10] the post-Han penal codes were successively revised in accordance with Confucian norms and mores and such government practices and institutions as the recommendation, examination, and school systems originated from Confucian principles. All in all, Confucianism did have considerable softening and humanizing effect on the traditional Chinese state. But the fundamental character of the traditional Chinese state cannot be fully understood without an analysis of the components of the ideology which was for most periods of Chinese history officially and uncritically labelled as Confucian.

[9] During the period of political division, roughly 300–600 A.D., the influence of Buddhism and Taoism was very great, although Confucianism remained a useful political ideology.

[10] Manchu rulers paid Confucius unprecedented homage. While worshipping Confucius in Peking, the emperor usually knelt twice and prostrated six times. When worshipping Confucius at his birthplace, Ch'ü-fu, the emperors K'ang-hsi and Ch'ien-lung performed the same *kotow* as subjects did to the ruler, namely, three kneelings and nine prostrations.

We may further sharpen our perception by searching beneath the Confucian veneer and trying to discover what was the net function of the so-called Confucianism to the traditional state. In other words, was Confucianism a master or servant of the traditional state?

For the study of traditional Chinese state and government, no period is more important than the Western Han (B.C. 206–8 A.D.). Even bearing later modifications in mind, it is small exaggeration to say that the fundamental character of the traditional Chinese state was determined in Western Han times, especially during and after the reign of Emperor Wu. For this reason, we will take special pains to dissect as precisely as possible the component schools of thought that were interwoven into Western Han statecraft and ideology, which in the later days of the greater triumph of Confucianism were usually regarded as Confucian.

First, since at its very inception the dynasty adopted the laws and institutes of Ch'in (221–207 B.C.), and Ch'in was known for its strict enforcement of its uniform law through heavy penalties, the principles of the one particular school of Legalism formulated by the Ch'in statesman Lord of Shang of the fourth century B.C. must be regarded as an important ideological component. And, since the despotic Ch'in empire was of such short duration and was hence discredited, early Han statesmen and scholars preferred to name this particular school after Han Fei, the famous synthesist of all earlier Legalist schools including that of Lord of Shang.[11]

Second, another important ideological component was derived from the particular school of Legalism formulated by Shen Pu-hai of the fourth century B.C., who systematically expounded the techniques of bureaucratic organization and administrative control. According to Shen, once the government machineries are set in order, all that the ruler needs to do is to prevent any single minister from gaining preeminent power and to hold in his own hands the two instruments of control, namely, reward and punishment. The highest level of administrative achievement is the one at which the ruler seemingly resorts to "non-action."[12] As a matter of fact, this highest art of administrative control was actually and successfully practiced by such rulers of real

[11] This is apparent from reading Ssu-ma T'an's preface to, and various biographies in, *Shih-chi* [Records of the Grand Historian].

[12] H. G. Creel, "The Fa-chia: 'Legalists' or 'Administrators,' " in *Studies Presented to Tung Tso-pin on His Sixty-Fifth Birthday* (Academia Sinica, 1961), pp. 607–36; for the origin of "non-action," see pp. 613–14.

political genius as Emperor Wen (179–157 B.C.) and Emperor Hsüan (73–49 B.C.).[13]

Third, for the first two-thirds of a century after the founding of Western Han, the prevailing ideology was Taoism. Though devoid of constructive political and social ideas, Taoism stressed laissez faire and "non-action," which certainly helped the nation to recuperate and the economy to revive.[14] But the Western Han state in its early years could afford to sponsor Taoism only because it had already adopted its laws and institutes from the Legalist schools. In reality, Taoism only supplemented, never overshadowed, Legalism.

Fourth, Confucianism helped theoretically to legitimatize the dynasty, to design elaborate rituals, ceremonies, and symbols which enhanced the emperor's charisma, and to humanize the harshness of a basically Legalist state by unceasingly exhorting the importance of moral suasion. While theoretically preferring moral influence to law as a principle of Government, the Han Confucianists were realists who no longer challenged the importance of law. In fact, they concurred with the Legalists on the necessity of treating commoners harshly with all the rigor of the law, and differed from the Legalists only on the latter's insistence on the universality of law and equity before the law.[15] As long as the Han Confucianists could revise the law—chiefly through legal commentaries—according to the Confucian concept of a clearly differentiated social order, they actually welcomed legal sanction, which was undoubtedly more effective than moral sanction. A basic reason why Confucian scholars who filled the bureaucracy during most parts of the past two thousand years were ardent supporters of the imperial system was because they were the main beneficiaries of the long process of "Confucianization" of law which had begun in Han times and was completed afterward.[16]

[13] Lao Kan, *Ch'in-Han shih* [History of Ch'in and Han Periods] (Taipei, 1952), pp. 29–36, 54–57.

[14] *Ibid.*, chap. 4.

[15] Etienne Balázs, *Le Traité juridique du "Souei-chou"* (Paris, 1954), *passim*, ably summarized by Arthur F. Wright, "The Formation of Sui Ideology," in John K. Fairbank, ed., *Chinese Thought and Institutions* (Chicago: University of Chicago Press, 1957), p. 81. Although Balázs' study deals with the penal law of the Sui period, his conclusion holds in the main for the Han as well as for all post-Sui periods.

[16] For the history of the "Confucianization" of Chinese law, see Ch'en Yin-k'o, *Sui-T'ang chih-tu yüan-yüan lüeh-lun kao* [Studies of the Origins of Sui and T'ang Institutions] (Chungking, 1943), pp. 73–81; and T'ung-tsu Ch'ü, *Law and Society in Traditional China* (Paris: Mouton, 1961), pp. 267–79. For an

In economic and social matters the Han Confucianists generally took the typically Taoist stand of laissez faire and "non-action,"[17] except that they advocated state intervention in the increasingly unequal distribution of landed property. Otherwise, they were passionately opposed to large-scale state trading and monopolies.[18] Because of its more catholic taste and its non-sectarian heritage, Han Confucianism was able not only to absorb the schools of Legalism and Taoism but also to work out a philosophical syncretism by which to rationalize the whole realm of human relationships and cosmic order.[19] The all-embracing nature of this "Taoist-Legalist-Confucian amalgam that is known as 'Han Confucianism,' "[20] coupled with the fact that Confucianism became a state orthodoxy during the reign of Emperor Wu, makes it not entirely illogical for modern students to say that the Western Han ideology was "Confucian."

But the fundamental character of the Western Han state and the relative importance of its ideological components are nowhere better and more authoritatively discussed than by Emperor Hsüan, one of the ablest Chinese rulers of all times. Upon hearing the remonstrance of his heir apparent that the severity of the laws be alleviated and that more Confucians be appointed to high office,

> Emperor Hsüan changed color and remarked: "The Han dynasty has its own laws and institutes, which embody and blend the

illuminating discussion of the relationship between traditional Chinese bureaucrats and Confucianized penal code, see Balázs, *Chinese Civilization and Bureaucracy* (New Haven: Yale University Press, 1964), pp. 13–27.

[17] It is well known that Confucius first associated "non-action" with the government of idealized legendary sage-kings.

[18] My generalization is based on the famous Han work, Huan K'uan, *Yen-t'ieh lun* [Discourses on Salt and Iron] and Pan Ku, *Han-shu* [History of the Former Han Dynasty], chap. 27, especially the introduction. Both these works are available in English. See E. M. Gale (trans.), *Discourses on Salt and Iron* (Leiden: E. J. Brill, 1931), which translates 19 chapters of *Yen-t'ieh lun,* and Nancy Lee Swann (trans.), *Food and Money in Ancient China* (Princeton: Princeton University Press, 1947).

[19] Such a philosophical syncretism is best represented by the famous Han work, *Po Hu T'ung: The Comprehensive Discussions in the White Tiger Hall,* trans. Tjan Tjoe Som, 2 vols. (Leiden: E. J. Brill, 1949–52).

[20] Arthur Wright, "The Formation of Sui Ideology," p. 85. For an authoritative analysis of Han political thought, see Hsiao Kung-ch'üan, *Chung-kuo cheng-chih ssu-hsiang shih* [History of Chinese Political Thought], 2 vols. (Shanghai, 1947), vol. 2, chaps. 8–10.

principles of realistic statecraft as well as those of ancient sage-kings. How could I rely entirely on moral instruction which [is alleged to have] guided the government of the Chou dynasty? Moreover, the ordinary Confucians seldom understand the needs of changing times. They love to praise the ancient and to decry the present, thus making people confused about ideals and realities and incapable of knowing what to abide by. How could the Confucians be entrusted with the vital responsibilities of the state?" Thereupon he sighed and said: "The one who will confound my dynasty will be my heir-apparent."[21]

From Emperor Hsüan's uniquely candid and profound remarks it is clear that the Western Han state was substantively Legalist and only ornamentally Confucian.

What Emperor Hsüan said of the fundamental character of the Western Han state more or less holds for the Chinese state of subsequent periods and is relevant even to an understanding of the nature of the modern Chinese state. Space does not allow a detailed analysis of the ideological components of all post-Han dynasties. Suffice it here to point out that there was a remarkable continuity of ideologies and institutions from the Sui reunification in 589 A.D. to the end of the imperial age in 1912. It is true that in formulating an ideology the Sui founder Wen-ti (581–604) had to take cognizance of the strengths of Buddhism and Taoism which had prevailed during the three previous centuries of political division and profoundly affected the life and faith of the Chinese and their alien conquerors in north China. But since Buddhism and Taoism offered relatively little that was truly useful for the reconstruction of state and society, the core of the Sui ideology had to be Confucian. As to the Sui founder's true attitude toward Confucianism, an able modern historian concludes:

> He used its sanctions to legitimize and consolidate his empire, but his character and background, his advisers, and the urgency of his many problems inclined him toward the authoritarian rigor associated with Legalism and inclined him at the same time to Buddhism, which salved his personal conscience and provided its special sanctions for a supreme autocrat.[22]

[21] This translation is partially based on and modified from that by H. H. Dubs. Pan Ku, *History of the Former Han Dynasty*, trans. H. H. Dubs, 3 vols. (The American Council of Learned Societies, 1944), vol. 2, pp. 300–301.

[22] Arthur Wright, "The Formation of Sui Ideology," p. 88. The usefulness of Buddhism to the Sui founder is explained on p. 82: "The build-up of Wen-ti

It is well known that, with the exception of the Mongol Yüan inter-
lude (1279–1368), the traditional Chinese state during the past millennium became increasingly more Confucian, thanks to the rise and ever-
increasing influence of Neo-Confucianism. Despite its rich contribution to Chinese philosophy, Neo-Confucianism's theories of human
relationships—especially those between the ruler and his subjects,
father and son, husband and wife—are largely passive. Although Confucius' original theory of human relationships is also based on the
principle of superordination and subordination, he never ceased to
stress the importance of the ruler's obligations to his subjects. Confucius' theory that human relationships are necessarily two-sided in
terms of the rights and obligations of the superior and the inferior is
carried to its logical extreme by Mencius, who even justifies the people's
right to revolt against the ruler who has abused his power. While outwardly rehashing the same theory, such Sung Neo-Confucian philosophers as Ch'eng Hao (1032–85), Ch'eng I (1033–1108) and Chu Hsi
(1130–1200) avoid the Mencian line of reasoning and make the subject's loyalty, the son's filiality, and the wife's obedience almost one-
sided moral imperatives.[23] This was the main reason why the Ch'eng-
Chu school of Neo-Confucianism was made the official orthodoxy during the Yüan, Ming, and Ch'ing periods, which witnessed an intensification of autocracy.

The net function of Confucianism—interpreted in the light of the
Ch'eng-Chu school—to the Chinese state of later dynasties is seldom
better and more frankly discussed than by the Yung-cheng emperor
(1723–35), the ablest of the Manchu rulers:

> Ordinary people know only that Confucius' teaching aims at dif-
> ferentiating human relationships, distinguishing the rights and

---

into a Cakravartin king—the ideal Buddhist monarch, who, using the true teaching, builds a universal and happy empire—was, in the times in which he lived,
one of the most effective ways to gain one of the primary goals of authoritarian
statesmen: recognition of the supreme and unchallengeable authority of the
Monarch."

[23] This is my own impression based on sampling the collected works of the
Ch'eng brothers and Chu Hsi. It may not be an exaggeration to say that Ch'eng
Hao was responsible for ethically justifying the subjection of women. It is significant to note that the view that for the subjects absolute loyalty was a one-
sided moral imperative was expounded by the conservative statesman and historian Ssu-ma Kuang and by an anonymous Sung author of *Chung-ching*
[Classic on Loyalty]. See Hsiao Kung-ch'üan, *Chung-kuo cheng-chih ssu-hsiang
shih*, vol. 2: 168–70, 188–89.

obligations of the superior and the inferior, rectifying human minds and thoughts, and amending social custums. Do they also know that after human relationships have been differentiated, the rights and obligations of the superior and the inferior distinguished, human minds and thoughts rectified, and social customs amended, the one who benefits the most [from his teaching] is the ruler himself?[24]

It thus becomes abundantly clear that, for all its ornamental value and humanizing effect, Confucianism was always a tool, never the master, of the traditional Chinese state, which during the entire imperial age remained highly authoritarian. Small wonder, then, that, in spite of the loquacity of Western-trained Chinese intellectuals, Western democratic thoughts and institutions could find no congenial soil in twentieth-century China. The only foreign ideology that has struck root in present China is Marx-Leninism, which not only fits China's unbroken tradition of autocracy but has helped to make the Maoist state more authoritarian than ever before.

The main institutional characteristics of the traditional and modern Chinese state shall be further analyzed.[25] First, the prevailing of the civilian ideal in traditional Chinese government administration should not blind us to the hard fact that every dynasty was founded on mili-

[24] *Ch'ing Shih-tsung shih-lu* [Veritable Records of Ching Emperors, Yung-cheng], chap. 59, pp. 20b–22a. I owe this illuminating passage to Professor F. C. Chang of the University of British Columbia.

[25] There are a fair number of highly useful Western studies on various aspects of traditional Chinese government and administration, of which we may mention: Derk Bodde, *China's First Unifier: A Study of the Ch'in Dynasty as Seen in the Life of Li Ssu* (280?–208 B.C.) (Leiden: E. J. Brill, 1938); Wang Yü-ch'üan, "An Outline of the Central Government of the Former Han Dynasty," *Harvard Journal of Asiatic Studies,* June, 1949; Robert des Rotours, *Traité des Fonctionnaires et Traité de l'Armée, Traduits de la Nouvelle Histoire des T'ang,* 2 vols. (Leiden: E. J. Brill, 1947–48); Edward A. Kracke, Jr., "The Chinese and the Art of Government," in R. Dawson, ed., *The Legacy of China* (Oxford: Oxford University Press, 1965), and *Civil Service in Early Sung China* (Cambridge, Mass.: Harvard University Press, 1953); and Charles O. Hucker, "Governmental Organization of the Ming Dynasty," *Harvard Journal of Asiatic Studies,* December, 1958. The Chinese and Japanese literature on traditional Chinese government is so vast as to make even a partial listing difficult. The purpose of this section is merely to study the fundamental character of the traditional Chinese state, hence I will deal only with the apex rather than with the vast bureaucracy.

tary strength or by the transference of military power. It is true that every dynastic founder had to make full use of available ideological factors to legitimize his throne and that in cases of more stable and enduring dynasties the military element had to be subordinated to the civilian. But the success and duration of a dynasty depended primarily on the ability of the founder and his successors to keep the imperial army effectively centrally controlled and to design various institutional checks by which to forestall the rise of regional military contenders. From the dawning of the first empire in 221 B.C. to the founding of the People's Republic of China in 1949 there has not been a single exception. In spite of the three stages of political evolution toward constitutionalism expounded by Dr. Sun Yat-sen, the fact that the Nationalist government—whether on the mainland or on the island of Taiwan—has yet to go beyond the first stage of military dictatorship is too well known to need any explanation. It seems more than coincidental that Mao Tse-tung owes his success less to Leninism than to the very peasant army which he himself has created and expanded, and that amid the current far-reaching purge Mao's last recourse is once again the army. In explaining the necessity of carrying on the purge to the army, *Liberation Army Daily* recently said: "If the ideology of the men behind guns changes, the guns will serve a different object, a different master."[26] In contrast to the weakness of European monarchies which aided the rise of democracy, the persistent historical fact is that the Chinese state has always derived its ultimate power from the army, and this has largely predetermined its authoritarian character.

Second, another characteristic of the traditional Chinese state was the emperor cult, which still has its bearing on the post-imperial state. Almost as soon as the plebeian Liu Pang ascended to the Han throne, various attempts were made to strengthen his claim by cloaking him with divine attributes. By 201 B.C. the court adopted the elaborate rituals and ceremonies suggested by Confucianist officials which, by making the emperor lofty, aloof, and almost unapproachable, further enhanced his prestige and charisma. As additional symbol of the ruling dynasty, the Han founder had his ancestral temples erected in every province of the empire. From the founder's death in 195 B.C. until 40 B.C., every deceased emperor had his temples in the capital city and provinces. From the third emperor to the eighth, each erected his temples during his lifetime. By about the middle of the first century B.C., there were 176 imperial temples and 30 temples for empresses and crown princes

[26] *Chicago Sun-Times,* June 20, 1966, p. 18.

throughout the empire, which required 24,455 victuals and sacrifices annually, 45,129 temple guards, and a government staff of 12,147 in charge of sacrificial ceremonies and music.[27] Although it is questionable whether during the highly superstitious Western Han period the Chinese nation actually believed that emperors were gods, there can be little doubt that by the latter half of the first century B.C. the emperor cult had successfully served its purpose. As a result of the debate of 40 B.C., imperial temples in the provinces were abolished. From Eastern Han (25–220 A.D.) onward there was usually only one temple erected for the dynastic founder after his death, to which all later emperors of the same dynasty were posthumously attached. For since Western Han times, the emperor's charisma had been generally taken for granted and an elaborate system of imperial temples was no longer needed. During the past millennium when imperial prestige enhanced almost progressively, there gradually had come into being a rich folklore which, if it did not outright regard the emperor as a god, nevertheless portrayed him as divinely ordained, and led to such common appellations for the emperor as "Lord of Myriad Years," "Real-Dragon Son of Heaven," and "Son of Heaven with Real Mandate of Heaven."

One of the reasons why the early Republican periods ranks among the most chaotic in Chinese history was the passing of the emperor system—a symbol of common allegiance for more than two thousand years. After the Nationalist government established itself in Nanking in 1927, it systematically cultivated the Sun Yat-sen cult by requiring all government offices and schools to hold a Sun memorial session each Monday, which ceremoniously consisted of three bows to Dr. Sun's photograph, the reading by the chairman of Dr. Sun's will, and the observance of three minutes' silence. From the early 1930's onward the Nationalist government began to cultivate the Chiang Kai-shek cult as well. Since then it has become customary that wherever the names and titles of Sun and Chiang appear in print, they are to be elevated in exactly the same way as were the names and canonized titles of emperors. Some China experts have interpreted the reason for the refusal of Mao's China to follow Khrushchev's de-Stalinization movement to be that China, politically, economically, socially, and ideologically, is in a stage roughly comparable to that of the Soviet Union in the early Stalin era. For students of Chinese history, however, a more valid explanation is the stark historical fact that for more than two thousand years the

[27] Lei Hai-tsung, "Huang-ti chih-tu chih ch'eng-li" [The Establishment of the Emperor System], *Ch'ing-hua hsüeh-pao* 10, no. 4 (October, 1934).

Chinese nation has never experienced any system of state and government which is not easily identifiable by a single charismatic leader, whether the emperor or his modern counterpart. The relentless cultivation of the Mao Tse-tung cult since 1949 answers a deep-rooted political need of the Chinese nation. The recurrent thought-rectification movements, based strictly on Maoism, further exalt him to a status comparable to those of the much idealized ancient sage-kings, who are alleged to have been infallible rulers as well as political philosophers. However strong at the moment the anti-Mao forces may be, and however much Mao's policies may be changed after his death, there will probably be no "whipping of the corpse" because modern Chinese political leaders must have learned from history that no one would gain from the destruction of the emperor or leader cult. The system of state and government which focuses on the concrete symbol of a single strong man has naturally inclined itself toward authoritarianism.

Third, perhaps the most important characteristic of the traditional Chinese state which is relevant to an understanding of the nature of the modern state was the absence of any effective institutional check to the doctrine of imperial absolutism. For one thing, ever since the Western Han the emperor was in theory, and often in fact if he was energetic, the final authority and the ultimate source of all laws. It is true that, as some Western scholars have pointed out, the penal codes of various dynasties were "not an arbitrary creation of a despot but a codification of earlier customary or other rules."[28] But, increasingly guided by Confucian moral precepts from Han onward, the penal codes of various dynasties often did not reflect social realities and were relatively simple and brief. For our study of the emperor's power they are far less useful than the voluminous collections of administrative law of various dynastic periods. The testimonial of Tu Chou, a famous law-enforcing official of Western Han, is most illuminating.

> Once one of his (Tu Chou's) guests chided him about this, saying: "You are supposed to be a dispenser of justice for the Son of Heaven, and yet you pay no attention to the statute books, but simply decide cases in any way that will accord with the wishes of the ruler. Do you really think that is the way a law official should be?

[28] Wolfram Eberhard, "The Political Function of Astronomy and Astronomers in Han China," ed. John K. Fairbank, *Chinese Thought and Institutions*, p. 41. Eberhard is based on K. Bünger, "Die Richtsidee in der chinesischen Geschichte," *Saeculum*, 3, no. 2 (1952).

"And where, may I ask, did the statute books come from in the first place?" replied Tu Chou. "Whatever the earlier rulers thought was right they wrote down in the books and made into statutes, and whatever the later rulers thought was right they duly classified as ordinances. Anything that suits the present age is right. Why bother with the laws of former times?"[29]

Tu Chou's remark hits upon the very crux of the question of imperial authority and holds for later dynastic periods as well. From all extant collections of administrative laws from T'ang to Ch'ing we find the perpetuation of the Han practice—whenever a ruler wanted to depart from certain established precedents he had merely to issue a new edict by which automatically to supersede the related old statutes. The fact that the administrative laws of various dynasties indicate in the main a remarkable continuity and steady amplification and rationalization could only be accounted for by the immensity and complexity of the task of governing a huge empire through bureaucracy—this virtually ruled out the possibility of a complete break with the past. In the case of an unusually energetic and despotic ruler like the Ming founder T'ai-tsu (1368–98), all three series of his injunctions to civil officials and one series to military officers not only had the force of law but were required to be studied and memorized by all officials and students of government schools. One is not likely to be too far wrong in saying that outside of the force of tradition there was never any effective check to the emperor's supreme authority. For all the cumulative ingenuity of Confucian officials and scholars throughout the imperial age, they failed to contrive any more effective means to check imperial authority than the late feudal theory of "Mandate of Heaven" and the Western Han theory of portents of nature, which, being purely moral-cosmological, had rather limited restraining effect on the autocratic ruler.

For another, the unchallenged supremacy of imperial authority made it impossible for traditional China to develop a cabinet system comparable to those of the modern West. It is true that during the first seventy years of Western Han the Imperial Cabinet, headed by the Chancellor, who was ipso facto a marquis and enjoyed power and prestige denied to others, was a real policy-making body. But the absolute

---

[29] Burton Watson, tr., *Records of the Grand Historian of China, Translated from the Shih chi of Ssu-ma Ch'ien,* 2 vols. (New York, 1961), 2: 449. The reason for slight modification of Watson's translation is given in Ping-ti Ho, " 'Records of China's Grand Historian' Some Problems of Translation—A Review Article," *Pacific Affairs,* 36, no. 2 (1963): 176.

monarch and his cabinet were compatible only when the former was willing to delegate full power to the latter, or when the latter was entirely subservient to the former. The tension between the two came to a head during the reign of Emperor Wu, who bypassed the cabinet by delegating more and more power to a newly created regency, which consisted of a devoted close relative and an ex-slave of alien origin. The results are ably summarized by a modern scholar:

> First, the Chancellor and the Imperial Secretary were both rele-gated to the post of mere administrators and lost their power to influence decisions regarding major state affairs. Second, replacing the Chancellor, an official close to the Emperor was now at the helm of the state. Third, the Imperial Cabinet, or the Outer Court as it was called, was replaced by the Inner Court, and the government was transferred to the Palace.[30]

Further to undercut the power of the Imperial Cabinet, Emperor Wu elevated the office of Masters of Documents, originally lesser officials of the Small Treasury, or the Emperor's private bursar, by charging its holders with such vital tasks as transmitting memorials and rescripts, advising on policies, and drafting decrees and directives. In contrast to the Chancellor who could not enter the palace and usually had an audience with the Emperor once every five days, the Masters of Docu-ments had constant access to the Emperor's person. Consequently their power steadily grew until by the latter half of the first century B.C. the office of Masters of Documents had become, as contemporaries who knew the inner workings of the central government observed, "the foundation of all offices."[31]

Although specific circumstances differed from one dynasty to an-other, the transfer of vital government function from the cabinet to the Inner Court repeatedly occurred, especially during Eastern Han, T'ang, and Ming. The Inner Court of Eastern Han consisted of members of imperial consort families and eunuchs, with the latter eventually gain-ing an upper hand. The early T'ang Inner Court was dominated by members of consort families and that of the latter half of T'ang by

[30] Wang Yü-ch'üan, "An Outline of the Central Government of the Former Han Dynasty," p. 169. For a broader study of the inner and outer court in Former and Later Han times, see Lao Kan, "Lun Han-tai ti nei-ch'ao yü wai-ch'ao" [On the Inner and Outer Courts of Han Times], *Bulletin of the Insti-tute of History and Philology, Academia Sinica,* 13 (1948): 227–67.

[31] Wang Yü-ch'üan, "An Outline of the Central Government of the Former Han Dynasty," p. 170; also Lao Kan, *Ch'in-Han shih,* chap. 13.

eunuchs. The Inner Court of Ming was dominated by eunuchs only. In any case, by virtue of its constant access to the Emperor's person the Inner Court dominated the cabinet.

There was yet another method by which the autocratic ruler could weaken the power of the cabinet. However much curtailed was the power and function of the Western Han cabinet during and after Emperor Wu, the Chancellor was still the sole head of the bureaucracy, or the premier. In Eastern Han the office of the Chancellor was split into three, namely, *ssu-t'u* (Grand Minister for Civil and Financial Affairs), *ssu-k'ung* (Grand Minister for Public Works), and *t'ai-wei* (Grand Commandant in Charge of Military Affairs.)[32] This organizational change in the cabinet system left a permanent imprint on the cabinet structure of later periods. The cabinets of all later dynasties were organized after the Eastern Han model, which was—to use a modern expression—in the nature of a committee rather than of the premier system.[33] The reason is not far to seek, for the division of the functions among the component offices of the cabinet constituted a system of checks and balances within the cabinet itself, a system which facilitated the ruler's control. The effectiveness of this committee system of cabinet depended in general on the basic dynastic policy, the ruler's willingness to delegate power to the cabinet, and the absence of obstruction from the Inner Court. During early T'ang, for instance, when the emperors were able and shared a sense of strong group solidarity with cabinet officials who came from the hereditary aristocracy of the metropolitan region, the system worked reasonably well.[34] During the Sung, when the hereditary aristocracy was a thing of the past and when the primary concern of the dynasty was to prevent the revival of regional militarism and the usurpation of power by civil and military officials, the cabinet as a committee fell a victim to its built-in system of checks and balances. Generally speaking, autocracy and a strong cabinet system were incompatible.[35]

[32] Lao Kan, "Lun Han-tai ti nei-ch'ao yü wai-ch'ao," final remark on p. 267.

[33] The basic difference between the premier system of the early years of Former Han and the committee system that characterized post-Han cabinet structure is thoroughly discussed in Ch'ien Mu, *Chung-kuo li-tai cheng-chih te-shih* [The Merits and Demerits of Chinese Governmental System during Various Dynasties] (Hong Kong, 1952), *passim.*

[34] Ch'en Yin-k'o, *T'ang-tai cheng-chih-shih shu-lun kao* [Studies on the Political History of the T'ang Period] (Chungking, 1943), Part I, especially concluding remarks on pp. 36–37.

[35] To be sure, there were in post-Han times a number of cases in which the cabinet did have policy-making function and even a strong leader reminiscent

During much of the period roughly from 300 to 700 A.D., the political influence and social prestige of the hereditary aristocracy had somewhat constricted the practice, though not the ideal, of the autocratic system of government. The historical trend in the past millennium, however, was the intensification of autocracy, which reached an all-time peak in early Ming. Between 1368 and 1380 the Ming cabinet was organized after the Western Han model of premier system. In 1380 the Ming founder did away with the cabinet entirely and doggedly tried to run the government personally. Rare statistics show that in an eight-day period from 29 September to 6 October, 1384, there were 1,660 memorials dealing with 3,391 govenment matters submitted to him.[36] This killing burden of government made it necessary for him to create a personal secretariat to help with the sorting of memorials and the drafting of imperial rescripts. Although in due course this secretariat became a de facto cabinet, it became increasingly circumscribed by the Inner Court composed of eunuchs. The Ch'ing cabinet system was much better institutionalized. Briefly, the Grand Secretariat handled administrative problems of regular and routine nature, and the Grand Council, which was created in 1729, participated in the deliberation of confidential matters. But it was an unmistakable sign of intensified autocracy that all confidential memorials were delivered direct to the Emperor in the palace and that they were not shown to grand council-

---

of the chancellor of the early years of Former Han. Wang An-shih (1021–86) and Chang Chü-cheng (1525–82) are outstanding examples. Wang's virtual "premiership" was due entirely to the wholehearted support of the Shen-tsung emperor, who felt an urgent need for systematic reform, in order to revitalize the empire. This was clearly a case of delegation of power by the ruler. That Chang Chü-cheng was able to take up real leadership in the cabinet and to carry out a series of useful administrative reforms was accounted for largely by his ability and by his skill at cultivating a harmonious working relationship with the chief eunuch, Feng Pao, who dominated the Inner Court. In fact, these and a few other similar cases rather help to deepen our understanding of the basic fact that power could be derived only from its ultimate source, namely, the emperor, not from the cabinet itself. For Wang, see Ch'i Hsia, *Wang An-shih pien-fa* [The Reforms of Wang An-shih] (Peking, 1958) and James T. C. Liu, *Reform in Sung China: Wang An-shih and His New Policies* (Cambridge, Mass., 1959); for Chang, see Chu Tung-yün, *Chang Chü-cheng ta-chuan* [Biography of Chang Chü-cheng] (Wuhan, 1957), especially chaps. 7 and 8.

[36] *Ming T'ai-tsu shih-lu* [Veritable Records of Ming Emperors, T'ai-tsu] (Kiansu Sinological Library photostat ed.), chap. 165, p. 3a. The dates are converted from the Chinese lunar calendar.

lors until after they had been perused by the Emperor. From a recent detailed study of types of Ch'ing memorials and their different procedures and channels of transmission, it is quite clear that Ch'ing emperors held the helm of government in their own hands and that both the Grand Secretariat and the Grand Council were the Emperor's personal secretariats rather than policy-making cabinets.[37]

Yet another sign of intensified autocracy was the secret services of the Ming and the secret memorial system of the Ch'ing. It is true that as early as 91 B.C. the office headed by the *ssu-li chiao-wei* (Colonel of Censure), who was empowered "to seize practitioners of witchcraft and investigate important treacherous elements," was already Emperor Wu's secret service, and brought death to thousands including the heir apparent.[38] Even in the much more humane Northern Sung period there was the *huang-ch'eng-ssu* (Palace Guard Commission), which employed agents provocateurs to trap critics of government policy.[39] But these were dwarfed by such Ming secret services as the *chin-i-wei*, literally "embroidered-uniform guard" or the emperor's special *gendarmerie*, and its special torture chamber called *chao-yü*, and the special intelligence services, *t'ung-ch'ang* (Eastern Depot) and *hsi-ch'ang* (Western Depot), headed by eunuchs.[40] Although the Ch'ing brought an end to these appalling secret services, from 1693 onward the K'ang-hsi emperor instructed a few of his confidants to send secret memorials, in which to report on the behavior of certain officials, direct to him in the palace. During the Yung-cheng period (1723–35) the secret memorial system became more general and the employment of ad hoc secret agents kept the Emperor well informed about the conducts of high officials and cases of administrative laxity at practically all levels.[41] With the creation of the chancery of palace memorials during the

[37] Silas Hsiu-liang Wu, "The Memorial Systems of the Ch'ing Dynasty, 1644–1911," *Harvard Journal of Asiatic Studies*, 27 (1967).

[38] Wang Yü-ch'üan, "An Outline of the Central Government of the Former Han Dynasty," pp. 156–61.

[39] James T. C. Liu, *Reform in Sung China*, pp. 89–90.

[40] A detailed treatment of Ming secret services in the broadest sense is Ting I, *Ming-tai t'e-wu cheng-chih* [Government by Secret Services during Ming Period] (Peking, 1951); also Charles O. Hucker, "Governmental Organization of the Ming Dynasty," pp. 11, 25, 60.

[41] This is my impression gathered from sampling the 60 *ts'e* of selected rescripts of the Yung-cheng emperor, *Yung-cheng chu-p'i yü-chih*, and other collections of his edicts and decrees, such as *Shang-yü nei-ke* and *Shang-yü pa-ch'i*.

reign of Chia-ch'ing Emperor (1796–1820), the system by which all memorials of personal and confidential nature were submitted directly to the throne was further regularized.[42] The Ch'ing palace-memorial system, therefore, served in part the purpose of secret intelligence, although it was less obtrusive and much subtler than those of the Ming. Besides, several literary inquisitions in the latter half of the seventeenth and particularly in the eighteenth century struck such terror in the hearts of officials and scholars that they became ideologically strictly conformist, at least outwardly.

Two thousand years of autocracy and five and a half centuries of intensified autocracy could not fail to leave its mark on modern China. As has been shown, the traditional Chinese government usually gravitated toward the ruler; even when the functions and power of the cabinet were well defined, the ruler could bypass it by creating a small informal or partially institutionalized Inner Court. To a certain extent, this remains true in modern times. In principle, the cabinet of the Nationalist government during its twenty-two years on the mainland was always the Executive Yüan, the policy-making power of which was well defined. To those who know the inner working of the Nationalist government, however, the Executive Yüan was on most occasions little more than Chiang Kai-shek's shadow. What relatively little policy-making power it retained was frequently undermined by the Personal Secretariat of the Chairman of the Military Affairs Commission, which in a sense may be regarded as Chiang's Inner Court in modern disguise. Further in keeping with the tradition of intensified autocracy, the Nationalist government created in the 1930's a number of secret services which in 1938 were metamorphosed into two, namely, the Central Intelligence and Statistical Bureau (commonly known by its abbreviation *chung-t'ung*) and the Intelligence and Statistical Bureau of the Military Affairs Commission (*chün-t'ung*).[43] That the working and the spirit of the Nationalist government on the island of Taiwan still bear some resemblance to those of the traditional imperial state scarcely needs elaboration.

While the actual working of the cabinet of the Nationalist government has always been profoundly affected by the whims of one strong man, the present Communist regime in mainland China has taken pains to define and institutionalize the functions of vital organs of the

[42] Silas Wu, "The Memorial Systems of the Ch'ing Dynasty, 1644–1911."

[43] Ch'en Shao-chiao (Major Ch'en, pseudonym), *He-wang lu* [Records of Black Rackets] (Hong Kong, 1965), *passim*.

state, also a characteristic of better organized dynasties of the past. (This partially explains why the current political struggle is so protracted.) Although it is impossible at our present stage of knowledge to describe accurately the inner working of the Peking government at its very apex, it seems fairly evident that the State Council, with its Premier and Vice-Premiers and a large number of ministries and special committees, is only the highest executive or administrative branch of the government. While it has often been called the cabinet, it is not the ultimate policy-making organ. The real policy-making organ is the Politbureau of the Chinese Communist Party (CCP) which strictly speaking is not a government but a party organ. Its current membership totals sixteen, of whom a mere seven constitute its all-powerful Standing Committee. From what relatively little we can verify, the chairman of the Standing Committee of the Politbureau, Mao Tse-tung, has been its dominant figure and hence the main architect of China's vital policies. To be sure, the immensity and complexity of administrative problems of a country as large and teeming as China makes the present regime much less monolithic than is usually believed. But the recurrent ideological-rectification campaigns and the relentless organization, both of which reach the nation at its grassroots and for which imperial China could offer no parallel,[44] have made the Chinese state more authoritarian than ever before. In this sense, the historical trend of intensification of autocracy, which started unmistakably from the founding of the Ming in 1368, is going on at an accelerated pace. While the Maoist ideology and the unprecedented power of organization are distinctly new wine, this new wine is contained in a two-thousand-year-old bottle of authoritarianism.

IV

If the passive aspects in the Confucian theory of political and social relationships were a servant of the traditional Chinese state, Confucius nevertheless turned out to be its tutor insofar as the theory of social equity was concerned. As will be shown, the central tenet of Confucius'

[44] Although available data does not enable us to know the inner working of the subcounty grassroots control apparatus during all major periods of Chinese history, I tend to believe that it is in the organization for controlling the nation at its grassroots that the Communist regime is incomparably more effective than the traditional government. The Communist aptitude for mass organization and mass control is so strikingly new that I feel it superfluous to trace in detail historical precedents. This is why Professor Franz Schur-

theory of social equity, especially his proposed means by which to bring about social equity, still guides the Chinese Communist state amid a full-scale transformation of the Chinese society.

The point of departure of the Confucian theory of social equity is that all things, including human beings, are by nature unequal. That men differ in intelligence, ability, and moral character is taken for granted by Confucius and his chief exponents. The Confucian concept of a natural hierarchy of men thus fitted in nicely with the feudal hierarchy of the times. Yet, on the other hand, Confucius and his exponents all realized that the feudal order which had long been in process of decay could be salvaged only when the injustice inherent in it was effectively redressed. Confucius found that the natural hierarchy of men, based on differences in intelligence, ability, and moral character, came into direct conflict with the feudal hierarchy, based on status at birth. An effective way to rationalize the hierarchical society, as Confucius suggested, was to select members of the ruling class on the basis of individual merit. But under feudalism most men, including many who were naturally gifted, lacked the opportunity for education. Confucius' proposal was therefore to offer the high and the low equal opportunities for education, for only thus could superior men be distinguished and selected from the rest and recruited for government service. Hence Confucius' immortal saying: "In education there should be no class distinctions." When it is remembered that up to his lifetime education had practically been a monopoly of the hereditary feudal aristocracy, Confucius, who endeavored to implement his doctrine by offering equal instruction to all his disciples irrespective of their social origin, should indeed be credited with the first step toward social and intellectual emancipation. While upholding a hierarchical society, he and his followers concerned themselves with the means to tackle its inherent injustice and bring about social equity mainly through education. This is why the true spirit of Confucian social ideology transcends feudal boundaries and has remained useful long after the breakup of the feudal system. Though Confucius and his followers were attempting to perpetuate the feudal system, they actually heralded the arrival of a new social order, based not on hereditary status but on individual merit.[45]

mann's *Ideology and Organization in Communist China,* quite aside from its extensive documentation and analytical acumen, should take on special significance.

[45] This subsection on the influence of Confucian social ideology on education and social mobility is taken freely from my book, *The Ladder of Success*

Since a certain amount of social equity and social circulation could only contribute to the stabilization of society, the traditional Chinese state during the long imperial age did attempt to implement by stages the true spirit of Confucian social ideology—witness the recommendation system and the founding of the Imperial Academy and of some local schools in Western Han, the permanent institutionalization of the competitive civil-service examination system from early T'ang onward, and the establishment after the founding of the Ming of a rudimentary but nationwide state-school and scholarship system. Wherever state effort fell short, the nation itself carried on. We need mention only the beginnings in Sung times of private academies and clan charitable schools which underwent mushrooming growth throughout Yüan, Ming, and Ch'ing, and the establishment after the founding of the Ming of local community schools. While private academies usually dealt with higher education, clan charitable schools and community schools were concerned exclusively with primary education. Consequent upon the examination and school systems, the political monopoly of the early T'ang aristocracy was broken up after the late seventh century, the Sung society became distinctly more open and mobile, and the Ming period on the whole offered more chances for commoners of above average intelligence and determination to ascend the social ladder than probably all previous dynasties. It was not until Ch'ing times that the opportunity-structure in socioacademic mobility for commoners drastically declined, owing mainly to the natural advantages enjoyed by members of official and rich families and especially to the increasingly acute academic competition caused by fixed or reduced quotas for various academic degrees and by sustained and unprecedented growth of population. This drastic shrinkage of the opportunity-structure for commoners seems to have accounted in part for the increasing social unrest and revolutions that have characterized nineteenth- and twentieth-century China.

The abolition of the time-honored examination system in 1905 and the accompanying decay of the traditional school system, the inadequate number of modern schools and their expensiveness as compared to the traditional, not to mention political anarchy and disintegration of the old order, have further narrowed the opportunities of social advancement for the majority of the nation. Although systematic data for elite mobility during the early Republican and the Nationalist periods

in *Imperial China: Aspects of Social Mobility, 1368–1911* (New York: Columbia University Press, 1962).

are unavailable, a perusal of *Who's Who in China* and other desultory biographical literature seems to suggest that rather few prominent Chinese of the early Republican and Nationalist periods originated from truly humble families—with the exception of some army men who rose from the ranks. For all Dr. Sun Yat-sen's admiration for the social equity embodied in the traditional examination system, the power elite of the Nationalist government and party was largely closed to outsiders. The increasing social inequity and the accentuation of the historical trend of shrinking opportunity-structure seems to have been one of the reasons for the vehemence and persistency of the revolutionary movement which culminated in the Communist victory in 1949.

The Chinese Communist movement, which has derived its strength first from the peasantry and then from the proletariat, seems to have ushered China into a chapter of social mobility on a scale entirely unprecedented. This can be conveniently surmised from the present mainland educational system. Detailed up-to-date statistics on mainland schools and school population are unavailable. If, in spite of minor inaccuracies and irregularities, the age data of the 1953 census are any guide, then boys and girls of the age group from 7 to 19 constitute slightly less than 25 per cent of the total population,[46] which is currently believed to be in the neighborhood of 700,000,000. Since school age begins at 7, this group of some 170,000,000 may roughly be regarded as one of school age. As a recent Canadian journalist reports, "It is estimated [that] there are 150 million Chinese attending school, not including part-time students."[47] However interpreted, these rough figures indicate that mainland China is rapidly approaching universal education. It is true that the main problems are the generally poor quality of a vast number of rural schools and the limited facilities for secondary and higher education, but education at all levels is highly competitive and based on academic merit, save for a very few institutes of higher learning where political ideology is a primary criterion for admission. In addition, the Peking government has earnestly been trying to help young people of proletarian origin to go through university. This can best be indicated by a speech made by one of the vice chancellors of the National Peking University on the occasion of the sixtieth anniversary of its founding on May 4, 1958. He revealed that although students of

[46] John S. Aird, *The Size, Composition, and Growth of the Population of Mainland China* (U.S. Bureau of Census, 1961), p. 66.

[47] Richard Harrington, "Young China: Is This Tomorrow's Enemy?" *Parade Magazine* (*Chicago Sun-Times*), June 5, 1966, p. 5.

peasant and working-class origin already constituted a significant 19.5 per cent of the entire student body, their drop-out rates were considerably higher than those of students of bourgeois origin. He therefore made a plea that more lenient academic standards be adopted and more financial aid be provided for them so that their proportion in the total enrollment could be rapidly increased.[48] It is likely that in recent years this policy may have applied to other universities and colleges. Against this background we may find a rationale underlying the otherwise chaotic "Great Proletarian Cultural Revolution."

It seems a historical irony that while Confucianism has been vehemently attacked by twentieth-century Chinese radicals and Communists, it is under the Communist rule that the Chinese society is approaching the ultimate Confucian goal that "in education there should be no class distinctions." Even mainland Chinese children's main worry of "academic failure,"[49] as a highly-trained Canadian child psychiatrist has observed, is typically traditional and Confucian. To further facilitate mass education, the Peking regime has taken steps to cope with China's most important cultural heritage—the written language. Since the inordinate difficulty involved in learning the written language has been a main cause of mass illiteracy, Peking has simplified an increasing number of written characters and hopes to carry out by stages phoneticization of the Chinese language. As is well known, the initial simplification of hundreds of more commonly used written characters has already helped in the nationwide campaign to wipe out illiteracy.

Twenty-five centuries of Confucius' teaching, much of which deals with human relations, psychology, and education, cannot fail to influence present-day China in a yet more important way. While it is true that all Communist states realize the importance of education as an instrument to bring about ideological and social changes, none has gone as far as Communist China in regarding education as the very pivot of total social transformation. Certainly no other Communist state has worked out more sophisticated psychological techniques and more relentless organization with which to carry out thought reform and brainwashing on a mass scale.

[48] *Hsin-hua pan-yüeh k'an* [New China News Agency Fortnightly], no. 11, 1958: 121–24.

[49] Denis Lazure, "The Cheerful Children of Red China's Communes," *MacLean's Magazine*, March 11, 1961.

Even more fundamental than redressing the social inequity of feudal China, education in the form of intellectual and moral instruction was viewed by Confucius as the sole long-range effective means to improve human environmental influence, which in turn would shape man's character. The philosophical point of departure is Confucius' theory of human nature, which is best described in his own words: "In their original natures men closely resemble each other. In their acquired practices they grow wide apart."[50] That Confucius' theory of human nature does not give a clear-cut answer as to whether human nature is originally good or evil ought not to concern us here. What is of abiding importance is the implication of its second sentence—that practices acquired from different human environments account eventually for the shaping of different moral characters. Hence Confucius' stress on the selection of neighborhood[51] and the Western Han legend that Mencius' mother had changed her domicile thrice before her son began to amend intellectually and morally, a legend which, through its perpetuation and integration with Confucian theories of human nature and of human environment in a primer universally used in schools since the thirteenth century, must have exerted incalculable influence over the Chinese during the past seven hundred years.[52] According to Confucius, the only way to improve human environmental influence is through education in the broadest sense, which includes both intellectual and moral instruction. Such is the power of education, as Confucius believes, that it can change the thoughts, conducts, and characters of all except a relatively few of superb intelligence and wisdom (who no longer need ordinary instruction to think and act properly) and the truly stupid and retarded.[53] Implied in the Confucian theories of human

[50] Feng Yu-lan, *A History of Chinese Philosophy,* trans. Derk Bodde, 2 vols. (Peiping: Henri Veteh, 1937), 1:75.

[51] *The Chinese Classics,* vol. 1, *Confucian Analects,* trans. James Legge (Hong Kong, 1861), bk. 4, chap. 1.

[52] Legends about Mencius' mother's careful selection of neighborhood had arisen during Former Han times at the latest, because they are told in *Han-shih wai-chuan* and Liu Hsiang's *Lieh-nü chuan.* See *Meng-tzu i-chu* [Annotations on the Works of Mencius] (Department of Chinese, Lanchow University, Hong Kong, 1965), vol. 1, Introduction. These legends were later perpetuated in the *San-tzu ching,* the authorship of which is attributed to the great encyclopedist Wang Ying-lin, 1223–96. Herbert A. Giles, in the preface to his translation, *San Tzu Ching* (New York, 1963 reprint), says: "It is the foundationstone of a Chinese education." The view that human nature is originally good is, of course, not Confucius' own but that formulated by Mencius.

[53] *Analects,* bk. 17, chap. 3.

nature and human environment is, therefore, a basic Confucian optimism and confidence in man's ability to improve human environment and hence also man's character—a contrast to the reliance of various religions on God. So profound and persistent has been this influence of Confucius that during the past millennium famous Chinese writers on human, family, and clan affairs, however much they might otherwise be susceptible to religions and superstitions, unanimously took this down-to-earth Confucian theory of human environment as the basic explanation for the rise and fall of individual and family fortunes.[54]

Besides, Confucius and his exponents throughout the ages all took special pains to understand, and succeeded in gaining deep insight into, human psychology.[55] The following observation made by an American psychiatrist who has interviewed Chinese intellectual refugees in Hong Kong is worth noting:

> Chinese culture has—possibly at the expense of technological advance—always emphasized the *human* aspects of life, and particularly the nuances of personal relationships. Children are taught to be sensitive to psychological currents about them, in order to learn how to behave appropriately toward others. In the educated adult, this sensitivity is expected and required. Most Chinese intellectuals whom I knew, as subjects or as friends, impressed me with their consistent skill in perceiving the emotion at play between one person and another, as well as their tendency to make use of this understanding in seeking their life objectives. They conducted human relationships as one practices a highly refined art. In this sense, I believe that thought reform could be viewed as the totalitarian expression of a national genius.[56]

The techniques and processes used in brainwashing in order to achieve catharsis-like effects are well known. What remains to be explained is why the repeated nationwide thought-reform movements are conducted through small "study groups." Even this is due to a peculiarly Chinese heritage of social institutions and of methods of intellectual discourse. As Professor Franz Schurmann has pointed out, "The Chinese Communists have also taken advantage of certain traditional behavior patterns, most important of which are the strong associative

[54] See my *Ladder of Success in Imperial China,* chap. 4.

[55] Feng Yu-lan, *A History of Chinese Philosophy,* 1:75.

[56] Robert J. Lifton, "Brainwashing in Perspective," *New Republic,* May 13, 1957, p. 25.

tendencies of the Chinese."[57] Outside of the basic social unit of family, there has been the modern-type patrilineal clan, which first came into being in 1050 and which became more and more common during Ming and Ch'ing, especially in the southern provinces. There have also been neighborhood and village organizations, guilds, and various *Landsmann* groups, which first appeared in early Ming and became increasingly common in all parts of China in Ch'ing times. While all these organizations transcend biological ties, they have nevertheless offered their members a face-to-face intimacy that usually characterizes primary social associations. Supplementing the family and the clan, they have provided the Chinese with a much-needed sense of belonging, helped them to settle disputes between individuals, families, and occupations, and performed an important function of educating them on the art of getting along with their fellow men and of understanding and satisfying each other's emotional and psychological needs.

The serious traditional Chinese intellectual discourse was, as a rule, conducted through small groups. It is highly probable that the *Analects* is basically a summary of various small group discussions presided over by Confucius and a few of his important disciples. The *Book of Mencius* is essentially of a similar nature. We can see more clearly the perpetuation of the method of an intellectual and philosophical discourse through small groups in the collected works of various Sung and Ming Neo-Confucian philosophers who gave rise to and lectured in private academies. Even in Ch'ing times, when private academies in general shifted their intellectual interest from philosophy to techniques of literary composition, not a few famous ones kept alive the Sung-Ming tradition of serious intellectual dialogue through small groups. In fact, so strong has been the tradition of small group discussion that it played a central role in the political indoctrination program instituted by the Nationalist party.

Thus, from Confucius' guarded optimism in man's ability to improve human environment and man's character, the Chinese Communists have developed an unshakable faith in the omnipotence of man to remold man's mind; from the nation's cumulative fund of skill in handling human relations, the Chinese Communists have perfected the sophisticated psychological techniques of thought reform; and from the highly useful role which various small associations have played in the life of the people and from the traditional methods of intellectual dis-

[57] "Organization and Response in Communist China," *Annals of the American Academy of Political and Social Science,* January, 1959, p. 59.

course, the Chinese Communists have instituted nationwide small "study groups" as the most effective long-range means to bring about total social transformation.[58]

V

In discussing China's economic heritage there is less need to go very far back. This is because in the course of China's long history its economy underwent several periods of remarkable expansion but also suffered many serious setbacks. Only certain salient features of China's economy during the recent and relatively recent past have a more direct bearing on the present.

First, as has been pointed out briefly in Section II of this paper, and discussed more systematically in my *Studies on the Population of China, 1368–1953,* the existence of unusually favorable economic and institutional factors during the century following the dawning of *Pax Sinica* in 1683 brought about a population explosion that created a set of new economic problems with which China's existing fund of technological knowledge failed to cope. That present-day China's most pressing economic problem is overpopulation and mass poverty—a phenomenon which had come into full play by 1850 at the latest—is too well known to require further discussion.

Second, while much of the present Chinese economy is yet to be fully modernized, there is little doubt that China is at least an economic entity. That China, a country so large and so varied, has become an economic entity is the result of centuries of inter-regional economic integration. Although it is true that the various geographic regions of China tended to integrate to a certain extent during practically all periods of political unification, the work of integration that had taken place during a certain dynasty was often offset by the effect of war and political division of a following period. It was from the founding of the Ming in 1368 that the work of inter-regional economic integration has become most noticeable and consistent, despite brief interruptions caused by large-scale peasant rebellions in the middle of the seventeenth

[58] Coincidentally, the key Chinese Communist slogan and movement of *"hsüeh-hsi,"* literally "to study and to practice," is precisely what Confucius advocated (*Analects,* bk. 1, chap. 1). The aims of Confucius' education are, of course, entirely different from those of the Communists. For a good etymological discussion of bk. 1, chap. 1 of the *Analects* which refutes Chu Hsi's commentary, see Yang Po-chün, *Lun-yü i-chu* [Annotations on Confucian Analects] (Peking, 1958), p. 2.

century, by the Taiping and Nien wars of the mid-nineteenth century, and by the recent Sino-Japanese war.

There are convenient "indices" with which to gauge the work of inter-regional economic integration in Ming-Ch'ing and modern times. From the late sixteenth century to the 1840's, the Jesuits, who had the rare opportunity of observing and comparing China and Europe at first hand, were unanimously impressed by the greater volume, frequency, and consistency of the inter-regional trade and commerce in China as opposed to that in contemporaneous Europe. While much of their description referred to the vast Yangtze region of rivers, lakes, and canals, they were equally struck by the "astonishing multitudes" of men, asses, mules, carts, and wheelbarrows that were engaged in the inter-local and inter-regional trade in the landlocked North China.[59] And the Jesuits' impressions are corroborated by more detailed findings of Japanese and Chinese economic historians on several important regional merchant groups who in Ming-Ch'ing times carried trade to practically every corner of the vast country.[60]

By far the most systematic set of indices is the records on various *Landsmann* organizations. From the early fifteenth century onward, there came into being in Peking various types of voluntary associations based on common geographic origin. By the late sixteenth and early seventeenth centuries, *Landsmann* halls established by merchants and craftsmen of various geographic origins began to appear in major cities and prosperous towns of the lower Yangtze. They became much more widespread and they greatly multiplied during the Ch'ing. In the lower-Yangtze city of Soochow, for example, there were in Ch'ing times forty-one *Landsmannschaften* which can be identified from recently published inscriptions and many more trade and craft guilds established by various *Landsmann* groups who came from practically all parts of China. By late Ch'ing and early Republican period, the city of Hankow alone had as many as fifty-two *Landsmannschaften* and *Landsmann* guilds, not to mention scores of merchant and craft associations whose precise geographic origins cannot be identified but which are likely to have been established by non-natives. In my recent book *Chung-kuo hui-kuan shih-lun* (An Historical Survey of *Landsmannschaften* in

[59] See my *Studies on the Population of China, 1368–1953*, chap. 9, sec. 1.

[60] Notably the study of Hui-chou merchants in Ming times by Fujii Hiroshi, "Shinan shōnin no kenkyū" [Studies of Hui-chou Merchants], *Tōyō gakuhō*, 36–38, and Fu I-ling, *Ming-Ch'ing shih-tai shang-jen chi shang-yeh tzu-pen* [Merchants and Commercial Capital during Ming-Ch'ing Times] (Peking, 1956).

China),[61] it is shown that by late Ch'ing times *Landsmannschaften* existed in Peking, all provincial capitals, dozens of major and minor coastal and inland ports, and many obscure inland counties noted neither for their trade nor craft. The highest density is found in the upper-Yangtze province of Szechwan, where practically every county had at least a few *Landsmann* halls and temples established by immigrants from afar and some counties had as many as forty or fifty.

In Szechwan and elsewhere in major cities where detailed local-history and new inscriptional data are available, we learn that various *Landsmann* groups tended to merge into what in modern terms may be called chambers of commerce, and to take part in matters concerning the welfare of the entire local community. Constant contacts between various *Landsmann* groups and natives often resulted in intermarriage and brought about social assimilation as well. Contrary to the impressions of Western and Japanese scholars that the prevalence of *Landsmann* organizations in Ch'ing times reflected an unusually strong local particularism in China, and has hence retarded the modernization of Chinese economy and society, the existence of thousands of *Landsmann* organizations in all parts of China and the coexistence of various *Landsmann* groups in the same major and minor cities could not but have facilitated inter-regional economic and social integration—a process which went on apace even during the late Ch'ing and early Republican period of political disintegration. Without centuries of inter-regional economic integration, modern China would not have been an economic entity.

Third, by far the most immediate economic heritage was the growth of the government-controlled modern sectors of the economy during the twenty-two years of Nationalist rule on the mainland, a period which has been called bureaucratic capitalism by leftist Chinese writers.[62] It is true that state control of sectors of the economy dates back to Ch'in-Han times. From the late second century B.C. onward the minting of coins was made a state monopoly and in late Sung, Yüan, and early Ming times the state had also the exclusive right of issuing

[61] Taipei, 1966.

[62] The amount of leftist Chinese literature on "bureaucratic capitalism" is quite considerable, but its raw data are all based on official figures released by the Nationalist government. Unless otherwise noted, much of the data and facts given herein is based on Meng Hsien-chang, *Chung-kuo chin-tai ching-chi-shih chiao-ch'eng* [Economic History of Modern China for Class Use] (Shanghai, 1951) and *Chung-kuo chin-tai kuo-min ching-chi-shih chiang-i* [Economic History of the Modern Chinese Nation] (Hupei University, 1958).

paper currency. The range of state-monopolized or state-controlled industries and trading varied from one period to another and peak state
activity was reached in the latter half of Western Han and during the
administration of the Sung statesman Wang An-shih (1069–74; 1075–
76). But the Ming-Ch'ing period as a whole witnessed a shrinkage of
governmental control and a tremendous expansion of the private sector of the economy. This tendency became clearer during late Ch'ing,
when under Western impact the government loaned a part of the
capital to merchants for the establishment of a few modern private
enterprises which, owing to the government loan, were in principle
managed by the government. The political anarchy of the early Republican era and the circumstances during and immediately after World
War I provided opportunities for private enterprises to expand significantly, especially in banking and in such light industries as textiles and
flour-milling.

Soon after its inception, the Nationalist government in 1928 established the Central Bank and exerted such strong pressure to bear on
three major private banks that they became virtually government
banks. These major banks were the government's main agencies for
speculative activities, particularly for selling government bonds at
sharp discounts from their face value and for high-cost credit. In the
early 1930's they also gained control of the once flourishing textile industry of lower Yangtze, then suffering from the Great Depression. The
nationalization of silver in 1935 further gave them the exclusive right
of issuing bank notes.

After the outbreak of the Sino-Japanese War in July, 1937, the Nationalist government established various new agencies by which to
monopolize the trading in silk, tea, cotton, cotton yarns and fabrics,
t'ung oil, hog bristles, tungsten, antimony, tin, mercury, etc. Moreover,
the National Resources Commission, government arsenals, and several
ministries owned or dominated most of the significant modern-type industries in areas not occupied by the Japanese. Although the war
period witnessed a mushrooming growth of private industries in the
southwest and northwest, most of them were small and even the larger
ones could not compete against the government-controlled enterprises,
which enjoyed various advantages. A leading Chinese newspaper estimated in 1946 that "during the war government capital accounted for
approximately 70 per cent of all the industrial capital."[63] It ought to be
mentioned that the above estimate did not include the portion of the

[63] Cited in Meng, *Chung-kuo chin-tai ching-chi-shih chiao-ch'eng*, p. 237;
date given in *Chung-kuo chin-tai kuo-min ching-chi-shih chiang-i*, p. 444.

capital which was theoretically "private" but actually came from a very few high bureaucrats who enjoyed Chiang Kai-shek's confidence.

Immediately after War War II, the surrender by Japan of publicly and privately owned economic enterprises in wartime Japanese-occupied areas increased the sector of the economy controlled by the Nationalist government even further. In contrast, the more important pre-1937 private industries in major seaports which had suffered severely from the war were decimated by the runaway inflation. The Central Bank index for the period from July 1, 1937, to April 30, 1949, shows that the commodity prices in Shanghai multiplied by 151.73 (10^{12}) times and that the volume of note issue expanded by 1.62 (10^{12}) times.[64]

It ought to be pointed out here that historically the Chinese concept of property was considerably weaker than that of the pre-modern and modern West. This was partly because of the absence of the capitalistic type of institutionalized channels for investment and partly because of the relative insecurity of private property.[65] The rise of the patrilineal clan system and of Neo-Confucianism in Sung times exerted so strong an influence on social customs that during the past millennium it became increasingly common for a man of success to share his property with his brothers and even with collaterals and remoter kin and relatives. The above factors, together with the generally mobile and competitive character of the Sung and post-Sung society, gradually gave rise to a typically fatalistic view that wealth and honor are inconstant.[66] By ruining what little that was left to the private sector of the modern economy and by reducing professional and salaried classes to an economic nonentity, the wartime and post-war inflation further diluted the Chinese concept of property and softened up the country for Communism. With such abuses and evils, bureaucratic capitalism not only dug its own grave but also led imperceptibly to bureaucratic collectivism.

[64] Shun-hsin Chou, *The Chinese Inflation, 1937–1949* (New York: Columbia University Press, 1963), p. 260. The other good treatments on the same subject are Chang Kia-Ngau, *The Inflationary Spiral: The Experience in China, 1939–1950* (Cambridge, Mass.: M.I.T. Press, 1958) and Arthur N. Young, *China's Wartime Finance and Inflation, 1937–1945* (Cambridge, Mass.: Harvard University Press, 1965).

[65] For a detailed discussion, see my *Studies on the Population of China*, pp. 204–207; my *Ladder of Success in Imperial China*, chap. 1, sec. 3.

[66] See my "The Salt Merchants of Yang-chou: A Study of Commercial Capitalism in Eighteenth-Century China," *Harvard Journal of Asiatic Studies*, 17, no. 1–2 (1954) and my "An Historian's View of the Chinese Family System," in *Man and Civilization: The Family's Search for Survival* (New York: Mc-Graw-Hill, 1965), sec. 3.

Comments by Arthur Frederick Wright

The Conference is fortunate indeed to have laid before it this lucid and forceful interpretation of the legacy of Chinese history. Though we approach these great problems from very different backgrounds and research interests, I find myself in broad agreement with Professor Ho's argument. In what follows I do not challenge the main line of interpretation, but offer some restatements and amplifications on the major themes.

On the extension of China's internal frontiers, I would like to add a word on the centuries-long drama of internal colonization and settlement. When one considers the great mountain ranges, the inhospitable lowlands, the formidable rivers of this subcontinent, its settlement takes on the epic quality of the exploits of the Brazilian Bandeirantes or the taming of the North American West. This is what made the late René Grousset speak of the Chinese as "a race of pioneers." It was in this long process that the Chinese developed a remarkable arsenal of techniques for the assimilation of minorities. One of these was the establishment of schools for aborigines which taught simple Chinese and the rudiments of classical learning. The local official made visits of inspection to the school, picked out the best students and had them sent to the capital for further training (indoctrination in the Chinese way of life). The best of these were then returned as officials to their home districts to carry forward the process of acculturation, certain of the superiority of what they had learned over tribal ways and determined to "make good" under the Chinese system. Another was the substitution of Confucian or state-approved Buddhist festivals for native observances, so that the aborigines would be drawn into the orbit of Chinese symbolism. Another was the introduction of the superior technology of Chinese agriculture, demonstrating how much more productive it was than native methods. There were other, harsh and punitive devices, but taken together they constitute a formidable body of techniques for dealing

38

with settlement problems. They are still being drawn on for the handling of the minorities of "Greater China."

I am skeptical about the influence of Taoism on public policy in the Han or later, though we know that monarchs of all ages were susceptible to the appeal of Taoism as a personal faith or body of arcane knowledge. Looking at the "Annals" of Emperor Wen and Emperor Hsüan, one finds them to have been wise, able, but *busy* monarchs. And do we need Taoism to account for the laissez faire attitude taken by run-of-the-mine Confucians of all ages? The tension seems to me better understood as between two sets of attitudes and policies, both encompassed in "Confucianism." One was tough-minded, centralizing, insisting on law, the use of force, government action. The other favored decentralized power (leaving it to the great families at the local level), suasion, precedent and the force of custom, minimum intervention by the state, a weak monarch. Both could find yards of Classics to support their position, both were "loyal" to the monarchy, though one would build it up and the other hoped by education and moral suasion to restrain the monarch. It is the tough-minded Confucians of all ages who read Shen Pu-hai for his ideas on the effective use of power, on administrative technique. In the long run of course, it is the tough strain that wins out, though the "soft" Confucians do not easily surrender. I return to this in a later paragraph.

I would be inclined to stress, in the rise of Neo-Confucianism, the zeal, the puritanical attitudes, the intolerance of the revival. (The notion that the Chinese are *always* tolerant, rational, etc., is a myth that dies hard.) The new Confucianism not only updated Confucian thought, it added new imperatives unknown in the more permissive and amorphous Confucianism of earlier centuries. It is the *new* Confucianism that insists on the segregation of sexes and the complete subordination of women. It is the new Confucianism that gradually develops the concept of loyalty from what it was—a relationship ultimately determined by the conscience of the subject—into what it became— an imperative to unquestioning and total subordination to any ruler, however idiotic or amoral he might be. The new Confucianism was more totalitarian in intent than the old had been, in that it gave the monarch authority to police all private as well as public morals and customs, to extirpate heresy, etc. No wonder that later emperors found in it the justification for gathering to themselves more and more of the power they formerly shared with the literati.

This brings me to another point. The tension between the Inner Court and the Outer Court needs a broader frame of reference than failure to develop a cabinet system. Essentially, the Inner Court consisted of the Emperor and the people who worked for him personally: different groups in different periods, for example, Buddhist monks, eunuchs (T'ang, Ming), imperial princes, empresses, family members, favorites, bond servants (the Manchu Dynasty), etc. The Outer Court consisted of ranking capital officials whatever the changes in rank and nomenclature. The relation between the Inner and the Outer Court was really a tension between the power of the monarch and the power of officialdom. Officials were needed to carry on the complex functions of government, to legitimize imperial power with appropriate symbolism, and to keep the records and fiscal accounting, while their more humble colleagues were performing analogous functions at the local level. The Emperor was needed as cosmic pivot, as the apex of the social and political pyramid, the final arbiter and judge, and as supreme commander in time of war. Neither officialdom nor Emperor could survive without the other, once the basic Han system was established. One could devise a "fever chart" that would show the ebb and flow of power across the years between the Inner and the Outer Court. This would show that the power of the Outer Court was probably at an all-time high in the Northern Sung (960–1127), but that from the Mongol period onward, the balance moved steadily towards the Inner Court, towards monarchical supremacy.[1] The forces that made for such an outcome have been admirably outlined by Professor Ho. Yet one would not be fair to Confucian officials of many generations if one did not say that many fought against this trend with wiles and guile and sometimes with raw courage. Partly this was self-interest—the defense of the power and privilege of the Confucian elite against steady erosion by the Inner Court. But partly it was idealism—the vision of monarch and officialdom working together in harmony for the common good.

On the passing of the Emperor system, I would be inclined to emphasize the many interlocked parts of the millennial system that collapsed along with it. It is true, as Professor Ho points out, that many attitudes have survived, but the end of the imperial system really meant the collapse of a civilization. The Confucian ideology that was so interwoven

[1] A modern parallel is the Gaullist system. The Elysée Palace staff, divided into four organs, works intimately with the President. De Gaulle makes the important policy decisions after memoranda and advice from his staff. Liaison with various ministries is parceled out among the staff who see to it that the appropriate ministers give effect to the policy decisions. The President's annotation on policy papers is "Seen," which parallels the usual Imperial notation on memorials: "Chih-tao-le." Cf. Brian Crozier, *Encounter,* October, 1965, pp. 62–65.

with monarchy went down with it, and the use of Confucianism by ideologues since has the hollow sound of ornamental rhetoric. The two-class society of Emperor and elite at the top and masses of peasants below, eroded by time, now disintegrated into a chaos of warlords, upstarts, new-style entrepreneurs, modern intellectuals, etc. The family, long regarded as the microcosm of the state—the paterfamilias being the analogue of the emperor—disintegrated. Respect for the aged gave way to exaltation of youth. A landslip of such proportions that is so long in coming and comes after centuries of glory and a century of frustration and failure leaves terrible psychic scars. These may account for some of the more extreme xenophobia and other pathological behavior that shows itself in China today.

Comments by Herbert Franke

To comment upon Professor Ho's paper is indeed a hard task. Any reader of his paper will be greatly impressed by its comprehensiveness and perspicacity, combining grasp of detail with insight into the structural patterns of historical development in China. It has proved more or less impossible to do what the present author originally had in mind, that is, to write something like "variations and fugue on a theme by Ho Ping-ti," but it was equally impossible to prepare a whole new composition, for the simple reason that there is hardly any point in Professor Ho's paper where I would have to raise objections or which could be the basis for a basically different presentation of the subject. There remained not much else but to try to supplement Professor Ho's observations with some additional arguments and historical details. It will be seen that most of these tend to stress the *déjà vu* aspect with regard to contemporary Communist China.

The problem of China's multinational character and the treatment of the minorities by the Chinese Communist Party (CCP) government reveal a peculiar Chinese definition of what constitutes a *shao-shu min-tsu*. The third largest minority, according to official sources, is the Hui

(Moslem) group, numbering already in 1953 more than 3,500,000. These Hui are, of course, linguistically and also ethnically pure Chinese (the Turkish-speaking Uighurs are listed separately). In the early twentieth century, particularly in the early years of the Republic, the term Hui meant actually the Turkish-speaking minorities, but contemporary usage makes a national minority out of a religious minority. This is not without precedent in history, apart from the fact that the "professional" clergy like Buddhist and Taoist monks had always been registered apart from the tax-paying population. We find already in the Yüan dynasty this curiously floating attitude to minorities. The famous Chen-chiang census, for example, of the early fourteenth century lists in addition to foreigners with a distinct ethnic character like Mongols, Uighurs, Khitan, etc., also the *Yeh-li-k'o-wen* as a separate group, but these were not a people but a religious group, namely, the Nestorian Christians.[1] It seems that this lack of differentiation between ethnolinguistic and religious groups reflects a tendency in traditional China which makes it difficult to speak of a Chinese nation. This concept is, obviously, of rather recent origin even in Europe and as far as China is concerned the foreign origin of this notion could be seen in the fact that the word *kuo-chia* seems to be a modern coinage. China was in the past a culture, not a nation in the modern sense. Everybody who lived a way of life different from the Han Chinese—and this is exactly what the Moslems did to a certain degree—seems to have been considered as alien, regardless of language and anthropological features. These traditional criteria seem to have survived until today. In traditional China all minorities, whether ethnic or religious, had to submit as far as possible to Chinese cultural values, and acculturation was regarded as one of the paramount duties of the enlightened ruler of the Middle Kingdom. This basic unwillingness to let people of different habits live as they pleased within the boundaries of China proper has effectively influenced the constitution makers of the Republican and the Communist era. In contrast to the Soviet constitution, China never has shown a tendency toward federalism. The state is always, today as throughout more than two millennia, conceived as unitarian. Democratic centralism (Art. 2 of the Chinese People's Republic Constitution) has replaced bureaucratic and monarchic centralism of the past. A state within a state was and still is incompatible with Chinese political thought.

[1] For a detailed discussion of the Chen-chiang census, see A. C. Moule, *Christians in China before the Year 1550* (London: Society for Promoting Christian Knowledge, 1930), pp. 145–65, and the works quoted there.

It is, as Professor Ho has pointed out, true that the Chinese Communists' attitude towards their national minorities is different from the former uncompromising Sinicization policy. This reorientation has had, ironically, some results which show in minority areas sometimes a greater degree of modernity than among the Han majority. Chinese children still have to cope in school with hundreds and thousands of characters, whereas the Thai-speaking Chuang minority has received the blessing of an alphabet. It is significant that the existing national scripts have not been replaced by the Latin alphabet. The Mongolian People's Republic has adopted the cyrillic alphabet, whereas in the Inner Mongolia Autonomous Region the ancient Mongol-Uighur script is still used in spite of its obvious shortcomings. This unexpected traditionalism contrasts sharply with the revolutionary changes brought about in almost every other field of life by the Communists since 1949.

In his section on the ideological foundations of traditional China, Professor Ho has demonstrated the overwhelming influence of Han Confucianism, which itself was strongly tainted by Legalist elements with an admixture of Taoism. The role of "non-action" in this curious mixture of Legalism and Taoism has been correctly described; philosophical Taoism has indeed strong links with Legalism insofar as the idea of "non-action" could be interpreted as the ultimate result of an inexorable functioning of legal measures, but also as the highest state of perfection within an individualistic and quietist philosophy (Taoism as ideological basis for absolutism and dictatorship). It is true as Professor Ho points out that Taoism as a philosophy has not developed constructive political and social ideas. But this statement does perhaps not quite apply to religious Taoism. Taoist religion has been repeatedly in Chinese history used by rebels as the ideological fundament of a "church state," particularly in the second and third centuries A.D. The mere existence of states like those of the Yellow Turbans in Shantung, or of Chang Chio and his followers in Szechwan, shows that Taoism as an organized religion, if not as a philosophy, could be construed as a tool for statecraft.[2] The relentless persecution of these communities

[2] Recently a considerable number of studies has been devoted to religious Taoism and Taoist rebellions, e.g., W. Eichhorn, "Description of the Rebellion of Sun En and Earlier Taoist Rebellions," *Mitteilungen des Instituts für Orientforschung,* 2 (1954): 525–52; "Bemerkungen zum Aufstand des Chang Chio und zum Staat des Chang Lu," 3 (1955): 291–527; H. S. Levy, "Yellow Turban Religion and Rebellion at the End of Han," *Journal of the American Oriental Society,* 76 (1956): 214–27; P. Michaud, "The Yellow Turbans" *Monumenta Serica,* 17 (1958): 47–127; R. A. Stein, "Remarques sur les mouvements de Taoisme politico-religieux au IIe siècle ap. J.-C.," *T'oung Pao,* 50

by the existing, more or less Confucianist authorities could be taken as evidence to what degree the "establishment" of China considered these Taoist rebel states and communities as a potential rival both in power and ideology. Sectarianism as a rebel ideology has a long history in China and its fate had always been determined by the fear of the ruling class that it would lose its monopoly in political thought and education. Also the anti-Buddhist movement must be seen in this context. Chinese history as a whole might well have taken a different course if one or even several of these unorthodox political entities had survived and a sort of politico-religious pluralism had supplanted monocracy. Reluctant coexistence with states regarded as barbarian or illegitimate did not affect the monocratic tradition of China.

Internal opposition as something legal or tolerated was likewise absent throughout Chinese history. There was, of course, room for opposition within the state machinery, with the Censorate as one of its centers. But even the Censorate had in some ways the effect of strengthening authoritarianism.[3] The numerous factionalist struggles at court never had the character of conflicting and basically different alternatives. In other words, conflicting social realities were virtually never at the bottom of political struggles within the metropolitan bureaucracy. This is markedly different from Europe where even before the invention of parliamentary government social forces could find an expression within the existing bodies, social or institutional. And there was, in Europe, always the Christian church and creed where social tendencies could take shape, disguised sometimes, but nevertheless tangible. But in China social realities were seen only in the light of Confucian political thought and never recognized as real factors. Economy, for example, is not a sphere of life with a *Lebensrecht* of its own; wherever possible economic powers developing outside the state machinery are either rigidly controlled or absorbed by the omnipotent state institutions. Accumulation of capital was always viewed with suspicion by the scholar-literati, perhaps because classical Confucianism had no place for wealth and economic success in its system. This again is in sharp

(1963): 1–78. Some general remarks will also be found in V. Y. C. Shih, "Some Chinese Rebel Ideologies," *T'oung Pao*, 44 (1956): 150–226. From all these studies it becomes clear that Taoist sectarianism had a strong potential of political organization, and developed into a definite rival of Confucianism as a state ideology.

[3] The recent study of the Censorate by Charles O. Hucker, *The Censorial System of Ming China* (Stanford, Cal.: Stanford University Press, 1966) demonstrates clearly the ambivalent function of the Censorate as a tool of the authoritarian ruler and as a check upon the ruling group at court.

contrast to Europe in the Middle Ages and the absolutist period where a conspicuous display of wealth was not only tolerated but even an indispensable part of grandeur and prestige.[4] As was befitting a country endowed with few natural riches, Chinese ideologies of all persuasions, not only Confucians, invariably extolled frugality. The modern Communist asceticism in China does, in this respect, follow a tradition which has deeply affected Chinese society.

One could, in this context, also draw attention to the fact that the concept of freedom never played a great role in Chinese civilization. The modern word (tzu-yu) is relatively young, and the term tzu-jan (which one could translate as "self-determination") has a distinctly individualist if not anti-social and even anrachic ring.[5] Tzu-jan was never a concept which lent itself to institutionalization. Eremitism was mostly regarded as something abnormal, permissible only in times of trouble or under barbarian rule. But still more important seems, at least to the present writer, another difference between Occidental and Chinese social thought. The position of law has been incomparably stronger in classical antiquity, particularly in Rome and in medieval Europe, than in China. The vast bulk of Chinese juridical literature and the highly developed systematism of traditional Chinese law cannot obscure the fact that law was regarded (similar to economy) not as an entity in itself and potentially superior even to the ruler, but as a mere governing tool. This does not invalidate Professor Ho's pertinent remarks on the Legalist character of the Chinese state since the Han, but what is important is that the administrator of law never developed into a position comparable to that of the juridically trained adviser who played such a role in early modern history in Europe. It is significant, that apart from some abortive reforms (Wang An-shih), a special training in law was never attempted, and that juridical reasoning, based *solely* on the letter of the law, did not develop. Again and again ideology and ethics, that is, extra-legal considerations tend to appear in juridical texts and documents.[6] In one word, Legalism did not produce a class of jurists in China. Law remained but one of the many-faceted activities of the scholar-official.

[4] For a period roughly coeval with the early Ming, a masterly description of the splendor and open display of wealth may be found in J. Huizinga's classical work *The Waning of the Middle Ages.*

[5] E. Balázs, *Chinese Civilization and Bureaucracy* (New Haven and London: Yale University Press, 1964), pp. 166–67, 247 (n. 25).

[6] This feature is revealed already by Sung collections of legal cases such as the recently republished *Ch'ing-ming chi* (Tokyo, 1964); cf. the review in *Zeitschrift der deutschen Morgenländischen Gesellschaft,* 115 (1965): 433–34.

Regarding the institutional characteristics of the Chinese state, Professor Ho states that "in contrast to the weakness of European monarchies which aided the rise of democracy, the persistent historical fact is that the Chinese state has always derived its ultimate power from the army, and this has largely predetermined its authoritarian character." This predominant role of the army in traditional China has certainly played its part in the founding of a dynasty or in quelling a rebellion. But it might be argued to what extent the state and its institutions rested on the power of the army in normal times. For centuries China's armies were for the greater part stationed at the frontiers and at the capital, and it is by no means sure that the army was the chief guarantee for maintaining peace and order and the existing social structure. At the present time we have not yet a reliable study of the military history of China.[7] Under Manchu rule, the banner garrisons were strategically distributed over the whole empire and therefore constituted a permanently available power tool of the Manchu court and the ruling minority as such. But one would like to know to what extent the army has been a major and omnipresent power factor in the provinces of Sung or Ming China. For in pre-modern times and without fire-weapons (which invariably and automatically give the soldiers power over those who do not have them), the technological equipment of the ruling is not superior to that of the ruled. There was no monopoly on tanks and machine guns in periods where man-to-man fighting could take place with more or less homemade weapons. This line of thought—that is, the problem of how power was maintained against a suppressed majority—belongs to the questions which historians very seldom ask. What is it really that perpetuates a minority rule? What we lack at this moment is a comprehensive and comparative study of the physical mechanism of power and its enforcement. It will perhaps be found that actual force (or, to be more explicit, the use of military power) has been in various civilizations and in past periods a less important factor than others, among which psychological conditioning should be mentioned. These remarks are not meant as a criticism of Professor Ho's thesis, only as the expression of the desirability of research on the lines mentioned.

The ruler cult has been ably and convincingly described by Professor Ho and I am, like him, certain that there is a line of tradition from the almost deified emperor to the present leader cult devoted to Mao

[7] I would like to draw attention to a study by Paul Demiéville where the author gives a clear and detailed account of the Buddhist attitude towards war and the military as such, "Le bouddhisme et la guerre," *Mélanges publiées par l'Institut des Hautes Études Chinoises*, t.1 (Paris, 1957): 347–85.

Tse-tung. The emperor's role as chief and infallible ideological leader is paralleled by the similar role of the party Chairman, and the regular lessons in classical exegesis at court by the meetings of the central committee or the political bureau. Nothing can be added to the poignant and lucid remarks of Professor Ho on the inherent authoritarianism of imperial rule in China.

I equally agree with Professor Ho's description of the role of guilds and similar associations in traditional China. Their function as conflict-settling groups has weakened the state influence on civil law to a considerable extent. Law is, within Chinese tradition, mostly administrative and penal law. And even where civil cases were brought before a mandarin, hierarchical and ideological reasoning prevails over purely legal argumentation. A corollary of this rather inferior position of civil law is the weakness of the concept of property,[8] with the resulting instability of property which was never an absolute right as it has been throughout most periods of Western history. This in turn facilitated downward social mobility, together with the traditional customs of inheritance. "Wealth and honor are inconstant,"[9] partly because there were no lasting safeguards for fortunes except for a rise in the official hierarchy—our understanding of social and economic ups and downs would be much clearer if we knew more about family budgets and commercial enterprise in pre-modern China.[10]

As an economic entity, China—as Professor Ho has pointed out—was much earlier a unity than comparable states in Asia and Europe. This has not only been remarked by the Jesuits in the late sixteenth and seventeenth centuries but much earlier by observers like Marco Polo in the thirteenth, who was deeply impressed by the amount of interregional trade in "Cathay." Without going into the complicated problem of the social and economic class structure of pre-modern China, one parallel between the past and the present should be brought to attention. The concept of "people" has in China never been understood as a conglomeration of individual human beings as such but rather in a certain restrictive way. The word *min* shows a curiously floating sphere

[8] See Wolfgang Bauer, "Die Frühgeschichte des Eigentums in China," *Zeitschrift für vergleichende Rechtswissenschaft,* 63 (1961): 118–84.

[9] See E. Balázs, *Chinese Civilization and Bureaucracy,* pp. 150–51.

[10] The charitable family estates were one of the means landowning gentry used to overcome the inherent instability of property. For a famous case see D. C. Twitchett, "The Fan Clan's Charitable Estate, 1050–1760," in *Confucianism in Action,* ed. D. S. Nivison and Arthur F. Wright (Stanford, Cal.: Stanford University Press, 1959), pp. 97–133.

of connotation in traditional China; it was used often as a negative term (*min* is who is not *kuan*, "official") and also sometimes tacitly understood as meaning a fraction only of the actual population.[11] Today the Marxist-Leninist theory equally seems to favor a restrictive meaning of "people," namely, restricted to the "toiling masses" of the proletariat. In other words, the concept of "citizen," as an individual possessing certain inherent or explicit subjective rights, has no roots in Chinese tradition, nor has the legal protection of social minorities.

A more difficult problem is how far there was authoritarianism present in the Chinese family system. Without going into details, I would like to draw attention to an opinion voiced some time ago to the effect that collectivization on Communist lines in China was not felt as basically different from the lack of individualism and a private sphere within the traditional family system.[12] To consider the People's Communes as merely replacing one collective by another is certainly extreme, but the problem merits discussion in more detail. This cannot be done without delving into social psychology and behavioral patterns, as H. F. Schurmann, quoted by Professor Ho, has done. For traditional and pre-modern China, we have remarkably few materials for a research which would, inter alia, show how actually the "people" reacted and felt towards government authority in general. My personal opinion is, contrary to that of some scholars, that the value of literary fiction must not be overrated, particularly because of the high degree of stylization even in those works where admittedly an anti-governmental attitude or social criticism is displayed. The *real* voice of the "people" has, to my knowledge, never been recorded, and we simply do not know how a peasant or artisan of, say, the Ming period, expressed himself. Everything we know has already been filtered in some way through a literary medium.[13] This makes it difficult to generalize about social motivation

[11] In the thirteenth century Chia Ssu-tao's adversaries complained that the agrarian reform laws had caused resentment among "the people," which can in this context mean only "rich land-owners."

[12] Wolfgang Franke, "Die Rolle der Tradition in heutigen China," *Moderne Welt*, 2 (1961–62): 164.

[13] Even in trials and lawsuits the sources never record the actual speech of defendants, not even when the records are written in colloquial language, as in *Yüan-tien chang* [Statutes of the Yüan]. The gulf between actual speech and written records is in China particularly wide. For the late Middle Ages in Europe we have enough records which have preserved the immediate, undiluted, and unstylized speech of individuals other than upper-class. See, for example, the fascinating *Oxford Book of English Talk* (London: Oxford University Press, 1955).

in the psychological sphere. I am not informed as to what extent modern sociological and psychological research can tell us more about the reactions of individuals towards political and social stress, but the importance of this question remains, and a more or less reliable answer could perhaps also furnish more clues about the effect of a change of regime on the average man.

The basic question is, of course, how the salient aspects of China's heritage affect the recent and contemporary developments. It is at this point that the difficulties of interpretation begin. Any reader of Professor Ho's paper will come to the conclusion that there were quite a number of governmental, ideological, social, and economic tendencies in traditional and pre-modern China which facilitated the acceptance of Communism, or rather, acquiescence and attentiveness. This must not mean that, as Chinese Communist historians would have it, there is a determinism at work which inevitably would lead to Communism. The factors which have favored the Communist takeover (unless we regard Mao's victory as due to a sinister machination of the Kremlin) cannot, either individually or cumulatively, be regarded as determining the course of history as it has developed. The best proof is that hardly anybody in the 1920's and 1930's predicted the ultimate victory of the Communists (except, again, the Communists themselves). A partial answer is perhaps to be found in J. K. Fairbank's statement: "The Confucian monarchy was a peculiarly non-national institution. It rested on a Confucian-Chinese social and cultural base but could be seized and manipulated by barbarian invaders quite as well as by Chinese rebels, sometimes indeed even more easily."[14] This is not to be understood as an expression of the all too facile thesis that the Communists represent only a phase in a quasi-dynastic cycle. But it remains nevertheless significant that Communism has come to power in China and in Russia—that is, in two states with a strong monarchic and authoritarian, absolutist tradition.[15] These traits undubitably survive in China, but others, working in a different direction, may also survive. But it is a probability that these other, non-authoritarian factors of Chinese tradition will remain marginal and that the Communists have brought about a deep

[14] John K. Fairbank, *Trade and Diplomacy on the China Coast* (Cambridge, Mass.: Harvard University Press, 1953), p. 23.

[15] It will be interesting to watch the development of Communism in Cuba, a country which had known something like absolutist rule (Batista) but which was conspicuously lacking in institutional traditions which could be compared to those of Russia or China. Cuba could be a test case of how far Communism can be influenced by the existing infrastructure and developed into something basically different from the brand of Communism in Russia and China.

and drastic deviation from tradition as far as the center of civilization is concerned. The present, "Great Proletarian Cultural Revolution" seems to be aimed at a still stronger deviation from traditional values and the cultural heritage of the past. There seems to be a chance that the features which made the foreign student of China still feel somewhat at home in Communist China will gradually weaken or disappear altogether.[16]

Comments by Derk Bodde

Professor Ho's paper is something of a *tour de force*. Within less than fifty typed pages it surveys a vast span of Chinese history from the point of view of geography and ethnology, demography, political ideology and institutions, social and educational thought, and economics. For each of these broad fields it adduces numerous specific examples on

[16] It remains a matter for discussion to what extent the knowledge of the former state of affairs in a country can be helpful for evaluating its conditions under Communist rule. The "old China hand" will, in many cases, discover much that has remained unchanged, but there is also the danger that in a search for similarities between the past and the present he will tend to overlook the drastic changes that have occurred. Nostalgia for a past state of affairs may produce a tendency to minimize the effects of Communism. One should perhaps not go so far as to say that the intimate acquaintance with a country in its pre-Communist stage must lead to a misjudgement, but we should not forget all those China experts who have maintained that the Chinese will never become Communist because they are "too individualistic" and family-minded. The present writer had personal experience with similar problems regarding Russia and the Soviet Union. The fatal and disastrous failure of Hitler's campaign against the Soviet Union is in no small degree the result of a thoroughly unrealistic image of Russia, largely due to the underestimation of Soviet achievements on the part of Germans from the Baltic countries and Russo-Germans who worked in German *Wehrmacht* staffs. These "experts" spoke Russian perfectly and had known pre-Soviet Russia but had failed to realize that the passive and fatalistic *muzhik* had been replaced by a different type of Russian since 1917.

whose foundation it formulates generalizations which it then proceeds to apply to the modern scene. Probably only a Chinese could approach his country's history so encyclopaedically, and few besides Professor Ho could demonstrate competence in all five fields by citing significant writings in each of them.

Of course Professor Ho knows that by choosing to write with such sweep he inevitably makes himself vulnerable to charges of omission, contradiction, or lack of balance. Though it is my obligation as a commentator to point these out when I think I see them, I do so keenly aware that equal or stronger charges could surely be made against me or any other scholar bold enough to undertake Professor Ho's difficult task.

Geography and Ethnology

Professor Ho is of course thinking in concrete physical terms when he states that the geographical shift from China Proper to "Greater China" really took place only under the Manchus. But I feel that in so saying he underrates the consequences of the great conquests of earlier major dynasties. More than this, however, I think the Manchus should not cause us to forget that long before a "Greater China" physically existed, a *concept* of empire was present in the Chinese mind. Its age-old epitome is the term *t'ien hsia*, "all under Heaven," used to express the concept of an all-embracing Chinese polity coextensive with the civilized world, and from there radiating its civilizing rays upon the darker reaches beyond. A succinct expression of the political side of the idea is found in a saying widely attributed to Confucius:

> Just as the sky has no two suns,
> So the earth has no two rulers.[1]

Historically, Chinese insistence upon the national need for political and cultural oneness contrasts, for example, with its absence in India and points to a major distinction between the two civilizations. Today it may still hold relevance for helping to explain China's attitude toward the outside world.

Coming back to the Manchus, it would seem that their role as con-

[1] The saying appears three times in the *Li chi* or *Book of Rites* (chaps. 5, 27, 46), with direct attribution to Confucius in the first two instances but no attribution in the third. See translation of James Legge in *Sacred Books of the East,* vol. 27, p. 323, and vol. 28, pp. 285 and 467. A fourth citation, again with attribution to Confucius, occurs in *Mencius, Va,* 4, where the second line is slightly modified to read: "So the people have no two rulers."

solidators of "Greater China" places scholars and ideologues in mainland China today in a somewhat anomalous position: on the one hand,
they are called upon to reject Manchu rule in China Proper as imperialistic and reactionary, but on the other, to accept Manchu conquests beyond the Great Wall as legitimate. That the latter is a purely Chinese
and not Marxist judgment is shown by the fact that all Chinese of the
mainland or Taiwan alike agree on China's legitimate suzerainty over
Tibet, even though it was a Manchu and not a Chinese ruler who first
sent troops into Lhasa in the early eighteenth century. I believe this
Conference might have benefited from a session devoted to Chinese
nationalism, past and present.

Professor Ho continues by discussing the Ch'ing policy of Sinicization
of China's ethnic minorities from the 1720's onward, and its possible
present-day parallels. Here I cannot agree with his conclusion that "the
present Peking government's policy toward national minorities is an
amplification rather than a reversal of the traditional." On the one
hand, the exploitative nature of the traditional Sinicization policy is
well known.[2] On the other, we are told by Professor Ho himself that the
present Peking regime has conferred "constitutional rights of self-rule
and regional administrative and cultural autonomy" on its racial
minorities, and has made "some genuine efforts to help them in agriculture, stock-raising, industry, education, public health, and social
reform." I am puzzled why all this should not be called a "reversal"
rather than merely an "amplification" of traditional policy.

Demography

On this topic I shall only call attention to the importance of what
Professor Ho calls the "almost progressive deterioration in the national
standards of living since the late eighteenth century," and express surprise that this Conference has not included a session on population—a
subject to which Professor Ho has made important contributions.

[2] Concerning the Miao tribesmen of Kueichow, we are told by Herold J.
Wiens: "Oppression and extortions by the Han-Chinese bureaucracy had reduced the Miao in 1735 to such a poor state that they undertook the most
desperate measures. . . . The armies of seven provinces crushed the Miao,
massacring 18,000 Miao warriors. . . . During the next half century the Miao
were subjected to further oppression, deception, and misgovernment at the
hands of the Han-Chinese officials. Their better lands were gradually taken
over by Han-Chinese landlords who brought in their own Han-Chinese tenant
farmers. The embittered Miao sought refuge in the sterile lands of the deeper
mountain recesses." (*China's March toward the Tropics* [Hamden, Conn.:
Shoe String Press, 1954], pp. 190–91.)

Political Ideology and Institutions

In this important section, the author's major theme is that of the strongly autocratic nature of imperial Chinese rule. To this I shall return in my conclusion. Here let me say that while agreeing with a great deal of Professor Ho's argument, I would myself prefer an analysis more in terms of broadly based social and institutional configurations, and less in terms of narrower political factors, notably the power relationships between the emperor and his bureaucracy.

I question, for example, how much the author's rather equivocal treatment of the emperor as not really divine yet almost divine really advances the discussion. If autocracy does in fact go with divinity, we would expect to find it best exemplified in Japan, yet as everyone knows, the Japanese emperors were anything but omnipotent.

In discussing the absence of effective institutional checks on autocratic rule, Professor Ho quite properly points to the failure of a real cabinet system to develop in China, and the harmful effects of heavy reliance upon the secret service. Very strangely, he says not a word about a remarkable and uniquely Chinese institution which did, to some extent, impose checks on the abuse of power. I am referring of course to the Chinese Censorate, on which we now have an excellent study in English.[3]

Professor Ho also speaks disparagingly of Confucian failure to devise psychological curbs upon autocracy more effective than the "Mandate of Heaven" theory and the theory of portents of nature. What he disregards is that the main ethical focus of Confucian political philosophy as a whole was always upon the responsibility of officials to provide moral and intellectual guidance for their sovereign, and of the latter to listen to them and strive for enlightened rule. Of course, as in any system relying heavily on moral suasion, injunctions of this sort were often ignored in practice.

It does not seem fair to me, however, to cite as a general pattern for all dynasties the story of about 100 B.C. concerning the Han jurist who followed the wishes of his sovereign rather than the statute books when deciding cases. Professor Ho quite correctly points out that an Emperor could always modify or bypass an old statute by issuing a new edict. I do not think, however, we have to conclude from this that the result was invariably or even usually arbitrary, especially under later dynasties when the whole legal process became more and more institutionalized. My own researches on Ch'ing law point to the development by

[3] Charles O. Hucker, *The Censorial System of Ming China* (Stanford: Stanford University Press, 1966).

then of what I am tempted to call a Chinese kind of "due process," with which the Emperor usually did not interfere. As against the above-mentioned Han jurist, for example, I might cite a legal case of 1796 in which the Chia-ch'ing Emperor, after initially wishing to lighten the penalty for a homicide case, desisted from so doing on being warned by the Board of Punishments that there was no statutory precedent for such action.[4]

In summary, I would not want it to appear that I deny the existence of a strong authoritarianism in traditional China. My difference from Professor Ho lies not in its denial but in definition of its primary characteristics. To this I shall return in my conclusion.

Professor Ho ends his third section by describing the present Peking government's system of organizational controls as a logical outgrowth of a long tradition of autocracy, differing from the past primarily in its infinitely greater effectiveness at the grassroots level. This is true as far as it goes, but I feel it does not go quite far enough. In imperial China an enormous gap traditionally separated the intellectual from the hand worker.[5] The result was that "public opinion" meant primarily the thinking of bureaucrats, landed gentry, and other privileged members of the ruling elite. In China today, however, a major Communist achievement has been the breaking down if not elimination of the traditional gap. Of course the government uses its effective communications channels to pump forth its own version of "public opinion" to the grassroots, but at the same time and via the same channels it is constantly receiving opinion back from the grassroots in a never-ending interchange. Here again, as in the treatment of racial minorities, continuities between past and present should not blind us to discontinuities.

Social and Educational Thought

In this section I feel that Professor Ho has somewhat over-idealized what he calls the Confucian theory of social equity. Like many other translators, he interprets the so-called "immortal saying" of Confucius as meaning: "In education there should be no class distinctions." It is

---

[4] The case is discussed in Derk Bodde and Clarence Morris, *Law in Imperial China* (Cambridge, Mass.: Harvard University Press, 1967), p. 175, and translated on pp. 298–300.

[5] Perhaps the earliest clear enunciation of the gap is in *Mencius*, III *a*, 4: "Some labor with their brains and some labor with their brawn. Those who labor with their brains govern others; those who labor with their brawn are governed by others. Those governed by others, feed them. Those who govern others, are fed by them. This is a universal principle in the world."

far from certain, however, that the four characters of the highly ambiguous original really carried the sweeping connotation now commonly given them. And even if they did, this by no means signifies that education in imperial China was ever seriously intended to reach a significantly broad sector of the population. This would have been impractical in any case, since the civil service, which was the prime user of educated men in traditional China, could never supply jobs to more than a tiny percentage of the total population. Of course there is a sharp contrast here with China today, which Professor Ho finds to be "rapidly approaching universal education." Neither he nor we, however, should see "historical irony" in this fact, for Confucianism and Marx-Leninism are as different in their educational ideals and aims as are the agrarian and industrial environments from which they spring.

In the second part of this section, on the other hand, Professor Ho convincingly demonstrates the exceedingly important psychological continuity between traditional Confucian beliefs in the goodness and perfectability of human nature, and Chinese Communist beliefs in the power of education and example to change the individual's social outlook and behavior. At this point, I doubt whether there is really much similarity between the small-group intellectual dialogues described by Professor Ho as having existed in traditional China, and the various thought-reform techniques used by the Chinese Communists (and also practiced in varying degrees in other Communist states). But it is the underlying philosophical view of human nature which is important here, and Professor Ho deserves much credit for making this clear, especially as it implies something unpalatable to many: the fact that Communism too has a system of moral and spiritual values. The widespread failure of Americans to realize this basic fact probably lies at the heart of our national failure to comprehend the psychological reasons for the appeal of Communism.

Economics

Here I venture only two brief comments: (1) In emphasizing as he does the way in which Kuomintang (KMT) governmental control of much economic enterprise paved the way for Chinese Communist nationalization of private enterprise, does not Professor Ho underemphasize the significance of the long previous history of governmental controls and monopolies in imperial China (possibly traceable, as he himself says, as far back as the seventh century B.C.)? (2) In his discussion of the traditional weakness of the concept of private property in China, Professor Ho cites the growth of the clan system and of Neo-Confucianism in

Sung times as inhibiting factors. By contrast, he says that in the Ming and Ch'ing there was on the whole "a shrinkage of governmental control and a tremendous expansion of the private sector of the economy." These statements seem very plausible to me, a non-specialist on this topic, yet apparently some scholars would interpret the situation rather differently. The Sung, for example, has been cited as precisely the period when a marked development of the concept of free property took place, resulting in a corresponding development of large-scale landlordism, whereas later dynasties allegedly saw a weakening of this concept.[6]

Conclusion

The main thesis of Professor Ho's paper, varyingly expressed in different places, is that: (1) authoritarianism was strong in traditional China, and (2) it has progressively increased during the last several dynasties—say from Sung or Yuan onward—thus leading naturally to the acceptance of Marx-Leninism in the twentieth century.

With the first half of this thesis I heartily agree, though with the reiterated proviso that I wish Professor Ho's analysis had given more emphasis to certain broad sociological factors. To me, Chinese authoritarianism means much more than the arbitrary behavior of the emperor toward his high officials. *All* of Chinese society from top to bottom was essentially authoritarian, the family as much so, or even more than, the governmental structure.

Among various broad factors that might be cited as relevant to this authoritarianism, I would like to call special attention to three:

1) A tendency to think and act in bureaucratic terms is discernible in China long before the creation of the first bureaucratic empire in 221 B.C. It parallels, and is interlinked with, the tendency to think in terms of political centrality already noted at the beginning of these comments. Today it is becoming increasingly apparent that even though the Chinese did not invent bureaucracy, they certainly believed in and developed it to a degree unknown in any other society before the Industrial Revolution.[7] And bureaucracy, to be effective, has to have a clearly demarcated chain of command, in other words, an authoritarian structure. It is significant that the three philosophical schools most con-

[6] See H. F. Schurmann, "Traditional Property Concepts in China," *Far Eastern Quarterly*, 15 (1956): 507–16, especially 513.

[7] Significant research on this subject is being done at the University of Chicago. See H. G. Creel, "The Beginnings of Bureaucracy in China," *Journal of Asian Studies*, 23 (1964): 155–84.

cerned with political thought in pre-imperial China—Confucianism, Mohism, Legalism—were all in varying degrees authoritarian.

2) The focal importance of the ruling bureaucracy in Chinese society prevented any other group from effectively challenging its prestige, power, and scale of values. This dominance by administrators who were at the same time scholars resulted in the governmental controls upon commercial enterprise to which I have already alluded. Here I particularly regret Professor Ho's non-mention of what to me is the greatest single sociological difference between China and the West: China's failure to develop a mercantile bourgeoisie like that in the West—with all the profound consequences this entailed—despite promising beginnings in the Sung dynasty.[8]

3) Professor Ho begins his essay by deciding to ignore China's traditional tributary relations with the outside world, in part because they are already so familiar to Western scholars. True enough, and yet as I have already suggested, Chinese political and cultural egocentrism not only predates the formal institutionalizing of tributary relationships, but may today still have relevance for understanding modern Chinese foreign policy. More than this, I think it bears importantly upon the question of the status of the Emperor to which Professor Ho has devoted considerable attention. In Europe the existence of numerous competing nation-states inevitably imposed external limitations upon the strength of the rulers of these states, and by the same token lessened their internal status vis-à-vis their own people. In the case of China, where the closest approach to the European system of competing nation-states was the Warring States period ending in 221 B.C., only very feeble international checks could be placed upon the assumption of autocratic power by the Chinese Emperor.

Turning now to the second part of Professor Ho's thesis—the progressive growth of authoritarianism from approximately Sung times onward—I know that this idea is widely held and may well be true. As I have written elsewhere,[9] however, I would be more ready to accept it if I saw it subjected to really rigorous analysis rather than commonly asserted in the form of rather vague generalizations. Professor Ho is no

[8] Here again important research is being conducted at the University of Chicago. See Robert Hartwell, "A Revolution in the Chinese Iron and Coal Industries during the Northern Sung, 960–1126 A.D.," *Journal of Asian Studies*, 21 (1962): 153–62, and "Markets, Technology, and the Structure of Enterprise in the Development of the Eleventh-Century Chinese Iron and Steel Industry," *Journal of Economic History*, 26 (1966): 29–58.

[9] Review of David S. Nivison (ed.), *Confucianism in Action*, in *Journal of Asian Studies*, 19 (1960): 447–48.

doubt right in saying that Sung Neo-Confucianism made "the subject's loyalty, the son's filiality, and the wife's obedience almost one-sided moral imperatives." Yet were these not already moral imperatives under the Han, when all emperors were posthumously designated *hsiao*, "filial," and such didactic texts as the *Classic of Filial Piety* and Liu Hsiang's *Biographies of Distinguished Women* enjoyed wide popularity? Professor Ho seems to link the growth of authoritarianism with Neo-Confucianism, yet within a single paragraph he states that the secret service of Emperor Wu of Han "brought death to thousands," whereas the Northern Sung was "much more humane," and under the Ch'ing "these appalling secret services" were brought to an end. Having first said that autocracy reached its height in early Ming, he later states that "the Ming period on the whole offered more chances for commoners of above average intelligence and determination to ascend the social ladder than probably all previous dynasties." As evidence of how Confucianism became a tool of authoritarianism, he cites the statement of the Yung-cheng Emperor (eighteenth century) that the person who benefits most from the Confucian teachings is the ruler. I think it possible to interpret this statement in a more Confucian way: The ruler is supremely responsible for the people's welfare; hence whatever benefits them benefits him too to an even greater degree. It is my own feeling—and only a feeling—that Chinese authoritarianism, rather than having followed a fixed course, has tended to fluctuate with the times according to particular individuals and circumstances.

In conclusion, let me express hearty agreement with another basic assumption underlying Professor Ho's whole paper, namely the existence of significant continuities between past and present in China. Yet as I have tried to show in several instances (treatment of racial minorities, techniques of grassroots control, education), formal similarities may conceal conceptual differences. For example, I believe there is a great difference between Confucian authoritarianism—a (theoretically) benevolent paternalism directed from above by a dominant elite upon a passive populace—and the authoritarianism of Marx-Leninism, which maintains continuing interchange between the dominant elite and the general populace and engages the latter in active participation toward the achievement of shared social goals. In a country in revolution it is inevitable that iconoclastic change and past tradition should both be present. We should not lose sight of the one in our search for the other.

I am deeply grateful to Professor Ho for the stimulus and insight his broadly conceived paper has given all of us, but I must apologize for the resulting undue length of my commentary.

Supplementary Notes by Herrlee G. Creel

China's heritage is so vast and so complex that it is difficult, in a brief paper, to do justice even to its most salient aspects. I should like, as a supplement to Professor Ho's paper, to call attention to some additional facts and factors that may be of help in arriving at a picture of China's past that can be of maximum usefulness for understanding its present.

Much of Professor Ho's paper concerns two related subjects: militarism and autocracy. Concerning the first he says that "the persistent historical fact is that the Chinese state has always derived its ultimate power from the army, and this has largely predetermined its authoritarian character." Concerning autocracy he says that "the relentless cultivation of the Mao Tse-tung cult since 1949 answers a deep-rooted political need of the Chinese nation. . . . The system of state and government which focuses on the concrete symbol of a single strong man has naturally inclined itself toward authoritarianism."

No one can question that military force and autocratic rule have played roles of importance in China's history, and it is undoubtedly necessary to look far back into China's past, as Professor Ho does, in order to appreciate those roles. But in fact these elements have been important in the history of every empire. If we are to appreciate their function in the specifically Chinese context we must examine their *relative* importance, in comparison with other forces that may have modified or even opposed them. In fact, such forces have been very significant, not only in the longer sweep of history but even in the brief history of Communist China. It is necessary, in my opinion, to examine the historic role of these additional forces in some depth, even in order to understand certain aspects of the struggles that have been going on inside Communist China in recent months.

Every sovereign state depends, and has depended, upon military force as an ultimate recourse; China is no exception. Every such state has also made some use of another potent force: psychology. Professor Ho has

59

not overlooked it. He speaks of the importance, for the present situa-
tin, of "twenty-five centuries of Confucius' teaching, much of which
deals with human relations, psychology, and education," and says that
no other Communist state "has gone as far as Communist China in
regarding education as the very pivot of total social transformation.
Certainly no other Communist state has worked out more sophisticated
psychological techniques and more relentless organization with which
to carry out thought reform and brainwashing on a mass scale."

Since every government has used both military force and psychological persuasion, the crucial question concerns the relative balance
between them. S. N. Eisenstadt, in his broad survey of many political
systems, writes: "In China, though in different periods, it enjoyed relatively great political significance, the army did not constitute a permanent, semi-legitimate (or at least accepted) factor in the political
process."[1] John King Fairbank says that "the Chinese military system
is of a different type from the European or Japanese. Once an imperial
regime has been instituted, civilian government has been esteemed over
the military. It took a soldier to found a dynasty but he and his
descendants invariably found it easier to rule as sages, through civilian
officials . . . the bureaucratic polity of China sought constantly to avoid
domination by any independent military power."[2] Joseph Needham
writes that China has been ruled "basically by the prestige of literary
culture, enormously important in Chinese traditional society, and not
by open dominance and force."[3]

When Confucius was asked what were the essentials of government
he replied that they were: first, the confidence of the people; second,
adequate food; and third and least essential, adequate military force.
He concluded, "If the people do not believe in the government, it cannot stand."[4] While Confucius was sometimes quite impractical, he was
here voicing a conviction that has been a working principle of government in China, beginning many centuries before his time and still very
much in force in Communist China. There is a clear echo of Confucius'
dictum in the statement of Mao Tse-tung to Edgar Snow, in 1965, that

[1] S. N. Eisenstadt, *The Political Systems of Empires* (London: Macmillan, 1963), p. 172.

[2] John King Fairbank, *The United States and China*, rev. ed. (Cambridge, Mass.: Harvard University Press, 1958), pp. 50–51.

[3] Joseph Needham, "The Past in China's Present," in *The Centennial Review*, 4 (1960): 154.

[4] *Analects*, 12.7.

the Chinese Communists triumphed because "the People's Liberation Army was strong and able and people believed in its cause."[5]

If for instance we compare the Chinese with the Western Roman Empire, it is apparent that the Romans took far more care, with highly trained and strategically located garrisons that could move quickly over superb military highways, to counter internal disorders with swift chastisement. Such disorders were not very frequent because the Romans were always ready, and punished those that did occur with a savagery that could not be forgotten.[6] On the other hand, the Romans, as compared with the Chinese, made relatively little use of psychological persuasion. The Romans are often praised for their tolerance of various religions and of local customs, and some of this praise is doubtless deserved. But this tolerance was in part a reflection of the fact that the Romans were not greatly concerned to assimilate their subjects ideologically (except for the urban aristocrats, whom they allied with themselves, and used as their instruments of local administration). Roman emperors did, in their public pronouncements, make much of Roman tradition and Roman virtue and the benefits of Roman rule. But as compared with the Chinese, the rulers of Rome did not expend great efforts upon causing the mass of their subjects to believe that their rule was benevolent and just, if only they kept the peace, paid their taxes, and never doubted that Roman power would meet disobedience with swift and terrible punishment. And testimonials to the lack of cultural and ideological solidarity in the Roman Empire—beyond the thin upper crust of the urban aristocracy—are legion.[7]

[5] Edgar Snow, "Interview with Mao," *The New Republic*, 152 (February 27, 1965): 22.

[6] Plutarch's account, written nearly two centuries after the event, of the sack of Athens in 86 B.C. by a Roman army under Sulla taking vengeance for the revolt of the Greeks, still rings with horror. "There was no numbering the slain," he says; "the amount is to this day conjectured only from the space of ground overflowed with blood." See Plutarch, *The Lives of the Noble Grecians and Romans*, trans. John Dryden (Modern Library ed.; New York, n.d.), pp. 556–57. Sulla ravaged and looted Greece so that she never fully recovered; see A. E. R. Boak, *A History of Rome to 565 A.D.*, 4th ed. (New York: Macmillan, 1955), p. 199.

[7] Testimony on this point is particularly convincing when it comes from the pen of a Roman official; see *The Letters of Cicero*, trans. Evelyn S. Shuckburgh, vol. 1 (London: G. Bell and Sons, 1920), pp. 78, 81–82; vol. 2 (London, 1917), p. 67. See also *Cambridge Ancient History*, 12 vols. (New York: Macmillan, 1924–39), 9:446–51; 10:209, 219, 845–46; 11:706; 12:708; M. Rostovtzeff, *The Social and Economic History of the Roman Empire*, 2d ed. (Ox-

The Chinese, on the other hand, have always—for as long as we have any detailed knowledge of their history—been intensely concerned with cultural and ideological solidarity. The Chinese Communists, following up their military conquest with an energetic campaign to convince the whole population of the justice of their cause, through education and propaganda, have acted according to a pattern that is at least three thousand years old. In fact, the very solidarity and identity of the Chinese people can be traced, in no small measure, to such a campaign.

Professor Ho mentions, among common appellations for the Emperor that have come into use during the past millennium, one that is both curious and significant: "Son of Heaven with Real Mandate of Heaven." For three thousand years China's rulers have claimed to possess the Mandate of Heaven. And there can be little doubt that this potent concept was originated as a propaganda slogan.

When the Chou people moved eastward from the Wei valley—in 1122 B.C. according to the traditional chronology—and conquered the Shang dynasty, they were a relatively less sophisticated but immensely vital and capable people. They pressed their conquests so far as to claim, and to some degree to control, a territory possibly larger than modern Spain. It included men of diverse backgrounds, all disposed to be hostile to the Chou and to regard them, in fact, as "barbarians." The Chou established a regime that was in large part feudal but also, insofar as the royal government was concerned, proto-bureaucratic. Critical scholarship has inclined to dismiss much of what traditional history says about the early Chou rulers as legend, and certainly they were glorified in legends that became an essential part of the *mystique* of the Chinese people. But very recent research and discoveries, both in Taiwan and in Communist China, have shown that these legends have a more solid substratum than has been supposed, and that for some three centuries the Chou Kings exercised a degree of control over much of their broad territories that was much greater than most critical scholars have been willing to credit.[8]

---

ford: The Clarendon Press, 1957), chap. 1, 192–94, 252–54, 334, 347–49; A. H. M. Jones, *The Later Roman Empire 284–682* (Norman, Okla.: University of Oklahoma Press, 1964, vol. 2:988, 996–97).

[8] My statements about the Western Chou period (1122–771 B.C.) are based upon my current research, which involves not only consideration of recent discoveries and research but also a complete reexamination and reevaluation of all of the sources. New light has come particularly from intensive study and analysis of inscriptions on bronze vessels. My results will be published in the first volume (now nearing completion) of my work on the origins of statecraft in early China.

The achievements of the Chou were truly extraordinary. They built, certainly, upon a foundation that was partly derived from their Shang predecessors, yet if we carefully compare what little we know of Shang government with that of the Chou, it is apparent that much of Chou practice was original and some of it was present in their own institutions before the conquest. Ever since their day, the ruler of China has been known as "the son of Heaven," and Heaven (*T'ien*) was a Chou deity, never mentioned in the Shang inscriptions. The foundations of China's traditional governmental structure were in considerable measure a Chou creation. The religious background of that government was in large measure Chou religion. The literary basis of what we know as Chinese culture was chiefly Chou literature. Although the Chou were at first considered barbarians, they created a large degree of cultural and ideological unity. The great Yangtze valley state of Ch'u was rich, powerful, and cultured, and was militarily an active and dangerous rival of the Chou power, yet even Ch'u regarded Chou culture with admiration.[9] The early welding of the peoples of much of the area we know as China into an ideological whole, with an intense consciousness of their cultural unity and historical role, was very largely a Chou achievement.

The Chou empire was won by conquest, and the Chou rulers placed garrisons at strategic points to maintain it. But the rather remarkable documents that are preserved to us, from the very beginning of the dynasty,[10] show that the earliest Chou rulers were intensely preoccupied with the desire to conciliate their subjects and convince them that their rule was just and benevolent. The actual conqueror of the Shang, King Wu (the "Martial King") is celebrated in early poems for his military prowess—"terrifying and strong was King Wu!" Yet this mighty conqueror is insistent upon the necessity for conciliation, and says that a wise ruler "fears . . . the little people," and does not "dare to mistreat even the helpless and solitary." His brother, the famous Duke of Chou, says that the ruler must seek good understanding with "the little people," and must "fear the danger of the people."[11] It was clearly as a

[9] For partial, but by no means complete, citation of evidence on this point, see my "The Beginnings of Bureaucracy in China: The Origin of the *Hsien*," in *Journal of Asian Studies*, 23 (1964):174–78.

[10] Not all, by any means, of the documents that purport to come from that time can be accepted. My recent research has altered some of my own previous opinions concerning the dating and authentication of purportedly Western Chou documents.

[11] "The Book of Documents" [*Shu-ching*], trans. Bernhard Karlgren, in *Bulletin of the Museum of Far Eastern Antiquities*, Stockholm, 22 (1950):

result of this concern that the Chou launched an intensive propaganda campaign to secure the confidence and adherence of those they had conquered. When we consider that this campaign was carried on three thousand years ago, without even the help of printing to say nothing of other technological devices, its success is surely one of the more remarkable and momentous facts of history.

Its most inspired and enduring doctrine was that of the Mandate of Heaven. There is reason to doubt that anything closely comparable to it had existed before the Chou conquest. It alleged, however, that each of three dynasties—of which the Chou was the third—had been entrusted by Heaven with its Mandate to rule, which was withdrawn from each of the earlier two when the final ruler of the dynasty fell into evil ways. The Chou, for their part, had had no desire to conquer the Shang, but Heaven had given them the Mandate and ordered them to attack and replace the Shang house in order to end the sufferings of the people and restore good government to the people. (Compare the Chinese Communist doctrine of their "liberation" of the Chinese people from Nationalist misrule.) The Chou had been unable to refuse the sacred mission. Within a short time this version of history was accepted even by the former subjects of the Shang, and it has remained orthodox ever since.[12]

To do justice even to the early history of political propaganda in China would require a volume. Confucius, although he would have rejected the imputation with scorn, was a master propagandist, all the more effective because his propaganda was subtle and probably unconscious.[13] His disciples, and later Confucians, were more obvious propagandists, and they succeeded in enlisting the sympathy of a large seg-

---

39, 45, 49. Here as elsewhere I have cited what seem to me to be the best available translations of Chinese works, but my quotations are in every case based upon my own study of the Chinese text, and may or may not wholly agree with the translation cited.

[12] On the Chou propaganda, see my *Studies in Early Chinese Culture* (Baltimore: Waverly Press, 1937), pp. 51–52, 57–63, 80–93, 105–6, and *Confucius, the Man and the Myth* (New York: John Day, 1949), pp. 13–14, 146–48. My earlier views on this subject are modified and further developed in the work on early statecraft which I am now writing.

[13] An example is his redefinition of the terms *chün-tzu* and *hsiao-jen,* which before his time usually meant "hereditary nobleman" and "plebeian." Confucius used them to mean—as they most commonly have ever since—"gentleman" in an ethical sense, and "mean man." Thus he appropriated the traditional connotations of these terms, honorific in the one case and derogatory in the other, to reinforce the standards of conduct that he advocated.

ment of the population. By Han times this sympathy had become so widespread that Emperors, whatever their private views might be, found it expedient at least to appear tolerant toward Confucianism, and highly inexpedient to oppose it openly.[14]

It is undoubtedly true that, as Professor Ho writes, "for the study of the traditional Chinese state and government, no period is more important than the Western Han (B.C. 206–8 A.D.). Even bearing later modifications in mind, it is small exaggeration to say that the fundamental character of the traditional Chinese state was determined in Western Han times. . . ." The beginning of this dynasty, which for the first time saw a plebeian enthroned as Son of Heaven, was a pivotal period. It was not at all easy for the Han to win acceptance and establish stable rule. This was done, in no small measure, by means of propaganda. The Han rulers alleged (and not in all respects falsely) that they were reestablishing the kind of rule that had existed in Western Chou times, bringing order and justice after the turmoil of the Warring States period and the "wickedness" of the Ch'in dynasty.

The founder of the Han dynasty was a peasant, Liu Pang, who rose from bandit chief to general to Emperor. After the Ch'in dynasty had been destroyed, two of the revolutionary generals, Liu Pang and Hsiang Yü, contested for the empire for four years. Hsiang Yü was a superb general; it was said that he never lost a battle that he personally commanded. But he was a ruthless and arrogant autocrat. He could not understand why his followers gradually melted away, and just before his death he cried out, "It is Heaven that destroys me; I have committed no military error!" In the following century China's most famous historian condemned him in these words: "He boasted of his military prowess, vaunted his superior wisdom, and would not learn from history. Under the guise of acting as supreme ruler, he wished to conquer the world and rule it by sheer force."[15] This might stand as a vignette of a kind of ruler who has usually been deplored in China for thousands of years.

His adversary, Liu Pang, was nothing like so good a military commander, and readily admitted the fact. He gave full credit for his success to his advisers and generals, claiming for himself only the ability

[14] Creel, *Confucius, the Man and the Myth*, pp. 161, 203, 222–53. The term "Confucianism," as applied with regard to Han and later times, is ambiguous and at times of dubious usefulness, but in order to avoid complexity I am using it in the rather loose sense in which it is commonly employed.

[15] *Les Mémoires Historiques de Se-ma Ts'ien*, trans. and annotated by Édouard Chavannes (Paris: E. Leroux, 1895–1905), 2:266–323.

to select men of capacity and make use of them. And he was a brilliant psychologist. He made it clear that if he became Emperor the people might expect mild rule. Personally, he had no use for Confucians and sometimes humiliated them with vulgar tricks. But he came to realize that Confucianism was popular, and used Confucian language in his proclamations. At one point, in very Confucian language, he preached a "crusade" against Hsiang Yü, and dramatized his denunciation by the vivid propaganda stroke of dressing his whole army in the color of mourning, for his enemy's crimes.[16]

Motion pictures of Chinese Communist ceremonies showing thousands upon thousands of individuals executing elaborate and precise maneuvers are most impressive, and must have great psychological impact upon participants and spectators alike. These undoubtedly derive much of their sophistication from the long Chinese experience—which we can trace back for more than three thousand years—with elaborate ceremonial. Such ceremonies were very early intended to, among other things, impress the ruler's subjects (and visiting foreigners as well). After the plebeian Liu Pang became Emperor he was at first inclined to be contemptuous of traditional behavior. He told a Confucian adviser that he did not have to bother with such things, for he had won the empire on horseback. "Yes," was the reply, "but can you govern it from horseback?" At first the peasant Emperor abolished court ritual as so much troublesome nonsense, but he quickly came to see that it was indispensable to the maintenance of his position.[17]

All of this effort directed toward propaganda clearly indicates concern with public opinion. "Sometimes it is said," Joseph Needham writes, "that in medieval China there was no such thing as public opinion. I am well satisfied that this is a wholly mistaken idea."[18] But, it may be asked, when one speaks of public opinion in China is this not something quite different from what we speak of as public opinion in the West? Is this not merely the opinion of the intellectuals, the "gentry," the "elite," who were out of touch with the mass of the people?

In my opinion it is important, in assessing political phenomena in

[16] *The History of the Former Han Dynasty, by Pan Ku*, trans. and annotated by Homer H. Dubs (Baltimore: Waverly Press, 1938–1955), 1:27–150.

[17] Takigawa Kametaro, *Shih-chi Hui-chu K'ao-cheng [The Historical Records* with Collected Commentaries and Critical Studies] (Tokyo, 1932–1934), 97.16, 99.13–18.

[18] Needham, "The Past in China's Present," p. 166.

China, to bear in mind that China has had a remarkable degree of cultural homogeneity. China has had a definite class structure, with marked class differences. But as compared with many societies, this structure has been characterized by a good deal of vertical mobility, both upward and downward, and the ideological differences between classes have consisted chiefly in variations in complexity rather than in content. An extremely difficult literature, embodying the history and the legends central to the culture, was read by statesmen and scholars. And simplified and embellished versions of the content of many of *these same books* were recited by professional storytellers in the market-places.[19] They could still be heard in this century, listened to eagerly by crowds of whom many were doubtless illiterate; they paid by tossing coppers to the storyteller, and those who were penniless needed only to stand well back. In such ways the central ideology of the culture became remarkably diffused; anyone who has lived in China has heard Confucius quoted, perhaps unconsciously, by donkey drivers and boatmen.

Various mechanisms churned this stratified culture. Polygamy took poor but comely women into rich houses, sometimes even into the palace itself. The same institution also produced so many offspring of the wealthy and powerful that many of them soon dropped to low estate. Before the beginning of the Christian Era it was observed that the grandsons of rulers might be seen weeding the fields. In the middle of the nineteenth century Tseng Kuo-fan, born into a peasant family of very modest means, who rose to be viceroy and a marquis, gave his sons a spartan upbringing to save his family from the fate of going "from shirt sleeves to shirt sleeves in three generations"—a common fate, he believed, of families that experienced good fortune in his day.

The broad recruitment of the civil service, especially through the competitive examinations, was extremely important as an avenue of vertical mobility. When a former swineherd was appointed Chancellor of the Empire in 124 B.C., this created a profound impression. Of all the chancellors who held office during the Former Han dynasty 22 per cent of those for whom we have biographical data came from "poor" or "lowly" families. (In comparison, C. Wright Mills found that only 18 per cent of the men who held the highest offices in the United States of America between 1789 and 1953 came from "lower-

[19] J. I. Crump, Jr., "P'ing-hua and the Early History of the San-kuo Chih," *Journal of the American Oriental Society*, 71 (1951): 249–56.

class families.")[20] Such mobility may well have been greater in the Former Han than in some later periods, and certainly it was difficult in practice for a peasant to become educated and rise high in the government. But in theory, and to some degree in fact, it was possible, and psychologically this was tremendously important. The one great prize, in the estimation of almost everyone, was to achieve high office. If a merchant became very wealthy, he still hoped that at least some member of his family might bring luster to it in this way. And the one avenue to such success was learning—office attained by any other means carried little prestige.

All this means that there was not, in China, generally speaking, such an "alienation of the intellectuals from the masses" as is sometimes supposed. There are those who seem to believe that Confucians have been, for the most part, well-to-do individuals who looked with disdain on the humble. But Professor Ho cites "Confucius' immortal saying: 'In education there should be no class distinctions.'" And he comments:

> When it is remembered that up to his lifetime education had practically been a monopoly of the hereditary feudal aristocracy, Confucius, who endeavored to implement his doctrine by offering equal instruction to all his disciples irrespective of their social origin, should indeed be credited with the first step toward social and intellectual emancipation.

Not all "Confucians" held this same attitude with the same zeal, yet many of them identified themselves with the popular cause. After the reign of the Han Emperor Wu (140–87 B.C.), an autocrat who terrorized his officials and exhausted the country, popular discontent was so great that the next Emperor felt constrained to give it a hearing. He therefore ordered his officials to inquire of a group of scholars from various parts of the country—who were in fact Confucians—as to "what were the grievances of the common people." In the ensuing debates, which lasted for days and attracted widespread attention, the court officials made fun of the protesting scholars as men "straight from the farm or from poverty-stricken alleys," "wearing plebeian

[20] Wang Yü-ch'üan, "An Outline of the Central Government of the Former Han Dynasty," *Harvard Journal of Asiatic Studies*, 12 (1949): 179:80; C. Wright Mills, *The Power Elite* (New York: Oxford University Press, 1957), pp. 400–401.

clothes and tattered shoes."[21] Obviously these intellectuals were not sleek aristrocrats.

Needham is clearly correct, I believe, in thinking that public opinion has been a far more potent force in China than is sometimes supposed. There seems to be an impression that the great bulk of Chinese peasants composed an illiterate, uninformed mass, uninterested in what was going on in the world. Certainly many were; many are today, in Europe and America. No quantitative study of this point is possible, but many incidents in history suggest that there was wider political awareness, and even more literacy, than is sometimes supposed. Late in 1935 I traveled somewhat extensively through rural sections of several Chinese provinces, and was quite surprised at the degree of literacy I encountered even among those who made their living by manual labor. Even more surprising, at this time when Chinese Communism had as yet had virtually no impact on these areas, was the widespread concern over the tensions that were building up in the world. A little Taoist priest, on a remote mountaintop in the west, told me that another world war was coming soon—of which I was skeptical. Two months later I was in London, where the attitude was one of business as usual and Hitler was still a joke.

Throughout history people in general in China have had an interest in government such as can be found in few other countries. For government has been the great activity, even the great game; and success in government has been the great prize, which few could win but almost everyone could dream of, if not for himself then for his son or his cousin. And government has been the business of the intellectuals, who for this reason have enjoyed a degree of empathy with the people not often found elsewhere. The popular attitude toward officials varied; they might be hated as oppressors, or admired and even loved, but they were seldom looked upon with indifference. People tended to identify themselves with scholars and with popular officials, much as some Americans identify themselves with movie stars or television personalities. Officials and even private scholars who had the courage to speak out against the court, or even against an Emperor, sometimes at the risk of their lives, became heroes. It was with good reason that Emperor Chao told his officials to ask the scholars about the people's grievances; the scholars knew, and they were generally regarded as the articulate representatives of the people.

[21] *The History of the Former Han Dynasty,* 2:160; Huan K'uan, *Discourses on Salt and Iron,* trans. and annotated by Esson M. Gale (Leyden: E. J. Brill, 1931), pp. 77, 103.

One of the most troublesome problems that the Chinese Communists have had to face is that of the relationship between the intellectuals and the regime. This is nothing new in Chinese history. Almost every dynasty—even those founded by foreign invaders—has found it necessary to enlist the cooperation of the intellectuals, because of their prestige with the people. Only in this way could final acceptance and tranquillity be achieved. But once a regime was entrenched it often tended to become more dominating. The intellectuals, who composed the great body of officialdom, resented the limitations this imposed on their freedom. Furthermore, time-honored tradition has ascribed to the intellectuals the *duty* of criticizing the ruler. Confucius said that it was a minister's duty to oppose his ruler to his face.[22] The *Classic of Filial Piety*, studied and quoted as a guide to conduct even by emperors themselves, has a chapter devoted to the duty of remonstrance, and says that a Son of Heaven will not go astray so long as he has ministers who will remonstrate with him and keep him on the right path.[23]

The function of criticism was even institutionalized, in what is known as the "Censorate." Although it is certainly true that censors were at times the subservient agents of dominant rulers, they have at other times functioned as harsh and effective critics of those who controlled the government, even including the Emperor himself.[24] C. P. Fitzgerald, writing of a period in the seventh century A.D. that was characterized by an unusual degree of imperial autocracy, says that nevertheless "the Censors were often fearless in carrying out their thankless and sometimes dangerous duty. They, and the rest of the hierarchy, were fortified by the strong tradition of government by moral precept rather than naked force which informed all Chinese thought."[25] James T. C. Liu, writing of the eleventh century, says that "when an emperor ignored both the power of remonstrance and the power of

[22] *Analects*, 14.23.

[23] *Hsiao-ching Chu-su* [*The Classic of Filial Piety* with Commentaries] in *Shih-san Ching Chu-su* [The Thirteen Classics with Commentaries] (Nanchang, 1815), 7.3a–5b. *The History of the Former Han Dynasty*, 2:160, 204.

[24] E. A. Kracke, Jr., "The Chinese and the Art of Government," in *The Legacy of China*, ed. Raymond Dawson (Oxford: Clarendon Press, 1964), pp. 309–39; Charles O. Hucker, "Confucianism and the Chinese Censorial System," in *Confucianism in Action*, ed. David S. Nivison and Arthur F. Wright (Stanford, Calif.: Stanford University Press, 1959), pp. 182–208; Joseph Needham, "The Past in China's Present," pp. 166–67.

[25] C. P. Fitzgerald, *The Empress Wu* (Melbourne: Cheshire, 1955), pp. 10–11; see also pp. 178–79.

opinion, he would be stripped of ideological authority and might actually find his ultimate power left naked and much weakened politically."[26]

Not only officials were expected to criticize. Edward A. Kracke, Jr., in his essay on "The Chinese and the Art of Government"—undoubtedly the best concise account of China's government that we have—devotes much attention to "the duty of the scholar as political critic."[27] Although China was in theory a despotic monarchy, it was far more customary than in our own government for officials even of low rank to address, to the chief of state, memoranda criticizing governmental procedures and proposing innovations—and to have them, in many cases, considered with care. Fairbank says that "all business was in form originated at the bottom and passed upward to the Emperor for decision at the top, memorials from the provinces being addressed to the Emperor at the capital."[28] And not only officials wrote such memorials. Private scholars wrote to the Emperor, too, and occasionally the author of such a communication was rewarded with an appointment to office—a Chinese civilian counterpart, perhaps, to the "battlefield commission."

When China's intellectuals took seriously the injunction of Mao Tse-tung to "let the hundred flowers bloom," and criticized the regime, they were obeying an imperative that was thousands of years old in their culture.

Conflict between the intellectuals and the regime could disturb and sometimes weaken the government. Conversely, the approval of the intellectuals, and the popular sympathy they could command, were a powerful support to an Emperor—and also to rebels seeking to overthrow him. New dynasties were commonly, though by no means always, established by military force.[29] But even in such cases the role of the intellectuals was greater than is sometimes recognized. Rebels courted them to win popular approval. When the standard of rebellion was

[26] James T. C. Liu, "An Early Sung Reformer: Fan Chung-yen," in *Chinese Thought and Institutions,* ed. John K. Fairbank (Chicago: University of Chicago Press, 1957), p. 124.

[27] Kracke, "The Chinese and the Art of Government," p. 333 and *passim.*

[28] Fairbank, *The United States and China,* pp. 91–92.

[29] Lien-sheng Yang points out that in a significant number of cases new dynasties were founded by powerful ministers whose "influence became so overwhelming that the last ruler of the old dynasty was obliged to abdicate" (*Studies in Chinese Institutional History* [Cambridge, Mass.: Harvard University Press, 1961], p. 5).

raised against the first notoriously despotic dynasty, the Ch'in, in 209
B.C., by the peasant Ch'en She (who was killed a few months later)
he had with him as adviser the direct heir of Confucius in the eighth
generation. And intellectuals of various schools flocked to his support.
This was in part a revolt of the intellectuals against despotism.[30] And
the peasant who subsequently succeeded in founding the Han dynasty,
Liu Pang, while he had no personal inclination toward Confucians,
had some of them as important members of his entourage; in fact,
his own brother, a member of a peasant family, had studied with a
prominent Confucian.[31]

In our own twentieth century it was intellectuals—a new breed, to
be sure, in large part foreign educated—who prepared the way, ideologically, for the downfall of the Manchu dynasty and for the subsequent establishment of the Nationalist government. By a process common to revolutions, control of the government passed in considerable
measure to men who were less intellectuals than practical politicians.
The fall of the Nationalists is sometimes attributed to their alienation
from the masses, but not less important is the disaffection that quickly
ensued among many intellectuals, who became anti-Kuomintang long
before they were specifically pro-Communist.

The support of a very large segment of the intellectuals was a most
important factor that helped to make possible the victory of the
Chinese Communists. Many professors and students fled from the
classroom to join the Communists, and their prestige did much to
win over the peasants. The leaders of the Chinese Communist Party
were for the most part intellectuals. As recently as 1956 Mao Tse-tung
said that he had "begun life as a primary school teacher."[32] In 1951
Robert C. North wrote:

> Although the Chinese Communists hail their party as the van-
> guard of the proletariat, no Politburo member is known to
> have come from a working-class family. . . . The educational level
> of these [thirteen] men is generally high. Nine have attended
> advanced institutions. Three received part of their education in
> Japan, two in Germany, and one in France. . . . Eight or more

30 *Mémoires Historiques*, 5:132; *Shih-chi Hui-chu K'ao-cheng*, pp. 48, 121.5;
Discourses on Salt and Iron, pp. 122–24.

31 *The History of the Former Han Dynasty*, 1:15–22.

32 Snow, "Interview with Mao," p. 23. In fact, Mao was much more of an
intellectual, if a frustrated one, than this rather humble statement might suggest. See Stuart R. Schram, *The Political Thought of Mao Tse-tung* (New
York: Praeger, 1963), pp. 7–24.

have studied at one time or another in the Soviet Union; two, and perhaps more, have served on the faculties of Russian educational institutions.[33]

In view of the long tradition of the independence of Chinese intellectuals, and their belief that it is their duty to criticize the government, it is not surprising that it has been hard to bring them under strict party discipline and into complete conformity with "the thought of Mao Tse-tung." The policies of the leadership, and of Mao, have varied, but there have been evidences of increasing tension. A South American editor has quoted Chen Yi, Vice-Premier and Foreign Minister, as saying, in May 1966: "To defend ourselves against deviation, we are trying to eliminate the three differences: Between manual labor and intellectual work; between the city and the country; between peasants and workers." "We are attempting to eliminate the intellectual class."[34] This is a strong statement, to be received with due reserve. Yet some of the confused reports that come out concerning China's current "cultural reform" are not incompatible with it.

No previous Chinese ruler ever tried to eliminate the intellectual class, with the possible exception of that great ogre of Chinese tradition, the "First Emperor" of the Ch'in dynasty (221-210 B.C.). He attempted complete totalitarian regimentation, and sought to forbid the possession of most classes of literature by any but his officials. He also put many scholars to death, but whether he actually intended to destroy the intellectuals as a class is uncertain.[35] If this was his intention, he did not succeed. His dynasty, which he said would last for ten thousand generations, outlasted him by three years.

Has the Chinese Communist regime, today, the power to make of China a country without an intellectual class? Could such a country develop and maintain the science, the hydrogen bombs, the industry to which the regime appears to be committed? These are interesting questions, to which the future may provide some answers.

For years there have been reports, often vague and unconfirmed, of disputes within the inner circle of the Communist hierarchy, and of criticism within that circle of the policies of Mao Tse-tung. Of

[33] Robert C. North, "The Chinese Communist Elite," *The Annals of the American Academy of Political and Social Science,* 227 (September, 1951): 67–68.

[34] Carlos Maria Gutierrez, "Peking's Obsession: Nuclear War with the U.S. Is Inevitable," *The National Observer,* 5 (November 28, 1966): 26.

[35] See Creel, *Confucius,* pp. 216–18, 223–25.

late "the thought of Mao Tse-tung" has been declared sacred, and a number of those who have been closest to him have been denounced as daring to disagree with it. Can this be regarded as a reappearance, in contemporary garb, of the age-old tendency in China for tension to develop between any ruler who attempts to monopolize the initiative, and his ministers?

There seems to be no political tradition, other than the Chinese, in which the role of the able minister has been so long and so consistently exalted—so much so as sometimes to cast the ruler he served into relative obscurity. It has commonly been supposed that the special position of the minister in China was essentially Confucian in origin, but recent discoveries and research have shown that it was present long before Confucius, in the second millennium B.C. The sacrifices mentioned in the Shang oracular inscriptions were normally made only to deceased members of the royal family, but along with them sacrifices were also made to a few deceased ministers considered especially meritorious. And like royal ancestors, these deceased ministers were considered spirits of great power, able to affect rainfall, harvests, and even the welfare of the reigning King.[36]

There was even a tradition that the most famous Shang minister, I Yin, disapproving of his ruler's conduct, deposed and banished him until he reformed, when he restored him to the throne.[37] We cannot certainly trace this tradition to a time earlier than around 300 B.C., and it may be false; but it was believed, and would influence later history. Around 1100 B.C. the Duke of Chou ascribed a large share of the credit for the achievements of a number of famous rulers of the past to their ministers, without whose help, he said, they could have accomplished little.[38]

We have already noted the significance of the Western Han period as providing the basic pattern for China's governmental institutions. During the reign of the first Han Emperor, Homer H. Dubs says, it became the practice "that the Emperor acts only at the suggestion of

---

[36] Kuo Mo-jo, *Pu-tz'u T'ung-tsuan* [Studies on the Oracle Bone Inscriptions] (Tokyo, 1933), Pieh 1.11ab; *Yin-hsü Shu-ch'i Ch'ien-pien* [Oracle Inscriptions from the Yin Ruins, first series], comp. Lo Chen-yü (1912), 4:15.4; Ch'en Meng-chia, *Yin-hsü Pu-tz'u Tsung-shu* [A General Account of the Yin Oracle Inscriptions] (Peking, 1956), pp. 346–50, 362–65.

[37] *The Ch'un Ts'ew* [*Ch'un-ch'iu*], *with the Tso Chuen* [*Tso-chuan*], *The Chinese Classics*, vol. V, trans. James Legge (London: Trübner and Co., 1872), p. 488 (translation, p. 491); *Mencius*, 5(1) .6.5; 7(1) .31.

[38] "The Book of Documents," p. 61.

others." And this custom, Dubs says, "was a real and often effective limitation upon the imperial power"; he cites concrete examples.[39]

The widow of the Han founder enthroned a child of her own choice. The ministers, who did not approve the choice, were unable to prevent this action but did not sanction it. When the Empress Dowager died, in 180 B.C., the ministers killed the young Emperor and, choosing from among various candidates, enthroned their own choice as Emperor Wen. He proved, as Professor Ho says, to be a ruler of "real political genius."[40]

Emperor Wu (140–87 B.C.) was one of the most autocratic emperors in China's history. His fifty-four-year reign gave him time to learn how to outmaneuver his ministers. He was undoubtedly brilliant, and some of his fame is deserved, though he is often given credit for constructive developments that were chiefly the culmination of the work that less flamboyant emperors, working quietly with their ministerial advisers, had long been prosecuting.[41] Wu terrorized his subjects, from the humblest to the most exalted civil and military officials. He was bitterly criticized in his own day and later, and there have been many who would agree with the verdict of Dubs that "the final result of Emperor Wu's overtaxation, wastage, and misgovernment was civil disorder." Whether the Han dynasty could have survived two such emperors is doubtful.[42]

In 74 B.C., thirteen years after the death of Emperor Wu, the reigning Emperor died without an heir. The principal ministers chose, from among possible candidates, Liu He, who was escorted to the capital and invested with the imperial seals. He gave himself up to unrestrained enjoyment and acted in a totally irresponsible manner. He gave promise of being an Emperor even more autocratic, if that were possible, than Wu. The chief ministers consulted together and agreed that his reign might be the end of the Han dynasty. Seeking a precedent for action, they cited the tradition that the Shang minister, I Yin, had deposed his ruler. Dubs says that this tradition, which is

[39] *History of the Former Han Dynasty*, 1:16–17.

[40] *History of the Former Han Dynasty*, 1.170–72, 198, 209–10, 221–22.

[41] See my "The *Fa-chia*: 'Legalists' or 'Administrators'?" *Bulletin of the Institute of History and Philology, Academia Sinica*, extra vol., no. 4 (1961): 631–32.

[42] *History of the Former Han Dynasty*, 2:1–25, 120. Wang Hsien-ch'ien, *Ch'ien-Han-shu Pu-chu* [History of the Former Han Dynasty with Commentaries] (1900), 24B.6b–20b, 75.4a; H. G. Creel, "The Role of the Horse in Chinese History," in *American Historical Review*, 70 (1965):657–64.

embodied in the Confucian work *Mencius,* was "part of the state constitution." After Liu He had ruled for twenty-seven days the ministers met together and deposed him. In his stead they set up another candidate as Emperor Hsüan, who became, as Professor Ho justly observes, "one of the ablest Chinese rulers of all time."[43]

Interplay between the ruler and his ministers continued to characterize China's government. At some times the ministers, or a particular minister, were so influential that the Emperor became impotent. Toward the end of the Former Han dynasty an able minister built up his power for decades, maneuvering his enemies out of positions of power and his supporters into them, winning the support of the intellectuals and the people through an elaborate propaganda based on Confucian ideology. In 9 A.D. he deposed the last ruler of the Former Han and became the first Emperor of a new dynasty. This was not the last time that a powerful minister succeeded in taking over the empire.[44] At other times the preponderant power lay with the Emperor—or an Empress. But much of the time there was a reasonable balance of power, and ruler and ministers operated with a good deal of harmony.

The "Great Proletarian Cultural Revolution" now under way is designed, we are told, to abolish all traditional ways of thinking and substitute "the thought of Mao Tse-tung." At the same time current reports make it clear that rumors that have persisted for years are certainly correct, and some of those who have been among Mao's closest advisers are in some respects in disagreement with him, and do not favor some of the changes he is seeking to promote.

It can be argued that Mao occupies the place of the Emperor, and that the Emperor has always had the power to break with all precedent simply by issuing a new decree, regardless of all dissent. But it is hard to say whether this is true or not. Even very energetic emperors were often greatly concerned about the reception which their edicts might encounter. In 627 A.D. T'ai-tsung, the virtual founder of the T'ang dynasty and one of China's ablest emperors, issued a decree in which he chided his ministers for automatically promulgating all of his edicts, with never a word of remonstrance. "From now on," he told his ministers, "if there is anything in a decree that you suspect is not as it should be, you must definitely bring it up for further dis-

[43] *History of the Former Han Dynasty,* 2:180–84, 203–205; *Ch'ien-Han-shu Pu-chu,* 63.17*b*–22*a*, 68.5*a*–10*b*.

[44] *History of the Former Han Dynasty,* 3:88–259; Yang, *Studies in Chinese Institutional History,* p. 5.

cussion."[45] In the tenth and eleventh centuries the "Document Reviewing Office" had the power to prevent the Emperor's edicts from going into force if it believed them in any respect erroneous, unwise, or unjust, pending reconsideration.[46]

Most Chinese seem to have known for thousands of years that "politics is the art of the possible." And most emperors have been glad to let the responsibility for taking the initiative, and the onus in case of failure, fall on their ministers. Wise emperors have usually hesitated to break markedly with precedent unless they were assured of adequate support.

It is less than seventy years since another ruler of China attempted a sweeping "cultural reform." In 1898 the Emperor Kuang-hsü, with the help of advisers who were brilliant and idealistic but not, unfortunately, widely influential, undertook to modernize China by fiat. A "cataclysmic series of reform edicts" ordered the remaking of many of the most fundamental aspects of the administration and of the governmental institutions. Fairbank writes:

> Seldom has the untrammeled power of an Emperor been more vividly exemplified, at least on paper. The Hundred Days of 1898 produced consternation among the officials high and low . . . too many officials felt themselves too closely endangered by these sudden changes. The Manchu Empress Dowager, Tz'u-hsi, who had been in retirement for the past decade, was able with military support to effect a *coup d'état*, depose the unfortunate Emperor, declare herself regent, and rescind all his edicts.[47]

The Emperor remained a prisoner for the rest of his life, and "when the Empress Dowager finally died in 1908, he somehow predeceased her by one day."[48]

It is evident that Mao and his closest associates hope that they have, in the "Red Guard," supporters who are untainted by traditional pat-

[45] Wang P'u, *T'ang Hui-yao* [A Digest of Governmental Institutions of the T'ang Dynasty] (Taipei, 1960), p. 926.

[46] E. A. Kracke, Jr., *Civil Service in Early Sung China—960–1067* (Cambridge, Mass.: Harvard University Press, 1953), p. 34.

[47] Fairbank, *The United States and China*, pp. 148–49. Meribeth E. Cameron, explaining the failure of the reformers, says that "what militated most against them was the inability of Kuang Hsu to inspire the official class with confidence" (*The Reform Movement in China 1898–1912* [Stanford, Cal.: Stanford University Press, 1931], p. 50).

[48] John K. Fairbank, Edwin O. Reischauer, and Albert M. Craig, *East Asia: The Modern Transformation* (Boston: Houghton Mifflin, 1965), p. 393.

terns of thought. They are reported to range in age from 12 to 19; if so, the oldest of them was only two years old when the Communists won China. They are the creatures of Communism; it is hoped that they will be responsive only to the thought of Mao Tse-tung. But such forces are notoriously easier to call into being than to control, and there are persistent reports that some Red Guards are controlled by anti-Mao elements. Whether Red Guards loyal to Mao, with others who support his claim to sole power, can win the day, remains to be seen.

There are many who hold that China has now been so transformed that its history is irrelevant for understanding its present and its future. This may be true, but up to this time many of the patterns that have been developing in China for thousands of years seem, if not to persist, at least to have interesting counterparts in the brief history of Communist China. Whether the Communists have now succeeded in eradicating Chinese history, as a factor influencing the conduct of the Chinese people, only history can decide.

Addendum by Ping-ti Ho

Being a host member and a co-planner of the Conference on China's Heritage and the Communist Political System, I purposely finished my paper early—on June 18, 1966, to be precise. Consequently, some significant events in mainland China since that date have not been integrated with my analyses of aspects of China's past. The thoroughness with which several other papers convergently tackle the recent developments makes it unnecessary for me to bring mine up to date. It is necessary, however, to prepare this addendum[1] for the following reasons. First, although the first two of the four written comments on my paper are mainly in the nature of an amplification of mine, they contain a number of remarks which either go beyond the scope of, or

[1] This addendum has been sent to the four discussants of my paper, none of whom has decided to comment further.

add depth to, mine. I will therefore call the reader's attention to those brilliant remarks made by these discussants which are most helpful to a deeper understanding of China's past. Second, the scope of China's heritage being extremely broad, I have had to select a few of the many aspects for discussion. Those significant aspects which are not covered in my paper and those perceptive remarks made by its discussants which materially help to make my analyses more balanced can only be pointed out in an addendum. Third, since discussions on a topic as broad as this are bound to result in some differences in opinion and judgment, those major points of divergence between the discussants and me ought to be further pursued. I am deeply grateful to all four scholars who prepared their written comments and shall comment in return on each of their papers in the order I received them.

Professor Arthur F. Wright not only graciously consented to serve as a discussant in absentia but also sent in his comment first. His paper is in many ways an excellent amplification of mine. I wish to point out very briefly the following points he has made which strike me as being particularly helpful to students of Chinese history. First, in only a few sentences he clearly and successfully explains the complex administrative, educational, religious, and technological means by which late imperial Chinese government carried out a policy of Sinicization of the various non-Han ethnic minorities in China proper. Second, I heartily agree with his incisive remark: "I am skeptical about the influence of Taoism on public policy in the Han or later, though we know that monarchs of all ages were susceptible to the appeal of Taoism as a personal faith or body of arcane knowledge. Looking at the 'Annals' of Emperor Wen and Emperor Hsüan [of Western Han], one finds them to have been wise, able, but *busy* monarchs." The first part of this remark greatly strengthens my observation that the main reason why the Western Han state in its early years nominally sponsored Taoism was "because it had already adopted its laws and institutes from the Legalist schools." The latter part of his remark shows how the theory of the monarch's "non-action" was a pious administrative ideal rather than reality. Altogether, his remark concurs with the opinions of the late Etienne Balázs and mine that the traditional Chinese state was substantially Legalist (largely of the metamorphosed Shang Yang school) and only ornamentally Confucian.

Perhaps the most important point made by Professor Wright is the one on the effect of Neo-Confucianism. "The notion," he writes in parentheses, "that the Chinese are *always* tolerant, rational, etc., is a myth that dies hard." He goes on to say:

The new Confucianism not only updated Confucian thought, it added new imperatives unknown in the more permissive and amorphous Confucianism of earlier centuries. It is the *new* Confucianism that insists on the segregation of sexes and the complete subordination of women. It is the new Confucianism that gradually develops the concept of loyalty from what it was —a relationship ultimately determined by the conscience of the subject—into what it became—an imperative to unquestioning and total subordination to any ruler, however idiotic or amoral he might be. The new Confucianism was more totalitarian in intent than the old had been, in that it gave the monarch authority to police all private as well as public morals and customs, to extirpate heresy, etc. No wonder that later emperors found in it the justification for gathering to themselves more and more of the power they formally shared with the literati.

This iconoclastic remark will help us in a systematic reassessment of Neo-Confucianism's many-sided effect on the Chinese state and society. I would like to supplement it further by pointing out that it was Neo-Confucianism that accounted for the rise of xenophobia,[2] a factor with which historians of Ch'ing are so concerned.

Professor Herbert Franke has likewise made important contributions to our study of China's heritage even through the much-confined medium of a short written comment. First, being an authority on Mongol Yüan and other dynasties of conquest, he has pointed out in a very succinct way that China's many ethnic minorities have their own languages, cultures, social systems and are in different stages of evolution. Implied in this remark is the important fact that the present Peking regime, instead of having an overall policy toward all ethnic minorities, must have been working out complex and varied policies to meet the different needs of the various ethnic minorities. I very much hope that Professor Franke will someday write on this subject so as to benefit those of us who are interested in studying China's growth as an ethnic entity.

Second, with his intimate knowledge of both European and Chinese history, Professor Franke has pointed out a significant difference between these two cultures which is not mentioned at all in my paper, namely, the underdevelopment of juridical thought and administration in traditional and contemporary China. He says:

[2] T. F. Tsiang, "China and European Expansion," *Politica*, 2 (March, 1936).

> The position of law has been incomparably stronger in classical antiquity, particularly in Rome and in medieval Europe, than in China. The vast bulk of Chinese juridical literature and the highly developed systematism of traditional Chinese law cannot obscure the fact that law was regarded (similar to economy) not as an entity in itself and potentially superior even to the ruler, but as a mere governing tool. This does not invalidate Professor Ho's pertinent remarks on the Legalist character of the Chinese state since the Han, but what is important is that the administrator of law never developed into a position comparable to that of the juridically trained adviser who played such a role in early modern history of Europe. . . . In one word, Legalism did not produce a class of jurists in China. Law remained one of the many-faceted activities of the scholar-official.

This difference between China and Europe is not only important to historians but also highly relevant to an understanding of certain peculiarities of Communist Chinese law.

Third, no student concerned with realities in traditional China can afford to overlook Professor Franke's remark on the difficulty in discovering the people's real opinion from literary sources—a remark which I shall cite later in my response to one of the major points raised by Professor Creel.

Last but not least, although Professor Franke was too polite to mention it in his written comment, he has kindly made his opinion known to me in conversation that this Conference has not afforded any opportunity for a systematic assessment of what may indeed have been China's most important heritage, namely, the Chinese language. I can hardly agree more with him that it is the Chinese language that has, among other things, shaped Chinese thoughts and philosophy, determined the nature and styles of Chinese literature and arts, acounted at least in part for the failure of traditional China to develop science, and contributed to the molding of a civilization that is uniquely Chinese. It is hoped that someday a group of authorities on Chinese language, philology, literature, history, philosophy, and art could gather together, under different auspices, to do a systematic assessment of the many-sided effect of the Chinese language. Its findings might sharpen our perception of various aspects of Chinese civilization and culture as few other conferences could.

Professor Derk Bodde's comment is full of pertinent remarks and insights, many of which help to make my generalizations in a crowded paper more balanced. There are some differences of opinion between him and me which, in the light of my following answers, are mostly reconcilable.

First, although Professor Bodde disagrees with my conclusion that "the present Peking government's policy toward national minorities is an amplification rather than a reversal of the traditional," actually his views and mine are not irreconcilable. It is true, as he points out, that the traditional policy of forced Sinicization often brought with it "increased exploitation" of the national minorities. But, as I have pointed out in my paper, the ideal of the statesmen of the 1720's was not further to exploit the minorities but rather to stabilize the minority areas by removing certain social and economic grievances of the downtrodden formerly under tribal rule. That the working of the traditional policy of forced Sinicization often brought hardship to the minorities does not mean that the ideal of such a policy differs categorically from that of the present Peking regime. Moreover, although the present government has granted cultural and administrative autonomy to the minorities, in carrying out its policy it sometimes has been forced by circumstances to use coercion and military force. In terms of the ideals and actual practices, therefore, the present Peking policy toward the national minorities looks more like an improvement and amplification rather than a reversal of the old.

Second, Professor Bodde is entirely justified in criticizing Section III of my paper for dealing only with "narrower political factors, notably the power relationships between the Emperor and his bureaucracy." I have done this with a purpose because within limited space the best way, it seems to me, to discover the character of the traditional state is to analyze the power relationship between the monarch and the apex of the bureaucracy. I do not entirely agree with Professor Bodde, who thinks the Censorate "a remarkable and uniquely Chinese institution which did, to some extent, impose checks on the abuse of power." It is true that in rare periods of Chinese history, such as during the reign of T'ang T'ai-tsung (627–49), the emperor did listen patiently to the advice and accepted with grace the remonstrances of high officials who were not necessarily members of the Censorate. To my limited knowledge, for most periods of Chinese history the Censorate fell considerably short of the level of moral courage and integrity that had been theoretically required of it. The main reason was that the censors enjoyed no immunity of life, and throughout the ages not a few censors martyrized themselves by impeaching the emperor's favorite courtiers. I can say more positively that during the intensification of autocracy in Ming-Ch'ing times the Censorate was more often than not a tool for strengthening, rather than an institution to check, the emperor's authority. At its worst it became an instrument of powerful unscrupulous ministers. I think that Professor Franke holds a view similar to mine.

Third, with regard to traditional Chinese law there is actually no fundamental difference in opinion between Professor Bodde and me. From his detailed study of Ch'ing law, especially the Ch'ing penal code, he is impressed by the development of what he calls "a Chinese kind of 'due process,' with which the emperor usually did not interfere." This is indeed to be expected because the penal code was substantially an embodiment of Confucian moral ideals, by which the monarch usually abode. But I have always been more interested in the traditional Chinese administrative law and have therefore pointed out a basic fact that ever since the Han the Emperor had the power to modify or bypass an old statute by issuing a new edict. This not infrequently happened even in Ch'ing times, when the administrative law, as compared with those of earlier periods, "appears to have been more meticulous, regularized, and rational."[3] All this does not mean that I believe that traditional Chinese rulers usually interfered with the law, although cases of real abuse are by no means rare. My original qualification should, I hope, dispel any possible difference in opinion between Professor Bodde and me:

> The fact that the administrative laws of various dynasties indicate in the main a remarkable continuity and steady amplification and rationalization could only be accounted for by the immensity and complexity of the task of governing a huge empire through bureaucracy—this virtually ruled out the possibility of a complete break with the past.

Fourth, Professor Bodde is not certain as to whether the famous saying of Confucius, "yu-chiao wu-lei," really means: "In education there should be no class distinctions." Granted that "class distinction" is a modern concept and expression, I still think that the above translation is probably the best we could think of, especially when this translation is not made by me but by James Legge and accepted by others including Professor Bodde himself.[4]

Fifth, Professor Bodde regrets my lack of mention of what seems to him to be "the greatest single sociological difference between China and

[3] Ping-ti Ho, "The Significance of the Ch'ing Period in Chinese History," *Journal of Asian Studies*, 26, no. 2 (February, 1967): 193.

[4] James Legge (trans.), *The Chinese Classics*, vol. 1: *Confucian Analects*, (Hong Kong, 1861), bk. 15, chap. 38; Fung Yu-lan, *A History of Chinese Philosophy*, 2 vols., trans. Derk Bodde (Peiping: Henri Vetch, 1937), 1:49.

the West: China's failure to develop a mercantile bourgeoisie like that in the West. . . ." I fully agree with him on this great sociological difference between China and the West and must happily remind him that I have attempted a systematic analysis of the factors that seem to have accounted for China's failure to develop a capitalistic system like that which characterized Europe from the sixteenth to the eighteenth century. This article, "The Salt Merchants of Yang-chou: A Study of Commercial Capitalism in Eighteenth-Century China," is in *Harvard Journal of Asiatic Studies*, 17, no. 1–2 (June, 1954): 130–68.

Finally, I am deeply grateful to Professor Bodde for throwing into our discussion his profound and many-faceted knowledge on Chinese philosophy and thought, ancient Chinese political institutions, traditional Chinese law, and his impressions derived from unique opportunities for observing in Peking the rise of the Communist regime. It is this rare combination of learning with firsthand observation that makes his commentary in many ways a healthy counterweight to my analyses and generalizations.

I feel honored by Professor Herrlee Creel's choice of my paper for a long commentary. The greatest value of his paper is his tracing of an important heritage in political thought back to the Western Chou period, a period to which he has dedicated much of his intellectual life. His discussion on the Chou begins with a remark made by me that one of the appellations used by commoners during the past millennium for the Emperor was "Son of Heaven with Real Mandate of Heaven." Being concerned with the ancient origin of the theory of Mandate of Heaven, he finds my remark "curious." What I need to explain is this: whereas in ancient times the theory of Mandate of Heaven had been worked out by early Chou kings and statesmen, and systematized by philosophers of the Confucian school, not until the intensification of autocracy during the past millennium did it really become deep-rooted in the *folklore*. The genius of Western Chou political propaganda (the propaganda cloaking its harsh military and political control of the Shang people), and the progressive shift from a religious reverence of Heaven as a supreme deity to an increasing reliance on man's wisdom and effort to solve human problems are important ingredients of Confucius' humanism, as were systematically discussed by some leading Chinese scholars decades ago.[5] In an over-congested paper such as mine

[5] For a brilliant study of the realistic and harsh Chou military and political control of the Shang nobility, army, and people, see Fu Ssu-nien, "Ta-T'ung Hsiao-T'ung shuo," *Bulletin of the Institute of History and Philology, Academia Sinica*, 2, no. 1 (1930); for an illuminating study of the genius of West-

I could not but choose the Western Han as a datum for my discussion of China's political heritage, for tracing the origin of everything would take us back to prehistory and call for a multiple-volume history of China.

Professor Creel and I differ on the importance of military force as an ultimate determinant in the rise and fall of dynasties in Chinese history. He insists that in our study of the roles played by military force and autocratic rule "we must examine their *relative* importance." It is curious, I think, that he should have begun his comment by saying: "Much of Professor Ho's paper concerns two related subjects: militarism and autocracy." Although I devote one of the five sections to discussing the character of the traditional and modern Chinese state, I allot only a single paragraph to what he calls "militarism." And even in this lone paragraph—not to mention elsewhere in Section III—I point out "the prevailing of the civilian ideal" in normal times and that "in cases of more stable and enduring dynasties the military element had to be subordinated to the civilian." But our more important difference lies in the fact that he questions the validity of my generalization that "every dynasty was founded on military strength or by the transference of military power." I have checked the source on which Professor Creel's questioning of my generalization is based. The source is Professor Lien-sheng Yang's article, "Toward a Study of Dynastic Configurations in Chinese History," which says:

> . . . Internal overlapping is typical in dynastic changes by way of abdication. First, the founder of the new dynasty, or his father, served as a powerful minister under the old dynasty. Finally, his influence became so overwhelming that the last ruler of the old dynasty was obliged to abdicate. This was the normal process of passing on the throne from the Han to the Sung dynasties inclusive.[6]

Professor Creel does not search for the fundamental cause for abdication. May I ask why was the founder of a new dynasty, or his father, so

---

ern Chou political propaganda and the beginnings of "humanistic" thought, see Kuo Mo-jo, *Ch'ing-t'ung shih-tai* [The Bronze Age] (1962 Peking reprint of 1945 ed.), art. 1, "The Evolution of the Concept of Heaven in Pre-Ch'in Times," which was written in 1935, pp. 1–51, especially, pp. 13–25.

[6] Lien-sheng Yang, *Studies in Chinese Institutional History* (Cambridge, Mass.: Harvard University Press, 1961), p. 5. Professor Yang was the only non-commentator of my paper to whom I had shown the preliminary draft. He took my generalization on the relationship between military power and the rise and fall of dynasties for granted.

overwhelmingly powerful as to force the last ruler of the old dynasty to abdicate, if the power of the former was not derived, in the last analysis, from his control of the major, or of all, military forces? I can see no reason to retract from my generalization that "every dynasty was founded on military strength or by the transference of military power" and that "from the dawning of the first empire in 221 B.C. to the founding of the People's Republic of China in 1949 there has not been a single exception."

Professor Creel's paper shows the influence of "public opinion" on the traditional Chinese government. At one point he says that "public opinion has been a far more potent force in China than is sometimes supposed." To comment fully on this point would require a separate paper. Suffice it here to cite the opinions of two discussants of my paper. Professor Herbert Franke says at one place:

> Internal opposition as something legal or tolerated was likewise absent throughout Chinese history. There was, of course, room for opposition within the state machinery, with the Censorate as one of its centers. But even the Censorate had in some ways the effect of strengthening authoritarianism. The numerous factionalist struggles at court never had the character of conflicting and basically different alternatives. In other words, conflicting social realities were virtually never at the bottom of political struggles within the metropolitan bureaucracy. This is markedly different from Europe where even before the invention of parliamentary government social forces could find an expression within the existing bodies social or institutional.

Professor Franke says at another place:

> For traditional and pre-modern China we have remarkably few materials for a research which would, inter alia, show how actually the "people" reacted and felt towards government authority in general. My personal opinion is, contrary to that of some scholars, that the value of literary fiction must not be overrated, particularly because of the high degree of stylization even in those works where admittedly an anti-governmental attitude or social criticism is displayed. The *real* voice of the "people" has, to my knowledge, never been recorded, and we simply do not know how a peasant or artisan of, say, the Ming period, expressed himself. Everything we know has already been filtered in some way through a literary medium.

Professor Bodde independently arrives at a similar conclusion:

> In imperial China an enormous gap traditionally separated the intellectual from the hand worker. The result was that "public opinion" meant primarily the thinking of bureaucrats, landed gentry, and other privileged members of the ruling elite.

All these do not, however, mean that the members of the ruling elite in traditional China did not, for their self-interest or for the interest of the dynasty in which theirs was invested, urge the throne to take the wishes of the nation into account. One of the modern sources from which Professor Creel has cited is Professor John K. Fairbank's *The United States and China*. Professor Creel quotes Fairbank's observation that "all business was in form originated at the bottom and passed upward to the emperor for decision at the top, memorials from the provinces being addressed to the emperor at the capital." What Professor Fairbank discusses here is obviously the administrative procedures and the procedures in the transmission of government documents, not procedures by which "public opinion" was reported to the throne. Moreover, the key word "bottom" refers to the bottom of the administrative machinery, that is, the county government, between which and the grassroots of the nation there was always an enormous gap. As Professor Bodde further explains:

> In China today, however, a major Communist achievement has been the breaking down if not elimination of the traditional gap. Of course the government uses its effective communications channels to pump forth its own version of "public opinion" to the grassroots, but at the same time and via the same channels it is constantly receiving opinion back from the grassroots in a never-ending interchange. Here, . . . continuities between past and present should not blind us to discontinuities.

In concluding my response to Profesor Creel's remark on the importance of "public opinion" in traditional China, I should like to mention in passing that there was no such "long tradition of the independence of Chinese intellectuals . . . ," as Professor Creel believes there to have been. Indeed, ever since the impending collapse of the feudal order during and after Confucius' lifetime the scholars or literati *as a class* were always characterized by their necessity to seek individual patrons or offices by every conceivable means. If anything, the highest career goal of the intellectuals was always government office, which in fact was their main "estate." This can be abundantly documented with biographies in various dynastic histories, novels, and social satires, especially the incomparable *An Unofficial History of the Literati* by Wu Ching-tzu (1701–54). Since they regarded government office as their main estate, how could they have developed a long tradition of independence?

The Chinese social structure, in Professor Creel's opinion, "has been characterized by a good deal of vertical mobility, both upward and downward...." At another place in his paper he says:

> Of all the chancellors who held office during the Former Han dynasty, 22 per cent of those for whom we have biographical data came from "poor" or "lowly" families. (In comparison, C. Wright Mills found that only 18 per cent of the men who held the highest offices in the United States of America between 1789 and 1953 came from "lower-class families.")

Since answers to the nature and extent of social mobility provide a deeper understanding of the character of Chinese society, I must take this oportunity to reply to Professor Creel's generalization more specifically. Let us first put into proper light the statistics worked out by a modern Chinese scholar cited by Professor Creel. There were altogether only 46 chancellors during a period of 214 years. Of this total, 36 have a biographical entry in the dynastic history. Eight of the 36 are described as being from "poor" or "lowly" families. My own checking of all these entries[7] shows that three of the eight who are described as being from "poor" or "lowly" families were followers of the Han founder. Since an unusual amount of social mobility often accompanied a nationwide rebellion and the rise of a new dynasty by military victory, the opportunity-structure through which the three early chancellors climbed up the social ladder was atypical rather than normal.

My more serious concern is about the accuracy of Professor Creel's unqualified generalization that the Chinese society has always been characterized by "a good deal of vertical mobility." To make our discussion meaningful, we have to be as specific as possible with social-mobility data of the major periods of Chinese history. It ought to be pointed out here that systematic quantitative data are available only for the study of elite mobility—that is, entry into officialdom. For periods which have not been studied quantitatively, we have to analyze their main social and institutional characteristics.

[7] Pan Ku, *Han-shu* [History of the Former Han Dynasty] (ed. with Wang Hsien-ch'ien's syncretic commentaries), chap. 40, p. 12a (Ch'en P'ing); chap. 40, p. 17b (Chou Po); chap. 41, p. 11b (Kuan Ying); and all the chapters on "Biographies."

First, the founder of the Later Han dynasty (A.D. 25–220) owed his throne to the support of various local magnates and powerful clans.[8] The consistent dynastic policy was therefore one of continually winning the support of these powerful interests. No wonder that this period witnessed the rise of hereditary aristocracy and a curtailment of the chances for commoners to move up the social ladder. It is true that the Later Han recommendation system was more regularized than that of the Western Han and that recommendation was based largely on "public opinion." But "public opinion" was manufactured almost exclusively by members of the elite and toward the end of the dynasty there finally emerged a system of rating of candidates for office based on family status.[9]

Second, in more than three and a half centuries after the fall of Later Han, the whole social order tended to congeal and the high statuses in particular became hereditary.[10] A recent excellent study of the social composition of the ruling class during the period from the founding of Western Chin in 265 to the Sui reunification in 589, based on an exhaustive analysis of 4,021 biographical entries in dynastic histories, shows that 67.1 per cent of the officials originated from hereditary aristocracy, 18.2 per cent from lower ruling-class families, and 14.7 per cent from "humble" (han-su) families. Be it noted, however, that the word "humble" must be interpreted in the contemporary social con-

[8] Yü Ying-shih, "Tung-Han cheng-ch'üan chih chien-li yü shih-tsu ta-hsing chih kuan-hsi" [The Interrelationship between the Founding of the Eastern Han and the Prominent Clans], *Hsin-ya hsüeh-pao*, 1, no. 2 (1956): 209–280.

[9] Yang Lien-sheng, "Tung-Han ti hao-tsu" [The Aristocracy of the Eastern Han Period], *Ch'ing-hua hsüeh-pao* (Tsing-hua Journal), 11, no. 4 (1936); Miyazaki Ichisada, *Kyūhin Kanjin-hō no konkyū—kayko zenshi* [Studies on the Chiu-p'in-kuan-jen System] (Kyoto, 1956); T'ang Chang ju, *Wei Chin Nan-Pei-Ch'ao-shih lun-ts'ung* [Essays on the History of the Wei-Chin-Nan-Pei-Ch'ao Periods] (Peking, 1955), pp. 85–126; Lao Kan, "Han-tai ch'a-chü chih-tu" [The Han Recommendation System], *Bulletin of the Institute of History and Philology*, 1948; K'ung Yü-fang, "Tung-Han chao-chü chih-tu k'ao" [The Eastern Han Recommendation and Examination System], *Chung-kuo wen-hua yen-chiu kui-k'an*, vol. 3 (September, 1943).

[10] The literature on the gradual freezing of upper statuses during the period of political division is very sizable. We need mention only a few: T'ang Chang-ju, *Wei-Chin-Nan-Pei-Ch'ao-shih lun-ts'ung*; Miyazaki, *Kyūhin Kanjin hō no konkyu—kakyo zenshi*; Wang Chung-lao, *Wei-Chin-Nan-Pei-Ch'ao Sui ch'u-T'ang shih* [A History from the Wei-Chin to the Early T'ang Periods], vol. I (Shanghai, 1961); Wang I-t'ung, *Wu-ch'ao men-ti* [The Hereditary Aristocracy during Five Southern Dynasties] (Ch'eng-tu, 1943), 2 vols.; Yang Yun-ju, *Chiu-p'in chung-cheng yü liu-ch'ao men-fa* [The Chiu-p'in chung-cheng System and the Hereditary Aristocracy of the Six Dynasties] (Shanghai, 1930).

text, for according to usage of that time any family below the hereditary aristocracy was considered "low." Fortunately for modern students,
the compound Chinese adjective "*han-su,*" which may for convenience
be translated as "humble," was defined by contemporaries. A "humble"
person or family was one which did not have "a hereditary estate" in
the broad institutional, social, and economic sense.[11] As to what percentage of the so-called "humble" were humble by the criteria I have
used to classify the much more massive and precise Ming-Ch'ing data, it
is hard to say. But these impressive statistics certainly do not indicate
"a good deal of vertical mobility."

Third, even when China was reunified briefly under the Sui and
more lastingly under the T'ang (618–907), the upper strata of the
bureaucracy was still filled largely with members of prominent aristocratic houses.[12] To be sure, the permanent institutionalization of
the examination system did bring into the ruling elite certain able commoners.[13] But the aggregate number of *chin-shih* (doctors of letters) was
only 6,620 in 288 years, to which we may add 1,621 who obtained less
distinguished and unusual degrees,[14] as compared to a total of 14,774
ranked civil officials and 4,031 ranked military officers in a single average year after the rebellion of 756.[15] While there is no gainsaying the
socio-institutional significance of the examination system, it is doubtful
that the examination system could have drastically altered the nature
of medieval Chinese society. Another excellent modern study, based
also on dynastic history, shows that during the latter half of T'ang, that
is, between 756 and 906, out of a total of 718 officials, 68.8 per cent came
from great aristocratic families, 14.5 per cent from families of less distinguished civil and military officials and local magnates, 19.6 per cent
from families whose exact statuses are unspecified but which were likely
plebeian, and only 2 per cent from proven lowly families.[16]

[11] Mao Han-kuang, *Liang-Chin Nan-Pei-Ch'ao shih-tsu cheng-chih chih
yen-chiu* [A Study of the Aristocracy, 265–589 A.D.], 2 vols. (Taipei, 1966);
see especially vol. 1, p. 8, for contemporary definition for "humble" and summary table on p. 362.

[12] Liang Mao-t'ai, "Kuan-yü T'ang-ch'u cheng-ch'üan hsing-chih te chi-ke
wen-t'i" [Social Composition of Early T'ang Ruling Class], *Li-shih yen-chiu,*
no. 6 (1959), pp. 63–78.

[13] Ch'en Yin-k'o *T'ang-tai cheng-chih-shih lüeh-lun kao* [Studies on T'ang
Political History] (Chungking, 1942).

[14] Ma Tuan-lin, *Wen-hsien t'ung-k'ao* (Commercial Press ed.), chap. 29.

[15] Tu Yu, *T'ung-tien* (Commercial Press ed.) chap. 40.

[16] Sun Kuo-tung, "T'ang-Sung chih-chi she-hui men-ti chih hsiao-jung"
[The Decline of the Aristocracy during Late T'ang and Early Sung], *Hsin-ya*

Fourth, not until the founding of the Sung in 960, when most of the T'ang aristocratic houses had become extinct amid the wars and turmoil of the Five Dynasties (907–60), did the Chinese society become more mobile. From biographies of the Northern Sung period (960–1126) in the dynastic history, a Chinese scholar has found that out of a total of 1,194 cases, 23.6 per cent came from high official families, 28 per cent from less prominent official and local-magnate families, 48.6 per cent from families whose statuses are unspecified but presumed to be plebeian, and 3.3 per cent from peasant families and families without fixed profession or residence.[17] These interesting findings are confirmed by Professor Edward A. Kracke's analysis of two extant *chin-shih* lists of the Southern Sung period, which show that in both examinations more than 50 per cent of successful candidates were from non-official families.[18] There can be little doubt about the significant changes in the social mobility pattern in Sung times, but I should like to express a word of caution. Most of the commoners who made good in the examinations might have originated from reasonably well-to-do families or from families which, though economically poor, had considerable scholastic tradition. The reason for this word of caution is that after desultory though fairly extensive sampling of Sung biographies, I have yet to discover a prominent Sung official whose family was originally truly poor and also lacking that vital scholastic tradition.

Fifth, for the 544 years of the Ming-Ch'ing period we have massive data on elite mobility which are of superior quality. They are lists of successful candidates at various levels, all with precise information on the candidates' ancestry which, as a rule, goes back three generations. Besides, these data are cross-sectional, not like the biographies in dynastic histories which are achievement-biased. It is unnecessary to repeat what I have systematically explained in my book, *The Ladder of Success in Imperial China: Aspects of Social Mobility, 1368–1911*, that my criteria for "commoner" are very strict and for "ruling class" extremely lenient, in order to avoid the possibility of exaggerating the mobility rates. Of a total of 14,562 *chin-shih* with ancestral data, 31.1 per cent originated from families which during the three preceding generations had had no holder of office or of any academic degree. For the Ming

---

hsüeh-pao, 4, no. 1 (1959), *passim*, and especially table between pp. 278 and 279.

[17] *Ibid.*

[18] Edward A. Kracke, "Family vs. Merit in Chinese Civil Service Examinations under the Empire," *Harvard Journal of Asiatic Studies*, 10, no. 2 (1947).

period, such candidates constituted as much as 46.7 per cent of the total; for the Ch'ing period, they accounted for 19.2 per cent. These candidates were from commoner families which had no tangible scholastic tradition. In addition, for the entire Ming-Ch'ing period, 11.6 per cent of *chin-shih* originated from commoner families which had produced a holder or holders of the lowest degree during the three generations preceding the attainment of the highest *chin-shih* degree. The *chin-shih* series are supplemented by a number of Ch'ing *chü-jen* (successful candidates of provincial examinations) lists, which comprise a total of 23,480 cases with ancestral data, and also by three extant *sheng-yüan* (successful candidates of county examinations or holders of the first and lowest degree) lists, which comprise a total of 11,504 cases. It is from an aggregate of 49,546 cases, then, together with my detailed analysis of many types of partially quantifiable and qualitative data and of the various institutionalized and non-institutional channels of mobility, that I have reached the conclusion that the Ming period was one of remarkable fluidity and mobility. It is from my analysis of the long-range mobility trend that I have pointed out the probable causal relationship between the shrinking opportunity-structure and declining mobility rates in the Ch'ing and the social unrest and revolutions that characterized nineteenth- and twentieth-century China.[19]

From the statistics for major post-Han dynasties presented above, it becomes abundantly clear, I think, that the Chinese society has not always been characterized by a great deal of vertical mobility and that the nature of Chinese society has undergone several important changes.[20]

[19] Ho, *The Ladder of Success in Imperial China* (forthcoming second printing), especially chap. 3.

[20] Professor Creel's inclination to idealize China's past is reflected, among other things, in his determination to abide by the erroneous impression that the late Ch'ing statesman Tseng Kuo-fan was from a "poor peasant family." From the standard chronological biography of Tseng and also from Tseng's own literary works, cited in detail in Ho I-k'un, *Tseng Kuo-fan p'ing-chuan* [A Critical Biography of Tseng Kuo-fan] (Shanghai, 1947), pp. 17–24, we know that Tseng was born into a substantial landlord-scholastic family. His grandfather as a young man used to sleep very late and fooled around with local playboys. At the age of 35 he was so shamed by a local elder that he changed his life habit drastically. Henceforth he insisted on doing farming symbolically and frankly admitted that real farming was done by his tenants. Tseng Kuo-fan's great-grandfather began to become prosperous so that his grandfather, the repentant playboy, was able to establish and strengthen the Tseng clan. Tseng Kuo-fan's father was a scholar all his life and never tilled the land. After teaching as a family tutor for more than two decades, Tseng Kuo-fan's father obtained his first degree.

Kwang-Ching Liu $\mathcal{2}$

Nineteenth-Century China:
The Disintegration of the
Old Order and the
Impact of the West

Few will deny that without knowledge of imperial China, one cannot hope to understand China today. For it was not just the land and the people that were inherited by the People's Republic. Despite the many-sided revolution that has occurred, certain basic patterns of power and policy, of ideology, and even of the economy, are as evident today as in the dynasties of the past. One may be sure that the study of China's long and complex history could yield useful insight into that country's current problems and potentialities.

There is, however, a phase of Chinese history that particularly attracts our attention. This is the nineteenth century—not the heyday of the old order, but a period of administrative deterioration and severe social strain. This was, as it happens, also the period when China entered into more extensive contact with the West, when nationalistic sentiment developed, and when certain new values were introduced. An understanding of the crisis and ferment of that time is crucial to our understanding of the China of the twentieth century.

This essay surveys the history of nineteenth-century China from two viewpoints: (1) the problems that confronted the old order, and (2) the new tendencies and movements born of indigenous as well as external forces. I hope to develop the following themes:

1. The breakdown of the old order began in the late eighteenth century in the crucial sector of government administration. This fell, on the whole, within the pattern of the declining periods of previous dynasties. However, the effects of misgovernment were made much worse by the unprecedented growth of population. The consequent overall scarcity of opportunities, together with the tensions created by

administrative and social disruption, produced particularly widespread dissident movements. The increase of literacy and semi-literacy among the people, due partly to the expansion of internal commerce since the eighteenth century, further added to the unrest.

Among Chinese rebels of the nineteenth century, the Taipings, inspired by their version of Christianity, did have an ideology that contained elements of social and political revolution. But their utopian programs were not seriously pursued and in any case they were defeated. Many millions of lives were lost in the civil wars of the third quarter of the century, but the rebellions did not leave any distinct ideological legacy.

The restoration of the Ch'ing order was, however, incomplete. While the governors-general and governors continued to be loyal, vested interests became entrenched within the provincial governments and the *chou* and *hsien* administrations continued to decline. The officials and *shen-shih* (sometimes translated as the "gentry") were, on the whole, more demoralized than ever, and economic and social strains persisted. That major rebellions did not soon occur again was due mainly to the loyalty of new Ch'ing armies in possession of Western weapons.

2. Contacts with the West during the nineteenth century did add impetus to the secular trends of growth in Chinese history—commercial development, improvement of the merchant's status, integration between various parts of the empire. But the most profound result of the West's impact was on the minds and sentiments of the officials and literati. Western encroachments brought a new dimension to the Ch'ing dynasty's crisis. Blind xenophobia arose early and recurred sporadically over local issues, and a great deal of cultural pride continued to exist. But a genuinely nationalistic sentiment nevertheless affected an expanding circle among the elite, and the aim of "wealth and strength" (*fu-ch'iang*) for the state was eventually widely accepted.

Meanwhile, cultural and economic contacts with the West, as well as the undeniable Western power, produced an unprecedented respect for technology, a new view of the world, and fresh concepts of government and political action. Greater facility of communications, resulting from new means of transportation, the new periodical press, and the new schools, added to the ferment. The result was a radical reform movement among the literati elite—one which emphasized political change as well as general enlightenment and liberalization of the society. A new type of revolutionary movement also came into being before the end of the century.

How a new political and social order was to grow out of these movements is the story of the next phase of Chinese history. It is certain, however, that nineteenth-century China had bequeathed a legacy of its own—severe social stresses within a disintegrating body politic and the rise of nationalistic and democratic sentiments. These tendencies were to grow and affect Chinese politics in the first half of the twentieth century. Today, a new, centralized political system has come into being and nationalism has become more pronounced than ever; greater "wealth and strength" for the state have also been achieved. Confucianism is destroyed and the country looks to the future, rather than the past. But despite the thoroughgoing revolution, it is still a question whether the new and expanded structure of opportunities is adequate to meet the aspirations of the people. Social equality has been effected to a remarkable degree, but it remains to be seen whether the latent desire for democracy can be ignored, even though it has long been effectually suppressed.

Administrative Disintegration and Social Strain

Despite the numerous weaknesses of the culture and institutions of imperial China, the *ancien régime* was capable of remarkable stability. For a century after the Manchu victory in 1683, domestic peace and order were so complete that the population multiplied at an unprecedented pace. Imperial control was being extended by the 1750's to all of Sinkiang and to Tibet, while China's supremacy over surrounding areas was regularly celebrated by the coming of tribute missions. The weaknesses of the old order were many. The autocracy and the conformity that characterized the traditional polity were enhanced under the astute rulers of the early and middle Ch'ing. The elaborate system of checks and balances in administration, while supporting monarchical power, made any innovation difficult. The literary examinations, as well as the rigid neo-Confucian orthodoxy, sapped the sources of creativity. Meanwhile, the tax-farming system, along with the Manchu recklessness in selling substantive offices, made many local officials potential enemies of the people. (The Ming-Ch'ing policy of never appointing officials to serve in their home provinces, which made the *chou* and *hsien* magistrates more dependent on the unprincipled clerks and runners, probably made the abuses of government even worse than in previous dynasties.) Yet the idealistic and conscientious side of the Confucian culture continued to be strong. On the whole, the officials were tending to their duties, and there were a sufficient number of *shen-shih* who concerned themselves with local welfare. The life of the majority of the people was hard, but for the better part of the eighteenth century, the living standard in many areas was actually rising.

The long period of stability permitted economic and institutional growth. The increase in the population, up to a point, was favorable to the economy. Large-scale internal migration testified to agricultural expansion. Especially on the lower Yangtze, there was a remarkable growth of commerce and handicraft industry (stimulated partly by the silver brought in through the trade with the West), but as trade developed, there was undoubtedly a great increase in the number of traders and artisans in all parts of the empire. Guilds and *hui-kuan* ("*Landsmann* halls") in hundreds of towns and counties indicate a high degree of inter-regional integration. Literacy or semi-literacy increased more widely than before in towns and even the countryside. While bureaucracy remained dominant, more and more merchant families attained *shen-shih* status through their sons passing the examinations or through purchase of degrees and offices. And there were also signs, however dim, of changes in the world of scholarship and thought. While the stupendous labors of the Han and Sung schools were largely irrelevant to real life, by the late Ch'ien-lung reign, a man like Chuang Ts'un-yü (1719–88), from his study of the "new texts" among ancient classics, had arrived at fresh concepts of history and scholarship.[1] There were also men who, in the tradition of Ku Yen-wu of the early Ch'ing, maintained a scholarly interest in the technical problems of administration, thus anticipating the nineteenth-century "studies of statecraft" (*ching-shih chih hsüeh*).

The equilibrium of the old order was first upset, however, in this crucial area of government administration. Decision-making on personnel and policy being so heavily concentrated in the throne, once the quality of imperial leadership slackened, the entire system began to sink under the effects of inertia and corruption. By the 1770's, in the Ch'ien-lung emperor's old age, the essential communication between the monarch and the principal officials of the empire was no longer maintained. With Ho-shen, the notorious former imperial bodyguard, in the top posts at court (1776–99), corruption was rampant in the metropolitan administration, in the armies, and in the provinces. Evidence abounds of Ho-shen exacting large bribes from governors-general, governors, and finance commissioners, and it fell upon the *chou* and

[1] Ch'ien Mu, *Chung-kuo chin san-pai nien hsüeh-shu shih* [History of Scholarship in China in the Last Three Hundred Years], 2 vols. (Taipei: Shang-wu, 1957), 2: 523–26; Hsiao I-shan, *Ch'ing-tai t'ung-shih* [A General History of the Ch'ing Period], 5 vols. (Taipei: Shang-wu, 1963), 4: 1750–52.

hsien magistrates to produce the funds by imposing irregular levies on the people. The abuses of the yamen underlings became much worse; justice was in abeyance; and the practice became common that the more unscrupulous among the *shen-shih* would so manipulate matters that their tax burden would be transferred to small landowners. Socio-economic abuses, such as concentration of landownership, were aggravated by the unequal tax burden and the lack of recourse to justice, resulting in widespread tenantry and pauperism.

It was at this juncture, as it happened, that China's population, which had been multiplying rapidly, outstripped the land and technological resources. While it was the tyranny of the tax collectors and the landlords that was most resented by the peasants, the sheer weight of numbers added to the general privation and reduced opportunities of employment. Under these circumstances, banditry and peasant riots in protest against taxation occurred more frequently. Strong, rebellious leaders would emerge, usually as organizers of some secret society group, from a stratum of society consisting of monks and priests, shopkeepers and artisans, itinerant merchants and smugglers, dismissed yamen underlings, and even some disgruntled landlords and literati-commoners (that is, scholars who failed to win the *chü-jen* degree or any degree at all).

Beginning in the 1770's, riots, brigandage, and risings led by secret societies were frequent in many parts of China. The first large-scale outbreak linked with the White Lotus sect occurred in Shantung in 1774 and the first insurrection inspired by the Triads, a freemason-like society that advocated "overthrowing the Ch'ing and restoring the Ming" (*fan Ch'ing fu Ming*), took place on Taiwan in 1786. There were risings among the Moslem Chinese in Kansu in the early 1780's and among the Miao aborigines of the Hunan-Kweichow border in the mid-1790's. Although these insurrections were quickly suppressed, the major rebellion led by the White Lotus sect broke out in central China in 1796 and was to last eight years and spread to five provinces. It was only by relying on temporary local armies that the dynasty managed eventually to win out.

The deterioration of the Ch'ing administration continued, however. Again we see the pattern of weaknesses at the top resulting in general malaise. The two emperors who ruled in the first half of the nineteenth century, Chia-ch'ing (1796–1820) and Tao-kuang (1821–50) were well-intentioned enough, but both surrounded themselves with either incompetent timeservers or men who were outright corrupt.[2] Nothing

[2] Hsiao, *Ch'ing-tai t'ung-shih*, 2: 280–83, 885–88.

was done to correct the abuses of the Ch'ing armies, and governors-general and governors were not encouraged to try the reform of local administrations. Banditry and local riots were more frequent than ever. Secret societies linked with the White Lotus staged risings in Shantung in 1807 and in Honan and Chihli in 1813 (the last even found allies among the palace eunuchs in Peking). Similar groups, as well as local bands of outlaw adventurers known as the Nien, staged frequent risings in several North China provinces—for example, in Honan in 1822, Shansi in 1835, Shantung in 1837, and Honan and Shantung in 1842–43. In South China, the loosely connected but seldom concerted Triad groups spread rapidly among the itinerant merchants, boatmen, transport coolies, and bandits in several areas. In Kwangtung, Triad-led revolts were particularly frequent in the 1800's and the 1830's and 1840's. In Hunan, the major rising under Lan Cheng-tsun lasted from 1836 to 1841, and throughout the forties, revolts were staged by other Triad groups of the province. They found response in Hupei and Kiangsi, and some of the Hunan groups eventually spread to Kwangsi in the late 1840's.[3] The disastrous effects of misgovernment and population increase were evident in many parts of China and were aggravated by the serious drought and floods that affected many provinces in the late 1840's. A major upheaval was at hand.

China's trade with the West and with India had meanwhile further expanded, of course, and the Opium War of 1840–42 resulted in the opening of the treaty ports. While the domestic crisis was due principally to indigenous causes, the West also contributed to the process. The sharp decline in the 1830's of the value of the copper cash in terms of silver hurt all taxpayers who had to pay in copper cash. Although brought about perhaps chiefly by the defects in mintage and by Gresham's law, the cash's declining worth was also caused by the outflow of silver that resulted from the growth of the opium trade. The multiplication of the Triad groups in the first two decades of the century was very likely aided by the increased volume of the tea and silk trade in Canton's hinterland. The intensification of their activities after 1820 was undoubtedly connected with the illicit opium traffic. And the Opium War itself was to have many disturbing effects. The dynasty's defeat meant loss of its prestige; but the victory which the Cantonese militiamen claimed in their brief encounter with the British in

[3] Hsiao, Ch'ing-tai t'ung-shih, 3: 3–4; Hsieh Hsing-yao, T'ai-p'ing t'ien-kuo ch'ien-hou Kuang-hsi ti fan-Ch'ing yün-tung [Anti-Ch'ing Movements in Kwangsi Before and After the Taiping Heavenly Kingdom] (Peking: San-lien, 1950), pp. 2–5.

1841 resulted in a popular belief that "the officials are afraid of barbarians, but the barbarians are afraid of the people."[4] When these militiamen (who were organized initially by the *shen-shih* of the Canton area) were disbanded, many moved inland as marauders. Several bands of them, as well as Cantonese pirates who were driven up the river by the British navy, moved to Kwangsi in the late 1840's, adding another element to the many ills of that province—official delinquency, a worsening population-land ratio, community feuds, widespread Triad organization, banditry, and the invasion of marauders from Hunan.[5]

The Taiping Rebellion broke out in Kwangsi in 1850 among the community of Hakka landlords, farmers, charcoal burners, and miners who had been discriminated against by the Kwangsi natives and who came under the spell of Hung Hsiu-ch'üan's "God-worshipping faith" (*pai Shang-ti chiao*). These were to form the nucleus of the armed bands which declared their rebellion in 1851. Only 30,000 strong (including Kwangsi natives who were converted) when they left the province in 1852, the rebel armies had grown to more than two million by the time they reached the lower Yangtze a year later. Meanwhile, a second major rebellion was taking form on the North China plain among the Nien bandits in the famine area north of the Hwai River. A federation of the scattered groups was formed between 1853 and 1855. They declared themselves in rebellion, and a "nest" area of about 200 miles radius was built up. Meanwhile, several Triad groups in Fukien, Kwangtung, and Kwangsi attacked and even occupied important prefectural towns and established small, independent regimes. The Ch'ing dynasty thus faced the prospect of rebellions spreading through all of eastern China, and soon the long pent-up grievances of the Moslem Chinese in Yunnan and in Kansu and Shensi were also to lead to major revolts.

1. The Challenge of the Rebellions

Did the rebellions of the mid-nineteenth century offer an alternative to the old order in China? It must be emphasized that the popular rebellions in Chinese history, although deriving their strength from peasant

---

[4] Lo Erh-kang, *T'ai-p'ing t'ien-kuo shih-kang* [Outline History of the Taiping Heavenly Kingdom] (Shanghai: Shang-wu, 1936), p. 36, quoting Hsia Hsieh's *Yüeh fen chi-shih* [A Record of the Miasma in Kwangtung and Kwangsi] (1869). See Frederic Wakeman, Jr., *Strangers at the Gate: Social Disorder in South China, 1839–1861* (Berkeley: University of California Press, 1966).

[5] Hsieh, *T'ai-p'ing t'ien-kuo ch'ien-hou*, chaps. 1–4.

participation and often inspired by heterodox religious faiths, seldom aimed at the overturn of traditional institutions. The White Lotus Rebellion of 1796–1804 was violently anti-Manchu. But despite its slogan "The people are forced by the officials to revolt" (*kuan p'i min fan*), it did not raise a new dynastic standard, much less contemplate any change in China's political system. Beyond promising the advent of the Bodhisattva Maitreya, who was to bring happiness to all in an unspecified future, the White Lotus rebels, who included landlords among their supporters, had no social message. They believed that wealth or poverty was predestined, although to followers who contributed funds, they pledged future "land awards in proportion to the original assessment."[6] The Triads had, of course, their slogan of "overthrowing the Ch'ing and restoring the Ming," which was often included in their membership oath. There is a question, however, whether this aim was ever taken seriously. In any case, their vision seldom went beyond the model of Ming T'ai-tsu, the iron-fisted monarch remembered also for his concern for the people's livelihood. The Triad rebels of the 1850's did, however, include in their proclamations condemnation of the corruption and tyranny under the Manchu rule—the sale of offices, the failure to restrain yamen clerks and runners. They also claimed that their looting and killing were for the sake of the masses—"to eliminate the tyrannical and to bring peace to the good people" (*ch'u pao an liang*) or "to comfort the people and to attack the criminals" (*tiao min fa tsui*). But the only extant Triad document of the period that contains radical ideas about rents, taxes, and local government, issued in 1862 in Kwangsi, seems to have been influenced by the program of the Taipings.[7]

Like the traditional rebels, the Taiping forces were made up largely of discontented peasants. Their leaders were men of varied backgrounds —scholars who failed the examinations (for example, Hung Hsiu-ch'üan

---

[6] Shao Hsün-cheng, "Pi-mi hui-she, tsung-chiao, yü nung-min chan-cheng" [Secret Societies, Religion, and Peasant Wars], in *Chung-kuo feng-chien she-hui nung-min chan-cheng wen-t'i t'ao-lun chi* [Symposium on the Problem of Peasant Wars in the Chinese Feudal Society], ed. Shih Shao-pin (Peking: San-lien, 1962), pp. 374–79. See also Li Kuang-pi *et al.*, eds., *Chung-kuo nung-min ch'i-i lun-chi* [Collected Essays on Chinese Peasant Risings] (Peking: San-lien, 1958), pp. 346–55.

[7] Chien Yu-wen, *T'ai-p'ing t'ien-kuo ch'üan-shih* [Complete History of the Taiping Heavenly Kingdom], 3 vols. (Hong Kong: Meng-chin shu-wu, 1962), 2: 935–50. See also Hsiang Ta *et al.*, eds., *T'ai-p'ing t'ien-kuo* [The Taiping Heavenly Kingdom], 8 vols. (Peking: Shen-chou kuo-kuang she, 1952; hereafter cited as *TPTK*), 2: 891–99.

himself and his cousin Feng Yün-shan), leaders among charcoal burners and miners (Yang Hsiu-ch'ing and Hsiao Ch'ao-kuei), wealthy landlords who collected more than a hundred thousand piculs of rice in rent annually (Wei Ch'ang-hui and Hu I-kuang), the educated sons of rich peasants (Shih Ta-k'ai), even former yamen clerks (Huang Yü-k'un) and pawnshop owners (Chou Sheng-k'un). Like the White Lotus rebels, the Taiping movement was inspired by a religious faith as well as the ambitions of its leaders. But by a historical accident, the Taiping religion was a Christian heterodoxy, and from the very beginning the movement also had the character of a disciplined military hierarchy.

The Taiping religion must be traced, of course, to Hung Hsiu-ch'üan's famous hallucinatory experience of 1837, when he saw the "venerable old man" in heaven, who berated Confucius and bade Hung exterminate the demons. Six years later, Hung identified this old man with the Christian God portrayed in the pamphlets written by China's first Protestant convert, Liang Ah-fa. Hung undoubtedly had suffered from mental illness, and symptoms of abnormality were to remain with him all his life. But it is nevertheless true that his mental state had enabled him to transcend the bounds of China's cultural heritage.[8] We must hasten to add that he did not rid himself of all his cultural conditioning. The "emperor fixation" that he developed was partly inspired by the typical Chinese admiration for imperial and bureaucratic grandeur, and throughout his career he never disparaged such Confucian virtues as filial piety, loyalty, and rectitude (cheng). Yet Hung was a genuine convert to at least certain elements of Christianity. He subscribed wholeheartedly to the Old Testament image of the only God who created heaven and earth, who is jealous of false deities and relentless in punishing sins against His commandments. Hung also accepted certain attributes of God the Father as described in the New Testament of whom all, of whatever sex, station, or nationality, are the children. It is true that Hung's Heavenly Father was austere rather than loving and that the Chinese prophet had little use for the Sermon on the Mount or the Pauline doctrine of salvation as an inner experience.[9] Yet Hung did devote himself with fervor to the propagation of

[8] P. M. Yap, "The Mental Illness of Hung Hsiu-ch'üan, Leader of the Taiping Rebellion," *Far Eastern Quarterly*, 13 (1953–54): 287–304.

[9] Eugene Powers Boardman, *Christian Influence upon the Ideology of the Taiping Rebellion, 1851–1864* (Madison: University of Wisconsin Press, 1952); Chien Yu-wen, *T'ai-p'ing t'ien-kuo tien-chih t'ung-k'ao* [Studies on the Institutions of the Taiping Heavenly Kingdom], 3 vols. (Hong Kong, 1958), vol. 3, chaps. 18, 19.

his new faith and the destruction of idols—not just the Buddhist and Taoist deities but Confucius as worshipped in the temples and even ancestral tablets in clan halls. Hung's zeal was so infectious that soon after his own conversion in 1843 he began to make converts among his relatives. The simple monotheistic faith, reinforced by the promise of heavenly bliss and warnings of damnation, was powerful enough to induce hundreds of villagers in southeastern Kwangsi to join the Society of God-worshippers in the late 1840's.

As the Society developed military units for the defense of the local landowning and laboring communities (mostly belonging to the Hakka people), other factors played a role. The God-worshipping faith itself was corrupted by wizardry, practiced by Yang Hsiu-ch'ing and others who claimed to speak with the voices of God and Jesus in trances and seizures. In putting together the defense force of the God Worshippers, the leaders borrowed their table of organization from the ancient Chinese classic the *Rites of Chou,* which provides for a centrally controlled hierarchy, combining civil and military functions. When the Heavenly Kingdom of Great Peace (*T'ai-p'ing t'ien-kuo*) was created in 1851, with Hung as the Heavenly King (*t'ien-wang*), it was intended to be a dynasty ruled by a hereditary monarch assisted by some six brother-kings. Yet the monarchy was also a theocracy, with Hung and the other kings claiming to be no more than the instruments of revelation. The Manchus were clearly identified with the devil. They were attacked in the Taiping proclamation of 1851–52 for their demonic origins as well as the corruption and tyranny of their government. While the Taipings appealed to the peasant's discontent as well as to the literati's ethnic sentiments, there is no doubt that they relied on their religion to maintain the discipline of their troops. Faith and comradeship as well as the severe punishments prescribed by Taiping martial laws accounted for the remarkable bravery and self-denial of their soldiers, at least in their early years. The idea of God as the proprietor of all material goods was behind the system of a "sacred treasury" (*sheng-k'u*) to which the earthly possessions of the convert-soldiers were committed (although the system might have owed its origins to the common kitchens maintained by many outlaw groups in Kwangsi).[10] The idea of women being as much children of God as men bolstered the former's status as active members of the Taiping forces. Although Hung and the other kings, exercising their prerogative as imperial rulers, early collected harems,

[10] Franz Michael, *The Taiping Rebellion: History and Documents,* 3 vols. (Seattle: University of Washington Press, 1966–), 1:60–64; Hsieh, *T'ai-p'ing t'ien-kuo ch'ien-hou,* chap. 4.

they succeeded in inducing their troops to observe the strict segregation of the sexes. The puritanical zeal of the Taiping fighters is seen in their remarkable abstinence from looting and rapine. Even in the late 1850's their discipline was superior to that of the imperial troops.[11]

Fighting their way to the Yangtze, the Taipings never occupied the numerous walled cities they captured for long. However, after settling down in their Heavenly Capital, Nanking, in the spring of 1853, they faced the problem of administering this city as well as the considerable territories in the lower Yangtze region which they were to conquer and control. They governed Nanking like an army camp. Men and women were drafted into military and labor services and put in segregated hostels; property was freely commandeered for the "sacred treasury." Elsewhere in their realm, the old administrative division of province, prefecture, and *hsien* was maintained under a new nomenclature. Examinations, in which Taiping scriptures were substituted for the Confucian classics, were held by Hung and other kings to recruit personnel for the central administration, and by commanders in major towns for the selection of provincial officials. Meanwhile, a program called "The Land System of the Heavenly Dynasty" (*T'ien-ch'ao t'ien-mou chih-tu*)[12] was proclaimed in 1853, providing for a drastic change in agrarian relationships as well as a new system of rural government.

This program called for redistribution of land among farmers. A new survey was to determine the productive capacity of each *mou* of land in the kingdom, and every farming family was to be awarded an amount of land (presumably to be held on a hereditary basis, although this was not specified) determined by the number of people in the family—each member more than sixteen years of age to receive one *mou* of the top-grade land and each boy and girl under that age to receive half that amount. Reminiscent of the "equal field" and other systems of land distribution practiced by previous dynasties, the program undoubtedly aimed at the realization of the egalitarian ideal implied in the Taiping religion: "to enable all under Heaven to enjoy the great blessings of the Lord God Almighty: land for all to till, food for all to eat, clothes for all to wear, money for all to spend; fairness and equality everywhere and no one who is not well-fed and warmly clothed." This noble ideal was qualified, however, by another principle based on the Taiping religion: that all property belonged to God and should be put at His disposal. The farming families were required to turn

[11] Chien, *Tien-chih t'ung-k'ao*, vol. 3, chap. 16.

[12] *TPTK*, 1:319–36.

over all their produce, except the amount needed for their own consumption and for the planting of new crops, to the treasury of the state (*kuo-k'u*), so as to prepare for "war and famine." The common treasury was also to provide for special individual needs such as marriage celebrations and funerals. It was plainly not the Taiping intention to foster a class of rich peasantry. In fact, the farmers were regarded as the lowest class in society. It was explicitly provided that officials found guilty of delinquency should be "demoted to being farmers" (*chuo wei nung*).

For the administration of the rural areas, the Taipings envisaged a civil-military hierarchy that would penetrate to the grassroots. The officers at the several levels were to bear the same titles as those of the mobile Taiping army, borrowed from the *Rites of Chou*. The basic unit of twenty-five families was administered by a sergeant (*liang ssuma*); every hundred families were headed by a lieutenant (*tsu-chang*); 500 families by a captain (*lü-shuai*); 2,500 families by a colonel (*shih-shuai*); and 12,500 families by a corps general (*chün-shuai*). The corps generals in an area equivalent to the *hsien* were supervised by a civil administrator called the corps supervisor (*chien-chün*). The long arm of the state thus reached down to the villages. Each sergeant was to be responsible for collecting grain from the twenty-five families in his charge, for the administration of justice, for sabbath services, and for the daily Bible school for children. The higher officers were to transmit the grain, to hear appeals, and to serve as itinerant preachers. Each farming family was, moreover, to furnish one person for the local defense force, commanded by the hierarchy. With the *shen-shih* and other local notables wiped out by the redistribution of land, this system—which reflected the religious as well as the military concerns of the Taipings—would regiment the Chinese countryside. The officers of the entire hierarchy were to be centrally controlled and appointed by the Heavenly King himself. But an egalitarian aspect was introduced by the provision that those same officers were to be chosen from the farmers who distinguished themselves in agricultural pursuits and in military service (an emphasis reminiscent of Legalism in ancient China). The candidates for such offices must, however, be approved by each level of the hierarchy, beginning with the sergeant, who was to submit the initial "recommendation" (*pao-chü*).

Although the "Land System of the Heavenly Dynasty" would have wrought vast changes in the Chinese social and political scene, it was never put into effect. Given the continued warfare and the insuperable obstacles to a thorough land survey, it is not surprising the Taipings never actually attempted land redistribution. The military commanders of the Taiping-controlled areas did, however, set up new *hsien* officials with the title of "corps supervisor" and charge them with the responsibility for producing revenue. Some of these new officials were successful candidates in the local Taiping examinations and included men of various backgrounds—monks and priests, boatmen and peddlers, and sometimes scholars who had previously won lower degrees under the Ch'ing. Others were former yamen secretaries and clerks and, in rare cases, even former *hsien* magistrates. The new *hsien* chief, under the close supervision of Taiping military men, would, in turn, appoint "village officials" (*hsiang-kuan*) using the titles stipulated in the "Land System"—corps general, colonel, captain, lieutenant, and sergeant. These were actually tax-farmers, however, and they were almost always chosen from powerful local figures (*t'u-hao* or *t'u-pa*), sometimes even men of *shen-shih* status. While this system undoubtedly gave opportunity to certain elements hitherto not prominent in society, it seems that in most cases it was the landlords and former yamen underlings that were the beneficiaries of the new regime. There are instances where the Taipings collected revenue directly from the tenants and freed them of the obligation to pay rent to the landlord. But the general practice was to support the agrarian status quo. Taiping proclamations even exhorted the tenants to pay their rents dutifully.[13]

If the Taipings had been more successful militarily and their regime had lasted longer, it is conceivable that the "Land System" would have been carried out in earnest. As it was, even though a fair degree of morale was long maintained among their troops, especially those who originally came from Kwangsi, their idealism was rather shortlived. Taiping Christianity became further corrupted and Hung's idiosyncrasies more marked, while Yang Hsiu-ch'ing, claiming to be not only God's spokesman but the Holy Ghost incarnate, was preoccupied with the enhancement of his personal power. The Taipings made serious strategic errors. They employed only a light force in their northern expedition toward Peking and meanwhile overextended themselves in campaigns toward the upper Yangtze. Discipline among the troops became lax. After the great purges of 1856, when Yang and Wei Ch'ang-hui, together with many of their followers, were murdered, the court was for a time almost leaderless. What maintained the regime was the

---

[13] See the numerous contemporary accounts, as well as tax documents, cited in Chien, *Tien-chih t'ung-k'ao*, vol. 1, chaps. 8, 9.

loyalty toward the monarch of the principal commanders—a traditional Chinese sentiment.[14] The ethical message of the Taipings was further diluted, as may be seen in the fact that the theoretically equal status of women was not maintained. Few women served in official positions, except in palaces and the "women's hostels" (*nü-ying*). While bound feet were prohibited, the high officials were permitted (and sometimes awarded) concubines, and the troops recruited camp followers.[15]

Idealism was rekindled at the Taiping court when Hung Jen-kan, the Heavenly King's cousin and one of his earliest converts, after several unsuccessful attempts, finally came to Nanking in 1859 and was made the monarch's chief adviser. Having lived in Hong Kong for more than four years as a catechist of the London Missionary Society, Hung Jen-kan, without negating the Heavenly King's bizarre doctrines, sought to inject a more inward, personal faith into Taiping religion. He also sought to restore unity of command in the government and to rid it of such abuses as the sale of titles and offices. He had a vision of industrialization through private enterprise—steamships, railways, mines that would use machines, banks financed by private capital. He lamented the lack of communication between the people and the monarch. He praised the governments of the West, including that of the United States, and advocated the publication of newspapers and the installation of "secret chests" (*an-kuei*) where the people could deposit complaints anonymously. He also favored "public associations of the literati and the people" (*shih-min kung-hui*) for the promotion of education and philanthropy.[16] Hung Jen-kan's brilliant strategic scheme of a two-pronged attack on the Yangtze area between Nanking and Hankow with a view to saving the key city of Anking was frustrated by the lack of coordination between the two chief commanders, Li Hsiu-ch'eng and Ch'en Yü-ch'eng. Hung Jen-kan himself fell from power in 1861. Thereafter, although Li Hsiu-ch'eng, in the parts of Kiangsu and Chekiang which he controlled, was able to inspire high morale among his troops and even developed the reputation of being a solicitous governor, the Taiping cause was already doomed. The courage of the old Kwangsi soldiers, intensified by the fear of extermination by Ch'ing forces, assured strong resistance until the very end. But with the fall of Nanking in 1864 and the massacres

[14] See, for example, Li Hsiu-ch'eng's confession, *TPTK*, 2:787–840.

[15] Chien, *Tien-chih t'ung-k'ao*, vol. 2, chap. 15.

[16] *Tzu cheng hsin-pien* [A New Work for Aid in Administration], in *TPTK*, 2:532–35.

and mopping-up campaigns that followed, the core of the Taiping movement and its ideology as well were effectively wiped out.[17]

Unlike the Taipings, the Niens did not have a distinct religious faith, although they used the oaths and symbols of secret societies and at least some of the Nien bands appear to have been affiliated with the White Lotus sect in the past. That the Niens did have vague dynastic aspirations is indicated by the title "King of the Great Han with Manifest Mandate" (*Ta-Han ming-ming wang*) adopted by Chang Lo-hsing in 1855. But the Niens, with their loosely federated commands under banners of different colors, never developed more than a military organization. Morale was maintained chiefly by the solidarity among the clans that participated in the movement. In the earth-wall communities of their "nest" areas, it was the clan leaders who were also large landowners that served as "masters" (*chu*), charged with responsibility for mobilizing manpower and resources. Some of the Nien leaders were illiterate (for instance, Chang Lo-hsing himself, who was the head of a salt-smuggling gang); others were landowners and even holders of lower degrees. They put into practice the ideal of "robbing the rich and relieving the poor" (*chieh-fu chi-p'in*), and won peasant support by distributing food and money. While they treated Ch'ing officials with vengeful cruelty, it seems that the landlord-tenant relationship in their communities was generally undisturbed, although the "masters," in order to raise provisions, could force the landowners to make large contributions from their harvests. The fact that many local *shen-shih* cooperated with the Niens seems to indicate the latter's lack of a drastic social program.[18] In any case, with the final defeat of their main forces in 1868, whatever radical ideas the Niens might have entertained disappeared without trace even among the secret societies that continued to be active in North China. For a few years after 1868, the Ch'ing dynasty continued to be faced with the revolt of the Moslem Chinese in Yunnan and in Shensi and Kansu. In the Shensi-Kansu area, especially, the rebels were inspired by the so-called

[17] The Taiping legend remained, of course. Sun Yat-sen heard stories about the Taipings in his boyhood and later remembered a good many details of the movement. See P'eng Tse-i, *T'ai-p'ing t'ien-kuo ko-ming ssu-ch'ao* [The Revolutionary Ideas of the Taiping Heavenly Kingdom] (Shanghai: Shang-wu, 1946), pp. 127–31.

[18] S. Y. Teng, *The Nien Army and their Guerrilla Warfare, 1851–1868* (Paris: Mouton, 1961), pp. 69–71, 100–112; Siang-tseh Chiang, *The Nien Rebellion* (Seattle: University of Washington Press, 1954), pp. 44–58; Fox Butterfield, "The Legend of Sung Ching-shih: An Episode in Communist Historiography," *Papers on China*, 18 (1964): 140–41.

New Teaching, a sect of Chinese Islam that had been developing since the eighteenth century. But neither the Moslem kingdom in Yunnan, nor the more widespread movement in the northwest under the fiery "generalissimo" (*ta tsung-jung*) Ma Hua-lung ever hoped to win control of more than a corner of the Ch'ing empire.[19] With the suppression of the Moslem revolts in 1873, the influence of the New Teaching declined. Whatever new ideologies had emerged in the mid-nineteenth century, they had failed to overturn China's old order.

2. Restoration and Continued Disintegration

That the dynasty managed to suppress the rebellions testifies to the continued strength of the old order. The crisis had brought about a greater realism on the part of the Manchu court. Although the emperor Hsien-feng (1851–61) was young and inexperienced, he listened to his Manchu advisers' admonition that in order to defeat the rebels it would be necessary to give greater authority in the provinces to Chinese officials of ability. Such officials were asked to organize local militias (*t'uan-lien*) in the Yangtze area against the Taipings, and Chinese were appointed as governors of the key provinces—for example, Hu Lin-i in Hupei and Lo Ping-chang in Hunan. Tseng Kuo-fan (1811–72), realizing that local militiamen were useless in major campaigns, organized a large and well-disciplined temporary imperial army (*yung* or *yung-ying*) in Hunan and won crucial victories against the Taipings. By the end of the decade, in 1860, the throne, on the advice of the Manchu nobleman Su-shun,[20] appointed Tseng Governor-General of Liangkiang with authority to control four provinces in the lower Yangtze area. After the Hsien-feng emperor died in 1861, a mere boy succeeded him and two empresses dowager were regents. But Prince Kung and Wen-hsiang, two Manchu statesmen of unusual sagacity, were for a few years the chief advisers to the throne. They continued the wise policy of relying on talented Chinese and responded creatively to many of their proposals. The more enlightened leadership from Peking led to a remarkable release of energy among provincial officials.

Such men as Tseng Kuo-fan were deeply loyal to the Ch'ing dynasty and were concerned over the Taiping challenge to the Confucian order. Their careers testified, moreover, to the versatility of the Confucian personality. Despite their literary training and habits, they proved

[19] Pai Shou-i, ed., *Hui-min ch'i-i* [The Moslem Risings], 4 vols. (Peking: Shen-chou kuo-kuang she, 1953), 1:52; 2:131; 4:plate.

[20] Hsiao, *Ch'ing-tai t'ung-shih*, 3:413–15.

themselves capable of organizing armed forces and arranging for their financing. They frankly accepted utilitarian aims (*kung-li*) as defined by such Confucians as Wang An-shih and Yeh Shih of the Sung Dynasty (who were considered unorthodox under the Ch'ing). Unfortunately, they could also be completely ruthless, as evidenced by their policy of exterminating the Taiping and other rebels so as to prevent any possibility of their recrudescence—thus making the civil wars of the nineteenth century among the cruellest in history. Tseng's frequent exhortations to himself and others that "severe punishments" and "harsh laws" must be employed were reminiscent of ancient Legalism.[21] Yet Tseng and his colleagues were faced with the tasks of rehabilitation as well as war, and in the areas recovered from the rebels they strove to realize the Confucian ideal of good government through properly trained men. There emerged in the 1860's many truly conscientious governors-general and governors who, within the limits of inherited institutions as well as their own restricted social vision, did work for benevolent and just government. It was this resurgence of Confucian idealism that made the T'ung-chih reign (1862–74) a period of restoration as defined by Mrs. Wright—not just an epoch of dynastic survival, but one in which the inherited civilization was reinvigorated.[22]

The question remains, however, whether—despite the outburst of energy on the part of scholar-officials—the process of administrative disintegration that had started in the late eighteenth century was arrested, and whether the severe economic and social tension that had been apparent since then was relaxed. Could it be that despite the surface calm of the late nineteenth century, the old order actually deteriorated further and that the potentiality for revolution actually increased?

Michael, in his influential writings, has argued that there never was a T'ung-chih restoration. Instead, he has emphasized the growth of "regionalism," by which is meant the increased military and financial power of the governors-general and governors born of the new armies raised initially to combat the rebels (the *yung* or *yung-ying*

---

[21] Chiang Shih-jung, ed., *Tseng Kuo-fan wei-k'an hsin-kao* [Unpublished Letters of Tseng Kuo-fan] (Shanghai: Chung-hua, 1959), p. 205; Tseng Kuo-fan, *Tseng Wen-cheng kung ch'üan-chi* [Complete Papers of Tseng Kuo-fan], 5 vols. (Taipei: Shih-chieh, 1965), vol. 5; *Pi-tu* [Replies to Petitions], p. 5; *Tsa-chu* [Miscellaneous Writings], pp. 75, 85, 87.

[22] Mary Clabaugh Wright, *The Last Stand of Chinese Conservatism: The T'ung-chih Restoration, 1862–1874* (Stanford: Stanford University Press, 1957).

forces) and the new commercial tax of likin.[23] This much is certainly true: the new armies and the new taxes were less subject to the effective supervision of the Board of War and the Board of Revenue than the traditional armies and taxes. Large breaches had therefore been made in the elaborate system of checks and controls that was built up in the early Ch'ing, and in this sense the old political order had been weakened. Moreover, the *yung* forces and the likin collectors soon formed strong vested interests within the provincial administration. The *yung* forces were organized on the principle that the commanders (*t'ung-ling*) would personally choose the battalion officers (*ying-kuan*), who in turn had complete responsibility for the 600 or so men in their respective battalions. The personal allegiances between the several levels within a large unit became so strong that it was difficult to reorganize the forces by changing the commanders and officers. Similarly, certain personnel in the provincial likin bureaus and their many branches developed such special connections and such expertise as tax-farmers that they became indispensable to any bureau commissioners (*tsung-pan*) which the governors-general and governors might appoint.[24] The relaxing of central control over armies and taxes was eventually to contribute to the collapse of the Ch'ing dynasty in 1911.

All this does not mean, however, that in the period between the suppression of the Taipings and the fall of the dynasty, the court had lost control of the provinces. Despite the greater administrative leeway[25] enjoyed by the governors-general and governors, the throne never

[23] Franz Michael, "Military Organization and Power Structure of China During the Taiping Rebellion," *Pacific Historical Review*, 18 (1949): 469–83; "Regionalism in Nineteenth-Century China," introduction to Stanley Spector, *Li Hung-chang and the Huai Army* (Seattle: University of Washington Press, 1964). See also Michael, *The Taiping Rebellion*, 1:198.

[24] Lo Erh-kang, *Hsiang-chün hsin-chih* [A New History of the Hunan Army] (Shanghai: Shang-wu, 1939), pp. 222–32; *Ch'ing-ch'ao hsü wen-hsien t'ung-k'ao* [Encyclopedia of the Historical Records of the Ch'ing Dynasty, Continued], 400 *chüan* (Taipei: Hsin-hsing, 1959), 49.8042–46, 8052–53. Further evidence may be found in the published papers of Li Hung-chang, Shen Pao-chen, Ting Jih-ch'ang, Chang Chih-tung, and Liu K'un-i.

[25] This administrative leeway is further seen in the domination of post-Taiping governors-general and governors over the provincial financial and judicial commissioners, who had the statutory authority to memorialize the throne and to communicate with the metropolitan boards. In the post-Taiping period, the two commissioners were often appointed at the recommendation of the governor-general or governor. Their authority was frequently bypassed by new commissaries (*liang-t'ai*) and other bureaus. See Lo, *Hsiang-chün hsin-chih*, pp. 243–44.

lost its power of appointment of all regular civil and military officials, including the governors-general and governors themselves. It is true that there were not a few governors-general and governors who owed their rise in officialdom to their having organized and commanded the *yung* forces during the rebellions—for example, Li Hung-chang, Tso Tsung-t'ang, Liu K'un-i, Liu Ming-ch'uan. But this does not mean that these men could direct or employ these forces independently of the throne. Although the practice developed that the governors-general and governors would nominate the commanders (*t'ung-ling*) of such armies, the throne's approval was required for the appointments. The Board of War controlled the Green Standard titles of general-in-chief (*t'i-tu*) and brigade-general (*tsung-ping*) which the commanders of the *yung* forces were expected to have, as well as the lesser titles— colonel (*fu-chiang*), lieutenant-colonel (*ts'an-ch'iang*), and the rest— so coveted by the subordinate officers. The court also controlled the appropriations for these armies and it frequently transferred the units of such forces from one province to another.[26] Likewise, the governors-general and governors were not free to dispose as they saw fit of the likin revenue. As soon as the Taiping wars were over, they were re-quired to report to Peking annually the amounts they obtained from the likin. While a considerable portion of the reported sums was re-tained in the provinces, especially for the support of the *yung* forces as authorized by the throne, often even larger sums were remitted either directly to Peking, to meet such imperial expenses as construc-tion of palaces or payment of indemnities, or to other provinces at the court's direction—to be used, for example, for financing Li Hung-chang's Anhwei Army, stationed in several provinces, Tso Tsung-t'ang's expedition to the northwest, or the war against the French in Vietnam or Taiwan. A favorite method by which the court raised funds in the post-Taiping period was to request large lump sums from the provincial likin revenue. While a governor-general or a governor could sometimes employ dilatory tactics in meeting such demands, they could not be disregarded, especially when the request was urgent, without jeopardizing his own position.[27]

[26] Kwang-Ching Liu, "Li Hung-chang in Chihli: The Emergence of a Policy, 1870–1875," in Albert Feuerwerker, Rhoads Murphey, and Mary C. Wright, eds., *Approaches to Modern Chinese History* (Berkeley: University of Califor-nia Press, 1967), pp. 70–81.

[27] David Pong, "The Income and Military Expenditure of Kiangsi Province in the Last Years (1860–1864) of the Taiping Rebellion," *Journal of Asian Studies*, 26 (1966–67): 49–66; Lo Yü-tung, "Kuang-hsü-ch'ao pu-chiu ts'ai-

The striking fact is that the more flexible procedures concerning the new armies and taxes bolstered rather than weakened the Ch'ing regime. Since the Banner and the Green Standard armies never recovered (and the effort to give special training to selected units of these forces proved ineffective), it was the *yung* forces that guarded internal peace and security. Commenting on the complaint by officials in Peking that the support of the *yung* forces in the entire empire cost as much as twenty million taels annually (largely from the likin) out of the total imperial revenue of fifty million, Li Hung-chang commented to a colleague in the early 1870's that without the *yung* forces, "there would decidedly be no peace and order and the fifty million would not be in existence."[28] Li's Anhwei Army was used during that decade to suppress brigandage and risings in Chihli, Shantung, Kiangsu, and Hupei. The *yung* forces maintained in almost every province were used for similar purposes. One should note that several governors-general who were also leaders of large *yung* forces were given extraordinarily long tenure—Li Hung-chang for twenty-five years in Chihli, Liu K'un-i a total of nine years in Liangkiang, Chang Chih-tung a total of fifteen years in Hukwang. But these and indeed all the governors-general and governors continued to be absolutely loyal.[29]

While the "regionalism" thesis must therefore be modified, there is still the question whether the government as a whole did not further deteriorate. For a few years after 1861, with Prince Kung and Wen-hsiang enjoying great power, the quality of the imperial decisions did improve. But even in the best years of the T'ung-chih period, the spirit of innovation hardly ever touched the Board of Revenue and the Board of Civil Appointments. By the late 1860's, the Empress Dowager Tz'u-hsi had managed to cut down Prince Kung's influence, and she was even more dominant by the time another boy emperor,

cheng chih fang-ts'e" [Remedial Financial Measures of the Kuang-hsü Reign], *Chung-kuo chin-tai ching-chi shih yen-chiu chi-k'an* [Journal of Modern Chinese Economic History], 1, no. 2 (1933): 189–270. Further evidence appears in the published papers of Li Hung-chang, Shen Pao-chen, Chang Chih-tung, and Liu K'un-i.

[28] Li Hung-chang, *Li Wen-chung kung ch'üan-chi* [Complete Papers of Li Hung-chang], 100 *ts'e* (Nanking, 1908), *p'eng-liao han-kao* [Letters to Friends and Colleagues], 13.31*b*.

[29] The decision of a number of governors-general and governors not to recognize the imperial edict declaring war against the powers in June, 1900, was due to exceptional circumstances and was justified by the fact that adherence to the pro-Boxer decree would bring disaster to the dynasty itself.

Kuang-hsü (1875–1908), ascended the throne. Tz'u-hsi was skillful in manipulating power and personalities. While she continued to rely on the Chinese to serve as governors-general and governors, she sought to restrain them, not only by balancing one Chinese faction against another, but also by enforcing the control exercised by the metropolitan boards. The elaborate regulations of such boards as Revenue, Civil Appointments, and War were by no means to be disregarded.[30] The Board of Revenue still controlled the land-tax system, the Board of Civil Appointments all the regular posts of the local government, and the Board of War the dispensation of Green Standard titles. Even when occasionally a good man served as board president or vice-president, the permanent staffs of these ministries, who were notoriously corrupt and were sticklers for the inherited regulations, were still to be reckoned with.

The governors-general and governors of the T'ung-chih period did make an effort to rehabilitate the agricultural economy and to reassert the traditional principles of government. But their success, comparatively speaking, was greater in the former than in the latter. The partial recovery of the war-torn areas was due chiefly to the industry of the peasants, including the new settlers from other provinces. But such measures as the remission and reduction of taxes, work relief, and the distribution of seeds and tools did contribute to the recuperation of the areas concerned. One should note that due to the obstruction of the Board of Revenue, tax-reduction programs were applied to only a few areas and were not as generous as had been originally proposed by provincial officials. Moreover, due to the deterioration of the *chou* and *hsien* administration, surtaxes and irregular levies were soon revived—in Kiangsu as early as the 1870's—thus negating the effects of the beneficent measures.[31]

Many governors-general and governors were indeed worried about the quality of local government and as far as they could they did seek ways to improve it. They administered the civil service examinations that were promptly revived in places formerly occupied or disrupted by the rebels and introduced questions that could better test the candi-

[30] Evidence may be found in the published papers of Li Hung-chang, Chang Chih-tung, and Liu K'un-i.

[31] Hsia Nai, "The Land Tax in the Yangtze Provinces before and after the Taiping Rebellion," *Ch'ing-hua hsüeh-pao* [Tsing Hua Journal of Chinese Studies], 10, no. 2 (1935), 409–74; summary translation in E-tu Zen Sun and John de Francis, *Chinese Social History* (Washington: American Council of Learned Societies, 1956), pp. 361–82.

dates' aptitudes. They took advantage of the system of "recommendation on the basis of military merit" (*chün-kung pao-chü*) and nominated men for local government posts. The fact remains, however, that
the power of appointment regarding such posts rested with Peking.
The number of men who won *chou* and *hsien* offices through "recommendation" was very few. Statistics discovered by Ho show that in
1871, of the 1,790 local officials in all the empire between the fourth
and the seventh ranks (which included circuit intendants, prefects,
and *chou* and *hsien* magistrates), only about 4 per cent were recommended by the provincial authorities on the ground of military and
other merits or promoted from subofficial positions. By 1895, the percentage of officials who belonged to those two categories had dwindled
to 1.5 per cent.[32] The bulk of the local appointments were, in fact,
determined by the Board of Revenue as well as the Board of Civil
Appointments. Despite the criticism voiced by many governors-general
and governors, the practice of the Board of Revenue's inviting "contributions toward substantive offices" (*shih-chih chüan-shu*) remained
in force throughout the century. Such regulations on this matter as
were approved during the Hsien-feng reign were not suspended until
1879, and four years later, in 1883, they were restored and not rescinded until 1901. During the last three or four decades of the century,
roughly half of the local officials in all the empire between the fourth
and the seventh ranks qualified by purchase. In 1871, of the total
number of 1,790 such officials, 51 per cent qualified by contributions.
In 1895, when the total number had increased to 1,975, 49 per cent
still bought their way into office. Moreover, among those who qualified
by holding regular degrees, there were also men whose appointment
or promotion was facilitated by a money donation.[33] It is true that

[32] Ping-ti Ho, *The Ladder of Success in Imperial China: Aspects of Social
Mobility, 1368–1911* (New York: Columbia University Press, 1962), pp. 48–49.
It should be noted that among officials who qualified by degree or by purchase,
a number in particularly vital posts were actually appointed on the recommendation of the governors-general or governors. These posts, known as "important posts to which officials are transferred by memorial from the province
concerned" (*pen-sheng t'i-tiao yao-ch'üeh*) were few in number. It seems that
the circuits, prefectures, and *chou* and *hsien* that included a treaty port were
always designated important posts. See *Ch'ing-ch'ao hsü wen-hsien t'ung-k'ao*,
135.8949–56.

[33] *Ch'ing-ch'ao hsü wen-hsien t'ung-k'ao*, 93.8530–35; Ho, *Success in Imperial
China*, pp. 48–50. The practice of selling offices was revived in 1903 and prohibited again in 1906. Even when it was prohibited, those who donated more
than Tls. 10,000 could still get offices.

some governors-general and governors of the T'ung-chih reign, including Tso Tsung-t'ang, Shen Pao-chen, and Ting Jih-ch'ang, did obtain the throne's approval for requiring those who bought offices to take simple tests before allowing them to assume their posts. But the boards at Peking were too solicitous of their authority and concerned about the loss of revenue to allow the appointments to be questioned, and these tests were soon dropped. Among those who purchased office were holders of the *shen-yüan* degree, whose literary and moral training was not necessarily inferior to that of men who passed the higher examinations. There cannot be any doubt, however, that numerous purchasers of the *chou* and *hsien* offices regarded the several thousand taels they paid as an investment. It is a matter of record that many merchants and even former yamen clerks thus rose to be magistrates.[34]

While it is not possible to say with certainty that the Ch'ing local government was worse in the late than in the early nineteenth century, this hypothesis seems to be supported by the fact that as of 1840, only 29 per cent of the 1,949 local officials between the fourth and the seventh ranks qualified by purchase,[35] whereas in 1895, as we have seen, the figure was 49 per cent of 1,975 such officials. When administration of *chou* and *hsien* was in the hands of unscrupulous men, the abuses of the yamen underlings undoubtedly became more unrestrained. Even the most vigorous of the T'ung-chih officials acknowledged that they could do little or nothing to improve the quality or conduct of the *chou* and *hsien* clerks. While the governors-general and governors continued to make periodic reports to the Board of Civil Appointments on the performance of the *chou* and *hsien* magistrates, there were so many rules that protected the latter (and the tenure of these officials in any one place was so short) that as long as they produced the annual land-tax quotas, it was difficult to take effective action against them.[36] The general atmosphere of the entire provincial bureaucracy became increasingly poisoned. Blatant corruption became common even among those *chou* and *hsien* magistrates who qualified by success in examinations. The supervision over them exercised by

[34] *Ch'ing-ch'ao hsü wen-hsien t'ung-k'ao*, 93.8531–35; Wright, *Last Stand of Chinese Conservatism*, pp. 83, 85–86.

[35] Ho, *Success in Imperial China*, p. 49.

[36] For example, an impeached official could be asked to redeem himself by future service, and a "dismissed" official might be allowed to remain at his post without title (*ko-chih liu-jen*); see Wright, *Last Stand of Chinese Conservatism*, pp. 88, 427.

prefects and circuit intendants was often merely nominal, particularly since many of these officials had themselves bought their way into office and expected monetary gifts from the magistrates.

One can further hypothesize that the social strains in the late nineteenth century were just as serious as in the period before the Taiping Rebellion. For the literati of the empire, opportunities had shrunk. Since as many as 49 per cent of the local officials had qualified by purchase—and many central government functionaries also obtained their offices in this manner—given the limited number of regular official posts, many men who were qualified to become officials by having won the *chü-jen* and higher degrees must have been passed over. It is true that many new bureaus were established in the provinces in the post-Taiping period, such as those administering likin, military supplies or industrialization projects. But these new bureaus were more often than not staffed by men who purchased honorary titles or degrees;[37] meanwhile, the number of regular degree-holders was increasing. As a reward for large donations during the war against the rebels, the quotas for the *chü-jen* and the *sheng-yüan* degrees were increased for some localities. While the number of *chü-jen* scholars probably increased only slightly, the number of *sheng-yüan* is believed to have been some 20 per cent larger in the post-Taiping period. It has been estimated that there were, at any given time in the late nineteenth century, about 10,000 *chü-jen* and 600,000 *sheng-yüan* in the empire.[38] These figures represented, of course, only a fraction of the literate population of the country, which must have been increasing with the expansion of commerce. The scarcity of official posts is reflected in the frenzied competition for every bureaucratic opening, so vividly described in such novels as *Kuang-ch'ang hsien-hsing chi* (Phantom Shapes in Officialdom [1901]) and *Erh-shih nien-lai mu-tu chih kuai hsien-hsiang* (Strange Phenomena Seen in the Last Twenty Years [1902]).

Even more acute tension existed, however, in rural society, where many factors that plagued the pre-Taiping period continued to exist. As a result of the loss of millions upon millions of lives during the Taiping wars, the conditions of peasant life in the Yangtze provinces

[37] This was true, in any case, of many of the new bureaus under Li Hung-chang. Biographies of many men who served in Li's economic enterprises are given in Albert Feuerwerker, *China's Early Industrialization: Shen Hsuan-huai (1844–1916) and Mandarin Enterprise* (Cambridge, Mass.: Harvard University Press, 1958).

[38] Ho, *Success in Imperial China*, pp. 181–84.

were easier than before. At least temporarily, the ravages of war served to reverse the trend toward concentration of landownership and gave opportunity to settlers from other provinces. But the benefits of tax reduction in the Yangtze area seem to have gone chiefly to the more unscrupulous *shen-shih* (many of them having obtained this status by purchasing degrees and titles), who were also the big landlords. Despite the proposal made by Li Hung-chang and others in the early T'ung-chih period that there should be no discrimination between "big" and "small" households in the collection of taxes, the former continued to be favored. Ting Jih-ch'ang, who was governor of Kiangsu 1867–70, was as shocked by the disparity between the tax rates applied to the big and small landowners as he was by the many cases of collusion between the yamen underlings and the *shen-shih* at the expense of poorer landowners. Those who could not pay their taxes and debts soon had to sell their land, and large estates were again common in the Yangtze provinces by the late years of the century.[39]

In localities affected by the Nien wars and in the areas of the Moslem revolts, particularly Kansu, the great loss of life had similarly resulted in a breathing spell for those who inherited the land. But elsewhere in the empire, the population pressure continued; in some parts of North China, population increase was even more rapid than in the first half of the century. Natural calamities were frequent and sometimes extremely serious. The floods in Chihli in 1871–72 were the worst of the century for that area,[40] and the great drought famine of Shansi and Shensi in 1877–78 was one of the most destructive in history. However, for the country as a whole, the chief causes of rural tension continued to be excessive and unequal taxation, the tyranny of the yamen underlings, landlordism and usury—social injustice reinforced by administrative abuses.

The more extensive foreign trade in the second half of the century must have had some beneficial effects in the hinterland. The export of tea, silk, and other goods stimulated the economy of the growing areas, while the greater volume of trade, both import and export, gave opportunity to a large number of merchants inland. But there were also offsetting effects. The land devoted to the cultivation of

[39] Ting Jih-ch'ang, *Fu Wu kung-tu* [Official Letters of the Governor of Kiangsu], 50 *chüan* (Canton: Hua-ying shu-chü, 1877), *passim*. See Kung-chuan Hsiao, *Rural China: Imperial Control in the Nineteenth Century* (Seattle: University of Washington Press, 1960), especially pp. 113–39, 382–407.

[40] Li Hung-chang, *Li Wen-chung kung ch'üan-chi, P'eng-liao han-kao, chüan* 11 ff.

poppies—stimulated initially by the market for Indian opium—was a net loss to agriculture. Foreign cotton yarn, imported in large quantities after 1870, while replacing some Chinese yarn, actually seems to have stimulated handicraft weaving. But the importation of heavy cotton cloth that competed with the peasant's product (in a particularly large quantity in the 1890's) must have had some adverse effects on village handicraft.[41] The change in trade routes caused by the opening of the treaty ports and the development of steamships and eventually railways brought hardship to transport coolies and boatmen. Insofar as the expansion of internal trade helped to spread literacy, it helped to foster disappointment with the existing opportunity structure, for the commercial growth was plainly not rapid enough to create a commensurate expansion of employment opportunities. The urbanization of the treaty ports, while significant, was also not extensive enough to absorb all the men that were dislocated or discontented.[42]

Although major rebellions were suppressed, serious banditry continued to be reported at frequent intervals by governors-general and governors.[43] Secret societies continued to flourish. In north and central China, the various groups linked to the White Lotus sect were often behind outbreaks of brigandage. In South China, Triad-led bandits were entrenched in many areas, and one particularly vigorous branch, the Elder Brother Society (Ko-lao hui), had spread by the 1870's to all the Yangtze provinces and even Yunnan and Kweichow. The membership of this society included some literati and many veterans of the yung armies in the war against the great rebellions. By the 1880's, the society was fomenting risings in Hunan and Hupei, and in 1891– 92, it planned revolts in several places along the Yangtze, from Anhwei to Szechuan. The slogan that urged "overthrowing the Ch'ing and restoring the Ming" continued to be sounded and at least one leader

[41] Yen Chung-p'ing, Chung-kuo mien-fang-chih shih-kao [A Draft History of Chinese Cotton-spinning and Weaving] (Peking: K'o-hsüeh, 1955) should be read together with Chi-ming Hou, Foreign Investment and Economic Development in China, 1840–1937 (Cambridge, Mass.: Harvard University Press, 1965), chap. 7.

[42] The Chinese population of Shanghai in 1905 has been given as 650,000, including 452,716 in the International Settlement and 84,792 in the French municipality. The estimated total populations around this date of Canton, Hankow, and Tientsin were 900,000, 870,000 and 750,000, respectively; see Hosea Ballou Morse, The Trade and Administration of the Chinese Empire (Shanghai: Kelly and Walsh, 1908), pp. 214, 230, 240, and 253.

[43] See, for example, the published papers of Shen Pao-chen, Chang Chih-tung, and Liu K'un-i.

styled himself "King Who Obeys Heaven's Will" (*shun-t'ien wang*). The Elder Brother Society was also behind a number of the particularly violent anti-missionary riots in the early 1890's.[44]

Why was it that the strains of the post-Taiping period did not lead immediately to a great eruption such as those in the 1850's? It should be pointed out that although the restoration of the old order was not complete, the cohesive role played by many a *shen-shih* in the society continued. While many rural notables merely exploited the poor, there were others who, while closing an eye to the conduct of their relatives and rent collectors, contributed both funds and leadership to the welfare of their communities. The particularly eminent *shen-shih*—who had had illustrious official careers and had many friends in high places—could even serve as a check on the abuses of the *chou* and *hsien* personnel. Experience gained during the rebellions had strengthened the local militia corps (*t'uan-lien*) organized by the *shen-shih*. Whenever these continued to be maintained, they could help at least to cope with local riots and small bandit groups.

The major factors that accounted for the stability of late nineteenth-century China were, however, first, the comparatively high quality of many governors-general and governors, and second, the effectiveness of the *yung* forces equipped with modern weapons. It was no accident that as long as Li Hung-chang was governor-general of Chihli, banditry in Chihli and even in Shantung (where units of the Anhwei Army were also stationed) was kept under control. As governor of Kwangtung (1884–89), Chang Chih-tung, who had no previous military experience but learned to work with the commanders of the *yung* forces, effectively crushed the Triad strongholds around Hui-chou, as well as serious outlawry on Hainan Island.[45] Later, when he was governor-general of Hukwang, the *yung* forces under him, as well as those under Liu K'un-i, Governor-General of Liangkiang, subdued the Elder Brother risings of 1891–92 with little difficulty. Relying on *yung* forces, Huang Huai-shen, Governor of Kwangsi, defeated the

[44] Shen Pao-chen, *Shen Wen-su kung cheng-shu* [Political Papers of Shen Pao-chen], 7 *chüan* (Soochow, 1880), 6.17–18; Chang Chih-tung, *Chang Wen-hsiang kung ch'üan-chi* [Complete Papers of Chang Chih-tung], 228 *chüan* (Peiping: Ch'u-hsüeh ching-lu, 1937), 30.19–22; 31.1–10; 32.13–18, 27; Lo, *Hsiang-chün hsin-chih*, pp. 212–14; Edmund S. Wehrle, *Britain, China, and the Anti-Missionary Riots* (Minneapolis: University of Minnesota Press, 1966), pp. 25–27.

[45] Chang Chih-tung, *Chang Wen-hsiang kung ch'üan-chi*, chüan 14, 17, 19, and 21, *passim*.

widespread Triad risings in that province in 1898–99, which were perhaps potentially no less explosive than the revolt of the Society of God-worshippers in 1850.[46]

Paradoxically, contact with the West helped to prolong the life of the dynasty. As in the years before the Taiping rebellion, the loss of imperial prestige as a result of defeats and humiliating treaties did contribute to the growth of disaffection. But, at least for the time being, the dynasty stood to benefit by Western trade and technology. Despite the low tariffs stipulated by treaty, the revenue collected by the Inspectorate General of Customs (including duties paid on foreign trade as well as trade between treaty ports carried by foreign vessels) increased from about Tls. 8,000,000 in 1864 to Tls. 22,000,000 annually in the early 1890's. This revenue was invaluable in the suppression of the rebellions and the financing of *yung* forces. Although the Ch'ing armies did not take full advantage of the latest Western weapons until the last years of their war against the Taipings—particularly after 1862, when Li Hung-chang went to Shanghai—the Hunan as well as the Anhwei armies did have the use of more modern weapons than those available to the Taipings.[47] In retrospect, Western cannon and rifles played a greater role in the suppression of the Taipings than did the help rendered by such Western commanders as Ward and Gordon. The Ch'ing campaigns against the Niens and the Moslem Chinese in the northwest undoubtedly would have been much more prolonged without the use of Western armament. It may be assumed that few secret-society groups of the late nineteenth century had access to similar weapons, although in the 1880's and 1890's, the Elder Brother Society in Hunan did try to smuggle arms from the treaty ports to its bases and hiding places.[48] Breechloading rifles and howitzers, either foreign made or manufactured at China's new arsenals, were a crucial factor in the Ch'ing dynasty's surviving into the twentieth century.

Indigenous Change and the Western Impact

We have discussed the many ills of the Ch'ing order, the great rebellions, and the dynasty's survival amidst continuing social tension. There were, however, other developments in nineteenth-century China.

[46] *Shih-erh-ch'ao tung-hua lu* [Tung-hua Records of Twelve Reigns], 30 vols. (Taipei: Wen-hai, 1963), Kuang-hsü 24, pp. 4151, 4208; Tai Wei-kuang, *Hung-men shih* (Shanghai: Ho-p'ing, 1947), pp. 68–69.

[47] Li Hung-chang, *Li Wen-chung kung ch'üan-chi, P'eng-liao han-kao, chüan* 2–5, *passim*.

[48] Chang Chih-tung, *Chang Wen-hsiang kung ch'üan-chi*, 31.2.

Even in the first half of the century, under conditions that led to the rebellions, secular growth and change were not arrested. In certain areas of Chinese life—particularly commerce and scholarship—there was significant growth, and there were even signs of new intellectual attitudes and dissenting opinions. The more extensive contacts with the West in the second half-century were, moreover, to introduce further innovations. Commercial growth, as well as a new social outlook, were stimulated by the trade and shipping at the treaty ports. Meanwhile, although cultural conservatism dominated the scene, there were among the literati-official elite those who were affected by new sentiments and values. Consciousness of China as an entity, along with a growing recognition of her weaknesses, were behind the new movements that began in the nineteenth century and continued into the twentieth.

Before describing these movements, it is necessary to consider the indigenous trends toward change in the first half of the century. Despite the worsening rural problems, China's immense domestic trade continued to develop. The junk trade on the Yangtze and on certain coastal routes seems to have reached its fullest extent during the second quarter of the century.[49] The Shansi and Ningpo banks, which financed trade as well as handling transfer of funds, also flourished in this period. Such indigenous trends as population increase, internal migration, and the expansion of handicraft textile production accounted for much of this growth. The tea and silk trade with the foreigners in Canton and in the early treaty ports, as well as the new opportunities arising from the opium traffic, formed only a part, although an increasing one, of the ongoing development. Wealthy merchants were common in the big towns. While few could rival the fabulous affluence of the government-licensed salt merchants or the hong merchants of Canton, the Shansi and Ningpo bankers and the owners of the Kiangsu seagoing junks undoubtedly accumulated considerable capital. The merchant's social status further improved. During the Taiping years, especially, many a wealthy banker or trader took advantage of the dynasty's sale of official titles and became an honorary prefect or magistrate, sometimes even brevet depart-

[49] In 1825 there were in Shanghai alone more than 3,000 Kiangsu seagoing junks (*sha-ch'uan*), the bigger ones carrying as much as 3,000 piculs. See *Chiang-su hai-yün ch'üan-an* [Complete Record of Kiangsu Sea Transport], 12 *chüan* (preface, 1826), 1.8–9. The junk guild (*ch'uan yeh hui-kuan*) in Shanghai seems to have been established as early as 1715, but the pulse guild (*Ts'ui-hsiu t'ang*), composed of the largest group of merchants in Shanghai trading by seagoing junk, was not founded until the Tao-kuang reign. See *Shang-hai hsien hsü-chih* [Gazetteer of the Shanghai District, Continued], 32 *chüan* (Shanghai: preface, 1918), 3.1, 6.

ment chief of a board at Peking. Merchants and officials met more and more on an equal footing—typically at the functions of the *Landsmann* halls.[50]

There were, moreover, striking new trends in the world of the scholar-officials. It is difficult, at this stage of research, to say what relationship existed between the growing capitalism and the new intellectual effort. In any case, there was a distinct reaction against the sterile Han learning and an awareness that some reform was necessary in order to arrest the obvious dynastic decline. More scholar-officials now devoted themselves to knowledge of "practical use in administering society" (*ching-shih chih-yung*) and believed that administrative techniques should be adapted to current circumstances and not be confined by ancient examples. The "school of statecraft" had come into existence certainly by the time *Huang-ch'ao ching-shih wen-pien* (Writings on Statecraft under the Reigning Dynasty) was published in 1827. The editors of this anthology, Ho Ch'ang-ling (1785–1848) and Wei Yüan (1794–1856), demonstrated in their careers absorbing interest in certain governmental functions that particularly required financial and managerial planning—for example, the salt monopoly and tribute grain transport. Adhering to the Mencian view of the government's obligation to the people, the "school of statecraft" nevertheless would not avoid considerations of "profit" (*li*) to the state, and it even appropriated certain Legalist emphases—witness Wei Yüan's glorification of the early Ch'ing military campaigns and his insistence that laws and decrees must be strictly and universally obeyed.[51] Several able and outstanding statesmen of the early nineteenth century, including T'ao Chu and Lin Tse-hsü, had similar ideas about learning and government. While serving as a metropolitan official (as vice-president of five boards

[50] Degrees (mostly purchased) and titles held by 37 large shipowners in 1826 are listed in *Chiang-su hai-yün ch'üan-an*, 4.54–61. An example of the sale of higher brevet offices to merchants in the Taiping period is the case of Hsü Jun. See his *Hsü Yü-chai tzu-hsü nien-p'u* [Hsü Jun's Chronological Autobiography] (postface, 1927), pp. 11*b*, 13*b*, 16*b*. For the close social relations between the Cantonese merchants in Shanghai and the Shanghai taotai and magistrate in the 1860's, see *ibid.*, 12*b* and 16*b*.

[51] Arthur W. Hummel, *Eminent Chinese of the Ch'ing Period*, 2 vols. (Washington: Library of Congress, 1943), 1:281–83; Hou Wai-lu, *Chin-tai Chung-kuo ssu-hsiang hsüeh-shuo shih* [History of Thought and Ideology in Modern China] (Shanghai: Sheng-huo, 1947), pp. 603–4; Ch'i Ssu-ho, "Wei Yüan yü wan-Ch'ing hsüeh-feng" [Wei Yüan and the New Trends in Late Ch'ing Scholarship], *Yen-ching hsüeh-pao* [Yenching Journal of Chinese Studies], no. 39 (1950), pp. 188–201.

in succession before 1853), Tseng Kuo-fan devoted himself not just to classical studies, but also to the concrete problems facing the tottering administration—the lack of conscientious and able local administrators, the deterioration of the armed forces, the hardship caused the peasant by the decline in value of the copper cash. While he put the greatest emphasis on the throne's responsibility for the selection of upright and capable officials, he also recommended the use of strict discipline to maintain efficiency and probity among them.[52]

While numerous officials were concerned with "statecraft," there were at least a few who championed reform. Both Pao Shih-ch'en (1775–1855) and Kung Tzu-chen (1792–1841) were in favor of abolishing the eight-legged essay in civil service examinations, and Kung particularly wanted to do away with the calligraphy test (which he himself failed when he reached the stage of the palace examination). Both men, moreover, traced the distressing administrative problems of the time to the dilemma at the very top—the lack of any assurance that the autocratic power of the throne was used properly or wisely. In an essay written in 1801, Pao, then a struggling young scholar, suggested that specially designated censors should be authorized to "refute" (*feng-po*) imperial edicts and that scholars of the imperial academies should be permitted to discuss matters of policy. Kung, who was also an unusually gifted poet, emerged from his studies of the classics with a philosophy of change. He subscribed to the "new text" school and the concept of institutions as defined in the *Kung-yang Commentary on the Spring and Autumn Annals*. In essays written in 1815–16, he warned of great disaster for the dynasty, should it fail to undertake reform (*kai-ko*). He bitterly attacked emperors who turned themselves into "enemies of the literati," who would even encourage corruption and shamelessness. He wanted to restore what he believed to be the ancient Chinese system under which the monarch not only treated officials with respect but shared with them his decision-making power.[53] Not all scholars who championed the "new texts" were outspoken critics of despotism; many were quite content with academic polemics. On the other hand, Tseng Kuo-fan, who revered the orthodox Sung interpretations of the classics, was convinced that the existing autocratic practices needed to be modi-

[52] Han-yin Ch'en Shen, "Tseng Kuo-fan in Peking, 1840–1852: His Ideas on Statecraft and Reform," *Journal of Asian Studies,* 27 (November 1967): 61–80.

[53] Hsiao Kung-ch'üan, *Chung-kuo cheng-chih ssu-hsiang shih* [History of Chinese Political Thought], 6 vols. (Taipei, 1961), 5:657–59; Hsiao I-shan, *Ch'ing-tai t'ung-shih,* 4:1764–92; Hou, *Chin-tai Chung-kuo ssu-hsiang hsüeh-shuo shih,* pp. 609–17.

fied if dynastic decline was to be averted. He regarded the lack of communication between official and emperor as the chief cause of the
administrative paralysis of his time. In memorials dated 1850–51, he
advised the throne to encourage criticism of policy from all officials
who were entitled to submit memorials, and he went so far as to suggest that the prior concurrence of all the censors should be sought by
the throne in making appointments.[54]

The few men who had hoped that the Ch'ing autocracy would correct
its own faults could do little more than write essays, and in Tseng's case,
memorials. But the campaigns against insurgents in the third quarter
of the century gave many officials, including Tseng himself, opportunity to practice their ideas on "statecraft." Greater utilitarian emphasis was called forth by the effort to defeat the rebellions. Military experience was gained and new methods of organization within the
bureaucratic framework were tried. Talents were recruited for the
many wartime tasks requiring managerial ability. While the scope of
"statecraft" was thus increased, there were at least a few exceptional
men who had not forgotten the more basic reforms needed. In essays
written in 1861 and circulated privately in the early T'ung-chih years,
Feng Kuei-fen (1809–74) stressed that the great weakness of the Ch'ing
system lay in the lack of channels through which the literati could communicate with the monarch. He recommended that all degree-holders
of the realm be invited to submit topical verses (an ancient Chinese
medium of expression) to the court. Showing his concern for local
government problems, he proposed the creation of a new grassroots
institution—the "village official" (hsiang-kuan), to be nominated by the
clans in each community for certain public services.[55]

There were, therefore, many developments that stemmed primarily
from indigenous sources. But the more extensive contact with the West
in the second half of the century was to result in movements of a new
kind. For the sake of trade, Britain fought two wars with China, in
1840–42 and 1856–60, and France joined in the second war, seeking, in
particular, the extension of missionary privileges. The Sino-foreign
treaty system, perfected between 1842 and 1860, guaranteed many
rights and privileges to the foreigners, including extraterritoriality,
residence in settlements policed and taxed by foreign municipal authorities, the determination of tariffs by treaty, foreign participation in

[54] Tseng Kuo-fan, Tseng Wen-cheng kung ch'üan-chi, vol. 1, Tsou-kao
[Memorials], pp. 3–5, 12–15; Shen, "Tseng Kuo-fan in Peking, 1840–1852."

[55] Feng Kuei-fen, Chiao-pin-lu k'ang-i [Straightforward Words from the
Lodge of Early Chou Studies], 2 chüan (1898 ed.), 2.12–14.

the administration of the Chinese customs service, operation of foreign ships between the treaty ports, and missionary residence in the interior. At the end of the Sino-Japanese War of 1894–95, the foreigners won the further privilege of operating factories in the treaty ports. The scramble for concessions soon brought foreigners the right to build railways and to work mines in the hinterland, and in 1898 four European powers obtained exclusive leaseholds on the China coast.

It is plain that down to the end of the nineteenth century, the West's economic impact did not alter the main pattern of Chinese society. But especially within the confines of the treaty ports, commercial growth was accelerated and a new social attitude emerged. Stimulated by Western example and benefited by the environment created by Sino-foreign treaties, private enterprise flourished in these cities. Many Chinese merchants had been associated with foreign firms at one time as compradors or agents; others were old-fashioned traders or bankers who adapted themselves to new opportunities. They were outside of the Ch'ing government's control and acquired the outlook of the independent merchant, gradually discarding certain old values, for example, the desire that their sons should become scholars and officials.[56] They also pioneered in acquiring Western entrepreneurial and technical skills. From the treaty ports, foreign trade spread to the interior. While certain effects were disruptive—such as the harm done by imported textiles to rural handicraft—there is little question that the areas that produced export goods stood to benefit, while the distribution of imports and the forwarding of produce for export opened up opportunities to merchants in the interior. The new trade, as well as rapid communication made possible by the coastal and Yangtze steamers, contributed to the existing trend toward inter-regional integration. Merchants from Kwangtung, Fukien, Kiangsu, and Chekiang who dealt in the foreign-trade goods were very active in all the treaty ports and in the tea and silk areas in the interior.[57]

Athough Christian proselytism, through a historical accident,

[56] For numerous biographies of second- or third-generation compradors in Shanghai, see Arnold Wright, ed., *Twentieth Century Impressions of Hongkong, Shanghai, and Other Treaty Ports of China* (London: Lloyd's, 1908), pp. 525–72.

[57] See the references to Chinese merchants in Imperial Maritime Customs, *Reports on Trade at the Treaty Ports in China* (Shanghai, 1864 ff.); Ho Ping-ti, *Chung-kuo hui-kuan shih-lun* [A Historical Survey of *Landsmannschaften* in China] (Taipei: Hsüeh-sheng, 1966), pp. 40–53; Kwang-Ching Liu, "Tong King-sing: His Compradore Years," *Ch'ing-hua hsüeh-pao* [Tsing Hua Journal of Chinese Studies], n. s. 2, no. 2 (1961): 151–53, 172–76.

afforded inspiration to the Taiping insurgents, its effectiveness was not conspicuous in the remaining decades of the century. The scattered Chinese Christian communities in the interior, fostered by austere Protestant evangelism as well as by the Catholic Church, were slow to spread their influence beyond their own members. Missionary schools, hospitals, and colleges—the last getting under way only in the 1880's— sowed the seeds of new knowledge and a new morality, but did not directly initiate a broad movement.[58] On the whole, Christian proselytism was more of an irritant than an inspiration to the post-Taiping generation—witness the frequent and violent anti-missionary riots in many parts of China after 1860.

While the direct effects of foreign trade and of the missionary effort were thus limited, the new external challenge, taken as a whole, was not long ignored by the crucial class of the officials and literati. With the support of the court at Peking, a movement was inaugurated in the 1860's by some governors-general and governors for China's "self-strengthening" (tzu-ch'iang)—the building up of military and financial strength, chiefly by adopting Western technology, so as to meet the threat of future foreign aggression. Meanwhile, contacts with the West increased, and the last two decades of the century saw an intellectual ferment among an increasing number of the literati which produced new concepts of social concern as well as new political criticism. Given further impetus by China's humiliating defeat in the Sino-Japanese War of 1894–95, a radical reform movement came into being which, in turn, paved the way for a republican revolutionary movement that was initiated before the end of the century.

1. Self-strengthening and Its Failure

Despite the overwhelming British power displayed in the Opium War of 1840–42, the Ch'ing government took very few steps after the Treaty of Nanking to prepare itself against the Western military threat in the future. This must be explained by the blind inertia at the court of the Emperor Tao-kuang and that court's preoccupation with the deepening internal troubles. It is also noteworthy that for twenty years after the conflict, few among the officials and the literati were convinced or even informed of the invincibility of Western ships and guns. Commissioner Lin Tse-hsü, who had become persuaded of the necessity of adopting Western ships and guns during his stay in Canton, could not effectively convey his newly gained knowledge of the British to the

[58] Kwang-Ching Liu, "Early Christian Colleges in China," *Journal of Asian Studies,* 20 (1960–61): 71–78.

throne, or to other high officials, since he was censured for bringing about the war and was soon exiled.[59] It is true that Lin passed on the materials he had had translated to Wei Yüan, who published them in 1844 in his *Hai-kuo t'u-chih* (Illustrated Gazetteer of the Maritime Countries). But it is doubtful whether either this work or Hsü Chi-yü's more up-to-date *Ying-huan chih-lüeh* (Brief Account of the Maritime World [1850]) conveyed a convincing picture of the West's military strength or of the complex civilization that lay behind it. The voluminous treatises by Wei and Hsü demonstrated the ease with which scholars of "statecraft" could turn their attention to the challenge from abroad. But except for Hsü, who was deprived of his post as Governor of Fukien a year after his book was published, there was hardly a high official of the time who saw the need for a major new policy to safeguard China from external danger.

This does not mean, however, that strong anti-foreign feeling did not come into being. For fourteen years up to the outbreak of the Anglo-French war against China in 1856, the officials of the Canton area, supported by the *shen-shih* and the populace, stubbornly refused to admit the foreigners into their city. After 1860, anti-foreign sentiment was vented by *shen-shih* and commoners in many parts of the empire in numerous riots against the Christian missionaries and their converts. Such xenophobia was inspired by local issues, by the *shen-shih*'s abhorrence of what was to him uncouth or heterodox, and by his jealous concern for his own privileges. But in the Cantonese anti-British placards or the Hunanese anti-Christian tracts, one finds references to "China" (*Chung-hua* or *Chung-t'u*), perhaps already implying more than a consciousness of the cultural differences between the Chinese and the "barbarian."[60]

By the 1860's, however, there was a fuller awakening among at least a small number of scholar-officials to the implications of Western encroachment. Disturbed as they were by the deterioration of the Ch'ing administration and by the rebellions, some influential men of the T'ung-chih period became convinced that the greatest threat to China and to the dynasty was from abroad. It is significant that such men of insight all had resided at least for some time in the vicinity of the treaty ports; they had personal knowledge of the Western administra-

[59] Lin Ts'ung-yung, *Lin Tse-hsü chuan* [Life of Lin Tse-hsü] (Taipei: Chung-hua ta-tien, 1967), pp. 463–67, 527–28.

[60] See Lü Shih-ch'iang, *Chung-kuo kuan-shen fan-chiao ti yüan-yin, 1860–1874* [The Causes of the Anti-missionary Movement among Chinese Officials and Gentry] (Taipei: Academia Sinica, 1966), pp. 21, 25.

tion there as well as the devastating effectiveness of Western weapons used against the Taipings. While they took pride in China's past, they realized that she was now only one of the countries in a larger world and that, moreover, the Western nations patently had the advantage over her in many ways. Writing in the last year of the Hsien-feng reign, Feng Kuei-fen declared that the West was not only superior in technology and in science (ko-chih); it was also ahead of China in its utilization of human as well as material resources and even in its government, since in the Western countries communication between the ruler and the ruled was easier, and practice was more in conformity with theory. Feng regarded China's defeat by two small European nations in the *Arrow* War as the "greatest outrage since creation, which should infuriate every red-blooded person." He argued, however, against the blind impulse to expel the Westerners and against the stratagem of "using the barbarians against the barbarians," advised earlier by Wei Yüan. Instead, he urged the recognition of China's inferiority to the West and the fostering of a sense of shame. "When we are ashamed," Feng wrote, "the best thing to do is to strengthen ourselves." Feng's idea of self-strengthening was plainly more than the mere adoption of Western technology. In the tradition of the "school of statecraft," he believed that by improving upon existing institutions, China could make greater use of her human talents and economic resources, increase the communication between monarch and people, and make practices conform to ideals: China needed to learn from the West, however, on matters concerning technology and science. Feng advocated the use of Western methods in arsenals and shipyards, the teaching of mathematics and sciences in government schools, and the modification of the examination system so as to encourage technical personnel as well as to strengthen the administration itself.[61]

While Feng merely evolved a theory, many of his ideas were advocated by such influential officials as Li Hung-chang, Tso Tsung-t'ang, Shen Pao-chen, and Ting Jih-ch'ang. Distressed by the fact that foreign settlements had become practically alien territory and that Chinese merchants were being "enticed away" by foreigners,[62] these men requested and obtained Peking's approval for concrete measures designed

[61] Feng Kuei-fen, *Chiao-pin-lu k'ang-i*, 2.40–44.

[62] See the letters of Li and Tso written between 1862 and 1866 and preserved in their published papers and Ting's writings in Ting Chung-ch'eng chengshu [Political Papers of Governor Ting] (manuscript, Sterling Library, Yale University).

for China's self-strengthening. Such men as Li and Tso were un-doubtedly aware of the fact that arsenals and naval fleets under their own auspices would enhance their position in the Ch'ing government; these were valuable, in any case, to the dynasty's internal security. Yet it cannot be gainsaid that there was a nationalistic element in their proposals. Li, Tso, and others probably never distinguished the Chinese nation from the Ch'ing dynasty. But when they emphasized the state's "wealth and strength" (fu-ch'iang), it was not for the sake of the monarch's power as the Confucian-Legalists would have it, but for the protection of China's land and people. While they were loyal to the dynasty, they were nevertheless equally committed to the entity they referred to as Chung-kuo or Chung-t'u.[63]

Since they were impressed primarily by Western equipment for war, their earliest efforts at self-strengthening were in this field. Li, with the assistance of Ting, set up new arsenals in Shanghai as early as 1863, two years before they founded the larger Kiangnan Arsenal. In 1866, Tso founded the Foochow Navy Yard, which Shen was to administer through the mid-1870's. Effort was not confined, however, to arsenals and shipyards. Training of technical personnel was emphasized, as was economic competition with foreigners. Almost at the same time that the arsenals and shipyards were established, new government schools were founded in Shanghai and Foochow, where sciences as well as foreign languages were taught. Li and Ting, especially, were impressed by the aggressiveness of Western economic enterprises. They aspired to recover China's "economic control" (li-ch'üan)—a nationalistic concept[64]—and they recognized the value of Western technology from the standpoint of the state's wealth. As early as 1864, they sought to encourage Chinese merchants to own and operate steamships, so as to compete with for-eigners in trade and shipping in Chinese waters. In 1867, Li recom-mended to the throne that Western techniques be employed in develop-ing China's mines.[65] Both ideas, however, remained unrealized until the 1870's.

[63] See, for example, Li Hung-chang, Li Wen-chung kung ch'üan-chi, P'eng-liao han-kao, 1.44, 46b; 2.46; Tso Tsung-t'ang, Tso Wen-hsiang kung ch'üan-chi [Complete Papers of Tso Tsung-t'ang], 134 chüan (1888–97), Shu-tu [Let-ters], 7.14, 17, 25, 36; 8.50, 55.

[64] Li-ch'üan is, of course, a traditional term referring to control over revenue as well as merchants' activities. But in the 1860's, it was increasingly used in the context of Western encroachment in these fields.

[65] Hai-fang tang [Archives on Maritime Defense], 17 vols. (Taipei: Acade-mia Sinica, 1957), Chi-ch'i chü [The Arsenals], 1:3–5; Lü Shih-ch'iang, Chung-

Li and others also proposed reforms that would facilitate the acqui-
sition of Western technology—ideas which unfortunately were not
heeded by the court. As early as 1864, Li had suggested to the Tsungli
Yamen that new categories (*k'o*) be established in the civil service
examinations so as to encourage men who specialized in science and
technology. In the early 1870's, Shen and Li put before the throne
similar proposals together with recommendations that a large number
of "schools for Western studies" should be established in the provinces.
Li also proposed plans for military reorganization, including the dis-
banding of the Green Standard units.[66] Through the 1860's, the arsenals
and shipyards proposed by Li and Tso had enjoyed the support of
Prince Kung and Wen-hsiang. After 1870, when Li became governor-
general of Chihli and imperial commissioner for the northern ports,
his influence in Peking was even greater. However, all that he and
others could persuade the throne to accept in the 1870's were an educational mission to the United States, where Chinese students were
trained in science and technology, a Chinese steamship company, the
use of machines in coal and iron mines in several provinces, a projected
cotton textile mill in Shanghai, the plan for a naval fleet, consisting of
modern ships built in Europe, and the training in Europe of naval personnel. In the mid-1870's, Li also advised the throne to consider promoting telegraph and railways. But it was not until the 1880's that the
court approved a telegraph system and a short railroad to connect
Peking with the Manchurian border.

In the 1880's, several new leaders of self-strengthening emerged. As
Governor of Kwangtung, 1885–89, and after that as governor-general
of Hukwang, Chang Chih-tung made grandiose plans for trunk railways that would connect Peking with the Yangtze, as well as for an iron
and steel industry. As governor of Taiwan, 1884–91, Liu Ming-ch'uan,
a former Anhwei Army commander, combined an energetic program
of railway construction, mining, and export trade with remarkable
innovations in the fiscal system of that island.

---

kuo tsao-chi ti lun-ch'uan ching-ying [Early Chinese Steamship Enterprise]
(Taipei: Academia Sinica, 1962), pp. 150–80; Knight Biggerstaff, "The Secret
Correspondence of 1867–1868: The Views of Leading Chinese Statesmen Re-
garding the Further Opening of China to Western Influence," *Journal of
Modern History,* 22 (1950): 132.

[66] *Ch'ing-tai ch'ou-pan i-wu shih-mo* [Complete Record of the Ch'ing
Dynasty's Management of Barbarian Affairs], 260 *chüan* (Peiping: Palace
Museum, 1930), T'ung-chih, 25.9–10; Biggerstaff, *The Earliest Modern Gov-*
ernment Schools, pp. 25–26; Liu, "Li Hung-chang in Chihli," pp. 93–97.

Did the self-strengthening movement involve the acceptance of new values? Interest in technology had always been maintained to a certain degree in the traditional Chinese society, and Wei Yüan's book of 1844 shows that scholars of "statecraft" were not reluctant to encourage "learning from the techniques of the barbarians." But the enthusiasm with which such officials as Li, Tso, Shen, and Ting greeted Western weapons and machines unavoidably implied a depreciation of virtue and culture as the sources of power. It is not surprising that a stalwart of the "Sung school" like Wo-jen should denounce the study of technology and even mathematics as incompatible with good government. Even Tseng Kuo-fan, despite his pragmatic tendencies, was uneasy about stressing implements (ch'i) over men (jen). But such doubts did not exist in the mind of Li Hung-chang. In a letter dated 1876, Li went so far as to say that "when implements reach a state of perfection, they touch upon the truth [tao]." Shen Pao-chen, famous as an official of model Confucian integrity, once declared that science should be regarded as "the gateway to the realm of the sages."[67] Li and Shen would probably have subscribed to the formula later enunciated by Chang Chih-tung: "Chinese learning for the essential principles, Western learning for practical applications." But the matters assigned to "practical applications" were extensive, including not only armament but also industrialization and new policies regarding the training and selection of personnel.

The program for economic self-strengthening, especially, opened up a vista of growth made possible by machines. While the "school of statecraft" merely sought the more efficient management of existing economic functions of the state, such as the salt monopoly, Li and others would expand these functions. "The only way to create new revenue at present," Li wrote in 1875, "is to seek it through the bounties of nature" —referring in particular to coal, iron, and other mines.[68] Criticism of the traditional static economy is implicit in the writings of such men as Hsüeh Fu-ch'eng and Ma Chien-chung, both members of Li's staff. Despite his eagerness to defend the traditional ideology, Chang Chih-

[67] Li Hung-chang, Li Wen-chung kung i-chi [Works of the Late Li Hung-chang], in Li Kuo-chieh, comp., Ho-fei Li-shih san-shih i-chi [Works of the Three Past Generations of the Li Family of Ho-fei], 24 chüan (1904), 5.12b. Shen is quoted by Wang Erh-ming, Ch'ing-chi ping kung-yeh ti hsing-ch'i [The Rise of Armament Manufacturing in the Late Ch'ing] (Taipei: Academia Sinica, 1963), p. 55.

[68] Li Hung-chang, Li Wen-chung kung ch'üan-chi, P'eng-liao han-kao, 15.8, referring to similar views expressed by Ting Jih-ch'ang.

tung pointed out that mines, factories, and railways could help to expand the profits (*li*) of farmers, artisans, and merchants.[69]

Self-strengthening gave greater honor to the military—although this was only a continuation of the trends created during the Taiping upheaval. As the rebellions were suppressed, many commanders of the *yung* forces were given high posts, such as that of Provincial Finance Commissioner. After 1875, when the Court initiated a policy of "coastal defense" (*hai-fang*), a number of former commanders, such as Chang Shu-sheng and Liu Ming-ch'uan, became governors-general or governors on account of their ability to organize defense against foreign encroachment. Meanwhile, even the middle-grade officers of the *yung* forces won higher social standing, if only because of their handsome pay and perquisites.

The programs for economic self-strengthening accorded greater prestige to entrepreneurial pursuits. This is indicated, first of all, by the fact that comprador-merchants were accepted as officials administering the government-sponsored steamships and mines.[70] The fact that Tong King-sing and Hsü Jun previously had purchased brevet titles helped their transition to the new status. But in terms of traditional institutions, their becoming the Commissioners (*tsung-pan*) of the China Merchants' Steam Navigation Company (1873) and the Kaiping mines (1877 for Tong and 1881 for Hsü) may be compared to a merchant of Yang-chou being appointed the Liang-huai Salt Commissioner! Unlike the salt monopoly, Li's steamships, mines, textile mills, and telegraph lines were operated directly by government bureaus under the arrangement of *kuan-tu shang-pan* (literally, "supervised by the government and undertaken by merchants").[71] Traditional practices were maintained to the extent that the enterprises were for private profit and at private risk, the government providing only loans that must be repaid. But it was government officials who actually directed the operation of the enterprises, their joint-stock form of organization notwithstanding. In fact, members of Li's staff who already had the status of officials soon

[69] *Ch'üan-hsüeh pien* [An Exhortation to Learning] (1898), in Chang Chih-tung, *Chang Wen-hsiang kung ch'üan-chi*, 203.30–34, 40–44.

[70] Feuerwerker, *China's Early Industrialization*, chap. 4; Kwang-Ching Liu, "British-Chinese Steamship Rivalry in China, 1873–85," in C. D. Cowan, ed., *The Economic Development of China and Japan: Studies in Economic History and Political Economy* (London: George Allen and Unwin, 1964), pp. 53–54.

[71] My reason for preferring this translation is indicated in Liu, "British-Chinese Steamship Rivalry," p. 53. I am preparing a detailed monograph on the early history of the China Merchants' Company.

aspired to replace the comprador-officials as managers of the enterprises. In 1885, Sheng Hsüan-huai, who was already the head of the Imperial Telegraph Administration established at Li's recommendation in 1881, became the Director-General (*tu-pan*) of the steamship company as well. He not only actually directed business operations, but also became the owner of controlling shares in each enterprise—the imperial telegraph, curiously enough, also had a body of shareholders. Sheng had never been a merchant prior to this. In terms of traditional institutions, he was like a man who started out as an official but was appointed to serve both as the Liang-huai Salt Commissioner and as a licensed salt merchant at the same time. Business had become such a respectable pursuit that Sheng never tried to hide the fact that he bought large shares in these enterprises.

Despite its many innovations, it is plain that the actual achievements of the self-strengthening movement were restricted, and that it could not attain its objectives. The rifles and howitzers made at the new arsenals were invaluable to the maintenance of the dynasty's internal security. But the shipbuilding program was never a success; Li's Peiyang navy was made up chiefly of vessels built in Europe. His steamship company, which purchased British-built vessels as well as the fleet of the American firm of Russell & Co., could at least hold its own against British firms in China. The Kaiping mines produced good coal in increasing quantity, and in the 1880's the imperial telegraph was extended to the coastal and Yangtze provinces.[72] But other projects suffered delays; the first cotton textile mill in Shanghai operated successfully only after 1891, and the first railway in China (from Peking to the Manchurian border, about 240 miles) was completed only in 1894. Meanwhile, comparatively well-equipped *yung* forces enabled the dynasty at times to adopt a firm stand in foreign policy—witness Tso Tsung-t'ang's campaigns in Sinkiang in the late 1870's, undertaken chiefly to back up China's claims on Russian-occupied Ili, and Li Hung-chang's use of a small expeditionary force to bolster his Korean policy in the early 1880's. But the Ch'ing government was not able to insist on its claims of suzerainty over Liu-ch'iu (formally annexed by Japan in 1879). Its long-delayed intervention in Vietnam came to nothing after the French warships destroyed the Foochow naval fleet with ludicrous ease in 1884. It was perhaps Britain's dominant interest in China, rather than the army and navy Li maintained in North China, that dis-

---

[72] Liu, "British-Chinese Steamship Rivalry," pp. 51–77; Ellsworth C. Carlson, *The Kaiping Mines, 1877–1912* (Cambridge, Mass.: Harvard University Press, 1957), p. 23; Feuerwerker, *China's Early Industrialization*, p. 196.

suaded the French from attacking that region. The final test of Li's efforts came with the Sino-Japanese War of 1894–95 over the control of Korea. China was defeated disastrously at sea and on land. The Ch'ing tributary empire finally disappeared, and the gates were opened to further imperialistic activities in China itself.

The failure of self-strengthening cannot be blamed exclusively on the few leaders of the movement. Despite the Western encroachments, inertia and conservatism were still strong throughout officialdom. It is true that by the mid-1870's the governors-general and governors almost to a man paid lip service to self-strengthening.[73] In addition to the efforts of the leaders mentioned above, by the late 1880's at least six arsenals for the manufacture of Western weapons had been established in different provinces, and five or six provinces had also attempted to introduce machinery into their mines, at Li's repeated urging. But few governors-general and governors, as Li bitterly commented in 1875, could escape the influence of their long training in writing the eight-legged essay and see themselves actually promoting "Western learning."[74] For some twenty years after "foreign-language schools" were established in Peking, Shanghai, Canton, and Foochow between 1862 and 1867, it seems that the only new government institutions founded that taught foreign languages and sciences, not counting those attached to the new military and naval academies, to the telegraph administration, and to the mines, were one associated with Li's torpedo works in Tientsin, one started by Chang Shu-sheng in Canton, and one by Liu Ming-ch'uan in Taipei.

Conservatism of the xenophobic variety was indeed as strong in Peking as in the provinces. A person who dared to write in praise of Western institutions, such as Kuo Sung-t'ao, who went to England as China's first minister to that country in 1877, was roundly denounced by many Peking officials. The journals Kuo kept were so severely attacked that the court ordered them destroyed. One should note that by the mid-1870's there were few men who believed, as did Wo-jen in the 1860's, that "propriety and righteousness" were sufficient defense for the empire. Despite the existence of such a man as Hsü T'ung, who was successively President of the Board of Rites and Board of Civil Appointments 1878–96 and who "hated Western learning as the enemy," there were very few who actually used the Confucian ideology itself to impugn the desire for a more efficient technology. Yet the ingrained cultural pride, the habits of a lifetime devoted to examinations and

[73] Liu, "Li Hung-chang in Chihli," pp. 97–98.

[74] Letter to Liu Ping-chang dated February 13, 1875, Li, *Li Wen-chung kung ch'üan-chi, P'eng-liao han-kao,* 15.3–5.

office-seeking, and considerations of factional politics made high officials reluctant to support innovations. The young moralists of the so-called Purity Group (*Ch'ing-liu*) demanded immediate war with Japan over Liu-ch'iu and with the French over Vietnam. They had no lack of respect for Western technology and sometimes memorialized in support of new arsenals and mines.[75] Yet it was only after the shock of defeat in the Sino-French War of 1884–85 that some of these men were awakened to the wider implications of self-strengthening. From the *Ch'ing-liu* group arose a latter-day leader of self-strengthening who did a great deal to promote "Western learning"—Chang Chih-tung.

The deep-seated inertia could perhaps have been broken down if imperial leadership had been more farsighted. Kuo Sung-t'ao could have been given a high post in Peking or the provinces instead of being banished to retirement. Fresh attitudes would have been introduced if the examination system had been modified as Li and Shen Pao-chen recommended. Such imperial leadership was not forthcoming, however. Empress Dowager Tz'u-hsi was not opposed to self-strengthening, and within certain limits often gave Li encouragement in his work. But although she did not hesitate at times to depart from tradition, she ruled by maintaining a paralyzing balance between the conservatives and the innovators. Li, in his position as governor-general of Chihli and Imperial Commissioner for the northern ports, was allowed in the 1870's to coordinate preparations for coastal defense. But his power waned after 1880, as indicated by the facts that he could no longer influence the choice of men to serve as governor-general or governor in the vital Liangkiang area and that the financial support for the Anhwei Army declined.[76] The Empress Dowager's court grew increasingly corrupt, particularly after 1884, when Prince Ch'un and Sun Yü-wen became her principal advisers and when Li Lien-ying, her chief eunuch, commanded wide informal power. In order to obtain funds for his navy, at a time when the Sino-Japanese competition in Korea had reached a critical stage, Li Hung-chang found it necessary to enter into collusion with Prince Ch'un to obtain funds through the Navy Yamen

[75] Biography of Hsü T'ung in *Ch'ing-shih* [History of the Ch'ing] 8 vols. (Taipei: Kuo-fang yen-chiu yüan, 1961), 7:5056; Yen-p'ing Hao, "A Study of the Ch'ing-liu Tang: The 'Disinterested' Scholar-Official Group (1875–1884)," *Papers on China*, 16 (1962): 47, 52.

[76] Stanley Spector, *Li Hung-chang and the Huai Army*, pp. 201–7. The governors-general of Liangkiang after Shen Pao-chen died in 1879 were Liu K'un-i (1880–81), Tso Tsung-t'ang (1881–84), Tseng Kuo-ch'üan (1884–90), Liu K'un-i (1891–94).

(created in 1885). The naval appropriations, including special levies on the provinces, were increasingly diverted to the notorious peculation in connection with the construction of the Empress' pleasure palace. After 1888, the sums received by Li were inadequate for the purchase of new warships.[77] Despite the considerable power enjoyed by Li, he plainly still was dependent on the throne's uncertain support in any major undertaking.

If the court had been more enlightened and less demoralized, could the self-strengthening efforts have achieved more? Such a hypothetical question cannot be answered, but the basic weaknesses of a deteriorating administration would, in any case, have been difficult to overcome. It would have been almost impossible, for example, to change the fiscal system so as to produce the capital necessary for full-scale, state-sponsored industrialization. Such change would have required a reorganization of the local and provincial administrations and of the regulations of the boards of Revenue and Civil Appointments. While such writers as Feng Kuei-fen had advocated reforms that could help to reduce corruption—the suspension of sales of offices, replacement of the existing yamen clerks by a new branch of the civil service, and the simplification of certain procedures in fiscal administration[78]—the chances of such measures being successfully carried out were extremely remote. Shen Pao-chen and Ting Jih-ch'ang, who were, in the early Kuang-hsü reign, governor-general of Liangkiang and governor of Fukien, respectively, were convinced that the prerequisite for a successful self-strengthening program was the reform of local government, which presumably could enable the state eventually to obtain more from the land tax. They themselves could do no more, however, than expose the most flagrant cases of peculation in the *chou* and *hsien* under their jurisdiction. (It was the unique conditions on Taiwan, which was made a province formally only in 1887, that enabled Liu Ming-ch'uan, its first governor, to reorganize the land-tax procedures there, with moderate success.)[79] Li had early dismissed basic fiscal reform as outside the realm

[77] Pao Tsun-p'eng, *Chung-kuo hai-chün shih* [History of the Chinese Navy] (Taipei: Hai-chün, 1950), pp. 209–15; John L. Rawlinson, *China's Struggle for Naval Development, 1839–1895* (Cambridge, Mass.: Harvard University Press, 1967), pp. 140–45.

[78] Feng Kuei-fen, *Chiao-pin-lu k'ang-i*, 1.15–26.

[79] The views of Shen and Ting are reflected in Li's replies to their letters, in Li, *Li Wen-chung kung ch'üan-chi, P'eng-liao han-kao, chüan* 10–19. On Liu, see William M. Speidel, "Liu Ming-ch'uan in Taiwan, 1884–91" (Ph.D. diss., Yale University, 1967).

of possibility, believing, in the first place, that a new land-registration could not be achieved. Instead, he looked to the existing commercial taxation—the maritime customs and the likin—for the financing of new undertakings, until such time as mines and other industrial projects could yield income to the state.[80] While Li was perhaps only being realistic, a heavy likin tax was plainly contradictory to his own professed aim of building national wealth through commerce. The expansion and the abuses of the likin levies were in fact a chief impediment to more rapid commercial development in Li's time.

Even in the programs that enjoyed the support of the throne, many weaknesses were obvious. As compared with the Green Standard forces, the Anhwei Army (like its predecessor, Tseng Kuo-fan's Hunan Army), by concentrating authority in the battalion officers, could operate with greater cohesion and efficiency. But under the system of assigning complete responsibility to these officers, it was almost impossible to remove them (as we have noted), or, without their concurrence, their subordinates. Despite Li's use of German instructors and the establishment of a military academy (*Wu-pei hsüeh-t'ang*) at Tientsin in 1885, no real reorganization ever took place within the Anhwei Army.[81] Meanwhile, during long years of peace, corruption and loose habits developed among the battalion officers themselves, as well as the commanders who supervised them. Even in the Peiyang Navy, where the high officers were men freshly trained in Europe, a vested interest quickly developed within the command of each warship. The vast system of ordnance and supply serving Li's army and navy was similarly riddled with interests which Li himself could not completely control.

Compared with certain other Ch'ing agencies handling funds and dealing with merchants (such as the Canton maritime customs before 1842 or the bureaus in charge of the transport of tribute grain), Li's bureaus for steamships, mines, and telegraph were the less corrupt. But the *kuan-tu shang-pan* companies were private enterprises in name only, and were inevitably tied up with officialdom. When the steamships and mines were under the management of comprador-officials, a policy of continuous expansion of capital equipment was followed, even though patronage, nepotism, and misuse of funds were common. But after

[80] Li Hung-chang, *Li Wen-chung kung ch'üan-chi, P'eng-liao han-kao,* 6.45, 10.35b, 16.25b.

[81] Yen Fu, "Chiu-wang chüeh-lun" [Crucial Proposals for China's Salvation], in Chien Po-tsan *et al.*, eds., *Wu-hsü pien-fa* [The Reform of 1898], 4 vols. (Shanghai: Jen-min, 1953; hereafter cited as *WHPF*), 3: 68.

Shen Hsüan-huai took over the steamship company in 1885, he depended chiefly on "pooling agreements" with the British firms to maintain profits, and little new tonnage was added. The Kaiping mines likewise stagnated after 1892, when Li had to accept Prince Ch'un's protégé, Chang Yen-mao, as Director-General.[82] The new economic enterprises, like Li's army and navy, could not escape the weaknesses of an almost universally worsening bureaucracy.

There was, moreover, the fact that it was not easy, at least initially, to shift from the literary to the warrior culture, from the rentier to the entrepreneurial spirit. Li and others sought to train personnel through the new government schools and by sending students abroad. Using the device of "recommendation on military merits," they did bring into prominence talented men who did not necessarily have the benefit of high degrees. Yet such men as Feng Chün-kuang were plainly better bureaucrats than arsenal managers.[83] Sheng Hsüan-huai had, to be sure, as good a business mind as could be found anywhere, but it was natural for him to seek perquisites through built-in opportunities rather than profits through risk and continuous investment. In Admiral Liu Pu-shang, Li had a naval commander of literary taste as well as capability for intrigue. It was he, however, who was the first to lose his nerve when the Chinese fleet confronted the Japanese in the fateful Battle of the Yalu.[84]

2. Intellectual Ferment and the Reform Movement

The term "self-strengthening movement," according to the usage of historians (which we have followed above), refers to the effort made by a few Ch'ing statesmen in the period 1860–95 to build up China's power so as to cope with the external threat, mainly by adopting Western technology. But the aim of self-strengthening was shared by many among the literati and officials who did not have a direct influence on policy. These included residents of the treaty ports who were often mere spec-

[82] Feuerwerker, *China's Early Industrialization*, chaps. 4, 5; Kwang-Ching Liu, "Steamship Enterprise in Nineteenth-Century China," *Journal of Asian Studies*, 18 (1958–59): 435–54; "British-Chinese Steamship Rivalry in China," 51–76; Carlson, *The Kaiping Mines, 1877–1912*, chap. 3.

[83] Feng, who directed the Kiangnan Arsenal in the 1870's, had been criticized as boastful, suspicious, and lacking in leadership. Li, *Li Wen-chung kung ch'üan-chi, P'eng-liao han-kao*, 11.23b, 31b.

[84] Chiang (Tsiang) T'ing-fu, *Chung-kuo chin-tai shih ta-kang* [Outline of Modern Chinese History] (Taipei: Ch'i-ming, 1959), pp. 104–5; Rawlinson, *China's Struggle for Naval Development, 1839–1895*, pp. 178–80.

tators of the national scene, lesser officials who did not have the opportunity to make policy themselves, and young scholars who were yet to gain high degrees and office. These still constituted a small minority among the literati and officials. They were the leaven of change, however, since they had broad views on the means by which nationalistic aims could be achieved. There were, moreover, among them men who were genuinely affected by new values and were concerned with liberation of the society and the individual, not just the wealth and strength of the state. Going beyond the scholar of "statecraft" or of the "new texts," at least a few men of the Kuang-hsü period experienced a transvaluation of values before the disaster of the Sino-Japanese War stimulated wider acceptance of the new thought. Out of this ferment grew a radical reform movement that sought to influence politics.

The two decades before the Sino-Japanese War saw a series of mortifying events—China's inability to take a firmer stand against the Japanese when the latter landed troops on Taiwan in 1874, further extension of foreign treaty rights in the Chefoo Convention of 1877, the final loss of Liu-ch'iu, the panic created by French naval attack during the Sino-French War, and the subsequent loss of Vietnam itself. Meanwhile, the growth of national consciousness was facilitated by the improved communications that resulted from Western innovations. By the 1870's, regular steamship service had been established between all Yangtze and coastal ports.[85] A person could travel from Hankow to Shanghai in three days, or from Canton to Tientsin in eight. The *Shun Pao*, the Chinese-language newspaper founded in Shanghai in 1872, was distributed in other provinces, and similar papers were founded in the 1880's in other treaty ports.[86] By the end of that decade, telegraph lines had been extended as far inland as Szechwan and Yunnan.

Moreover, there were, by the 1880's, many more opportunities for the Chinese to obtain a closer knowledge of the West. While they resented foreign aggression, many among the literati began to be affected by new influences, often in spite of themselves. Young scholars, en route by steamship to take the examination in Peking, would visit Shanghai and Hong Kong and be impressed by the clean streets and new buildings. Chinese who traveled abroad, such as Wang T'ao, brought back adula-

[85] Kwang-Ching Liu, *Anglo-American Steamship Rivalry in China, 1862–1874* (Cambridge, Mass.: Harvard University Press, 1962).

[86] Roswell S. Britton, *The Chinese Periodical Press* (Shanghai: Kelly and Walsh, 1933), chaps. 6, 7; Chang Ching-lu, *Chung-kuo chin-tai ch'u-pan shih-liao* [Materials for the History of Publishing in Modern China], 2 vols. (Shanghai: Shang-tsa and Ch'ün-lien, 1953–54), 1:72–75, 85–86.

tory reports of Western government and law. Works on Western science and technology and on current affairs were increasingly available in the Chinese language—for example, the more than ninety works translated by John Fryer and others and published by the Kiangnan Arsenal between 1871 and 1885, and the *Hsi-kuo chin-shih hui-pien* (Digest of Recent Events in Western Countries), published by the Arsenal between 1873 and 1898.[87] Publications of the mission presses now attracted more attention from the literati, especially the *Wan-kuo kung-pao* ("The Globe Magazine," or "The Review of the Times"), founded in 1874 by the American Methodist, Young J. Allen. Devoted to the propagation of science and "general enlightenment," no less than of Christianity, the *Wan-kuo kung-pao* presented many thought-provoking themes: that the Western peoples looked to the future for fulfillment while the Chinese wished to return to the past; that the Confucian moral culture was defective in that it did not emphasize the autonomy (*tzu-chu*, literally "being one's own master") of each individual; that many literati-bureaucrats were in fact vain, greedy, and hypocritical; that the Ch'ing regime ignored the two main tasks of government—the education (*chiao*) and livelihood (*yang*) of the people.[88]

It is not surprising that it was the Chinese literati who resided in Shanghai and Hong Kong who early put forward a broad program for "reform of institutions" (*pien-fa*). Cheng Kuan-ying, who had had a Chinese education in his youth and who worked in the 1860's and 1870's as agent and comprador of British firms in Shanghai, found time, apart from his business pursuits, to write and publish essays on China's manifold problems. Wang T'ao, a well-trained classical scholar, worked for missionaries as a translator and amanuensis before he visited Britain in 1867–70 under the auspices of the Christian sinologist James Legge. Thereafter, his chief activity was writing editorials for the Chinese newspapers in Hong Kong and Shanghai.[89] Although friendly to for-

[87] Britton, *The Chinese Periodical Press*, chap. 5; Adrian Arthur Bennett, *John Fryer and the Introduction of Western Science and Technology into Nineteenth-century China* (Cambridge, Mass.: Harvard University Press, 1968).

[88] See Wang Shu-huai, *Wai-jen yü wu-hsü pien-fa* [Foreigners and the Reform of 1898] (Taipei: Academia Sinica, 1965), pp. 9–98. An article by Alexander Williamson published in *Chiao-hui hsin-wen* [Church News] in 1871–72 and reprinted in *Wan-kuo kung-pao* [Globe Magazine], 9 (1876–77): 344–46, recommended gradual participation by the people in government through a parliament-like institution (*i-yüan*).

[89] Cheng Kuan-ying, *I-yen* [Facile Words] 2 *chüan* (preface, 1875); *Sheng-shih wei-yen* [Warnings for a Prosperous Age], 8 *chüan* (preface, 1892; en-

eigners, both Cheng and Wang called for China's reassertion of her national rights—abolishing extraterritoriality and regaining economic control (*li-ch'üan*) through tariff autonomy and the exclusion of foreign vessels from the inter-port trade. They advocated a broad program of military preparedness and industrialization—military academies for officers, new ships for the navy, railways, textile mills, banks, modern mints. They also advocated agricultural improvement through, for example, the use of new irrigation techniques. They were more emphatic than the high officials of the time in demanding reform of the examination system—the abolition of the eight-legged essay and the creation of a category of degree-holders specializing in science and technology. They also wanted a new system of schools. In the economic realm, they defended private initiative, while stressing the need of governmental protection for Chinese enterprise, to enable it to compete with foreign firms. Cheng, who was to become Associate Commissioner of Li Hung-chang's steamship company in 1882, felt that the managers of the *kuan-tu shang-pan* companies should be chosen from among merchants rather than officials. Both Cheng and Wang wanted the abolition of the likin, in view of the great harm it did to commerce and the many abuses involved in its collection. They recommended that the import duties be increased while export duties be kept low.[90]

Cheng and Wang stressed the importance of administrative reforms and, moreover, raised the question of political reform. They were aware of the problems of local government. They called for the suspension of the sale of offices and a more genuine supervision by the governors-general and governors over the local officials; they hoped that the clerks at the *chou* and *hsien* yamens and at the metropolitan boards could be replaced by literati; they also wanted the complex rules and regulations of the six boards to be simplified so that greater efficiency might be gained. Like earlier political critics, they realized that the monarch's isolation from the officials and the literati was the source of the existing administrative paralysis. Wang was convinced from his study of European history that her parliament (*i-yüan*) accounted for England's

larged ed., 1900). Many major essays in *Sheng-shih wei-yen* were written in the 1880's; see "Fan-li" [General Plan], pp. 2–3. A copy of *I-yen*, which seems to have been published in Hong Kong by Wang T'ao (who wrote a preface and a postface) is in the writer's possession. Wang's essays were reprinted in *T'ao-yüan wen-lu wai-pien* (Hong Kong, 1883). See Paul A. Cohen, "Wang T'ao and Incipient Chinese Nationalism," *Journal of Asian Studies*, 26 (1967), pp. 559–74.

[90] Cheng, *I-yen*, 1.2–7, 9–12, 22–25, 39–46; *Sheng-shih wei-yen*, *passim*; Wang, *T'ao-yüan wen-lu wai-pien*, *passim*.

superiority in government. Cheng explicitly recommended a two-house parliament consisting of officials and *shen-shih* "elected equitably and universally from among the people"; while the emperor was to retain a veto over the decisions of the *i-yüan,* the latter should be empowered to consider administrative innovations. Both writers emphasized that such a deliberative body could help the country to achieve "a united mind and will" (*hsin-chih ju i*), particularly regarding the goal of self-strengthening. This unity of purpose was not to be imposed from above, however, but to be achieved through initiative from below. Cheng and Wang laid great stress on the value of the newspaper, as well as of parliament, as a vehicle for public opinion (*min-ch'ing*), believing that the press could serve as a check on the parliament as well as the bureaucracy. They urged the government to encourage the establishment of newspapers in all provinces and to allow them to expose official abuses.[91]

Neither Cheng nor Wang ever questioned Confucian moral principles. They believed that the Chinese heritage held the *ta-tao* ("great truth"). But they urged their readers to learn the "substance" (*t'i*) of the Western civilization as well as its "application" (*yung*), the latter including such institutions as public schools and parliaments. Showing the influence of missionaries, Cheng and Wang advocated equal educational opportunity for women and the unbinding of their feet; they also recommended humanitarian enterprises such as prison reform and relief for the disabled and the destitute.[92]

While Western influence was strongest among writers of the treaty ports, in the 1880's and the early 1890's an increasing number of officials of little renown put forward ideas often similar to those of Cheng and Wang. Among Li Hung-chang's advisers, Hsüeh Fu-ch'eng, who had had few contacts with foreigners at that point in his career, advocated, in his essays of 1879,[93] that China should seek treaty revision in order to rid herself of extraterritoriality and to raise the import tariff. He urged government protection of Chinese merchants but non-inter-

[91] Cheng, *I-yen,* 1.1–2, 38–39, 46–49; 2.39–43; *Sheng-shih wei-yen,* 1.4–33; 2.58–63; Wang, *T'ao-yüan wen-lu wai-pien,* 1.19–23; 2.9, 12–13, 19–21; 3.7–8; 7.21–22.

[92] Cheng, *I-yen,* 2.48–50, 53–55; *Sheng-shih wei-yen,* author's preface, 1.1–2, 60–68; 2.35–38; 3.7–28; 8.72–82; Wang, *T'ao-yüan wen-lu wai-pien,* 1.1–2, 10–11, 20–21; 3.11; 4.17–18.

[93] *Ch'ou-yang ch'u-i* [Simple Proposals Regarding Foreign Affairs], in Hsüeh Fu-ch'eng, *Hsüeh Fu-ch'eng ch'üan-chi* [Complete Works of Hsüeh Fu-ch'eng], 3 vols. (Taipei: Kuang-wen, 1963), vol. 2.

ference in their pursuits. Hsüeh argued that just as there had been a great change of institutions (*pien-fa*) at the time when the ancient Ch'in dynasty was founded (221 B.C.), another great change was due two thousand years later, particularly since China had entered into a new international system. He recommended reform in the examination and civil service systems and in the rules and regulations of the six boards to permit less encumbered efforts toward the achievement of "wealth and strength." Even more remarkable than Hsüeh, however, were a few officials whose work did not involve self-strengthening problems and who nevertheless wrote books on reform in the early 1890's—T'ang Chen, a *hsien* magistrate in Anhwei in 1890; Ch'en Ch'iu, an official temporarily at home in Chekiang in 1892; Ch'en Ch'ih, a department director of the Board of Revenue in 1896.[94] The three men were as worried as Hsüeh was about further foreign aggression; they were for modifying the examination system, for industrialization, and for the promotion of "Western learning." They showed deeper knowledge and concern, however, regarding the paralyzing administrative problems of the time, both at the metropolitan and at the local level. (Ch'en Ch'ih, drawing on his experiences at the Board of Revenue, made particularly concrete proposals on how the power of the clerks at the six boards ought to be reduced.) It is significant that all three were in favor of some form of deliberative assembly (*i-yüan*). T'ang Chen made the unique suggestion that a two-house parliament might be created out of the existing metropolitan bureaucracy. Ch'en Ch'iu proposed local consultative assemblies for each *chou* and *hsien*, while Ch'en Ch'ih favored both local assemblies and a national parliament, the lower house of which was to be composed of elected representatives.[95]

While far-reaching reforms were advocated by a number of writers, it remained for a young scholar of a more philosophical bent to break with the orthodox ideology and, moreover, to take a lead in political action. Even before the youthful K'ang Yu-wei (1858–1927) had any contact with "Western learning," he was already revolting against his own education—Sung learning which he considered "bigoted and narrow" and Han learning which he found to be merely "trifling details."

[94] T'ang Chen, *Wei-yen* [Warnings] (Shanghai, 1890); Ch'en Ch'iu, *Chih-p'ing t-ung-i* [General Proposals Concerning Government] (preface, 1892); Ch'en Ch'ih, *Yung-shu* [A Utilitarian Discourse] (preface, 1896). Several major essays in *Yung-shu* were written before 1894. That Ch'en Ch'ih was familiar with Cheng Kuan-ying's writings is indicated by the fact that in 1893 he wrote a preface to the *Sheng-shih wei-yen*.

[95] See *WHPF*, 1:177–78, 228, 234, 245–47.

K'ang recalled in his autobiography[96] that in 1878, when he was not yet twenty, he became convinced that truth did not lie in the words of the learned teacher he once venerated, but in understanding revealed in Zen-like meditation: "In a great release of enlightenment, I beheld myself a sage and laughed for joy; then suddenly I thought of the sufferings and hardships of all living beings and wept in melancholy." The Buddhist strain in K'ang's thought was subtly transformed by his contacts with things Western. On a trip to Hong Kong in 1879, he was so impressed by the colony's orderly administration, as well as the architecture, that he concluded that the Europeans must have had the benefit of good laws (fa-tu) and could not be compared with the barbarians of China's past. He began to study world geography and collect books on "Western learning." Three years later, in 1882, when he visited Shanghai, he purchased "all the books translated by the Kiangnan Arsenal and by Western missionaries."[97] K'ang began to formulate a moral and political philosophy that represented a radical departure from Ch'ing thought, as evidenced in two of his earliest extant manuscripts—K'ang-tzu nei-wai pien (The Esoteric and Exoteric Essays of Master K'ang) and Shih-li kung-fa (Substantial Truths and Universal Laws), written between 1884 and 1887.[98] It was not just that he used many Western scientific terms (such as ether and electricity) and wrote one of the books in the form of Euclidean theorems and axioms. K'ang did no less than to redefine the Confucian concept of jen ("benevolence" or "love") and to expand its implications in society. In K'ang-tzu nei-wai pien, he attacked the Confucian virtue of i ("righteousness" or "sense of duty") as having been so corrupted by "practices and customs" as to become incompatible with jen. "I say in a hundred years this will

[96] "K'ang Nan-hai tzu-pien nien-p'u" [K'ang Yu-wei's Chronological Autobiography] in WHPF, 4:107–69. A fully annotated English translation is in Jung-pang Lo, K'ang Yu-wei, 1858–1927: A Biography and a Symposium (Tucson, 1967). See also K'ang's preface to his Li-yün chu [The Evolution of the Rites Annotated] (dated 1884 but probably written later), quoted in Kung-chuan Hsiao, "K'ang Yu-wei and Confucianism," Monumenta Serica, 18 (1959): 104–5.

[97] See Liang Ch'i-ch'ao's biography of K'ang in WHPF, 4:9. K'ang was reading the Wan-kuo kung-pao at least by 1883. See WHPF, 4:116.

[98] Richard C. Howard, "K'ang Yu-wei (1858–1927): His Intellectual Background and Early Thought," in Arthur F. Wright and Dennis Twitchett, eds., Confucian Personalities (Stanford: Stanford University Press, 1962), pp. 305 ff. See Kung-chuan Hsiao, "The Philosophical Thought of K'ang Yu-wei: An Attempt at a New Synthesis," Monumenta Serica, 21 (1962): 129–69; "K'ang Yu-wei and Confucianism," passim.

certainly change. . . . The ruler will not be exalted nor his subjects demeaned; woman will be treated with the same respect as man; and gentleman and commoner will be deemed alike." K'ang wanted above all to affirm human equality (*p'ing-teng*)—the fact that each person was endowed with soul and intelligence, even though the intelligence of one person "is different from that of another." In *Shih-li kung-fa*, K'ang set forth the principles of his ideal society: that each person should have the right to autonomy (*tzu-chu chih ch'üan*), that laws should be applied to everyone in an identical way, that all social and political institutions should be determined by all the people concerned after public discussion. Details of K'ang's utopia included elections and parliament, freedom to depart from the teachings of sages and mentors, free choice of husbands and wives, even the raising of children in public institutions. K'ang may have been inspired by the ancient altruistic philosophy of Mo-tzu and by the intuitionists among the Sung, Ming, and Ch'ing scholars. He himself ascribed his ideas to ancient Confucian texts, to Mahayana Buddhism, and to "Western learning."[99]

K'ang meant his philosophy to be universal in application. He regarded the essential truth of Confucianism, Buddhism, and Christianity to be the same and saw no distinction between the natural endowments of "barbarians" and Chinese. Yet he was also nationalistic. The Sino-French War of 1884–85, which threatened his city, Canton, left a deep impression on him.[100] He was sure that more serious crises awaited China, and what he had seen of the complacency and corruption of the government led him in 1888, while in Peking, to try to have a memorial presented to the throne. Already he was arguing that the prerequisite for self-strengthening was political reform—the broadening of the imperial counsels so as to allow easy communication between the subjects and the sovereign. (K'ang regarded the lack of communication between subject and throne as the principal cause of maladministration and widespread misery, as well as the inability to cope with the foreign threat.)[101] No official at Peking was willing to forward

[99] *WHPF*, 4:114–20; Hsiao, "The Philosophical Thought of K'ang Yu-wei," p. 131.

[100] In a letter dated 1883, K'ang wrote with great feeling on the Opium War, the Anglo-French occupation of Peking in 1860, and the current French threat to Yunnan and Kwangtung as well as to Vietnam. K'ang criticized Chang Shu-sheng, who resumed his governor-generalship at Canton in the summer of 1883, for making only feeble defense preparations. *Wan-mu ts'ao-t'ang i-kao* [Unpublished Works from the Thatched Hut among Ten Thousand Trees], 4 vols., mimeographed (family ed., 1960), 4.1–3. See also *WHPF*, 4:117.

[101] *WHPF*, 4:123–31.

K'ang's memorial, however, and returning to Canton, he devoted himself chiefly to teaching and writing.

It was at this point that he finally clarified his own thinking on what the original Confucius stood for. He found in the *Kung-yang Commentary* (the classic particularly venerated by the "new text" school) the idea of a three-stage progress toward the era of the "great peace." He also rediscovered, somewhat later, the passage in the *Book of Rites* that describes the ideal society where men "not only regard their own parents as parents and their own sons as sons," but share a common concern for humanity—a passage which, it should be noted, was also quoted in Taiping literature.[102] Believing that the teachings of the sages had long been distorted, K'ang sought in his *Hsin-hsüeh wei-ching k'ao* (On the Forged Classics of the Wang Mang Period [1891]) to prove that a number of classics, regarded as canonical since the first century A.D., were actually spurious. Since these works had often been respectfully cited by Sung neo-Confucianists, the authority of the latter —and of the orthodox Ch'ing ideology—was challenged by implication. In *Kung-tzu kai-chih k'ao* (Confucius as a Reformer, written in 1896 but not published until the winter of 1897–98), K'ang argued that the great sage, instead of looking to the past for inspiration, actually worked for the future, and that instead of being a defender of feudalism, he was a champion of "rule by the people" (*min-chu*). Confucius was, according to K'ang, using an idealized antiquity as a justification for institutional reform (*t'o-ku kai-chih*); he was an uncrowned king (*su-wang*) who legislated for the ages. While a long period of monarchical despotism had intervened, China would eventually advance to the era when each individual's right to autonomy was to be amply safeguarded. To his new views on morality in society, K'ang thus added a theory of progress.[103]

By the time he completed the *Kung-tzu kai-chih k'ao*, K'ang was, of course, very much involved in the political issues of the day. In Peking in April, 1895, for the metropolitan examination, he drafted the famous "ten thousand word memorial," which recommended continuation of the war and immediate adoption of sweeping reforms. The

[102] Hsiao, "K'ang Yu-wei and Confucianism," pp. 106, 113–16. Hung Hsiu-ch'üan quoted the identical passage from the *Book of Rites* in his "Yüan-tao hsing-shih hsün" [Instructions on Rousing the World with the Basic Doctrine] (written between 1845 and 1846), *TPTK*, 1:92.

[103] Hsiao, "K'ang Yu-wei and Confucianism," pp. 136–43, 150–75. K'ang's famous *Ta-t'ung shu* [Book of the Great Unity] was not completed until 1902 during his sojourn in India.

memorial was co-signed by some thirteen hundred candidates for the examination at Peking, although it was never permitted to reach the throne. Drawing upon the ideas of such men as Cheng Kuan-ying and Ch'en Ch'ih, the views of Timothy Richard and Young J. Allen published in the *Wan-kuo kung-pao,* and the experience of Meiji Japan about which K'ang learned from Huang Tsun-hsien's *Jih-pen kuo-chih* (History of Japan [1890]) and works in Japanese which he struggled to read himself,[104] K'ang presented a comprehensive program of reform that centered on certain political innovations. He called for rapid industrialization for the purpose of building up "national wealth," but argued that it was also necessary to improve the life of the peasants— for example, by introducing new agricultural techniques and promoting internal migration. He recommended immediate changes in the examination system so as to encourage specialization in science and technology, but he also wanted educational facilities made available to all the people. He visualized schools and libraries in every village, where illiteracy would be eliminated and where Confucianism (presumably K'ang's version) was to be energetically propagated. All these measures must be preceded, however, by reform in the government itself. K'ang proposed that the sale of offices be discontinued; that a governor (*hsün-fu*) be appointed to every circuit (*tao*) so that he might effectively supervise a smaller area than a province; that the rank of the *hsien* magistrate be raised; and that clerks, either in the local or in the metropolitan administrations, should be chosen from among the holders of the *chü-jen* degree. Like Feng Kuei-fen, K'ang recommended that "village officials" nominated by each community should help in local administration, but he also wanted a body of elected representatives that could serve as a national legislature. He suggested that every 100,000 households elect a representative from among men of either official or non-official status, to serve as *i-lang* (a Han dynasty title meaning "deliberative official"). The *i-lang* should take turns attending upon the emperor in groups. They were, moreover, to meet as a body to consider matters concerning reform and revenue; proposals receiving a two-thirds vote from this body were to be "put into effect by the six boards." K'ang believed that such a representative body not only would bring before the throne the grievances of the populace, but would rally support for self-strengthening. "When four hundred million people are of one mind, how can the country not be strong?"[105]

[104] See Richard C. Howard, "Japan's Role in the Reform Program of K'ang Yu-wei," in Lo, *K'ang Yu-wei, 1858–1927,* pp. 279–312.

[105] *WHPF,* 2:131–66.

While K'ang's ideas and proposals epitomized the new ideology of reform, others added certain emphases more directly Western in origin. Ho K'ai, a physician and a prominent citizen of Hong Kong who had spent some twenty years in England studying medicine and law, wrote a series of essays on reform between 1887 and 1895, in collaboration with Hu Li-yüan, another resident of Hong Kong who had more training in Chinese.[106] Ho and Hu presented many proposals for "new policies," ranging from increased salaries for officials to railroad construction, and emphasized the need to change China's antiquated legal system. They particularly stressed the role of a parliament as the author of laws that protect life and property. "Since government is the affair of the people, authority should belong to the people. . . . As to laws and decrees regarding the means by which life and property are to be protected, the people themselves know best."[107] The book by Ho and Hu envisioned a parliament under the Ch'ing although as of 1895, Ho was actually giving assistance to the young Cantonese revolutionaries who plotted against the dynasty from Hong Kong.

While Ho and Hu introduced essentially Lockian ideas, Yen Fu, the dean of Li Hung-chang's naval academy at Tientsin, propagated social Darwinism in his non-official role as editorial writer and translator. Having learned English and the sciences as a student at the Foochow Navy Yard school, Yen was fascinated by English political thought, especially after his two-year sojourn in Britain in the late 1870's. In elegant yet pungent essays published between 1895 and 1898 and in his *T'ien-yen lun* (an annotated translation of T. H. Huxley's *Evolution and Ethics*, 1897), Yen expanded on an idea that won immediate acceptance among many of his readers—the survival of the fittest in the perpetual struggle for existence. In the world of man, Yen emphasized, the struggle was chiefly among communities (*ch'ün*), which, in the modern context, were the nation-states. A community could prosper, however, only when its individual components were superior—physically, intellectually, and morally. Yen called for a more robust Chinese race, for an educational policy that emphasized scientific method and independent inquiry, and for the inculcation of a public morality that included concern for individual liberty as well as a sense of honor. He was mortified by the lethargy and hypocrisy

---

[106] Hsiao Kung-ch'üan, *Chung-kuo cheng-chih ssu-hsiang shih*, 6:795–803. I have consulted Lloyd E. Eastman's paper, "The Early Institutional Reformers, 1885–1895," presented at the 18th Annual Meeting of the Association for Asian Studies, New York, April 4, 1966.

[107] *WHPF*, 1:196–201.

among the Chinese; he wanted, above all, to see his fellow literati transformed into dynamic, responsible citizens. Yen appears to have been less contemplative than K'ang on deeper moral issues; he was on the whole less concerned with the worth of the person than with the wealth and power of the state.[108] Nevertheless, he was definitely committed to the democratic as well as the nationalistic ideal, there being, in fact, no apparent conflict between the two in the Victorian England that he so admired. Yen asserted unequivocally that "the state is the property of the people," and he sternly condemned the monarchical tyranny in Chinese history. Though he believed in gradual and not precipitate change, he did want the local officials of China—prefects as well as *chou* and *hsien* magistrates—to be elected officers, and he wanted to see a national parliament in Peking.[109] Yen's Darwinian message was used, in fact, by himself and others in the 1895–98 period to reinforce the arguments for constitutionalism and reform.

The ideas sketched above are significant in themselves as events in intellectual history. While elements of democratic thought can be found in Chinese classics, notably *The Works of Mencius,* earnest intellectuals such as K'ang and Yen must have learned about democratic institutions with a sense of discovery. Certain deep-rooted Chinese problems, such as that of agrarian relationships, were neglected by the reform writers discussed above. Nevertheless, some of these men did visualize a continuous liberalization of the society. Their ideas represented, in any case, the hope for a new political order. But of course, a tremendous gap existed between the ideals of the few and the realities of a deteriorating yet still entrenched authoritarian government.

Operating from the British colony of Hong Kong, an insurrectionary movement of a new type had appeared. During the Sino-Japanese War, Sun Yat-sen (1866–1925) organized a semi-secret patriotic society in Hawaii, where his brother lived and where he had sojourned twice before, and in Hong Kong, where he had attended school and medical college and enjoyed many friendships. The objective of the Hsing Chung Hui ("Revive China Society"), according to its formal declaration, was to "pursue the study of wealth and strength so as to revive China and uphold her national dignity." But it was chiefly a conspiratorial group, aiming ultimately at overthrowing the Manchus and

[108] Benjamin Schwartz, *In Search of Wealth and Power: Yen Fu and the West* (Cambridge, Mass.: Harvard University Press, 1964).

[109] Yen Fu, *Yen Chi-tao shih-wen ts'ao* [A Collection of Yen Fu's Poetry and Prose], 6 *ts'e* (Shanghai: Kuo-hua, 1922), 1.25–26; 3.7–8.

immediately, as of 1895, at organizing the Triad bandits and country militiamen around Canton with money and weapons supplied from Hong Kong, with a view to seizing control of the former city by a surprise attack on the principal yamens. It is not certain whether the society, at this time, required its members to take an oath affirming the ideal of "a federated republican government" (ho-chung cheng-fu). Ho K'ai, whom Sun had long known and who solicited British help for the conspirators, represented them as a "reform party," aiming at replacing the Manchus with a new ruling house, a step which was to be followed by a "constitutional upheaval." But Sun himself, at this point in his career, appears to have been more interested in action than in ideology. So were the handful of other leaders of the Hsing Chung Hui, who, like Sun, were men educated in Hong Kong or abroad and more in touch with the local commercial society (and in the case of Cheng Shih-liang, the Triad groups as well) than with the world of the Chinese literati.[110] After the "Canton revolt" aborted in October, 1895, the principal leaders went overseas, and Hsing Chung Hui activities were not resumed in Hong Kong until 1899.

Meanwhile, the literati reform movement on the mainland had expanded and gone through tumultuous days. Even the administration at Peking had been stimulated by the Sino-Japanese War into taking a slightly broader attitude. Back in 1889, when the young emperor Kuang-hsü, began his personal rule, Weng T'ung-ho, the imperial tutor, had presented to him Feng Kuei-fen's reform essays of 1861. As a member of the Grand Council and president of the Board of Revenue, Weng advocated war against Japan in 1894. With China's defeat, he was belatedly converted to self-strengthening. Reversing his former stand, he urged the construction of railways, and he was highly pleased when he was appointed a director of the T'ung-wen Kuan (Interpreter's College).[111] In the few months after the Treaty of Shimonoseki, numerous officials in Peking and the provinces memorialized the throne, advising new economic and educational policies. In the winter of that year the court, in addition to making plans for new armies, authorized plans for new banks and ordered the provinces to establish "bureaus of commerce" (shang-wu chü).[112] In June, 1896, the throne asked the

[110] See Harold Schiffrin, Sun Yat-sen and the Origins of the 1911 Revolution (Berkeley: University of California Press, forthcoming in 1968).

[111] Kung-chuan Hsiao, "Weng T'ung-ho and the Reform Movement of 1898," Ch'ing-hua hsüeh-pao, n.s., 1, no. 2 (1957): 121.

[112] See WHPF, 2:1–5, 269–97, 397–402.

provinces to establish schools of Western learning and to consider sending students abroad. At least some governors-general and governors
took effective action. Chang Chih-tung, besides raising his "Self-strengthening Army" and continuing to be interested in railways and steel
works, took steps in 1895–96 (first at his temporary post at Nanking and
later at Wuchang) to promote cotton textile mills, establish schools that
taught Western subjects, and send students abroad. In Hunan, under
Governor Ch'en Pao-chen, a series of innovations were introduced—
telegraph lines connecting with a neighboring province, steam launches
in Tungting Lake, electric lights in the provincial capital, Changsha.
Ch'en's educational commissioner, Chiang Piao, who had studied at the
T'ung-wen Kuan in Peking and worked in the Chinese legation in
Japan, introduced an additional test on "current affairs" into the provincial examination, using the books written or translated by Young
J. Allen and Timothy Richard as texts. Chiang founded an academy in
Changsha which taught mathematics, sciences, and foreign languages,
about a year before the School of Current Affairs (Shih-wu hsüeh-t'ang)
was established in the same city in the autumn of 1897.

While the sponsorship of provincial administrators was essential to
industrial and educational progress, the shen-shih often played an
active role. In the case of Chang Chien (1853–1926), who won the top
distinction in the metropolitan examination of 1894 but forsook the
official's career thereafter, we know from his writings that he was
anxious for China to develop her industrial and agricultural capacity
and to carry out administrative reforms. He believed, however, that
scholars should turn themselves into practical men organizing production, instead of merely indulging in "empty talk," and that they should,
moreover, work independently of the government, even though it was
necessary, in major enterprises, to have the latter's assistance. In his
native Nantung, in Kiangsu province, he often took the lead in local
affairs—petitioning the authorities for reduction of surtaxes, promoting
sericulture, organizing poor relief and militia.[113] With the encouragement of the governor-general of Liangkiang—Chang Chih-tung and,
later, Liu K'un-i—he organized in 1896 the Dah Sun Cotton Mill, and
proved himself a highly competent entrepreneur. In Hunan, prominent
retired officials, including Wang Hsien-ch'ien (a former Libationer of
the Imperial Academy) and Chang Tsu-T'ung (a former Department
Director of the Board of Punishment), were among the founders of a

---

[113] Chang Hsiao-jo, Nan-t'ung Chang Chi-chih hsien-sheng chuan-chi [Bi-
ography of Mr. Chang Chien of Nan-t'ung] (Shanghai: Chung-hua, 1930), pp.
50–54.

company running steam launches and an industrial school. Before he became its violent critic, Wang, a classical scholar of repute, was a sponsor of the School of Current Affairs.[114]

While there was now greater *shen-shih* participation in the programs for innovation, the younger and more idealistic literati were not satisfied. They wanted broad institutional reforms, such as the abolition of the eight-legged essay in the examinations, and political reforms in the direction of constitutionalism. Like the Tung-lin group of the late Ming, K'ang Yu-wei and his followers were political protestants who acted on ideological grounds. The K'ang group was, of course, more concerned with the threat of foreign aggression than the late Ming partisans ever were; also, their new Confucianism incorporated "alien" elements in a way that the Tung-lins would surely have detested. While the Ming reformers were primarily concerned about the moral quality of officials in high places, K'ang and his friends were armed with a whole range of policy proposals, which included modifying the structure of the government. While the nucleus of the Tung-lin group was composed of high officials, the late nineteenth-century activists were young men who had either only recently or not yet won higher degrees. K'ang's friends never really became a faction at court. But they aspired to do so through the organization of *hsüeh-hui* ("study societies") among scholar-officials. Moreover, they extended their influence among the literati of the empire through periodicals produced by lithographic process and dwelling on nationalistic themes.

As early as 1895, K'ang had adopted a two-pronged approach to reform. On the one hand, he hoped to influence the policies of the throne itself, by writing memorials and by presenting his views to high officials like Weng T'ung-ho. On the other hand, he sought to exert an educational influence among officials high and low—K'ang's self-confidence being unbounded—and on the literati of the empire at large. Together with his disciple, Liang Ch'i-ch'ao, he founded in July, 1895, a small newspaper in Peking, at first under the guise of the missionary publication *Wan-kuo kung-pao* and later under the title of *Chung-wai chi-wen* ("Chinese and Foreign News"), which was produced in an edition of a thousand copies and distributed to officials at Peking. In August, K'ang, with the assistance of Ch'en Ch'ih (who was still a department director of the Board of Revenue) and others, founded the Self-strengthening Study Society (*Ch'iang-hsüeh hui*), defying the interdiction against literati associations which the dynasty had maintained

---

[114] *WHPF,* 2:585–89. See Charlton M. Lewis, "The Reform Movement in Hunan, 1896–1898," *Papers on China,* 15 (1961), 62–90.

since its earliest days. K'ang undoubtedly hoped to widen his contacts with officials of influence through this society. Among the men approached were Sun Chia-nai, President of the Board of Civil Appointments, Wen T'ing-shih, Expositor of the Hanlin Academy, and a large number of censors and members of the Hanlin Academy; donations were also solicited from important governors-general like Chang Chih-tung and even military commanders like Yüan Shih-k'ai. K'ang also aimed at a broad membership among the capital bureaucracy and among the officials and *shen-shih* of the provinces. He wanted not only to create reform sentiment, but also to achieve genuine discussion at the society's meetings, to promote the translation of Western and Japanese works and to sponsor schools, libraries, and study abroad. Late in 1895, he founded a branch of the society in Shanghai. Prominent officials and *shen-shih* of several provinces were invited to be members, including Chang Chih-tung, Chang Chien, and the sons of Tso Tsung-t'ang, Shen Pao-chen, and Ch'en Pao-chen.[115]

Although one of his memorials did reach the emperor in the summer of 1895, K'ang's stay in Peking during that year plainly did not affect imperial policy. Weng T'ung-ho, though he befriended K'ang, would not follow his advice and recommend the abolition of the eight-legged essay.[116] Attacked by a censor, the Self-strengthening Study Society was banned by imperial edict in January, 1896. K'ang returned to Canton, but he and his students continued their campaign. In the *Shih-wu pao* ("China Progress"), founded in August, 1896, in Shanghai and edited by Liang Ch'i-ch'ao, the reform movement had an influential organ, each issue (published every ten days) selling some 12,000 copies in 1897.[117] Liang's eloquent editorials hammered on the theme of "reform of institutions," particularly emphasizing the need for thorough reform of the examination system and the establishment of new schools. Desiring not to offend such officials as Chang Chih-tung, Liang only brought up such issues as the parliamentary system and the rights of the people (*min-ch'üan*) in an inconspicuous fashion and did not propose immediate action. But he did argue for the inclusion of Western "social principles" (*kung-li*) in the curricula of the new schools, and urged with

[115] *WHPF,* 4:384–94; John Schrecker, "The Pao-kuo Hui: A Reform Society of 1898," *Papers on China,* 14 (1960): 51–52.

[116] See K'ang's account in *WHPF,* 4:135–36.

[117] Chang P'eng-yüan, *Liang Ch'i-ch'ao yü Ch'ing-chi ko ming* [Liang Ch'i-ch'ao and the Late Ch'ing Revolution] (Taipei: Academia Sinica, 1964), pp. 266–67. In the summer of 1897, the *Shih-wu pao* had 109 distributing agencies in seventy towns or *hsien.*

enthusiasm that "study societies" of all kinds be established widely in the empire. Liang was for equality of the sexes and advocated schools for women and the liberation of their bound feet. He suggested that children should learn to read, not immediately from the classics, but from simpler material that would not "suffocate the mind."[118] Liang warned that innovation was a "universal law" which a nation could defy only at its peril. Unlike K'ang, who was preoccupied with classical sanctions, Liang would also justify reform by invoking the example of the West, as well as the Darwinian concepts of Yen Fu.[119]

The years between 1896 and 1898 saw a quickening tempo to European imperialism in China. These years also saw the first blooming of "Western learning" there. The circulation of *Wan-kuo kung-pao* and of the Kiangnan Arsenal publications increased many times. Books by Young J. Allen and Timothy Richard gained wide currency.[120] More officials and *shen-shih* began to sponsor schools that taught modern subjects. By early 1898, there were established in eight provinces—but with the highest concentration in Kiangsu, Hunan, and Kwangtung— some twenty-six literati associations which were varieties of *hsüeh-hui*. These, in turn, often founded new schools and put out new publications.[121] The K'ang-Liang group acted as catalysts. K'ang's brother, Kuang-jen, was the chief organizer in Shanghai of a society for the

[118] See Liang's articles reprinted in his *Yin-ping shih wen-chi* [Collected Writings from the Ice-drinker's Studio] (Taipei: Chung-hua, 1960), especially 1:14–34, 37–64, 69, 79–80, 93–96, 99–102, 105.

[119] *Ibid.*, pp. 2–8, 106–10. Liang wrote in a letter to Yen Fu in 1897: "I have always had an extreme abhorrence of people who cite ancient Chinese practices in order to uphold Western political institutions and claim that all the West's strong points were our own. This is a habit that comes from the empty vanity of our countrymen. I originally did not intend to follow the custom. But in the magazine [*Shih-wu pao*] I had to preach to people of mediocre caliber and I often could not avoid the custom myself." Cf. Joseph R. Levenson, *Liang Ch'i-ch'ao and the Mind of Modern China* (Cambridge, Mass.: Harvard University Press, 1953), chap. 2.

[120] *Wan-kuo kung-pao* sold about 4,800 copies per issue in 1897, not counting the large pirated editions put out by Chinese merchants. Timothy Richard's translation of Robert Mackenzie's *The Nineteenth Century*, under the title of *T'ai-hsi hsin-shih lan-yao* (Shanghai: Kuang-hsüeh hui, 1895), appeared in 19 pirated editions in Szechwan province alone in 1898. Allen's book on the Sino-Japanese War and its lessons was likewise a best seller. See Wang, *Wai-jen yü wu-hsü pien-fa*, pp. 40–42.

[121] Liang Ch'i-ch'ao, *Wu-hsü cheng-pien chi* [The Coup d'État of 1898] (New York: Yu-fang, 1958), pp. 240–45; Chang Ching-lu, *Chung-kuo chin-tai ch'u-pan shih-liao,* 1:77–86.

preparation of translations, a girl's school, an association for the prohibition of foot-binding, and a group devoted to the publication of new reading materials for children. K'ang, aided by his students, founded a new reform periodical and a school in Macao. While visiting Kwangsi, he helped T'ang Ching-sung, former governor of Taiwan, establish a study society in Kweilin. However, the K'ang-Liang group were directly responsible for only a few of the twenty-six new societies. In Shanghai, for example, Lo Chen-yü, who did not sympathize with radical views on reform, founded a group for the study of agricultural techniques; and in Soochow, scholars inspired by the writings of Liang and others founded a Kiangsu Study Society (*Su hsüeh-hui*). At all events, word of such new societies was broadcast in Liang's *Shih-wu pao*, and we find independent *hsüeh-hui* formed in Hunan, Hupei, Chekiang, Fukien, and even Shensi. Unlike the banned Self-strengthening Study Society, which sought the support of influential officials partly for political purposes, most of the new *hsüeh-hui* were merely academic in nature. They all emphasized "Western learning," even though some were also devoted to classical studies.[122]

In Hunan, the reformers soon had the opportunity to develop a new political approach. Governor Ch'en Pao-chen, assisted by his reform-minded son, San-li, continued to be interested in innovation. In July, 1897, Huang Tsun-hsien, who had served many years in the Chinese legations and consulates in Japan, the United States, and England, and who wrote the *Jih-pen kuo-chih* (History of Japan [1890]), became judicial commissioner of Hunan. He agreed with many of the ideas of K'ang and Liang and at his suggestion Liang was invited to be the chief instructor of the newly founded School of Current Affairs at Changsha.[123] The gathering of such men as Huang, Liang, Hsü Jen-chu (the new educational commissioner after September 1897), and two young Hunanese of exceptional talent and vigor—T'an Ssu-t'ung and T'ang Ts'ai-ch'ang—made Hunan for a time the principal center of new activities, including an unsuccessful experiment in *shen-shih* "self-government."

Liang, who arrived at Changsha in November, 1897, had further developed his political thinking. He now wanted to propagate "people's

---

[122] *WHPF*, 4:136, 377–83, 427–28.

[123] Ting Wen-chiang, *Liang Jen-kung hsien-sheng nien-p'u ch'ang-pien ch'u-kao* [Materials for the Chronological Biography of Liang Ch'i-ch'ao: A Tentative Compilation], 3 vols. (Taipei: Shih-chieh, 1958), 1:37; T'an Ssu-t'ung, *T'an Ssu-t'ung ch'üan-chi* [Complete Works of T'an Ssu-t'ung] (Peking: San-lien, 1954), p. 366; *WHPF*, 4:185–86.

rights" more explicitly, citing Western achievements such as the American Revolution and proposing to reevaluate the Confucian tradition from the standpoint of certain concepts found in *Mencius* and in the *Kung-yang Commentary.* The evils of despotism, including the particular misdeeds of the Manchu rulers, were earnestly discussed by Liang and other teachers before the more than forty students of the School of Current Affairs.[124] The reformers did not confine themselves to teaching, however. The German occupation of Kiaochow in mid-November created an atmosphere of acute crisis that heightened their fervor. They now wanted to organize the more enlightened *shen-shih* into a "study society" that could turn itself into a provincial assembly. Liang even suggested to Governor Ch'en that Hunan might survive as an independent base in the event that the empire was overwhelmed by further foreign aggression.[125]

The chief inspiration behind the radical movement in Hunan came from T'an Ssu-t'ung (1865–98), who returned to the province the same November from a sojourn of about two years in the Shanghai-Nanking area, where he had frequently exchanged views with Liang Ch'i-ch'ao. The gifted son of the governor of Hupei, T'an indulged himself in poetry and in antiquarian studies in his youth, but was by the early 1890's increasingly attracted by the ideas of the early Ch'ing radical Wang Fu-chih. He developed a contempt for most of the famous Ch'ing scholars since Wang's time.[126] Rudely shocked by China's defeat in the Sino-Japanese War, he began to read such publications as the *Ko-chih hui-pien* ("Chinese Scientific Magazine," edited by John Fryer) and *Wan-kuo kung-pao;* as early as the autumn of 1894, he tried without success to establish a school of mathematics in Liu-yang, his native place in Hunan.[127] In the latter part of 1895, while visiting Peking, he met Liang and through him became acquainted with K'ang Yu-wei's teachings. T'an read further on Mahayana Buddhism and Christianity, as well as Western sciences. His *Jen-hsüeh* ("On Love"), completed in 1896 and circulated among friends although not published at that time, was a remarkable testament of his new cosmology and moral philosophy, as well as a tract for the times. Like K'ang, T'an saw in concern for hu-

---

[124] Ting Wen-chiang, *Liang Jen-kung,* 1:42–46.

[125] Liang's letter to Ch'en in Liang, *Wu-hsü cheng-pien chi,* pp. 249–62.

[126] Yang T'ing-fu, *T'an Ssu-t'ung nien-p'u* [Chronological Biography of T'an Ssu-t'ung] (Peking: Jen-min, 1957), pp. 54–61; letters and essays in T'an, *T'an Ssu-t'ung ch'üan-chi, passim.*

[127] See letter to Pei Yüan-cheng dated the 7th month, 1894, in T'an, *T'an Ssu-t'ung ch'üan-chi,* pp. 386–430.

manity, or *jen*, the vital force of the universe. He likewise regarded *jen* as implying the imperative of human equality—that every person is entitled to self-realization and autonomy. T'an was more violent than K'ang in attacking conventional morality. He bitterly resented the three cardinal relationships ("*san-kang*") of the Chinese tradition—between monarch and subject, father and son, and husband and wife. The relation between monarch and subject was to him "particularly dark, stultifying, and oppressive of humanity." While the rulers of antiquity, T'an believe, were chosen by the people, now "the life and blood of the empire are being drained, so that the monarch can be indolent, arrogant, licentious, and murderous."[128]

Although often absorbed in abstract problems of religion and ethics, T'an was convinced of the necessity of drastic reforms if China was to be saved. He believed that the secret of self-strengthening lay in unceasing innovation (*jih-hsin*). Endorsing the reform program outlined in K'ang's memorials, he further suggested, for example, that Chinese dress should be changed to something like the Western style, and that the traditional virtue of frugality (*chien*) should be discarded, since increased consumption was a sign of dynamism and would serve to stimulate trade and industry. T'an despaired of the prospects for achieving self-strengthening under the Manchus, whom he deeply resented. He believed, however, that the spread of knowledge (*hsüeh*) was bound, in time, to generate enough "heat and light" to compel change.[129] Himself the product of *shen-shih* culture, T'an believed that progress toward "rule by the people" could be achieved by the more enlightened *shen-shih* participating fully in government affairs. "Even when it is not possible to realize rule by the people," he wrote in a letter of June, 1897, "the *shen-shih* and the elders should be accorded the right (*ch'üan*) to deliberate on government affairs."[130] Having returned to Hunan in November 1897 at the invitation of Governor Ch'en and Commissioner Huang, T'an saw an opportunity to put his ideas into practice.

T'an, together with his close friend T'ang Ts'ai-ch'ang, edited the reform periodical *Hsiang-hsüeh hsin-pao* ("The New Journal of Hunan") and took part in planning mining and other enterprises. His major interest lay, however, in the plans for a province-wide association to be called the Southern Study Society (*Nan hsüeh-hui*). It was hoped

---

[128] *Jen-hsüeh* [On Love], in T'an, *T'an Ssu-t'ung ch'üan-chi*, especially pp. 6–7, 11–13, 26–28, 53–69.

[129] *Ibid.*, pp. 38–44, 71–73, 78–80.

[130] *Ibid.*, p. 307.

that this society, besides serving as a training ground for future officials, could help to found schools and industrial enterprises, collect likin, build roads, compile and publish a guide to legal precedents, and supervise the local police and *pao-chia* systems. With the approval of Governor Ch'en, ten prominent *shen-shih* of the province were asked to be sponsors and to nominate other "public-spirited and patriotic men" to the society, each *chou* and *hsien* to be represented by three to ten members.[131] Inaugurated in March, 1898, the Southern Study Society showed promise, at least for a few weeks. Criticizing his own class in a speech given before a meeting of the society, Huang Tsun-hsien pointed out that while officials were "monopolizing power as well as dignity," the people had long been victimized. He urged the *shen-shih* members of the society to practice "self-government" (*tzu-chih*) in their counties or towns, taking greater responsibility for such matters as education, commerce, irrigation and other public works connected with agriculture, industrial production, and the control of banditry. As an earnest of his intention, Huang, in his capacity as provincial judicial commissioner, created a "bureau of security" (*pao-wei chü*) and invited the members of the Southern Study Society to help create a police system for each of their communities.[132] Meanwhile, lectures on "Western learning" were held for members of the society; a daily newspaper, *Hsiang-pao* ("Hunan News"), edited by T'an and T'ang, was distributed; and branches of the society were planned for at least six places in the province.[133]

Whatever hope there was for the society to develop into a provincial assembly was dashed, however, when smoldering criticism among the prominent *shen-shih* developed into vociferous opposition in the late spring of 1898. Although Wang Hsien-ch'ien and Chang Tsu-t'ung had been in favor of the establishment of the School of Current Affairs as well as new industrial projects, they had no idea, at first, that such un-Confucian notions as "people's rights" would be taught in the school. It was early March when they found out about the radical ideas taught by Liang and other teachers at the school—Liang himself having, on account of his health, left for Shanghai, whence he soon proceeded to Peking. By April or May, such men as Wang and Chang—to say nothing of their *shen-shih* friend Yeh Te-hui, an extreme conservative who even doubted the efficacy of Western technology—were incensed by T'an

[131] *Ibid.*, pp. 93–102; Liang, *Wu-hsü cheng-pien chi*, p. 262; *WHPF*, 4:50–51.

[132] *WHPF*, 4:423–25; T'an, *T'an Ssu-t'ung ch'üan-chi*, 167–68.

[133] T'an, *T'an Ssu-t'ung ch'üan-chi*, pp. 136–48, 301, 303–4, 306; *WHPF*, 4:195.

Ssu-t'ung's laudatory comments on K'ang Yu-wei, published in the *Hsiang-pao*. K'ang's work on Confucius as a reformer (published the past winter) was only then being read in Hunan and his heretical views fanned the resentment of the Confucian stalwarts.[134] There was, moreover, opposition in other parts of the province besides the capital, Changsha. Fan Ts'ui, a senior licentiate and a member of the Southern Study Society from the town of Shao-yang, was expelled from his own community by the local notables because he distributed tracts that included such phrases as "equality" and "people's rights" and favored imitating the West. In May, P'i Hsi-jui, who was giving a series of lectures to members of the Southern Study Society, was attacked so violently that he had to leave the province, as were several teachers whom Liang had brought to the School of Current Affairs. Although Governor Ch'en continued to support the society, its many plans had to be shelved; only a series of academic lectures was maintained through the summer of that year.[135]

Even as their hopes dimmed in Hunan, the radical reformers had the opportunity, ephemeral and unreal as it may now seem, to introduce their ideas at the court itself. Returning to Peking in 1897, during the Kiaochow crisis, K'ang again tried to present memorials to the throne and to win the attention of high officials. As it happened, there were now officials, like the censor Kao Hsüeh-tseng, who spoke in favor of K'ang in memorials and recommended him for imperial service. There were also two powerful imperial advisers who, inclining toward their own versions of reform, could use K'ang to defend new policies in the factional struggle at court. Chang Yin-huan, member of the Tsungli Yamen and Vice-President of the Board of Revenue, was much in the Emperor's confidence at this time. He had served as Chinese minister in Washington and had an enlightened outlook. He undoubtedly had spoken favorably about K'ang before the Emperor.[136] Weng T'ung-ho, who had befriended K'ang during the latter's sojourn in Peking in 1895, found in the early winter of 1897–98 that the Cantonese scholar's views on foreign policy—namely, that China should befriend Britain and Japan and open more treaty ports in North China and Manchuria —were particularly useful in his own maneuvering at court (since some of Weng's rivals for leadership were for a pro-Russian stance, even after

---

[134] *WHPF*, 2:637–40; T'an, *T'an Ssu-t'ung ch'üan-chi*, 337–38.

[135] *WHPF*, 4:195, 315–18; Yang, *T'an Ssu-t'ung nien-p'u*, pp. 110–11.

[136] Ping-ti Ho, "Chang Yin-huan shih-chi" [The Career of Chang Yin-huan], *Ch'ing-hua hsüeh-pao*, 13, no. 1 (1941): 202–8.

the Russian seizure of Port Arthur that followed upon the German occupation of Kiaochow). Weng himself had become increasingly disposed toward moderate administrative reforms and could visualize himself as the leader of a group pressing for innovation, with K'ang as his chief lieutenant. The senior statesman was indeed to change his views on K'ang before long (probably as early as January 24, when K'ang uttered what Weng described as "extremely unrestrained" statements in an interview with the ministers of the Tsungli Yamen, Weng himself being present).[137] But before this date, the Emperor had been persuaded by Chang, Weng, and others to read one of K'ang's memorials, and the monarch now ordered K'ang to submit his further views, as well as the books he had promised on the reform experiences of Russia and Japan.

K'ang continued his propaganda campaign, particularly attempting to rally support for his cause among officials who could memorialize the throne. In January, he organized the Kwangtung Study Society (Yüeh hsüeh-hui) at a Cantonese Landsmann hall. He also helped to plan several other provincial "study societies," including two that had Manchus as members. In April, after the humiliating Ch'ing capitulation to the demands of Germany, Russia, and France for leaseholds, K'ang sought to mobilize sentiment among the degree candidates then gathering at Peking, as well as the metropolitan officials, by organizing the Society for Preserving the Nation (Pao-kuo hui), which, according to his plan, was to establish branches throughout the country. Three well-attended meetings were held (in the first of which more than two hundred persons participated). K'ang and Liang made fervent speeches on the urgent need for action to save "the nation, the race, and the [Confucian] teaching." However, while K'ang won many friends, he also antagonized many people. His heretical book on Confucius as a reformer was then attracting attention in Peking. By May, the new society had come under severe attack, particularly by Hung Chia-yü, a functionary of the Board of Civil Appointments, who in a vitriolic pamphlet, which was widely distributed, distorted a sentence in K'ang's book and accused him of harboring the ambition to become "the lord of the people and the monarch of the faith" (min-chu chiao-huang).[138]

[137] Ping-ti Ho, "Weng T'ung-ho and the 'One Hundred Days of Reform,' " Far Eastern Quarterly, 10 (1950–51): 127–30; Hsiao, "Weng T'ung-ho," pp. 166–72.

[138] WHPF, 4:138, 142–43; Schrecker, "The Pao-kuo Hui," 56–64; Ho, "Weng T'ung-ho and the 'One Hundred Days of Reform,' " pp. 130–33; Hsiao, "Weng T'ung-ho," pp. 173–79.

The pamphlet touched off a flurry of memorials impeaching K'ang and his society. There were men like Hsü Chih-ching, a sub-chancellor of the Grand Secretariat, who continued to admire K'ang and recommend him for imperial service. But Weng T'ung-ho now warned the Emperor of K'ang's "unpredictable intentions." Although at the monarch's command Weng drafted the famous edict of June 12, declaring "reform and self-strengthening" (*pien-fa tzu-ch'iang*) to be national policy, he did so reluctantly and produced a document that was a masterpiece of ambiguity.

The Emperor himself, however, had determined on a more drastic course. This was the key factor behind the "one hundred days of innovation" (*wei-hsin*), between June 12 and September 20, 1898. Since attaining his majority in the late 1880's, the Emperor Kuang-hsü (who was twenty-seven in 1898) had been resentful of the Empress Dowager's continued domination over personnel and policies. He undoubtedly saw in reform a chance to assert himself against his "foster mother." But the Emperor was also an idealist. He had long shown a liking for Western mechanical gadgets, had once wanted to learn English (which the Empress and Weng T'ung-ho discouraged), and often had his eunuchs purchase Chinese books from the mission bookshop in Peking.[139] Weng and another imperial tutor, Sun Chia-nai, had shown him the reform writings of Feng Kuei-fen, Ch'en Ch'ih, and T'ang Chen. The monarch had been genuinely grieved by China's plight since 1894; and he was now stirred by the examples of Peter the Great and the Meiji Emperor as portrayed in the short books K'ang wrote specially for him. On June 15, an edict dismissed Weng T'ung-ho from office—an act which, even if it originated with Tz'u-hsi (who had her own reasons for disliking Weng) very likely also accorded with the Emperor's wishes, since he had found Weng's recent criticism of K'ang irksome. The very next day, he gave K'ang a long audience. The Emperor had probably, at that particular juncture, secured a tacit understanding from Tz'u-hsi that he could take some reform measures. But the Empress Dowager saw to it that she would remain in control. On the same day Weng was dismissed, Jung-lu, her most trusted Manchu, was made Governor-General of Chihli, in charge of the best imperial forces. Another edict of that day required that all newly appointed officials of the second rank or above must have an audience with the Empress Dowager. The Emperor still had to work through a Grand Council dominated by such conservatives as Kang-i. Nevertheless, he began to

[139] Hsiao, "Weng T'ung-ho," pp. 143, 150.

respond energetically to reform proposals that K'ang and his friends were encouraged to submit.

What did K'ang's group propose in 1898? Almost all the measures contemplated in Chinese reform writings since the 1870's were brought forth—reform of the examination system, new schools, encouragement of enterprise and invention, simplification of the six boards' regulations, abolition of sinecures, liberation of bound feet—to mention only a few. But the core of K'ang's program was political. He wanted to open channels of communication between subjects and sovereign, to add new machinery to the metropolitan as well as the local administration, and eventually to realize constitutional monarchy (*chün-min ho-chih*). In his 1897 memorial, written after the German occupation of Kiaochow (the one that the Emperor never saw), he had envisaged a parliament (*kuo-hui*), "to which all affairs of the state are to be turned over for deliberation and decision." In his memorial of January 29, 1898, which did reach the monarch, he urged that the latter take three immediate steps: make a dramatic declaration for reform; allow all officials and subjects to submit memorials; and establish a Bureau of Government Institutions (*Chih-tu chü*), which would draft a constitution. Realizing that it was impossible to abolish the existing organs of government, K'ang proposed the creation of twelve new ministries, some of which were to duplicate the functions of the six boards. Among the new ministries was one that would rewrite Chinese law, the new statutes to be adopted first at the treaty ports. K'ang proposed the establishment of a Bureau of People's Affairs (*Min-cheng chü*) in every circuit of the empire, and suggested that the officials of these bureaus take over certain functions currently in the hands of governors-general and governors. Branches of the bureaus were to be set up at the *chou* and *hsien*, where new officials, in consultation with the *shen-shih*, were to expand the existing functions of government by undertaking land surveys and the census, promoting health and education, and assisting agriculture, industry, and commerce—leaving the administration of justice and the collection of taxes "in the charge of the magistrates for the time being."[140] Although many of K'ang's ideas show the influence of Meiji Japan, they represented K'ang's own convictions that had been developing since the 1880's.[141]

Given Tz'u-hsi's position as the imperial foster mother, and the temper and bureaucratic self-interest of the men whom she had put in

[140] *WHPF*, 2:194, 199–202, 204–5.

[141] Cf. Howard, "Japan's Role in the Reform Program of K'ang Yu-wei," in Lo, *K'ang Yu-wei, 1858–1927*, pp. 279–312.

high places, it is plain that the Emperor could not undertake any major innovations against her will. It is remarkable that he did issue so many edicts providing for a great variety of reforms, including the abolition of the eight-legged essay and the calligraphy tests from the examinations (June 23 and 30). The two hundred or so edicts of the "hundred days" included many which dealt with educational and economic matters. An imperial university was established, and an elaborate system of provincial schools was envisaged; newspapers and translation services were planned; new industrial and agricultural techniques were encouraged; a central bureau for railways and mines was established and another for the promotion of agriculture, industry, and commerce. At least some of these edicts produced immediate effects. During the "hundred days," preparations were begun in the provinces to comply with the new rules on the examinations; new schools were founded; and bureaus of commerce (shang-wu chü) were established in Kiangsu.[142]

K'ang and his friends, upon whose suggestions the Emperor had acted, would perhaps have been wise to be satisfied with educational and economic reforms and not insist on measures of a more strictly political nature. In fact, soon after the eight-legged essay was abolished, K'ang's brother, Kuang-jen, had strongly urged him to forego the rest of his program and leave the capital. K'ang Yu-wei, however, was determined to push on with his plans. In late June and in July, he drafted memorials for four of his censor friends (including Yang Shen-hsiu and Sung Po-lu) and for Hsü Chih-ching of the Grand Secretariat, urging the creation of the proposed Bureau of Government Institutions. Liang Ch'i-ch'ao drafted a memorial for his relation Li Tuan-fen, Superintendent of Government Granaries, recommending a new advisory body for the throne and revision of the regulations of the six boards. Still other men, not linked to the K'ang group, also stressed political and administrative reforms. Chang Yüan-chi, a functionary of the Board of Punishment, memorialized recommending the abolition of the Censorate and the Hanlin Academy; and Tsen Ch'un-hsüan, a sub-director of the Imperial Stud, the reduction of sinecures and duplicate offices.[143] In mid-August, K'ang drafted for Kuo-p'u-t'ung-wu, a Manchu sub-chancellor of the Grand Secretariat, a memorial requesting the immediate promulgation of the constitution and the convening of a

[142] WHPF, 2:409–10, 435, 466–70; 4:149, 201; Liang, Wu-hsü cheng-pien chi, p. 53; Wolfgang Franke, The Reform and Abolition of the Traditional Chinese Examination System (Cambridge, Mass.: Harvard University Press, 1960), p. 46.

[143] WHPF, 2:206–8, 214–16; 4:152–53.

parliament. K'ang himself followed with a series of memorials recommending that, pending the convening of a parliament, a new body of
imperial advisers be created by asking each prefecture to nominate one
person, whether of official status or not, who was to take turns in groups
of twenty advising the Emperor at the Mou-ch'in Court (the imperial
library which had been used by previous Ch'ing emperors for meetings
with officials). K'ang suggested that the practice of earmarking certain
offices for Manchus or Chinese should be discontinued, and he dwelt on
the advantages of the "separation of the three powers" (san-ch'üan t'ing-
li)—the legislative, executive, and judicial.[144]

If only to assert himself against the power of Tz'u-hsi, the Emperor
favored measures that could help to break down the barriers surrounding him. He repeatedly asked the Tsungli Yamen and the Grand Council to implement K'ang's proposals concerning a Bureau of Government
Institutions, which would in turn consider changes in the governmental
structure. He received evasive replies.[145] The Emperor did not neglect
the many suggestions he received about correction of administrative
abuses. In late July, he ordered the six boards to revise and simplify
their regulations, and in subsequent edicts, he exhorted the governors-
general and governors to exercise proper supervision over local administration, and asked them to send to Peking for imperial audience chou
and hsien magistrates who were "enlightened about current affairs, in-
dustrious, and loving toward the people." In late August, he ordered
the abolition of certain sinecures and duplicate offices in Peking and in
the provinces (including governorships in Hupei, Kwangtung, and
Yunnan). In an action without precedent in the history of the dynasty,
he gave permission, on August 2, to all functionaries of the government to communicate with the throne, their memorials to be forwarded by their respective offices; and to all other subjects to do the
same, their memorials to be forwarded by the Censorate. Meanwhile,
the Emperor began to show resentment toward the high officials. He
issued periodic edicts berating the presidents of the boards and governors-general and governors (occasionally mentioning names, including
that of Jung-lu) for lack of promptness and diligence in discharging
their duties. On September 4, the monarch precipitately dismissed the
two presidents and four vice-presidents of the Board of Rites, on the

[144] WHPF, 2:236–42, 251–52; 4:153–56; Kuo-chia tang-an chü Ming-Ch'ing
tang-an kuan [Ming-Ch'ing Archives Institute of the National Archives], ed.,
Wu-hsü pien-fa tang-an shih-liao [Archival Materials on the Reform of 1898]
(Peking: Chung-hua, 1958), pp. 172–73.
[145] WHPF, 4:153–54.

ground that they had refused to forward a memorial from a minor official of the board and did so only when the latter threatened to submit it through the Censorate. The edict of August 2, reaffirmed several times, resulted, by early September, in dozens of memorials from low-ranking officials and from the people being received daily by the throne, but the monarch plainly lacked real power. He did choose pro-reform officials to be the new presidents and vice-presidents of the Board of Rites, but could only give them acting status, since otherwise the approval of the Empress Dowager would have been necessary. On September 5, he appointed T'an Ssu-t'ung (who had been summoned for service from Hunan) and three others of K'ang's sympathizers secretaries of the Grand Council, with the lowly fourth rank. These men were, however, designated as the throne's assistants in "matters concerning new policies."[146]

The Emperor himself now championed "people's rights." He asked for a meeting of the ministers at court to consider Kuo-p'u-t'ung-wu's proposal that plans for a parliament should be formulated at once. When Sun Chia-nai pointed out that the parliament would deprive the monarch of his power and give it to the people, the Emperor replied: "I want only to save China. If I can save the people, what does it matter that I have no power?"[147] T'an Ssu-t'ung was eager to pursue the parliamentary plan, but the group that held daily meetings at K'ang's residence decided that the first step should be the creation of a new advisory body for the throne—that is, the Mou-ch'in Court idea. A remarkable edict issued on September 12 (known to have been drafted by T'an) praised Western "political learning" (cheng-chih chih hsüeh) which aimed at the enlightenment and enrichment of the people and at their getting "the advantages to which they are entitled in life." It declared that China could learn from the West on the matter of "instituting a government for the people" (wei-min li-cheng).[148] T'an also drafted an edict embodying the Emperor's decision to "open the Mou-ch'in Court," citing the precedents of previous Ch'ing monarchs meeting with officials there. On September 14, the Emperor took the draft with him to see Tz'u-hsi in her summer palace, on the outskirts of the capital.[149]

What followed is well known. Despite the Kuang-hsü Emperor's

[146] WHPF, 2:45, 48, 52, 59–61, 63, 65–66, 68–73, 75–76, 78, 81–82.

[147] The Emperor's exchange with Sun is cited in K'ang's memorial submitted sometime after August 19; see WHPF, 2:237; cf. note 144 above.

[148] WHPF, 2:84–85.

[149] WHPF, 4:51, 159; Shih-erh ch'ao tung-hua lu, Kuang-hsü 24, p. 4176.

exalted position as the Son of Heaven, Confucian ideology, with its emphasis on filial piety, approved the ascendancy of the Empress Dowager over her adopted son. K'ang's ideas on the classics and on politics had, of course, appalled many. Even officials who favored the adoption of "Western learning," like Chang Chih-tung, drew the line when it came to the question of democracy. "If the idea of the people's rights arises," he declared in his *Ch'üan-hsüeh pien* ("An Exhortation to Learning"), written in April, 1898, in reaction against the reform newspapers published in Hunan, "the ignorant people will be pleased, the rebellious people will rise, and there will be great disorder everywhere."[150] Even some of the most upright officials who, in the past, had been unhappy about the Empress Dowager's power, felt that as between the Empress and the misguided Emperor, the former was to be preferred, since he was corrupted by heretical doctrines and she was, after all, his (foster) mother.[151] Even more important than the ideological considerations was the fact that a preponderant number of the metropolitan officials—and provincial ones, too—had identified their own interests with Tz'u-hsi. While the abolition of the eight-legged essay created resentment among those who had long been trained in this medium (particularly those who were soon to take the examination themselves), the proposed reform in the structure of the government threatened many interests. During July, word spread in Peking that the

[150] *Ch'üan-hsüeh   pien,*   in   Chang,   *Chang   Wen-hsiang   kung   ch'üan-chi,* 201.24. Chang's telegram to Governor Ch'en of Hunan dated May 11, 1898, attacked the reform paper *Hsiang-pao* [Hunan News] and said that he had written a book called *Ch'üan-hsüeh pien. (Ibid.,* 155.20.) The work, which was in favor of educational and economic reforms, was presented to the throne by a sub-expositor of the Hanlin Academy on July 25. On the same day, the Emperor ordered that the forty extra copies submitted be sent to governors-general, governors, and provincial educational directors, to be republished in the provinces. It was not until August 22 that he asked the Tsungli Yamen to have the book printed in an edition of 300 copies, presumably for officials in Peking *(WHPF,* 2:43, 59).

[151] Ch'en Ch'iu, "Wu-hsü cheng-pien-shih fan pien-fa jen-wu chih cheng-chih ssu-hsiang," [Political Thought of the Opponents of Reform During the Coup d'État of 1898] *Yen-ching hsüeh-pao,* 25 (1939): 79–80. Ku Hung-ming, an ideological conservative, wrote that "by the first fundamental law of state in China, resting upon the principle of absolute obedience of children to parents, the supreme authority in the Chinese body politic of Her Imperial Majesty the Empress Dowager as the mother of the nation or country, admits of absolutely no question or doubt." Ku, *Papers from a Viceroy's Yamen* (Shanghai: Shanghai Mercury, 1901), p. 3, quoted in Hsiao, "Weng T'ung-ho," p. 218.

Emperor meant to reorganize the entire administration through a Bureau of Government Institutions which would probably "abolish all the six boards and the nine courts." To such powerful Manchu officials as Governor-General Jung-lu and Grand Councillor Kang-i, who owed their prominence to the Empress, it was apparent that the Emperor's plans could only mean their own downfall. The summary dismissal of the presidents and vice-presidents of the Board of Rites on September 4 created a crisis for power-holders, big and small. The cashiered officials, as well as Manchu sycophants of the Imperial Household department and eunuchs who had helped Tz'u-hsi to tyrannize over the young Emperor in the past, gathered at the summer palace and begged her to arrest the new trend.[152] There were, moreover, Chinese officials who saw their interests as bound up with hers. Grand Secretary Hsü T'ung, head of the so-called "northern faction" among the high Chinese officials at court, and former President of the Board of Rites and of the Board of Civil Appointments, had been particularly disliked by the Emperor, who had granted him only one audience from 1889 on. The Chinese censors whom Hsü patronized, no doubt following his wishes, had made particularly venomous accusations against K'ang and Liang before and during the "hundred days." Yang Ts'ung-i, a partisan of Hsü, a relative of Li Hung-chang, and also a protégé of Jung-lu, was among the first to memorialize the Empress Dowager, begging her to assume the regency again.[153]

While the imperial mother's dominant role was acceptable to Confucian ethics, what doomed the Kuang-hsü innovations was, of course, the monarch's lack of military and even eunuch backing, despite his being Son of Heaven. When, on September 14, the Empress made known to him, while he was kneeling before her, that his own position would be in jeopardy if he pursued the reforms further, the young monarch's resentment was mixed with fear. He made one more desperate attempt to assert himself. Since late July or early August, disturbed by rumors of an impending coup d'état in favor of Tz'u-hsi as regent, K'ang and his friends had tried to enlist the support of Yüan Shih-k'ai, the vigorous Chinese commander who had been training the dynasty's crack troops near Tientsin under Jung-lu's general supervision. On September 14, in an eleventh-hour attempt to save his cause, the Emperor, on the advice of K'ang and T'an, summoned Yüan

---

[152] Liang, *Wu-hsü cheng-pien chi*, pp. 109, 123–24; *WHPF*, 4:160; Ch'en Ch'iu, "Wu-hsü cheng-pien-shih," pp. 75–77.

[153] Ch'en Ch'iu, "Wu-hsü cheng-pien–shih," pp. 69, 71–74.

for audiences, which took place three times between September 16 and 20.[154] Whether Yüan, who was apprised by T'an of all the reformer's plans, reported to Jung-lu what he was told will perhaps never be known. In any case, upon Yüan's return to Tientsin on the 20th, Jung-lu hurried to Peking to see the Empress Dowager, and on the next day, Tz'u-hsi returned to the palace in Peking, made the Emperor a prisoner, and began to arrest the reformers. K'ang and Liang luckily escaped, with British and Japanese help, but T'an Ssu-t'ung and five others died martyrs. In the few weeks that followed, most of the reform edicts of the "hundred days" were rescinded, at the wish of Tz'u-hsi as regent. Men like Kang-i and Hsü Tung and Manchu princes of even greater ignorance gained power. The way was prepared for the impassioned and self-righteous imperial sponsorship in 1900 of the Boxers, the pro-Manchu secret society, who sought to exterminate foreigners and all things Western.

The failure of Kuang-hsü's efforts reflects the great gap between the ideals of the reformers and the realities of Ch'ing politics. Given the autocratic power of the Empress Dowager, backed as it was by Confucian notions of filial piety and loyalty no less than by naked force, there was plainly no chance at that particular juncture that any significant political change could be achieved. Nevertheless, the reform movement initiated by such men as K'ang and T'an was of great consequence. The growing sentiment among the literati and the *shen-shih* for educational and other reforms eventually pushed the Empress Dowager's court toward innovation, after the Boxer fiasco had revealed the stupidity of her erstwhile advisers. Meanwhile, the political awakening of the literati gave impetus to the revolutionary movement. Not a few admirers of K'ang and Liang, including students and teachers of the School of Current Affairs at Changsha, now sympathized with Sun Yat-sen's Hsing Chung Hui in Japan.[155] K'ang and Liang organized a Society for the Protection of the Emperor (*Pao-huang hui*) and remained constitutional monarchists. But Liang, in the magazines he began to publish in Japan in late 1898, bitterly attacked the Ch'ing court, besides arguing eloquently for Western political institutions and ideas. The popularity of his writings, circulated widely in China, helped the revolutionary cause.[156] T'an Ssu-t'ung's *Jen-hsüeh*, published

[154] *WHPF*, 4:51–52, 159–60; Ting Wen-chiang, *Liang Jen-kung*, 1:69–72.

[155] See Feng Tzu-yu's list in Ch'ai Te-keng *et al.*, eds., *Hsin-hai ko-ming* [The Revolution of 1911], 8 vols. (Shanghai: Jen-min, 1957), 1:150–72. Note especially Ou Chü-chia, Pi Yung-nien, Ch'in Li-shan, and Chou Hung-yeh.

[156] Chang, *Liang Ch'i-ch'ao yü Ch'ing-chi ko-ming*, pp. 81–118, 273–85.

in Japan in 1899, likewise stimulated anti-Manchu sentiment. In August, 1900, T'an's devoted friend, T'ang Ts'ai-ch'ang, in cooperation with the Elder Brother Society in Hupei, staged a shortlived revolt "in the service of the emperor," a few weeks before the Triads and other groups financed by the Hsing Chung Hui fought the government troops at Hui-chou in Kwangtung. Within two or three years, revolutionary societies founded by the young scions of *shen-shih* sprang up in Kiangsu, Hunan, and Chekiang, and with the Chinese students flocking to Japan for study, a better-organized movement soon was started there. Many of the young literati revolutionaries now attacked K'ang and Liang for their belief that constitutionalism could still be achieved under the Ch'ing, once the Empress Dowager was removed from the scene. But in historical perspective, the anti-Manchu republican revolution must be regarded as an extension of the efforts made by the reformers in the 1890's. Both movements sought to open up more effective communication between the government and the governed. Both sought political transformation as a prerequisite for national self-assertion as well as for the liberalization of society.

The Nineteenth-Century Legacy and China Today

This paper is primarily historical. I have set myself the task of answering two broad questions: (1) In what manner did the traditional social and political order deteriorate during the nineteenth century? and (2) What were the most important results of the West's impact upon China during this transitional period? Before these questions can be answered, one must ascertain the facts. From a fresh reading of the sources, I have tried to clarify the issues relating to the following crucial historical problems: the class character of the Taiping rebellion; the extent to which the traditional order was restored after the hopeful T'ung-chih era; the nature of the late Ch'ing "regionalism"; the significance of the "statecraft school" among Ch'ing scholars; the ideological innovations of the self-strengthening movement; the influence of missionary publications and of Chinese reform writings beginning in the 1870's; the nature and scope of the movement for political reform in the 1890's.

While these inquiries are chiefly historical, reflection on the current Chinese scene has persuaded me that the peculiar legacy of the nineteenth century, no less than the more basic heritage of China's long past, is of great relevance to our understanding of the China of the 1960's. Some seventy years of accelerating and drastic change have intervened, of course, between the coup d'état of 1898 and the Great Proletarian Cultural Revolution. But certain broad social and administrative situations have persisted. Moreover, certain new tendencies and movements that began in the nineteenth century have played a part in shaping the Chinese Communist society, while others have survived as latent forces that might affect its future. In conclusion, I should perhaps recapitulate some of the facts brought out above and try to relate them to the China of today.

China's problems have been basically internal. Although many developments of the late Ch'ing fall within the pattern of the declining periods of the previous dynasties, the social strains from the late eighteenth century on had been more severe than in previous times. The abuses of local government during the late Ch'ing must have been at least as bad as in any comparable period in the past, considering the Manchu recklessness in selling local offices and the unrestrained practices of the yamen clerks and runners. While the humane aspects of the *shen-shih*-dominated society continued to evidence themselves, there is reason to believe that in an environment of increasing cynicism, the behavior of the local elite reached a new low during the nineteenth century. There were, moreover, other and extraordinary pressures on the society. The unfavorable effects of the unprecedented population growth cannot be overstated. Moreover, the remarkable commercial expansion during the dynasty, ironically, added to the stress of the times. Literacy grew with commercial wealth, and with it the level of expectations. On the other hand, the economy did not develop nearly fast enough to produce commensurate opportunities. The growth of mercantile employment could not satisfy all the aspiring men, while bureaucratic openings remained extremely limited as always.

Social tension plainly existed on two levels in nineteenth-century China. Among the peasants, tenantry and pauperism on the whole tended to increase, leading to frequent riots and brigandage. Inspired and led by the secret societies, which absorbed restless literate or semiliterate elements, the uprooted peasantry could provide the force that made for large-scale rebellion—as indeed they did during the nineteenth century. Although among the rebels of that century, the Taipings were the only ones to have conceived a drastic program of institutional change, social grievances and resentments were widespread and long-continued after the rebellions were suppressed. We must note, however, that throughout the century there was also great tension among the literati elite themselves and even among the high degreeholders that constituted the ruling class. There was increasingly hectic competition for the limited number of official posts, and abuses were rampant among those who did get these positions, particularly when they won them by purchase or bribery. While the immediate result was the greater demoralization of the literati, the situation also created potential for revolution, once there was enough ideological and institutional change to provide the stimulus. This was, of course, exactly what happened in the last decade of the Ch'ing.

Since coming to power, the Chinese Communists have achieved a thoroughgoing reorganization of the local government in China. Administrative mechanisms have been extended fully to the village level, and as long as the party cadres are disciplined and their morale high, the masses that have been organized for production, although hard-driven, might perhaps be assumed to be equitably treated. Yet although the old landed elite has been ruthlessly destroyed and even the "rich peasants" have been repressed, discontent among the socialized peasantry must still exist. The continued growth of population has put pressure on the "private plots" that farmers have been allowed to have. Moreover, the potentiality of unrest has been increased by the unprecedented expansion of literacy, which has outstripped the enormous expansion of the opportunity structure since 1949. The number of youths who graduate from the middle schools each year, for example, is many times the number of new openings at the urban industrial establishments or in the party or state bureaucracy. The rate of economic growth plainly has lagged behind the multiplication of aspiring men. This situation lends logic to the fervent call of the Maoists for continuous leveling of the society and for self-denying service by all. The question for the future is whether Mao's demand for self-sacrifice is to be accompanied by economic and other policies that might cancel out the long-term results of the self-denying labor performed by so many. We may further observe that serious strains undoubtedly exist among the ruling elite of seventeen million party members. At any level, there are bound to be men who hold more favored positions and those in less attractive ones—the "ins" and the "outs." Plainly, it is upon those who are the "outs" that Mao pins his hopes for his "revolutionary rebel groups." But the chances of unrest may be expected to increase as long as the ideological and political rift continues.

A second theme I have stressed regarding nineteenth-century China is administrative disintegration—disintegration in the sense that the elaborate system of control so carefully built up earlier in the dynasty was no longer fully maintained, even though the dynasty had not yet collapsed. To the society as a whole, the most serious consequence of the administrative disintegration was the worsening quality of the *chou* and *hsien* government. But from the standpoint of the power structure, the most significant development was the growth of provincial vested interests—chiefly a new type of imperial army raised and stationed in the provinces and a new group of administrators and agents who collected the likin. It has been stressed in this paper that through the nineteenth century, Peking did possess means for the control of such armies and over the likin revenue. The actual coordination of the *yung* forces and of the bureaus collecting the likin was in the hands of the provincial governors-general and governors, who were invariably loyal to the throne. But we must also note that the governors-general and governors could seldom tamper with the internal organization of the *yung* forces, once their commanders were chosen. Neither could the governors-general and governors easily overhaul the permanent staffs of the likin bureaus and they had to be satisfied with such proceeds of the likin as their experienced and well-connected collectors turned over to them. We may therefore distinguish two facets of the late Ch'ing "regionalism": On the one hand, the governors-general and governors, while loyal to the dynasty, enjoyed more administrative leeway than before. On the other hand, deep-seated vested interests were formed, which the governors-general and governors could only imperfectly control. When the revolution broke out in 1911, elements in the provincial military and financial establishments forsook not only the dynasty, but also the governors-general and governors.

While the government of the People's Republic is organized very differently from that of imperial China, the centralized mechanisms developed by Peking since 1949 are perhaps reminiscent of the elaborate system of checks and controls devised by such emperors as K'ang-hsi and Yung-cheng in the heyday of the Ch'ing. Yet for some years before the current crisis, Peking's policy had been—or had this been a matter of necessity?—to allow considerable leeway to the regional and provincial committees of the party. That the provincial leaders have enjoyed great personal power is indicated by the fact that not a few of them have held the same offices since the early 1950's.[157] Recent events have demonstrated that the loyalty of some of these men to Chairman Mao is not as firm as that of the late Ch'ing governors-general and governors to the Empress Dowager! Although full-fledged warlordism is not likely to

[157] See Frederick C. Teiwes, *Provincial Party Personnel in Mainland China, 1956–1966* (New York: East Asian Institute, Columbia University, 1967).

arise, whatever regional or provincial leaders survive or emerge from the current intra-party strife will probably continue to enjoy great authority in their areas. We may expect the basic ideological allegiance to survive, and the various parts of the nation will continue to be interdependent. With the regional and provincial leaders—political or military—coordinating the activities of the lower echelons, centralization may still be maintained to a large degree. But it will be interesting to see whether there is a layer of entrenched committees or agencies below the level of the provincial committees, staffed by men who, through long experience or local connections, have become difficult to replace.

While such problems as social tension and regional vested interests were created chiefly by forces within the Chinese society itself, China's development since the mid-nineteenth century has plainly been affected by contacts with the West. It is a thesis of this paper that despite the strong inertia among the Chinese officials and literati, the impact of the West produced new sentiments and ideas that were of great long-term significance. There was, first of all, the rise of nationalistic feelings. Resentment of Western intrusion arose quite early among the *shen-shih*—witness the organization of anti-British militia near Canton in the 1840's and the anti-Christian agitation that began in the 1850's. Blind xenophobia was to persist through the century, but in the 1860's, with the emergence of the self-strengthening movement, national consciousness—as opposed to a mere conviction of cultural superiority—may be said to have come into being. Although the self-strengthening movement represented the efforts of comparatively few officials and their advisers, it marked a clear ideological break with the past. Such men as Li Hung-chang and Chang Chih-tung, despite their continued loyalty to the Ch'ing dynasty and the narrowness of their social and political vision, were genuinely aware of the Western and Japanese threat to China's territory and people. Moreover, they recognized the shortcomings of China's own culture—primarily in technology, but also in several other matters—and they sought a positive program for the defense of the country and for economic competition with foreigners. Nationalistic thought continued to gain strength from the 1870's on, and after the Sino-Japanese War of 1894–95, with the appearance of reform periodicals, "study associations," and new schools, it may be said that nationalism (which implies the sharing of nationalistic sentiment by a large sector of the community) had come into existence among China's upper classes.

There were, however, several kinds of intellectual outlook that accompanied the early Chinese nationalistic sentiment. Advocates of self-strengthening inherited certain beliefs of the "statecraft school"—that the state need not avoid pursuing utilitarian aims and that government business should be managed not only with due attention to technical details, but in a pragmatic manner without reference to ancient precedents. In their eagerness for China to acquire "wealth and strength," certain of those who championed self-strengthening had begun, perhaps unconsciously, to put less emphasis on the Confucian ideology itself. Despite his often-quoted statement that Confucian teachings should serve as the "foundation . . . to be supplemented by the methods of various nations for the attainment of wealth and strength,"[158] Feng Kuei-fen devoted most of his essays of 1861 to proposals for innovation and not to cultural and moral exhortation. In fact, he praised Western government as well as technology and felt that the Chinese had cause to feel "ashamed" on both counts. Like Feng, Li Hung-chang never questioned the orthodox ideology. But he was extremely critical of China's literary culture. He simply gave Confucianism little thought and concentrated rather on the military and economic undertakings to which he attached great value, as well as the bureaucratic and political problems (including the conduct of foreign relations) that had become routine to him. With Chang Chih-tung, however, matters of ideology were accorded primary emphasis. Chang was eager for China to acquire science and technology and he even favored the imitation of Western administrative techniques and commercial institutions.[159] But on the other hand, he would still give priority to moral training and classical studies, and unlike Feng, he never criticized the defects of the autocratic imperial system.

While no less patriotic than Chang, reformers like K'ang Yu-wei found serious fault with the orthodox moral and political doctrines. By the early twentieth century, the practical patriotism of Li Hung-chang had been adopted by many an official, while the iconoclasm of K'ang had grown into a profound movement of cultural criticism.

Today, nationalism has become a part of Chinese Communism. "Wealth and strength" are being achieved for the state. The country has been industrialized, and exactly a century after the founding of the Kiangnan Arsenal in 1865, China had developed its first nuclear device.

[158] Feng, *Chiao-pin-lu k'ang-i*, 2.39.

[159] Chang Chih-tung, *Chang Wen-hsiang kung ch'üan-chi*, 203.2–3, 12, 19–22, 30–34.

Nationalism as well as the aspiration for greater "wealth and strength" seem certain to persist, but we may perhaps assume that there is more than one kind of intellectual outlook among the Chinese Communists. Fervidly patriotic and interested as he is in scientific and technological advancement, Mao Tse-tung nonetheless believes that history is best served by the particular moral and political doctrines that he wishes to perpetuate. As Schwartz has emphasized, to Mao, "the only desirable modernization is a modernization which can be incorporated into the Maoist vision."[160] This is perhaps not unlike Chang Chih-tung, who believed in a modernization that could be incorporated into the Confucian vision. The question arises whether there are not within the Peking leadership today, men more like Li Hung-chang, who despite his thorough Confucian upbringing would not bother with ideology too much; and, moreover, whether there are not potential reformers who would want to modify the ideology itself, once it stood in the way of patriotic aims. It is safe to say that many in China do not agree that the present Maoist policies are necessarily in the country's best interest. Just as nationalism contributed to the decline of Confucianism when the two became incompatible, will nationalism also help to modify Maoism when they conflict?

Nationalism was, however, not the only result of the West's impact on the Chinese literati. In this paper, I have emphasized the rise of democratic values (as distinguished from nationalistic values) in the last decades of the nineteenth century. Contacts with the West served to accentuate certain latent ideas and, furthermore, point up new institutional possibilities. It is not entirely true, as many writers have implied, that when Confucianism proved inadequate or sterile, a vacuum was thereby created in the intellectual life of the literati. As the formerly entrenched orthodoxy began to weaken, many Chinese did form new and real commitments. There was first of all an assertion of the importance of the individual—an attitude not necessarily in conflict with the growing nationalism. The outlook of the Chinese merchants at the treaty ports may well have been infectious. Moreover, there was an awakening among the literati to the fact that comparatively independent careers were possible outside of the bureaucracy. The famous decision made by Chang Chien in 1895 favoring private entrepreneurship over government service is only one example. Many Chinese came

[160] Benjamin Schwartz, "Modernization and the Maoist Vision—Some Reflections on Chinese Communist Goals," *China Quarterly*, no. 21 (1965), p. 14.

to feel that they could pursue their careers with self-respect and security even within the bureaucracy, if they worked in a technical or expert capacity. Such attitudes marked the beginning of the bourgeois and professional spirit, so different from the ethos of a mere bureaucrat or a parasitic merchant. It must be stressed that the sense of moral obligation, so long nurtured by Confucianism, continued strong among the young literati. Moreover, the reform and revolutionary movements were to stimulate a new spirit of self-sacrifice, which was already evident in the writings of T'an Ssu-t'ung and was to become so pronounced in the pages of the revolutionary journal, *Min-pao*.[161] But the bourgeois and professional ethos continued to develop in the first half of the twentieth century, even as many Chinese youths became affected by new revolutionary ideas that called for self-denial. It is apparently the persistence and revival of individualistic aspirations that Mao now seeks to combat.

The emphasis on the individual, however, did not preclude the rise of new social concerns. In the early writings of K'ang Yu-wei and in T'an Ssu-t'ung's *Jen-hsüeh*, we see the broadening of the Confucian virtue of *jen* to include the concept of equality—a concept which, to K'ang and T'an at least, implied the recognition that all persons are entitled to self-realization and autonomy. From these premises stemmed the new social ideas broadcast in the reform journals of the 1890's—the attack on parental and male tyranny and on the stultifying methods by which the classics were taught to the young; the advocacy of a school system that would spread to every village and educate women as well as men; the championing of humanitarian reforms as well as "people's rights." Such themes of social liberation were, of course, to be expanded in the early decades of this century, even though new authoritarian and collective doctrines developed at the same time.

Today, under a totalitarian system, at least some Western social ideals have been incorporated into Chinese society. The opportunities for education have been increased more than ever before, the energies of women liberated more than ever before. The land reform, which involved the loss of many hundreds of thousands of lives, destroyed the pre-1949 elite, and since then the "rich peasants" have also been repressed. Economic equality was thus achieved to a large degree in the countryside. To be sure, the priority given to defense and to industrial development has prevented the continuous improvement of living conditions. But the subsistence and the minimum welfare of China's more

---

[161] T'an, *T'an Ssu-t'ung ch'üan-chi*, pp. 60–61, 87–89; *Min-pao* (Tokyo, 1905–10), *passim*.

than six hundred million have been maintained, which is no mean achievement. It is apparent that the Chinese Communists would particularly encourage only a narrow and harsh type of personality to rise through their ladder of success—although the Liu Shao-ch'i faction would presumably give more recognition than the Maoists to men who are "more expert than red." The intrinsic worth of the person is, in any case, not respected. As is well known, the pervasive measures of surveillance and the cruel techniques of "thought reform" amount to a total rejection of any free play of the individual's intellect or personality. And yet it cannot be said that in the society as a whole, the desire for self-realization or autonomy has been entirely eliminated, partly because this desire is rooted in human nature, and partly because it is too early to say that the pre-Communist Western influences have been wiped out.

Finally, I wish to stress a particularly neglected subject in the history of nineteenth-century China—the desire for greater communication between the literati and the throne and for the amelioration of autocracy. In the early nineteenth century, quite independent of Western influences, Pao Shih-ch'en and Kung Tzu-chen were already criticizing the abuses of despotism and suggesting that the throne should share its decision-making power with the ministers and the scholars of the imperial academy. Feng Kuei-fen regarded the isolation of the monarch from his subjects as the principal defect of the government of his day, and beginning in the 1870's, Chinese reform writers in the treaty ports and elsewhere advocated not only the publication of newspapers which would give vent to public opinion, but also the establishment of a parliament which could give effective advice to the monarch. Constitutionalism was in fact at the core of the program advocated by K'ang Yu-wei and his followers, backed as it was by their concept of the people's right to "autonomy." The Kuang-hsü emperor, who took the unprecedented step of permitting all officials and subjects of the Ch'ing empire to memorialize the throne, actually planned toward the end of the "hundred days" for a new imperial council that would prepare for the convening of a national parliament.

The ideal of a parliamentary democracy was, of course, to be discredited as being impractical. The Empress Dowager's suppression of Kuang-hsü's plans in 1898 was followed by the many misfortunes that befell the constitutional experiment in the early Republican era. Yet even though representative institutions proved to be of little immediate relevance, surely the desire for the amelioration of autocracy did not disappear. Through the warlord period and the Nanking and Chung-king eras, the demand for greater communication between the governed and the government continued in many forms—the demonstrations staged by students, teachers, and the citizenry; magazines of liberal opinion; actual organization of political groups. In the quarter-century before 1949, the Chinese Communist movement profited by the many voices that were critical of the foreign and domestic policies of what-ever regime was in power.

Like the authoritarian government of China's past, the Communist state that was established in 1949 does not allow for dissent. The quasi-legislative functions of the several levels of government congresses do not include the making of policy. Policy is made by a few at the top, and the differences in views at the top are currently being resolved by a desperate political struggle. It must be pointed out that there is great-er general awareness of public affairs in Communist China than in the past. Popular "participation" in the implementation of policies has indeed been made compulsory. Through the endless "struggle" and "criticism" meetings connected with the mass organizations, resident committees, and production units, the directives of the state or party are seriously discussed by many. Yet such discussions, which involve face-to-face meetings between the cadres and the people, must be re-garded chiefly as a device to manipulate the individual and to insure conformity.[162] For those who are dissatisfied with the policy directives themselves, neither the meetings and congresses nor the press provide an outlet for their views. Even among the elite of party members and party officials, effective communication with the policy-maker at the top appears to have been very meager. Until the recent split in the leadership, the airing of dissenting opinion had been rare indeed. Even a high official such as Wu Han had to disguise his criticism of Mao's policies in a historical play, which he published at his peril.[163] It is not unlikely that many in China today have become dissatisfied with the Communist system of "democratic centralism" and that the desire for the liberalization of the autocracy is as strong in the present as in the days of K'ang Yu-wei and T'an Ssu-t'ung. One can only hope that out of the current internal crisis, a political system will eventually emerge that will allow for orderly expression of public opinion, as well as a more all-around recognition of humanitarian values.

[162] See James R. Townsend, *Political Participation in Communist China* (Berkeley: University of California Press, 1967), especially chap. 7.

[163] See Stephen Uhalley, Jr., "The Cultural Revolution and the Attack on the 'Three Family Village,' " *China Quarterly*, no. 27 (1966), pp. 149–61.

Comments by Albert Feuerwerker

A major theme of Professor Liu's paper is that the nineteenth century saw a "breakdown . . . in the crucial sector of government administration." This he tends to interpret largely as "misgovernment." I find no fault with either his formulations or the evidence he adduces, except to suggest that the pattern of decline which he describes might also profitably be treated in a broader context of the general question of political integration in late-imperial China. The comments which follow bite tentatively at that tempting problem.

The "disequilibrium" introduced by foreign encroachment in the nineteenth century was not confined to the Chinese economy. It may be that the effects of imperialism on the remarkable political integration that had made imperial China the longest-lived political system in human history were even more potent. This supposition calls for some elaboration on the nature of that integration, and on the kinds of political change that were possible within its parameters.

My point of departure is the multiform character of Confucianism. At one and the same time, Confucianism was a component of the religious (normative) and philosophical (cognitive) symbols which provided the ultimate ground of legitimacy for Chinese social values and the general cognitive framework within which these values "made sense"; Confucianism expressed itself directly in the social values that governed the institutionalization of the social patterns characteristic of Chinese society; and, finally, Confucianism contributed to the ideology which mediated between these values and the empirically observable institutions which they shaped. Thus we may consider Confucianism simultaneously under the guise of a religion, of social values, and of a political ideology.

In the broadest sense, the role of religion is one of supplying the source and definition of the ultimate values which provide the individual personality the means for managing his "existential" tensions, and which give a meaningful coherence to the central social values

179

which define the structure of society. Religious ideas refer to intrin-
sically untestable first princples, as do the metaphysical postulates of
any philosophical system. For our purposes and as regards their function in legitimizing social values, we do not need to distinguish the
two sharply, especially in regard to China, where the moral or normative aspect of religion and the cognitive orientation of philosophical
speculation tended to be merged.

The first principles of Confucianism as religion and philosophy center on the postulation of the universe as a self-created, infinite, and
"harmoniously functioning organism consisting of an orderly hierarchy
of interrelated parts and forces, which, though unequal in their status,
are all equally essential for the total process."[1] By the time of the Neo-
Confucian synthesis, these parts and forces have been ordered in an
elaborate metaphysics focusing on the permutations and combinations
of *li*, "principle," and *ch'i*, "physical substance." The universe is a functioning organism, a process; inherently it is characterized by change.
But this mutation is not random, nor is it linear or evolutionary. It is
either of the nature of polar oscillations (the alternation of *yin* and
yang) or it follows a cyclical pattern in a closed circuit (the five elements, colors, etc.).

Moreover, the universe is good. ". . . Even what we humans regard
as evil—for example, death—is, from a higher point of view, an integral
part of the total cosmic process and therefore inseparable from what
we choose to call goodness. In short, whatever is in the universe must
be good, simply because it *is*."[2] Man's nature is the essential link between the human and non-human worlds, and this nature is equally
good for all, human evil arising either from a failure to realize the
potentialities of that nature or from an inadequate understanding of
how the universe operates.

These first principles are, so to speak, the templates that determine
the parameters of the social values which in turn define the structure
of Chinese society by controlling the formation of its basic institutional
patterns. "Social values" as used here refers to such phenomena as the
preponderance of "loyalty," of performance in relationships of inferior
to superior in the central value system of Tokugawa Japan; or of the
omnipresent "success ethic," of achievement for its own sake, in present-
day America. The comparable social values in the case of traditional

[1] Derk Bodde, "Harmony and Conflict in Chinese Philosophy," in Arthur F.
Wright (ed.) *Studies in Chinese Thought* (Chicago: University of Chicago
Press, 1953), p. 68.

[2] *Ibid.*

China, which derive their legitimacy ultimately from the above-mentioned religious and philosophical ideas, are summed up but of course not adequately presented by such phrases as the primacy of order, of cooperative human harmony, of social integration. In short, human society should be a reflection of the ordered harmony of the universe. The emphasis is not on achievement or on fulfilling the obligations defined by one's position in a hierarchy of relationships. Though these aspects are present as well—in particular the political value of loyalty—they are nevertheless secondary to order, harmony, and the reconciliation of opposites.

The overriding importance of kinship, of the family, and its deep interpenetration with the political, occupational and other institutional sub-systems in traditional Chinese society may be taken as one evidence of the primacy of human or social harmony.

It is not sufficient to prove this by quoting the *Analects* or *Mencius*, though these works would support the position I am taking, since pre-Han Confucian writings cannot provide a full picture of what Confucianism became as a result of later accretions of metaphysical, Legalist, and Buddhist ideas. For Ch'ing China, I suggest that the famous "Sixteen Maxims" of the K'ang-hsi Emperor may be a useful source for determining the dominant social values. We may recall that in the first of these injunctions the Emperor exhorted the people to "Pay just regard to filial and fraternal duties, in order to give due importance to the relations of life." An eighteenth-century official paraphrased this instruction as follows:

> Well, what then is filial piety? It is great indeed! In heaven above, in earth below, and among men placed between, there is not one that excludes this doctrine. Well how is this proved? Because filial piety is the breath of harmony. Observe the heavens and the earth! If they do not harmonize, how could they produce and nourish so great multitudes of creatures? If man does not practice filial piety, he loses [his resemblance to] the harmony of nature—how then can he be accounted man?[3]

[3] William Milne (trans.), *The Sacred Edict, containing Sixteen Maxims of the Emperor Kang-He, amplified by his son, the Emperor Yoong-Ching; together with a paraphrase on the whole, by a Mandarin* (London: Printed for Black, Kingsbury, Parbury, and Allen, 1817), pp. 35–36. The "Sacred Edict" is, of course, the 10,000 word *Sheng-yü Kuang Hsün* issued by the Yung-cheng emperor in 1724 as a commentary on the sixteen maxims or injunctions proclaimed by his father in 1670. These in turn were an elaboration of the six maxims of the first Ming emperor (see *Ta-Ch'ing hui-tien shih-li* [Collected Statutes and Precedents of the Ch'ing Dynasty], Kuang-hsü ed., *chüan* 397).

The commentator then proceeded to show how filial piety was inextricably related to every other facet of life:

> If in your conduct, you be not correct and regular, this is throwing contempt upon your own bodies, which were handed down to you from your parents: this is not filial piety. When doing business for the government, if you do not exhaust your ideas, and exert your strength; or if in serving the prince, you be unfaithful, this is just the same as treating your parents ill:—this is not filial piety. In the situation of an officer of government, if you do not act well, but provoke the people to scoff and rail; this is lightly to esteem the substance handed down to you from your parents:—this is not filial piety. When associating with friends, if, in speech or behavior you be insincere: this casts disgrace on your parents:—this is not filial piety. If you, soldiers, when the army goes out to battle, will not valiantly and sternly strive to advance; but give persons occasion to laugh at your cowardice; this is to degrade the progeny of your parents;—this also is not filial piety.[4]

While social values control the formation of basic institutional patterns, it need hardly be stressed that the world of human collectivities and the personalities who in their several roles constitute them are not merely the passive reflection of these values. The postulation of such and such values is in any case an abstraction by the observer from endless streams of action; in the nature of the case, few or none of the actors themselves could, if called upon to do so, reproduce the same abstractions. Religious and philosophical ideas and symbols may be explicitly stated; social values in most cases must be inferred from these, and also from explicit statements of ideology made by the actors. Ideology (and science as source of empirically relevant theories, which I ignore here) differs from religious ideas in that it necessarily involves an element of contingency. Its referrent is not to the basic principles of existence or of conduct, but to empirically observable states in the natural world, and its validity depends above all upon its success in operating in that world. The role of ideology (I am concerned here primarily with political ideology) is that of mediation between social values and the institutions of society. It is concerned with adjusting these two to one another. This it does in two ways: first, by a process of exegesis, of interpreting the meaning of social values; and second, by means of exhortation, by invoking a normative commitment to work toward shaping the actual world in terms of these values.

4 *Ibid.*, p. 39.

The main body of Confucian political writing, I believe, can best be considered under the heading of ideology, all the way from Mencius' dialogues with King Hui of Liang to K'ang Yu-wei's invocation of Confucius as a reformer. Exegesis implies both an explanation of the meaning of the social values in question and the construction of explicit social theories justifying specific institutions asserted to embody these values. Such ideological constructs as the famous "five relationships," the traditional rank order of *shih, nung, kung, shang,* the "Mandate of Heaven," the role of the emperor as intermediary between Heaven and the people, provided detailed content to the valued social harmony and simultaneously justified particular political institutions as promoting that harmony.

For the literati—at least for many of them—exegesis also involved an element of exhortation or persuasion. The two were relatively undifferentiated in the traditional examination system and the course of education in preparation for it. For the mass of the non-literate, persuasion might be carried on by formal argumentation and propaganda, for example in so-called village lectures (*hsiang-yüeh*). But I would suggest that much more important was the employment of powerful expressive symbols to persuade the masses. Local sacrifices, the local veneration of Confucius and other sages, ancestor "worship," and above all the quasi-magical, quasi-divine aura surrounding the local magistrate himself were important means of gaining at least the acquiescence of the populace to the political ideology studied and expounded by the literati.

The political institutions formed and upheld in this manner were a glory to behold. What accounts for their long life and their capacity to unite a sub-continent—in contrast to India, for example, where Hinduism was rarely able to provide the basis for a stable political integration? There is of course no single or simple answer. One line of approach would be to consider the combination of detailed prescriptive regulation and discretionary flexibility that characterized China's political synthesis. It might almost be said that we are dealing with two sets of political institutions whose overlapping and interplay contributed to the long-lived stability of political power in traditional China.

From the top looking downward to the vast millions of the Chinese peasant population, there was the imperial political system. The traditional political ideology justified the primary bifurcation of society into the ruling literate elite and the various sub-groupings of the ruled as the means of realizing social harmony. The classical exposition of this polarity may be found in *Mencius:*

Some labor with their brains and some labor with their brawn. Those who labor with their brains govern others; those who labor with their brawn are governed by others. Those governed by others, feed them. Those who govern others, are fed by them. This is a universal principle of the world (IIIa, 3).

Political ideology also justified a centralized administration organized around the person of the Son of Heaven, to whom in theory all paper work was directed and from whom all decisions emanated. So long as the emperor effectively performed the indispensable ritual functions of his office, and so long as he retained Heaven's mandate, his absolute power could not in theory be challenged. His role was not only that of ruler; even more important, perhaps, it was a representative one symbolizing the postulated harmony of the non-human and human worlds.

The administration of his empire was carried on through a rationalized bureaucratic structure spreading outward from the capital into the provinces and the 1,500-odd *hsien*. Elaborate rules governed the recruitment and employment of the officials who filled these posts. On paper, at least, the administrative structure was characterized by a high degree of rationality. Its operations too were subject to detailed prescriptions, covering 1,320 *chüan* in the last edition of the *Ta-Ch'ing hui-tien shih-li* (Collected Statutes and Precedents of the Ch'ing Dynasty) alone, leaving aside the multitude of regulations of the several ministries, etc. From the top looking down, then, the political system of traditional China was centralized, bureaucratic, and governed by detailed regulations. From this viewpoint, the employment of political power in the traditional state tended to be universalistic, that is, directed toward the governed as members of empirically defined classes, rather than on the basis of their personal relations with those who governed. Moreover, from the viewpoint of the center, the content of the regulations to be applied tended to be specific and detailed, comprehending all possible cases, rather than diffuse and open to adjustment and manipulation.

Now if this seems to run counter to the common description of Chinese government as being a "government by men rather than government by laws," it is precisely because the complex of political institutions centering on the emperor and his bureaucracy represented, as I have suggested, only one-half of the Chinese political synthesis. The long-lived and much remarked political stability should be seen as the product of a continuing equilibrium between institutions that can be described as tending in the direction of universalism and specificity and emanating from the political center, and a competing or overlapping set emanating from the local governmental and kinship level that tended in the direction of particularism and diffuseness.

The existence of these two elements is symbolized by the way in which the fiscal pie was divided. The *Hui-tien,* the regulations of the Hu-pu, the provincial and local taxation guides set forth in great detail the fiscal obligations of the populace. It is well known,[5] however, that the sums collected and disbursed in accord with these regulations accounted for only a part, perhaps only 50 per cent, of the total tax burden of the empire. This half was the half reported to and subject to the control of the central fiscal organs; the detailed and rationalized prescriptions which governed its collection, forwarding, and disbursal in a sense paralleled and interpenetrated with the rationalized bureaucratic structure I have described. But on top of this 50 per cent was an additional collection for the most part not provided for in the statute books and taxation guides. This was customary, local, and variable. It was composed of payments of all kinds (whether denominated as tax, surtax, fee, fine, gift, favor, or bribe) largely to local officials which may be subsumed under the heading *lou-kuei,* "customary exactions." While acknowledged, and often sanctioned by the central authorities so long as the burden was not so heavy as to give rise to protests and disorder, these exactions were the principal source of funds for local administration and for the local officials whose stipends as set forth in the regulations were completely inadequate for the duties they were expected to perform and for the staffs they were required to employ.

The political administration, formal and informal, financed by this *lou-kuei,* in contrast to the centralized, rationalized, and regulated central administration, tended to be local, personal, and customary. In its formal aspect it was represented by the *hsien* magistrate, a product of the rationalized examination system, of course, and an appointee of the emperor at the center. But in the performance of his office and in the sources of his effective power he was intimately tied to local, personal, and customary institutions. Being by law a stranger to his district, and with his incumbency likewise usually limited to three or at most six years, the magistrate was dependent on local experts and on the goodwill of the local gentry for the efficient discharge of his responsibilities. The staff that served under him for the most part was a personal staff, provided for in the statutes but recruited and paid by the magistrate from his personal allowance and other perquisites. Fi-

[5] Ch'ü T'ung-tsu, *Local Government in China under the Ch'ing* (Cambridge, Mass.: Harvard University Press, 1962).

nally, the duties which he performed, though broadly defined in the law code and tax regulations of the empire, contained a very large element that was either customary or discretionary. There was a certain looseness and informality about the structure and operation of government at the local level which contrasted sharply with the center. If government by men and not by laws had any meaning at all, it was in reference to this second half of the Chinese political synthesis.

What was true of the local magistrate, who was nevertheless the "formal" administrator of his district, was truer still of the local gentry (and village elders) whose political roles were less "formalized" than his. The manifold functions of the gentry (*shen-shih*) carried an unmistakable political tint, though these activities (for example, local arbitration, the organization of charity, grain storage, planning and execution of public works, teaching in the local schools, upkeep of temples, etc.) were not formally governmental and were not performed in consideration of any charter of local government issued by the official authorities.

The "economy" of local political power, from the bottom looking up to the center, was, then, particular and diffuse. At every turn, its "expenditure" tended to be governed by the personal ties between governor and governed, while the price asked and finally paid was one that could be haggled over, depending on the occasion and the circumstances.

The long life of China's traditional political institutions may be seen as in part the product of an equilibrium in tension between these two levels of the polity. Whatever the claims of the center, government of a country of China's size and population from a single center and by means of detailed prescriptive regulations—what one today would call a centralized authoritarian state—was an impossibility before the twentieth century, if for no other reason than because pre-modern technology, especially in the means of communication, ruled it out of the question. Conversely, a political system founded entirely on the above-mentioned local complex of institutions would simply not provide an adequate basis for sub-continent wide political integration. Both hemispheres were needed; the problem was to see that they fitted properly, a problem that runs through the whole of China's imperial history. Level I and Level II, if I may call them so in the interest of brevity, overlapped in a narrow area, a middle ground where there was room for movement and a change of balance. So long as the change was kept within this overlap, the basic political system was able to maintain a relative stability. Should either level impinge too deeply onto the domain of its co-tenant, the stability of the overall political system itself, which depended on the maintenance of an equilibrium between the two, was imperiled.

The foregoing remarks are obviously in need of some elucidation. What is meant by "equilibrium," what kind of "change" is possible within "stability," how could the overall political system be "imperiled"? This brings me back to the question of ideology, from which I earlier departed in order to discuss the political institutions justified and propagated by Confucianism as a political ideology.

I would suggest that the institutions of Level II were governed by ideological constructs which diverged in some important respects from those that governed Level I. It is not that these two ideological foci stood in stark opposition to one another; it is in fact their overlapping that is the key to understanding the overlapping of Levels I and II discussed above. And, above all, "social harmony" remained for both the ultimate value in whose interest the ideological functions of justification and exhortation were carried on. The point is that the same ultimate reference, the same social values, may yet give rise to divergent and sometimes competing ideologies. It is at the level of the interplay and conflict of ideologies that we should look for one of the causes of institutional changes within the basic framework of a society governed by social values which remain largely intact. (Let me emphasize that I do not believe that this mechanism of change is always the most important one in the sense of being an ultimate cause, but as an efficient cause it must always be present.) In traditional Chinese society, where it is generally agreed that at least some basic features remained constant over very long periods, the appearance, and disappearance of particular institutions—above all, institutions for the exercise of political power— has always been closely correlated with the movement of ideologies.

By "equilibrium" I mean a condition in which none of the competing or divergent ideologies gives rise to prolonged instability as a result of adopting a completely uncompromising position vis-à-vis the others; in which in general the several ideologies serve adequately to square existing institutions with social values; and into which no external pressure has been introduced sufficient to lay the social values themselves directly open to question. A drastic change in any of these conditions raises the possibility of a solution that goes beyond the mere change of institutions within a generally stable society. Here a whole society, and above all its political system, is imperiled.

One way of describing the different developments of the same ideological theme at Level I and Level II is to suggest that the first tended to select for emphasis those elements of the Confucian ideology that were primarily political, that corresponded to the interests of the Chinese state as a highly organized bureaucracy. While the term "Legalist" may be misleading, it carries the overtones that I want to convey. Level II, although it shared much of the ideology of Level I, was more inclusive. In a sense it can be seen as expressing what might be called the Confucian "general will," which was broader and more diffuse than the interests of the bureaucratic state per se. The Confucian "general will" tended to oppose to the detailed prescriptive regulation of the bureaucratic state the old ideal of rule by moral example, by personal excellence, that perhaps was more in line with the interests of the overwhelmingly large part of the educated elite ("gentry," "literati") who were not actually in office, or not in office at the political center. The idealization of the specific role of the *chün-tzu* (read "gentry," etc.) and of local officials as *fu-mu kuan,* and the preoccupation with one's kinship obligations indicate this emphasis.

In addition, this "general will"—much more than the political ideology of the center—had absorbed elements from the non-rationalized Taoist, Buddhist, and animistic streams which through the centuries flowed parallel with Confucianism. These tended to reinforce its predisposition to more informal methods of social control. The "excesses" of Buddhism and Taoism were condemned (as they were in the "Sixteen Maxims"), but their utility as an expressive outlet for the populace was acknowledged. Even the central government never made any real effort to wipe out these "heretical" beliefs. At Level II, they sometimes coalesced with institutions that clearly were primarily the product of Confucian ideology. The not uncommon assimilation in the popular mind of the local official to the local deity is perhaps the best example.

In sum, then, the ideological differences at Levels I and II were correlated with a bureaucratic emphasis on the one hand, and an extra-bureaucratic emphasis on the other—a Confucian *raison d'état* and a Confucian "general will." The mutual interplay, the tensions, the changing equilibria between these political hemispheres, and more broadly between the ideological emphases that justified them, constituted a permanent feature of China's political integration.

Within a generally stable society, preserving intact its basic social values, institutional change could occur when one or another of these two trends was in the ascendant. One of the clearest examples of this process is provided by James Liu's study of Wang An-shih.[6] Wang's

[6] James T. C. Liu, *Reform in Sung China: Wang An-shih (1021–1086) and His New Policies* (Cambridge, Mass.: Harvard University Press, 1959).

reforms represented par excellence the interests of the center, of the bureaucracy, of what I have called Level I, rather than those of the Level II and the Confucian "general will." That they may incidentally have been beneficial to the "people" is secondary. His opponents, the anti-reform party, stood in the other camp. Their opposition to Wang was based primarily on the centralizing, overtly bureaucratic character of the measures he proposed; this was not the way China had been governed by the sage-kings. Again, the fact that the position of the anti-reformers may be interpreted as socially conservative is an incidental matter. Social harmony, the highest value, was to be achieved by less bureaucratic, more informal means.

In the nineteenth century, we may see these same features in the conflict between the "reformers" of several different shades and their opponents. The apparent paradox that it was the leaders of local or regional foci of power, Li Hung-chang or Chang Chih-tung, for example, who were most concerned with "self-strengthening" is resolved in part by seeing these regional leaders as proponents of the same bureaucratic *raison d'état* that motivated Wang An-shih. K'ang Yu-wei, Liang Ch'i-ch'ao, and the reformers of 1898 can be seen in a similar light. All hoped to insure social harmony by new departures—including new political institutions—that could be justified as strengthening Level I, but were opposed by those to whom Level II was the sine qua non of Confucian rule.

Emphasis on Level II and its "general will" ideology was a common characteristic—I here go way out on my limb—of such apparently diverse persons and groups as Ku Yen-wu, Huang Tsung-hsi, and Wang Fu-chih of the early Ch'ing, the opponents of "self-strengthening" and of the reforms of 1898, and the local resistance to the centralizing reforms of the Manchu government at the end of the dynasty. Such a grouping produces strange bedfellows, but it is a warning against the easy application of such labels as "progressive" and "conservative" as a technique for probing the political process in traditional China.

Whether or not all my examples are appropriate—this requires careful study—I believe that it still holds true that the kind of shifting equilibrium I have described was a means whereby some institutional change could occur while maintaining unchanged the basic values of the Chinese political order. If it happened—as it sometimes did as a result of natural disasters, manifest political incompetence and corruption, burdensome fiscal exactions, and the like—that neither version of the Confucian ideology proved able to square existing institutions with these basic values, the political integration of the society as a whole was threatened. In the modern period the uprisings of the White Lotus sect, the Taipings and Nien, and the Boxers presented just such threats. But these were overcome with greater or lesser effort, and in their aftermath the ideology was refurbished and institutions and values were squared again, if only temporarily.[7]

The "evil" wrought by foreign encroachment, by imperialism if you will, was to present a permanent threat to the Chinese political equilibrium that could not be overcome within the parameters of the traditional society. Compounding the increasingly difficult internal task of squaring existing institutions with basic social values—this I take it is what is meant by the downward turn of a dynastic cycle—external foreign pressure introduced two additional disequilibrating elements. It induced a questioning of the values themselves, of the viability of the traditional society as a whole, and it brought in its train new uncompromising ideologies whose irresoluble conflict resulted in a prolonged and fatal instability.

The challenge to the basic values of traditional China was both direct and indirect. Directly it was a byproduct of the Christian missionary movement, and of the actual presence of foreigners and the establishment of foreign-type institutions in the treaty port areas. While the explicit aim of the missionaries was still to preach the truth of the Gospel, it is evident that by the latter part of the nineteenth century European and American evangelists, doctors, and teachers in China were, with varying degrees of awareness, performing in a much more inclusive role as transmitters of European culture in general. The best known example, of course, is the influence of Timothy Richard on Liang Ch'i-ch'ao and others involved in the Reform Movement of 1898. In a similar manner, Western-type commercial, manufacturing, financial, judicial, and educational institutions in the treaty ports exercised an attraction to some Chinese who were exposed to them, and raised a question about the comparative worth of traditional institutions and the values on which they were based.

This relatively peaceful acculturation, however, did not occur in isolation from the forceful application of superior Western power to gain and secure commercial and political prerogatives in China. The sheer confrontation of Western strength and Chinese weakness could not but accelerate the doubting of tradition that was simultaneously being induced by the more pacific penetration of foreign ideas.

7 This is a major theme of Mary C. Wright's magisterial work on the post-Taiping period, *The Last Stand of Chinese Conservatism: The T'ung-chih Restoration, 1862–1874* (Stanford: Stanford University Press, 1957).

The Ch'ing government was indeed "in the middle," between two forces, millstones as it were, whose conflicting demands eventually ground it out of existence. On the one hand were foreign demands for the expansion of trading opportunities, spheres of influence, the protection of their missionary nationals, indemnities, and railroad and mining concessions. On the other was the increasingly importunate reaction of the Chinese populace to the fact of the Western role in China, a reaction that by the last quarter of the century could be seen in two forms, though they were sometimes difficult to differentiate: a "reactionary" xenophobia, and a budding nationalism directed against the Manchu dynasty. The progressive undermining of traditional institutions and values was evident all across the board as a result of the interplay of these forces.

We may note, first, the loss of China's peripheral territories and nominal dependencies. The process included Russian penetration into Chinese Turkestan (Sinkiang), the French seizure of Annam, British annexation of Upper Burma, and successful assertion of Japanese suzerainty over the Ryūkyū Islands; and it culminated in the Sino-Japanese War, the loss of Formosa, and the effective alienation of Manchuria first to Russia after the Boxer uprising and then to Japan after her victory in the Russo-Japanese War. The significance of this humiliation lay not only in the exposure of China's weakness, but perhaps more important in the final collapse of the traditional tribute system of foreign relations which even in the 1880's Li Hung-chang was still seeking to shore up in Korea.

The missionary movement itself was a two-pronged threat. While Western ideas and ideologies were slowly filtering their way into Chinese consciousness, the presence of missionaries—in particular their activities in the interior, far from the treaty ports where Western influence had been relatively far-reaching—had more immediate consequences. This whole period is punctuated with incidents involving violence directed by the Chinese populace either against Christian converts or against the missionaries themselves. The result of these disorders was nearly unbearable strain on the Manchu government as a consequence of the growing xenophobia of the local gentry and people whose resentment of missionary interference in local affairs for the protection of converts was exacerbated by the repeated yielding of Peking to foreign envoys in the capital and Western gunboats on the Yangtze. In 1900 came the Boxer uprising, the greatest of these anti-foreign disturbances, in whose wake followed a further attrition of the traditional Ch'ing state. Not only did the "native customs" now also come under the control of the foreign Inspectorate as security for the Boxer indemnities, but the "Manchu Reform Movement," in a last desperate effort to preserve the dynasty, abolished the examination system (that central arch of the Confucian bureaucratic state) and took hesitant steps toward constitutional government.

Finally, these decades saw the ideological disintegration of Confucianism itself in face of the need to rationalize what was happening to China. The first major step along the path to oblivion for Confucianism, as we can see now, was the famous *t'i-yung* dichotomy which the "self-strengtheners" of the post-Taiping period used to rationalize the introduction of Western arms and military technology. *Chung-hsüeh wei-t'i, Hsi-hsüeh wei-yung* ("Chinese learning for the fundamental structure, Western learning for practical application") seemed safe enough to Feng Kuei-fen and Li Hung-chang. But as Joseph Levenson in particular has pointed out, *t'i* and *yung* as used in the great philosophical tradition could not be so easily separated, with the former remaining Chinese while the latter became Western. In the next stage, though they did so under the cover of Confucius himself, the reformers of 1898 explicitly questioned the validity of the Chinese *t'i* that was supposed to be protected by the controlled application of Western techniques. And then the question became merely academic (as we say): with the abolition first of the examination system, and a few years later of the imperial system itself, the search for central values passed beyond the confines of Confucianism onto a new battleground where Mr. Science and Mr. Democracy were the men of the day, and nationalism and then communism contended for men's allegiance.

The diffusion of Western political ideas in China against a background of sometimes violent confrontation with the nations from which these ideas came, did not result in the transformation of China into a Western-style political entity. The equilibrium of the old order was irretrievably lost, but a new integration was slow in emerging. This we may note bears a remarkable similarity to the half-way effect of Western economic penetration of China. *Some* political change introduced into China from outside her society seems to have had the effect of making *further* change in the direction of stability more difficult for the moment. The "problem of partial development" seems to be relevant to the political as well as to the economic effects of imperialism. Of course, the causes of this delay were manifold and complex. I would suggest that so far as the political impact of the West is concerned, this hiatus of forty years was in part due to the ensuing prolonged conflict within China between uncompromising political ideologies whose origin was

Western. Only when Chinese Communism had finally overcome its rivals, was a new political integration achieved.

Let me conclude with even wilder speculation on the nature of integration in the political system of Communist China. Maoism, too, we may decompose into Maoist "general will" and Maoist *raison d'état*. By the former I mean "the thought of Mao Tse-tung" as a general integrative ideology for post-1949 Chinese society analogous to Confucianism as the ideology of Level II in late-imperial China. The latter subsumes the particular policy lines followed by the Peking regime since its inception, and is perhaps more correctly identified with the party and state bureaucracies headed and shaped by Liu Shao-ch'i and Teng Hsiao-p'ing and by Chou En-lai than with Chairman Mao himself. It is the functional equivalent of the ideology of Level I in our earlier discussion.

As in nineteenth-century China, the Maoist Level II, although sharing much of the ideology of Level I, is broader and more diffuse and opposed to bureaucratic rationality with its inevitable tendency toward routinization and even "revisionism" the ideal of rule by moral example, by personal revolutionary commitment, that is part of the mythology of Yenan and the party's incredible victory in 1949. Maoist "general will," I suggest, is also essentially anti-urban, fearful that the integrative revolutionary élan may be diluted by the ineluctable "bourgeois" character of China's modernizing sector.

The seventeen years of Communist rule in China have seen a tension and interplay between the Maoist "general will" and the Maoist *raison d'état* reflected in the advances and retreats of policy which has in rough alternation emphasized normative exhortations and rational incentives in its attempts to transform Chinese society. The basic values and goals are shared, but the means have been fought over. So long, however, as neither sub-ideology adopted a completely uncompromising position vis-à-vis the other—which implies that both in some combination were effectively able to square existing institutional arrangements with Marxist-Maoist social values, that is, that the regime was relatively successful in its domestic development programs and in its foreign policies—no prolonged political instability was experienced. It is now precisely the apparent inability since the Great Leap to repeat the impressive economic achievements of the First Five Year Plan, together with the manifest foreign policy difficulties of the regime, that have introduced a situation in which the basic integration of the political system is called into question.

Comments by Philip Kuhn

Modes of Change in
Nineteenth-Century China

The question of the relative importance of cyclical change (that related to the so-called dynastic cycle) and of non-cyclical change (including "secular" or long-term factors as well as wholly new factors from outside) is a particularly vexing one to specialists in the "modern" period. It is interesting that the title of Professor Liu's paper uses the phrase "the disintegration of the old order" rather than "the decline of the Ch'ing Dynasty"; for many of the events Professor Liu describes, such as the decline of administration, the spread of corruption, and the eruption of rebellion, are clearly, as he points out, "within the pattern of the declining periods of previous dynasties." However, as they blend into the events of the late nineteenth and early twentieth century, they seem also to be the first steps in the disintegration of traditional Chinese society itself. Cyclical devolution leads imperceptibly into secular evolution, until the two appear a single process. The outcries of Kung Tzu-chen are but an overture to the radical reformism of K'ang Yu-wei. The quality of local government, which had begun seriously to decline by 1800, continues its unbroken descent into the rural chaos of the Republican period. Looking back at the nineteenth century from our superior historical perspective, we see a period of crisis in the old tradition as the initial stage of the destruction of that tradition.

Several historical interpretations would have us see in nineteenth-century history certain trends that transcend the dynastic cycle and herald the end of the traditional order as a whole. A relatively convincing case can be made for the importance of the population rise as a factor that jarred Chinese history from its traditional track. The emergence of a "semi-feudal, semi-colonial" society as a result of Western encroachments, or its companion theory, the development of capitalist "burgeons" in the Ming period, are other, less convincing hypotheses.[1] Surely there were developments in nineteenth-century Chinese society

[1] Albert Feuerwerker and S. Cheng, *Chinese Communist Studies of Modern Chinese History* (Cambridge: Harvard University Press, 1961), pp. 181–89.

that were in various ways unprecedented, as there had been in every other period of Chinese history. Yet we cannot resist the temptation to ask, as a purely theoretical exercise, whether there was not some point during the nineteenth century at which the Chinese state could still have been reconstructed along traditional lines; whether, if the Western powers had for some unimaginable reason failed to intensify and expand their assault, there were not elements of stability and continuity within China that would have enabled a new, strong, but traditionally ordered regime to replace the faltering Ch'ing; whether, in other words, the "old order" did not contain the seeds of its own perpetuation, a perpetuation forestalled by factors largely exogenous to the Chinese system.

The Survival of the Traditional Elite

Despite our best efforts to do away with it, the "dynastic cycle" seems to persist as a useful element in our historiography. The dynastic cycle theory is useful in that it postulates elements of continuity in local society that make it possible to explain the long-term stability of Chinese political institutions; it envisages the possibility that administrative entropy and dynastic change do not permanently affect the substructure of Chinese life. Clearly some inter-dynastic crisis periods have had greater, and others less effect upon local society.[2] At the time of the Manchu conquest, at least, a key element of stability appears to have been the continued dominance of the local elite. It was this elite that, by virtue of its undiminished community influence, its tradition of orthodox learning, and its ethic of administrative service, made possible the reintegration of the traditional state in a shape similar to that of its predecessor. The elite provided the pool of talent and education from which the new regime could staff its bureaucracy. It assured the maintenance of those customary community services without which Chinese local government could not operate; and, through its devotion to the social status quo, it made possible the reestablishment of local order, without which a reliable registration and taxation system could not be built. Finally, on a national scale, it served as the vital link between the bureaucracy and the local communities, between the urban administrative centers and the rural hinterland.

If the nineteenth century exhibited in some respects "the pattern of the declining periods of previous dynasties," then we should expect to find that the decline in the effectiveness of the formal governmental apparatus and the weakening of central imperial control were not

[2] Ho Ping-ti, *The Ladder of Success in Imperial China: Aspects of Social Mobility, 1368–1911* (New York: Columbia University Press, 1962), pp. 216–17.

matched by an equally serious decline in the position of the local elite. There is inded considerable evidence that the mid-century rebellions, despite their terrible destructiveness in some areas, left the power of the local elite undiminished and, in some instances, even enhanced. The lower levels of degree-holders, aided frequently by merchants, sometimes succeeded in maintaining their control over rural areas even in districts whose administrative centers had fallen to the Taipings.[3] In some districts the Taipings chose local militia leaders among the indigenous elite as local headmen (hsiang-kuan) for lack of locally powerful cadres of their own.[4] The campaigns of the new provincial armies were complemented by the local-control and fund-raising activities of gentry militia organizers.[5]

That the mid-century rebellions left the rural elite solidly entrenched is further suggested by the tendency of the pao-chia system to come under its control. The pao-chia system under the early Ch'ing was supposed to be administered by commoners; and was probably thought of, at least in part, as a counterweight to the power of the elite. Like other aspects of local government, pao-chia had begun to founder by the early decades of the nineteenth century, and probably even earlier, and was in a shambles by the time of the Taiping Rebellion. To rebuild pao-chia was clearly essential if order and local security were to be recovered after the rebellions. Early in the Kuang-hsü reign there was a noteworthy effort in Hupeh to reinvigorate pao-chia by entrusting its leadership to members of the elite. Though the p'ai and chia units were to be managed by commoners, the higher units were to be managed by gentry (shen-shih). The nomenclature embodied in this system makes it clear that pao-chia was being turned over to those members of the local elite who were already the de facto power in their communities: those in command of local militia associations.[6]

The configurations of the pao-chia system in the late nineteenth century still require much research. Instances such as the above are worth our close attention, particularly because they seem to be the initial stages of a process that continued into the twentieth century: the integration of elements of the local elite into the formal machinery of

[3] See my article, "The T'uan-lien Local Defense System at the Time of the Taiping Rebellion," Harvard Journal of Asiatic Studies, 27 (1967): pp. 218–55.

[4] Ihara Hirosuke, "Taihei Tengoku no gōson tōji," Shigaku Kenkyū, 86, (1962): 50.

[5] Such as the powerful local machine of Liu Yü-hsun in Kiangsi; see Nan-ch'ang-hsien chih [Gazetteer of Nanchang hsien] (1870) chüan 28.

[6] Li Yu-fen, Wu-chün pao-chia shih-i che-yao [Selected Materials on Pao-chia Administration in Wuchang] (1887), chüan 3:1–2b.

county government. Consider as an example the sub-*hsien* administrative division called the *ch'ü* as it existed during the early 1930's. We find that the headship of these rural divisions was commonly held by members of the indigenous elite, in whom were vested formal civil governing powers of considerable scope. In some areas they also had military authority through their control of the local security militia. These powerful local figures had ample opportunity for either public betterment or private enrichment. A survey of rural conditions in Kiangsu during the early 1930's found that the *ch'ü* office was the only significant locus of power below the level of the *hsien*.[7] Apart from their participation in the lower echelons of the bureaucracy, the elite was able to protect its local power through control of militia units. During the early thirties it was estimated that the province of Fukien had more than 40,000 militiamen under the control of "powerful gentry (*hao-shen*), landlords, and merchants."[8]

The composition and character of the local elite underwent a certain amount of change between the late nineteenth century and the mid-twentieth, particularly because of the gradual influx of men who got their start through trade or soldiering.[9] However, though research on this subject is still exceedingly sparse, there is also evidence of considerable continuity; the group whose formal status was jeopardized by the abolition of the traditional examination system in 1905 seems to a large extent to have maintained its position in local society and even to have forged new links to the state apparatus. It appears that the so-called "local self-government" (*ti-fang tzu-chih*) movement that played such a prominent part in twentieth-century administrative theory served in some respects simply to ratify the power and influence of the local elite. Thus there are some reasons to doubt that the "disintegration of the old order" affected the lower reaches of society as thoroughly as it did the superstructure of the state itself.

[7] Hsing-cheng-yuan nung-ts'un fu-hsing wei-yuan-hui [Executive Yuan, Committee on Rural Reconstruction], *Chiang-su-sheng nung-ts'un tiao-ch'a* [Investigations of Rural Villages in Kiangsu Province] (Shanghai: Commercial Press, 1934), pp. 65–77. Also, *Shen-hsi-sheng nung-ts'un tiao-ch'a* [Investigations of Rural Villages in Shensi Province] (Shanghai: Commercial Press, 1934), pp. 148–49. See also Ch'ien Tuan-sheng, *Min-kuo cheng-chih shih* [A History of Governmental Institutions during the Republican period] 2 vols. (Changsha: Commercial Press, 1939), 2:666–72.

[8] Feng Ho-fa, *Chung-kuo nung-ts'un ching-chi tzu-liao* [Materials on the Economy of China's Rural Villages] (Shanghai: Li-ming shu-chü, 1935), pp. 880–81.

[9] Chow Yung-teh, *Social Mobility in China* (New York: Atherton Press, 1966), chaps. 4 and 5.

The Social Impact of Modernization

Though much of the "old order" in rural China remained intact as the nineteenth century drew to a close, and indeed persisted into the Republican period, there were obviously new forces at work that prevented the reconstruction of the Chinese polity along traditional lines. It can be argued that these forces came principally from outside China and cannot logically be connected to the disintegrative trends within. A useful catchall for these forces has been the term "modernization," the early stages of which Professor Liu has described. A prime subject for research is the effect of modernization upon the Chinese elite, which survived the nineteenth-century rebellions with local roots so strong and provincial power so impressive. What was it about the modernization process that rendered this elite powerless to halt the political fragmentation of the twentieth century and to reconstitute effective government on a national basis?

Here I suggest we look beyond the actual content of modernization—the particular values and techniques involved in this confrontation of cultures—and consider the gross structural effects of the process upon Chinese society. We confront first the fact that early modernization was mainly a phenomenon of the cities, especially the treaty ports, and left rural China largely untouched; and second, that the gap between the modernizing and pre-modern cultures tended to become coterminous with the gap between city and countryside. The emergence of the self-strengthening movement and new-style economic enterprise, though clearly needed for China's national survival, were the first steps in a process that was to place severe strains on China's internal cohesion. The emergence of a modernizing Chinese urban culture helped to produce a new urban elite who, despite their notable attainments in the modern sectors of industry, politics, journalism, and scholarship, were less and less capable of playing a role in the central task of Chinese government: the administration of a predominantly rural society from an urban administrative base.

What Fei Hsiao-t'ung has called the "social erosion" of rural society was exacerbated by the process of modernization.[10] As the cities entered further into the new culture, they stimulated the flow of talent out of the villages and towns of the interior; and this traffic was increasingly one-way. Those of the elite who found careers in the modernizing sector of urban life found it hard to retain their ties with the pre-modern

[10] Fei Hsiao-t'ung, *China's Gentry: Essays in Rural-Urban Relations* (Chicago: University of Chicago Press, 1953), pp. 127–42.

culture of village or county seat. This was even more the case with those who went abroad for study.[11] Even the most politically radical among the young urban elite had little to offer toward solving the deepening crisis in rural China. The divisive effects of modernization upon the elite drew warning cries from such radical rural reconstructionists as Liang Sou-ming and T'ao Hsing-chih, both of whom sought to reidentify young, progressive urbanites with the problems of the countryside.

It appears that the ability of the late Ch'ing literati to hold the old order together under the stress of internal rebellion stemmed partly from the ability of high-ranking bureaucrats such as Tseng Kuo-fan to participate to some extent in both urban and rural cultures, to bind the national elite with a chain of common values. But the drastically widened cultural gap between city and country in the twentieth century precluded the emergence of such figures. It is not surprising that the reintegration of the national polity, when finally it came, should have been accompanied by drastic efforts to bridge that gap; and to produce a new elite with cultural roots in both modern and pre-modern sectors of Chinese life.

Notes by Dwight H. Perkins:
China's Economic Heritage

In a number of papers at this conference and in much of the discussion there is a generally held belief that changes in the economy in the century prior to 1949 played a significant part in the rise of the Chinese Communists to power. Without dealing explicitly with the effect of economic performance on politics, I should like to challenge the com-

[11] The divisive effects of modern schooling, and particularly of foreign schooling upon the Chinese elite are explored in their many aspects by Y. C. Wang in his *Chinese Intellectuals and the West, 1872–1949* (Chapel Hill: University of North Carolina Press, 1966).

monly accepted pre-1949 economic picture. In addition, I should like
to point out some of the major changes that have occurred in the
economy since 1949 that have an effect on such issues as the possible reemergence of regional political-military power bases.

Economic Conditions, 1800–1949

Put simply, the commonly held view is that living standards deteriorated markedly and fairly steadily after 1800 until the Communists came
to power in 1949. This declining trend in per capita income was, it is
believed, accompanied by increasing tenancy and greater instability
and loss of life from famine. These conditions in turn were a major
factor in the Communists' rise to power.

Any one of these issues could properly be the subject of a book. To
date, however, most political scientists and historians have appeared to
feel that the economic picture was clear and hence required little
further questioning or analysis. On the basis of work that various economists, including myself, have been doing, it has become apparent that
the commonly held view, if not wholly misleading, is at least subject to
serious question.

It is impossible to compare with precision per capita income in the
1930's or the 1950's with any period in the eighteenth or nineteenth
century. We do know, however, that per capita income in the 1930's
and 1950's was well above that in India in the 1950's and Japan in the
Meiji period. In particular, grain output per capita in China in the
twentieth century was roughly comparable to that in the grain-surplus
countries of Southeast Asia. If per capita grain output in eighteenth
century China had been much higher than it was in, say, the 1930's, one
would expect that more of the grain would have been used as fodder
and there would have been far more animals, meat consumption, and
the like than there are today. But there is no evidence that this was the
case and some evidence to the contrary.

For the twentieth century one has more data available. A very crude
index of agricultural output which I have constructed for the 1914–57
period suggests that there was little change in per capita farm output
during this period. Estimates by John Chang for modern industry suggest that growth in that sector between 1912 and 1942 averaged 8.2 per
cent a year. This industrial growth may have been entirely at the expense of handicrafts, but it doesn't seem likely. The presumption is,
therefore, that average per capita income rose in the twentieth century,
although only very slightly.

What information we have on tenancy also suggests little significant change in the nineteenth and twentieth centuries. North China had little tenancy in either the nineteenth century or in the twentieth. Certain areas of heavy tenancy in south China in the past few decades were also largely controlled by landlords a hundred years ago. The Taiping Rebellion, to be sure, reduced tenancy in many areas of southern Kiangsu and northern Kiangsi, but a more typical pattern reasserted itself. There may also have been some change in the more recently settled areas of the southwest, but evidence is scarce.

The evidence regarding the impact of famine on human life is more clear-cut. Because of the railroad, harvest fluctuations in north China caused much less loss of life in the twentieth century than in the nineteenth. In this respect, people in the eighteenth century were probably better off than in the nineteenth because the eighteenth was apparently a period unusually free from major weather disasters and one when water control activity was quite vigorous. How the twentieth century compares with the eighteenth would be difficult to say.

If people were objectively better off in terms of economic conditions in the twentieth century than in the nineteenth and perhaps even the eighteenth century, it does not follow that they believed this to be the case. There is considerable evidence to suggest that the opposite belief was commonly held. In particular, the uncertainty caused by political disruption may have made economic conditions seem worse than they were.

The implications of this line of reasoning are quite different from the more commonly held view. If real economic conditions were fairly good but political instability made them seem poor, then the restoration of political stability would, at least temporarily, give to the political organization responsible an image of being highly competent in the economic sphere as well. This image would in turn reinforce the new government's political strength.

Economic Discontinuities After 1949

Whether or not economic conditions prior to 1949 necessitated any radical change in economic policy, there is no question that such changes did occur and that most of them have implications for the political system.

Perhaps the most important change is that the Chinese Communists, by collectivizing agriculture and socializing the other sectors, have taken over virtually complete responsibility for the performance of the economy. Economic success or failure today is thus certain to have a much more profound effect on politics than it has had in China's past or than it has in less centralized economies in other parts of the world today.

Centralization of economic controls together with the rapid industrialization that occurred in the 1950's also has major implications for the possibility of a return to anything approximating the warlord era of the 1920's. As Professor Wilbur has pointed out, Peking was a prize for any warlord in the 1920's in large part because control of Peking meant control of the customs revenues. The Western powers controlled where these revenues would go and they decided that they should go to Peking.

Overall government revenues under the Communists are 10 to 20 times higher than under any previous government. More important, the principal sources of revenue have changed. Today most revenue comes from profits and taxes on industrial enterprises. Unlike the agricultural tax, this industrial revenue is not evenly spread across the country but is heavily concentrated in Manchuria, Hopei, and Shanghai. Any group in firm control of these areas would have overwhelming financial power vis-à-vis such areas as southwest China, Sinkiang, and Inner Mongolia. If the customs revenues gave Peking governments in the 1920's considerable power, how much more power would a government in control of Peking have today. In terms of real output, this same government would also control a disproportionate share of the nation's industry, particularly its heavy industry. Such power was a determining factor in the American Civil War. With the advances in conventional weaponry since that time, I suspect that control of the industrial base would be even more important in a protracted struggle in China today.

To make use of such power, of course, a government in control of Peking would have to be unified within itself. It would also have to be determined enough to impose great destruction on areas of China held by its opponents, far greater destruction than was ever perpetrated by warlords in the 1920's. If the greatly enhanced scale of military operations and resulting destruction would inhibit action by the authorities in Peking, however, it would presumably also tend to deter local leaders elsewhere from attempting to set up a regime independent of Peking.

There are many other major economic discontinuities in the pre- and post-1949 situation. Changes in the transportation network particularly in northwest China would be another of considerable political significance. A full discussion of these issues, however, is a proper subject for a paper, not a brief comment.

C. Martin Wilbur   3

Military Separatism and the Process of Reunification under the Nationalist Regime, 1922–1937

Introduction

The decade of the 1920's appears to have been a turning point in modern China's political history, the period in which a trend toward regional military separatism was reversed by the Kuomintang (KMT) or Nationalist Party. National unity was not effectively restored by the KMT: the armies and government it created could not impose political unity upon the country before they were driven from the mainland in 1950. The reasons for this failure are complex and debatable, but one of the most important probably was the nature of the system of military separatism itself. It is the purpose of this essay to analyze the system and to describe the efforts of the KMT to overpower it. If the system has been crushed by the Communist regime, then the turning point in the 1920's may come to be regarded as a decisive historical development.

Militarism was one of the three cardinal problems confronting the Chinese nation during the first half of the twentieth century. It was indissolubly linked to the solution of the other two—alien control over important aspects of Chinese life and the need to modernize the Chinese state and society. By "militarism" I mean a system of organizing political power in which force is the normal arbiter in the distribution of power and in the establishment of policy. In China from 1912 onward this was the case.

Militarism in China before 1950 characteristically had another feature, the regional distribution of power to an extent that no one military authority was able to subordinate all rivals and create a unified, centralized, and hierarchical political structure. This was an old and recurrent Chinese problem.

A unified, centralized, and hierarchical political system had become the traditional norm for the Chinese state. Most Chinese leaders of the twentieth century, including some militarists themselves, perceived that unless such a system were re-created, it would be impossible to deal effectively with foreign interference or to move significantly toward a modern society. Military separatism encouraged foreign domination of China in several major ways, and foreign power was too great to be withstood in the absence of a unified and centralized state. Military separatism was a major obstacle to modernization of the society because militarists, the final arbiters in their own realms, were either little concerned with modernization or primitive in conceptualizing the process. They were primarily interested in the consolidation and perpetuation of their own power, either locally or on a national basis if possible. Furthermore, the internecine wars characteristic of the militarist system diverted a large proportion of the talent, energy, and resources of the country away from use in the modernization of society.

Realists understood that the regional aspect of militarism could be overcome only by an overwhelming concentration of military power within one regional group that participated in the political system. There was no other way. This concentration would have to be supported by other forms of power—articulated public opinion, mobilized financial and other economic resources, and power imported from abroad. Power imported from abroad was dangerous: it was used by rivals and it was difficult to control. The essence of statecraft in this aspect of the power struggle was to control and use available foreign power—financial, technical, industrial, and military—and to prevent or neutralize its use by rivals. Yüan Shih-k'ai and his successors in the Pei-yang Army system and both Chiang Kai-shek and Mao Tse-tung were realists in their attempts to use foreign power to re-create a unified and centralized state.

We shall amplify and illustrate these generalizations after discussing two other matters: the essence of the Chinese system of regional separatism and the factors which had brought the system into existence.

An Anatomy of the Regional Militarist System

In the decade centering on 1920, regional militarism was dominant in China. Throughout the country there existed independent military-political groupings, each of which controlled territory and exploited local resources. Each, as a system, was similar to all the others; they differed primarily in scale. Yet each system was flavored by the geographical and cultural characteristics of its particular region and by the personalities of its leaders.

The Crucial Problem: Centralized vs. Decentralized Control

The Chinese military regimes in the 1920's were structured hierarchies usually organized for both civil administration and warfare. They seem to have been held together in varying degrees by strong leaders, organization and discipline, bonds of personal loyalty between leaders and followers, ideological commitment, local ties, and personal advantage. These military groupings were characterized by two conflicting tendencies: centralization vs. decentralization of control. Most armies were, in theory, parts of a national army under the central government in Peking, or were provincial armies. In fact, many were independent of any higher authority. But within any independent system the same problem—centralized control against lower-unit autonomy—existed. Divisions and brigades might in theory be subordinate to the higher authority of the system of which they were parts, yet they separately garrisoned cities or districts and might attempt to secure and control their own finances. Usually the center was unable to procure adequate finances for the entire system and had to allow the subordinate units to secure their own revenues. The same conflict occurred in procurement of arms, the basic stuff of all military units. Were they to be procured and allocated by the center, or by each unit for itself? How far down within a system could autonomy go and the system still retain unity?

Strong and relatively enduring systems seem to have been characterized by centralized control over primary resources—money and arms—and particularly by control over their allocation to subunits. This meant collection of taxes, requiring bureaucracy, and management of arsenals or procurement from abroad, both requiring experts. A centralized system needed powerful personalities as leaders, strong and reciprocal loyalties between leaders and subordinates, and expertise in management. Military groups in which decentralized tendencies predominated were often mere alliances among units making up a fictitious system. Both tendencies existed in all of China's militarist systems in the 1920's, in varying combinations.

Territorial Base as Fundamental Determinant of Autonomy

The territorial base was the fundamental determinant of the power and endurance of an independent militarist regime. It provided the financial resources for recruitment and pay of troops and for procurement and replenishment of arms. Dissatisfaction over allocation of bases often accounted for the breakdown of a system, while attempts of ambitious groups to secure better bases caused innumerable civil wars.

Geographical location and resources within the base were primary and inter-connected considerations. A most desirable base should be defensible, have ready access to the sea, and be rich in resources. Necessary resources consisted of population, agriculture, industry, and money. Usable wealth was concentrated in cities, which were also the centers from which surrounding territory was taxed in money and grain. Cities contained the industrial plant necessary to equip armies. Yet a broad territory around cities must also be held for security, manpower, and food.

Manchuria was an excellent base, easily defended. During the entire Republican period, Manchuria was never taken from a Chinese army based there by Chinese armies from the neighboring provinces. Its population was numerous and sturdy, with a strong sense of regional identity. It was rich in agricultural products, had well-developed cities, commerce and modern industry, an excellent arsenal, relatively good internal communications, and easy access to the sea. Japan's privileged economic position in the south and Soviet Russia's growing power in the north provided both benefits and hazards for the local regime headed by Chang Tso-lin till June, 1928. Szechwan, both populous and productive, was far from the sea; the Yangtze River was a precarious route for arms procurement even though most of its steam-powered shipping was under foreign register. Apparently the province was too large and its internal communications too inadequate for Szechwan to be controlled by a single indigenous regime. It was a theater of internecine wars and was frequently invaded.

Kwangtung was rich and prosperous, with good access to the sea and many well-developed cities and towns, but it was difficult to defend from the west or east. It was repeatedly invaded by extra-provincial armies, usually aided from within.

The lower Yangtze region was extremely prosperous, with many wealthy cities in addition to Shanghai, China's center of foreign business and modern industry. But the Yangtze Delta was difficult to defend. This great prize changed hands repeatedly.

Shansi provided a base for the longest-lasting single regime of the Republican period. It was difficult to attack, had the resources for a modest industrial plant, was relatively poor in population and agriculture, and had no access to the sea except through rival bases. Yen Hsi-shan generally stayed aloof from China's internecine wars but was tempted to involve his regime twice when Peking was the prize.

Peking, in Chihli, was the supreme prize for many reasons. It had been China's capital city continuously for five hundred years. The regime which controlled Peking could dominate a government which clothed itself in the mantle of legitimacy. The government could confer a certain symbolic legitimacy to military regimes throughout the country; this was of some advantage to them in gaining public support. More important was the fact that, between 1912 and 1928, foreign governments recognized or at least dealt with whatever government was established in Peking. Such Chinese governments had to accept China's existing treaties and were responsible for the national foreign debt. But they also received a steady income from the centrally administered Maritime Customs Service, which was effectively under foreign protection, and they derived some revenues from the salt *gabelle* and government-owned railways. Using these assets as security, governments at Peking regularly contracted foreign and domestic loans. They also contracted foreign loans by granting rights to exploit parts of China's mineral resources or to construct railways. Such loans were regularly used to strengthen the military power of the regime behind the government. Furthermore, the government at Peking could grant permits for importation of foreign arms and munitions by local regimes which it recognized as legitimate. Insofar as foreign powers exercised control over their nationals in the arms business and upheld the Maritime Customs Service in its efforts to prevent the smuggling of arms, this central government authority was an important asset. It was used by the controllers of a Peking government to build up and tie together military factions, and it might tip the balance in internecine wars. Chihli, with Tientsin as its major port and Peking as the national capital until 1928, was fought for many times between 1911 and 1930. As a territorial base, Chihli was not easy to defend; as a prize, it was the object of many temporary coalitions among military regimes based outside.

Any populated bit of Chinese territory could serve as a military base. It might consist of a few districts around Yü-lin in southeastern Kwangsi, which served as Li Tsung-jen's base in 1922 and 1923 and which gave him a start toward provincial leadership. It might be the impoverished but easily defended "bad lands" of western Honan which was the base for a powerful bandit gang which raided widely in 1925; or, it might consist of no more than a few villages along part of a mountain range between two provinces such as the base which gave Mao Tse-tung his start as a militarist in late 1927. A poor and remote base was only a starting place. No militarist system could endure on slender resources.

Ambitious military leaders tried to improve their bases at the expense of systems occupying neighboring territory. To do so, a leader usually had to exploit his base to the utmost. For example, when T'ang Chi-yao in Yunnan attempted to capture Canton early in 1925, he secured arms through Indochina for his invading army, provided the force with opium grown in Yunnan, and is alleged to have sent a million dollars to Canton to buy out Yunnan and Kwangsi troops encamped in that city and neighboring towns.[1] The men, arms, opium, and money for this unsuccessful venture were all extracted, ultimately, from Marshal T'ang's base, Yunnan. To defend a base likewise required administering it effectively enough to procure the stuff upon which military power existed.

A militarist system was only one of many social systems within its territorial base. There were towns with their complex social structures; the local "gentry" with their codes of behavior, economic institutions, and enforcement devices such as control of militia and influence over local courts; there were merchants' associations, secret societies, "clan" organizations in south and central China, farmers' self-defense organizations, bandit groups, etc. A militarist system that lasted for any period in a particular base was intimately related to the local society. Very likely it had emerged from it. Every successful militarist must be an expert Chinese politician, particularly when in alien territory. He had on his staff or quickly developed a staff of locally influential people to advise him on local power relationships and how best to govern and milk the territory.

To administer a base required civil bureaucracy. Throughout China civil administration continued on the pattern inherited from the Ch'ing dynasty, which had inherited it from the Ming. During the Republican period it had simply become much more decentralized. Most militarist regimes used the existing administrative system, putting their own men in key positions. The object was to secure as much as possible of the tax revenue normally produced by the base, and to develop new sources of revenue. This had to be done without creating irrepressible turmoil or revolt within. There were limits beyond which it was dangerous to extract revenue. Sun Yat-sen tried his best during 1923 and 1924 to maximize revenues coming to his own system, so he could expand his base around Canton and participate in internecine war for the control of Peking. He created so much opposition among Cantonese

---

[1] U.S., Department of State, microfilm 893.00/6039, *Report of American Consul at Yunnan-fu,* January 22, 1925 by M. S. Myers.

merchants that they organized a defense force and some of them contributed financially to Ch'en Chiung-ming in the hope that Ch'en would drive Sun out. Sun suppressed this merchant opposition with the military units nominally under his authority; they could not tolerate merchant independence. Sun then went off to Peking to participate in national politics without having solved the problem of getting revenues under his own control.

The Problem of Finances

A militarist system that had grown beyond the most rudimentary stage needed adequate funds for at least four purposes: to compensate the leadership echelons in order to strengthen loyalties and counteract centrifugal tendencies; to provision and pay troops; to procure adequate supplies of arms and munitions; and to pay off rival power groups or bribe their subcommanders. The inexhaustible need for funds by militarist regimes is one of the most evident facts about modern China till the end of the Nationalist period on the mainland. The following examples of military financing are meant only to illustrate problems.

A study of local taxation in the 1920's is found in Gamble's book on Ting *hsien,* a county some thirty miles south of Paoting in Chihli. In 1925 Ting *hsien* had sixty-four tax-collecting units located in twenty-two different centers throughout the county. Any militarist capturing the area would be compelled to use existing institutions and to employ local people to collect taxes for him. The system of tax-farming—letting out taxes to professional collectors by competitive bidding—produced many abuses so far as the taxpayers were concerned but was convenient for an army in need of quick revenue. Land taxes were collected in some regions many years in advance. In the critical years of 1927 and 1928, extra emergency land taxes were collected in Ting *hsien* amounting to 200 per cent and 61 per cent of the normal tax.[2]

Likin was a lucrative and convenient form of taxation on goods in transit. There was a tendency for each regime to set up likin collection stations in its territory, so that during the 1920's China was dotted with over seven hundred such stations. Seven collected tolls in the eighty miles between Tientsin and Peking.[3] In 1927 Fukien province had 41 likin stations collecting a reported Ch. $3,336,000 through tax-farmers.

[2] Sydney D. Gamble, *Ting Hsien: A North China Rural Community* (New York: International Secretariat, Institute of Pacific Relations, 1954), pp. 166–84.

[3] R. H. Tawney, *Land and Labour in China* (London: Allen & Unwin, 1932), pp. 18, 56.

The tax on opium was an indispensable source of revenue for militarists who controlled areas of opium production, transit, or heavy consumption. Opium Suppression Bureaus were agencies to monopolize sale and taxation of opium for the local authority.

Another typical form of raising revenue was to assess a city a certain amount of money with the threat that, if it did not pay, the troops would be permitted to loot. The local merchants' association might be delegated to collect the ransom at a price settled by negotiation.

Powerful regimes settled in favorable territory were able to raise a great deal of revenue by sequestering income from railways or telegraph. An official report of the Chinese Minister of Communications, submitted in September, 1925, estimated that up to the end of 1924 no less than Ch. $180,000,000 had been appropriated from China's railway revenues by different militarists.[4]

The Peking government borrowed large amounts against the security of the Maritime Customs revenue. This allowed the various regimes which controlled Peking to lay hands on immediate cash by contracting debts to be paid from future customs revenues. Nine of these loans, floated between 1914 and 1924 under the guarantee of the Inspector-General of Customs, Sir Francis Aglen, totaled nearly 134 million Chinese dollars.[5]

A militarist regime controlling a province might issue paper currency through the provincial bank. This currency was inadequately secured but would be forced upon the local population. In short, it was a form of tax. Chang Tso-lin had a special currency, the *Feng-p'iao*, which circulated in Manchuria. It was so insecure that Japanese currency tended to become the standard for business transactions. In June, 1927, there were about $55 million worth of Shantung provincial banknotes in circulation in Chang Tsung-ch'ang's satrapy, issued against original silver reserves of only $1.5 million. As Chang's fortunes declined with the approach of the Nationalist armies, the currency depreciated rapidly, and Shantung merchants refused to accept it at par. Chang had a few merchants and local bankers shot as a warning. In re-

[4] Silas H. Strawn, "China Today," *Annual Report, 1926–27,* China Association (London), pp. 13–24.

[5] London, University of London, School of Oriental and African Studies, Sir Frederick Maze Papers, Confidential Vol. 2 (1926–29), copy of a letter from L. A. Lyall, dated 28 May 1927. In the same years the government floated other loans totaling $198 million which Sir Frederick later undertook to repay from Customs revenues. Much of the money, according to Lyall, was spent on armaments.

sponse, the private banks closed and merchants either declined to do business or raised their prices.

Whether a militarist system could acquire a major share of the tax revenues produced in its base depended upon whether it controlled the territory on sufferance of a more powerful organization demanding a share. This was one of the crucial problems of relations within militarist systems.

The case of the salt *gabelle* will clarify the point. This was theoretically a centralized collecting system with all revenues going to the government in Peking. In 1913 a mixed Chinese and foreign inspectorate was established, somewhat on the model of the Maritime Customs Service, to attempt to provide efficient collection and transmission to Peking of all revenues over those owed to bondholders for principal and interest on the 1913 Reorganization loans. By 1927 the system had broken down. All provincial military governors demanded the salt revenue collected in their particular territories. In Fukien during 1926 eight separate armies were independently preying on the salt revenue, and the Salt Inspectorate decided to close the Amoy office because it could collect no revenues.

A similar problem occurred in the Maritime Customs Service. The problem was, who was to control the "Washington surtaxes" added to conventional tariffs? In October, 1926, the Canton government imposed a 2½ per cent surtax to be collected by itself. Thereafter, practically every local regime controlling a port added the surtax and appropriated it regardless of the Peking government, provincial governments, or even the Nationalist government, which was trying to monopolize this revenue in areas under its control.

We may generalize that militarists needed money in large amounts continuously and used all traditional methods to extract it from their bases. If someone discovered a new method, it spread rapidly to other areas where it could be employed. Yet there were two checks, at least, upon the efficacy of various revenue devices—local resistance when pressure became unbearable and the drying up of sources of revenue.

The Problem of Arms

A second indispensable source of power for a military regime was its arms. There were essentially three ways an army could procure arms and munitions: by seizing or buying stocks held by other militarists, by manufacture within the base, or by purchase abroad.

By the 1920's, China had large stocks of rifles, machine guns, and cannons of a great variety of makes which had been produced in Chinese arsenals or purchased from abroad during the process of modernizing China's armed forces. Many wars and suppressions of weaker bands were essentially arms procurement drives.

In the mid-1920's there were about twenty arsenals in China. The most productive seem to have been those at Mukden, Taiyuan, Hanyang, Shanghai, Foochow (naval), and Canton. Possession of a well-operating arsenal was a strategic asset. Yet arms and munitions were imported in great quantity and it was generally cheaper to buy them than to make them.

Importation of arms, munitions, and material destined exclusively for their manufacture was illegal after 1919 for subjects and citizens of Great Britain, Spain, Portugal, the United States, (Czarist) Russia, Brazil, France and Japan, and soon thereafter the Netherlands, Denmark, Belgium, and Italy. The governments party to the Chinese Arms Embargo Agreement abided, on the whole, by the provisions of the agreement. However, certain arms-producing powers were under no obligation to prevent shipment and sale of arms to China—for example, Soviet Russia, Czechoslovakia, Sweden, and Norway. Soviet Russia provided both the southern Nationalist military forces and Feng Yü-hsiang with large amounts of arms and munitions during 1925–27. Smuggling of munitions is a subject which by its nature is difficult for the historian to uncover. There were many foreign agents in Shanghai and other cities who could, for a price, arrange for imports of arms and delivery to a militarist with the money to buy them and the connections to assure their transit inland. There were also a number of British, Japanese, German, American, and other trading firms in China eager to sell machinery and chemicals useful for arsenals, as well as airplanes, trucks, and other equipment of potential military importance. In short, arms procurement was part of the larger complex of foreigners in China.

Some regimes employed foreigners to help in the technical management of arsenals, as advisers or as instructors in their academies, and a few hired foreign mercenaries, White Russian or Japanese, to operate armored trains and artillery, or to serve as shock troops.

Inter-Regime Politics

Practically every base was surrounded by bases controlled by other regimes. This called for a high degree of political skill on the part of a military leader to protect his own base and to manipulate the larger political situation for aggrandizement. Every military leader had to count on the possibility of his rivals combining against him, and he had to protect his rear if he launched a campaign to improve his position.

He must be alert to every conference, troop movement, or arms shipment in a neighbor's regime. He also must keep a sharp eye on his own subordinates and their secret negotiations. Only the crafty and the well-connected could survive. This was an additional reason why militarists employed old bureaucrats skilled at factional intrigue and having wide personal connections.

Many of the stronger military leaders kept ambassadors in other Chinese centers of power to conduct negotiations and to report on conditions and plans in the rival camp. The situation was not unlike international relations, with alliance systems and balances of power. But the system was unstable because military bases were not well-defined and institutionalized nation-states. Few of the important regimes were actually secure in their "own" bases; they might be toppled from within by defection of subordinates. Few bases had clearly demarcated boundaries. The two outstanding exceptions were those of Yen Hsi-shan in Shansi and Chang Tso-lin in Manchuria.

Another great difference between a nation-state and the province-wide bases in China was the absence of institutionalized nationalism. In spite of strong provincialism, the provinces were not nations but parts of the greater China. Provincial regimes could not be buttressed by national loyalty. Defection and treachery were not inhibited by patriotism. Preceding every military campaign there was likely to be extensive secret negotiation to form alliances, neutralize potential rivals, and secure the defection of subunits in the camp of the regime against which the war was to be fought.

The party which was persuaded to turn over required assurance that he and his troops would either be incorporated as an independent unit into the other system or be left in control of his sub-base or given a better one. He must also be promised money and arms.

Some Impressions

The documents and the press of the period leave several strong impressions. One is of political instability—of alarms, threats, and counter-threats, of alliances, defections, and realignments, of campaign after campaign in various parts of China. The second impression is of the brevity of civil wars, if actually fought, and their indecisive nature. Few regimes were permanently knocked out or their troop units destroyed. Defeated brigades or regiments were either incorporated into stronger systems or driven into poorer bases. The line between "banditry" and "legitimacy" was arbitrary.

These impressions evoke an image of constant turmoil, with only one clear line of development—that toward an ever-increasing number of military units and men under arms, and a growing burden of taxes. Estimates of the number of men under arms rise from about 500,000 in 1913 to 1.2 million in 1920. At the end of 1925 the figure may have reached 1.8 or 1.9 million. By July, 1928, at the end of the Northern Expedition, KMT forces were thought to number about 1.6 million and those of the whole country more than 2.2 million.[6]

Rural China provided an unlimited supply of young males eager to enlist for the promise of regular pay. Demobilization was difficult not only because commanders usually refused to reduce their capital—that is, their reputed troop strength—but also because demobilized troops might simply turn to banditry. In a sense, armies were a form of relief for the unemployable. But they were a drain on the nation's scanty resources and contributed very little to the economy.

Another impression is that the turmoil caused by civil wars from 1911 onward, and the increasing but unpredictable taxation, so exhausted the Chinese people that they were prepared to accept any government that seemed likely to end such disorder. During the 1920's, every important commander proclaimed his intention to restore peace and denounced his rivals for fomenting wars. Apparently appeals to public opinion had some importance in inter-regime politics. From 1924 onward, the southern Nationalists expended great efforts in propaganda to persuade the public that they could and would suppress the "northern warlords." This appeal won wide support for their side in internecine conflicts.

Militarists as Products of Their Day

The above discussion is not meant to imply that military leaders in the 1920's were merely power-hungry rulers who had no thought for the good of their country. They may better be characterized as the natural products of their time in China. Many regarded themselves as heirs to a proud tradition of past military heroes who had united the country or preserved the peace in their own regions. Some had had a classical education and aspired to be regarded as officials of culture and learn-

[6] *China Year Book, 1919–20*, (Peking and Tientsin: Tientsin Press) pp. 318–30; *ibid., 1921–22*, pp. 518–19; *ibid., 1926–27*, p. 1065; Kao Yin-chu, *Chung-hua-min-kuo ta-shih-chi* [A Record of Important Events during the Chinese Republic] (Taipei, 1927), p. 300, "July 2, 1928." For a more detailed estimation as of the end of 1928, see the report of Ho Ying-ch'in in *Ke-ming wen-hsien* [Documents of the revolution] vol. 24 (Taipei: 1953 onward), pp. 4856–63 (hereafter cited as KMWH).

ing; they tried to gather intellectuals into their entourages. They were infused with the Confucian idea of benevolent rule. Some believed themselves to be serving the cause of republicanism in "protecting the constitution" or "upholding legitimate government." All were doubtless inspired by sentiments of nationalism.

Wu P'ei-fu, one of the greatest militarists of the decade before 1926, had been educated in the classics. One of the virtues he held to most strongly and demanded of his subordinates was loyalty. He remained loyal to his superior, Ts'ao K'un, although by 1923 he overshadowed him in power and disagreed with him in important policies. As a ruler, General Wu acted very much like a nineteenth-century viceroy. Yet he had a growing sense of modern nationalism. In 1918 Wu P'ei-fu issued a circular telegram expressing the hope that civil officials would not be avaricious nor traitors to the country, that military officials would not contend for territory. He stated his personal law, never to be a military governor, seek sanctuary in a foreign settlement, negotiate with foreigners, or seek a foreign loan. In his manifestoes he urged reunification of China, convocation of a national assembly, and resistance to Japan. In 1924 Wu attempted to reunify China by the only means then possible: through an elaborate chess game of alliances, judicious use of money, and bit-by-bit destruction of rival systems. He might have succeeded but for the defection of one of his most powerful subordinates, Feng Yü-hsiang. This betrayal simply overturned the chessboard. Thereafter Wu P'ei-fu did not entirely live up to one of his announced ideals: he did seek British assistance in 1926 against Feng Yü-hsiang and the Nationalists, who were receiving military supplies from Soviet Russia. But he refused to the last to become a puppet ruler of north China under the Japanese.[7]

Feng Yü-hsiang, who came from a peasant family and had no early formal education, tried to acquire one and to help his troops become literate. He demanded a spartan life from his officers. In the areas he administered, he discharged corrupt officials, promoted public education, established public libraries, orphanages, and rehabilitation centers, and prohibited gambling, prostitution, and the use of opium. He used his troops to repair city walls, build roads, plant trees, and work at flood control, all in the fine tradition of viceroy Tso Tsung-t'ang during the 1870's. His credo was benevolent rule on behalf of the common people. Though strongly nationalistic in his outlook, he compro-

[7] Odoric Wou, "Wu P'ei-fu" (M.A. thesis, University of Hong Kong, 1965).

mised this position by accepting aid first from Japan and then from Soviet Russia.[8]

Ch'en Chiung-ming of Kwangtung received both a classical education and a period of training in Japan, where he came under revolutionary influences and became an advocate of constitutional government. When in control of south Fukien in 1918–20, he supported the new culture movement, financed study abroad for at least eighty students, supported the KMT organ *Chien-she* ("Reconstruction") in Shanghai, and invited a group of anarchists to assist his educational work. When he won military control of Kwangtung in 1920 he undertook the educational modernization of the province and invited Ch'en Tu-hsiu to preside over these reforms. He also took steps to inaugurate representative government and clean administration, and even had published a draft constitution for Kwangtung which expressly forbade military interference with civil rule, and established a limit of 30 per cent of the budget for military purposes, with at least 20 per cent of the budget to be spent on education—which was to be compulsory at the elementary level.[9] His conflicts with Sun Yat-sen and military defeat by Chiang Kai-shek have obscured from popular knowledge this interesting reformer and cast him into the role of a "warlord."

These examples will serve to show that military leaders were influenced in various degrees by the ideological currents and the reformist plans of the early Republican period. Such men and the military-political regimes over which they presided could not, however, produce a reunified country. No such regime was powerful enough to prevail over the rest. How had such a situation come about?

Factors Giving Rise to Twentieth-Century Separatism and Militarism

No *single* explanation for the emergence of militarism in China will get us far in understanding how the phenomenon arose or why it has arisen many times during China's long history.

[8] James E. Sheridan, *Chinese Warlord: The Career of Feng Yü-hsiang* (Stanford: Stanford University Press, 1966).

[9] Winston Hsieh, "The Ideas and Ideals of a Warlord: Ch'en Chiung-ming (1878–1933)," *Papers on China,* from Seminars at Harvard University, vol. 16 (Cambridge, Mass.: East Asia Research Center, Harvard University, 1962), pp. 198–252.

Latent Factors

Several factors inherent in China's geography and history might conduce to the rise of autonomous military-political regimes if the general political situation made such a development possible. Differences in topography and climate throughout the great land mass we now call China resulted in varying cultural adaptations that are evident from the dawn of Chinese history. The gradual expansion of the Chinese realm brought into one nation peoples of diverse cultures, while the frequent invasions of China by peoples from outside its frontiers brought in other groups with non-Chinese attributes. These historic processes left residues of ethnic and linguistic differences between the populations in various parts of the empire, as well as separate traditions, which presented obstacles to political unity. Merely to call to mind the differences in speech and customs between the peoples of Shantung and Kwangtung or of Szechwan and Chekiang will make this evident. Even such adjoining provinces as Kwangtung and Hunan had markedly different dialects and historical traditions. Thus centrifugal tendencies were always powerful, and the area we think of as China was divided for periods nearly as long as those in which it was united. Yet the historical trend from Mongol times onward was toward national unity; periods of disunity were brief.

China's size and poor communications created great obstacles to centralized control over the diverse regions, provinces, and local districts. Statesmen tried to solve this problem through the device of the imperial institution acting through civil and military bureaucracies recruited and controlled by the imperial government and infused with a common ideology. This ideology, "Confucianism," was also purposely inculcated in the vast population in order to internalize a spirit of social harmony and obedience to the imperial will.

The ethic of loyalty to closely related individuals—parents, kin, teachers, sponsors—and to small collectivities such as family, clan, village, and common-interest associations, was stronger in China than loyalty to abstract ideals such as impartial justice or the nation; it was probably stronger even than loyalty to the emperor. This ethic often expressed itself in the tendency toward cliques and factions in bureaucracies and other large collectivities. Such factions were organized along lines of personal attachment or common provincial origin for mutual protection and advancement of the members. In a society characterized by intense struggle for advancement and security, and lacking a system of impartial law or strongly developed institutions outside the state which could protect the individual, the control of military power—from local militia or bandit gangs up to provincial forces or regional armies —was extremely important for ambitious men and cliques.

Thus the geographic expanse and diversity of China, the cultural and linguistic differences and separate historic traditions among its people, and the ethic of particularistic loyalty conduced in times of stress to regional separatism and military autonomy. Such tendencies might prevail against the counter-tendency of political unity and centralized control if the one over-arching institution—the imperial government—was weak. When the central government was weak, power gravitated to men with the sword—a phenomenon not peculiar to China. Such was the case during the closing decades of the Ch'ing dynasty.

Recent Historical Developments

China's military regimes as they existed in the 1920's were the outgrowth of a long development in which we may distinguish several important strands.[10] One was the creation of provincial or regional armies under such leaders as Tseng Kuo-fan, Tso Tsung-t'ang, and Li Hung-chang in the 1850's and 1860's to combat the Taiping and other rebel forces attempting either to overthrow the Manchu dynasty or to detach border areas from imperial control. These provincial armies were internally unified by ties of personal loyalty within their officer corps. The commanders who organized these forces and who then were appointed as provincial governors and viceroys gained considerable control of local finances, and organized their own staffs of experts and infiltrated them into the imperial bureaucracy. The armies gradually declined in military effectiveness and were replaced by more modern forces trained along Western lines and equipped with modern arms. They had left, however, an important legacy—erosion of centralized control over military power. The imperial government no longer firmly controlled the armed forces or disposed the finances of the separate provinces.

The modernization of China's armies during the last three decades of the Manchu dynasty was carried out by Chinese viceroys such as

[10] The following is based on W. L. Bales, *Tso Tsung-t'ang: Soldier and Statesman of Old China* (Shanghai: Kelly and Walsh, 1937); Stanley Spector, *Li Hung-chang and the Huai Army: A Study in Nineteenth Century Chinese Regionalism* (Seattle: University of Washington Press, 1964); Ralph L. Powell, *The Rise of Chinese Military Power, 1895–1912* (Princeton: Princeton University Press, 1955).

Li Hung-chang, Chang Chih-tung, and Liu K'un-i. These men operated in their various domains with some coordination between their efforts and yet with much factional rivalry. They created separate military academies to train officers, built arsenals, hired Western instructors and technicians, and purchased arms abroad using such provinicial finances as they controlled or, with permission of the Court, percentages of specified customs revenues. The form of army building strengthened the trend toward regional autonomy. This autonomy was evident during the Sino-Japanese War of 1894–95, and was clearly shown during the Boxer disturbance of 1900.

After the military disasters of 1900, Yüan Shih-k'ai began to rebuild the Peiyang Army in the north. It became China's strongest force. Yüan used senior officers loyal to himself and trained junior officers in his military academies. The Peiyang Army played a crucial role in the elimination of the Manchu dynasty and the imperial institution and made possible Yüan's ascendancy as China's first president from 1912 to 1916.

Parallel to the development of the Peiyang Army, other modern armies had been formed in Hunan and Hupei by Chang Chih-tung, in the Nanking viceroyalty by Liu K'un-i, and in Fukien, Kwangtung, Szechwan, and the southwestern provinces. After the Revolution of 1911–12, these southern units, outside the Peiyang system, tried to maintain their independence from Yüan's control. Many of them opposed Yüan's effort to make himself emperor in 1915–16.

After Yüan's death, his generals became the principal holders of military power throughout most of China. Then the Peiyang Army itself broke apart into several contending factions. There were many other armies in China with long histories and independent territorial bases of power, and new ones were quickly formed. Thousands of Chinese had been trained as military officers in the provincial military schools, the Paoting Academy, or Japan. China had many arsenals operating in separate provinces and foreign-made arms had been imported in large amounts. Thus a once unified political system became fragmented.

This account of the development of military separatism does not imply an autonomous process. Other important historic processes closely interacted with it and with each other in the nineteenth and early part of the twentieth century. We may mention the gradual breakdown of the Chinese social fabric in the nineteenth century under the pressure of a rapidly growing population and increasing economic inequality between social classes; the decay of the imperial institution and decline in the efficiency of the Ch'ing bureaucracy; and foreign competition for paramountcy over parts of China's territory and wealth. Western imperialism challenged the old order while Western nations and Japan provided new models for government and social organization. Confucianism as the national ethical system withered under the competition of many alien ideologies such as Christianity, republicanism, social Darwinism, socialism, Marxism-Leninism, and, above all, nationalism. Nor should we forget the influences exerted by individuals upon events and popular attitudes, individuals such as the Empress Dowager Tz'u-hsi, and Kuang-hsü Emperor, K'ang Yu-wei, Yen Fu, Liang Ch'i-ch'ao, Sun Yat-sen, Ch'en Tu-hsiu, and Hu Shih, to mention only a few. Likewise the rulers of military satrapies were Chinese human beings. They were the products of their environment, thought as Chinese, had aspirations for their country as well as for themselves. To use the term "warlord" to embrace such a diversity of human personalities as Wu P'ei-fu, Chang Tso-lin, Yen Hsi-shan, Ch'en Chiung-ming, Feng Yü-hsiang, Li Tsung-jen, or Chiang Kai-shek and a great many other leaders of military-political regimes may conceal more than it reveals. They all operated within a system which none of them had created.

Nationalist Efforts to Overcome Regional Separatism, 1922–1926

By 1922 it was evident that China could not be reunited through establishing the imperial system again, nor through agreement among the great military factions, nor through federation of independent provinces. National unity could be reimposed only through military force. Wu P'ei-fu, fresh from a victory over the Manchurian army in the first Chihli-Fengtien War, and Sun Yat-sen, spurred by defeat in an internecine struggle with Ch'en Chiung-ming, each began an attempt to achieve national unity. Wu failed. Sun died while the process he inaugurated with Russian help was in its embryo. His main successor, Chiang Kai-shek devoted twenty-five harassed years struggling to unify the country and might have succeeded except for Japanese, American, and Russian interference.

Unification of China and re-creation of central authority could begin only from within the militarist system itself. Sun's minimum requirements were a strong base, adequate finances, arms and disciplined troops, and, above all, strong cohesion within his system. Foreign aid would add an element of power, depending upon its nature and extent. Sun had always searched eagerly for foreign financial and technical support. He also played the Chinese alliance game, seeking help from holders of real regional power in the effort to topple whatever faction held Peking—that mystic center of legitimacy, whose government received foreign recognition and steady revenue almost automatically.

But military power, foreign aid, and alliances were not enough. Every major faction attempted to utilize these, yet none had been able to accumulate enough preponderance to break the system of regional separatism, not even Yüan Shih-k'ai with his Peiyang Army and foreign financial support. Some additional power would be necessary. This power was ideology. In China after 1919 nationalism was undoubtedly the most potent ideological force. It could galvanize educated youth, appeal to urban dwellers and overseas Chinese, and infuse officers and troops with a unique élan. If nationalistic spirit could be mobilized in support of one military faction against its rivals, the balance of power might be overturned.

It was the combination of mobilized nationalism, concentrated military power, and adequate initial finances which allowed the Canton regime to push to the Yangtze in 1926, toppling rival factions. Then, after consolidating a base in the lower Yangtze, a reorganized nationalist coalition—but a coalition of still independent military factions—succeeded in capturing Peking. This success was not enough to overcome regional military autonomy. We shall offer an explanation after describing the general trends in a complex process by which Sun and his successor built their preponderant power between 1923 and 1928.

Sun Yat-sen: The Man and His Program

Dr. Sun Yat-sen[11] was a man of broader vision than any of his major rivals who headed military factions. He was personally more nationalistic and more sympathetic to social reformist currents than such men as Wu P'ei-fu, Tuan Ch'i-jui, or Chang Tso-lin. He dreamed large dreams for China—its reunification, emancipation from foreign controls, and modernization. The man of destiny at the center of those dreams was Sun himself. Though rather shallowly educated in both Western and Chinese thought, Sun had been a world traveler before 1912, and he was an eager reader of foreign and Chinese books. Probably he understood social and intellectual trends in China better than

[11] This and the following section condense my papers "Sun Yat-sen and Soviet Russia, 1922–1924," prepared for Columbia University's University Seminar on Modern East Asia: China, March 1965; and "Forging the Weapons: Sun Yat-sen and the Kuomintang in Canton, 1924" (issued privately, 1966). Each is documented (Columbia University).

most of his rivals, and he knew the outer world much better than any of them. Nevertheless, he was notably unsuccessful in his efforts to enlist foreign power, except toward the end of his life when he won the aid of revolutionary Russia. Till 1923 he was a failure as a leader of military coalitions; he could never get the substance of power under personal control. Yet he had other bases of strength—a nationalistic political organization, continuous financial support from overseas Chinese, and a name widely revered in his native Kwangtung and generally respected among persons of modern education throughout China. He usually kept around himself—partly because of his magnetic personality, partly because of his control over the Chunghua Kemingtang and then the Chungkuo KMT—a group of talented men, skillful in money-raising, in propaganda, and in contacts with influential men throughout the country such as secret society leaders, influential gentry, businessmen, labor-union organizers, military leaders, local politicians, and student activists.

In August, 1922, Sun's power was at low ebb; he was a refugee in Shanghai with no regional base and very little military support. He immediately set about to reestablish his tarnished reputation, to secure foreign support, to revitalize the KMT, to gather money from overseas Chinese, to form alliances, to smuggle arms, and to get money to military groups which might win back his base in Canton.

In these efforts Sun succeeded rather remarkably. His KMT comrades rallied and helped him plan the party's rejuvenation. By judicious use of funds raised mainly from his overseas supporters, some of Sun's aides were able to buy the support of small Yunnan and Kwangsi armies which, in collaboration with a Kwangtung division loyal to Sun, succeeded in driving Ch'en Chiung-ming out of Canton. Soviet Russia, which was seeking a Chinese nationalist movement to turn against "the imperialists" and which was having difficulties in negotiating a treaty of recognition with the Peking government, agreed to come to his aid—under certain conditions. Dr. Sun thus was able to return to Canton on February 21, 1923. He then began the slow and difficult process of building a base of military power and a national strength resting upon organization and ideology. He died on March 12, 1925, while the process was still in its early stages.

Main Trends and Crucial Problems

The general trends up to July, 1926, were these: In the field of organization, a nationalistic party was re-created with a hierarchical structure resting upon a broad membership throughout the nation and among

Chinese overseas, but with a small group of leaders at the top making policy and directing the party's activities. This top leadership began gradually to direct a government and the military forces in the base area, and it aspired to direct a variety of mass organizations that were created throughout the country. The party membership was infused with an ideology. This called for a national revolution to end foreign domination, to destroy rival military regimes and create a single national government, and to introduce social reforms which would gradually correct economic inequities among various sectors of the population and set the nation on a process of modernization. The leadership publicized these nationalistic goals through a revitalized propaganda organization in order to attract new members and broad support for the party's goals. In the gradually enlarged base area of Kwangtung, the leaders created a governmental system which succeeded in enlarging revenue and centralizing control over its collection and distribution. They created a military organization, relatively well armed, trained, disciplined, and indoctrinated; but their most important accomplishment was to bring all the units in this military system increasingly (though not entirely) under centralized control. These accomplishments resulted from strenuous efforts by party veterans and newly recruited younger activists—many from the Chinese Communist Party (CCP) and its Youth Corps—and from Russian assistance.

The main weakness was disagreement among the leaders concerning the social goals of the national revolution and disagreement over priorities as between social revolution and national unification. Among the KMT leaders there was a broad spectrum of opinion ranging from mildly reformist to social revolutionary, between conservatism and radicalism. This was the result not so much of the mixed class character of the party as of competing ideologies among intellectuals throughout China. These ideologies ranged from advocacy of the restoration of the Confucian value systems, pragmatic step-by-step social and economic reform, anarchism, and reformist socialism, to radical social revolution according to Marxist-Leninist prescriptions. The various leaders of the party differed (depending upon their personal educational experiences, temperaments, clique alignments, economic interests, and previous efforts to articulate an ideological synthesis) on the issues of how much social revolution China needed and what means should be used to bring about change. Sun Yat-sen, through considering himself a Socialist and a revolutionary, was unable to articulate a consistent set of social goals or to clarify the methods to be used in revolution. By temperament he was a reformist and gradualist, and he disapproved of violent struggle between classes as the means to refashion Chinese society. He favored "broadening" the revolution to include as many classes and segments of the population as possible as against "deepening" the revolution in favor of certain classes at the expense of others.

Yet Dr. Sun, acting under the pressure of Russians from whom he sought material support, admitted and even welcomed into the KMT the members of a small CCP numbering only a few hundred nationalistic, idealistic, and activist intellectuals. This party was dedicated to social revolution, became more and more committed in practice to class struggle, and had as its goal a second-stage revolution which the CCP rather than the KMT would direct. The ideas and goals of the Communist leaders could not be hidden from other Nationalist leaders. In working toward them the CCP tried to maximize its influence within the KMT; to expel the more conservative KMT leaders who, for their part, attempted to expel the Communists; and to monopolize control over mass movements among labor, farmers, and youth, which previously had been fields in which older KMT leaders worked.

In short, the CCP, within the revolutionary alliance, was attempting to gain control over the national revolutionary movement. Its leaders favored some social revolution during the course of national unification. Yet the strategic decision to work within the KMT—based upon the theory of a two-stage revolution (first national-bourgeois, then proletarian-socialist)—compelled the Russian and Chinese Communist leadership to moderate the drive to power within the KMT and to restrain the mass movement as far as possible from disruptive violence.

Thus the broader goals of the national revolution were ambiguous, and the movement was permeated by conflict. After Dr. Sun's death in March, 1925, the movement was marked by struggles for power to direct the national revolution. These struggles impeded, though they did not block, the trend toward accumulating real power and centralization of control outlined above.

Nationalist Accomplishments in Building Power

In the period from autumn of 1923 to January, 1926, KMT membership within China increased from a few thousand to a figure possibly in excess of 200,000 that could be numerated by the Canton center.[12]

[12] Membership figures for the Kuomintang (KMT) were reported by T'an P'ing-shan, head of the KMT Organization Department, at the Second Kuomintang Congress in January 1926. He used round numbers and left out enrollments in army units, ships, and police, as well as those enrolled in some provinces (e.g. Chihli, Anhui, Fengtien, Shansi, Shensi, Kewichow, and Yun-

A central structure was created which had several small policy-making bodies—the Standing Committee of the Central Executive Committee, a Political Council, a Government Council, and a Military Council— as well as functional operating bureaus concerned with Party Organization, Propaganda, Overseas Chinese, Youth, Labor, Farmers, Women, and the Military. There were also party organs in China's major cities charged with enlarging the membership and directing its activity in regions, provinces, and the largest urban centers. The KMT expanded its publications and increased their effectiveness in propaganda. The principal architects of this rejuvenation and expansion were Dr. Sun, Liao Chung-k'ai (assassinated August 20, 1925), Hu Han-min, Wang Ching-wei, and Borodin (Mikhail M. Grusenberg); but many other party veterans and new recruits used their creative energy, organizing talents, contacts, financial skills, and gifted pens to bring it about.

Expansion, more effective organization, and increased militancy characterized the mass movements after 1924. These movements were unionized labor, farmers' associations, and organized students. Membership in unions under the direction of a National General Labor Union grew from a reported 540,000 in May, 1925, to a reported 1,241,000 in May, 1926.[13] All such figures are suspect, but great growth is not. The national body and several of its major constituent federa-

---

nan) and some cities (e.g. Shanghai, Hankow) for which reports were unavailable. The figures given come to 148,700, of which 23,000 were in Canton and 48,000 in the rest of Kwangtung. *Chungkuo Kuomintang ti-erh-tz'u tai-piao ta-hui hui-chi-lu* [Records of the Second Kuomintang Congress of Representatives] (Central Executive Committee of the Kuomintang, April, 1926), pp. 31–32. A somewhat more complete numeration, based upon reports made by provincial and municipal branches at the Second Congress, is found in *Chung-kuo Kuomintang cheng-li tang-wu chih t'ung-chi pao-kao* [Statistical report on the work of party adjustment of the Chinese Nationalist Party] (Organization Department of the Central Executive Committee, March, 1929). A supplement gives a total of 212,281 persons registered, but figures for most provinces are in suspiciously round numbers and there are no figures for three provinces and three major cities. Kwangsi is alleged to have 96,367 members!

[13] The May, 1925, figures appear in *Ti-i-tz'u kuo-nei ke-ming chan-cheng shih-ch'i ti kung-jen yun-tung* [The labor movement during the period of the First Revolutionary Civil War] (Peking: Peoples Publishing Company, 1963), p. 50, from an article published in *Hsiang-tao chou-pao* [The Guide Weekly], May 17, 1925; and in the Manifesto of the Congress quoted by Teng Chung-hsia, *Chung-kuo chih-kung yun-tung chien-shih* [A brief history of the Chinese labor movement] (Hua-chung Hsin-hua shu-tien, 1949), p. 136. The May, 1926, figures appear in an article by "Lo-sheng" (a pseudonym), entitled "Ti-san-tz'e ch'uan-kuo lao-tung ta-hui chih ching-kuo chi ch'i chieh-

tions were controlled by Communists. There were many other unions, however, whose leaders refused to permit them to fall under Communist control. The Farmers Movement grew from practically no organized membership in 1924 to 626,457 members in May, 1926 in Kwangtung alone.[14] These associations were knit together in a hierarchical structure whose directing organs, the National Farmers Association and the Kwangtung Provincial Farmers Association, were controlled by Communists. The national student movement became strong and militant. But the competition was intense by late 1925 between rival KMT centers in Canton and Shanghai and between the KMT and the CCP for control of the student movement. The remarkable growth of these mass organizations from mid-1925 onward was partly a result of the anti-imperialist movement, which KMT and Communist leaders directed particularly against British interests in China. The spurs were the May 30th Incident in Shanghai and the June 23rd Incident in Canton.

These events, in which Chinese were shot down on their own soil by foreign-controlled police and foreign troops, had a tremendous emotional impact in China. They intensified hostility to foreigners and their special privileges, enhanced the image of Soviet Russia, drew popular support to the KMT, which had been promising to end the "unequal treaties," and damaged the reputations of northern military factions and the credibility of the Peking government, which showed itself unable to protect China and was accused of being in league with imperialists.

Young Communists, working under the banner of the national revo-

kuo" [The Experiences and Results of the Third National Labor Conference], published in *Hsiang-tao chou-pao,* no. 155, May 5, 1926, and reprinted in [The labor movement during the period of the First Revolutionary Civil War], p. 219.

[14] The May, 1926, figures on the Kwangtung Provincial Farmers Association come from *Chung-kuo nung-min wen-t'i* [The problem of Chinese farmers] (January, 1927); reprinted in *Ti-i-tz'u kuo-nei ke-ming chan-cheng shih-ch'i ti nung-min yun-tung* [The farmers' movement during the period of the First Revolutionary Civil War] (Peking: Peoples Publishing Company, 1953), pp. 38–39. A figure for June 3, 1926, shows 647,766 members in Kwangtung and 981,441 nationally (*ibid.,* pp. 17–18). A careful study by T. C. Chang of Lingnan University in Canton, made in the spring or early summer of 1927, shows itemized enrollments of members in 6,442 village unions which total 823,338 members, but the precise date is not given. I judge it to be late 1926 or early 1927. *The Farmer's Movement in Kwangtung* (Shanghai: National Christian Council of China, 1928), p. 16.

lution, were exceptionally active in the anti-imperialist movement; as a consequence, the party grew from less than a thousand members in January, 1925, to about 10,000 by the end of the year, according to an inside Communist history. It continued to grow rapidly and increased its grip on the labor-union movement and the Farmers Association. The Communist Youth organization grew from 2,365 members in the summer of 1923 to about 9,000 by September, 1925.[15] By July, 1926, there were approximately 30,000 members in the CCP. Its members were still far fewer than those in the KMT, but the latter included enrollments en masse of some army units, the Canton police, schools, etc.

The Creation of a Base

The KMT excelled in building governmental and military power in its base around Canton. To put it most simply, governmental power meant the ability to collect taxes and control the distribution of revenues. This required centralized control over military forces. So long as military commanders were subordinate to no other power, they appointed their own tax collectors and dispensed revenues within their own systems. In 1924, Canton and the surrounding towns in the delta were garrisoned by autonomous military groups, mostly extra-provincial. Dr. Sun's Generalissimo's Headquarters, the provincial government, and the Canton municipal government received only a small part of the taxes collected. Large parts of Kwangtung were not even nominally under the Generalissimo's control. In 1924, the provincial revenues collected by the government at Canton, or at least under its notice, totaled about eight million Chinese dollars. For the first six months of 1925 revenue collection was running at the same rate—$4,099,254. In the last six months of 1925, after the organization of a national government, receipts from Kwangtung were $14,913,247. In July, 1926, income of the "national" and Kwangtung provincial treasury was $14,731,207— nearly as much as the entire income of the last half of 1925.[16]

[15] C. Martin Wilbur and Julie Lien-ying How, *Documents on Communism, Nationalism, and Soviet Advisers in China 1918–1927* (New York: Columbia University Press, 1956), pp. 90, 94.

[16] George Sokolsky, "A Visit to Hongkong and Canton," *China Express and Telegraph* [1926, London], reprinted from *North China Herald*, April 24, May 1, and May 8, 1926. Information supplied by T. V. Soong, who became Minister of Finance after the assassination of Liao Chung-k'ai in August, 1925. The figures are supported in a Japanese report of the Investigation Section of the Taiwan Government-General, based on investigations by Kiwata Ide, a customs officer of the Taiwan Government-General in Taiwan. Sotōku Kanbō Chōsaka, *Shina no kokumin kakumei to kokumin seifu* [The Chinese

These financial improvements were made possible by the creation of new fiscal institutions and tightening up of the entire revenue system, the subjugation of some extra-provincial armies, and enlargement of the base through conquest. In August, 1924, the KMT established a Central Bank in Canton, initially financed by a Russian loan. This bank was proclaimed to be the government's financial agent, with exclusive rights to float foreign and domestic bonds, issue banknotes, and serve as the government's treasury for all receipts and disbursements.[17] Under the management of Dr. Sun's Harvard- and Columbia-trained brother-in-law, T. V. Soong, the bank gradually was able to assume these powers. After suppressing the Yunnan and Kwangsi forces of Generals Yang Hsi-min and Liu Chen-huan in Canton during the second week of June, 1925, the triumphant KMT leaders decided that no military commander would be permitted to collect taxes and that all funds must go through the civil treasury. The Second Kuomintang Congress in a Resolution on Finance, passed on January 19, 1926, strongly affirmed the necessity for centralized control of all taxation and government spending, and strict adherence to adopted budgets.[18] When George Sokolsky visited Canton in March, 1926, he was told that Mr. Soong, by then Minister of Finance, had brought all financial agencies under one department and had set up an espionage and anti-smuggling bureau to prevent corruption; Sokolsky also learned that over 90 per cent of the provincial revenue was being collected by the government

---

National Revolution and the Nationalist Government of China], Minami Shina oyobi Nanyō Chōsa [Investigation of South China and the Southern Seas], vol. 2, no. 152, p. 216. (I am indebted to Mr. Akira Kurihara for translating this item.) *The British Chamber of Commerce Journal* (Shanghai) 12 (May, 1927): 131, gives a figure of $7,896,000 as receipts of the province of Kwangtung in 1924, less than 1/12 of the revenue collected in 1926, which it lists as $100,136,000. Also *Ts'ai-cheng pao-kao* [Financial reports], a collection of reports of the Nationalist government, mostly from 1925 to 1934, given by Mr. Ch'en Kuo-fu to the KMT Archives, no. 444/19. This is the fourth item in the collection.

[17] *Kuo-fu nien-p'u* [A chronological biography of the Father of the Country] (Taipei: 1965), pp. 1044–45, August 2, 1924; *North China Herald,* August 23, p. 287. In a speech at the opening of the Bank, Dr. Sun Yat-sen stated that its establishment had been made possible by a foreign loan of $10 million. *Kuo-fu ch'üan-chi* [Complete works of the Father of the Country], vol. 3 (Taipei: 1961), p. 488. The exact figure is given in a later Russian source. I. Ermashev, *Sun Yat-sen,* ed. S. L. Tikhvinskii (Moscow: 1964), p. 295.

[18] *Chungkuo Kuomintang ti-erh-tz'u tai-piao ta-hui hui-chi-lu,* pp. 184–88.

and that banknotes of the Central Bank were always valued at par and were accepted by the Customs to the exclusion of all other currency. Mayor C. C. Wu showed Sokolsky one day's reports of cash receipts, expenditures, and the municipal bank balance, all duly signed by the appropriate officers; he informed Sokolsky that every municipal department had to deposit collected revenues in the provincial treasury within twenty-four hours.[19]

The KMT organized in Kwangtung a National Revolutionary Army, which by mid-1926 numbered approximately 100,000 officers and men who were, in varying degrees, well trained, armed, battle-tested, and indoctrinated. An important institutional step had been the creation of an officers academy at Whampoa Island near Canton. The academy had enrolled some 4,900 cadets by mid-1926, mostly drawn from high schools and colleges all over China.[20] These cadets, under the general supervision of their commandant, Chiang Kai-shek, were systematically indoctrinated with the KMT's ideology of a national revolution to unify the country and drive out foreign imperialism, and were exhorted to love and protect the common people. They were given military training by Chinese instructors who were products of the Paoting Military Academy, lesser Chinese military schools, or the Japanese officers academy. A group of Russian military officers also gave valuable training in low-level command, military tactics, the use of various types of weapons, engineering, and communications. Upon graduation from their short-term course these cadets were commissioned as junior officers in the "Party Army" which was gradually expanded into three divisions making up the First Army Corps of the National Revolutionary Army. This Party Army, commanded by General Chiang Kai-shek, gained battle experience in three campaigns during 1925: the First Eastern Expedition in February and March against a coalition of militarists under Ch'en Chiung-ming; the liquidation of the mercenary armies holding Canton under Generals Yang and Liu in June; and a Second Eastern Expedition in October and November which finally

[19] Sokolsky, "A Visit to Hongkong and Canton."

[20] There are many accounts of Whampoa Military Academy. The figure is based on a "Student Directory" published in 1938, cited in Richard B. Landis, "The Origins of Whampoa Graduates Who Served in the Northern Expedition," *Studies on Asia, 1964* (Lincoln, Neb.), p. 150. See also A. I. Cherepanov, *Zapiski Voennogo Sovetnika v Kitae; iz Istorii Pervoi Grazhdanskoi Revolutsionnoi Voiny, 1924–1927* [Notes of a military adviser in China: From the history of the First Revolutionary Civil War in China, 1924–1927] Moscow: Academy of Sciences of the USSR, Institut Narodov Azii, "Nauka," 1964) pp. 92, 126.

suppressed the coalition under Ch'en. Nationalist official historians have attempted to create the impression that these battles were won by Chiang and the Party Army almost single-handedly, but that impression does not accord with the facts. Other armies supporting the KMT participated in all three campaigns and in the conquest of south Kwangtung in November and December and the capture of Hainan Island in January, 1926. By early 1926, the KMT and its creations, the Nationalist Government and the National Revolutionary Army, were becoming masters of Kwangtung, and the government was striving to gain full control over provincial revenues.

Yet the National Revolutionary Army was still something of a patch-work early in 1926, without consistent organization and lacking standardized equipment. The First Army Corps had three divisions and numbered about 10,600 men. The Second Army Corps, mostly made up of Hunanese Troops and under the command of T'an Yen-k'ai, consisted of some 15,000 troops organized merely into nine regiments and three independent battalions. The Third Army Corps, commanded by Chu P'ei-te and made up largely of Yunnan and Kwangsi troops, numbered about 14,000, of whom about half had rifles; it had two divisions, two independent brigades, and one independent regiment. The Fourth Army Corps, the old Kwangtung Army, was commanded by Li Chi-shen; it consisted of two divisions and three independent regiments, but its size was uncertain, for it was campaigning and incorporating defeated troops. The Fifth Army Corps was the private preserve of the one-time bandit chief Li Fu-lin; it garrisoned Honam Island south of the city of Canton, but General Li did not report his troop strength to the Military Council, of which he was a member. There were also three independent divisions of unknown strength. The head of the Russian military advisers in Canton, General Nikolai V. Kuibyshev, who went under the name of Kisan'ka, reported in late 1925 to the Military Attaché of the Soviet Embassy in Peking that "it is difficult at present to ascertain the total number of men in the National Revolutionary Army because most of the smaller units are in contact with the Operations Department only when requesting funds from the Military Council."[21]

The Military Council was the policy-making and coordinating body for military affairs, made up of the most prestigious political leaders of the KMT and the more powerful military commanders. Its member-

[21] Wilbur and How, *Documents on Communism*, pp. 191–92. Kisan'ka's Report was probably dated around the end of December, 1925.

ship shifted with changes in political influence and military power. Under it there was a General Staff with a Chinese head and a Russian adviser for each department and General Victor P. Rogachev as actual Chief of Staff. It was a technical group with the objective of standardizing and unifying the armed forces; it had theoretical power to determine army sizes and finances, though as yet it could not do so.[22] The Military Council attempted to gain control over the Kwangtung Arsenal by appointing a supervisor and legislating an end to the practice of each general ordering and paying for arms and munitions independently. The Council was not yet able to enforce this order.[23]

There were two other devices for improving the quality of the armies under the National Revolutionary Army. One was schools for lower officers. Four of these varied greatly in quality. In January, 1926, the Military Council decided to create a Central Military and Political Academy directly under itself, with the goal of a centralized and standardized system of training lower officers and retraining higher ones; the training was to be supervised by the party and was to include political indoctrination. Separate schools were to be abolished and their resources and students concentrated in the one Academy.[24]

The second device was creation of Political Training Departments in the National Revolutionary Army "to promote political education, instill a national revolutionary spirit, raise fighting capacity, solidify discipline, and realize Sun Yat-senism in the Army."[25] Kuomintang Party Representatives were to work at all levels of the armed forces, from army headquarteres down to platoon. They had authority in political affairs equal to that of officers in military matters. In higher-level military organs, the Party Representatives were to have powers and duties identical with those of the respective commanding officers and were to countersign their orders, which would otherwise not be valid. This effort to introduce the Soviet Russian commissar system was loaded with potential conflict. Nevertheless, Party Representatives were appointed

[22] *Ibid.*, pp. 167, 190, 212.

[23] *Ibid.*, p. 193.

[24] *Ibid.*, pp. 168, 202–4.

[25] *Ibid.*, p. 200, quoting "Regulations of Political Departments in the National Revolutionary Army," probably dated December, 1925, or January, 1926. A somewhat modified and expanded set of Regulations was officially promulgated on March 19, 1926. *KMWH*, vol. 12, pp. 1818–21. The March 19 Regulations are preceded by "Organizational Outlines of the Political Training Department of the Military Council" in four chapters and 26 articles. *Ibid.*, pp. 1814–18.

throughout army corps and divisions, and Political Training Departments were organized in many units before the Northern Punitive Expedition began.

Since this work of military reorganization was carried out with the advice and financial support of a group of Russian military officers, it may serve to paraphrase a part of a history of the National Revolutionary Army[26] sent by one of them to the Russian Embassy in Peking, probably in March, 1926. Summarizing accomplishments since December, 1925, he reported: (1) A military tribunal was established to curb arbitrary actions of commanders. (2) Functions of the KMT Political Bureau, Military Council, General Staff, and army administrative organs had been clearly defined. (3) One of the most influential generals, Li Chi-shen, had been appointed Chief of the General Staff. (4) The Commission for Reorganization of the Army had completed its work in two corps. Army units were being reorganized in accordance with the new consolidated budget of the National Revolutionary Army, staff work of the armies was being set in order, and efforts were underway to enumerate personnel, arms, and munitions. (5) A new grouping of armies was nearly complete. The Central Military and Political Academy had been established, and other schools were being abolished; courses of instruction were being given officers in several army units; a great volume of books, pamphlets, and handbills on military and political topics had been issued, and a daily army newspaper was being published in 18,000 copies and sent to the various military units. (6) The ranks were being cleared of bandits, opium smokers, and old soldiers, and preparation of training programs for garrison and field service and rifle practice had been started. (7) The Central Administration of Supplies had been set up, while local organs of supply and a system of accountability and control had been started. A fixed military budget had been put into effect, and budgets for all army units were fixed. The work in the arsenal had been improved so that the problem of munitions supply was solved. (8) Political sections, the system of political commissars, and KMT nuclei had been instituted in almost all army units, while cultural and educational work was being started in all units. "It must be recognized," so the report concluded, "that with regard to the reorganization of the army, its centralization, and closer connection with the Kuomintang, a great work has been accomplished, in spite of the limited financial resources of the Government and the

[26] This report probably was one of those discovered in the office of the Soviet Military Attaché raided by Peking police on April 6, 1927.

great difficulty and obstacles with which it was confronted when carrying through even minor innovations."

In short, the National Revolutionary Army early in 1926 was in the process of being centralized, rationalized, and politicized.

Other Factors and Developments

Russian aid to the KMT was highly important in strengthening the party in its bid for national power. This aid was shrouded in secrecy at the time and the facts seem to have been obscured since then by both sides, so it is difficult to present a clear picture of its scale.

Russian advisers, both political and military, assisted in strengthening the KMT and its army from the beginning. Borodin had two young Russian graduates of Frunze Military Academy on his staff when he began work with Sun Yat-sen in October, 1923. Russia provided four military instructors for Whampoa Academy when it opened in May, 1924, and the number increased in July and October as new groups of Russians arrived in Canton. When the Academy Army participated in the first campaign in eastern Kwangtung in February–March, 1925, twenty Russian officers—headed by the talented General Vasilii K. Blücher (known in China as Galin, Galen, or Galents) and numbering an admiral, six other generals, and five colonels—assisted in developing strategy as well as in directing artillery, managing communications and commissary, and operating an armored train. In the Second Eastern Expedition in October–November, 1925, Russian military officers were on the staffs of most participating Chinese divisions. In January, 1926, there were more than 140 Russian advisers in and about Canton, working in the highest organs of the party and government, serving at Whampoa and in Chiang's First Army Corps and in the Navy and Aviation Bureaus, aiding in intelligence, propaganda, and the farmers movement, and attached to the Kwangtung–Hong Kong Strike Committee.[27] This was probably a larger establishment than the entire diplomatic corps in Peking.

[27] Information on advisers at Whampoa and on the First Eastern Expedition derived from a participant, A. I. Cherepanov, *Zapiski Voennogo Sovetnika v Kitae.* (I am indebted to Mrs. Lydia Holubnychy and Mrs. A. Kisselgoff for translations from this source.) On May 2, 1925 General Galin sent General Hsü Ch'ung-chih, commander of the Second Kwangtung Army in the First Eastern Expedition, a list of the 19 Russian officers, in addition to himself, assisting the Academy Army. See *Su-lien yin-mou wen-cheng hui-pien* [Collection of documentary evidence of the Soviet conspiracy] (Peking: Metropolitan Police Headquarters, 1928), vol. 3, "Canton," pp. 104–6. A participant in the Second Eastern Expedition, N. I. Konchits, has left a detailed account of his role and

Soviet Russia, or the Comintern, gave financial support to the KMT as a party early in 1924, if not earlier, and financed Whampoa Military Academy to an amount of over 2,500,000 Chinese dollars, although Chinese taxpayers also paid for its support. Russia also made a loan of 10,000,000 Chinese dollars to establish the Central Bank. Russian organizations, as well as Communist and leftist groups in other countries, sent contributions in support of the strike against Hong Kong, which began in the summer of 1925. A large shipment of Soviet arms to Canton in October, 1924, may have been a gift, but sometime thereafter the Canton government was expected to pay for arms deliveries.[28]

---

mentions many other Russian military advisers. N. I. Konchits, *Sovietskiie Dobrovoltsy v Pervoi Grazhdanskoi Revolutsionnoi Voine v Kitae; Vospominaniia* [Soviet volunteers in the First Revolutionary War in China: Reminiscences] (Moscow: Academy of Sciences of the USSR, Institut Narodov Azii, 1961). (I am indebted to Mrs. Holubnychy for a translation.) Information on the number of Russians and their functions in Canton early in 1926 is derived from a variety of newspaper and intelligence reports as well as from documents captured in a raid on the offices of the Soviet Military Attaché in Peking on April 6, 1927; see particularly Wilbur and How, *Documents on Communism*, nos. 16, 22, and Glossary C; "A list of Names and Positions of Members of the Soviet Group in South China," *Su-lien Yin-mou Wen-cheng Hui-pien*, vol. 3, "Canton," pp. 97 ff.; and "Minutes of a Meeting of the Military Council of Russian Advisers at Canton, July 1, 1925, Covering Plan for Employment of Personnel, etc.," reprinted in *Chinese Social and Political Science Review*, 11 (1927): 160–66.

[28] Early financial assistance to the KMT, Tsou Lu, *Chung-kuo Kuomintang shih-kao* [A draft history of the Kuomintang], 2d ed. (Chungking: 1944), pp. 390 and 399 (n. 22). Borodin told Louis Fischer that the Soviet government made a grant of three million rubles for organizing Whampoa Military Academy and its initial running expenses (*The Soviets in World Affairs*, vol. 2 [New York: J. Cape & H. Smith, 1930], p. 64). This was equivalent to approximately 2,700,000 Chinese dollars at current rates of exchange. N. Mitarevsky, *World-Wide Soviet Plots, as Disclosed by Hitherto Unpublished Documents Seized at the USSR Embassy in Peking* (Tientsin: Tientsin Press, 1927?), p. 39, quotes a letter from Moscow, dated March 17, 1925, to Comrade Soustchefsky in Peking, which states that Galin had been given 100,000 rubles for upkeep of the school at Whampoa for two months, as well as 450,000 for the formation of new military units.

The first shipment of Russian arms arrived at Whampoa October 7, 1924; it included artillery, machine guns, and 8000 or more rifles. Chiang Kai-shek, *Min-kuo shih-wu-nien i-ch'ien chih Chiang Chieh-shih hsien-sheng* [Mr. Chiang Kai-shek before 1926], ed. Mao Szu-ch'eng, 2 vols., reprint (n.p.: n.d. [but after 1948; original edition probably 1936]), p. 336; F. F. Liu, *A Military History of Modern China, 1924–1949* (Princeton, 1956), p. 14; and Sokolsky, "A Visit to Hongkong and Canton." Sokolsky learned from a foreign source

Even if arms had to be paid for after delivery, the National Revolutionary Army was greatly advantaged by receiving them. They supplemented the inadequate production of Kwangtung's arsenals; their allocation tended to enforce centralized control; and their use to defeat enemies within Kwangtung enlarged the territory from which the government might collect taxes. It is not yet possible to construct an overall figure for the value of arms and munitions delivered by Soviet Russia to Canton. Here is a revealing example. The Soviet Military Attaché in Peking, Egoroff, telegraphed General Galin in Canton about July 4 (probably 1926) that supplies already handed over to Canton as of the previous December were valued at 2,500,000 rubles. He then listed supplies concentrated at Vladivostok, the greater part apparently already en route to Canton, valued at two million rubles. This concentration included more than five million rifle cartridges, twenty machine guns with ammunition, fifty-eight artillery pieces with large quantities of ammunition, and nine airplanes. Galin was told that Canton must pay now for supplies already delivered, and that, in the future, orders would be executed as far as possible only for cash.[29]

In providing this assistance, Soviet Russia was, naturally, pursuing national interests as then conceived. It was supporting a national revolution directed against "imperialism," and particularly against Russia's number one enemy of that era, Great Britain. Inevitably Borodin and other Russians in the mission at Canton favored those Chinese leaders who, so far as could be determined, accepted Russian ideas concerning the social revolution within the national revolutionary movement. The weight of Borodin's personal influence and his control of Russian aid fell on the side of the "leftists" in the KMT. This was a price the KMT paid for the massive assistance Russia selectively provided.

---

that the shipment consisted of 12,000 rifles and 40 field pieces, all free of charge to the Canton government. Chiang, in the source quoted, says Sun Yat-sen had agreed to purchase the equipment; but in Chiang Chung-cheng (Chiang Kai-shek), *Soviet Russia and China: A Summing-Up at Seventy* (New York, 1957), p. 257, Chiang says that "When our revolutionary government in Canton was threatened by a revolt, we accepted Soviet Russia's proffered aid, totaling some 3,000 tons of material."

[29] This document, seized in the April 6, 1927, Peking raid, is reprinted in *Chinese Social and Political Science Review*, 11 (1927): 208–9; and *China Year Book, 1928*, p. 802; and in several other sources. Several similar documents were discovered. V. V. Vishniakova-Akimova, *Dva Goda v Vosstavshem Kitae, 1925–1927* [Reminiscences of two years in revolutionary China, 1925–1927] "Nauka" (Moscow, 1956) p. 200, states that seven ships running between Vladivostok and Canton supplied oil, arms, and planes.

A second important development was the rise of Chiang Kai-shek within the Nationalist military system. We shall have to concentrate upon the trend toward his rise and pass over the details. Chiang was not even a delegate to the First Kuomintang Congress, and Sun and the senior leaders of the party persuaded him only with great difficulty to take command of Whampoa Military Academy. Once he did so, however, he started to build what became a base of personal power. In this he was undoubtedly aided by Russian advisers and arms, whether wittingly or not. The Academy Army's contribution to the first victory over Ch'en Chiung-ming's coalition, and over Generals Yang Hsi-min and Liu Chen-huan in June, 1925, elevated Chiang's position in Nationalist councils. A turning point in his career came after the assassination of Liao Chung-k'ai on August 20, 1925. This was seen by KMT leftists and Borodin as part of a rightist plot to overthrow the newly created Nationalist government. The leaders appointed a three-man special committee consisting of Wang Ching-wei, by then the leading leftist politician, and two generals, Hsü Ch'ung-chih and Chiang Kai-shek, with unlimited emergency powers to deal with the crisis. Borodin was the committee's adviser. The committee arrested two generals suspected of being involved, and Chiang put Hu Han-min under detention. Hu was a leader of great prestige and Wang's principal rival. He was compelled to go on a Russian vessel for a tour of inspection of Russia, not even being permitted to stop in Shanghai. Almost simultaneously Chiang used his army to disarm some of the units of General Hsü Ch'ung-chih's Kwangtung Army and forced Hsü to retire to Shanghai. A number of the less radical KMT leaders departed or were sent away. Wang and Chiang emerged as the two most important leaders in Canton, the one holding all the top political offices and the other controlling preponderant military power. Behind the scenes Borodin played an important role in these arrangements.[30]

The veteran leaders of the KMT were badly divided over the radical trend which the social revolution was taking in Kwangtung and over the growing influence of the CCP and Russian advisers there. A prestigious group which had either withdrawn or been driven from Canton held a conference in Peking during November and December, 1925, which they asserted was a meeting of the Central Executive Committee. Actually, the Central Executive Committee was almost equally divided; neither side could muster a quorum. The Peking group resolved to dismiss nine Communists who were regular or reserve members of the Central Executive Committee, to separate the two parties, to suspend

[30] Wilbur and How, *Documents on Communism*, pp. 165–66.

Wang Ching-wei's membership for six months, and to dismiss Borodin as adviser to the party. They then set up a rival party center in Shanghai and planned to call the Second Congress of the Kuomintang there in March. But the Kwangtung group called *its* Second Congress first. This meeting, held in January, 1926, has passed into history as the official Congress.

This Congress affirmed the policy of alliance with Russia and admission of Communists into the KMT and elected a new Central Executive Committee. No leaders of the Peking-Shanghai group were elected, except Tai Chi-t'ao who, though probably anti-Communist by now, had played an ambiguous role in Peking and was a supporter of Chiang Kai-shek. Chiang was elected to the new Central Executive Committee; in fact, he was among four receiving the highest number of votes. He could not have achieved this mark of esteem had not most of the ninety-odd Communists attending the Congress voted for him. The other three who tied with Chiang were Wang Ching-wei, Hu Han-min (in exile), and T'an Yen-k'ai, commander of the Second or Hunan Army Corps and a prestigious party veteran. Communists won seven (possibly eight) seats on the Central Executive Committee of thirty-six, while "left" KMT members won seven seats and probably many more, depending upon the definition. The even more important Central Executive Committee Standing Committee of nine, elected January 22, had on it three leftists—Wang, Ch'en Kung-po, and Kan Nai-kuang; three Communists —T'an P'ing-shan, Lin Tsu-han, and Yang P'ao-an; and three others— Chiang, T'an Yen-k'ai, and Hu Han-min.[31] The leftists and Communists were ascendant, but Chiang and Wang were the two most powerful figures in Canton.

[31] The record of the vote for KMT Central Committees is found in *Chung-kuo Kuomintang ti-erh-tz'u tai-piao ta-hui hui-chi-lu*, pp. 145–46. Of 252 ballots cast, the top four elected to the Central Executive Committee received 248; T'an P'ing-shan received 246; Mme. Sun 245; and Sun Yat-sen's son, Sun Fo, was last with 142. The analysis is based upon the careful study by Li Yun-han, *Tsung Jung Kung tao Ch'ing Tang* [From the admission of the Communists to the purification of the (Nationalist) Party] (Taipei, 1966), pp. 472–73. Li identifies Chu Chi-hsün as a Communist, but he is not usually so listed in other studies. He does not list Ho Hsiang-ning (Mme. Liao Chung-k'ai) nor Sung Ch'ing-ling (Mme. Sun Yat-sen) as KMT leftists. Jerome Ch'en, "The Left Wing Kuomintang—A Definition," *Bulletin of the School of Oriental and African Studies, University of London*, vol. 25, pt. 3 (1962), pp. 557–76, counts 13 leftists in the 36-man Central Executive Committee, adding to Mr. Li's seven the following: T'an Yen-k'ai, Mme. Sun, Chu P'ei-te, Ching Heng-i, Sun Tse-wen (T. V. Soong), Mme. Liao, Ting Wei-fen, Wang Fa-ch'in, Liu Shou-chung, and Sun Fo. This seems to go too far.

Chiang, then aged thirty-nine, was both ambitious and suspicious. He apparently suspected the Communists and the Russian advisers of plotting against him in favor of Wang; apparently he was angered by increasing Russian control over the central military organs; and he became increasingly hostile to General Kisan'ka, who had replaced Galin as chief of the Soviet Military group. Borodin, whom Chiang may also have mistrusted, had left Canton shortly after the Second Congress for one of his periodic consultative trips to Peking. In March, Chiang suspected, possibly with some reason, a plot to force him to go to Russia (just as he had helped to send off Hu Han-min), even by kidnapping if necessary. Whether such a plot was being prepared or whether it was merely Chiang's pretext to curb the Russians and the Communists, he acted decisively on the early morning of March 20, 1926.

General Chiang declared martial law in Canton and used units of the First Army Corps and the Whampoa cadets to arrest the Communist Deputy-Chief of the Navy Bureau and to disarm the guards at the residences of the Russian advisers and at the headquarters of the Communist-dominated Strike Committee. Chiang then went through the formalities of contrition for his arbitrary act, but he had his way. The Russians decided upon a policy of conciliation, sending Kisan'ka, Rogachev, and Admiral Smirnov home, while the Chinese Communists withdrew their commissars from the First Army Corps and disbanded the Communist-controlled League of Military Youth. Wang Ching-wei, who was ill, both actually and politically, found it expedient to go into retirement, leaving Canton on May 9 for Paris. He sailed on the same vessel as Hu Han-min, who had returned to Canton with Borodin on April 29. Seeing how the wind was blowing, Hu retired to Shanghai.

Borodin and Chiang patched up their differences. Chiang's principal concession was to drive more KMT conservatives from Canton. Borodin agreed to continue Russian aid to the KMT, including support for the Northern Punitive Expedition which Chiang desired but which the Russian advisers and the Chinese Communists had opposed as not yet timely. The Communists agreed to Chiang's insistence upon restricting their activities in the KMT. As a result, they gave up control of the KMT's Organization Bureau, which was now headed by Chiang himself with his close associate, Ch'en Kuo-fu, as his deputy. Communists also relinquished important posts in the Propaganda Bureau, the Farmers Bureau, and the Secretariat. Furthermore, Chiang's supporter, the elderly Chang Ching-chiang, was elected to a new post as Chairman of the Standing Committee of the Central Executive Committee, although he was not even a member of the Committee. Thus were Chiang's rivals excluded, the Communists curbed, and the Russian advisers compelled to retreat.[32] It was merely the first round in the battle.

A third important development was incorporation into the National Revolutionary Army of autonomous military systems in neighboring provinces—a portentous move. The first was actually an alliance with Kwangsi forces put together by three young generals, Huang Shao-hsiung, Li Tsung-jen, and Pai Ch'ung-hsi. They had fought their way to the top in a series of wars which plagued Kwangsi during the early 1920's. By late 1925 they were able to set up a government for Kwangsi under Huang. Being products of late Ch'ing military schools and having participated in Tung Meng Hui activities, the revolution against the Manchus, or various "constitution-protection" wars, they were a nationalistically inclined trio. They enrolled in the revived KMT and permitted it to penetrate the regions under their control. During the spring of 1926, negotiations between the KMT and the Kwangsi power-holders resulted in an agreement by which Kwangsi came under the Nationalist government and the Kwangsi army was renamed the Seventh Army Corps of the National Revolutionary Army. General Li was named commander, Huang became Party Representative, and Pai, Chief-of-Staff. This appears to have been more an alliance than union,

[32] This summary interpretation of the "Chung-shan Gunboat Incident" and its aftermath is based upon the account writen by Miss Julie How in Wilbur and How, *Documents on Communism*, pp. 215–33. The incident is very obscure, and the inner facts may never be known. Vishniakova-Akimova, *Dva Goda v Vosstavshem Kitae, 1925–1927,* pp. 190–91, reports that antagonism developed between Kuibyshev-Kisan'ka and Chiang over the matter of finances, Chiang wishing to appropriate the lion's share for the First Army Corps and Kuibyshev-Kisan'ka insisting upon centralized control of the National Revolutionary Army and equal distribution of funds and supplies to all Army corps. This conflict led Kuibyshev-Kisan'ka to consult Wang Ching-wei on all problems and to ignore Chiang. (I am indebted to Mrs. L. Holub-nychy for this information.) Passages in Chiang Kai-shek's "diary" for January 19, February 7, 11, and 26, 1926, provide obscure indications of his growing hostility for Kisan'ka. Chiang Kai-shek, *Min-kuo shih-wu-nien I-ch'ien chih Chiang Chieh-shih hsien-sheng,* pp. 668, 678, 679, 686. The aftermath of the incident was a complex readjustment of political forces in the face of Chiang's military power. Chang Ching-chiang's election to the chairmanship of the Committee was made possible by a resolution passed on May 19 at the Second Plenum of the Central Executive Committee, held in Canton from May 15–25. The resolution, proposed by Chiang, established the post temporarily and permitted the Chairman to be elected from among party members in either the Central Executive Committee or the Central Supervisory Committee, of which Chang was a member. See Li Yun-han, *Tsung jung-kung tao ch'ing-tang,* p. 508, for the key resolution as found in the KMT Archives.

for the government in Canton contributed nothing to the maintenance of the Seventh Army, did not reorganize it according to the three-three system, and did not get control of Kwangsi revenues although it apparently tried to.[33]

The second such incorporation was the Fourth Hunan Division under T'ang Sheng-chih, with whom the Nationalists had long negotiations. General T'ang drove Governor Chao Heng-ti from Changsha in March, 1926, but was quickly driven out of the capital by forces supported by Marshal Wu P'ei-fu, who was again playing an important role in the military politics of the central provinces. T'ang retreated to his old base in southern Hunan and was barely saved by a brigade sent by Li Tsung-jen. Late in May the KMT, as a step toward the Northern Punitive Expedition, decided—after further negotiation with T'ang— to name his force the Eighth Army Corps of the National Revolutionary Army, with T'ang as commander.[34] Soon after, at T'ang's request, the KMT appointed his representative in Canton, Liu Wen-tao, as Party Representative in the Eighth Army. The revolutionary credentials of T'ang and Liu were virtually nil.

These alliances were only a part of a complicated series of negotiations with such other regional militarists as General Sun Ch'uan-fang, the greatest power in the lower Yangtze provinces, General Yuan Tsu-ming of Kweichow, and General Yang Sen, Military Governor of Szechwan, to induce them either to join in the coming war against Wu P'ei-fu or at least to stay neutral.[35] All sent representatives to Canton, as

[33] Based on Ch'en Hsun-cheng's account in *KMWH*, vol. 12, pp. 1798–1800; and Li Tsung-jen's reminiscences as told to Dr. T. K. Tong. A specific agreement was reached between March 15 and 25, 1926, during a visit of General Pai Ch'ung-hsi to Canton, for the formal accession of Kwangsi to the National Government. All Kwangsi financial organs were to be under the supervision of the Ministry of Finance of the Nationalist government, all financial officials to be appointed by the government, and all revenues to go into the national treasury. (See *KMWH* as cited; and *Canton Gazette,* March 19, 1926.) According to General Li there actually was no financial integration.

[34] The late General Pai Ch'ung-hsi told the writer that in March, 1926, he was sent to Ch'angsha to negotiate with T'ang Sheng-chih. Not until General T'ang was in defeat did he agree to his domain being invaded by troops from Kwangtung.

[35] Negotiations with Sun Ch'uan-fang, Yuan Tsu-ming, and Yang Sen were reported by Seifulin, Russian Military Attaché in Peking, on June 3, based upon Borodin's reports from Canton. See Wilbur and How, *Documents on Communism,* p. 269 in document 25. General Yang Sen told the writer that, before the Northern Expedition, Chiang Kai-shek sent Ch'en Pao-i, an old friend of Hsieh Ch'ih, from Kwangtung to negotiate with Yang in Szechwan and that Ch'en made several trips.

Feng Yü-hsiang may have done also. Chiang Kai-shek seems to have been the principal player moving the pawns in these preliminaries to the coming military chess game.

The Northern Expedition: First Phase

The Northern Punitive Expedition which began officially in July, 1926, was an enormously complicated revolutionary movement which sucked millions of Chinese as well as several major foreign powers into the vortex. Here we must emphasize those aspects which forwarded and inhibited national unification.

The Strategic Situation, July, 1926

There were three important military coalitions which stood in the way of the Nationalist government's hope of reunifying China through a military-political campaign—the forces clustered around Wu P'ei-fu, Sun Ch'uan-fang, and Chang Tso-lin.[36]

Wu P'ei-fu had been trying since mid-1925 to recruit a military coalition in central China that could overthrow both Feng Yü-hsiang in the north and the KMT in the south. By July, 1926, he had created a paper coalition in Hupeh, northern Hunan, and Honan which Nationalist historians portray as numbering more than 200,000 men—probably a greatly exaggerated figure. Marshal Wu's financial resources were slim, and the various divisions and brigades controlled their own bases and were little dependent upon him.

Marshal Sun Ch'uan-fang headed an "Alliance of Five Provinces" in east China—Fukien, Chekiang, Kiangsu, Anhui, and Kiangsi—also with a troop strength reported to number more than 200,000. The financial resources of this coalition, based upon the wealthy lower Yangtze area, were much greater than Wu's, but the alliance was one of convenience. Based upon Shanghai, Marshal Sun was a nominal supporter of Wu; both were Shangtung men, and Sun had been Wu's subordinate in the Chihli clique. But this did not cause Sun to provide much support for Wu's effort at a comeback; he apparently preferred to preserve and improve his own domain.

Chang Tso-lin, based on Fengtien, headed the most formidable coalition, whose members controlled Manchuria, Shantung, and much of Chihli. The relatively well-armed forces of this groupment allegedly

---

[36] For the list of these coalitions see *KMWH,* vol. 12, pp. 1780–89; *Pei-fa chan-shih* [A battle history of the Northern Expedition] (Taipei: Ministry of National Defense, 1959), vol. 1, pp. 62–68; and *Pei-fa chien-shih* [A brief history of the Northern Expedition] (Taipei: Ministry of National Defense, 1961), charts following p. 46.

numbered more than 350,000 men. Chang Tso-lin and Wu P'ei-fu, though old enemies, jointly supported a government in Peking and were attempting to drive Feng Yü-hsiang's forces out of their base around Nank'ou and at Kalgan.

The First Kuominchün, Feng Yü-hsiang's army northwest of Peking, was supported with Russian arms and advisers, though Feng himself was in Soviet Russia. At some date this army might become an ally of the National Revolutionary Army.

There were also other military groups in the west which could not be overlooked in strategic planning. T'ang Chi-yao in Yunnan and Yuan Tsu-ming in Kweichow could menace Kwangtung from the west, and Yang Sen in eastern Szechwan, an ally of Wu P'ei-fu, would be on the western flank if the Northern Campaign reached Wu-Han. Yen Hsi-shan in Shansi might be a useful ally, or possibly a rival, if the expedition should approach Peking. On the east coast there were two naval concentrations which might also play an important strategic role, one at Foochow, the other at Shanghai. The Shanghai force was particularly important because of the possibility of its interdicting the lower Yangtze from military crossings or transport of troops.

The National Revolutionary Army consisted of approximately 100,000 officers and men in Kwangtung province, organized in six army corps consisting of 20 divisions made up of 67 infantry regiments plus two regiments and six battalions of artillery. In addition, there were nine Kwangsi brigades of the Seventh Army Corps (18 regiments of infantry and two artillery battalions), perhaps 40,000 men; and the Eighth Army (Hunanese) with a paper organization of six divisions (22 regiments) but whose actual numerical strength can scarcely be estimated.[37]

The basic strategic objectives of the Northern Expedition were first to capture the Wu-Han cities, then to take Shanghai and Nanking, and finally to capture Peking. This plan called for the defeat of Wu P'ei-fu, Sun Ch'uan-fang, and Chang Tso-lin in succession. Naturally, it was essential to prevent their combining forces. Hence, throughout the Northern Expedition, Commander-in-Chief Chiang Kai-shek conducted continuous negotiations with some of his enemies to keep them neutral-

[37] *KMWH*, vol. 12, pp. 1802–5, as of May, 1926; and *Pei-fa chan-shih*, chart following p. 46, exact date not specified. Troop strengths are my estimates. Pai Ch'ung-hsi, who was Deputy Chief-of-Staff of the National Revolutionary Army during the period in question, told the writer that the Army consisted of eight armies, 26 divisions, and 9 brigades, made up of 110 regiments and nine battalions, and totaling 170,000 men. This, of course, includes the Seventh (Kwangsi) and Eighth (Hunan) armies.

ized till their turn came and to induce some of their armies to turn over to the revolutionary side. There existed enough rivalry among the three major constellations and enough attachment to the respective regional bases to make the task of keeping the enemies separated relatively easy. When and under what terms enemy units would defect and "join the revolution" depended, however, on the tide of battle and flow of silver bullets.

In July, 1926, the income of the "national" and Kwangtung treasury was 14.9 million, while expenses were 14 million (figures rounded).[38] Major expenditure categories were for: government, 1.5 million; military, 11.5 million; and reserves deposited for treasury bonds, 1 million —a ratio of civilian expenses of 10.7 per cent to military expenses of 81.5 per cent. How much more, if any, was concealed for purposes of buying enemy commanders is unknown. The government in Canton was using every device to raise emergency funds.

Defeat of Wu P'ei-fu and Sun Ch'uan-fang

The first objective, the capture of the Wu-Han cities, was accomplished by October, 1926, in a drive north through Hunan and Hupeh at the cost of several serious battles. Wu P'ei-fu had remained in the north to participate in the ejection of Feng Yü-hsiang's army from Nank'ou Pass, which was accomplished by August 14. By the time he came south, it was too late to hold Hunan. He was badly defeated at Ho-sheng Bridge in Hupeh on August 29, and the Nationalist forces were approaching the Yangtze.

Before Wu could gather his forces to defend the Wu-Han cities, Hanyang and Hankow had been taken (September 6–7) and Wuchang invested. Wu P'ei-fu beat a retreat to Chengchow in Honan, having been deserted by many units which turned over to the Nationalists. During this period Chiang Kai-shek kept up his negotiation with Sun Ch'uan-fang, who ignored until it was too late Wu's pleas to attack the Nationalist flank. Even before Wuchang was taken by negotiation on October 10, after a long and bloody siege, the Nationalists invaded Kiangsi, one of the "Five Allied Provinces" under Sun Ch'uan-fang.

[38] These and the following figures come from *Ts'ai-cheng pao-kao*, KMT Archives, no. 444/19. Income for August was 13.9 million and expenditures 13.9 million (69.4 per cent for military); in September, income was 10.8 million, expenditures 10.8 million (60.5 per cent for military); in October, income was 10.3, expenditures 10.4 (64.7 per cent for military). According to *British Chamber of Commerce Journal* (Shanghai), 12 (May, 1927): 131, total income and expenditures for 1926 were $100,136,000, of which $72,862,000 went to the military.

Though Sun rushed troops into the Kiukiang-Nanchang area and inflicted heavy losses on the Nationalists during September and October, his railway line was cut, his base at Kiukiang was taken on November 5, and Sun withdrew to Nanking with his personally led troops nearly intact. As late as October 28, he had been negotiating with Chiang. Another campaign was launched early in October through Fukien toward the second major objective, Shanghai. By late December the First Army Corps had taken Foochow and a Nationalist force sent from Kiangsi had captured a town in southwestern Chekiang that was on a route toward Hangchow.

Thus, by the end of the year the strategic situation had changed markedly. Most of Hunan, Hupeh, Kiangsi, and Fukien were in Nationalist hands. Wu was powerless, and Sun Ch'uan-fang had lost so heavily that he had had to beg Chang Tso-lin for help. The help was in the form of an army under Sun's old enemy, Chang Tsung-ch'ang, who arrived in Nanking in late December.

Three major factors may account for these successes. One was the valor of many of the divisions and brigades fighting on the Nationalist side, particularly those of the Fourth (Kwangtung) and the Seventh (Kwangsi) Army Corps, which suffered heavy casualties. A second was the assistance given by farmers, students, and workers in the enemy's rear, and the effect of Nationalist propaganda among enemy troops. Another was the strategic and tactical advice provided by Russian officers, as well as their radio communications and aerial reconnaissance.

Yet as important as any of these was the devastating effect of the turnover of enemy units.[39] Practically every division of the Hunan army switched sides; as a result T'ang Sheng-chih's Army Corps grew enormously. General Lai Shih-huang of the Fourth Kiangsi Division turned over even before the campaign in Kiangsi began, though the matter was kept secret so that he was able to pass on to Chiang's headquarters news of enemy troop movements. He was rewarded by being named Commander of the Fourteenth National Revolutionary Army. Hanyang, with its important arsenal, fell as a result of General Liu Tso-lung's betrayal; he was rewarded by being given the designation of Commander of the Fifteenth National Revolutionary Army, made up of his own Hupeh troops. The sudden withdrawal of part of General Chou Feng-chi's Third Chekiang Division at the last stages of the campaign to take Nanchang opened the way to the capture of Kiukiang, taken for the Nationalists by another defector, General Ho Yao-tsu. That Chou might defect was known to General Chiang, who re-

[39] The following reports of defections are found in Ch'en Hsun-cheng's account in *KMWH*, vol. 13, and in telegrams in vols. 12 and 13.

ported the prearranged signals to General Li Tsung-jen. The way into southern Fukien was eased for General Ho Ying-ch'in, commanding the First Army Corps, by the defection of two brigades which were promptly formed into the Seventeenth National Revolutionary Army. General Ho was able to secure Foochow partly due to the turnover of the naval units based there.

Naturally, the initial successes of the campaign induced many generals to switch when the time was still propitious, and some had to switch to avoid seeing their units absorbed into one or another of the southern divisions. The effect of this was to change the National Revolutionary Army into a large, unwieldy conglomeration of units, most of which had had no political indoctrination at all. In the first week in January, Chiang called a military conference at his new headquarters at Nanchang, which was attended by nearly all important commanders, including many who had only recently discovered the revolution. He pleaded with them to permit a numeration of their troop strength and arms and to allow his headquarters to standardize their divisions. General Galin spoke of the advantage of reorganizing divisions according to the Russian three-three system. The great variety of armies was an impossible expense to the Nationalist treasury. By March 1, 1927, a Table of Organization had been prepared which listed twenty-six army corps plus seven independent divisions and one brigade already organized as battle forces, numbering an estimated 500,000 men; there were eight other armies awaiting registration. However, the monthly income of the "national" and provincial treasury of Kwangtung was less from January through March, 1927, than it had been in July when the expedition began.[40] It appears the "national" treasury was losing control over revenue, and that many commanders were collecting revenues as of old.

Issues of Policy and Power

At the cost of great simplification, it may be said that as soon as the first successful burst of the Northern Expedition was over, the issues of "how much social revolution?" and "how much anti-imperialism?" became acute.[41] Would social revolution disrupt the military drive for

[40] I read the minutes of the Nanchang conference in the KMT Archives, as also the March 1, 1927, Table of Organization. Revenue figures are found in the *British Chamber of Commerce Journal*, 12 (May, 1927): 131–2: January, $12,451,000 (rounded); February, $7,140,000 (down because of the Chinese New Year): March, $11,476,000. Clearly these figures reflect income only from Kwangtung; revenues collected elsewhere were not entering the books.

[41] In the following discussion I have synthesized many notes taken in the KMT Archives, *North China Herald,* and reports from the American Consul-

unification, and would the anti-imperialist struggle cause the Powers to support the enemy? In the confusion of a complicated revolution in which there were widely differing views and no commonly accepted structure of authority, these issues could not be resolved by agreement. They would be settled only through a contest for power within the revolutionary camp.

In the anti-imperialist movement a major strategy had been worked out: concentrate attack upon British interests in China and keep the pressure off Japan, the United States, and other powers. This sensible strategy was difficult to execute, because foreign interests were interwoven. In attacks upon Christian churches, mission schools, and hospitals, it was scarcely possible to distinguish between British and American or French and Italian. In stimulating a strike movement against British-owned factories or banks, it was impossible to prevent labor organizers from demanding benefits from American and Japanese businesses also. If British concessions in Hankow and Kiukiang could be seized with ease by mob action, it was difficult to restrain xenophobic activists from turning the mobs on Japanese concessions and Japanese persons also. By early 1927, foreign missionaries and business people of all nationalities were fleeing the central provinces, and all the Powers were taking action to protect them and the great concentration point of foreign interests, Shanghai.

Foreign and Chinese business were symbiotic in the great trade centers of the middle Yangtze. When foreign banks were forced to close, many Chinese banks failed. When foreign factories were struck or foreign trading firms compelled to suspend in Changsha, Kiukiang, and Hankow, the economic impact spread throughout the Chinese mercantile community; it was felt far in the hinterland as markets for tung oil, tobacco, eggs, and other farm products withered. When British, Japanese, and American companies, fearing seizure of their shipping vessels, cut off their runs into Nationalist territory (about three-quarters of the steam shipping on the Yangtze was under foreign register), stagnation of business in Wu-Han grew more serious. This meant declining tax collections for the Nationalists just when the swollen armies required ever-increasing revenues.

The same issue arose as a result of the social revolution. In the labor movement, demands for higher wages and better working conditions in foreign and Chinese enterprises and for a union voice in manage-

General in Hankow during late 1926 and early 1927 and in Shanghai in 1927. See also *Papers Relating to Foreign Relations of the United States, 1927,* vol. 2 (Washington, D.C., 1942; hereafter cited as *FRUS*).

ment led to protracted strikes or lockouts which disrupted all business and put large numbers of workers on relief. Their relief became a drain on the Wu-Han treasury. In the rural social revolution, which Mao Tse-tung so greatly admired during his inspection tour in Hunan, assassinations of "local bullies and evil gentry" drove the local elite out of market towns, causing disruption of rural commerce in tea and rice. Under a theory that if rice were not exported from one county or one province to another, rice prices would remain low in rural areas to the benefit of the poor, the cities began to face rice shortages; there was even alarm about a rice famine in the temporary capital of the revolution, Wu-Han. When farmers' associations began to expropriate land of the propertied classes, some of the victims were families of officers in the armies of Hunan and Hupeh which had but recently joined the National Revolutionary Army.

Social revolution could not but stimulate counter-revolution. The danger lay in disruption of the revolutionary alliance, strengthening of the enemy side, and foreign support of moderates or counter-revolutionaries during the very process of national unification. A political report of the Central Committee of the CCP (dated January 26, 1927) analyzed the alarming situation:

> The Right Wing of the Kuomintang is daily becoming more powerful. . . . There is currently an extremely strong tendency within the Kuomintang to oppose Soviet Russia, the Communist Party, and the labor and peasant movements. . . . The tendency toward the Right is due to the belief of Chiang Kai-shek and Chang Ching-chiang that only one party should exist in the country, that all classes should cooperate, that class struggle should be prohibited, and that there is no need for a Communist Party. . . . The second reason is their belief that the National Revolution will soon succeed, that there will soon be a movement for class revolution, and that the greatest enemy at present is not imperialism or militarism but the Communist Party. . . . The most important problem . . . is the alliance of foreign imperialism and the KMT Right Wing with the so-called moderate elements of the KMT, resulting in internal and external opposition to Soviet Russia, communism, and the labor and peasant movements.[42]

The Central Committee advocated urging the masses to support the Nationalist government financially and militarily in order to allay the

[42] Wilbur and How, *Documents on Communism*, pp. 432–34, document 48.

KMT's fears of the CCP and of an early Communist revolution; it advocated propaganda strongly critical of bourgeois ideology and warning against KMT reliance upon the bourgeoisie which would place the Nationalist Party against "the real revolutionaries," the masses of workers and peasants; and it advocated concentration on the anti-British movement and delay in extending the anti-imperialist movement to Japan, France, and the United States, "in order to isolate Britain."

But who was to decide such complex issues of policy during a revolution that was both domestic and international in its scope—leaders in Soviet Russia, torn in a factional struggle? the Russian advisers on the scene? the more moderate leader of the CCP or its militant activists? or, within the KMT, the leftists, the moderates, or the rightists? There was no orderly way to decide. A plenary session of the KMT Central Executive Committee held in Wu-Han, March 10 to 17, 1927, was dominated by leftists, Communists, and Borodin. Chiang did not attend. The plenum tried to hammer out a policy both to restrain the social revolution and to curb the most feared leader in the party, Chiang Kai-shek. His supporters were attacked and his formal powers reduced. But this could not reduce his real power nor prevent his search for domestic allies and for foreign support as an alternative to Russia. When Chiang launched a military drive in March to gain control over the rich bases of Chekiang, Kiangsu, and Anhui, the power struggle within the alliance reached a climax.

Nationalist armies captured Shanghai on March 21–22 and Nanking on March 23–24. In Shanghai the labor movement, controlled and directed largely by Communists, rose in an insurrectionary general strike on March 21, after Nationalist forces under General Pai Ch'ung-hsi had arrived at the city's outskirts. Armed labor pickets and guerrilla groups seized control of the native cities from within, disarming police and attacking the garrisoning northern troops. Regular Nationalist army units then completed the military take-over of the Chinese parts of Shanghai.

Nationalist troops entered Nanking on the heels of retreating northern troops. On the morning of the day of the take-over, March 24, the "Nanking Incident" broke out. Groups of Nationalist soldiers of the Sixth Army Corps, and probably also from the Second and Fortieth Army Corps, looted the British, American, and Japanese Consulates, wounded the British Consul, attacked and robbed many foreign nationals in the city, and killed three Englishmen, an American, a French and an Italian priest, and a Japanese marine. At 3:30 in the afternoon, two American destroyers and a British cruiser laid a curtain of shells around the residences of the Standard Oil Company to assist the escape of some fifty foreigners, mostly American and British. The bombardment of this sparsely populated area may have killed six Chinese, though early reports published in China and Russia asserted that thousands had been killed. The bombardment quickly damped down the attacks on foreigners, General Ch'eng Ch'ien restored order among his troops and, on the 25th, all foreigners who wished to leave were evacuated without harm, although foreign properties were looted and burned for several more days.[43]

[43] There is an extensive literature on the Nanking Incident. The following are a few important collections and studies: *KMWH*, vol. 14, pp. 2378–92; *Kung-fei huo-kuo shih-liao hui-pien* [Collected historical sources on the Communist bandit's scourge of the country] (Taipei, 1964), vol. 1, pp. 235–55; Chiang Yung-ching *Boloting yü Wu-han cheng-ch'üan* [Borodin and the Wu-Han regime] (Taipei, 1963), pp. 117–24; Li Yun-han, *Ts'ung jung-kung tao ch'ing-tang*, pp. 584–88; Great Britain, Foreign Office, China No. 4 (1927), *Papers Relating to the Nanking Incident of March 24 and 25, 1927* (HM Stationery Office, London, 1927, vol. 26, Cond. 2953); *FRUS, 1927*, vol. 2, pp. 146–236; *The China Yearbook, 1928*, chap. 16, pp. 723–36, "The Nanking Outrages"; Alice Tisdale Hobart, *Within the Walls of Nanking* (London: Jonathan Cape, 1928), pp. 157–243; Dorothy Borg, *American Policy and the Chinese Revolution, 1925–1928* (New York: American Institute of Pacific Relations and Macmillan, 1947), pp. 290–317; Eto Shinkichi, "Nankin Jiten to Nichi Bei" [The Nanking Incident and Japan and America], in *Takagi Yasaka sensei koki kinen ronbunshū* [Articles commemorating Dr. Takaki Yasaka's seventieth birthday] (Tokyo, 1959), pp. 299–324. Akira Iriye, *After Imperialism: The Search for a New Order in the Far East, 1921–1931* (Cambridge, Mass.: Harvard University Press, 1965), pp. 126–33.

Responsibility for the incident is still uncertain. Were the Nationalist troops instigated to commit their attacks and, if so, by whom? If instigated, was the driving force anti-imperialist passions among some lower officers and political commissars on the spot, or was there an attempt by persons of higher authority to embroil part of the Nationalist armies in a conflict with the Powers? As early as March 25, Yang Chieh, Commander of the Seventeenth Nationalist Division, told the Japanese Consul, Morioka Shohei, that the soldiers had been instigated by Communists in Nanking. The Consul reported to his government that the acts of violence had been planned by party commissars and Communist officers of lower grade within Second, Sixth, and Fortieth Armies, and by members of the Communist Party's Nanking branch (Iriye, *After Imperialism*, pp. 128–29, based on official Japanese sources). Shortly, officials close to Chiang Kai-shek interpreted the event as a Communist plot to embarrass Chiang, and soon the finger of blame was pointed toward Lin Tsu-han, head of the Political Department of the Sixth Army and/or Li Fu-ch'un, head of the same Department in the Second Army—but without any substantiating proof so far as I have been able to discover. Lin was in Wu-Han at the time of the incident, while Li may have been with the Second Army, but not necessarily in Nanking. General Chiang stopped

The Nanking Incident, like the May 30th Incident and the Shakee Massacre earlier, immediately inflamed Sino-foreign relations. The Western Powers and Japan intensified their preparations to protect their nationals. The view that Communists had been responsible for the Incident quickly became an accepted interpretation. The Japanese Government through its Consul-General in Shanghai, Yada Shichitarō, encouraged Commander-in-Chief Chiang Kai-shek to suppress radicalism which might lead to further incidents.

In Shanghai, local Communist and leftist leaders, backed by the Wu-Han center, attempted to create a government in Shanghai under their own control and to persuade the incoming leaders of the Nationalist armies to accept this government. There followed a most complicated period of alignment of forces which placed on one side the Communists in Shanghai, most of the modernly organized labor unions, some left-inclined intellectuals, and a few Russian advisers and the Soviet Consulate. This group tried to generate popular support by whipping up anti-imperialist sentiment.

On the other side were ranged members of the KMT "Old Right Wing," who had long made Shanghai their stronghold and who had good connections with Chinese financial, industrial, and commercial leaders, who had reasons of their own to oppose the militant labor movement; Shanghai underworld gangs, which had a more traditionally Chinese system of organizing labor and hence were rivals of the General Labor Union; and, in varying degrees, the leaders of the Nationalist armies which had invaded and conquered Chekiang, Anhui, and southern Kiangsu or had switched sides to join the revolution on the eve of triumph. Benevolently inclined toward this side—on the side of "law and order"—were the foreign administrations and the police of the International Settlement and the French Concession; behind these, the foreign consular body; and behind them, the power of some 40 warships and 16,000 foreign troops which had been rushed to

---

at Nanking on March 25 for a few hours and, according to the Japanese Consul's account, "closed the Nanking branch of the Communist Party" (Iriye, *After Imperialism,* p. 129). In Chiang Kai-shek, *Soviet Russia in China,* pp. 46–47, is the following assertion: "Communists in the armed forces had created this incident in the hope of provoking a direct clash between the foreign powers and the Revolutionary Forces. I shall not enter into the details of their plot, the evidences of which were conclusive." Yet it is surprising that with the massive collections of documents from the Wu-Han regime and from the Communist party which are preserved in Taiwan, no documentary or testimonial evidence of Communist instigation of the incident has been produced, so far as I have learned.

Shanghai to prevent a recurrence of the seizure of the British concessions in Hankow and Kiukiang in January. The well-protected foreign
settlements were filled with Chinese and foreign refugees from the violence of the social revolution and the anti-imperialist struggles of the
Northern Expedition.

The contest was completely unequal. What the Communist Central
Committee in January feared had occurred—"the alliance of foreign
imperialism and the KMT Right Wing with the so-called moderate
elements against Soviet Russia, the Chinese Communist Party, and the
organized workers and peasants."

General Chiang Kai-shek was a strategist who usually planned far
ahead. He had maintained good connections with Shanghai leaders of
the KMT, the Chinese business community, and the underworld; he
had selected with care the armies that should invade Shanghai and had
negotiated the turnover of the Chinese navy; and he had cultivated
Japanese political leaders and sent reassuring messages to foreign con-
suls. It appears that Chiang was the principal architect of the purge of
the Communists from the KMT in Shanghai, Nanking, Chekiang,
Fukien, Kiangsi, and Kwangtung. Yet there were many other Chinese
of note who urged him on, supplied him with funds, and joined in the
"Party Purification" in the areas under their control. The purge began
in April and cost the lives of an unknown number of idealistic youths,
resistant laborers, and Communists who failed to escape.

After the establishment of a new and rival government at Nanking,
divisions of opinion wracked the leftists, the Communists, and the Russian advisers in Wu-Han on military strategy (who now was the main
enemy, Chang Tso-lin or Chiang Kai-shek?) and on the social revolution (whether to curb it or extend it?). The Nationalist armies of the
competing centers both launched campaigns northward toward Peking
and reached the Lung-hai railway. There the powerful National
People's Army under the overall command of Feng Yü-hsiang linked
up first with the Wu-Han armies under T'ang Sheng-chih and then with
the armies commanded by Chiang Kai-shek. Chiang's base in the lower
Yangtze was far richer than the Wu-Han base, which was cut off from
the sea and had not yet recovered from economic stagnation. Each side
courted Feng as its ally against the other, in the fashion of military
politics, but it appears that the financial inducements which Chiang
could offer gave him the bargaining edge.

The left KMT leaders in Wu-Han, now led by Wang Ching-wei,
gradually came to the conclusion that they too must expel the Communists from the KMT. They were pushed to this conclusion partly by

the counter-revolutionary tide which had developed in the Eighth Army Corps, one of their main props, and partly by their own uncertainties concerning the social revolution. Yet, most decisive was the issue of who was to be in control of the national revolution, the leftist KMT leaders or the Communists and the foreign advisers in their midst? Apparently Stalin's decision to try to capture control of the KMT by increasing the power of Communists and their mass movement within it, a decision revealed by M. N. Roy to Wang Ching-wei against the advice of Borodin, tipped the scales. Most of the leftist leaders decided a separation of the two parties must come and the Russian advisers must be sent away. Feng Yü-hsiang, who was as much indebted to Russia as were Wang and Chiang, consulted with them separately and then publicly urged the Wu-Han leaders to make the separation. This was done with restraint toward Communist colleagues at first and with great courtesy toward the Russian friends.

By late July the Soviet policy executed so brilliantly by Borodin and his hard-working associates had collapsed. Where lay the fatal flaw?

Perhaps it lay in three assumptions: That men in Russia, ignorant of Chinese conditions, could mastermind a revolution from afar; that Russians on the scene could control a nationalistic movement; and that they could manipulate Chinese holders of military power.

Yet collapse of policy did not wipe out the effects of seven years of Soviet effort. The Nationalist Party had been energized against Russia's enemies, the capitalist Powers. A generation of young leaders had been radicalized in their outlook and schooled to mobilize popular opinion and to create mass organizations as sources of power. The CCP, inspired by nationalism and devoted to social revolution through class struggle, was firmly rooted in China. Competition between the two parties—their dialectic relationship—had stimulated both.

After their split with the Nationalists, some of the Communist leaders were determined to build a military base of power under their own control. They tried to do so through the Nanchang Uprising, followed by a military campaign back to Kwangtung, where they apparently believed a revolutionary movement among farmers and workers still existed. But the organs of social revolution in Kwangtung had been nearly extinguished by then. The newly created Red Army was decimated and scattered near Swatow.[44] The last gasp of the insurrectionary policy in Kwangtung was the Canton Commune in December, 1927,

[44] C. Martin Wilbur, "The Ashes of Defeat," *The China Quarterly*, no. 18 (April–June, 1964), pp. 3–54, for primary accounts of the Nanchang Uprising.

when Communist-led violence was crushed with equal violence. The Kwangtung base proved to be an illusion; other bases would have to be found and developed.

The Northern Expedition: Second Phase, 1928

Papering Over the Cracks in the Kuomintang

Complicated political and military maneuvers took place after both the Nanking-Shanghai and the Wu-Han wings of the KMT had purged Communists from the Nationalist Party and ended the Russian alliance. Chiang Kai-shek had weakened his military position against Sun Ch'uan-fang by withdrawing troops from the Shantung front to guard against or to threaten Wu-Han; this permitted the enemy to sweep south and nearly capture Nanking. Chiang was forced into retirement by some of his ostensible subordinates, and a number of important leaders retired with him. Nationalist troops under Generals Li Tsung-jen and Ho Ying-ch'in then defeated the invading force of Sun Ch'uan-fang in the bloody Lung-t'an battle (August 25–31, 1927). Chiang's retirement and the restored security of Nanking opened the way for negotiations between the rival Nationalist centers. Apparently Wang Ching-wei could not get terms satisfactory to himself. He departed for Canton and set up a third center. In the meantime, a combination of forces under Generals Ch'eng Ch'ien, Chu P'ei-te, and Li Tsung-jen drove the Eighth Army Group out of Hupeh back to Hunan, and T'ang Sheng-chih fled to Japan. In the east, the First Army Group was able to link up again with Feng Yü-hsiang at Hsüchow, where the Lung-hai and Tientsin-Pukow railways meet near the southern borders of Shantung. Chiang Kai-shek went to Japan and on November 5 had a long talk with the Prime Minister, Baron Tanaka, who encouraged him to consolidate gains south of the Yangtze and thoroughly eradicate communism, but not to get entangled in the warlord politics of the north.[45]

After Chiang returned to Shanghai on December 1, he and Wang Ching-wei held discussions with other leaders to form a new government. But Wang suddenly felt compelled to take another trip to France due to the hostility of the Western Hills Clique and because some of his subordinates seemed implicated in the destructive Canton Commune of December 11–14. The improved military situation for the Nationalists, together with uncontrollable factionalism within the party, called for Chiang's reassumption of his military command. In January, 1928, he

[45] Akira Iriye, *After Imperialism*, pp. 157–58, based on Japanese minutes of the conversation.

resumed his posts as Chairman of the Military Council and Commander-in-Chief of the Nationalist Armies.

The way now seemed clear to plan the final drive on Peking. The KMT Central Executive Committee held a plenary session, February 3–6, 1928, in Nanking and elected a New Government Council and an enlarged Military Council. It voted to remove from its list Communists elected to the Central Executive Committee at the Second Kuomintang Congress, to re-register party members, to combat Communist activities, and to replace class struggle with mutual cooperation.[46] This was a complete reversal of the politics of the radical Second Congress. The KMT was on its way to becoming a cautious and conservative party. While still nationalistic and determined to win back full sovereign rights for the country, the leaders were also determined to avoid anti-foreign incidents during the renewed Northern Expedition.

Strategic Situation

If the Nationalist armies could be united, they now had a good chance of driving the Fengtien Army back to Manchuria. On the enemy side were the remainder of Sun Ch'uan-fang's and Chang Tsung-ch'ang's troops in Shantung, the weak forces of a former bandit, Ch'u Yü-p'u and the still powerful Fengtien Army in Chihli and Manchuria. The Ankuochün, as the combination under Chang Tso-lin was named, numbered some 400,000 men. They had the advantage of short lines of communication, especially the railways north of the Lung-hai, and a secure rear base in Manchuria.

The Ankuochün was faced by a much larger numerical force, consisting of three main groupings. The First Army Group under Chiang Kai-shek was based on the rich lower Yangtze provinces of Kiangsu, Chekiang, and Anhui. Its core element was the Whampoa Army, that is, the First Army Corps of the start of the Northern Expedition, but it had picked up a variety of armies and now lacked inner cohesion. Advance elements of the First Army Group stood at the southern border of Shantung on the Tientsin-Pukow railway. Chiang had his headquarters at Hsuchow. The Second Army Group under Feng Yü-hsiang was the old first Kuominchün. It was battle-tested and relatively well integrated but was dependent upon the inland base of Honan and Shensi. Feng needed all the money and munitions he could persuade Chiang to turn over. The Second Army Group faced the Ankuochün along a line

---

[46] Pin Su (comp.), *Chung-shan ch'u-shih-hou liu-shih-nien ta-shih-chi* [A record of important events during sixty years since the birth of Sun Yat-sen] (Shanghai: T'ai-p'ing-yang Bookstore, 1929), item dated January 7, 1928.

north of the Lung-hai. A vital third factor in the Nationalist strategic alignment was Yen Hsi-shan, with his armies based in Shansi. This province lay west of Chihli; if Yen entered the war in earnest, he might cut the Chihli section of the Peking-Hankow railway or menace Peking from the northwest along the Peking-Siuyuan line. Yen did join, and his armies were designated the Third Army Group. The Nationalists theoretically had yet another resource, the Fourth Army Group in Hupeh. This grouping, made up of the Kwangsi Army and parts of the Hunan Army, could not enter the fray without passing through Feng's base in Honan, and Feng opposed this. Furthermore, Li Tsung-jen and Pai Ch'ung-hsi had apparently become very hostile to Chiang and the Nanking center. They dared not weaken their hold on Hupeh for fear Chiang would induce some of their rivals to attack their rear. Nevertheless, some troops from the Fourth Army Group did join the campaign at its last stages. Thus there were some 700,000 troops in the Nationalist coalition, but the coalition was more deeply divided than the force which had begun the Northern Expedition nearly two years before. It was now spread over eleven provinces and had the riches of Shanghai with which to finance a quick campaign.

Finances for the Expedition

The financial problems of the Nationalist government in Nanking were serious. When T. V. Soong took up the post of Finance Minister on January 7, 1928, he reported that the monthly income of the government was only two or three million yuan, but its expenses were eleven million or more. He was referring only to revenues collectible in Chekiang and Kiangsu, for no other taxes were seen by the government. Mr. Soong hoped that by reorganizing the finances of Kiangsu and Chekiang, which would take several months, he could collect some ten million monthly.[47] That would be less than Kwangtung alone produced when he managed finances there. Payments to troops were several months in arrears, and various armies were pressing for funds. Chinese New Year was upon him and settlements had to be made. Soong was able, "with the confidence and support of the people" (as he put it), to raise more than twelve million dollars within ten days. But no sooner had the New Year crisis passed than he was faced with the costs of the renewed Northern Expedition. He was instructed to raise $1,600,000

[47] This information comes from the statement prepared by T. V. Soong for the Fifth Plenum of the Kuomintang Central Executive Committee, August 7–15, about two months after the capture of Peking. See *North China Herald*, August 11, 1928, pp. 217–18.

every five days for the Military Council and the headquarters of the Generalissimo. Chiang would not accept less. The Minister of Finance had to use every device to meet this quota. He floated treasury bonds issued against future Shanghai customs receipts (the $2\frac{1}{2}$ per cent surtax) and cigarette and kerosene taxes; he repeatedly borrowed from native banks against future receipts from the salt tax and flour tax. Soong alleged that what the Ministry of Finance collected he turned over to Commander-in-Chief Chiang, who used it as he saw fit; Soong had no say in its distribution. Presumably the Commander-in-Chief used the funds to pay troops under his direct command, to subsidize Feng and Yen, and to bribe units within the Ankuochün to defect. Military expenses used up 88 per cent of all Nationalist government disbursements of more than Mex. $150 million during the fiscal year, June 1, 1927, to May 31, 1928.[48]

The Drive on Peking

A series of negotiations typical of military politics took place before warfare actually began. Chang Tso-lin tried to create an alliance with Chiang and Yen against Feng, and he tried to encourage the Kwangsi group against Chiang. On the Nationalist side apparently no major faction wanted to be the first to commit its troops.[49] Yet by mid-April fighting began in earnest. The weakest units of the Ankuochün, those of Sun Ch'uan-fang and Chang Tsung-ch'ang in Shantung, were attacked first in a coordinated drive by part of Feng's army eastward and Chiang's army northward. Sun Ch'uan-fang was defeated in an attempt to capture Hsüchow, and this opened the way for a drive on the provincial capital, Tsinan, by Feng's cavalry and some units of Chiang's infantry. Tsinan was taken on May 1, and the next day Chiang Kai-shek set up his headquarters in the Governor's Yamen.

By this time, however, Japan had sent a contingent of troops to

---

[48] USDS 893.00 PR/10, Chargé in China (Perkins) to Secretary of State, September 14, 1928, reprinted in *FRUS, 1928*, vol. 2, p. 163. I believe the figure of Mex. $150 million and taels 2 million disbursed by the National Government did not include revenues collected in Kwangtung, Kwangsi, Hunan, Hupeh, Shensi, Kansu, Honan, and Shansi, for T. V. Soong in his Report (for the Fifth Plenum) said those provinces "were doing their best to meet their own military expenses"—i.e., the military regimes retained complete fiscal autonomy in their respective bases.

[49] *FRUS, 1928*, vol. 2, pp. 123–95, "Conditions in China, February 1928"; USDS 893.00/9851, Chargé Mayer to Secretary of State, Peking, March 1; *ibid.*, pp. 132–35, 893.00 PR/5, The Minister in China (MacMurray) to Secretary, Peking, April 17.

Tsinan to protect some two thousand nationals in the Japanese settlement, and a Japanese division had taken control of the railway from the capital to the port of Tsingtao. There is good evidence that the Japanese government intended only to protect its nationals from a possible recurrence of the Nanking Incident of March 24, 1927, although the Shantung Expedition has long been interpreted as a Japanese warning to the Nationalists to stay out of Manchuria.[50] The Nationalist government was determined to avoid a clash with Japan. Favorably impressed by the discipline of the Nationalist troops which entered Tsinan, the Japanese commander, General Fukuda Hikosuke, decided to grant General Chiang's request that Japanese troops be withdrawn from Tsinan. At the very time they were preparing for their evacuation on May 4, a clash broke out between a few Chinese and Japanese troops on the morning of the third, and this led to sanguinary fighting—the Tsinan Incident. Each side, of course, charged the other with responsibility, but Japanese and Chinese civil and military officials on the spot tried to stop the fighting. A truce agreement was concluded on the fifth. The Chinese side began withdrawing troops, and Chiang withdrew his headquarters to Taian. General Fukuda then presented harsh and humiliating demands under a twelve-hour ultimatum, apparently expecting that the Chinese would not accede. When Chiang and the Nationalist government refused to comply, General Fukuda reopened hostilities on May 8, which lasted for several days until all Chinese forces were killed or expelled from Tsinan. Even so, the Nationalist government did all in its power to prevent anti-Japanese incidents in cities under its control.[51]

Tsinan was merely a way station; the Nationalist armies were driving on Peking. During May the forces of Generals Yen Hsi-shan, Feng Yü-hsiang, and Chiang Kai-shek continued their advance "due to success in battle, adroit use of money, and manipulation of factional alignments." There was another reason. On the night of May 17/18, the Japanese government warned Chang Tso-lin that he should give up Peking and retire peaceably to Manchuria; otherwise his troops would be disarmed as they entered Shanhaikuan. This advice was irresistible, especially

[50] Iriye, *After Imperialism*, pp. 193–98, for the Japanese decision based upon Japanese records.

[51] *Ibid.*, pp. 201–4, 248–50; *FRUS, 1928*, vol. 2, pp. 136–39; *China Year Book, 1929–30*, pp. 878–93 for Chinese and Japanese documents on the Tsinan Incident; *KMWH*, vol. 19, pp. 2479 ff.; vol. 22, pp. 4443 ff.; and vol. 23, pp. 4783 ff. It was nearly a year before the incident was settled and Japanese troops withdrew from Shantung.

since the position of the Fengtien army was precarious. Apparently an agreement was reached between Chang Tso-lin and Nationalist agents to permit Yen Hsi-shan's troops to take Peking, thus keeping the prize from Chang's old enemy, Feng Yü-hsiang. Feng had reason to be incensed. Another agreement was reached for a peaceful transition period during which the capital would be administered by a group of elders, while a brigade of Manchurian troops would be left in the city to maintain order. The brigade's free departure after the takeover was, in effect, guaranteed by the Diplomatic Corps, certainly with the understanding of all Nationalist commanders.[52]

Chang Tso-lin and many of his top officials departed on a special train on the night of June 2/3. Generals Chang Hsueh-liang and Yang Yu-t'ing left June 4. A brigade of Yen's soldiers entered Peking on June 8, and Marshal Yen arrived on the 11th with General Pai Ch'ung-hsi. Thus, nearly two years after its official launching, the Northern Expedition had succeeded in its major objective, the capture of Peking.

Unresolved Problems

The success of the Northern Expedition appeared to open the door to an era in which China's new political leadership could tackle the three major problems confronting the modern Chinese nation—regional separatism, foreign domination, and socioeconomic maladjustment. During the ensuing nine years, there were some notable accomplishments. No one can say what more would have been achieved had not the Sino-Japanese War intervened in 1937. Historians will long debate whether accomplishments outweighed failures. They will also argue whether failures were fundamentally due to the intractability of the problems or to the incompetency of the men who tried to solve them. This is the interpretive debate centering upon social forces as opposed to individuals as shapers of history.

The major accomplishment of the National Government was progress toward political reintegration. Upon this problem Chiang Kai-shek, who dominated the government, invested his greatest energy and the major resources of the state. The problem of foreign domination was approached with skill and purpose; up to 1930 the National Government was able to win back control over maritime customs tariffs and

[52] *FRUS, 1928*, vol 2, *passim*. The quotation is from MacMurray's report of June 15, p 148. For an account of Minister Yoshizawa's warning to Chang Tso-lin, see Iriye, *After Imperialism*, p. 211, based on Yoshizawa's report to Tanaka. A Japanese warning was communicated to both sides on May 18 not to fight in Manchuria, and this was explained to the diplomatic corps in Tokyo on the 17th. *FRUS, 1928*, vol. 2, pp. 224–25 and 229.

some foreign concessions. But it confronted a foreign power, Japan, which it could not coerce and which became intent upon protecting and extending its privileged position in Manchuria. Thus after September, 1931, China lost ground in its effort to solve its second major problem. Accomplishments were least impressive in respect to the third problem, the creation of a modern and equitable society. Fundamental issues of social policy were neglected or misinterpreted by men in power —Chiang most of all—whose eyes were fixed upon other matters and who were conservative by temperament and training.

Political Reintegration

When the Northern Expedition ended, there were five nearly equally powerful militarist agglomerations, each controlling a separate base. The group which proclaimed itself the central government was based upon Chekiang, Kiangsu, and Anhui. Feng Yü-hsiang's coalition was based upon Honan and Shensi and contolled parts of Chihli. Yen Hsishan controlled Shansi, southern Chahar, and the areas around Peking and Tientsin. The Fourth Army Group possessed Hupeh and its native province, Kwangsi. Though Chang Tso-lin had been assassinated in an explosion arranged by some Japanese officers of the Kwantung Army, Manchuria was the base for a strong army which Chang Hsueh-liang brought under his authority. In addition, Kwangtung was held by a group of native generals and politicians, and the whole of west and southwest China was still under militarist regimes whose powers had been very little disturbed by the campaign. Reintegration would still be a formidable problem.

In July, 1928, the successful commanders of the Northern Expedition held a preliminary discussion of troop disbandment and the creation of a single national army. In January, 1929, representatives of the major Nationalist power groups held a formal conference in Nanking. The conference accomplished little except to make clear that military separatism would not be overcome by the voluntary relinquishment of power. The degree to which the failure was due to the strength of the separatist tradition (social forces) or may be ascribed to the ambitions of rivals (the personal factor) is contentious. Chiang Kai-shek did not succeed in persuading his rivals to subordinate their armies to the government of which he was President. He then launched a civil war against the Kwangsi group (Li Tsung-jen and Pai Ch'ung-hsi) and drove them back to their original territory. Next he eliminated T'ang Sheng-chih, who had made a brief comeback. Feng Yü-hsiang had declined to give support to the Kwangsi group, and his turn came next. The power of Feng's army was greatly reduced when Chiang purchased the defections of two of its important commanders, Han Fu-chü and Shih Yu-san. Finally, Feng and Yen Hsi-shan tried together to create a rival government in Peking with distant support from Li Tsung-jen and with Wang Ching-wei as the chief political figure. Chiang overcame this combination by purchasing the power of the Fengtien Army. Chang Hsueh-liang made the move which toppled the government backed by Yen and Feng exactly one year before his own power in Manchuria was overthrown by the Japanese Kwantung Army in the Mukden Incident of September 18, 1931.

Seen from the Nanking government's side, these civil wars were a success. By 1930 one militarist regime after another had been reduced to provincial proportions and Nanking's influence was spreading. Explained in materialistic terms, Chiang's success was due to the great financial resources of his base and to his easy access to foreign arms. The fact that the Powers quickly extended recognition to the National Government brought it the revenues of the efficient Maritime Customs Service. When the Powers granted China the right to fix its own tariff schedules, that income increased. The National Government hired a group of German military advisers who helped with strategy and trained the central army. Chiang's conviction was "military matters come first." He insisted that most of the government's resources be devoted to building the central army and suppressing rival regimes. He used the government treasury as his private checkbook whenever he felt it desirable to purchase the adherence of influential commanders. Yet, that simplification leaves out of account Chiang's consummate ability to play the militarist chess game and his devotion to the pursuit of personal power.

The Red Army

Political chaos in the wake of the Northern Expedition, the unresolved social crisis in rural areas, and the civil wars of 1928–30 provided several groups of Chinese Communist leaders with the opportunity to develop their own military regimes. In the initial stage, these regimes were like many a bandit army before; they were created in areas bordering two or more provinces, relatively inaccessible regions where provincial control was weak. But they were not simply bandit armies. Their leaders had strong convictions about the socioeconomic inequities of Chinese rural life and set about to correct them, using theories and methods absorbed during the previous years of Comintern influence. Experiments in rural social revolution and in guerrilla warfare began to pay off in the creation of larger inland bases and armies.

By mid-1930, these armies were strong enough to induce the Comintern's Executive Committee and Li Li-san in Shanghai to think there was a chance to seize control of three provincial capitals, Changsha, Nanchang, and Wuchang, and thus to start a new revolutionary wave. This was a miscalculation. The effort, however, caused the Nanking government and Chiang Kai-shek to fix their attention upon the Red Army as another potential rival and as a scourge to public order. After settling his score with Feng and Yen and turning north China over to Chang Hsueh-liang, Chiang Kai-shek set out to destroy the Red Army.

It was a protracted war in which each side learned how to use its power against the other. The Mukden Incident and the brief conflict of the Nationalists with Japan around Shanghai in early 1932 gave the Communist forces a respite. But once the National Government turned on the full power of its developing central army, the ill-equipped, poorly financed, and landlocked Red armies had no choice but to abandon their bases and retreat into the remote hinterland to save themselves. The retreat was epic, but it provided the Nanking government with the occasion to extend its power into areas it had never effectively controlled. By the middle of 1936, when remnants of the Red armies had gathered in an impoverished base in northern Shensi, the National Government had moved a respectable way toward reintegrating the country under a single regime.

Many developments other than military helped to make this possible. Some of these were foreign financial and technical assistance, improvements in the monetary system, creation of a centralized banking structure, revival of private industry and commerce, and extension of a modern transportation and communications network. Very little had been done toward solving China's rural social crisis. Civil wars probably intensified the crisis.

The Problem of Japan

A great obstacle to national reunification was the resurgent imperialism of Japan. The National Government's policy was to trade space for time: the space of Manchuria and parts of north China for time in which to build military power and unify the country. This was the meaning of the slogan "unity before resistance." It is difficult to see how the National Government could have adopted the reverse priority —resistance before unity. War against Japan in 1931, '33, or '35 would have been fatal to that government. But it is not difficult to argue in retrospect that the methods used to achieve unity did not produce it. In 1936 there still existed many separatist regimes, and the nation was be-

ginning to clamor against the government and to demand a united front
against Japan.

The Sian Incident of December, 1936, arose over this issue. Chiang's
decision at Sian to call off his war against the Red Army and accept the
policy of united front brought him and the Nanking government its
greatest public support. It also gave the Red Army time to recuperate.

China was not adequately prepared for war against Japan in 1937.
Nor was there any ally or combination of powers that would join it in
war. Soviet Russia feared Japan's rising power in northeast Asia, but it
feared Germany also. It was eager to see the Nationalist government
face Japan with as much unity as possible; hence Soviet insistence on a
united front in China. Britain and France were too absorbed with the
German problem, and their interests in China were too inconsequential
to justify conflict with Japan. The United States was militarily and
psychologically unprepared for war in the Pacific in China's defense.

The reasons for the National Government's decision to risk war over
the Japanese seizure of Peking in July, 1937, are still obscure. There are
too many imponderables to allow us to say that a compromise settlement could have been achieved, trading more space for further time.
After feelers toward a compromise, Chiang Kai-shek and his closest associates decided for war. In the rising tide of nationalism the decision was
undoubtedly popular. It immediately rallied all military groupings to
the government; every regime offered troops.

The war proved to be the National Government's undoing. For
Chiang and his military colleagues, this was an entirely new encounter.
Their experience with civil war had poorly prepared them to fight a
well-armed, well-organized foreign foe which could not be divided or
corrupted. Perhaps that is one reason why the war was so poorly
planned and so disastrously fought in its early stages. Stand-and-die
positional warfare scarcely suited the odds which China faced.

It is my impression that, after the first disastrous year, Nationalist
China relapsed into a more familiar type of warfare, and also that militarist politics revived. The social crisis deepened. China, alone, could
not solve its greatest foreign problem, Japan in China. Neither could
Chiang harness Russian or American power to the Nationalist leaders'
domestic goal, reunification without social revolution.

Some Possible Legacies

What were some of the legacies of this turbulent transitional period?

The Chinese people had had their fill of civil war and foreign intru-
sions. By the end of the Sino-Japanese War in 1945, they longed for

peace, reconstruction, and a unified state. Perhaps a majority of the urban and educated looked to the National Government with hope for the future. They were soon disillusioned and increasingly opened their minds to the Communists' appeals. The Nationalists and Communists fought one more civil war. By the end of 1949 when the outcome was clear, the Government of the People's Republic of China held out the prospect of peace and progress. It had won the "Mandate of Heaven" and most of the people were prepared to give it a chance.

The Nationalist interregnum helped to shape the future by its accomplishments before 1937. The National Government had reduced regional separatism and had started a process of modernization in some aspects of the society and economy. By 1945 it had engaged Japan in a long and costly war and had won back most "lost rights." The Chinese People's Republic inherited a somewhat modernized and professionally trained bureaucracy, an expanded public school system, an enlarged and improved transportation network, a modernized system of public information, the foundations of a coherent monetary and banking system, the beginnings of a national public health service, a rudimentary state statistical system and crop-reporting service, and many other elements of the infrastructure for a modern state and society. By the war's end, the "unequal treaty" system had been ended. There were no foreign-administered concessions, the government set its tariffs on foreign trade, and extraterritoriality was a thing of the past. These not inconsiderable achievements opened a path to the future.

The Communist leaders who assumed national responsibility in 1949 were themselves a product of the age described. They grew up in it and reacted against it. Military separatism had provided the CCP its chance to survive. Mao Tse-tung and his colleagues learned the power of the sword. The Red Army grew in the interstices of a fragmented state. It recruited manpower among the disaffected peasantry. The leaders learned to "go to the masses" and listen to their grievances, and to mobilize youth, peasants, workers, and women. They gained valuable experience in "United Front work."

The environment of militarism and foreign intrusion shaped Communist domestic and foreign policies after 1949 to an important degree. Communist leaders were determined to make China a strong and unified country, set on a course of forced-draft industrialization, and they were intent on correcting the social abuses of an archaic society as they conceived these abuses to be. The memory of this turbulent period may color the outlook of the Chinese people and influence the policies of their leaders for a generation to come.

Comments by Wang Gungwu

We are indebted to Professor Wilbur for this paper which contributes greatly toward the explanation of the most confusing events of the Republican period. The analysis of the key questions of "militarism" and "political disintegration" is excellent. In particular, his information concerning financial issues and military organization is most helpful toward illuminating the frequent shifts of power, alliances, and leadership.

The paper raises so many important questions that any attempt to comment on it must appear inadequate. I shall not try to cover all these questions but limit myself to the general theme of the Conference and comment only in terms of the heritage of China's past and its relation to modern historical change. In this context, I wish to draw attention to one of the most significant points in Professor Wilbur's paper. This is the point about the "power [of] ideology" and "the combination of mobilized nationalism [and] concentrated military power" which tipped the balance in favor of one group between 1923 and 1928. Again and again, Professor Wilbur returns to the importance of organization and ideology, and much of his analysis suggests that the type of organization which eventually succeeded was largely determined by ideology. He notes early in the paper "the absence of institutionalized nationalism" among the militarists in their province-wide bases and his discussion of the devastating effect of large-scale defections of their non-politicized and unindoctrinated troops to the National Revolutionary Army is particularly convincing. This helps to explain why the Kuomintang (KMT) forces failed to fulfill their *national* mission and how their leaders came to earn the name of "militarists" themselves.[1]

The emphasis on ideology is, I believe, very important because it best

[1] Professor Wilbur carefully avoids the loaded term "warlord" and defines "militarism" as a system in which force is the normal arbiter of power and policy. By this definition, Chiang Kai-shek, and even Mao Tse-tung, are militarists. This blurs the important differences between the KMT and CCP forces and the militarists of the 1916–28 period which are essential to our understanding of the KMT and CCP successes.

reveals the nature and extent of the "political disintegration" which marked the downfall of the Manchu Ch'ing dynasty.[2] It was not so much military separatism which characterized that disintegration; it was ultimately the response of the educated Chinese to the impact of Western power and ideas which brought the disintegration about. In other words, for China during the three decades from 1900 to 1930, the development of nationalism on the one hand, and universalist ideologies of Western origin on the other, determined the way political authority disintegrated and, as a result, also the way central authority was eventually to be reestablished. The conscious efforts, unprecedented in their intensity, to rouse the Chinese to realize that the crisis they observed was a national crisis of a fundamental nature engaged more and more of the Chinese people. It was this commitment of millions from all walks of life to support any leader who could free China from foreign domination which was decisive both in the KMT successes against the militarists and in the eventual victory of the Communists in 1949.

In short, by using "political disintegration" to mean the disintegration of political authority rather than the mere breakdown of central administration, we can see the qualitative difference between the loss of political direction following the fall of Confucianism and the imperial system after 1911 and the failure of earlier dynasties to control the machinery of a centralized government. Whether or not all the protagonists realized this, it was the need for a new *kind* of authority which gave the process of centralization its special problems in the 1920's.

By so defining "political disintegration," it is perhaps obvious why direct comparisons with what appear to be similar periods of distintegration in Chinese history may be misleading. Historical analogy, however, is a common Chinese failing, and, even if we are ourselves skeptical, we cannot ignore how Chinese observers may mentally and openly compare disparate periods of China's past. For our purposes, it is relevant to look at earlier periods of division or disintegration of central power, but it must be borne in mind that ultimately it is not comparable fragments of history which are important but the cumulative

[2] This disintegration is excellently summed up by Professor Wilbur, as "the gradual breakdown of the Chinese social fabric in the nineteenth century under the pressure of a rapidly growing population and increasing economic inequality between social classes; the decay of the imperial institution and decline in the efficiency of the Ch'ing bureaucracy; and foreign competition for paramountcy over parts of China's territory and wealth. . . . Confucianism as the national ethical system withered under the competition of many alien ideologies such as Christianity, republicanism, social Darwinism, socialism, Marxism-Leninism, and, above all, nationalism" (pp. 219–20).

effect of continuous historical experience which makes all the difference.

To begin with, let me suggest that there are nine identifiable periods of division or loss of central control since the Eastern Chou, as follows:

1. The Ch'un-ch'iu and Chan-kuo period, the classic example of centralization after centuries of division, but centralization with a new ideology (Legalism) and a New Order (the Ch'in Imperial System).[3]

2. The transition from Ch'in to Han and the swift reunification under Liu Pang, followed by modifications in the new ideology and New Order, especially after Confucianism was "established."[4]

3. The fall of Eastern Han and the division into Three Kingdoms, a period of disorder lasting almost a century and leading rapidly to another period of division.[5]

4. The Sixteen Kingdoms and the North-South division of about 260 years, periods of foreign invasions and conquest of North China accompanied by new feudal relationships and the new faith of Buddhism, with Buddhism failing to be a new state ideology and reunification eventually achieved in the name of a revived Confucianism in Northern Chou and Sui.[6]

5. The erosion of central power after the An Lu-shan rebellion (through *Chieh-tu shih* or military governors) to the re-centralization of the Northern Sung, a period of about 220 years during which 80 years (*circa* 890–970) represented a period of complete fragmentation.[7]

[3] I should refer at least to D. Bodde's *China's First Unifier* (Leiden: E. J. Brill, 1938), but the highly developed inter-state relations of these centuries distinguished the period from any other in Chinese history and deserve particular attention; see Richard L. Walker, *The Multi-State System of Ancient China* (Hamden, Conn.: Shoe String Press, 1953).

[4] The "establishment" of Confucianism and its use by Han Wu-ti and his successors is clearly outlined in Ping-ti Ho, "Salient Aspects of China's Heritage," pp. 9–15, this volume.

[5] It is possible to add another short period, the transition from Wang Mang to the Eastern Han (Hans Bielenstein, "The Restoration of the Han Dynasty," *Bulletin of the Museum of Far Eastern Antiquities* 26 [1954]: 1–209 and 31 [1959]: 1–287), but as the divisions were so brief, they need not concern us here.

[6] The unifying role which Buddhism played was important for Chinese society and culture (Arthur F. Wright, *Buddhism in Chinese History* [Stanford: Stanford University Press, 1959]), but the faith played little part in the political system.

[7] A full study of the period of fragmentation has yet to be made. For a study

6. The division of Sung-Khitan and Sung-Jurchen–Mongol empires, the latter of 150 years, followed by unification by the Mongol conquerors.[8]

7. The breakdown of Mongol government, a period of over 20 years before the reunification under Chu Yuan-chang.

8. The transition from Ming to Ch'ing dynasties, in several stages, over a period of 65 years (1616–81).[9]

9. The militarist period, 1916–1927, followed by a period of partial reunification, 1928–1949.[10]

It would be easy to argue from the nine periods of division, lasting almost 1,350 years out of some 3,000 years (from Western Chou to 1949), that division was as normal as unification in Chinese history.[11] Since each period of division was also dominated by armed struggles for power, Professor Wilbur may be justified in arguing that regional militarism was "an old and recurrent Chinese problem." But there are reasons why such a view could be misleading.

First, it should be noted that of the 1,350 years of division, about 1,100 years were of the periods before the eleventh century. Since about 975, for almost 1,000 years, there have been only 260 years of division, and since 1368, only about 50 years of serious division. Furthermore, during the past thousand years, all the divisions have involved foreign conquerors and the repulse of foreign conquerors, and perhaps only the

---

of the structural changes which preceded the re-centralization process in the North, see my *The Structure of Power in North China during the Five Dynasties* (Kuala Lumpur: University of Malaya Press, 1963).

[8] Professor Herbert Franke has drawn my attention to the fascinating developments in inter-state relations in east, north and central Asia during this period of China's weakness which he is now investigating.

[9] Neither periods (7) and (8) are listed as periods of division in the official histories, but it may be argued that central control was negligible during parts of each period. If they are not included, China would have to be described as being continuously unified for over 600 years (1276–1911).

[10] It is arguable if 1928–49 could be called an extension of the militarist period. It is perhaps less misleading to distinguish between a period of fragmentation and one of partially successful unification under one dominant regime.

[11] In Professor Wilbur's words, "centrifugal tendencies were always powerful, and the area we think of as China was divided for periods nearly as long as those in which it was united." I take him to mean China Proper, but as I point out later in this comment, regional forces in the *new* territories of Manchuria, Mongolia, Turkestan, and Tibet may well produce new military separatism. This, however, cannot be said to have been rooted in Chinese history.

20 years prior to the foundation of the Ming and the 12 years from 1916 to 1928 could be described as primarily periods of regional militarism. Once reduced to these two periods, it would be difficult to find useful analogies between Chu Yuan-chang and his rivals and the struggles of Sun Yat-sen, Chiang Kai-shek, and Mao Tse-tung against various "militarists."

Second, by returning to the question of "political disintegration" as defined earlier, none of the earlier periods except the first had anything to do with the decay of an Old Order and the emergence of a New Order. One may note that the twentieth century, compared with this first period, had its "Hundred Schools," albeit mostly foreign in origin, and its new ruthless centralizing ideology in communism (as compared with Legalism), but many historians will, I think rightly, regard such comparisons as far-fetched. We do not have equivalents of the complex *chu-hou* and multi-state relationships which were to last for over five centuries. It would be tempting to compare Mao Tse-tung with Ch'in Shih-huang-ti, hopefully wishing a new Ch'en She and Wu Kuang would appear soon. This, however, is not history and is well left to political aspirants. As for the other seven periods, the fourth produced some tantalizing possibilities with Buddhism as a new faith, and the fifth resulted in important changes in the social, economic, and political structure, but all three periods (first, fourth, and fifth) ended in the same basic imperial system which was established during the Western Han and persisted with modifications until 1911.

Third, I have implied above that division arising from foreign conquests may not be compared with the divisions of the twentieth century. If we take the partial Japanese conquests of 1932–45, it is obvious that Japan did represent a New Order which the T'oba and Sha-t'o Turks, the Khitans, and the Jurchens did not.[12] As for the total conquests, both the Mongols and the Manchus eventually succumbed to the Chinese imperial tradition. It should, however, be pointed out that the Mongols brought southwestern China (especially Yunnan) into the Chinese realm, while the Manchus doubled China's territorial extent by incorporating Manchuria, Tibetan lands, and key parts of Mongolia and Turkestan. These are new regions which the Chinese have never been able to hold in the past, and in the period 1911–49, the

[12] Although this is speculative, Japan, as a mutant of a New World Order, dominated by Western technology and political and economic values, might well have imposed a New Order directly on the Chinese had they succeeded in conquering China. They could then have been the instruments for a modernization no less ruthless than any the Chinese could themselves have established.

independence of Mongolia and Tibet and at least the regionalism of Manchuria and Sinkiang greatly influenced the key political developments within China Proper. This is undeniable and obviously provides new possibilities for military regionalism today and in the future before these territories break off or are wholly integrated.

The point about foreign involvements is also relevant here in confirming the uniqueness of the twentieth-century divisions (the ninth period). The impact of the West since the 1840's is qualitatively different in two significant ways. It offered a new international system based on superior force and a new kind of economics, and it offered new alternatives for China in its technology, its ideologies, and its educational institutions. And although this impact and the response it elicited from the Chinese contributed to the political disintegration of the Confucian Order, the two together also played their part in reducing the period of disunion.[13] For, indeed, if we are to measure the extent of change during this period, what is remarkable is not so much the long duration of division, but the speed with which the divisions were brought to an end. It did not really take the Chinese long to find new sources of authority, whether it be the new militant nationalism or the even newer, even more militant communism—both centralist and authoritarian in easily recognizable ways.

It seems to me that an equally useful approach toward the period of regional militarism is to seek the factors which speeded the partial reunification in 1928 and the successful reunification in 1949 (Taiwan is exceptional for obvious reasons). For such an approach, I would like to suggest certain broad categories for investigation: the first two represent cumulative historical experience stemming from continuities in China's past itself, and the next three from new factors of modernization derived from Western advances.

1. The long tradition of being *one* political system which is inseparable from Chinese civilization itself, reinforced by Neo-Confucianism, and more recently by anti-foreign, anti-imperialist feeling.
2. The last centuries of social, cultural, and economic integration, especially since 1368.

[13] The West has usually been depicted as the cause of China's disintegration. We should also examine it as a factor in the new unification—both as the protagonists (imperialists) to be fought and opposed at all costs and as the innovators, the revolutionaries, the messengers for a New Order. Certainly the more powerful, longer-range weapons of the past two generations and the new communications media have made traditional provincialism in China Proper a thing of the past.

3. The range and power of modern arms and transportation—the technological leap which shortened distances and reduced China Proper at least to manageable proportions.
4. The new economics of tighter financial control and more success-ful revenue collection, leading to the desire for more sophisticated and larger-scale financial manipulation and planned development.
5. Education and mass communication—the new ideologies and the rapid spread of new skills, all aimed at rapid modernization.

With these factors in mind, it is perhaps easier to understand why each "militarist" or any other kind of contender could find support as a potential unifier. It may not matter whether each one of them saw himself as a Liu Pang, a Chao K'uang-yin or a Chu Yuan-chang in modern dress, armed with modern weapons, financed by foreign banks, and indoctrinating his followers with the latest methods. What matters was the tendency to favor more and more the men who consistently saw the country's problems in *national* (anti-foreign, anti-imperialist) terms. From this point of view, it became clear that the only leaders with this objective in mind were those of the KMT and the Chinese Communist Party. These men had transcended militarism and offered themselves as bearers of the Mandate of Heaven to save the nation. They were men who looked as if they could fulfill their promise to "rightly govern the state and bring tranquillity to all" (*chih-kuo p'ing t'ien-hsia*).

Comments by Hsu Dau-lin

I think it is unnecessary for me to waste words here in praise of Profes-sor Wilbur's paper: its eminent scholarship speaks for it better than any commentator can do. It is a brilliant example of the work Western scholarship has produced on recent China. It has helped clarify a num-ber of problems of this little-studied period of great historical con-fusion. I would like to limit my comments to two topics: (1) the so-called "regionalism"; (2) defections and betrayals by Chinese generals.

Regionalism

Professor Wilbur refers to "regionalism" under the late Ch'ing and sees in the Chinese military regimes in the 1920's a "legacy" of the regional leaders who fought the Taiping rebellion. It is on this point that I would like to offer a different view.

Professor Wilbur describes various factors which, strongly centrifugal, kept China divided almost as long as it was united. My reaction to this is the other way around, because I am rather impressed by the strong integrating forces which, despite all the centrifugal factors, kept China united longer than it was divided.

There are, I believe, two important forces at work in China's unification: its cultural ideology and its political ideology. (Economy might be a third. Professor Ho in his paper in this volume [pp. 33–35] has called our attention to the integrating function of the *Landsmannschaften* in China.) In the face of cultural ideology, no local subculture was strong enough to become a serious obstacle to China's political unity. Again and again, enlightened magistrates destroyed local "superstitious temples," suppressed local "bad" customs in China's "less civilized" areas. The political ideology of national unity made no ruling house feel comfortable in coexistence with another ruler on China's territory. Even rebels and bandits, once they were masters of a region, dreamed of unifying China, either for themselves or for the coming "true Emperor."

It is true that in Chinese history, whenever a dynasty declined, military separatism emerged. But the Manchu Court in the 1860's, in my view, had not yet reached that point. It is also true that, as toward the end of the Taiping rebellion, the Court was "forced to accept the necessity of greater regional control by governors-general and governors. In the administration of provincial finance of Kiangsi, for example, the governor and provincial treasurer enjoyed a much greater degree of freedom than in normal times in directing the disposal of the tax revenue."[1] But the personal power of regional leaders was by no means unlimited in scope. But David Pong has shown that even "Tseng Kuofan, although bearing the title of Imperial Commissioner for military affairs in Kiangnan, was not able to exercise absolute authority over Shen Pao-chen" (who was a friend and protégé of Tseng). Tseng was annoyed to such a degree that he made

> a severe personal attack on Shen for being impertinent in his official capacity and showing a lack of consideration for a friend

[1] David Pong, "The Income and Military Expenditure of Kiangsi Province in the Last Years of the Taiping Rebellion," *Journal of Asian Studies*, vol. 1, p. 66.

and colleague. . . . There were still a number of factors which bound the provincial officials to the throne. Many regional leaders at this time still possessed a strong sense of loyalty to the Emperor who, after all, still retained the ultimate power of appointment.[2]

Pong concludes—

... "Regionalism" as it developed towards the end of the Taiping period, was a very limited one. It was still conditioned by central control in the sphere of official appointment, in directing the provinces to provide funds for other provinces; it was, in short, still serving the imperial interests in a large number of ways.[3]

We must, above all, not forget that Tseng Kuo-fan, Tso Tsung-t'ang, Li Hung-chang, as well as the other regional leaders after them, had held relatively long terms of office only because they were judged successful in their entrusted mission, not because they were unremovable. They were transferred to another trouble-shooting job or just to another corner of the empire as soon as the Court found it desirable. This firm control over regional officials prevailed even well into the last years of the dynasty: Yuan Shih-k'ai, powerful as he was, was simply forced into retirement once the Court chose to do so.

Even during the first Republican years Peking retained effective control over China's separate provinces. Yuan Shih-k'ai sent his military governors (Chang Hsi-luan and Tuan Chih-kwei) to Hupeh and Fengtien as late as August, 1915, though powerful local commanders were dying to get these posts. Only when he was engrossed in his dreams of reviving the imperial system and hence incurred the wrath of the nation, did Yuan capitulate. On January 8, 1916, Wang Chan-yuan got Hupeh; two months later, Chang Tso-lin got Fengtien. Since that date, every Chinese division commander dreamed of becoming a military governor.

With Yuan Shih-k'ai's death (June, 1916) and the split of the Peiyang group into factions, China started quickly to disintegrate. In February, 1918, Feng Yü-hsiang was ordered to fight in Hunan, but he stopped midway and published a "circular telegram" from Wuhsueh urging peace. When he, thereupon, was dismissed, his "brigade," 9,553 officers and men, published another "circular telegram" saying they would rather face a firing squad together than let him go. The government revoked his dismissal. In May, 1920, Wu P'ei-fu, fighting in Hunan, suddenly quit and marched his troops toward Peking. After defeating the

Premier's forces, he set up, in alliance with Chang Tso-lin, another cabinet (August, 1920). From that day on, the Peking government was no longer in control of the warlords, but instead was controlled by them.

"Military regionalism" in recent China thus started in the 1920's—at the earliest in the 1910's, but not, in my view, in the 1850–60's.

Defections and Betrayals by Chinese Generals

In the period covered in Professor Wilbur's paper, that is from the 1910's to the 1930's, military secessions, uprisings, defections and betrayals were frequent, at some times almost continuous, phenomena. They were of various duration, from a few days to a few months or a few years, but all shed an equal dishonoring light on Chinese generals. I have no intention of passing judgment on actions, but for a better understanding of the historical situation, a few comments on the changing background are in order.

Government's Authority and Rebellions

Military campaigns of a regional leader against government forces took on the nature of a "secession" or an "uprising" depending on both the authority of the government and the prestige of the opposing party. When the government's authority is high and the dissenting party has little or no prestige, then such action will appear simply as an "uprising"; it has no popular support and cannot last long. When, on the other hand, the government's authority is low and the opposing party enjoys high prestige, then it is the government which will collapse. But when both parties are equal in authority and prestige—when the government has lost much of its authority or its authority is not yet firmly consolidated, and is facing an opponent with certain prestige—then there will be a long period of continuous struggles between old adversaries, of emergence of new contenders, or of coexistence between several rival groups, peaceful or otherwise. Now let us review the historical period in question.

From 1912 to 1915 Yuan Shih-kai's government enjoyed unchallenged authority; Sun Yat-sen's armed opposition during the summer of 1913 was crushed in two months (July–August). A secessionist regime was set up in the southwest in opposition to Yuan's new empire (May, 1916), but it was dissolved as soon as Yuan died (July, 1916). Tuan Ch'i-jui, as premier, had inherited Yuan's position of power, but created a strong rival in Feng Kuo-chang who, once made China's President, refused to play the role of a puppet under Tuan and aligned his "Chihli" generals against Tuan. When Ts'ao K'un, the "Chihli" leader, and Chang Tso-lin, the new leader from Fengtien, together, defeated Tuan in summer, 1920, and set up a cabinet of their own choice, the Peking government lost all its prestige and China was subjected to continuous warfare between feuding warlords. This situation prevailed well into the final years of the third decade, although the Northern Expedition of the Kuomintang (KMT) claimed "national unification" in December, 1928, and actual fighting did indeed cease for a short while. This was the moment when the National Government in Nanking was transformed from a local regime into a national government. At the beginning it was set up only as an opposition organization (April, 1927) against the legitimate government in Wuhan (which was moved there from Canton in January 1927). But Nanking's power and prestige increased in proportion with Wuhan's confusion and weakness so that in December, 1927, Wuhan's leader simply joined Nanking. The regime in Peking led a still less respectable existence and, with Chang Tso-lin's departure on June 3, 1928, simply disappeared.

But the Nanking government, though theoretically achieving national unity in December, 1928, was far from having a fully respected authority. Various regional leaders, though on the surface submitting to Nanking's orders, were militarily more powerful than ever before and regarded Chiang Kai-shek (who as China's President received the first foreign envoys in Nanking on June 3, 1929) only as a parvenu. Here are the repeated attempts by the various leaders to overthrow Chiang:

1929	March	Li Tsung-jen's uprising in Kwangsi
	May	Feng Yü-hsiang's first uprising in Honan
	Oct.–Nov.	Feng Yü-hsiang's second uprising in Honan (Chiang commanded against Feng in person)
	Dec.–Jan.	T'ang Sheng-chih's mutiny in Chengchow
1930	March–Oct.	The Yen-Feng war: all the major anti-Chiang leaders, Yen Hsi-shan, Feng Yü-hsiang, Li Tsung-jen, Wang Ching-wei, T'ang Sheng-chih, united in their effort to overthrow Nanking. An anti-government was set up in Peiping (Sept. 1). Chiang suffered 80,000 casualties, his opponents 150,000.
1931	May–Oct.	"Military Government" in Canton (set up by Li Tsung-jen and Wang Ching-wei).

But the Mukden Incident of September, 1931, imposed a moral restraint upon all Nanking's adversaries and Chiang's prestige rose high. After the Mukden Incident, anti-Chiang drives became less frequent, less warlike and were invariably overcome quickly:

1933	May–Aug.	Feng Yü-hsiang's fourth uprising in Chahar
	Nov.–Jan.	Fukien uprising ("People's Government")
1934	May	Feng Yü-hsiang's fifth uprising (lasting two weeks)
1936	June–	The Kwangtung-Kwangsi Crisis (Ch'en Chi-t'ang and Li Tsung-jen in alliance against Nanking), ended by negotiation.

After the peaceful solution of the Kwangtung-Kwangsi Crisis, Chiang's prestige reached such an unprecedented height that it even forced his captors in Sian to release him and to obey him. But this probably also prompted the Japanese not to delay their attack any longer (July, 1937).

Defections for sale

Buying enemy subgenerals to defeat the enemy leader has long been a favorite device in the hands of Chinese conquerors, though it was hardly used in the nineteenth century: not during the Taiping Rebellion, nor in the 1911 Revolution, nor even by Yuan Shih-k'ai against Sun Yat-sen in 1913 or his Yunnan opponents in 1915.

The first purchase of defection in recent Chinese history was made by the Canton rival regime (Ts'en Ch'un-hsüan) in 1920, the first General for sale was Wu P'ei-fu. For 300,000 Canton dollars (Mex. $240,000), he concluded peace with his opponents and marched his troops against Peking.[4] The trick was soon learned in the north and Wu P'ei-fu's first subgeneral became his first pupil in defection. For 1,000,000 Fengtien dollars (Mex. $150,000) Feng Yü-hsiang rebelled against Wu P'ei-fu and brought about his quick collapse in October, 1924.[5]

But it is in the hands of Generalissimo Chiang K'ai-shek that buying enemy generals was developed to a formidable weapon which was put to uninhibited use. Professor Wilbur has shown us in his paper in this volume to what extent silver bullets and new titles contributed to the success of the Northern Expedition in its first phase. The same device helped to overcome a number of major domestic crises, as is shown in the table on the following page.

[4] See *Wu P'ei-fu hsien sheng chi* (Collections of Mr. Wu). Taipei, private print, 1960, p. 337.

[5] *Ibid.*, p. 497.

Date		Opponents	Defecting Enemy Generals
1929	April	Li Tsung-jen	Hu Tsung-to, T'ao Chün, Hsia Wei, Ch'eng Ju-huai
	May	Feng Yü-hsiang	Han Fu-chü, Shih Yu-san
	Dec.	T'ang Sheng-chih	Ho Chian
1933	Nov.	Fukien's "People's Government"	Shen Kuang-han, Mao Wei-sho, Ch'u Sho-nien
1936	June	Ch'en Chi-t'ang, Li Tsung-jen	Kwangtung's air force and Yu Han-mou

In times when the government enjoys high prestige, defections hardly appear as immoral. But it is entirely different with those who become addicted to defection and sell their allegiances back and forth a number of times. A notorious pair of such habitual defectors are Han Fu-chü and Shih Yu-san. The former, Han Fu-chü, was promoted from soldier to General by Feng Yü-hsiang, defected Feng in May, 1929, to become Governor of Honan (June), but in March, 1930, during the Yen-Feng war, fought again on Feng's side, defecting from Chiang. In September, when Feng's chances appeared slim, he again defected from Feng, this time becoming Governor of Shantung. In December, 1937, he conspired with the Japanese, thus defecting from Nanking for a second time, but his scheme was detected. He was executed in January, 1938, in Hankow.

Shih Yu-san was also a Feng-made general but he, too, defected from Feng in May, 1929. He became Governor of Anhwei only six months later (November 24). The Generalissimo officiated in person at his swearing-in ceremony. One week later, December 2, he rebelled, and attacked and almost took Nanking. Though he was defeated only after a bitter battle, he was allowed to "repent," and was even given a command post in Honan. This did not prevent him from defecting and fighting on the Yen-Feng side in 1930. A little later, in July, 1931, he attempted another uprising in Honan, was quickly defeated and he again "retired." In September, 1934, he attempted, for the fourth time, an uprising but accomplished nothing. During the Sino-Japanese War he was made Governor of Chahar but was executed for conspiracy with the enemy, on December 8, 1940 (in Chungking).

It is interesting to note that both these notorious defectors came from Feng Yü-hsiang's camp, both defected from their master, himself a master-defector (Feng was called "General Turncoat" from 1924 on), and both died before a firing squad.

Tang Tsou

4

Revolution, Reintegration, and Crisis in Communist China: A Framework for Analysis

Introductory Remarks

The totalitarian regime in China emerged as a reaction against the country's political disintegration during the early part of the twentieth century.[1] This response followed the failure of the Nationalists to build up a unified party and a reintegrated polity soon enough to withstand the disruptive effects of the Sino-Japanese War. One of the most re- markable achievements of the political leadership of the Chinese Com- munists up to 1959 was their ability to maintain the unity of their party and an adequate degree of political integration, despite both the un- precedented problems confronting them and the inevitable clashes of views on policy issues. They tried to promote political integration in their own way with policies entailing obvious economic and sometimes even political costs.

Total control and total mobilization, two distinguishing features of a totalitarian polity, were indispensable ingredients of the Peking re-

[1] This paper was completed in the first week of January, 1967. The written comments on it by Professors Charles P. FitzGerald and Jerome Cohen were completed in March on the basis of their oral remarks made at the conference in the first week of February. No extensive revisions have been made in the paper to take account of developments since early January and the voluminous new materials available. Some footnotes have, however, been added to include new materials which throw light on the Cultural Revolution.

The author wishes to acknowledge the research grant given him by the Rockefeller Foundation during the academic year 1965–66, and the research support given by the Social Science Divisional Research Committee, the Cen- ter for International Studies, and the Committee on Far Eastern Studies of the University of Chicago.

gime's stability and success. But the Chinese Communists seemed to have realized that total control without political integration would create tremendous reaction against them which would have to be dealt with by the intensified use of secret police and physical terror. Repression would soon reach a point of diminishing returns and control could break down during a period of prolonged crisis. Success in mobilization probably correlates with the degree of integration achieved within the elite and between the elite and the masses. Upon closer examination, measures undertaken to mobilize the masses are sometimes integrative measures as well. As Karl W. Deutsch defines it, social mobilization is "the process in which major clusters of old social, economic and psychological commitments are eroded or broken and people become available for new patterns of socialization and behavior."[2] The erosion of old social, economic, and psychological commitments is one aspect of the process of social disintegration. The development of new patterns of socialization and behavior is one facet of the process of social integration.

While the Chinese Communists succeeded in bringing into existence a polity with a higher degree of integration than the Nationalists, they have encountered mounting difficulties in adjusting their integrative measures to the trends toward functional differentiation, specialization, professionalism, and some amount of routinization which occur in all stable, modern, and industrializing societies. The achievement of a degree of integration enabled the regime to survive and to recover from the extraordinary crisis of three consecutive years of agricultural failure and the ever escalating dispute with the Soviet Union—difficulties which would have brought down most other governments. But the intensified attack on the intellectuals since November, 1965, the Great Proletarian Cultural Revolution, and the current purges make it clear that setbacks in both domestic and foreign policies activated two conflicting opinion groups which the integrative measures of the regime have failed to harmonize and harness. The struggle for power between these two groups has centered precisely around the issue of the extent to which the thought of Mao Tse-tung should be the integrative myth[3] of the political community and should shape policies and guide activities in various spheres of social life. This conflict raises the very question of how well the ideology and the pattern of integrative measures

[2] Karl W. Deutsch, "Social Mobilization and Political Development," *American Political Science Review,* 55 (September, 1961) : 494.

[3] For the term "integrative myth," see Chalmers Johnson, "The Role of Social Science in China Scholarship," *World Politics,* 17 (January, 1965): 268.

which had been developed in the revolutionary period in relatively backward base areas fitted the new situation and emerging trends.[4] Since Communist China offers an example of an experiment in one type of political integration, an examination of her past achievements enables us to see the conditions facilitating this type of political integration and to discern the methods employed to promote it. Insofar as this experiment has created its own problems, subjecting it to analysis helps us to discover the limits of its success and the roots of its difficulties.

The Political Community

Analytically speaking, political integration has three different aspects, although emipirically they are linked together: integration among the elite, integration between the elite and the masses, and integration of a political community. Logically and historically, one takes precedence over the other in the order given. Without integration among the elite, integration between the elite and the masses is difficult to achieve; without integration between the elite and the masses, there cannot be an integrated political community. In a disintegrated political community, the process of political integration begins historically with the integration of the elite or a counter-elite and ends with a reintegrated political community through the integration beween the elite and the masses. To the degree that integration is achieved, the reintegrated political community furnishes a general framework within which the elite and the masses find their places. Thus, a study of the process of integration must start with the elite, but a study of the system of integrative measures can start with the political community.

As Herbert Spiro suggests, "most communities are political systems."[5] Conversely, a political system is inseparable from a political community. As Talcott Parsons observes, "a relatively established 'politically organized society' is clearly a 'moral community' to some degree, its members sharing common norms, values, and culture."[6] But the choice of the political community rather than the political system per se as our focus of attention is a deliberate one. In a situation where profound

[4] John W. Lewis, "The Study of Chinese Political Culture," *World Politics*, 18 (April, 1966): 511.

[5] Herbert J. Spiro, "Comparative Politics: A Comprehensive Approach," *American Political Science Review*, 56 (September, 1962): 577.

[6] Talcott Parsons, "Some Reflections on the Place of Force in Social Process," in *Internal War*, ed. Harry Eckstein (New York: Free Press of Glencoe, 1964), p. 34.

changes take place in all spheres of human life (social, economic, political, intellectual, moral, ideological, cultural, religious, artistic, technological), the environment and the political system interact continuously. From the environment, demands arise which lead to the disruption of the traditional political system.[7] Then a new political system emerges which makes the restructuring of the environment its principal preoccupation. To encompass the interactions between the political system and its environment, the term "political community" is used.[8]

A political community presupposes a set of basic principles governing social and political life. In a democratic or a traditional community, there is an agreement on these fundamental principles, and the political system is based on this consensus. This agreement on fundamentals (political consensus) has its origin in the ideologies or schools of thought which once divided the politically active men into various groupings. After a revolution and through a long process of evolution and change, there then emerges an ideological agreement which, generally speaking, draws upon selected ideologies in different proportions to serve as the foundation of an integrated political community.

The collapse of the traditional order in China left in its wake a highly disintegrated political community. It produced a total response in the form of a totalitarian movement and regime with a total ideology which contained an all-inclusive criticism of the existing society and justified total change and reconstruction. In a totalitarian system, the official ideology backed directly by the coercive power of the state serves as a substitute for the agreement on fundamentals characteristic of both democratic and traditional political communities.

Ideology performs several important functions in a political community. It helps to integrate the various functional groups in the society by laying down the basic principles of social life which distinguish between "right" and "wrong." It prescribes the "rules of the game" guid-

[7] For a discussion of the political system and its environment, see David Easton, *A Framework for Political Analysis* (Englewood Cliffs, N.J.: Prentice-Hall, 1965), chap. 7.

[8] Presumably, the term "political system" may be used synonymously with the term "political community." But sometimes the former term is used in a narrower sense. For example, Gabriel Almond observes that every political system is embedded in a particular pattern of orientations to political action, i.e., political culture (Gabriel Almond, "Comparative Political Systems," *Journal of Politics,* 18 [August, 1956]: 396). Statements of this kind suggest that orientation to political action is not part of the political system per se as the term was used by Almond. The term "political community" has the advantage of encompassing "political culture" as well as other things which interest us.

ing competition for power and material resources. It sets the general orientation of the political community by defining the common purposes. It provides schematic images of social and political realities which enable the actors to "understand" their environment and to cope with it. It enlists commitments, motivates action, and creates a collective conscience to the extent that it is accepted by the actors and internalized in their personality through a process of socialization. Finally, it legitimizes the political system and transforms power into authority.[9]

These usual functions of ideology are magnified in the case of Communist China for the following reasons. First and most obviously, the possession of an all-embracing official ideology is a basic characteristic of totalitarian regimes. Second, Communist China has a newly established regime in which revolutionary dynamism and momentum have not entirely lost their force. The notion of "the end of ideology" is a view developed by intellectuals in a stable society to characterize a phenomenon which occurs typically in mature regimes. What it actually denotes is the decline of a particular *type* of ideology, that is, such total ideologies as Marxism and Leninism. Far from meaning the end of ideology, it refers to the achievement of an "ideological agreement" which has become "the ideology of the major parties in the developed states of Europe and America."[10] In a sense, the "end of ideology" signifies the triumph of one type of ideology. As applied to a mature totalitarian regime such as the Soviet Union, this notion refers to the process of ideological erosion, a process that in the Soviet Union has gone rather far under the impact of socioeconomic reality and emerging problems for which the ideology has provided no adequate answers. By contrast, Mao Tse-tung, Lin Piao, and their followers have been making a determined effort to reassert the thought of Mao Tse-tung in order to preserve the original revolutionary dynamism and momentum.

Third, in contrast to the Bolsheviks, the Chinese Communists came to power after a protracted political-military struggle within China.

[9] Clifford Geertz, "Ideology as a Cultural System," in *Ideology and Discontent,* ed. David Apter (New York: Free Press of Glencoe, 1964), pp. 47–71. Apter, "Introduction," *ibid.,* pp. 15–46. David Easton, *A Systems Analysis of Political Life* (New York: John Wiley & Sons, 1965), pp. 286–88, 289–90. Johnson, "Social Science in China Scholarship," p. 268. Talcott Parsons, *The Social System* (Glencoe, Ill.: Free Press, 1951), pp. 349–59.

[10] Seymour Martin Lipset, "Some Further Comments on 'The End of Ideology,'" *American Political Science Review,* 60 (March, 1966): 17. See also Joseph La Palombara, "Decline of Ideology: A Dissent and an Interpretation," *ibid.,* pp. 1–16.

The thought of Mao Tse-tung evolved out of practical actions and policy decisions undertaken in the past. It consists essentially of the rationale behind these undertakings and of the justification and rationalization of them. It is the codification of the revolutionary experience of the Chinese Communist Party (CCP). It guided the revolutionary struggle from defeat to victory. It gained its legitimacy and appeal by its proven effectiveness in the past. Furthermore, the CCP from 1927 to 1949 was a Communist party without a proletarian base. Instead of social origin, the Chinese Communists therefore stressed the acceptance of Marxist-Leninist-Maoist ideology as the criterion of a Communist. Ideological indoctrination thus became an absolute necessity and the sole guaranty of the self-identity of the party.

Fourth, in the traditional political system in China an explicit system of official ideology in the form of Confucianism played an important role in legitimizing the regime, in humanizing the autocratic rule, in determining the content of education, and in defining the proper rules governing human relationships. The rejection of the specific content of Confucianism created a moral and intellectual void, while the breakdown of age-old political institutions produced a long period of chaos. The Chinese were confronted with novel social situations which seemed unstructured and incomprehensible to them at a time when institutionalized guides for behavior and thought were weak or absent. It is during times like these that men urgently need what Clifford Geertz calls "maps of problematic social reality" and "a template or blueprint for the organization of social and psychological processes."[11] Marxism-Leninism and the thought of Mao constituted such a map and blueprint. Even today, the Chinese Communists stress the importance of ideological unity. Lin Piao in his important letter of March 11, 1966, states: "China is a great socialist state of the dictatorship of the proletariat and has a population of 700 million. It needs unified thinking. . . . This is Mao Tse-tung's thinking."[12] This continued emphasis on ideological unity may very well be a reaction against the moral and intellectual chaos which characterized the period of political disintegration. It may also represent the persistence of a cultural pattern.

Fifth, the Chinese Communists have undertaken to modernize and industrialize their country under more difficult material conditions, but with greater success, than any other underdeveloped nation after

[11] Geertz, "Ideology as a Cultural System," pp. 62–64.

[12] *Peking Review,* June 24, 1966, p. 6.

World War II. In overcoming the difficulties and achieving success, they have relied on mobilizing human resources in China, on creating new social, economic, and psychological commitments, and on transforming the attitudes, habits, and customs of the people. In these endeavors, indoctrination has played a principal role. The Chinese Communists' emphasis on the importance of ideological transformation indicates a recognition of a strategic or limiting factor in social change, that is, the moral basis of the society, to use Edward Banfield's term.[13] Without a drastic change in the ethos of the Chinese society, the rapid modernization and industrialization to date would have been impossible.

The political community in China has been held together by the elite through a structure of political institutions and mass organizations and on the foundation of a single faith. In questioning the concept of the elite as developed and applied to the American system by C. Wright Mills and Floyd Hunter, Robert A. Dahl has in effect outlined an operational definition of the concept and challenged us to apply it to any specific political system or community.[14] For the purpose of opening a dialogue between political scientists and specialists on China, one might submit the proposition that the political systems in both traditional and Communist China can pass the three tests proposed by Dahl for the existence of a ruling elite. First, in both systems the ruling elite can be shown to be a fairly well-defined group. In traditional China, the ruling elite—which was also the social elite—was composed of the emperor, the aristocracy, the emperor's personal retainers, and what Ping-ti Ho calls "the ruling class," consisting of "officials, people holding official ranks and titles, subofficials, and degree-holders above *sheng-yüan* for the Ming period, with the same definition for the Ch'ing period except for the exclusion of *chien-sheng*."[15] In Communist China there has been a bifurcation between a political and a social elite.[16]

[13] Edward Banfield, *The Moral Basis of a Backward Society* (Glencoe, Ill.: Free Press, 1958), p. 163.

[14] Robert A. Dahl, "Critique of the Ruling Elite Model," *American Political Science Review*, 51 (July, 1958): 463–69.

[15] Ping-ti Ho, "Aspects of Social Mobility in China, 1368–1911," *Comparative Studies in Society and History*, 1 (June, 1959): 342. See also Ping-ti Ho, *The Ladder of Success in Imperial China* (New York: Columbia University Press, 1962), p. 40. S. N. Eisenstadt, *The Political Systems of Empires* (London: Macmillan Co., 1963), pp. 116, 157, 160–61.

[16] Franz Schurmann, *Ideology and Organization in Communist China* (Berkeley: University of California Press, 1966), pp. 51–53, 171.

But there is still no question that the political elite of party leaders, cadres, and members constitutes the ruling elite or class. Second, there is a fair sample of cases involving key political decisions in which the preferences of the elite ran counter to those of any other likely group that might be suggested. Third, in each case, the preferences of the ruling elite have prevailed.[17]

In a totalitarian society, elite integration is the key to political integration. The governmental institutions and the mass organizations created by the elite are transmission belts which the elite use to mobilize, control, and integrate the people. But to a greater extent than in the Soviet Union, the CCP has created these institutions and organizations in its own image. Their structures and principles of organization parallel closely those of the party, with such modification as fits their specific functions. For example, the structure of the people's congresses of the state parallels the structure of congresses in the party. The Standing Committee of the National People's Congress and the State Council parallel the Central Committee, the Secretariat, and the various departments of the party. On the local levels, the structure of the people's councils parallels the structure of party committees. The principle of "democratic centralism," originally used in the party, is supposed to govern all state organs and mass organizations.[18] The method of "criticism and self-criticism," first developed within the party, is now extended to "all our factories, co-operatives, business establishments, schools, government offices, public bodies, in a word, all the six hundred million of our people. . . ."[19] The "small groups" in which some five to twenty people meet frequently for various purposes follow much the same procedures and have similar power structures as the party small groups. Thus the congruence of the patterns of authority, which is considered by Harry Eckstein as one of the keys to political stability, is fairly close, at least between the party and other secondary groups or organizations. One may lay down as an hypothesis that so long as the party remained united, this parallelism in the structures and organizational and operational principles facilitated the party's control over the government bureaucracy, the army, and all secondary organizations and groups. Party leaders who held leading positions in non-party insti-

[17] In the Great Proletarian Cultural Revolution, the ruling elite is split into two major groups. Intra-elite struggle is a different phenomenon from a conflict between the elite and any other group.

[18] Mao Tse-tung, *On the Correct Handling of Contradictions among the People* (Peking: Foreign Languages Press, 1957), p. 13.

[19] *Ibid.*, p. 18.

tutions and organizations could operate with familiar rules. Moreover, since the organizational and operational principles long established in the party served as the norms for other institutions and organizations, the bureaucracies in the latter could not easily obstruct or evade party control by laying down their own complex rules and regulations, or by creating their own traditions which contravened those of the party.

The fact that it was possible for the party to create or reshape the governmental institutions and mass organizations in its own image can ultimately be explained by the weakness and instability of the secondary associations and governmental institutions during the Republican period. The latter were developed in an institutional and organizational vacuum after the collapse of the traditional order. The Chinese Communists' victory in the civil war, together with the lack of strength, tradition, and stability on the part of these non-Communist organizations and institutions, gave the party a carte blanche to remodel them. During the revolutionary period, the party constituted a small political community tied together by ideological, organizational, and personal bonds. This small and tightly knit political community existed in a disorganized society. It attempted to create a reintegrated political community in its own image. Thus, political development in China can be understood as a process in which a small group of men accepted a modern ideology, adapted it to Chinese conditions, perfected a system of organizations, developed a set of practices, and then extended this pattern of ideology, organization, and practices to the whole nation.[20]

Insofar as this attempt achieved some degree of success, it was facilitated by the following factors. First, China is not sharply divided along religious or nationality lines. The Chinese have seldom taken their religion seriously. The problem of national minorities is also not very disruptive. The Manchus absorbed wholeheartedly the Chinese culture during their 267-year rule over China. During the Republican period of thirty-seven years, the barriers between the Manchus and the Hans

[20] Tang Tsou, "Stability and Change in Communist China," in *The United States and Communist China,* ed. William W. Lockwood (Princeton, N.J.: Princeton University Press, 1965), p. 21. For a more extended discussion of this point, particularly the use of mass line as a strategy of economic development, see Chalmers A. Johnson, "Building a Communist Nation in China," in *The Communist Revolution in Asia,* ed. Robert A. Scalapino (Englewood Cliffs, N.J.: Prentice-Hall, 1965), pp. 47–81. For an interpretation of the international behavior of Peking as a projection of Mao's revolutionary strategy, see Tang Tsou and Morton H. Halperin, "Mao Tse-tung's Revolutionary Strategy and Peking's International Behavior," *American Political Science Review,* 59 (March, 1965): 80–99.

were completely swept aside. The national minorities account for only 6 per cent of the total population. Second, in the past thousand years or so, regionalism or provincialism constituted a serious problem in traditional China mainly when a ruling dynasty was in decline. When the imperial government was strong, it could generally hold these divisive forces in check by a complex system of political and bureaucratic measures, perfected over several centuries. Third, on the whole it must be said that traditional China was characterized by a high degree of political integration. Although imperial power did not effectively penetrate below the *hsien* level, cultural and linguistic (as distinguished from dialectic) homogeneity was a powerful force uniting the Chinese empire. The Confucian tradition permeated to the level of the commoners. Upward social mobility enabled intelligent and hard-working commoners to become members of the ruling class. The gap between the elite and the masses was not wide. Fourth, political disintegration during the Republican period was associated with defeats and humiliations in foreign relations and with civil wars and political chaos in internal affairs. It brought about a deep yearning for a high degree of unity.

Many historical circumstances also helped to establish the legitimacy of the Communist regime. The total bankruptcy of the Nationalist government left the CCP as the only alternative to continued political disintegration and instability which had been the most striking phenomenon on the Chinese political scene after the collapse of the empire. The most salient characteristic of Chinese politics since the period of warlordism between 1916 and 1927 had been a drive toward the reestablishment of a strong central authority. The Nationalist movement and the formation of the Kuomintang (KMT) regime in themselves had been steps toward this historic aim. The KMT had succeeded in fashioning the largest coalition of forces in the 1930's under the existing pattern of political participation and rules of the political game. But the Sino-Japanese War intervened before the authority of the Nationalist regime could be fully consolidated. The war also undermined whatever achievements the regime had attained. At the same time, the war produced a chaotic situation in which the CCP could expand its power and influence by appealing both to Chinese nationalism and to a widespread desire for reforms. This contrast suggests the advantage which an ideologically motivated and effectively organized totalitarian movement has over a neo-traditionalist and disunited nationalist movement, even in the very attempt to capture nationalism as a source of power.

Using nationalism as an effective appeal and as one element in its program, the CCP succeeded in winning the cooperation of many groups and in forming a latent united front against the KMT within the broader united front with the Nationalists against the Japanese. In other words, Chinese Communist ideology directed the party's attention to the importance of social groups which had not been active participants in the political process. By changing the pattern of political participation and the rules of the political game, the CCP succeeded in organizing a coalition of social groups much larger and more powerful than that headed by the KMT. During the civil war from 1946 to 1949, this latent united front against the KMT came to the surface. As the military fortunes of the KMT ebbed and the inherent weaknesses of the Nationalist regime were glaringly revealed under the strain of the civil war, the progressive isolation of the KMT was accompanied by the building up of an even broader united front by the Chinese Communists, including, as the Communists put it, "90 per cent" of the Chinese people against a handful of reactionaries. To the lack of any other alternative to political chaos was added a second factor which helped the Chinese Communists to establish the "legitimacy" of their regime. This was the popular support which they gained at the time of the founding of the regime.

The third factor was the effectiveness of their military, political, social, and economic programs during both the Sino-Japanese War and the civil war. Obviously, nothing succeeds like success. But the point is that in a society in which most of the traditional rules of conduct had been called into question and new ones had not been established, success through effectiveness could not be challenged on the ground that this success was obtained by illegitimate means. Furthermore, success and effectiveness could themselves be used to justify new rules of conduct, new institutions, and a new ideology which contributed to this success.

It is generally agreed that the Chinese political system which emerged out of the period of disintegration is basically different from the traditional one. Yet traditions cannot and need not be quickly and completely discarded. Some of them will of necessity persist. Others may turn out, upon close examination, to be parallel to modern patterns and therefore make the latter acceptable. While a large part of the efforts of the modernizers or innovators must be employed to demolish those traditions which cannot be reconciled with modernity, their success in building a stable, modern political community will be fostered by a parallel between modern institutions and the persisting traditional patterns and sometimes even by the conscious use of these

288 Revolution, Reintegration, and Crisis in Communist China

traditions to support the modern system. Seen in this light, the contemporary question of tradition versus modernity which preoccupies many social scientists emerges as the perennial question of continuity and change in historical development.

As a preliminary framework for a study of the problem of tradition versus modernity, or continuity and change, in China (or elsewhere), a series of distinctions can be made. First, there is the distinction between *whole* and *part*. No doubt the nature of the political system in China, taken as a whole, has basically changed. The Marxist-Leninist-Maoist totalitarian regime is fundamentally different from the Confucian-authoritarian government of the past. The present system is characterized by total mobilization and active participation of the populace directed toward rapid social change, and by total political control which penetrates to the grass roots. In contrast, the traditional system was characterized by the domination of the elite over a passive population.

But certain parts of the Chinese tradition have persisted. The Chinese Communists distinguish between the "feudal" dregs and the "popular" elements in the cultural heritage of China. The former is considered reactionary and must be eliminated, but the latter is accepted as progressive and must be developed in the new culture. What the Chinese Communists call the "feudal" dregs embraces those components which gave the Chinese culture as a totality its character. What they call the "popular" elements consist of those ingredients which occupied a secondary position in the traditional society. Because the total system has changed, some of the surviving traditional elements occupy different positions, have different meanings, and entail different consequences in the new system. For example, anti-bureaucratism was a persistent strand in the peasant rebellions which flared up time and again in Chinese history. This is an element of the "people's culture" which Mao not only seeks to preserve but also to elevate to a central position in the political system. Anti-bureaucratism is now a constant feature in the theory and practice of the Maoist ruling elite. It is used by the top leaders to bridge the gap between the party and the masses, to bring the party and the people together, and to control the cadres through pressures exerted by the masses. In the present Cultural Revolution, Mao uses the masses to attack and destroy various party organizations. Another instance of the survival of a tradition which, however, belongs to a different category is the self-cultivation of the Confucian gentleman, paralleled by the Chinese Communist practice of self-criticism. But it is obvious that self-cultivation as an individual act and self-criticism in a collective setting are two different things. Of particular interest to students of social change in China is the persistence of parts of the traditional social system at the local level. The survival and resurgence (after the Great Leap Forward) of the natural villages, the traditional kinship ties, and the marketing systems in the rural areas constitute a remarkable phenomenon which raises difficult questions regarding the relationship between structural changes at the macro- and micro-societal levels. Moreover, the modern system and the surviving traditional elements may not always complement each other. Under certain circumstances, the tensions between them may become very sharp and contribute to serious disruptions. Some of these tensions underlie the Cultural Revolution.

Second, the traditional and the Communist political systems, including some of their respective components, are similar to each other in *form*, but basically different from each other in *content*. In both the traditional authoritarian system and the modern totalitarian system, ideology has a pervasive influence. Up to the Cultural Revolution which has disrupted the Communist political system, the ruling class in both the traditional and modern systems was a well-defined group, and a single bureaucratized organization played a dominant role in society.[21] All these structural forms have not changed. But, the traditional ideology—with its concept of harmony, with its notion of reciprocal relationships between those occupying superior and inferior positions, with the postulation of limited action by government as one of its strands—had during various periods the function of civilizing, harmonizing, humanizing, and restraining absolute imperial power, or at least could potentially be used for that purpose. In contrast, the Chinese Communist ideology—with its ethic of conflict, its doctrine of dictatorship of the proletariat, and its call for uninterrupted revolution—has the consequence of maximizing the use of power by the state and of vastly expanding the function of government. The parallelism of structural forms in the political system facilitated the acceptance of the totalitarian system and partly accounted for the Chinese Communists' capacity to make it work, but the environmental changes necessitated the replacement of one content by another.

Sometimes traditional forms are consciously used to support new

[21] In a remark criticizing the regime, Chou Yang pointed to one of the parallels but presented it in a different way. He said, "Old ideas sometimes appear in other forms, that is, old content in new form. The old content—feudal-patriarchal rule; the new form—the secretary of the Party committee in command" (*Peking Review*, August 19, 1966, p. 31).

institutions. In 1963, the Maoists began a major effort to use traditional art forms to propagate Communist ideas. The most conspicuous example is the staging of Peking operas on contemporary themes. Yet sometimes form is inseparable from content; old forms may have to be modified or discarded and new ones developed. As Chiang Ch'ing asked, "Isn't it necessary to make a revolution and introduce changes if the old literature and art do not correspond to the socialist economic base and the classical artistic forms do not entirely fit the socialist content?"[22] Chiang Ch'ing's concern about the lack of correspondence between traditional form and modern content in the realm of literature and art points to one of the causes of the Cultural Revolution—that is, the tension between some of the surviving traditional elements and the new, Maoist components in the sociopolitical system. The Maoists set out to destroy, among other things, the traditions of bureaucratism, regionalism, and localism which had persisted or re-emerged. Undoubtedly some of the long-standing Chinese traditions will survive even the Cultural Revolution. At the moment, however, it is difficult to foresee how and in what proportions the traditional and modern elements will again be integrated in the sociopolitical pattern which will emerge after the present crisis.

But the problem of form and content is much more complicated than the above remarks suggest. In such cases as the kinship system, the disruption of the structure may have gone farther than the erosion of the attitudes cultivated by it. In other words, the form of a social institution may have been disrupted, but the content may persist.

Third, one must make a distinction between *ends* and *means*—that is, between the *goals* of a political community and the *methods* of achieving those goals. Most if not all the goals espoused by the Chinese Communists are modern ones. But the Chinese sociopolitical tradition has conditioned their choice of methods or means. For example, the modern goal of industrialization is to be achieved through governmental effort rather than private enterprise. This choice of means is partly conditioned by the long tradition of the domination of the society by a political elite, and partly by the lack of a tradition of truly free enterprise on any large scale.

Fourth, there is the distinction between *values* and *style*. The major values espoused by the Chinese Communists such as progress, equality between men and women, political activism, are totally modern. But the style of leadership is traditional. For example, the Chinese Communists in exercising leadership among the masses use the traditional

[22] *Ibid.*, December 9, 1966, p. 7.

style of casual conversation, heart-to-heart talks, and intimate person-to-person relationships. When some people characterized Mao as the modern Son of Heaven, they were referring mainly to the continuation of the political style.

Finally, there is the distinction between *explicit orientation* and *implicit support*. The explicit orientation may be totally modern, but the implicit support may be traditional. For example, the explicit principle of foreign relations is "proletarian internationalism" and world revolution. The implicit support for this orientation comes from the tradition of a universal empire. Toward Southeast Asia, the explicit policy is to eliminate American imperialist influence by supporting national liberation movements in some cases and by promoting neutralism in others. The implicit support comes from the traditional cultural and political hegemony of China in that area.

The logical relationships among these theoretical distinctions await further examination and elaboration. It may very well be that these five distinctions are merely expressions of different aspects of a single pair of fundamental categories. If so, we would achieve a greater degree of economy and elegance in our solution of the problem of tradition versus modernity and the question of historical continuity and change. The present formulation may be a step forward in this endeavor.

In spite of the fact that the Chinese Communists established in their early years a political community with a higher degree of integration than that achieved by the Nationalist regime in the period between 1927 and 1949, the patern of political integration contained within itself disintegrative forces with which it could not cope. A tentative and perhaps over-simplified explanation of this paradox can be offered here.

In the Chinese Communist political community, an ideology in the form of the thought of Mao Tse-tung played an extraordinarily important role in setting the general orientation, in bringing about integration of the various functional groups, in legitimizing the regime, and in enlisting commitment. Because of the operational character of Mao's thought and because of the paramount role played by Mao in making the most important decisions, at least before 1959, there was a particularly close association between ideology and policies.

Policies may be associated with ideology in various ways. At one extreme, a policy may be a direct projection or a derivation of ideology, with perhaps some necessary adjustment to reality. At the other extreme, a policy and an ideology may have no other association except that they are formulated by and identified with one and the same leader. If a policy has led to success, it may establish a precedent and become incorporated into the ideology when it is subsequently rationalized in theoretical terms. The policy of establishing base areas and organizing a guerrilla army and the strategy of surrounding the cities with the countryside were not originally part of Marxism-Leninism. But they have subsequently become a central part of the thought of Mao, which also includes ideas borrowed from Marxism and Leninism. Between these extremes lie several other possible forms of connection between policy and ideology. Policy may flow from a convergence between practical and ideological considerations. Perhaps the commune system falls into this category. Or the policy goal may be a reflection of practical needs but may be pursued through methods which are rooted in ideology. The Great Leap Forward is primarily of this type. Or a policy may be adopted on purely pragmatic grounds but may be justified or rationalized by ideological arguments. Perhaps the policy of self-reliance is of this nature.

Given the close association between policy and ideology, criticisms of the regime's policy may easily become criticisms of the ideology. Differences over policy soon become divergences in ideology, and disagreements over policy cannot be resolved on pragmatic grounds alone. Under these circumstances, the failures of Mao's domestic and foreign policies since 1959 produced not only criticisms of these policies but also a questioning of specific elements of Mao's thought. For example, Lin Mo-han, a former Vice-Minister of Culture, is quoted as having said in 1960: "In studying the writing of Chairman Mao, there is no need to study their specific viewpoints because some of them have lost their timeliness."[23] The doubters of Mao's thought also resorted to the method of verbally reaffirming its validity but refusing to be guided by it in practice. Thus, the party charged that after 1963 there was a tendency for many party members to be outwardly "left" but to follow the rightist line in actuality and that they were "waving the red flag to oppose the red flag." The dissidents put forward ideas and values which were basically incompatible with a fundamentalist interpretation of the ideology but refrained from launching an open attack on it. Yang Hsien-chen's theory of "two combining into one," and the historian's view that theory or doctrine emerges from historical data are cases in point. Syncretism rather than doctrinal purity may come from this process of development. The dissidents tried either to insulate certain areas of activities from the influence of the ideology or even to establish

[23] *Jen-min jih-pao* [People's Daily], September 22, 1966, p. 6.

therein values and norms not in harmony with the Maoist doctrine. One example of such attempted insulation can be found in the notion of "purely academic discussion" to be conducted with standards different from those prevailing in the areas of political debate. Another example is the strict enforcement of academic standards at institutions of higher learning in disregard of a policy of favoring students of worker and peasant origin. These developments at once reflected and might accelerate the emergence of relatively well-defined and differentiated sectors in the society, whose norms and values might or might not be easily integrated with each other. The dissidents affirmed the validity of the ideology at a high level of generality but showed both reluctance to propagate it and doubt as to the advisability of extending its sphere of application. The Mao-Lin group charged that the party officials controlling the propaganda apparatus put countless obstacles in the way of printing and distributing Mao's works on a large scale.[24] All this questioning of Mao's thought seems to have taken place in a climate of opinion which was otherwise characterized by apathy and lethargy toward ideological or even political issues. Hence, Mao, Lin, and their followers have found it necessary to call on the people to be actively concerned with political and ideological questions. This questioning of Mao's thought at once reflected and aggravated the tendencies toward disintegration, disorientation, demoralization, and the erosion of the legitimacy of the regime which had been brought about by policy failure.

The association between Mao's thought and policy failures, together with the doubt about the applicability of Mao's thought to many areas of social life, raises the question of congruence between ideology on the one hand and social reality and emerging trends on the other. To answer this question, one must examine the characteristics of Mao's thought, the circumstances under which it was first evolved, and the changed environment under which it has been applied. We shall consider the following aspects of Mao's thought which have always been present but which he has pushed to the extreme since 1958 and particularly since the Cultural Revolution: first, the idea of conflict; second, the tendency toward polarization in the thought pattern; third, the concept of the centrality of man; fourth, the controlling importance of "politics"; and finally, the importance of ideas over material conditions.

The thought of Mao developed out of the imperatives of fighting a guerrilla war in economically backward parts of China against vastly superior KMT and Japanese forces. It is permeated by the ideas of con-

[24] *Peking Review,* August 12, 1966, p. 15.

flict, struggle, and combat.[25] Since the unfavorable balance of forces could be changed and victory achieved only after a long period of time, the concept of a protracted war emerged. The protracted civil war took the form of a series of KMT campaigns of encirclement and annihilation and Chinese Communist counter-campaigns. Except for the last one, each of the four sets of campaigns and counter-campaigns followed a cyclical pattern. The cycle began with the KMT's offensive and the CCP's retreat toward the center of the base area, reached a critical point in a decisive first offensive battle waged by the Chinese Red Army, moved toward a general offensive by the CCP with the KMT in retreat, and terminated in a voluntary halt by the Chinese Communist forces to prevent an overextension of their inadequate military power. During the stalemate phase in the Sino-Japanese War, the Chinese Communist forces also fought campaigns with similar features against the Japanese.

The ideas of combat and protracted struggle have continued to influence the thinking of the leaders since 1949. There has been a series of domestic campaigns, with the Great Proletarian Cultural Revolution as the latest one. At least four of these campaigns—the agrarian reform movement, the two campaigns to set up agricultural producers' cooperatives of the lower and higher types, and the Great Leap Forward—show a cyclical pattern.[26] The idea of combat, the concept of protracted struggle, and the series of campaigns have given content and substance

[25] It is obvious that the Marxist theory of contradiction was the intellectual source of this idea. The theory of contradiction was more congruent with political reality in the first half of the twentieth century in China than the Confucian theory of harmony. The unity of theory and practice of the CCP stood in sharp contrast to the wide discrepancy between the advocacy of Confucian virtues and the practice of *realpolitik* by Generalissimo Chiang.

To justify the attack on various high party officials and party organizations in the Great Proletarian Cultural Revolution, the Maoists repeatedly used Mao's assertion that "in the last analysis, all the myriad principles of Marxism can be summed up in one sentence: 'To rebel is justified' " (*Jen-min jih-pao* [editorial], August 23, 1966, p. 1). This assertion can be found in Mao's talk on December 21, 1939, celebrating Stalin's sixtieth birthday. This talk was reprinted in *Hsin-Hua yüeh-pao* (New China Monthly), 1 (January, 1950): 581–82. When it is used in the context of the Cultural Revolution, it means that to rebel is justified even in a state ruled by a Communist Party and in a socialist society. A Red Guard poster added to this idea a qualification: "We are permitting only the Left to rebel, not the Right." (I am indebted to Stuart Schram for giving me the exact reference to Mao's speech in 1939.)

[26] G. William Skinner, "Compliance and Leadership in Rural Communist China—A Cyclical Theory" (a paper delivered at the 1965 Annual Meeting of the American Political Science Association, Washington, D.C., September, 1965).

to the goal of building a socialist society and have led to a revival of the theory of uninterrupted revolution. The continued application of this idea, however, has taken place in an environment in which the popular desire for a measure of stability and routinization has increased with time. This desire is reflected in the writings of the dissidents and the Maoists' analysis of these writings. In a widely read book published in 1956, Feng Ting defined social history as the history of the pursuit of happiness by all men. He wrote:

> Happiness in normal life means peace and no war, good food and fine clothing, a spacious and clean house, love between husband and wife, parents and children. There is no doubt about this, and this is also what we all are seeking.[27]

This view was attacked in 1964 as incompatible with the proletarian notion that the highest purpose in life is to serve the majority of the peoples of China and the world, as well as to struggle for the complete victory of communism in China and in the entire world.[28] Teng T'o, a former member of the Secretariat of the Peking Municipal Party of the CCP Committee which was reorganized in June, 1966, wrote: "People's attention should be called to treasure one-third of one's life so that after a day's labor or work, everyone can learn some useful knowledge, both ancient and modern, in a relaxed mood."[29] Commenting on this sentence, Yao Wen-yüan, whose attack on Wu Han in November, 1965, signaled the prelude to the Cultural Revolution, wrote:

> In asking everyone to read *Evening Chats at Yenshan* "in a relaxed mood," they [Teng T'o and his friends] were trying to dull the people's revolutionary vigilance; beginning by corroding "one-third of the life" of those who were not firm in their revolutionary stand, they aimed at corroding the whole of their lives and making them serve as the organized force and social basis for the Three-Family Village clique in recruiting more and more people and promoting peaceful evolution.[30]

[27] Quoted in D. W. Fokkema, "Chinese Criticism of Humanism: Campaigns against the Intellectuals, 1964–1965," *China Quarterly*, no. 26 (April–June, 1966), pp. 71–72.

[28] *Ibid.*, p. 72.

[29] Teng T'o, *Yen-shan yeh-hua* [Evening Chats at Yenshan] (Peking: Pei-ching ch'u-pan she, 1961), p. 3. See also, Yao Wen-yuan, "On 'Three-Family Village,'" *Peking Review*, May 27, 1966, p. 13. This sentence appeared in the first article in Teng T'o's column, "Evening Chats at Yenshan."

[30] Yao Wen-yuan, "On 'Three-Family Village,'" p. 14.

Talks about "relaxation" in their writings were considered to be poisonous weeds.[31] The Maoists also acknowledged that in the literary circles there was "opposition to the 'smell of gun-powder.' "[32]

Second, there is a tendency toward polarization in Mao's thought which accompanies the ideas of conflict, combat, and struggle. Fighting a guerrilla war reinforced the Comintern's theory of "two camps" and sharpened the distinction between the "enemy" and "ourselves." To identify the enemy in changing circumstances became one of the main intellectual tasks of the party. In spite of the shifting alliance with various groups and the policy of the united front, there is in the thought of Mao a tendency to polarize all things into two opposites. The dichotomy set up between the "enemy" and the "people" has become the basis of the political system. Recently an editorial of *Jen-min jih-pao* (People's Daily), official organ of the CCP, declared: "Either you crush me or I crush you. Either the East wind prevails over the West wind, or the West wind prevails over the East wind. There is no middle road."[33] (An interesting question to be further explored is whether or not the tendency toward polarization in political struggle existed in traditional China and, to the extent it existed, whether or not it was related to bureaucratic life.) This thought pattern finds expression in the Maoists' policy toward literature and art which sets the writer's tasks as the portrayal of heroic characters and the exposure of the evil nature of the enemy and which condemns the "writing about middle characters."[34]

This tendency toward polarization in Mao's thought is partly an expression of the necessity of most ideologies, including Maoism, to simplify social reality in order to serve as a guide to action, but it has become an obstacle in coping with reality as the simple life of the base areas has been replaced by an increasingly complex society. Thus, the

[31] *Ibid.*, p. 13.

[32] "Long Live the Great Proletarian Cultural Revolution," *The Great Socialist Cultural Revolution in China,* Vol. 3 (Peking: Foreign Languages Press, 1966), p. 9.

[33] "A Great Revolution That Touches People to Their Very Souls," *ibid.*, p. 7. For a discussion of this "either-or" polarity as it affects Chinese philosophical discourse, see Donald J. Munro, "The Yang Hsien-chen Affairs," *China Quarterly,* no. 22 (April–June, 1965), pp. 75–82.

[34] "Hold High the Great Red Banner of Mao Tse-tung's Thought and Actively Participate in the Great Socialist Cultural Revolution" (editorial), *Chieh-fang-chün pao* [Liberation Army Daily], April 18, 1966, in *Great Socialist Cultural Revolution,* vol. 1, pp. 4–5, 18–19.

attempt by semieducated cadres and illiterate masses to apply the thought of Mao to specialized and technical fields of activity or to solve new problems has impressed Mao's critics as "oversimplification," "philistinism," and "practicalism."

The third aspect of Mao's thought relates to the centrality of man. In guerrilla warfare, popular support is the decisive factor in giving the poorly equipped partisans a chance to survive and to achieve ultimate victory. While the military technology is very simple, the human equation is rather complex. The idea that man is more important than weapons is thus a product of guerrilla war. Likewise, there has been a tendency for the Chinese Communists to overstress the role of sheer human effort in economic reconstruction in which the availability of material resources normally makes a crucial difference. The emphasis on the importance of manpower to compensate for the lack of material resources has necessitated a continued accentuation of the demand for personal sacrifice for the good of the collectivity—a demand which was also an essential ingredient in the success of a protracted guerrilla war. Thus, three articles written by Mao in the Yenan period—"In Memory of Norman Bethune," "Serve the People," and "The Foolish Old Man Who Removed the Mountains"—which stress the importance of personal sacrifice and human effort have been designated the *lao san p'ien* ("three constantly read essays").

But this demand for greater personal sacrifice and human effort could no longer be made on a populace which had once been readily mobilized by the party's promise to give it land or by the Japanese invasion. Rather, it had to be imposed on a people which primarily desired economic betterment. The dissidents therefore assumed the role of promoters of the interests of the people against the demands of the state and the party. In their historical writings and plays, they constantly praised those officials in the Chinese Empire who "pleaded for the people" (*wei min ch'ing-ming*) in their memorials to the throne. They commended highly the ancient practice of treasuring the labor power of the people.

Fourth, the thought of Mao calls for the politicization of almost all spheres of social life.[35] In turn, "putting politics first" means putting Mao Tse-tung's thought first, according to the Maoists in the last few years.[36] This process of politicization originated in guerrilla warfare, in

[35] Even friendship is being replaced by comradeship. See Ezra F. Vogel, "From Friendship to Comradeship: The Change in Personal Relations in Communist China," *China Quarterly*, no. 21 (January–March, 1965), pp. 46–60.

[36] *Peking Review*, January 21, 1966, p. 5.

which popular support must be won by a political program and the institution of a proper relationship between the army and the population. The underlying principles of the Ku-t'ien Resolution, drafted by Mao in December, 1929, were that political considerations must prevail in most policy decisions and actions and that the party must control the army.[37] In the "Talks at the Yenan Forum on Literature and Art," Mao stressed that literature and art must serve politics. During the Great Leap Forward, the slogan "let politics take command" was raised; and in the past few years, Lin Piao has urged that everyone give prominence to "politics" in all fields of activity.

The penetration of politics into almost every sphere of social life may have been a short-term expedient to reconstruct new patterns of social relationships in a disintegrated society. But it is basically incompatible with long-term human needs in a stable, modern community. These needs center around the preservation of an autonomous area of social and private life into which "politics" with its emphasis on conflict, struggle, and combat does not intrude. Hence, the orthodox Maoists have found it necessary to attack frequently the "bourgeois" theory of human nature.

Furthermore, giving prominence to politics in every sphere of activity requires that professional criteria be subordinated to political ones in making decisions and judging work performance. The demand for placing politics above expertise increased after the attack on the intellectuals was intensified in November, 1965. *Chieh-fang-chün pao* (Liberation Army Daily) criticized the view that "politics" is given prominence if "politics" produces concrete results in work (*cheng-chih lo-shih tao yeh-wu*). It advocated the notion that giving prominence to "politics" must produce concrete results in men, that is, it must produce men with correct political viewpoints and behavior (*cheng-chih lo-shih tao jen*). This emphasis on politics in the special sense fails to give technical skill its proper place and runs counter to the demands and needs of the professional groups in a society with increasing social differentiation and specialization.[38]

The fifth aspect of Mao's thought emphasizes the importance of ideas over material conditions. To institute a proper relationship be-

[37] *Chung-kuo Kung-ch'an-tang Hung-chün Ti-ssu-chün ti-chiu-tz'u tai-piao ta-hui chüeh-i an* [Resolution of the Ninth Conference of Delegates from the Fourth army of the Red Army of the Chinese Communist Party] (Hong Kong: Hsin-min-chu ch'u-pan she, 1949). Hereafter cited as *Ku-t'ien Resolution*.

[38] A. Doak Barnett, "Mechanisms for Party Control in the Government Bureaucracy in China," *Asian Survey*, 6 (December, 1966): 659–74.

tween the party and the army, between officers and soldiers, and between the army and the masses so that the army could fight a guerrilla
war successfully and also become an instrument in making a revolution,
Mao found it necessary to effect a basic change in the values, attitudes,
and political-military viewpoints of party members and military personnel. The Ku-t'ien Resolution already contained the rudiments of a
program of thought reform which was subsequently systematized in the
Cheng-feng Movement of 1942–44. The successful application of new
ideas by Mao and his followers to overcome objective difficulties and to
defeat his opponents during the revolutionary period left a permanent
legacy in the mentality of Mao and his loyal followers. This is reflected
in Lin Piao's concept of "four first," that is, the concept of giving first
place to man as between man and weapons, giving first place to political
work as between political work and other work, giving first place to
ideological work as between ideological and routine tasks in political
work, and giving first place to living ideas as between ideas in books
and living ideas.[39]

The Maoists claim that the creative application of Mao's thought
will in the long run overcome any objective difficulty. In effect, they are
standing Marxist materialism on its head. Ostensibly criticizing the
followers of Ernst Mach but actually pointing at Mao, Teng T'o wrote:
"The Machians imagined that through reliance on the role of the psychological factor, they could do whatever they pleased, but the result
was that they ran their head against the brick wall of reality and went
bankrupt in the end."[40] This charge raises the question of the applicability of the thought of Mao to Chinese society seventeen years after the
establishment of the regime, to an international environment in which
a certain degree of stability is maintained by two strong and dynamic
powers[41] and to a world in which the underdeveloped nations are beginning to tackle the various problems of political development. In this
connection, Teng T'o attacked by insinuation Mao's method of leadership in domestic affairs as "the arrogant, subjectivist, and arbitrary way
of thinking and style of work of one bent on acting wilfully." This was,
he said, "the tyrant's way."[42] Mao's thesis in international affairs that

[39] *Peking Review*, January 21, 1966, p. 5, n. 1.

[40] "Teng T'o's *Evening Chats at Yensan* Is Anti-Party and Anti-Socialist
Double-Talk," *Great Socialist Cultural Revolution*, vol. 2, p. 21.

[41] Tsou and Halperin, "Mao Tse-tung's Revolutionary Strategy," pp. 97–99.

[42] *Great Socialist Cultural Revolution*, vol. 2, pp. 13–15. Yao Wen-yuan,
"On 'Three-Family Village,'" p. 12.

"the East wind is prevailing over the West wind" was obliquely characterized as "empty talk."[43] By the admission of the Maoists, the dissidents indirectly described Mao's policy as "boasting," "indulging in fantasy," "substituting illusion for reality," and as resulting in "the total destruction" of "the family wealth consisting of one egg."[44]

It is obvious that failure in policies associated with an ideology and the criticisms of these policies leading to the questioning of the validity of the ideology ushered in a profound crisis in the regime. For the proper functioning of the Chinese political system depends more heavily on the general acceptance of an ideology than does that of other regimes, due to the unusually important role played by ideology in providing the basic principles of the political community, in setting the orientation of the regime, in legitimizing the political system, and in enlisting commitment. Political development up to 1965 does not seem to have reached a point where the legitimacy of the regime as distinguished from the correctness of its policy was seriously challenged. But Mao and his followers feared that developments similar to Khrushchev's denunciation of Stalin and the Hungarian Revolution might take place. Quite possibly, some of the Chinese leaders may have feared that policy setbacks and generational changes might at some future point undermine the political system itself. In his famous interview with Edgar Snow on January 9, 1965, Mao admitted the possibility that "youth could negate the revolution, and give a poor performance; make peace with imperialism, bring the remnants of the Chiang Kai-shek clique back to the mainland, and take a stand beside the small percentage of counter-revolutionaries still in this country."[45]

Seriously concerned with the weakening of the ideological foundation of the regime and its future orientation, Mao, Lin, and their followers see the solution in the reaffirmation of the thought of Mao Tse-tung which in their opinion ought to be the regime's basic ideology. They have attempted to dissociate failure from the policies adopted and to attribute it to extraneous factors and errors in implementation, thus absolving the thought of Mao from any responsibility for the failure. They have endeavored to attribute all kinds of successes—from the explosion of an atomic device to the accomplishments of the Tachai

[43] *Great /Socialist Cultural Revolution,* vol. 2, pp. 28–29; Yao Wen-yuan, "On 'Three-Family Village,' " p. 11.

[44] Kao Chu, "Open Fire at the Black Anti-Party and Anti-Socialist Line!" *Great Socialist Cultural Revolution,* vol. 2, pp. 2–4.

[45] Edgar Snow, "Interview with Mao," *The New Republic,* February 27, 1965, p. 23.

Brigade to the ideology itself, whether there was a connection or not. They have advocated the study and application of the ideology by everyone and in every field, thus intensifying their program of indoctrination and seeking to enlist the commitment of everyone to the ideology. They have sought to link up class struggle with the struggle for production and scientific experiment, thus endeavoring to cope with practical problems while being engaged in political combat with the dissidents. At a time when the ideology is being questioned and the party itself is divided, they have tried to emphasize "personal legitimacy" to compensate for the weakening of "ideological legitimacy" and to overcome the problems created by the split between ideological authority and organizational authority. These attempts have pushed the cult of personality to a new height. As the present crisis is without any precedent in the history of the Chinese Communist movement since Mao's capture of the party center, the Maoists have attempted to use new methods or new applications of familiar methods to deal with it. Hence, the Red Guards and the Great Proletarian Cultural Revolution.

This reassertion of Mao's thought has entailed a measure of radicalization in the ideological sphere which has found expression in the savage attacks on traditional, Western, and "revisionist" ideas. Yet the basic problem of how to strengthen the ideological foundation of the regime and yet at the same time cope effectively with political and economic realities remains. In most areas of social life, the Maoists seem to be at a loss to fashion new, constructive programs which are at once in accord with their interpretation of Mao's thought and which would not disrupt whatever progress has been made in the last seventeen years. Hence, the Cultural Revolution has thus far been justified partly by the slogan that without destruction there cannot be construction and that destruction must come before construction.

The Great Proletarian Cultural Revolution and the Red Guards are therefore the expressions of a profound crisis in integration. The Maoists and the dissidents represent two political forces which the integrative measures of the political system cannot reconcile because the integrative myth itself has become a subject of controversy. This divergence on this most fundamental question confronting the regime may have divided the Chinese people in every sector of social life into two opinion groups. But not every sector has been influenced by this controversy to the same extent, and the relative strengths of the two groups may be different in different sectors. In the struggle for power which has ensued, the thought of Mao has also become a symbol. The vested interests of a group in upholding or questioning Mao's thought link ideological debates with *realpolitik* and have accounted for the extreme claims made for Mao's thought. The policy debates, the political division, and the linkage between ideology and vested elite interests are the problems to be discussed in the next two sections.

The Ruling Elite and the Masses

The dynamics of a political community in which there is a recognizable power elite are provided by the relationship between this elite and the other social groups. When the regime was set up in 1949, the CCP succeeded in unifying all major social formations in China under its leadership and excluded from this coalition only the most uncompromising groups, labeling the latter bureaucratic capitalists, compradores, and reactionary landlords. This achievement in integrating the diverse social groups and the masses entailed the implicit, if not explicit, modification of some of the Marxist-Leninist tenets and departed from Soviet practices toward the bourgeoisie and the rich peasants. It was made possible by social conditions of an underdeveloped country in which the capitalist class was relatively weak and in which there was a tradition of bureaucratic domination of the merchants. It was produced by the circumstances confronting the CCP in its prolonged struggle for power. In this struggle, the CCP was forced by the objective conditions to adopt strategy and tactics that paved the way for the initial form and structure of political integration.

Chinese society was seen by Mao as having "a shape bulging in the middle while tapering off towards the two ends."[46] In more concrete terms, this imagery meant that both the proletariat and the "reactionary big landlord and big bourgeoisie" formed only a small minority of the Chinese population while the other intermediate classes constituted the vast majority.[47] Mao's political strategy in the revolutionary struggle was "to develop the progressive forces, to win over the middle-of-the-road forces, and to isolate the die-hards."[48] It formed the basis of Mao's concept of "new democracy" which was to be based on a "joint dictatorship of all the revolutionary classes."[49] In this new democracy, "the proletariat, the peasantry, the intelligentsia and other sections of the

[46] *Selected Works,* vol. 3 (London: Lawrence & Wishart, 1954), p. 239.

[47] *Ibid.,* p. 260; vol. 4 pp. 25.

[48] *Ibid.,* vol. 3, p. 194.

[49] *Hsin-min-chu-chu-i lun* [On New Democracy] (San Francisco: Cooperative Publishers, 1945), p. 8.

petty bourgeoisie are the basic forces determining her fate."[50] But the proletariat should not overlook the partially revolutionary quality of the "bourgeoisie" and the possibility of establishing with it a united front against imperialism and the government of bureaucrats and warlords.[51]

In 1949, these ideas crystallized into the notion of a united front of four classes: the working class, the peasantry, the urban petty bourgeoisie, and the national bourgeoisie under the leadership of the working class, which would create a people's democratic dictatorship.[52] The status of these four classes within the united front by no means gave equal weight to each. But the significant fact is that the national bourgeoisie was considered a component class of the "people" who exercised dictatorial power over the "reactionaries" and that the petty bourgeoisie was designated an ally of the working class. The inclusion of the national bourgeoisie within the ranks of the people paved the way for the peaceful transformation of the capitalists by turning the privately owned industrial and commercial enterprises into joint state-private enterprises and by turning the capitalists into managerial personnel under state control.

The concept of the united front and the strategy of uniting 90 per cent of the people against a small group of reactionaries alerted the CCP to the problem of establishing correct relations with other classes and integrating the various classes into a unified polity. But Mao's vision of a socialist society and the very nature of his totalitarian regime rendered it necessary for him to destroy the political influence of these social groups while integrating their members into the political community. Thus, methods had to be evolved to achieve this. The theory of class struggle and the precedent provided by Stalinist Russia favored the use of repressive methods. In the land-reform program, an unknown number of "local tyrants and bad gentry" were liquidated. After Peking entered the Korean War, it ruthlessly suppressed the so-called reactionaries within the country. Yet in comparison with Stalin, Mao employed violence more openly and selectively. This openness in the use of terror suggested that the regime had succeeded in legitimizing terror by the appeal of its political, economic, and social programs more effectively than had the Soviet government. This success can also be attributed to the strict political control over the use of violence, to

[50] *Ibid.*, p. 15.   [51] *Ibid.*, p. 14.

[52] Mao Tse-tung, *Selected Works*, vol. 4 (Peking: Foreign Languages Press, 1960), p. 415.

the careful selection of the targets to attack, to the policy not to use physical coercion except as a last resort (for example, in dealing with the intellectuals and the national bourgeoisie), and to the development of methods of "thought reform" as a functional substitute for terror and as a supplement to its use. Thus, although Mao's programs aimed at achieving social, cultural, and spiritual changes far more sweeping and radical than anything Stalin ever attempted, his methods of action were, at least until the Cultural Revolution, more moderate than Stalin's. Whether or not the Great Proletarian Cultural Revolution, the Red Guards, and the current purges constitute an exception to this generalization is still difficult to determine at the moment of writing early in January, 1967.

The use of violence, no matter how open, selective, and successfully legitimized, could have had seriously disruptive effects if carried too far. Thus, the Chinese Communists restricted the use of suppression and coercive methods to what were defined as contradictions between the people and the enemy, while proposing the use of "democratic methods, methods of discussion, of criticism, of persuasion and education" to resolve the contradictions among the people. It is, of course, quite true that the boundary between the two kinds of contradictions is not fixed. The line of demarcation between the people and the enemy is actually the political standard of supporting or opposing the regime and its policies. It was drawn by the regime itself according to Mao's six criteria.[53] Recently, an overriding criterion has been added—whether or not one wholeheartedly supports and applies Mao's thought and the Maoist line in everyday work. It must also be stressed that if a contradiction among the people cannot be resolved by the "methods of discussion, criticism, persuasion and education," it can become a contradiction between the people and the enemy and be resolved by suppression

[53] In the published and edited version of the speech, Mao said: "We believe that, broadly speaking, words and actions can be judged right if they:

"(1) Help to unite the people of our various nationalities, and do not divide them;

"(2) Are beneficial, not harmful, to socialist construction;

"(3) Help to consolidate, not undermine or weaken, the people's democratic dictatorship;

"(4) Help to consolidate, not undermine or weaken, democratic centralism;

"(5) Tend to strengthen, not to cast off or weaken, the leadership of the Communist Party;

"(6) Are beneficial, not harmful, to international socialist solidarity and the solidarity of the peace-loving peoples of the world.

"Of these six criteria, the most important are the socialist path and the leadership of the Party" (Mao Tse-tung, *On the Correct Handling of Contradictions among the people* [Peking: Foreign Languages Press, 1957], pp. 55–56).

and other forceful measures. Mao's method of coercive persuasion is still one form of coercion as we understand it, but it was less brutal and perhaps more effective than overt repressive measures. In short, the violent class struggle became a controlled form of class struggle. The aim was to achieve the desired social change with the least disruptive effects so that a relatively high degree of integration and unity could still be established after the contradictions or conflicts among the "people" had been resolved.

In dealing with the various social groups, the elite follows what is called a *mass line*. The mass line is defined by Mao as the principle of "from the masses, to the masses." In Mao's words, "this means summing up . . . the views of the masses (i.e., views scattered and unsystematic), then taking the resulting ideas back to the masses, explaining and popularizing them until the masses embrace the ideas as their own, stand up for them and translate them into action by way of testing their correctness."[54] The mass line legitimizes the programs and policies of the party because these are supposed to have come from the masses, the creators of history. It directs the cadres' attention to the need for ascertaining, articulating, and aggregating the interests of the masses. It goes without saying that in this process of systematizing and co-ordinating the views of the masses, the elite selects some and rejects others in the light of its own notion of the true interests of the masses. It then superimposes on the correct views of the masses its overall, long-term program and its ideological conceptions. The product of this process may or may not bear any resemblance to the "scattered and unsystematic" views of the masses. It is, however, presented to the masses as their own ideas. It is said to represent the demand of the masses. The mobilization of mass support and the mass participation in the execution of the program mark the final phase of the mass line. The mass line can be a highly effective method for achieving integration between the elite and the masses if the substantive programs adopted by the party reflect the genuine interests of the masses, as was the case in the Yenan period.[55]

To implement the mass line, the party must be able to penetrate the masses and their formal and informal organizations. It has developed a pattern of methods to facilitate this penetration. The cadres are urged to develop a style of work which will bring the party and the masses together. They are told to live the same kind of life as the masses, to share the same hardships, to develop intimate relationships with the

[54] *Selected Works*, vol. 4 (London: Lawrence & Wishart, 1956), p. 113.

[55] See Chalmers Johnson, "Chinese Communist Leadership and Mass Response: The Yenan Period and Socialist Education Campaign Period," in this volume, pp. 397–437.

masses, to set a personal example for them to follow, to be considerate of the feelings of the people, and to exhibit a selfless devotion to public duties. Party directives abound with injunctions against "isolationism," "bureaucratism," "warlordism," and "sectarianism," which create a gap between the masses and the power elite. This style of work has been institutionalized in various interesting methods of work which run counter to Western ideas of economic use of skilled manpower. The party experimented with a system under which the cadres must regularly participate in physical labor as ordinary workers on a fixed day or days in a week at a fixed job. Leading cadres were told to spend a period of time at the grass roots—in production brigades or teams of a commune, or in factory workships—so that they could learn intimately the conditions of work and the problems confronting the masses at the lowest level.

The Chinese Communists are highly conscious of the gaps between social groups which have been created by modern conditions. To a much greater extent than their counterparts in the Soviet Union, they have tried various methods to minimize the "three antitheses" between the working class and the peasantry, between the city and the countryside, and between manual and mental labor. One of the bases on which the regime formulates its wage policy is that the wages and living standards of the workers should not be too high in comparison with the earnings and living standards of the peasants. One of the many methods of reducing the antithesis between the city and the countryside is to mobilize the students in urban areas to help the peasants during the busy season. The Taching oil field was characterized as "a village-like city or a city-like village—a new social organization which helps eliminate the differences between industry and agriculture and between town and countryside."[56] The policy of participation of cadres in labor is partly based on the need to minimize the antithesis between mental and manual labor. The "half-work, half-study" schools and the "half-farm, half-study" schools are primarily means to provide an education to children from poor families in spite of a lack of financial resources on the part of the state. But they are also justified as a method to obliterate the differences between mental and manual labor. As Franz Schurmann has pointed out, the type of cohesion which the Chinese Communists seek to bring about is similar to Durkheim's notion of "mechanical" solidarity as distinguished from "organic" solidarity.[57]

[56] *Peking Review,* April 22, 1966, p. 20. See also *ibid.,* p. 17.

[57] Schurmann, *Ideology and Organization,* pp. 99–100. See also Lucian W. Pye, *Aspect of Political Development* (Boston: Little, Brown & Co., 1966), p. 60.

Yet despite the initial success of the CCP in organizing a united front embracing all the major social groups in the country, and despite the elaborate system of measures to integrate the elite and the masses, political development in Communist China during the past seventeen years has resulted in the vanishing of the united front, in fact if not in theory. At least during one period of time, it led to the alienation of the peasantry so vividly recorded in the *Kung-tso t'ung-hsün* (Bulletin of Activities). It has produced increasing tension between the Maoists and the intellectuals inside and outside the party, leading to the Great Proletarian Cultural Revolution and the current purges. These disruptions stand in contrast to the party's success during the Yenan period in gradually unifying all the major social groups under the party's leadership, and to the widespread popular support enjoyed by the party at the time of the establishment of the regime in 1949.

This political development has been paralleled by a radicalization of the domestic programs of the CCP which actually began in 1946, continued with its ups and downs after 1949, accelerated after 1955–56, and reached a climax in the Great Leap Forward in 1958. This trend toward radicalism superseded the moderation of the CCP in the Yenan period. The degree of radicalism can be measured first by the gap between the goal and reality, second, by the length of time in which a goal is supposed to be achieved, and third, by the scope of the radical program as indicated by the number of people affected and the areas to which it is applied.

There are two broad explanations for this radicalization which changed the party's relationships with the various social groups. First, Mao had always envisaged a sweeping transformation of the Chinese society. The deradicalized program adopted after 1935 was a tactical change and forced adjustment to political reality; the moderation of Mao's theory and practice was a function of the balance of forces within China in which the CCP was a minority party. While the CCP's methods of action persisted to a large extent, the changes in the balance of forces particularly since 1949 made it possible for Mao to adopt radical programs for the transformation of Chinese society. These radical programs entailed either the destruction of some of the social groups or the drastic weakening of their political influence. The landlord class was destroyed in the land-reform movement. The influence of the rich peasants was seriously weakened by the establishment of the system of agricultural producers' co-operatives, although there has been a tendency for new rich peasants to appear.[58] The economic foundation of

[58] Schurmann, *Ideology and Organization*, pp. 497–500.

the political influence of the national bourgeoisie was undermined by the system of joint state-private enterprises, although the social and political status of the individual capitalists was maintained by the continued payment of dividends.

The intellectuals constitute the social group which has caused the regime its greatest difficulties. The political influence of the Democratic League—to which most of the politically active non-Communist intellectuals belonged—largely disappeared in the aftermath of the period of "blooming and contending" and the subsequent anti-rightist campaign. But the influence of the old, individual intellectual in his capacity as a specialist, a writer, and a scientist remained. Furthermore, new intellectuals are found in growing numbers in many sectors of a modernizing and industrializing society.[59] Their general knowledge and special skills, which are needed by the regime, also constitute the sources of many ideas opposed to Mao's thought and policies. The conjunction of the old and newly emergent forces has been considered to be a serious threat by the regime, or at least by one group of its leaders. Chou En-lai was reported to have declared in December, 1964, in his report on the government:

> ... for quite a long period the landlord class, the bourgeoisie and other exploiting classes which have been overthrown will remain strong and powerful in our socialist society. ... At the same time, new bourgeois elements, new bourgeois intellectuals and other exploiters will be ceaselessly generated in society, in Party and government organs, in economic organizations and in cultural and educational departments. These new bourgeois elements and other exploiters will invariably try to find their protectors and agents in the higher leading organizations. These old and new bourgeois elements and other exploiters will invariably join hands in opposing socialism and developing capitalism.[60]

The difficult problem posed by the intellectuals is even more vividly reflected in Ch'en Yi's recent interview with an editor of a Uruguay newspaper. In trying to explain the "capitalistic degeneration" in the Soviet Union, Ch'en Yi was quoted as stating:

[59] John W. Lewis, "Political Aspects of Mobility in China's Urban Development," *American Political Science Review*, 60 (December, 1966): 899–912. The author regrets that he could not take full advantage of this article, since it appeared after the final draft of this paper had been completed.

[60] *Peking Review*, January 1, 1965, p. 12.

... At the Twentieth Party Congress, Khrushchev said that Stalin had killed many people. That's not important. That he had stimulated the cult of personality. That's secondary. Maybe Stalin made these mistakes. But there was a more serious one. By stimulating industry and technology [that is, urban work and the intellectuals] without resolving the agricultural problem, he contributed to the process of degeneration.

He did not take steps to eliminate the capitalist evils of intellectuality. He was too impatient to declare that there was no longer a class struggle in Russia. Stalin did not foresee the possibility of a turn toward capitalism. Because of this, the Soviet people were not prepared to confront revisionism. Molotov, Malenkov, Kamenev did not know how to fight it, and the revisionists reached the cruel extreme of burning [sic] Stalin's corpse. Afterwards, Khrushchev used the intellectuals to restore capitalism. And imperialism spurred him on. . . . We are attempting to eliminate the intellectual class.[61]

It is apparent that in China non-party intellectuals became a major, though unorganized, social force, that some party intellectuals posed a challenge to party ideologues, and that general knowledge and scientific expertise came to be a source of opposition to the thought of Mao. When the party dissident, Teng T'o, stressed the importance of the *tsa chia* ("eclectic scholars") in leadership work and scientific research, he was advocating the assignment of generalists-intellectuals to leadership positions in place of the party ideologues.[62] A series of policies adopted by the regime can be understood as measures to curb the influence of the intellectuals, specialists, and experts. The Cultural Revolution involved "a great debate on the relations between politics and particular profession" in every department or unit throughout the country, with the party insisting that "putting politics first is fundamental to all work."[63] Even scientific experiment must, according to Vice-Premier Nieh Jung-chen, Chairman of the National Scientific-

[61] *The National Observer*, November 28, 1966, p. 26.

[62] Teng T'o, *Yen-shan yeh-hua*, pp. 7–9. In the same article, Teng also denied that there was any pure school of thought in traditional China. He asserted that on the contrary the well-known scholars in the past were eclectics in various degrees. This view ran counter to the Maoists' insistence on the purity of ideology and preference for ideologues over men with broad knowledge and liberal viewpoints.

[63] *Peking Review*, April 22, 1966, p. 18.

Technical Commission, be guided by Mao Tse-tung's thought.[64] One of the two major targets of attack in the Cultural Revolution has been the "bourgeois 'experts,' 'scholars,' 'authorities' and respected masters and their like"[65] and "specialists and professors."[66] The understandable emphasis on the importance of techniques was caricatured as the "purely technical viewpoint" and as the idea that "technique decides everything."[67] The alleged monopoly of "technique" by the experts was denounced. The role of the workers in scientific and technical development and in running the enterprise in the "three-in-one combination" was exalted. The workers were praised for having done things "which bourgeois technical 'specialists' lacked the courage to do" and for having achieved "what bourgeois technical 'authorities' failed to achieve."[68] They were said to "have shattered the arrogance of the bourgeois technical 'specialists' and 'authorities' and deprived them of their power."[69] The policy of raising the level of literature and art by giving high salaries, high royalties, and high awards to creative writers and artists was condemned, as was the policy of relying on famous writers, directors, and actors.[70] The old system of enrolling students in institutes of higher learning through competitive examinations was abolished because "it places school marks in command" and "encourages the students to become bourgeois specialists by the bourgeois method of 'making one's own way' and achieving individual fame, wealth and position."[71] *Jen-min jih-pao* expressed warm support for the "revolutionary proposal" of several students that the period of schooling in the colleges of arts should be reduced from five to one, two, or three years.[72] The domination of the educational system by bourgeois intellectuals was to be changed.[73] Even a professor's exhortation for the students to read more, take more notes, and write more was condemned. Since the intellectuals, scholars, experts, and specialists are concentrated in the urban areas, the Maoists' attack on them

[64] "Speech at the Opening Ceremony of the Peking Physics Colloquium," *Peking Review,* July 29, 1966, p. 34.

[65] *Great Socialist Cultural Revolution,* vol. 5, p. 1.

[66] *Peking Review,* May 6, 1966, p. 30.

[67] *Ibid.,* p. 28.

[68] *Ibid.,* July 29, 1966, p. 26.

[69] *Ibid.*

[70] *Ibid.,* August 12, 1966, pp. 35–36.

[71] *Ibid.,* June 24, 1966, p. 16.

[72] *Ibid.,* July 22, 1966, pp. 20–22.

[73] "Decision of the Central Committee of the Chinese Communist Party Concerning the Great Proletarian Cultural Revolution," August 8, 1966, *ibid.,* August 12, 1966, p. 10.

was also an attack on an urban culture which was considered by them as "bourgeois" and as too heavily influenced by the West. Programs justified by the need to eliminate the three antitheses turned out to be directed against the urban intellectuals.

One group of intellectuals not attacked consists of those "scientists, technicians and ordinary members of working staffs," who are patriotic, work energetically, are not against the party and socialism, and maintain no illicit relations with any foreign country. Those scientists and scientific and technical personnel who have made contributions are to be handled with special care. Toward them the policy is to help them gradually transform their world outlook and style of work.[74]

The second explanation for the radicalization of the movement takes as its point of departure an understanding of the Yenan period. The structure of ideology, institutions, organizations, practice, attitudes, values, and style of work perfected during the Yenan period contained a balanced mixture of moderation and radicalism. In the years since 1949 during which this structure has been extended to the whole society, the relative prominence of its moderate and radical features has fluctuated with the passage of time until radicalism has become dominant in the Cultural Revolution and moderation has been overshadowed. Furthermore, the sociopolitical context in which this structure operates has undergone a basic change. With this change, the theory and practice of the Yenan era have taken on different political meaning. These brief remarks need to be amplified.

During the Yenan period, the CCP's theory and practice were developed and applied in the party, the army, and the front organizations which many people voluntarily joined. Their extension and intensified application in all spheres of sociopolitical life has taken place under the auspices of a party in power. Thus, their acceptance has lost the voluntary character of the revolutionary days and has become compulsory. For example, thought reform through criticism and self-criticism as applied in a party which members joined of their own volition and could freely leave is quite a different thing from thought reform as imposed upon everyone in the country. The method remains the same, but the program amounts to what Benjamin Schwartz calls the transformation of the whole Chinese people into a nation of spiritual proletarians. When the mass line was used during the Sino-Japanese War, the CCP's programs corresponded to the genuine interests of the masses in resisting the Japanese forces and in preserving order and security behind the Japanese lines. When the same method was adopted as a

[74] *Ibid.*

strategy of economic development in the period of the Great Leap Forward and in the establishment of the commune system, it was used to change the age-old work organization and habits of the peasants, to drive them to work harder, and to disrupt, in effect, the traditional system of marketing in the rural areas. Thus, it enlisted popular participation and support in the Sino-Japanese War but provoked hostility and slowdown during the Great Leap which contributed to the three years of agricultural crisis.[75]

Second, the theory and practice of the CCP took a comprehensive, coherent, and partially complete form during its revolutionary days, reflecting the simple, undifferentiated life of the guerrilla bands and party activists in the interior of China where division of labor was simple and a type of mechanical solidarity could be easily established. When they were applied in more highly developed areas of China, they clashed with what remained of the relatively complex socioeconomic institutions. When they are applied in a rapidly developing, industrializing, and modernizing society, there is the problem of how to reconcile their assumptions of mechanical solidarity with the principles of specialization and functional integration on which a modern complex society is based.[76]

For example, Mao's experience in the Yenan period reinforced his Marxist prejudice against sharp differentiation of functions among the various social groups. He was reported to have pointed out recently that each army unit should engage in one or two of the three fields of activity—agriculture, industry, and mass work; that where conditions permit, the workers should engage in agricultural production and side occupations; that the peasants should also collectively run some small factories; that the students should in addition to their studies learn other things, that is, industrial work, farming, and military affairs; and that where conditions permit, those working in commerce, in the service trades, and in party and government organizations should also do the same.[77]

---

[75] Chalmers Johnson, "Building a Communist Nation in China," in *The Communist Revolution in Asia*, pp. 57–58. On the relationship between the commune system and the traditional system of rural markets, see G. William Skinner, "Marketing and Social Structure in Rural China, pt. 3," *Journal of Asian Studies*, 24 (1965): 363–99.

[76] Schurmann, *Ideology and Organization*, pp. 97–101, 109, 233–38.

[77] *Jen-min jih-pao* editorial in commemoration of the Thirty-ninth Anniversary of the Founding of the Chinese People's Liberation Army, in *Peking Review*, August 5, 1966, p. 7.

The populist and anti-bureaucratic bias of the "democratic" half of the principle of "democratic centralism" challenges the increasingly large and complex system of bureaucracy and management.[78] The clash between the theory and practice of the Chinese Red Army and the Eighth Route Army on the one hand and the Soviet model of a modern, specialized fighting force on the other led to the gradual abandonment of the Soviet model from 1958 onward. The confrontation between the thought of Mao and the demands for specialization has produced "the three-unification movement" which aims at uniting cadres, technicians, and workers into a work team and in which each is expected to become the other. These developments are radical in the sense that the gap between Mao's policies and the emergent social reality is widened.

Third, the radicalization of the Chinese Communist movement stems from one particular aspect of the thought of Mao. This is best formulated by Vsevolod Holubnychy:

> Mao believes that practice reveals not only the correct or expected truth but also the wrong or unexpected truth. What his whole epistemology calls for is to push practice and experimenting to the utmost—up to the brink of error and failure . . . the rule of procedure is: In your search for truth, push incessantly forward until you come to the brink of the pit. . . . It is more probable than not that in every particular case, he [Mao] would be inclined to go a step farther than one would ordinarily expect and he would be disposed to explore extreme opportunities, advance radical propositions and push them hard until or unless they become utterly impossible.[79]

It has been in this spirit that Mao has tried to extend the application of his theory and practice in one area of social life after another. He did this in the area of agriculture and economic life with his Great Leap Forward and the system of communes. In the Cultural Revolution, characterized as a great innovation in the international Communist movement, he is attempting something analogous to the Great Leap Forward in the fields of education, art, literature, and politics. If fully implemented, the tentative proposals to reform the examination and educational system and the movement to discredit the "academic au-

[78] Schurmann, *Ideology and Organization,* pp. 113, 127, 265.

[79] "Mao Tse-tung's Materialistic Dialectics," *China Quarterly,* no. 19 (July–September, 1964), p. 27.

thorities" and "specialists" in various areas of intellectual life promise to produce results as disastrous to China's cultural life as the Great Leap Forward and the commune system were to China's economy, although the effects will not be as obvious and immediate.

If the radicalization of the Chinese Communist movement has come from the extension and selective and intensified application of the theory and practice as developed by the CCP during the revolutionary period, we must ask ourselves the fundamental question: What social condition has made it both necessary and possible for the CCP to do so?

The social condition in twentieth-century China which has made this extension possible can be described as the high degree of disintegration of the traditional sociopolitical system, coupled with the weakness of the emergent, transitional system. A high degree of disintegration meant not only that the core elements of the overall system had been destroyed but also that some of the substructures of the social system were no longer viable. Thirty years ago, we employed the elegant term "the collapse of a civilization" to describe such a condition. Today some of us prefer such terms as systemic and multiple dysfunction. The warlord period from 1916 to 1927 was the political expression of this disintegration. The new institutions and organizations which emerged in the aftermath did not last long enough to stabilize themselves. Collectively, they did not form a functionally integrated system. In the midst of this disintegrated society, the Chinese Communists built a small political community of their own, one tied together by ideological, organizational, and personal bonds. The dislocation in most sectors of social life and the relative weakness of some of the surviving institutions have made it both possible and necessary for the CCP to rebuild the overall sociopolitical system and many of the subsystems in its own image.

In this situation there could be no boundary between the state and the society or even the state and the individual. Political power of necessity penetrated to every sphere of social life, including the innermost thought of man. This development inevitably resulted in the radicalization of the Chinese Communist movement. Yet the only ideas, practices, and style of work which many of the Maoists have known and prized are those which they themselves developed in the long years of the revolutionary struggle. In a sense, the Maoists can be considered conservatives because they oppose new emergent things in order to perpetuate their original revolutionary tradition.

In sum, the trend toward increased radicalism which replaced the moderation of the Yenan period has brought about a basic change in the relationship between the party and the various social groups since 1949. The high degree of political unity and popular support enjoyed by the regime at the time of its establishment has been eroded as a result of the successive assaults by the elite upon many of these groups. While the capitalists as a class no longer exist and the non-Communist parties and groups have lost almost all their influence, the old ideas and attitudes of these groups have lingered on. These old ideas and attitudes have been reinforced by the trends toward differentiation, specialization, and professionalism in a developing society. While the peasantry has in the past several years been pacified by the restoration of the private plots, the revival of the rural markets, the reorganization of the commune system, and the allocation of a greater amount of resources to agriculture, the old and new intellectuals in and outside of the party have posed a serious challenge to the policies and ideology of the Maoist group. As the dissent of the intellectuals has been the reflection of unresolved problems in various sectors of the society, the tension between them and the Maoists serves as an indicator of the unsatisfactory relationship between the various social groups and a powerful group in the ruling elite. How the Maoists will handle the intellectuals will determine future political developments in China. In any case, the time when effective political integrations can again be achieved seems at this moment to be quite far away. It will probably come only after a long period of cessation of radical changes, of painful readjustment, and of peaceful economic evolution.

The Elite: The Charismatic Leader and the Routinizing Organization

In a political system in which there is a fairly clearly defined power elite, the unity achieved within this elite is at once a measure of the degree of political integration attained and a decisive factor in bringing it about. Similarly, the division and conflicts within the elite mirror the diverse forces within the political system and the society. For a limited period of time, a united elite can bridge the social gaps and control the centrifugal forces in the society without recourse to violent and repressive methods on a large scale. But the diverse interests of the various social groups inevitably find expression within the ranks of the elite. Unless these interests can at least be partially satisfied by the elite's policies and programs, they will, over a period of time, produce fissions within the elite itself. Furthermore, the members of an elite in power in a modernizing society work in different governing institutions which perform increasingly specialized and differentiated functions and which have diverse clienteles. Different sections of the elite may take on some of the attributes of what Western social scientists call institutional interest groups. The system of party committees and party secretaries at various levels is supposed to integrate the work and functions of the diverse institutions and organizations. Yet it may itself become a strongly entrenched vertical institutional group with its own interests and viewpoints. Even within each of these institutional groups, further functional differentiation takes place.[80] Individuals working within these specialized groups may develop diverse viewpoints because of their different social origin, education, experience, and location in the political and social system. How the conflicts and struggle for power will take shape depends on the effects of the policy pursued by the regime on these groups and individuals and varies with the relationship between the ideology and the functions performed by them.

The Chinese Communists succeeded in building up a highly unified party during the revolutionary period. This impressive solidarity persisted for many years after the establishment of the regime. Then in 1966, we learned all of a sudden that the unity of this elite had suffered the most serious breakdown in its whole history, or at least since 1935.[81] Furthermore, the "structural legitimacy"[82] of the party was weakened, if not destroyed, when the Red Guards were used to attack the top leaders, the various parts of the party apparatus, and the regional and local committees. While it is impossible at this moment of writing to give an adequate analysis of this development, some preliminary and highly tentative thoughts about the initial unity and its subsequent breakdown will be put forth to elicit discussion.

One of the greatest achievements of the Chinese Communists in the revolutionary period was their success in building up a highly unified party whose deep foundation has been seriously shaken and whose elaborate structure has been strongly buffeted by the Cultural Revolution. This achievement in the past was particularly remarkable in

[80] For a description of the existing functional "systems" in the Chinese Communists' political apparatus, see Barnett, "Mechanisms for Party Control," pp. 671–74.

[81] The Maoists declared that "the struggle between the two lines within the Party [in 1966] . . . is likewise the most profound struggle in the history of our Party" (*Peking Review*, December 23, 1966, p. 19).

[82] For the concept, see Easton, *A Systems Analysis of Political Life*, p. 287.

view of both the pattern of factional politics in twentieth-century China and the bloody purges used in overcoming factions in the Bolshevik party of the Soviet Union. Political factions in Republican China frequently stemmed from conflict between strong personalities and were based on the selfish interests of individuals or groups of individuals bound by personal ties of some sort, sometimes rationalized by ideology and program, and sometimes not. Frequently, they reflected regional, provincial, and local loyalties. In their most advanced form under the Nationalist regime, they rested upon functional differentiation among the various groups. For example, the Whampoa Clique had its foundation in the Central Army; the C.C. Clique, in the party bureaucracy; and the "Political Science Group," in some high echelons of the government. But even in its most advanced form, factional politics was still highly colored by issues of personality while the various factions themselves were divided into small cliques bound by particularistic ties. Although the factional struggle for power and preferment was very intense, the issues were seldom resolved on the basis of principles.

The CCP, as a product of Chinese society, was confronted with the same divisive forces that rent the other groups into conflicting factions, cliques, and individuals. In its attempt to build up a highly integrated party, it succeeded in reducing factionalism and personal conflicts to manageable proportions by rigorously implementing the Leninist principles of party organization, by developing a new pattern of inner-party life, by checking the divisive forces at their inception, and by firmly establishing the ideological and organizational authority of Mao Tse-tung. On the basis of the Leninist principles, it has tried to keep to a minimum what are called unprincipled disputes and struggles within the party. These are defined as disputes and struggles which are started not for the sake of serving the interests of the entire party but for the sake of promoting individual and factional interests. Also included in this category are disputes and struggles which do not follow organizational procedures but are characterized by secret scheming against some individual members.

The CCP was constantly on the alert for divisive forces within the party and endeavored to control them by achieving unanimity in thought. For this purpose, it waged frequent struggles against "erroneous" ideological tendencies on the basis of a set of principles, that is, Marxism-Leninism and the thought of Mao Tse-tung. In the conduct of inner-party struggle as a means of unifying the party and of combating ideological deviations, the CCP departed at an early date from Stalin's practice of bloody purges and developed a new style of inner-party life.

As early as 1941, Liu Shao-ch'i contrasted the conditions under which the Bolshevik and the Chinese parties were established. When Lenin was building the Bolshevik party, his most important consideration was, according to Liu, "the struggle against right opportunism" as symbolized by the Second International. In contrast, the CCP had from the very beginning been established on the basis of Leninist principles. But it had frequently committed the error of waging violent and excessive inner-party struggle and of moving toward "left deviation."[83] In accordance with this diagnosis, the CCP has established a practice of opposing "mechanical and excessive struggle" within the party. Instead of investigation, arrest, imprisonment, and trial in inner-party struggle, it has placed primary reliance on the method of "criticism and self-criticism" in order to resolve inner-party conflicts on the basis of principles, to achieve unanimity in thought, and to "cure the disease and save the person."

The development of this more moderate form of inner-party struggle took place at a time when the CCP was still a minority party constantly threatened with the outbreak of a new civil war and when the Communists had to achieve unity in order to survive. It departed from the Chinese political practice at that time in the party's insistence that no compromise of principles is permitted, but it conformed to that practice by allowing political opponents a route of retreat and a chance to come back to the fold. This moderate form of inner-party struggle was necessary to preserve party unity in the face of powerful enemies, and became a well-established practice. Although the party could not prevent serious challenges by oppositionist elements within the party, notably the "anti-party faction" of Kao Kang and Jao Shu-shih and the "right-wing oppositionists" in the P'eng Te-huai affair, there was no bloody purge from 1935 to 1965. What has happened to the individuals purged in the current crisis remains unclear.

It was no accident that this moderate form of inner-party struggle was institutionalized simultaneously with the establishment and consolidation of Mao's ideological and organizational authority. Indeed, the latter was probably the precondition of the former. For inner-party struggle can be controlled within set limits and can assume a moderate

[83] Liu Shao-ch'i, "Lun tang-nei tou-cheng," in *Cheng-feng wen-hsien* [Documents on the Rectification of the Styles of Work] (Hsin-Hua shu-tien, 1949), pp. 175–76.

form only when there is a recognized ideological authority to distinguish between "correct" and "incorrect" principles and an invulnerable
organizational authority to regulate and enforce the limits of the
struggle. In a Communist party, the ideological authority and the organizational authority must be identical in order for the authority to
be fully effective. This identity was achieved in the period between
1935 and 1945.

The historical circumstances under which Mao established and consolidated his ideological and organizational authority greatly facilitated
the development of a moderate form of inner-party struggle and the
achievement of a high degree of unity and continuity in the CCP leadership. It was Mao who had first developed the guerrilla bases in the
hinterland and formulated a pattern of political-military strategy and
tactics to guide the Communist forces in their early successes in expanding their control and in their war against the KMT's campaigns of
annihilation and encirclement. The Red Army was defeated in 1934
when the returned-student group controlled the party apparatus and
directed the war effort. Mao captured control over the party center in
1935 during the Long March when the fortunes of the CCP were at
their lowest ebb since 1927. Under his leadership, the CCP entered a
period of rapid expansion. His successes legitimized his ideological and
organizational authority while his opponents were discredited by their
failures. Thus, the establishment and the consolidation of his authority
were not accompanied by bloody purges. Most of the leaders in the
period from 1927 to 1935 remained the leaders of the regime up to the
autumn of 1965.

The conditions which governed the successful development of guerrilla warfare demanded full integration between the military and civilian officials, between the various functional groups within the party,
and between the elite and the masses. Thus, the CCP was intensely conscious of the various gaps within and outside the party and took action
to close them. In this integration, civilians were given the top positions.
Guerrilla warfare depends for its success on popular support, and this
is obtained by a political, economic, and social program which only
civilian leaders can formulate. The political aspects of fighting a successful guerrilla war are very complex, while the military aspects are
fairly simple. Therefore, the party leaders could guide the military
officers, but military officers could not guide the movement. At the same
time, the army took on many political and economic activities which
were inseparable from guerrilla fighting. It was, at the same time, a
fighting force, a working force, and a production force. Mao became the

military strategist and tactician as well as the ideological authority. He was the prophet armed and triumphant. This tradition of civilian control over the military soon became a very powerful force, sanctioned and strengthened by both the Chinese political tradition and Leninist principles, in spite of the fact that the military took active part in political affairs.

It is generally recognized that common experience and memories of the past contribute to the development of a common outlook on the basis of which the present is understood and a decision is made. Most of the top Chinese Communist leaders share the common experience and memories of fighting a guerrilla war in various base areas, although many, of them, particularly those who worked in the field of literature and art, in united-front work, and in student movements, lived for long periods of time in Nationalist-controlled cities and were exposed to the influence of Western ideas and way of life. To the extent that there is a sharing of common experience and memories, unity in thinking and action can be more easily achieved. The bulk of the writings of Mao is a summation of the political-military experience of waging guerrilla warfare. Its abstract principles generalize the lessons of past defeats and success to guide the party's actions. To the extent to which Mao's thought was not questioned, it enhanced the unifying effects of the common experience and memories by providing a systematic and authoritative interpretation of the past. At the time of the establishment of the regime, the Leninist principles of organization, the development of a new pattern of inner-party life, the firm establishment of the ideological and organizational authority of Mao, the continuity of leadership, and a systematic and authoritative interpretation of common experience provided by the thought of Mao helped to bring about a highly unified elite. Thus, an organic unity of the charismatic leader, the ideology, and the organization was created. The harmony among these three fundamental forces during a period of revolutionary upheaval helps to explain the effectiveness of the CCP then and for some time afterward.

In the first few years of the regime, party unity was one of the main factors contributing to the establishment of effective political control. This effective political control enabled the Chinese Communists to regulate the demands of the various groups in the society. It gave them a relatively free hand to establish a new political system, to formulate their socioeconomic programs, and to allocate resources in the light of their ideology, revolutionary experience, and estimate of the situation. It rendered feasible the adoption of unpopular policies such as the

entry into the Korean War, the campaign for the suppression of counter-revolutionaries and the Three-anti and Five-anti campaigns. These
and other unpopular policies inevitably depleted the capital of popular
support available to the regime. Yet circumstances helped the party to
balance this loss of popular support by demonstrating the effectiveness
of the regime and soundness of its policies. Its success in controlling
runaway inflation in the last years of Nationalist rule and in rehabili-
tating the war-torn economy within three years of assuming power made
the people's lives tolerable. The defeat of General MacArthur's drive
toward the Yalu stirred the national pride of the Chinese to the highest
point since the Opium War. The First Five-Year Plan of 1953–57 was a
good beginning for industrialization. The land reform program and the
establishment of agricultural producers' cooperatives caused relatively
little disruption in the countryside. So long as the policies of the regime
met with relative success, the struggle for power within the party could
be contained and the crisis of party unity minimized, for the issues
around which the struggle took place were relatively specific and narrow, as in the case of the purge of Kao Kang and Jao Shu-shih in 1954
and debate over the military line in 1958.

But the three years of crisis produced at least partly by the Great
Leap Forward and the commune system,[84] together with the drastic
deterioration in Sino-Soviet relations since 1959, had quite different
consequences for party unity. They raised a whole range of policy
issues which called into question the basic orientation of the regime in
both domestic and foreign affairs. Chou En-lai declared in his report in
December, 1964, on the work of the government:

> From 1959 to 1962 . . . the class enemies at home launched re-
> newed attacks on socialism, and consequently once again fierce
> class struggle ensued. In the domestic field, quite a few people
> actively advocated *"san-tzu i-pao"* (referring to the extension of
> plots for private use and of free markets, the increase of free enter-
> prises with sole responsibility for their profits or losses, the fixing
> of output quota based on households), *"tan-kan feng"* (referring
> to the restoration of individual economy), "liberalization," "re-
> versing previous decisions," and capitulationism in united front
> work; in the international field they advocated *"san-ho i-shao* (re-

[84] In an article written jointly by the editorial departments of the *Hung-ch'i*
and *Jen-min jih-pao*, Liu Shao-ch'i is charged with having said that the agricultural crisis was made up of "three parts natural calamities and seven parts
man-made disasters" (*Hung-ch'i* [Red Flag], no. 13, 1967, p. 11).

ferring to reconciliation with imperialism, reactionaries, and modern revisionism, and reduction of assistance and support to the revolutionary struggle of other peoples). They used their bourgeois and revisionist viewpoints to oppose our general line of socialist construction and the general line of our foreign policy.[85]

At the moment of writing, it is impossible to identify the dissidents, although we do know that, among others, Wu Han, Teng T'o, Chou Yang, and Sun Yeh-fang were accused of having expressed some of these views. Nor is it necessary to do so. All that is needed is for us to indicate that there was an intense debate within the party on all the important issues, that this debate led to the questioning of the extent to which Mao's thought can be vigorously applied in various areas of activities, and that the struggle for power within the party has evolved around this last question.[86] One group of leaders has advocated and undertaken an extensive and vigorous application of Mao's thought, while another group has in practice failed to do so or has tried to restrain the Maoists' attack on the dissidents. It is this contrast in approach that has created for the former a vested interest in upholding Mao's thought and for the latter a vested interest in limiting its application. This contrast has also made it possible for one group to use Mao's thought as a weapon to attack and purge its opponents.

One must probe more deeply, however, into the reason for this division within the party. Our explanation is twofold. The first part relates to what Max Weber calls the routinization of charisma.[87] The CCP has long been led by a charismatic leader and at the same time has developed a large organization with a long tradition going back to the

[85] *Jen-min jih-pao,* December 31, 1964, p. 2. For an English translation, see *Peking Review,* January 1, 1965, pp. 12–13.

[86] In his self-criticism, Liu Shao-ch'i stated that Teng Tzu-hui, Director of Office of Agriculture and Forestry of the State Council, advocated the fixing of output quota based on households at several meetings and that on another occasion Teng spoke on the merits of the "responsible farm system" and that "we did not oppose this view" (Liu's self-criticism as reproduced in a big character poster posted on December 26, 1966, in Peking by the Chingkanshan Red Guards of the Tsing Hua University.) Liu himself was accused of having advocated the fixing of output quota on the basis of households and of having actively encouraged "going it alone" (*Hung-ch'i,* no. 13, 1967, p. 11).

[87] Max Weber, *The Theory of Social and Economic Organization,* trans. A. M. Henderson and Talcott Parsons (Oxford: Oxford University Press, 1947), pp. 363–73. *From Max Weber,* trans. H. H. Gerth and C. Wright Mills (New York: Oxford University Press, 1946), pp. 53, 54, 262, 297.

revolutionary period. Certain developments in the party point to a process of routinization which diminishes the influence and the control of the charismatic leader over the organization. At the Eighth Party Congress in September, 1956, the statement that "the Communist Party of China takes Marxism-Leninism as its guide to action" was adopted to replace the statement in the Party Constitution of 1945 that "the Communist Party of China guides its entire work by the teachings which unite the theories of Marxism-Leninism with the actual practice of the Chinese Revolution—the thought of Mao Tse-tung." Not only had the phrase "the thought of Mao Tse-tung" disappeared in the new Party Constitution but also the statement that "no political party or *person* [italics added] can be free from shortcomings and mistakes in work" had been added.[88] At the same time, a provision was adopted under which the party can have an honorary chairman when necessary. This arrangement was apparently intended to give the charismatic leader an honorific post in the party but to remove him from day-to-day control over party affairs. The forces of routinization were headed by two persons engaged principally in organizational work in the party, Liu Shao-ch'i and Teng Hsiao-p'ing. At the 1956 Congress, they delivered, respectively, the political report of the Central Committee and the report on the revision of the party Constitution and were elected, respectively, the ranking Vice-Chairman of the party and the General-Secretary. It was they who would be the chief beneficiaries of Mao's relinquishment of power. This process of routinization was facilitated by Khrushchev's denunciation of Stalin at the Twentieth Party Congress which was a reflection of the same process in the Soviet Union. In December 1958, the Sixth Plenum adopted a decision approving Mao's proposal that he would not stand as a candidate for the chairman of the People's Republic.[89]

There are reasons to believe that during the period between 1959 and 1962 Mao's control over party affairs was further weakened as the party adopted a series of pragmatic policies to extricate China from the economic crisis. According to one report, Mao complained that during these years the party leaders treated him as they would treat a dead

[88] *Eighth National Congress of the Communist Party of China,* vol. 1: Documents (Peking: Foreign Languages Press, 1956), p. 143.

[89] For two different interpretations of this event, see Gene T. Hsiao, "The Background and Development of 'The Proletarian Cultural Revolution,'" *Asian Survey,* 7 (June, 1967): 395; Chün-tu Hsüeh, "The Cultural Revolution and Leadership Crisis in Communist China," *Political Science Quarterly,* 82 (June, 1967): 187.

parent at his funeral. The latent tension between the charismatic leader and the routinizing and bureaucratized organization increased after the economic recovery in 1962 when Mao began to raise the question of the ideological purity of some of the members of the organization and started a counter-offensive against his critics and the dissidents. This tension was brought to a head by the foreign policy crisis in 1965 and by the leader's attempt to purge the dissidents below the top echelons of the organization. The organization's effort to protect the dissidents and to restrain Mao's attacks led to a split between the leader and the organization. The basic conditions which had moderated the inner-party struggle since 1942, if not since 1935, and which accounted for the early effectiveness of the CCP no longer existed. The tremendous prestige of the leader was now pitted against a strongly entrenched organization. A prolonged and intense struggle ensued. Mao tried to divide the organization by using the leaders of a lower rank against the leaders of a higher rank and by setting one functional group within the party against another. He also promoted the formation of new groups, the Red Guard units, to attack the various party units. In this attempt, he exploited the enthusiasms and grievances of the underprivileged youth against the "establishment" and the more privileged groups of the society. His endeavor was facilitated by the revolutionary ideology and heritage which legitimized the spontaneous activism and revolt of the youth.[90] In these developments, the process of routinization of charisma and the struggle for succession in the political system were linked up with the process of functional differentiation in a modern society. This latter process constitutes a second explanation of the current crisis.

In both Chinese society and the CCP, the process of functional differentiation has gone very far in the past seventeen years. It has been facilitated by a policy, followed since the revolutionary days, of assigning the same individual to the same field of activity over a long period of time. But this process has come into conflict with the demands for doctrinal uniformity. The increasingly differentiated and specialized sectors of the society and the party are supposed to be guided in their work by a single ideology with rather specific operational rules. But the operation of Mao's thought may be functional for work in some spheres

[90] Throughout the Cultural Revolution, the following statement addressed by Mao to the youth has been frequently quoted: "The world is yours as well as ours, but in the last analysis, it is yours. . . . Our hope is placed in you" (*Peking Review*, March 31, 1967, p. 12).

of sociopolitical activities, dysfunctional for that in others, and quite irrelevant to that in still others. For many party leaders engaged in activities of the first type, for example military affairs, it is possible to retain faith in the ideology, to carry out policies intimately linked to it, to design programs in conformity with it, and even to devise new methods to apply it extensively and vigorously. For many leaders engaged in the second type of work such as literature, art, and higher education, it is difficult to be fully convinced of the validity of the ideology and to implement programs heavily influenced by it. For them, it is necessary to limit the application of the ideology and the policies associated with it in order that their work may be carried out successfully. For leaders engaged in activities of the third type, especially in science and technology (most notably the making of atomic weapons), it is possible to pay only lip service to ideology and to proceed in their work largely according to professional standards. In addition to such immediate considerations, historical circumstances have sometimes had differential effects on the intellectual outlook of those persons engaged in these three different types of work. Their previous education, training, and experience may be closely related to the thought of Mao as in the case of military leaders, unrelated to it as in the case of scientists, or associated with intellectual currents somewhat incompatible with it as in the case of those persons working in the fields of literature, art, and higher education. Finally, new experiences and new situations may affect still further the person's or the group's attitude toward Mao's thought. All the time, the formulator of the ideology has continued to insist on the universal applicability of his thought.[91]

These general propositions help to explain the different approaches toward the thought of Mao adopted since 1959 by many military-political leaders on the one hand and by most party leaders working in the fields of literature, art, and education on the other. The latter's views are apparently widely shared by leaders working in other areas. It is true, however, that there have been serious struggles even within the People's Liberation Army (PLA) over the issue of whether or not Mao's

[91] The intra-elite dissensus in this period provides many materials to support Edward Shils's generalization that "dissensus is apt to arise from persons whose occupational roles are concerned with perceiving and promulgating order and those whose roles are concerned with its conduct and management" and that "the most important [source of dissensus] arises from divergent conceptions of the locus and substance of charisma" ("Charisma, Order, and Status," *American Sociological Review*, 30 [April, 1965]: 209–10).

military line should be modified.[92] The first struggle was precipitated by the new experience gained by some high-ranking officers in the Korean War. Let us recall that Lin Piao was the commander of the first phase of China's operations in the Korean War and that P'eng Te-huai became the commander afterward. With his poorly equipped and inadequately supplied army, Lin Piao scored a smashing victory over General MacArthur by adopting a strategy which closely followed the principles laid down by Mao in his article, "Problems of Strategy in China's Revolutionary War" (1936).[93] In contrast, P'eng Te-huai conducted regular, positional warfare during the larger part of the war with new and more modern weapons purchased from the Soviet Union. It is perhaps not accidental that Lin Piao has continued to adhere closely to Mao's military thinking while P'eng became an advocate of regularization and modernization of the PLA along the lines of the Soviet army. A recent editorial in *Chieh-fang-chün pao* confirmed Western analyses of the struggles within the army and their relationship to the experience of the Korean War.

> The first big struggle started after the conclusion of the war to resist U.S. aggression and aid Korea. Under the pretext of "regularization" and "modernization," a handful of representatives of the bourgeois military line, making a complete carbon copy of foreign practice, vainly attempted to negate our army's historical experiences and fine traditions and to lead our army on to the road followed by bourgeois armies. . . . Responding to Chairman Mao's call of "Down with the slave mentality! Bury dogmatism!" the 1958 Enlarged Session of the Military Commission of the Central Committee of the Chinese Communist Party smashed their frantic attack and defended Chairman Mao's thinking and line on army building.[94]

Presumably, it was also some time in 1958 that Peking rejected Moscow's "unreasonable demands designed to bring China under Soviet

[92] For a thorough treatment of this subject up to 1960, see Alice Hsieh, *Communist China's Strategy in the Nuclear Era* (Englewood Cliffs, N.J.: Prentice-Hall, 1962).

[93] *Selected Military Writings* (Peking: Foreign Languages Press, 1963), pp. 75–145.

[94] *Peking Review,* August 5, 1966, p. 9.

military control."[95] But this first inner-party struggle in the military sector did not result in any serious purges.[96]

According to Peking, the second struggle took place in 1959. At an Enlarged Session of the Military Commission which took place after the Eighth Plenum of the Central Committee held at Lushan in August, P'eng Te-huai's "bourgeois, revisionist military line" was repudiated. At the Lushan Plenum, P'eng was dismissed from the post of Minister of Defense but was allowed to keep his membership in the Political Bureau. Yet, as John Gittings concludes after an exhaustive study, this major upset "involved only seven other leading officers at the most generous estimate."[97] The third struggle occurred in late 1965 or the first half of 1966. Lo Jui-ch'ing, Chief of Staff, was reported to have been purged. How many other leading officers were involved is still not clear.

What is important to us at the moment is the fact that a group of military leaders found it feasible to apply Mao's thought in the PLA and could claim immense success with at least some credibility. After Lin Piao replaced P'eng Te-huai as Minister of Defense and as the actual operating head of the Military Commission, a most significant development took place in the PLA. At the time of the dismissal of P'eng, the morale, discipline, ideological commitment, and political reliability of the army had sunk to a low point, partly due to the neglect of political work under P'eng's leadership and partly due to the impact of the Great Leap Forward.[98] Beginning with his famous article of September 29, 1959, and continuing through a series of meetings of the

[95] *The Polemic on the General Line of the International Communist Movement* (Peking: Foreign Languages Press, 1965), p. 77.

[96] General Su Yü, Chief of Staff, was dismissed during the Quemoy Crisis of 1958. We have no knowledge of the reasons for his dismissal. He was soon rehabilitated and appointed to another, though less important, post. During the Cultural Revolution, he appeared frequently on important public functions and was described by a New China News Agency dispatch as a member of the Standing Committee of the Military Commission of the Central Committee.

[97] John Gittings, "Military Control and Leadership, 1954–1964," *China Quarterly*, no. 26 (April–June, 1966), p. 100. Cf. Franz Michael, "The Struggle for Power," *Problems of Communism*, 16 (May–June, 1967): 14.

[98] John Gittings, "The 'Learn from the Army' Campaign," *China Quarterly*, no. 18 (April–June, 1965), p. 154. Ralph L. Powell, *Politico-Military Relationships in Communist China* (Washington, D.C.: Department of State, 1963), p. 1. John W. Lewis, "China's Secret Military Papers: 'Continuities' and 'Revelations,' " *China Quarterly*, no. 18 (April–June, 1964), p. 76.

Military Commission and PLA Political Work Conferences, Lin Piao vigorously upheld and applied Mao's thought on army building. He proceeded to devise a series of specific policies and to undertake concrete actions for this purpose. The decline in party membership in the companies was reversed, and party branches were established in the one-third of the companies which still lacked them. It was stipulated that every platoon must have a party small group and every squad have some party members. With this strengthened party apparatus, Lin launched a continuous and comprehensive program of political education for the individual soldier. In turn, the successfully indoctrinated soldiers were asked to undertake political work among the masses.

Lin Piao's endeavors met with great success. As John W. Lewis concludes: ". . . The 'revolutionary' leadership techniques must be credited in large measure for salvaging the crumbling social order in 1961 and then for progressively restoring morale and discipline in the army and in the general populace."[99] The application of Mao's thought produced the desired effects in the army for simple and obvious reasons. Military discipline and total control of personnel were again reinforced by intensified political work. The values of public service and self-sacrifice could be more easily instilled in the armed services than elsewhere. The soldiers were young and relatively uneducated men whose thinking was not too difficult to influence. The skills demanded of them were fairly simple; originality and creativity were not essential in day-to-day work in the army. It can be reasonably argued that the "people's war" is still the best method of defense against an American invasion of the mainland and a promising strategy for revolution in some underdeveloped countries. Whatever their causes, Lin's successes made him the leading advocate of the vigorous application of Mao's thought. To Mao, they must have seemed a vindication of his thought at a time when other policies associated with it had brought economic disaster upon China. In retrospect, it seems that in making himself the leading advocate of Mao's thought, Lin Piao followed essentially the same path to power that Liu Shao-ch'i had pursued in the early forties.

In contrast to the successful reassertion of Mao's thought in the PLA under Lin Piao's leadership, some of the party leaders found it impossible to implement vigorously Mao's thought and still carry out their duties successfully. Others became skeptical of the applicability of Mao's thought in various fields. These tendencies were more visible in the fields of literature, art, education, and academic affairs than in

[99] *Ibid.*, p. 75.

many others.[100] This development, following a direction contrary to the one in the PLA, finally led to the most profound upheaval within the party since 1935, alongside of which the P'eng Te-huai affair looks like a preliminary skirmish of minor proportions. These contrasting tendencies also determined the form of the current struggle for power.

It is to be recalled that at the Lushan Plenum in August, 1959, P'eng Te-huai criticized the commune system and the Great Leap Forward—with the prior knowledge and apparent support of the Soviet leadership. According to a Western report, Mao declared during a prolonged debate that should the dismissal of P'eng lead to a revolt of the army, he would go back to the villages and recruit another army.[101] If this report is correct, it is clear that Mao was willing to go to any lengths, including the risk of destroying the army, in order to preserve the basic orientation of the regime, to maintain his position of leadership, and to crush his opponents. In the event, this proved to be unnecessary. But seven years later in the Great Proletarian Cultural Revolution, Mao was quite willing to disrupt the party for the same purposes.[102]

[100] This point can be inferred from the long series of exaggerated charges made by the regime against these leaders. See, for example, editorial, *Hung ch'i* [Red Flag], no. 8, 1966; reprinted in *Peking Review*, June 17, 1966, pp. 7–13.

[101] David A. Charles, "The Dismissal of Marshal P'eng Teh-huai," *China Quarterly*, no. 8 (October–December, 1961), p. 63.

[102] New materials available have made it emphatically clear that the Cultural Revolution had its origin in the policy disputes and struggles for power in the P'eng Te-huai affair. On December 21, 1965, Mao once again pointed out explicitly that "the crux of *Hai Jui Dismissed from Office* was the question of dismissal from office. The emperor Chia Ching dismissed Hai Jui from office. In 1959 we dismissed P'eng Te-huai from office. And P'eng Te-huai is 'Hai Jui' too" (*Hung-ch'i*, no. 9, 1967). Chi Pen-yu, a member of the Cultural Revolution Group under the Central Committee, declared in a speech on May 23, 1967: "Particularly during the period of the country's economic difficulties between 1959 and 1962, the handful of counter-revolutionary revisionists, supported by the handful of top Party persons in authority, put out a large number of poisonous weeds such as *Hai Jui Dismissed from Office, Hsieh Yao-huan* and *Li Hui-niang*. In these they insidiously attacked and insulted our great Party in an attempt to reverse the verdicts on the Right opportunist P'eng Teh-huai and others dismissed from office at the Lushan meeting and to incite people to join them in activities aimed at a counter-revolutionary restoration" (*Peking Review*, May 26, 1967, p. 26). The May 16, 1966, circular of the Central Committee drawn up under the personal guidance of Mao reiterated his view that "the key point in Wu Han's drama *Hai Jui Dismissed from Office* is the question of dismissal from office." It attacked P'eng Chen, then the ninth

The fact that Mao found it necessary to disrupt the party in order to make his views prevail suggests the strong resistance within the party. This strong resistance in turn indicates that the process of bureaucratization and functional differentiation has gone very far. A review of the events leading up to and during the Great Proletarian Cultural Revolution shows that this is the case. During the period from 1959 to 1962, the economic disaster obliged Mao to acquiesce in a policy of liberalization in many fields and prevented him from acting against the dissidents. As Donald Munro points out, "there occurred in China a faint echo of the Hundred Flowers period of 1957."[103]

As soon as the economic crisis eased, Mao began his counterattack. At the Tenth Plenum in September, 1962, he warned the party: "Never forget the class struggle." Since then he has been reported as having pointed out that "some people were making use of the writing of novels to carry on anti-party activities and were creating a public opinion for the restoration of capitalism."[104] He launched the Socialist Education Movement and the three revolutionary movements of class struggle, of struggle for production, and of struggle for scientific experiment. He called on the Chinese people to learn from the PLA, which had successfully applied his thought.

Mao's endeavors encountered serious resistance in the field of literature and art. For the renewed and intensified application of Mao's doctrine that literature and art must serve politics would have imposed further limitations on the creative talents of writers and artists at a time when the quality of works produced had already been declining over a period of years, ever since Mao delivered his "Talks at the Yenan Forum on Literature and Art."[105] As Chou Yang was reported to have

---

ranking member of the Politbureau and the First Secretary of the Peking Municipal Party Committee, for covering up the serious political nature of the struggle and the heart of the matter, "namely, the dismissal of the Right opportunists at Lushan in 1959 and the opposition of Wu Han and others to the Party and socialism" (*ibid.*, May 19, 1967, p. 7).

[103] Donald J. Munro, "Dissent in Communist China," *Current Scene*, June 1, 1966, p. 3. In retrospect, it seems significant that the slogan, "Let a Hundred Flowers Bloom and a Hundred Schools of Thought Contend" was first proposed, in a speech on May 26, 1956, by Lu Ting-yi, Director of the Propaganda Department (who was later dismissed in July, 1966), to a gathering of scientists, social scientists, doctors, writers, and others.

[104] *Peking Review*, August 22, 1966, p. 36.

[105] T. A. Hsia, "Twenty Years after the Yenan Forum," *China Quarterly*, no. 13 (January–March, 1963), pp. 226–53.

told a group of young writers and scholars, the intellectuals of his generation were inferior to those of the preceding generation and the intellectuals of their generation were in turn inferior to those of his own. He asked what would happen if this trend continued.

Mao noted the resistance to his demands. He has been reported as having pointed out in 1963:

> In all forms of art . . . problems abounded; the people engaged in them were numerous. . . . Wasn't it absurd that many Communists showed enthusiasm in advancing feudal and capitalist art, but no zeal in promoting socialist art.[106]

While his efforts seem to have made some progress in other fields, for instance in the establishment of "political departments" within economic administration after the example of the PLA, his policies still failed to make much headway in the field of literature and art. Thus, a rectification movement was launched in June, 1964, within the All-China Federation of Literary and Art Circles and its affiliated association. At that time, Mao made his most serious warning to date, declaring

> In the past fifteen years the literary and art circles for the most part . . . had not carried out policies of the Party and had acted as high and mighty bureaucrats. . . . In recent years they have even slid to the verge of revisionism. If serious steps were not taken to remould them, they were bound at some future date to become groups like the Hungarian Petofi Club.[107]

[106] *Peking Review*, July 8, 1966, p. 18. It has become increasingly clear that Chiang Ch'ing (Mrs. Mao Tse-tung) has played a vital role in the debate in the field of literature and art and the power struggle which finally led to the attack on Liu Shao-ch'i. In this debate and power struggle, personal bitterness and jealousy were apparently intertwined with important policy issues. For some of the important articles and speeches revealing the role of Chiang Ch'ing, see "Patriotism or National Betrayal?" *Peking Review*, April 7, 1967, pp. 5–16; "On the Revolution in Peking Opera," *ibid.*, pp. 13–15; "Chairman Mao's 'Talks at the Yenan Forum on Literature and Art' Is a Programme for Building a Mighty Proletarian Cultural Army," *ibid.*, May 26, 1967; "Summary of the Forum of Literature and Art in the Armed Forces with Which Comrade Lin Piao Entrusted Comrade Chiang Ch'ing," New China News Agency dispatch (Peking), May 28, 1967; Speech by Comrade Chiang Ch'ing, *Peking Review*, December 9, 1966, pp. 6–9.

[107] *Peking Review*, August 12, 1966, p. 36.

Yang Hsien-chen, Shao Chuan-lin, Feng Ting, and Chou Ku-ch'eng were subject to devastating attacks.[108] Still this persecution of the party and non-party intellectuals was not extensive and far-reaching enough to satisfy Mao. This dissatisfaction is reflected in the recent charge made by the Maoists:

> In this so-called "rectification movement," Chou Yang in general forbade open criticism of a sinister gang in literary and art circles which was opposed to the Party, opposed to socialism, and opposed to Mao Tse-tung's thought. As for those few members of the sinister gang like Tien Han, Hsia Yen and Shao Chuan-lin for whom open criticism was inevitable, he played a series of tricks of sham criticism but actual defense.[109]

This conscious and unconscious resistance was possible because the process of bureaucratization and routinization had gone a long way in the party apparatus controlling the field of literature and art. Chou Yang was the Secretary of the League of Left-Wing Writers of China in 1931, and became the deputy director of the Propaganda Department of the Central Committee in 1949. He appointed his fellow writers in the 1930's to leading posts in the party propaganda apparatus.[110] This

[108] Fokkema, "Chinese Criticism of Humanism," pp. 68–81.

[109] *Peking Review*, August 12, 1966, p. 36. On January 14, 1965, a National Work Conference called by the Political Bureau adopted a Summary Minutes of Discussion, entitled "Some Current Problems Raised in the Socialist Education Movement in the Rural Area" (the twenty-three-article document), which was "drawn up under the personal leadership of Comrade Mao Tse-tung" (*Peking Review*, August 19, 1966, p. 6). This secret document was sent down to the Party committees at the level of the *hsien* and regiments. In it, the Party Center defined the problem confronting the movement as "the contradiction between socialism and capitalism." The focal point of the movement was to "rectify those persons in authority in the Party who are taking the capitalist road." According to this document, some of these persons acted openly; others operated behind the scenes. Some of their supporters were persons at low levels; others were persons at high levels. See, "Nung-tsun she-hui chu-i chiao-yü yün-tung chung mu-chien ti-chu ti i-hsieh wen-ti" ["Some Current Problems Raised in the Socialist Education Movement in the Rural Areas"]. Many of the essential points of this document were later incorporated in the Decision Concerning the Great Proletarian Cultural Revolution adopted on August 8, 1966, at the Eleventh Plenum of the Central Committee. In the twenty-three-article document, it was stated for the first time that "the main target of the present movement is those within the Party who are in authority and are taking the capitalist road" (*Hung-ch'i*, no. 9, 1967).

[110] *Peking Review*, August 12, 1966, p. 35.

group of party leaders shared the more liberal and critical traditions of the 1930's in literature and art. They were greatly influenced by Western ideas. For example, Chou Yang was reported, perhaps not without exaggeration, to have lauded "European bourgeois culture of the eighteenth and nineteenth centuries" as "the summit of human culture in the world" and to have advocated "the continuous introduction into China of the bourgeois literature and art of other countries."[111] They were also bound by intimate personal ties developed over a long period of time. This process of bureaucratization is indicated by the Maoists' accusation that "Chou Yang tried to recruit deserters and enlist renegades, to form a clique to serve their own selfish interests and to usurp the leadership in literary and art circles."[112] Routinization inevitably accompanies bureaucratization. Mao was reported to have said:

> In a revolutionary period those who only know how to follow routine paths cannot see this enthusiasm of the masses for socialism at all. . . . They can only travel the well-trodden paths. . . . That sort of person is always passive. . . . Someone always has to give him a poke in the back before he will move forward.[113]

Bureaucratization means command method of leadership. Thus, it was charged that these people "are merely accustomed to monopolizing everything themselves, giving orders and reducing the masses to inactivity."[114]

[111] Ibid., June 17, 1966, p. 7.

[112] Ibid., July 12, 1966, p. 36. There is little doubt that Chou Yang had reservations about Mao's policies in general and his doctrine of literature and art in particular. According to the Maoists, Chou Yang said that the correctness of the general line had not yet been proved, that the "all-round leap forward" in 1958 had caused a disproportion in the economy, that production would certainly be raised once the fixing of quota was based on the household, that if socialism does not lead to democracy it is the tyrant's way, that the dissemination of Mao's thought promoted "the cult of the individual and would strangle the people's initiative." He was said to have opposed Mao's policy that literature and art must serve the workers, peasants, and soldiers, and to have considered this idea outdated (ibid., p. 37; ibid., August 19, 1966, pp. 29–30, 36). Apparently, Chou Yang looked down upon the dominant form of drama and art during the Yenan period which consisted of using artists to do propaganda work among the soldiers and peasants. This form of art was apparently a main source of Mao's ideas on literature and art which, according to Chou Yang, were based on "art-troupe experience."

[113] Ibid., August 19, 1966, p. 20.   [114] Ibid.

Bureaucratic organizations have their own method of protecting themselves. They control the communications from the top leaders. Chou Yang was charged with the error of not transmitting Mao's and the Central Committee's instructions on, and severe criticisms of, literary and art work to people at the lower level. Bureaucratic organizations develop their own informal network of communications. Chou Yang was charged with having said one thing at the open session of a large meeting but to have expressed the opposite view at smaller meetings and outside the meetings.[115] Bureaucratic organizations can try to sabotage the policies of the top leaders. Chou Yang and others were said to have put numerous hindrances in the way of the Maoists' policy of staging Peking operas on contemporary themes and to have laid down numerous rules and regulations to prevent the effective implementation of other policies. Bureaucratic organizations can resist penetration by top leaders. The Peking Municipal Party Committee was accused of erecting a "tight barricade against the Central Committee" and of maintaining "an independent kingdom, water-tight and impenetrable."[116] An undercurrent of distrust between the party intellectuals and the party military leaders is reflected in Chou Yang's use of the old saying that "it is impossible for scholars to reason with soldiers."[117]

The materials brought to light by the Cultural Revolution and Mao's decision to stage it show the serious limitations of the much-vaunted method of thought reform, even when applied within the party. As the Maoists admitted, there are "a considerable number of muddled-headed people inside the Party whose world outlook has not been effectively remoulded."[118] It has become clearer than before that no matter how effective the technique, thought reform can only be successful when the ideology continues to demonstrate its validity by serving as a basis for successful policies and actions, shows its usefulness as a schematic image of reality, and retains its reliability as a crude map in an uncertain situation. When these conditions are not met, thought reform can even be counter-productive, for attempts at indoctrination merely sharpen the psychological conflicts of the individual without leading to the acceptance of the ideology. Mao's method of controlling the party bureaucracy through indoctrination, which had

115 *Ibid.*, August 12, 1966, p. 3.

116 *Ibid.*, July 8, 1966, p. 32.   117 *Ibid.*, August 19, 1966, p. 35.

118 *Ibid.*, November 4, 1966, p. 7. See also *ibid.*, August 19, 1966, p. 20.

at an earlier period of time been effective, could no longer produce similar results. The Stalinist method of controlling the party by secret police ran counter to his political style. In any case, many secret police units at various levels were under the control of the party organization rather than Mao himself.

In order to reassert the thought of Mao and to preserve the basic orientation of the regime, Mao was forced by the widespread dissidence and resistance to his policies in various sections of the party to broaden his attack until he had purged some of the highest party leaders. Lin Piao apparently took advantage of the same situation to strike down his competitors and to become the heir apparent to Mao. In the case of some of the leaders such as Liu Shao-ch'i and Teng Hsiao-p'ing, lack of reliable information prevents us from determining whether and to what extent they opposed specific policies of Mao, whether they were implicated primarily by the errors of their trusted subordinates, and whether their mistake lay mainly in trying to limit the extent of the purges and to moderate Mao's handling of the Cultural Revolution.[119]

Space does not enable us to review in any detail the more recent events, but there are several interesting points which deserve mention. First, Mao's policies continued to meet with resistance at every important juncture. In September, 1965, at a Central Committee meeting, Mao pointed to the need to subject the "reactionary bourgeoisie" to criticism.[120] Apparently, opposition within the party prevented him

---

[119] Materials available since the time of writing indicate that Liu Shao-ch'i came into serious conflict with Mao over the dispatch in June, 1966, of work teams to conduct the Cultural Revolution in various universities, units, and departments. Liu apparently tried to control the "revolutionary teachers and students" through the work teams, to protect some of the leading party officials under attack, and to preserve the integrity of the party organizations as much as possible. In contrast, Mao wanted to carry out a sweeping change of the leadership of the various party units. See "The Confession of Liu Shao-ch'i," *Atlas,* April, 1967, pp. 12–17, and *Mainichi,* January 28, 1967. It also becomes quite clear that Liu, as the manager of the party apparatus, has generally held less radical views than Mao, the leader of the movement and regime, although prior to the failure of the Great Leap Forward the differences between Liu and Mao had been resolved in one way or another and an effective unity between the leader and the party organization had been preserved. To Liu, the party is supreme; to Mao, the leader, his thought as the embodiment of revolutionary principles, is above the party as the final source of authority and truth.

[120] It is now known that this "work conference of the Central Committee" was a session of the standing Committee of the Political Bureau attended also by the leading party officials of all the regional bureaus of the Central Com-

from launching the attack until November.[121] By the Maoists' admission, "even after Comrade Mao Tse-tung criticized the . . . Peking Municipal Party Committee, they [the party leaders in Peking] continued to carry out organized and planned resistance in an attempt to save the queen by sacrificing the knight."[122]

On June 3, 1966, the Central Committee announced the reorganization of the Peking Municipal Party Committee, appointing Li Hsüeh-feng as its First Secretary to replace P'eng Chen.[123] Then, in spite of Mao's reservations, some party leaders hastily sent out work teams for the avowed purpose of carrying out the Cultural Revolution in various units and places.[124] In fact, the persons in charge of various units or

---

mittee. At this meeting in September and October of 1965, Mao gave his instructions regarding criticism of Wu Han ("Circular of Central Committee of Chinese Communist Party, May 16, 1966," *Peking Review*, May 19, 1966, p. 6).

[121] This attack took the form of an article by Yao Wen-yüan on Wu Han's historical play, *Hai Jui Dismissed from Office*, published in the *Wen-hui pao* in Shanghai on November 10, 1965, and not reprinted in the *Jen-min jih-pao* (pp. 5–6) until November 30. The Maoists now claim that this "first shot at the P'eng Chen counter-revolutionary revisionist clique" was "led by Comrade Chiang Ch'ing" (*Peking Review*, May 26, 1967, p. 27).

[122] *Peking Review*, July 8, 1966, p. 30. On April 16, *Frontline* (of which Teng T'o was the editor-in-chief) and the *Peking Daily* (an organ controlled by the Peking Municipal Party Committee) published a collection of materials with comments entitled "A Criticism of Three-Family Village and *Evening Chats at Yenshan*." The Maoists charged that this criticism was a sham and that its purpose was "to prevent the struggle from going deeper" by sacrificing Teng T'o. Yao Wen-yuan, "On 'Three-Family Village,'" pp. 5–8. This article was first published in Shang-hai's *Chieh-fang jih-pao* and *Wen-hui pao* on May 10, 1966.

Prior to mid-May, there existed an organ known as the "Group of Five in Charge of the Cultural Revolution." It was headed by P'eng Chen, of all people. P'eng prepared a report which was approved by the Central Committee for distribution on February 12, 1966. It minimized the political aspect of Wu Han's play. On May 16, 1966, the Central Committee issued a circular which sharply attacked P'eng's report, dissolved the "Group of Five," and set up a new Cultural Revolution Group directly under the Standing Committee of the Political Bureau (*Peking Review*, May 19, 1966, pp. 6–9). How the reversal of the position of the Central Committee between February 12 and May 16 came about remains obscure.

[123] *Jen-min jih-pao*, June 4, 1966, p. 1.

[124] *Peking Review*, December 9, 1966, p. 8. The decision to send work teams was made by Liu Shao-ch'i. *Atlas*, April, 1967, p. 13. See also note 86.

those in charge of the work teams "organized counter-attacks against the masses," "spearheaded the struggle against the revolutionary activists, encircled and attacked the revolutionary left and suppressed the revolutionary left and suppressed the revolutionary mass movement."[125] Thus, "an error on matters of orientation and an error of line took place during a short period."[126] Mao then convened the Eleventh Plenum which met from August 1 to August 12, 1966, and adopted the Decision Concerning the Great Proletarian Cultural Revolution. But the number of members and alternate members of the Central Committee who attended the meeting was not announced.[127] Instead, the communiqué reported that, among others, "representatives of revolutionary leaders and students from institutions of higher learning in Peking" were present.[128] A few days after the Red Guards were received by Mao in mid-August, "new problems cropped up."[129] Since then, there have been frequent reports of clashes between the Red Guards and other groups or even between Red Guards under different leadership.

The resistance encountered by Mao suggests that he was not in effective control of the party after 1959, that his orders were no longer followed as a matter of course, that he may not always have had majority support in the Political Bureau before August, 1966, and perhaps not even in the Central Committee, and that a politically unorganized majority of top party leaders had serious reservations about his policies. If these speculations are correct, not only was Mao's ideological authority seriously weakened, but also ideological authority and organizational authority were no longer united in one person or one organ of the party as they had been before 1959. This created a serious dilemma for the party, for Mao still had enormous personal prestige and considerable support within the party. Although the other leaders could attempt to persuade Mao to accept their views, argue with him, and could endeavor to restrain, resist, and even sabotage his moves, they

[125] *Peking Review*, August 19, 1966, p. 19. The translation used here is slightly different from the text as it appeared in the *Peking Review*.

[126] *Ibid.*, August 26, 1966, p. 7.

[127] According to Franz Michael, only 80 of the full Central Committee membership were present (47 regular members and 33 candidate members), with 101 absent (44 regular members and 57 candidate members). "The Struggle for Power," *Problems of Communism*, 16 (May–June, 1967) : 19.

[128] *Peking Review*, August 19, 1966, p. 4.

[129] *Ibid.*, December 9, 1966, p. 8.

could not take positive actions to oppose or attack him openly without undermining the foundation of the party and the regime. They also could not openly criticize the thought of Mao Tse-tung and formulate and propagate a counter-ideology. They were thus generally on the defensive. In contrast, Mao took the offensive by using Lin Piao and the Red Guards to intimidate and shake up the party organizations in different units and by reorganizing the Standing Committee of the Political Bureau together with the Political Bureau itself. By doing so, he seriously weakened the structural legitimacy of the party and established a precedent under which the all-sacred party organization can be attacked by other units. This will make governing the nation much more difficult from now on.

Second, Mao's attack was gradually broadened and focused at a fairly early stage on persons within the party itself. As the very perceptive report by the editor of *Current Scene* pointed out, "Opposition created during the previous phase became the principal object of attack during the next stage."[130] The Socialist Education Movement was intensified in November, 1965, with Yao Wen-yüan's attack on Wu Han's historical play, *Hai Jui Dismissed from Office*. The attack on Wu Han became the attack on the "bourgeois" intellectuals as a whole. By May, the attack was broadened to include Teng T'o, an influential member of the Secretariat of the Peking Municipal Party Committee, and Liao Mo-sha, the director of its United-Front Department. After the Peking Municipal Party Committee had been reorganized, the leadership in the Propaganda Department of the Central Committee was changed. Party leaders working in the field of literature, art, education, and propaganda in various localities were dismissed or severely criticized. The two concrete targets became first, "those in authority who have wormed their way into the Party and are taking the capitalist road" and, second, "the reactionary bourgeois academic 'authorities.' "[131] But the Maoists also recognized that their opponents enjoyed widespread popular support. By their own admission, the resistance to the Cultural Revolution also came from "the old force of habit in society,"[132] and "the bourgeois reactionary line has its social base which is mainly in the bourgeoisie."[133] Hence, it was necessary to organize such a large-scale "mass movement" as the Red Guards in order "to destroy the social basis on

[130] "A Year of Revolution," *Current Scene*, December 10, 1966, p. 9.

[131] *Peking Review*, August 26, 1966, p. 17.

[132] *Ibid.*, August 12, 1966, pp. 6–7.   [133] *Ibid.*, November 4, 1966, p. 7.

which the handful of bourgeois Rightists rests and to carry through the Great Proletarian Cultural Revolution thoroughly and in depth."[134] But as the Decision Concerning the Great Proletarian Cultural Revolution adopted by the Eleventh Plenum made clear, "the main target of attack in the present movement is those in the Party who are in authority and are taking the capitalist road."[135]

Third, as has been pointed out by many commentators, it was *Chieh-fang-chün pao*, the organ of the PLA rather than the party's official organ, *Jen-min jih-pao*, which took the lead in the Cultural Revolution. In one case, the army organ criticized a view expressed in an editorial of the party organ. This is only one of the many indications that the political influence of the army has increased greatly while that of the party itself has declined.

Fourth, at least up to the time of the completion of this paper in early January, 1967, there were efforts to preserve continuities with the past amidst the political upheaval. The PLA still has been kept in the background, and the principle of civilian control over the military, although weakened, has been maintained at least in theory. Despite many incidents involving the Red Guards and other groups, an attempt has been made to preserve the rule that reasoning and not violence should be used. An effort has been made to limit the number of persons against whom drastic action is taken. A way has been left open for the deviant party leaders to repent and to come back to the fold. Whatever the role of the secret police in the Red Guard movement, there has been no secret-police terror. For this, Red Guard terror has acted as a substitute.[136] Whether or not the attempts to preserve these traditions have

[134] *Ibid.*, September 23, 1966, p. 15. It is quite probable that the majority of the Red Guards consists of children from the less privileged groups in the society, i.e., workers, peasants, and lower cadres. They are motivated by jealousy of children from privileged groups. *Ibid.*, January 1, 1967, p. 10.

[135] *Ibid.*, August 12, 1966, p. 8.

[136] Under the slogan of eliminating old ideas, old culture, old customs, and old habits, the Red Guards resorted to violent action against some elements of the population. The Red Guards thus replaced the public security forces as the instrument of violence and coercion. The use of violence by these loosely organized and inadequately supervised Red Guard units was indiscriminate and non-selective. Whether or not this was intended by the Maoists, the effect of this indiscriminate use of violence was the creation of an atmosphere of terror in which the personal and organizational ties among individuals were cut or loosened. The expectations of individuals were destabilized, and the activities of the various established organizations were hampered and disrupted. Furthermore, the Red Guards denounced some of the leading officials in wall

been and will be successful remains in doubt. These traditions were established and further developed during a period when those opposed to Mao had been discredited by the failure of their policies, when Mao had offered the party a promising alternative program, and when Mao's ideological and organizational authority had been consolidated. They could be maintained only so long as there was a unity of the leader, the ideology, and the organizations. But these conditions no longer exist.[137]

---

posters or struggle meetings and subjected them to public humiliation, using some of the techniques which Mao described with high praise in his report on an investigation of the peasant movement in Hunan in 1927. The rampaging Red Guards intimidated the population and deterred them from rallying to the support of the officials under attack, while they undermined the prestige and authority of the latter. All the time the media of mass communication conducted an intensive propaganda campaign to discredit the oppositionists and their anti-Maoist views.

[137] Toward the end of 1966, when the Cultural Revolution was launched in the factories and the rural areas, there were many reports that the workers deserted their posts, demanded and received bonuses and supplementary wages, demanded and got better housing accommodations, an even went on strike in some cases. Other reports stated that the peasants wanted to divide up all the year-end surplus grain harvested by the production teams or even the grain reserves and to use up the public accumulation funds, and that the students and other urban elements sent to the countryside were returning to the cities. The Maoists charged that the oppositionists were using material benefits to bribe the masses to join them, to discredit the Cultural Revolution, and to disrupt the economy. This charge can only be partly correct. The basic explanation is the fact that the whole Chinese system of economy relies more heavily on political control over demands and performance of the workers and peasants for its effective functioning than do many other systems. This political control was imposed by the party committees at different levels and in different units. With some of the party leaders and party committees under attack by the Red Guards, this whole system of political control was weakened. The masses took advantage of this situation to advance their economic demands or simply to relax their efforts. With their political authority shaken, the party officials may have found it difficult to resist these demands or may have been unable to control the behavior of the masses. Because they themselves were under attack, they feared to take up responsibility and in some cases simply gave up their leadership roles. This must be the basic explanation which the Maoists did not mention.

The situation both as perceived by the Maoists and as it actually developed demanded the reimposition of political control by the Maoists. It brought about a new stage of the Cultural Revolution, the stage of the seizure of power in various localities and units by the Maoists from the established party committees. This stage began with the so-called January Revolution. Shanghai was the first city in which the seizure of power took place. This stage was characterized by several features. Mao called on the army to support the revolu-

Fifth, the timing of Mao's move seems to have been related to international events. When Mao called for criticism of the "reactionary bourgeoisie" in September and October of 1965, America's sharp escalation of the war in Vietnam had prevented a defeat of the government forces in South Vietnam. There was increasing fear of war with the United States. The Soviet Union was proposing "united action" to counter the American moves. On September 30, 1965, an army coup which was supported by the Communist Party of Indonesia took place and led within a few days to a counter-coup by the army which ended in the slaughter of hundreds of thousands of Indonesian Communists and their followers. In October, Peking failed to impose its views on the composition and tasks of the Second Bandung Conference, and the much

---

tionary rebels in their seizure of power. The army units paraded in the streets to demonstrate their power and, in the case of the city of Harbin, actually surrounded an opposition group and disarmed its members. Revolutionary rebels would first seize the public security bureaus and the mass media of communication, and then would assume the power of the party committee and the government organ of a particular unit or at a particular level. The provisional organ of power, now known as a revolutionary committee, was based on the principle of the three-in-one combination. In other words, it was to be composed of, first, the leaders of the revolutionary mass organization (that is to say, the revolutionary rebels or the Red Guards), second, the representatives of the army units stationed there, and third, the revolutionary leading cadres (that is, those party officials who originally supported Mao or were persuaded to join the Maoists to seize power from the oppositionists or their fellow colleagues on the party committee).

Since the army was the only organization which remained *relatively* unscathed in the Cultural Revolution, it was the only instrument which could supervise industrial production and farm work. Army units were ordered to support the work of industrial production and to help with routine farm work. The workers and the peasants were told to cooperate with them. In mid-March the seizure of power at the production-team and production-brigade level was suspended for the period of the busy spring farming season. Shortly afterward, the Maoists launched an intensive attack on the top party person in authority who was taking the capitalist road and on his book on self-cultivation, i.e., Liu Shao-ch'i and his book, *Lun Kung-chang-tang-yüan ti hsiu-yang* [On the Self-cultivation of a Member of the Chinese Communist Party] (Changchiak'ou: Hsin-Hua shu-tien, 1946). A revised edition was published in 1962 by Jen-min chu-pan she. English translations were published by the Foreign Languages Press in 1961 and 1964, under the title of *How To Be a Good Communist*.

Thus the January Revolution, Mao's call for the PLA to give active support to the revolutionary left, and the widespread violence in many localities indicate that the party traditions have become further eroded because the objective conditions necessary to their preservation no longer existed.

heralded meeting was postponed. The Pakistani-Indian War ended in a setback for Pakistan and in the Tashkent Conference which greatly enhanced Soviet prestige. This series of setbacks in foreign policy must have heightened Mao's sense of urgency regarding the need to take preventive action against the dissidents. Furthermore, during this period there must have been a great debate over the policy toward the Soviet Union. The issues may have been whether, in the face of an increased danger of war with the United States, Peking should modify, however slightly, her hostile policy toward the Soviet Union and whether the Soviet proposal of "united action" in Vietnam should be accepted. By November, a decision must have been made, with Mao insisting on the rejection of "united action," refusing to undertake large-scale intervention in the war but at the same time rejecting negotiation with the United States.[138] Presumably, Mao did not want another "Korean War" during which Peking ran the serious risk of an American attack and the Chinese army bore the brunt of the fighting. Instead, he preferred that the Vietnamese continue to conduct the "people's war" on a basis of "self-reliance." Probably he also hoped to embroil the Soviet Union and the United States in a confrontation so that the American-Soviet conflict would be more serious than the Sino-American conflict. By June 5, 1966, if not two or three months previously, the fear of war with the United States must have receded, either because the pattern of American escalation in Vietnam had been stabilized and had thus become clear to Peking, and/or because Peking, after her rejection of united action with the Soviet Union, had reassessed American intentions. Furthermore, the internal struggle for power had become critical by this time. An important document published by *Chieh-fang-chün pao* on June 6 asserted that "if we think only of dealing with the Chiang Kai-shek gang and United States imperialism but neglect the possibility that the bourgeoisie can still work for a come-back and subvert us from within, . . . then history will judge us a criminal."[139] It was only when the fear of an imminent war had receded that Mao and his followers decided to take such a drastic step as the purging of top party leaders and the launching of the Red Guard movement, thus disrupting openly the unity of the party and the nation which would have been imperative for defense in case of war.

[138] Editorial departments of *Jen-min jih-pao* and *Hung-ch'i*, "Refutation of the New Leaders of the C.P.S.U. on 'United Action,'" *Peking Review*, November 12, 1965, pp. 10–21.

[139] *Ibid.*, July 15, 1966, p. 20.

Finally, as everyone realizes, the struggle for power was intimately related to the problem of succession to Mao. Inability to provide for orderly transfer of power is an inherent weakness of all totalitarian regimes. But the crisis in China had certain features which distinguish it from the struggle for succession to Lenin's mantle. In China, the masses were mobilized by both sides. The mass-line method of the CCP had been so rigorously applied in the past that the various social groups had to be drawn into the power struggle in order to obtain even temporary results and to legitimize the outcome. In addition, the major political, social, and economic institutions became more deeply and actively involved in the struggle than in Stalin's fight against his opponents. The army played a central and active role, just as it was once the basis of Mao's power before he had gained control of the party apparatus. The tradition of the PLA as a work force in political affairs as well as a military organization apparently affected the nature of the struggle for succession. The party apparatus was strongly entrenched because of the long-established policies on the assignment and promotion of cadres and the tradition of continuity of leadership. At the same time, the thought of Mao still retained considerable influence. Thus, once there occurred a split between the ideological and organizational authority within the party, its early successes and its long traditions not only failed to prevent a rift in the political system but also magnified the scope and intensity of the crisis.

Summary and Conclusion

From 1935 up to the eve of the Great Leap Forward, the CCP was almost unique among all Communist parties and totalitarian movements in the continuity and solidarity of its leadership, in the flexibility of its political strategy and tactics, in the popular support it enjoyed, in its capacity to effect rapid socioeconomic transformation, and in its ability to bring about at least a minimum of sociopolitical integration of different regions and classes.

Many historical circumstances provided favorable conditions for the victory of the CCP and for the acceptance and consolidation of the political system which the party created in its own image. The Chinese Communist movement was the response of a group of men to the problems of a highly disintegrated political community which demanded a total solution and revolutionary change. Yet the repudiation of the old order and the rejection of the content of many traditions did not preclude the persistence of certain cultural patterns and traditional forms which made the new political system acceptable to the Chinese. The important role played by an explicit, official ideology in the Chinese Empire, the autocratic nature of the political system, the cult of the emperor, the existence of a well-defined elite, the submersion of the individual in a collectivity, are all cases in point.

During the revolutionary period, Marxism-Leninism was adapted to Chinese conditions in the thought of Mao Tse-tung. Marxism-Leninism–the thought of Mao became one of the few, if not the only, political doctrines which were Western in origin but took deep root in China. This body of Marxist-Leninist-Maoist ideas was congruent with Chinese reality at the time. Certain parts of Marxism-Leninism suited the conditions of a disintegrated society. The theory of contradiction justified the inevitable, violent conflicts which the absence of a stable and acceptable political order made ubiquitous. The sociological analysis of class and class struggle directed the Chinese Communists to the necessity of making the peasantry and other social groups active participants in the political process, thus enabling them to change the whole pattern of political participation and to defeat the ruling group. The concept of the unity of theory and practice corresponded to the great need for resolute action to achieve carefully defined goals. The principles of party-building fitted an environment in which the rebuilding of a new political community had to begin with a tightly organized group of men. Other parts of Marxism-Leninism, such as the concept of an organic tie between a Communist party and the proletariat, were discarded in practice. The thought of Mao itself evolved out of successful practice in handling political work and military affairs in the course of fighting a guerrilla war. Defeat suffered by the party when rival leaders were in power discredited them, while success achieved by the movement under Mao's guidance confirmed his leadership and legitimized his thought. His rivals' failure and his own success gave Mao control over the party without bloody purges. The unity of ideological and organizational authority in the person of Mao and his followers enabled the party to develop a moderate method of inner-party struggle. This united elite with its international orientation proved to be more capable of exploiting nationalism than the Nationalist party. Employing its united-front tactics, it succeeded in acquiring leadership over all the major social groups toward the end of the civil war. Similarly, circumstances and success in domestic and international affairs helped the party to consolidate its control and to legitimize the political system which it had brought into existence.

The early successes were made possible by a system of ideas and practices which contained within itself the seeds of policy failures occurring between 1958 and 1961 and the profound crisis of 1966. This system had made the thought of Mao the doctrinal basis of the regime, the cognitive framework for understanding reality, and a general guide in formulating policies. The more impressive the early successes and the longer the history of the movement, the more tenaciously one group of leaders, particularly the aging formulator of the ideology himself, held on to the doctrine and the memories of the past. But the ideology was no longer congruent with the social conditions of a developing, industrializing, and modernizing society. It no longer reflected the genuine interests and desires of the population. Policies associated with ideology in various ways proluced disastrous results. Among the dissident intellectuals inside and outside the party, criticism of these policies led to doubts about the ideology. The ideological authority of Mao was thus weakened, and effective organizational authority gravitated more than ever to another group of party leaders. A split occurred between ideological and organizational authority. At the same time, however, the first group of leaders continued to find the ideology a useful guide in some sectors of an increasingly differentiated society. They sought to reassert the ideology in order to preserve the general orientation of the regime and to strengthen its foundations.

Thus, two opinion groups emerged in opposition to each other. Their conflicts could not be reconciled, harmonized, or resolved on the basis of the ideology, because the applicability of this ideology was itself the central issue in the dispute. There were no longer any fundamental standards by which to judge right and wrong, for the standards as embodied in the ideology were the subject of the debate.[140] The ideology which had performed an integrative function at an early time became itself a disintegrative force. In the struggle for power, it was used as a weapon by one group to attack the other. *Realpolitik* was joined to a conflict over principles. Party unity disappeared. The persistent force of Mao and his followers was confronted with tenacious resistance or opposition by a politically unorganized majority of the party. This confrontation and the widening split between ideological and organizational authority could not be easily resolved by a political system in which it is almost impossible to remove the top leader and in which the

[140] An editorial by the *Jen-min jin-pao* and the *Hung-ch'i* charged that some responsible persons in the party "reversed right and wrong, juggled black and white . . ." (*Peking Review,* January 1, 1967, p. 9).

strongly entrenched party organizations at various levels were difficult to purge. At this point, the historical accident of the longevity but uncertain health of Mao may have become a factor. All these circumstances introduced a series of complicating factors into the process of routinization of charisma and turned that process into an open struggle between a charismatic leader and a routinizing and bureaucratized organization.

The Great Proletarian Cultural Revolution cannot properly be called a purge, since a purge is an institutionalized practice in the system. It is rather a profound crisis in the institutions of the party themselves. In this sense, the present inner-party struggle is different in nature from all the previous purges since 1935. The organizational legitimacy of the party center was weakened when, as the editor of *Current Scene* put it, Mao employed his enormous personal prestige and packed the Eleventh Plenum with outsiders "in order to overcome the resistance of what may have been a majority within Party leadership councils,"[141] and rammed through the revolutionary decisions on the Cultural Revolution. The organizational legitimacy of the party apparatus in various units and at different levels was destroyed when the Red Guards were used to attack them.[142] The long-established traditions and rules governing inner-party struggle were violated. In the process of the Cultural Revolution which has been justified by the thought of Mao and has been said to have been under his personal command, the excesses of the Red Guards, the naïveté of their actions, and the turmoil created by them may have further called into question the validity of Mao's thought and his wisdom. The ideological legitimacy of the regime and the personal legitimacy of the leader may have been further weakened. As the party and the ideology constitute the core of the regime, the political system as a whole has been badly shaken.

---

[141] "A Year of Revolution," *Current Scene*, December 10, 1966, p. 6. Chiang Ch'ing indirectly admitted that the Maoists did not constitute a majority. An official report of her speech on November 28, 1966, contained this intriguing sentence: "Referring to the question of 'minority' and 'majority' she said one could not talk about a 'minority' or 'majority' independent of class viewpoint" (*Peking Review*, December 9, 1966, p. 9).

[142] The Red Guards are probably under the very loose control of the Cultural Revolution groups and committees and the guidance of the PLA. There is also no doubt that the army protected and supported the Red Guards; the *Peking Review* reported that in the last few months of 1966, "the Chinese People's Liberation Army sent more than 100,000 commanders and fighters to take part in the colossal work involved in making the visitors feel at home in the capital" (*Peking Review*, January 1, 1967, p. 4).

A Maoist victory will establish a precedent under which the Chairman of the party may violate many, if not all, of its most important norms and prescribed procedures and ignore its regular structural arrangements, and under which personal legitimacy may be used to override structural legitimacy. It will restore the position of the charismatic leader and his thought and weaken the party as an institution. It will delay the process of routinization. The important change in the interrelationship of the leader, the ideology, and the organization will make institutionalization in the political sphere more difficult and the political stability achieved at any particular time more precarious than before. This precedent can, however, be nullified if Mao's successors repudiate implicitly or explicitly this particular aspect of the Cultural Revolution. This is a likely development in the long run. A victory by the opposition will make it necessary to reject, revise, or reinterpret the thought of Mao and/or to develop new doctrines to replace or to supplement it. In either case, the effectiveness and legitimacy of the regime will not be easy to re-establish quickly. Even if an uneasy compromise emerges out of a stalemate, the authority and capacity of the regime to act will be diminished, and public confidence in it will not be easy to restore soon. China's search for a reintegrated political community has suffered a setback. It will have to begin again with a battered political system.

Thus, just as the thought of Mao and his policies in the Great Leap Forward produced an economic disaster, the thought of Mao and his policies in the Great Proletarian Cultural Revolution seem likely to have serious consequences in the next few years not only for cultural and academic life but also for the political system as a whole. What we have witnessed is the tragedy of a once effective doctrine which has outlived its usefulness and the tragedy of a once impressive political system which has rested on the foundation of a total ideology rather than on a consensus or agreement on fundamentals. Only future events can reveal whether the current political upheaval represents the last gasp of a revolution or whether it represents a new totalitarian "breakthrough" in which a leader gains or regains absolute dictatorial control and, together with his heirs, pushes the revolution to a more radical stage of fairly long duration. What cannot be doubted is that the contrast between the early successes and the present turmoil places in high relief the universal problems and difficulties of transition from revolution to the establishment of a new integrated political community.

Comments by C. P. FitzGerald

The measure of Professor Tsou's penetrating and exhaustive study of the causes which have led to the Great Cultural Revolution in China today is given by the developments subsequent to the date at which the paper was written and presented to the Conference on China's Heritage and the Communist Political System. Almost every turn of the political wheel in China since then has conformed to the trends which Professor Tsou forecast. The basic cause of the movement is seen as the failure of a once effective ideology—the thought of Mao Tse-tung—to cope with the greater complexity of a developing society. In this sense Mao is paying the penalty for his own success. The ideology which guided China from confusion and civil war to the rebuilding of a centralized and strong state has in turn become outmoded by the character which the new society increasingly assumed, a character which is contrary to Mao's own ideals, and which he is determined to alter and to correct.

There is, as Professor Tsou sees it, a profound conflict between policy and ideology, which centers on the problem of the integration of the new Chinese society. Policy and ideology were supposed to be in harmony, but to an increasing extent they have drifted into antagonism. The ideology, the thought of Mao Tse-tung, is based essentially on the experience of the long guerrilla war first against the Kuomintang (KMT), then against the Japanese invaders, and then once more against the KMT in the final civil war. This record of more than twenty years covers the most active period of Mao's own life, the era of his greatest achievements, and not unnaturally returns to him as a constant inspiration when seeking solutions to current problems. The requirements of a guerrilla civil war are that every aim subordinate to victory and personal survival must be relegated to secondary consideration. A constant dedication and unremitting effort is needed from devoted followers, who can see for themselves that only by winning this struggle is any future assured to them.

This approach to the economic and social problems of a great nation, actually at peace, is bound to meet with skepticism and covert opposition from many who will doubt whether it is still appropriate, or adequate, in the changed circumstances brought about by the very triumph of the revolution nearly twenty years ago. Effort is demanded of a people who have toiled for all these years to build a new China, and now expect to see some at least of the fruits of their labor in the form of economic betterment. To be once more asked to sacrifice such hopes, and even to be told that the hopes themselves are a sign of backsliding, of bourgeois vices, must raise in many minds a new and disturbing question: What was the revolution for? If not to create a new, strong, and more satisfying economy, but merely to provide a platform for continuing revolution, for, it would seem, the sake of revolutionary zeal itself, without a further aim, this must be a daunting prospect to many intellectuals, managers, public servants, technicians, and scientists who had given wholehearted service to the task of national reconstruction.

The attack upon these classes or categories of people, and thus upon all urban culture, seems retrograde and destructive to outside observers, and must also appear disastrous to many of the affected people themselves: to political leaders, party hierarchs, and experienced civil servants who believed that the revolution, having achieved its first goals, was now ready to move forward to attain the satisfactions of improved standards of living, advancing technology, and an expanding educated class. The Great Proletarian Cultural Revolution thus calls in question the process of integration—the integration of a new society, which is one of the themes of Professor Tsou's paper. The problem of integration in China, a problem which is not new, is analyzed and the factors making for success as well as the obstacles are considered. The essential needs for a successful integration are listed as follows:

1. The nation should not be seriously divided on religious or nationality lines. This is certainly not a real danger in China. Religion is a minor factor in Chinese society; creeds such as Islam or Christianity have only relatively very small following, and in the case of Islam can be isolated as a culture trait of a national minority, the Moslems, and thus not likely to make an impact on the Han majority. Buddhism, with many more millions of practising followers, has never been a politically active faith, and has always been tolerant of rival systems.

The national minority peoples, although in aggregate numbering many millions, are scattered, and very largely, especially the numerous peoples of the southern and southwestern provinces, embedded in a Han population which has been settled in the areas for many generations. Cultural autonomy as introduced by the People's Republic is a sufficient outlet for their national sentiment. A minor problem could arise on the frontiers where, as in Sinkiang, there are national minority peoples in contact with foreign states in which people of their own ethnic group live, but it would not seem probable that this danger is very real.

2. There are no real regional divisions in China imposing a natural separation upon the possible unity of the state. This has been proved by all history—the instability of divisive regimes, the difficulty of basing them upon any consistent region, the lack of distinctive internal frontiers. North and South China may appear very different in Canton and in Peking, but no exact borderline can ever be determined; in the Yangtze region they shade into each other, rice giving place to wheat, straw sandals to cloth shoes, bamboo construction to mud brick, in a wide zone of interpenetration.

3. The tradition of imperial unity. The tradition is strong, and runs through all Chinese history. The tradition, especially as applied to the earliest times, may be—in fact is—much stronger than the facts, but this is not a political defect even if it is an academic error. In any case the tradition and the facts are closely in harmony for the past thousand years, since the T'ang period. This is already a very long time.

4. Republican confusion stimulated the yearning for reintegration. There can be no doubt that nothing so harmed the early Republic as the obvious fact that even the shaky unity maintained to the last by the Ch'ing dynasty speedily collapsed under their successors. To a very large number of Chinese, almost to all who had sufficient education to appreciate the distresses of the state, unity seemed much more important than the ideology on which reunion could be achieved. This was a profound factor in the victory of the Communist party.

5. The consequences of the Japanese War. This war was the first real threat of outright conquest by a foreign people, and one, moreover, whose homeland was beyond the seas, which had ever menaced China. Manchus and even Mongols, Toba or Hsiung Nu, had all been neighboring barbarians whose advanced culture, when they acquired it, was borrowed from China, whose rule was largely conducted through Chinese personnel on Chinese statecraft and civil service lines, and who moved into China to enjoy a privileged status as a ruling class but did not retain in their old homelands an alternative focus of loyalty and

alien tradition. The Japanese came as aliens who claimed an equal, or a higher place, had a more advanced technology and better weapons, and offered to China only the most conservative political development, largely based on the revival of institutions, such as the monarchy, which China had decisively rejected. In addition the Japanese were integrated in their own country, from which they certainly would not have migrated en masse, but would have ruled in China as an alien colonial authority. These were more than sufficient causes to unite the Chinese people against the invader as it had never before united against any alien enemy.

These, then, are the reasons why the Communist regime was able to go far in the task of integrating the Chinese people under the new regime, but the practical operation of this process reveals a dichotomy between modern and earlier ideas, a contrast between the explicit and the implicit, which Professor Tsou sees as probably a root cause of the present political crisis.

There is first the contrast between the whole and the part. The whole is explicit, the constant reiteration on the unity of all China at the popular level, "All China Federations" of this, that and the other, the collective ideal, the commune, and the mass movements. In contradiction stands the part, the elements described as "feudal remnants" (or "dregs"!), the sections of society who cannot easily be drawn into the popular mass, who were marked off by their former way of life and higher education, or who are still seen as distinct because of these characteristics and their inability to renounce the standpoint and outlook of their class origin. Such people have been used and were considered useful and necessary for their skills and their knowledge, and it was assumed that they would gradually lose their old-time outlook and character, and fade into the continuum of the new society. It seems as if one reason for the Cultural Revolution is that this expectation has proved false; advancing technology and more widespread higher education has tended to strengthen and revive the former "scholar" class and to underline the difference in its way of life and outlook from that of the peasantry and proletariat.

Second, there is the contradiction, or contrast between content and form. The explicit character of the regime is a modern totalitarian party dictatorship, denying, in theory, personal rule, but emphasizing, also in theory, mass popular participation in government. The reality shows that much of the traditional authoritarian state survives. Mao Tse-tung himself may avoid the archaic and picturesque trappings of imperial pomp, but he in fact has exercised personal power to a degree which many of his imperial predecessors would have envied. The party has acted as a parallel civil service, ruling under his guidance, while the civil service itself has continued many of the well-tried methods of bureaucracy, although cleansing itself of the former vice of corruption. Here again it seems that the purpose of the Cultural Revolution is to break up this crust of custom and free "revolutionary forces," which it is hoped will strike out a new line—rather undefined—and give the regime a wholly new character.

There is the contrast between ends and means—the aim socialism; the means, the use of small group discussions, the winning of consensus at all levels, the avoidance of the open conflict of opposed policies in assemblies subject to voting procedure. These latter methods, the dislike of straight confrontation, are certainly part of China's social tradition, and have proved a major obstacle to the realization of democratic forms of government. It does not appear, however, that the operation of the Cultural Revolution is making any very great progress in eliminating these methods or traditions. Denunciation of alleged opposition leaders without providing them with an opportunity or a forum for defending or justifying their actions is the rule; protesting, counter "Big Character Posters" may be a first step toward more freedom of expression.

Values and style are a further contrast. The values which the regime acclaims, education for all, a rising standard of living, industrialization and welfare are modern, and differ only in minor points of emphasis from the values proclaimed in other parts of the world. But style is still largely traditional. The great public works of irrigation and flood control are carried out by the mass mobilization of thousands of workers, as they have always been back to Han times and earlier. Campaigns of emulation, stimulants for enthusiasm, are more often traditional and moral than economically motivated; the style of Chinese life remains surprisingly close to many of the manners of the past. How far such activities as that of the Red Guard movement are expected or intended to alter this aspect of Chinese society cannot be easily assessed. It has seemed from outside China that some at least of the behavior of the Red Guards is violently anti-traditional, but that other aspects have very strong traditional roots. The belief that the very young were in some way possessed of an almost magical intuition on political matters is well documented from the earliest Chinese literature.

Thus the operation of the process of integration has had explicit, modern, revolutionary aspects, and implicit, traditional characteristics, which may have been harmonized for several years during which the new economy and new social system took shape but have increasingly come into conflict as the problem of how to strengthen ideological foundations and at the same time cope with new political and economic realities became urgent. There is a deep crisis in integration and this is the social condition which has impelled Mao to inaugurate the Cultural Revolution. Professor Tsou sees this crisis as a reflection of the unresolved problems in sections of Chinese society. First, the problem of the charismatic leader and the routinization of the bureaucracy. Mao stands alone, far above his contemporaries and colleagues. He alone increases the canons of Marxist thought by the addition of his own. The party and the state, run as it would seem to observers by very able men, has nonetheless had to run on lines, and these inevitably begin to turn into grooves as time goes on.

Resistance to changes of the kind Mao wishes to make come from within the party, especially in the fields of literature and art. It may well be that the Chinese Communists, who are drawn from a class and culture deeply committed to literature and art, can see that one of the aspects of the Russian Party which most offends even friendly observers, is the rigid control of literature and art, to the detriment of both. With this goes clear evidence that such restrictions do not in fact work; they fail to control thought. That this failure is also evident in China is easily demonstrated, and was exhibited in full view on the occasion of the "Hundred Flowers." Mao then mistook the genuine willingness of intellectuals and scientists to work for the reconstruction of China as evidence of conversion to his own ideology, which it was not. There is no reason to believe that in this respect things have changed very much; indeed, the insistence of the Cultural Revolution on the need to eliminate the remains of bourgeois thinking, and the general criticism of intellectuals and their aspirations, suggests that no real change in the attitude of the educated has come about. As before, many, or most, are willing enough to do a good job in their own profession, to help the nation to advance, and also to conform to the political tone in fashion, whether this be appreciative of Soviet Russia or violently critical. But there is no evidence that these groups hanker for a revival of revolutionary zeal or the ideals and manners of the guerrilla war period. That ideology is no longer felt to be congruent to the situation of China today, a situation in which major economic and demographic problems remain to be tackled, and one in which a false step might precipitate a disastrous war. Undoubtedly the opposition to the Cultural Revolution, probably quite unorganized and in no sense a coherent "anti-party," feels that these are the true priorities, and that the thought of Mao Tse-tung is no longer giving them their rightful place.

There is also the consideration that the present Cultural Revolution held up as the great movement in which the present generation of youth can prove its worth, is essentially a false analogy with the real revolution of hard and desperate military operations twenty years ago. The Red Guards are not in danger from hosts of counter-reactionaries; the opposition they are called upon to crush are not trained troops holding strong positions, but a group of hitherto respected leaders of the Communist party, or distinguished men of letters and science, who command, it seems, no coherent mass force of their own but still enjoy the confidence and respect of many members of the Communist party. Attacks upon these men, their public humiliation, and the hooliganism with which some Red Guard activity has been sullied are not glorious feats which the Red Guards themselves will remember with pride in twenty years' time, or wish their own sons to emulate. It may well be that this element of falsity in the Cultural Revolution will do more to devalue it as a future model of political mass action than any outright failure of the present policies.

There remains the question of how far China's setbacks and conflicts in foreign policy have motivated the Cultural Revolution, or influenced its course. It must appear very strange to a foreign observer that Mao Tse-tung should choose to loose the Cultural Revolution upon his country at a time when two dangerous foreign quarrels threaten China. On the one hand, the war in Vietnam could take a turn which might face China with the choice of open participation or open abandonment of her policy of supporting a "people's war." At the same time that this risk of war with the United States must still be considered real enough, China continues to exacerbate her ideological quarrel with Russia and to inject into it questions of strategic policy and national interest which are bound to render it still more intractable. The fact that Russia after a long period of comparative restraint has begun to launch counterattacks, which take the damaging form of exaggerating the confusions and conflicts of the Cultural Revolution itself, seems to make no impression on Chinese policy other than to sharpen hostility.

It thus seems that Mao is deliberately violating a rule of Chinese foreign policy which has proved its validity ever since China in the nineteenth century was forced into the community of nations. China should never at the same time quarrel with the great land power with which she shares a long common frontier and with the sea power which dominates the Pacific Ocean and China Sea. Failure to recognize this fact was fatal to the Manchu dynasty. Unaccustomed to seek the equal alliance of any foreign power they failed to use Russia as a counterweight to Britain, or to ally with Britain to check Russia. Yet during most of the period when China was under pressure from these two powers, they were themselves very suspicious of and hostile to each other. It may be that the Manchus could not have secured such an alliance had they tried, but they did not even try, and offended both (as in 1900) at the same time. The KMT did not learn the lesson any better: unwilling to make friends with Russia, then already a Communist power, in the years before World War II, they thus forsook the only possible counterbalance to the sea power of Japan, which directly threatened China with invasion and conquest. Even in the summer of 1938 when Russia and Japan clashed along the Manchurian frontier at Nomanhan, China made no attempt to obtain the alliance of Russia.

Mao Tse-tung, soon after the triumph of his party, made it clear that he had taken heed of these facts and would "lean to one side"—the side of the U.S.S.R. For the first time in history China entered into a voluntary alliance with a foreign power, instead of the chance associations brought about by the attacks of her enemies. From the point of view of China's national interests the Russian alliance gave great benefits. It deterred any foreign intervention, since this could have meant a widespread world war. It thus served to limit the character of the Korean War and prevent air attacks upon Chinese territory. It enabled China to follow her own interests in Tibet, to reintegrate Sinkiang under central authority, and later to regain full control over all Manchuria. It enabled her to profit from Russian technology and experience in the planning and construction of new industrial plants. It is true that Russia refused to give China the support she expected in the Offshore Islands crisis of 1958. Two years later the rising conflict between the two nations led to the withdrawal of Russian advisers and experts from China, with serious consequences upon the economy. So it seemed that the Russian alliance was after all not proving beneficial.

It is probably too soon, and the evidence still unrevealed, to know the degree to which these disagreements sparked off the later full-scale public dispute. But whatever the causes, the fact is patent today that China is at odds with the two powers who alone can be a danger to her national interests, the land power, Russia, and the sea power, the

United States. It may be asked whether the Cultural Revolution which needs enemies who can be identified and defied, also requires that these enemies be foreigners. It would be easy to answer this question if it could also be shown that the opposition in China was identified with a group who deplored the developing quarrel with Russia. But this identification is unconvincing. Liu Shao-ch'i, P'eng Chen, and others attacked or disgraced were known as hard-line opponents of Russia, men who had frequently joined in the chorus of vituperation. It can be argued that since Russia is "revisionist"—in Chinese eyes—and stands for all the trends which Mao seeks to eliminate through the Cultural Revolution, therefore Russia is an enemy who must be condemned regardless of the possible dangerous consequences. The United States, enemy number one, the spearhead of imperialism, must, of course, continue to be treated as a hostile power. There is no escape—the two powers, being hostile, must be faced at the same time, whatever the risks. "Come the Three Corners of the World in arms and we shall shock them," may be good rhetoric, but it is bad foreign policy. It would be a curious outcome to the thought of Mao Tse-tung if it proves to be in this respect all too similar to the thought of Empress Dowager Tz'u Hsi, who disliked, despised, and distrusted all foreigners and sought only to get rid of them.

Comments by Jerome Alan Cohen

More than Chinese courtesy compels me to note my admiration for, and fundamental agreement with, Professor Tsou's brilliant and thorough analysis. His essay is so comprehensive—providing an integrative interpretation of the Chinese Communist political system—that it is difficult to decide which aspects to select for this necessarily brief comment. I will therefore merely emphasize certain questions relating to the Great Proletarian Cultural Revolution and, in passing, raise a few caveats that are not intended to be pedantic or fatuous.

1. At the outset, I would urge caution in characterizing China's current crisis as a bipolar struggle. Professor Tsou, while recognizing the complexity of the power struggle and the impossibility of drawing even a reasonably complete picture of the political conflict, invokes phrases such as "the Maoists and the dissidents" and "two conflicting opinion groups." Undoubtedly, common opposition to Chairman Mao may be a factor that tends to unify all those leaders who have been attacked since November, 1965. Undoubtedly, also, one of the underlying causes of the crisis is the irrepressible clash between the forces of routinization and those of charisma. Nevertheless, it is far from clear how much consensus there was or is among the dissidents regarding the issues that precipitated the crisis, nor is it even certain what those issues were. P'eng Chen and Lo Jui-ch'ing, Liu Shao-ch'i and Teng Hsiao-p'ing, and T'ao Chu and Chu Teh appear to have left the Maoist campaign train at different stations. Although in retrospect it is possible to discern reasons for Liu's "falling out" with Mao, can we fairly incapsulate the views of other dissidents under a "Liuist" label? Even if we assume that Mao's attack on the party organization has driven many leaders to support Liu in defense of the party, will this unity endure if the party regains responsibility for the nation's affairs? We should, of course, ask similar questions about those leaders who, as of this writing, have not run afoul of the Cultural Revolution. To pick the obvious example, can we consign Chou En-lai to the Maoist opinion group? When more is known, surely we may expect the present struggle over policies and power to be revealed as no less complex than its many predecessors in twentieth-century Chinese history.

2. At the close of his essay Professor Tsou raises the fascinating problem of the impact upon party legitimacy of Mao's riding roughshod over the wishes of what appears to have been a majority of the Central Committee at the Eleventh Plenum: "A Maoist victory," he writes, "will establish a precedent under which the Chairman of the party may violate the norms and prescribed procedures of the party and ignore its structural arrangements, and under which personal legitimacy may be used to override structural legitimacy. It will restore the position of the charismatic leader and his thought and weaken the party as an institution. It will delay the process of routinization."

Of course, this is not a new problem in the Communist world; Stalin blatantly violated many of the rules of the Communist Party of the Soviet Union (CPSU). Because none of Stalin's successors had his immense power, prestige, and charisma, and because all of them had suffered under his despotism, they necessarily showed more sensitivity to the relation between adherence to party rules and the legitimacy of the party leadership. As Richard Lowenthal has written:

> In retrospect, it is possible to view much of the internal history of the Khrushchev era as having revolved around this institutional question [of the relative powers of the leader and the highest constituted organs of the ruling party]. In denouncing Stalin's arbitrary rule not only for its lawlessness and cruelty, but also for its failure to respect the party statutes and to submit all policy decisions to regular meetings of the party congress, Central Committee and Politbureau, Khrushchev had in fact given the party bureaucracy a double pledge: that he would not use the secret police against them, and that he would consult them according to the statutory rules.[1]

In striving to consolidate his power from 1953 to 1957, Khrushchev was a shrewd manipulator of party legalism. In 1957, when what he later termed "an arithmetical majority" of the party Presidium voted to unseat him, he refused to resign. Instead, having previously been successful in appealing policy disputes to the Central Committee, he argued that only the Central Committee, in whose behalf the Presidium was supposed to exercise authority, could force him to resign. A special session of the Central Committee was called, and it voted not only to continue Khrushchev's leadership but also to remove the hostile majority from the Presidium.

While we do not know whether they perceived any other options, the fact is that the so-called "anti-party group" and their supporters acquiesced in the Central Committee's decision, thereby establishing what may have become a precedent that facilitated the overthrow of Khrushchev himself in 1964. Khrushchev's removal remains shrouded in mystery, but it appears to have been achieved when the Central Committee affirmed the Presidium's demand for his resignation. Significantly, the change in the Central Committee's attitude toward Khrushchev between 1957 and 1964 has been attributed in part to his efforts during those years to shake off the shackles of the party rules, whose vindication he had championed on the road to power.[2]

[1] Richard Lowenthal, "The Revolution Withers Away," *Problems of Communism,* vol. 14:10, 11–12.

[2] *Ibid.*

Does this brief Soviet reference shed any light on the Chinese experience? If we know little about the rules governing decision-making in the CPSU we know less about them in the highest councils of the Chinese Communist Party (CCP). Like its Soviet analogue, China's 1956 Party Constitution provides only a bare framework of relevant rules. Moreover, Chairman Mao, like Stalin, has violated the few rules that are contained in that Constitution. For example, in the absence of "extraordinary conditions," Article 31 requires the National Party Congress (NPC) to be convened each year; yet there has been no NPC meeting since 1958. Similarly, although Article 36 calls for semiannual plenary sessions of the Central Committee, no such sessions were held between September 1962 and August 1966. Thus, by the time of the Eleventh Plenum, structural legitimacy was hardly in its pristine state.

It has been asserted, and Professor Tsou appears to agree, that Mao packed the Eleventh Plenum with outsiders who were fervent supporters of the Cultural Revolution, thereby inhibiting any open resistance by the majority of committee members who are believed to oppose him.[3] This tactic is reminiscent of Khrushchev's post-1957 effort to undermine the policy-making authority of the Central Committee by turning its meetings into semi-public shows.[4] Mao undoubtedly resorted to other tactics as well. For obvious reasons he probably did not invoke the provision of Article 16 of the Party Constitution that, in "conditions of urgency," authorizes the Central Committee to remove its own members upon a two-thirds vote. Since the Party Constitution gives the NPC exclusive power to elect Central Committee members, it is also unlikely that Mao attempted formally to add to the committee's membership. But he undoubtedly prevented some of his opponents from attending the meeting. It is particularly difficult to believe that P'eng Chen and Lo Jui-ch'ing were present. Mao may also have resorted to other techniques, possibly including articulation of the position subsequently advanced by his wife that "one could not talk about a 'minority' or 'majority' independent of class viewpoint."[5] (The Khrushchevian associations of the term "arithmetical majority" probably made that euphemism unacceptable.)

Plainly enough, Mao's recent tactics must have eroded still further the party's already diminished store of structural legitimacy. But such

[3] "A Year of Revolution," *Current Scene,* Dec. 10, 1966, p. 6.

[4] Lowenthal, "The Revolution Withers Away," p. 12.

[5] "Speech by Comrade Chiang Ching," *Peking Review,* Dec. 9, 1966, pp. 6, 9.

conduct by Chairman Mao does not necessarily establish a precedent for future party chairmen, for Mao has trained his heirs to appreciate the educational value of the negative example. This may be what Tsou means when he points out that "this precedent can, however, be nullified if Mao's successors repudiate implicitly or explicitly this particular aspect of the Cultural Revolution."

Mao's negative example may do even more. If the Stalinist experience is any guide, a dictator's charisma is not readily transferable, and his arbitrary acts may inspire his successors to insure bureaucratized party controls over the new leader through the increased assertion of party norms. This does not mean, of course, that Mao's successor as chairman will be chosen by a democratic vote of the Central Committee. Given the history of a nation whose "mandate of heaven" theory of political legitimacy was often merely an ex post facto rationalization, it would not be surprising for the Central Committee to have to legitimize a decision arrived at by other means. Once the new leader is ensconced, however, he is likely to have to pay far greater attention to party norms than Mao has done, both in consolidating his power and in continuing to assert it. I therefore tend to be less pessimistic than Professor Tsou about the long-range impact upon China's political stability of Mao's intra-party machinations.

3. Chalmers Johnson tells us that Mao may have to choose between revisionism and coercion.[6] Curiously, however, one of the most overlooked aspects of the Cultural Revolution has been the role of the public security force, the state's principal instrument of coercion. It is difficult enough, of course, to characterize the operation of the public security force during the years prior to the advent of the Red Guards. Professor Johnson writes of the "capricious" application of coercion.[7] Professor Tsou believes that, "in comparison with Stalin, Mao employed violence more openly and selectively," but he notes that "whether . . . the current purges constitute an exception to this generalization is still difficult to determine at this moment." He subsequently notes the efforts on the part of the Chinese leaders to preserve some of the party traditions, including the rule that reasoning and not violence should be used. Although he concludes that the conditions under which these traditions developed no longer exist, Professor Tsou writes

[6] Chalmers A. Johnson, "Chinese Communist Leadership and Mass Response: The Yenan Period and the Socialist Education Campaign Period," in this volume, pp. 397–437.

[7] Ibid.

that "whatever the role of the secret police in the Red Guard movement, there has been no secret-police terror."

Lately, however, there has been more and more evidence to show that segments of society, particularly the bourgeoisie and the intellectuals, have been terrorized since the Eleventh Plenum. And the gigantic struggle meetings convened against "demons and monsters" such as P'eng Chen and Lo Jui-ch'ing exemplify the use of terror rather than reasoning against the highest echelons of the party itself.

I agree with Professor Tsou, however, insofar as he implies that we do not know enough about the relation of the public security force to the Red Guard movement. Although there occasionally have been reports that the public security force has helped to organize and supervise Red Guard activities, at least in certain areas outside Peking, the Maoists have regarded the police as unreliable and even hostile. I will only cite a few bits of evidence. The use of Red Guards to detain and to inflict severe sanctions upon disfavored persons last summer and autumn constituted a usurpation of powers that have usually been reserved to the public security apparatus, even during mass movements. In Shanghai, the incubator of the great "January Revolution" that is said to be sweeping the country, the "urgent notice" issued by thirty-two "revolutionary rebel organizations" January 9, 1967, provided that those who violated its strictures "shall be punished by the Public Security Bureau." But its final paragraph laid down an unusual threat to the public security force itself:

> The Municipal Party Committee and the Public Security Bureau are enjoined to act upon the above points. Those who act against the above points shall, after investigations, be immediately punished on charges of undermining the great cultural revolution.[8]

Subsequent events do not seem to have enhanced the Maoists' confidence in the Shanghai police. The February 24 Draft Resolution of the newly-formed Shanghai Municipal Revolutionary Committee stated that "the armed core of the militia, the People's Liberation Army and other people's forces are the strong pillars of the provisional organ of power at each level" and exhorted "all true proletarian revolutionaries on the public security, procuratorate and judicial fronts" to ally with those pillars.[9] And in distilling their experiences in seizing power

[8] "Thirty-two Shanghai Revolutionary Rebel Organizations Issue 'Urgent Notice,' " *Peking Review*, Jan. 20, 1967, pp. 7–9.

[9] "Shanghai Municipal Revolutionary Committee Holds Grand Meeting," *Peking Review*, March 3, 1967, pp. 10–11.

from "those in authority taking the capitalist road," the revolutionary rebels of Heilungkiang province emphasized the importance of first seizing the Public Security Bureau and the newspapers and radio in order to prepare the final onslaught upon "the core of the reactionary stronghold"—the Provincial Party Committee.[10] Their description reflects the bitterness of the struggle in one of China's major cities:

> The power of the Harbin City Public Security Bureau was relatively thoroughly seized; the actual power was taken over from above and on down. Its basic experience is to rely on the Left forces both within and outside the Public Security Bureau forming a powerful united front and sweeping aside every obstacle set up by the enemy. At first, persons in the Public Security Bureau who were in authority and taking the capitalist road tried to resist the takeover of power, but their attempt was thwarted by the revolutionary rebels. Then, they colluded with outside forces such as the "Red Flag Army," the "Combat Preparedness Army" and the "Red Militia Detachment" to stage a counter-seizure of power, and this was also thoroughly smashed. At last, they attempted to exploit the complexity of public security work to force the young revolutionaries to retreat. This also was overcome by relying on the Left forces within the Public Security Bureau. Similarly, those people in the bureau who were misled for a time were helped to see the truth thanks to the efforts made by the revolutionary Left forces in the bureau to arouse the masses, energetically expose the sinister headquarters that had attempted a counter-seizure of power, and bring to light one by one all the chief and minor ringleaders who had committed various kinds of crimes. In this way, those among the masses who wanted to make revolution and the revolutionary cadres rallied around the revolutionary take-over committee. Thus, the revolutionary take-over committee stood on solid ground, consolidated its positions, and laid a firm foundation among the masses for the institution of an entirely new order in public security work.[11]

The anti-leftist orientation of important segments of the police apparatus should not surprise those who have studied contemporary China's public security system. Although loyalty to their former chief, Lo Jui-

---

[10] "Basic Experience of Heilungkiang Red Rebels in the Struggle to Seize Power," *Peking Review*, February 17, 1967, pp. 15–16.

[11] *Ibid.*, pp. 16–17.

ch'ing, and to other deposed leaders may motivate some police figures, there is probably a more fundamental explanation. Public security officers are law enforcement specialists who constitute a professional group, with all that the term implies. When in the late 1950's Lo Jui-ch'ing preached the need for public security forces at every level to obey the commands of local territorial party committees, he was not merely giving lip service to the general party line; he was genuinely seeking to overcome the resistance of bureaucrats who, although themselves party members, nevertheless resented political interference in their day-to-day work. Interviews with former public security officers suggest that "red" versus "expert" tensions grew especially strong during mass movements when the party frequently would order the police to detain or arrest particular people on insufficient evidence or simply prescribe quotas for the police to meet. This inevitably resulted in a large number of errors, which the police were left to sort out after the movement had subsided. Perhaps the most notorious example of the quota technique was the 1955 *su-fan* campaign to liquidate counter-revolutionaries, when the efforts of insecure cadres to overfulfill their quota led to excesses that even Chairman Mao subsequently had to acknowledge. Such excesses diminished the self-esteem of the law enforcement bureaucracy and seriously damaged its reputation with the masses, not an inconsiderable factor to an organization that during the past decade has annually sponsored a "love the people" month in an attempt to improve its image.

Nothing that has happened in China suggests that the withering away of the state is any nearer today than in 1949. A full-scale study of the public security apparatus is needed to help us understand the future as well as the past.

4. Implicit in Professor Tsou's paper is the suggestion that we may possibly be witnessing, from the last balcony to be sure, the playing out of a Greek tragedy, with Teng T'o as Cassandra and Mao as the hero who dimly perceives his fate but inexorably marches to his fall. If Mao persists in attempting to reshape man according to his revolutionary romantic image and if, as Teng T'o predicted, it leads to bankruptcy, the result may well be what social scientists like to call, for reasons best known to themselves, "systemic and multiple dysfunction." Civil war, chaos, and mass starvation could be tragic not only for China but also for international stability. The United States, like other nations, should consider whether such a turn of events would be desirable, and, if not, whether anything can be done to prevent it. One can conjure up a situation in which we may come to believe that the Chinese

Communists have been performing a public service in organizing, sheltering, and feeding the world's largest population. It is not inconceivable that the United States and others, rather than risk the unknown, may decide to shore up a sagging but irritating Chinese regime, as did the great powers a century ago. On the other hand, William P. Bundy, U.S. Assistant Secretary for East Asian and Pacific Affairs, may decide that the wise course is to "let the dust settle," as his father-in-law, Dean Acheson, did two decades ago.

I do not argue that such a melodramatic turn of events will occur. I do believe, however, that we ought to be prepared to face it. Most observers would grant that a more likely possibility is that the currently contending factions will reach some sort of compromise. My own inclination is to bet on one that leaves Mao nominally at the helm but that gradually responds to the felt needs of a modernizing society. We should not forget that Kadar put down the Hungarian Revolution, but shortly afterward began to respond to the forces that gave rise to it. If, as the Chinese charge, the Russians now have Khrushchevism without Khrushchev, the Chinese may soon have Mao without Maoism. Moreover, even Stalin died, and, when Mao passes from the scene, China may be freer to follow the path of Soviet and East European revisionism.

Benjamin I. Schwartz

5

China and the West in the
"Thought of Mao Tse-tung"

The moment hardly seems appropriate for calm reflection on the nature and function of "Chinese Communist ideology." In fact, the very concept of a unified "Chinese Communist ideology" maintaining its identity over time is now in great jeopardy. Are we to identify the ideology with the current version of the thought of Mao Tse-tung or with the views of the leader's illustrious opponents? In his *Ideology and Organization in Communist China*, Franz Schurmann defines ideology at one point "as a manner of thinking characteristic of an organization," presumably, in this case, the Chinese Communist Party (CCP). Yet, in a sense, at the heart of the Great Proletarian Cultural Revolution lies the vehement assertion on the part of Mao Tse-tung and his group that the thought of Mao Tse-tung is infinitely more than the ideology of any organization; that Mao's thought is not incarnate in any organization but rather transcends and breaks through the limits of all organizations. Indeed the definition of ideology "as a manner of thinking characteristic of an organization" seems far more applicable to the outlook of Mao's opponents—men such as Liu Shao-ch'i, Teng Hsiao-p'ing, and Lo Jui-ch'ing—than to the supreme leader himself.

Accordingly, in the following paper I shall concentrate my attention on the evolving thought of Mao Tse-tung even though it is now clear that his outlooks and orientations may not be the simple embodiment of Chinese Communist ideology. In dealing with Mao, we are dealing not with an organization, not with a movement, not with an embodiment of the "Chinese mind" or the "Chinese revolution" or any other abstract force. His outlook has been shaped by the Chinese past, by the turbulent history of modern China, by the ideas with which he has come in contact, and so forth, but with it all, he remains an existent individual and is not now and never has been the mere embodiment of transcendental forces. He is, to be sure, an enormously important individual who has had an impact on the course of recent Chinese history, but we certainly cannot preclude the possibility that the "Maoist" phase of Chinese history may soon be brought to an end and that many of his ideas and outlooks may not survive. In that event the study of his intellectual and political evolution will remain of enormous interest to the student of Chinese history and human affairs in general. On the other hand, if he continues to prevail in the current conflicts, his outlooks will, of course, continue to affect the course of events and therefore be of "operational" concern. The content of our reflections need not, I hope, be seriously affected by either eventuality.

The concern with the thought of Mao Tse-tung is, of course, open to many objections—the first and most obvious being that Mao is no thinker but rather a hard-bitten political leader who has been constantly preoccupied with his own political survival and with the necessity to respond to the "real" emerging military, political, and economic situations which confront him. The assumption behind this view of the role of ideas in human history is that (1) the only ideas to be treated seriously are those of people defined as great thinkers, and (2) the ideas of such great thinkers, perhaps precisely because of their depth and subtlety, probably never affect the "real world," which is run by practical people. What is overlooked in these assumptions is the fact that the ideas of the thinkers in their simpler, cruder, and more rudimentary form may have an enormous impact on myriads of people who have never heard of their writings, not to speak of those who know them second-hand. In this form, ideas may have an enormous impact on the manner in which "practical" people meet the "real" situations which confront them. A qualified version of this thesis which has come to my attention is that of a gentleman who, having made a content analysis of Mao's writings, finds that allusions to and quotations from Chinese literature far outweigh allusions to Marx, Lenin, or any other non-Chinese thinker. He derives from this the conclusion that the impact of Western ideas on Mao has been slight, and that Mao must be viewed wholly within a "Chinese context." This kind of analysis, I would again submit, is based on a thoroughly fallacious concept of how ideas may come to influence the lives of men.

It should also be added that there is no intention here of treating Mao's "thought" as a static set of propositions crystallized during the Yenan period and then applied as a kind of "operational code" to all the enormously shifting circumstances of the history of mainland China since 1949. In this view, while the Chinese world around Mao has undergone enormous, unanticipated changes, he has remained, as it were, the calm eye of the hurricane, applying his maxims and methods with enormous equanimity and self-possession to all shifting circumstances. The assumption here made is that Chinese circumstances have changed and that Mao has changed with them. The notion of the "Yenan syndrome" is an absolutely essential tool of analysis but only if it is not treated in a mechanical way. It is quite true that since 1949 Mao has remained more or less obsessed with the experience of his movement (1927–49, circa); it is true that much of his outlook has remained *related* to Yenan themes and motifs, that the Yenan thinking has established a certain context and drastically limited the range of his thought. It nevertheless remains a fact that the Hundred Flowers experiment, the Great Leap Forward ideology, and the Cultural Revolution cannot be simply deduced from Yenan propositions. They can only be understood in terms of the circumstances to which they are responsive and these responses themselves involve a certain hindsight reinterpretation of Yenan. The Cultural Revolution does not merely illustrate Yenan maxims; it also tends to isolate, universalize, and carry to the extreme certain Yenan maxims which at the time formed part of a more complex, ambivalent experience. It is now often forgotten that Yenan had its "soft" as well as its "hard" side. The soft side involved an attitude of patience and flexibility vis-à-vis political groups and intellectuals outside of the Yenan areas, a moderate land policy, a relatively affirmative attitude toward the Chinese cultural heritage, an approval of mixed economy, and so forth. It is true that this was all part of the New Democratic strategy and that thought reform, the guerrilla mystique, and totalitarian populism probably represented the deeper tendencies of Mao's outlook, but it is well to remind ourselves that the "softer" side of Yenan was invoked at the time of the Hundred Flowers experiment. It is interesting to note that the whole "soft" side of Yenan is now being attributed to the errors of Liu Shao-ch'i. It is also well to remind ourselves that Mao Tse-tung himself probably had a fairly modest conception of the range of applicability of his maxims when he came to power in 1949. He probably wholeheartedly accepted the notion that one must look to the Soviet Union as the model in vast areas of what we in the West call the "modernization process." It is the Great Leap Forward which marks the extreme extrapolation and universalization of Mao's Yenan maxims; in the ideological sense the Cultural Revolution is a yet more extreme and exclusivist expression of these maxims. It is this latest, most extreme, most utopian—and perhaps not inevitable —development of Mao's thought which I should now like to examine in terms of its filiations to strands of both Western thought and the Chinese heritage.

In my own writings in the past I have tended to stress the gradual disintegration of Marxism-Leninism as a unified ideology. I remain convinced of the basic validity of this view, but at the same time am aware that, as stated, it may have its misleading aspects. First, the disintegration of Marxist-Leninist ideology does not imply the disintegration of ideology as such or the triumph of "non-ideology." Certainly in the Cultural Revolution the *furor ideologicus* of Mao Tse-tung's thought burns more fiercely than ever. Second, the disintegration of Marxism-Leninism does not necessarily imply, as I hope to indicate, the disappearance of the "Western" components in Mao Tse-tung's vision of the world. This may therefore mark a good point at which to reexamine the disintegration of Marxism-Leninism and the relationship of that tradition to other aspects of modern Western thought.

Marx's mature doctrine of the "mode of production" may, from one point of view, be regarded as an effort to bring together in a kind of synthesis two interpretations of human history which emerged out of the Enlightenment and which were extremely prominent in early nineteenth-century thought. Both of these modes of thought share the concept of progress but interpret progress quite differently.[1] One interpretation, which probably comes out of the views of people like Turgot, Condorcet, Saint-Simon, and others, emphasizes technico-economic progress—the steady, cumulative, and irreversible "progress of the arts." Another strain which is exemplified by Rousseau and others tends to see history primarily as a moral drama in which the social good finally triumphs over social evil. The morality in question tends to be a social-political morality and the triumph of goodness manifests itself in terms of a good sociopolitical order. There are within this moral interpretation tendencies which lead to liberal democracy and others which lead to socialism and anarchism, but the pathos is one which stresses moral passion, indignation, and the hatred of social evil, oppression, and injustice. The pathos of the technico-economic interpretation on the other hand tends to be cool, "scientific," and dispassionate. Its adherents may believe in such goods as liberty, equality, and democracy, but they tend to see the achievement of these goods as fortunate by-products of technico-economic progress.

Those who viewed human history as a social moral drama were, at

[1] In a sense, what we are dealing with here are ideal types, and there are, of course, many individuals who do not fit neatly into either category.

least in the early period, often indifferent or even hostile to technology and economic development. One need but cite the writings of Mably or Rousseau's "Discourse on Inequality" to see how little connection was seen between technico-economic progress and the just society. In the early nineteenth century we find the left Jacobin, Buonarroti, still ardently committed to the "reign of virtue" of Robespierre and Babeuf, expressing utter contempt for the Saint-Simonist stress on what we now call industrialism:

> It is thus not in the unlimited development of industry and in the accumulation of individual wealth that one should locate the per- fectibility of the social order; happiness is more in the moderation of desires, the love of virtue and the peace of a good conscience than in the multiplication of needs. . . . To expect men who are increasingly occupied with manufacture, commerce and money to be friends of virtue and to devote themselves to their country is to expect streams to return to their source.[2]

In contrast to this, we might cite the statement of Buonarroti's contem- porary, D'Argenson, that

> thanks to the progress of the economic science all the questions of popular justice are discussed in terms of methodical arguments and a language that is moderated to the point of coldness while during the assemblies at the beginning of the Revolution these doctrines seemed to be the inseparable companions of hatred and passion.[3]

This coldness and hostility to technico-economic development of the early adherents of the moral view of history is, however, not a logically essential aspect of this view. One could urge, as many later were to do, that precisely the achievement of the reign of virtue and freedom would in itself release man's technical creativity and economic produc- tivity.[4]

When we turn to Marx, we find that in his earliest writings he is cer-

[2] Elizabeth L. Eisenstein, *The First Professional Revolutionist: Filippo Michele Buonarroti (1761–1837), a Biographical Essay* (Cambridge: Harvard University Press, 1959), p. 107.

[3] *Ibid.*, p. 113.

[4] The conflict between these two orientations has by no means been resolved even in contemporary America. The technico-economic approach still finds its adherents in the ideology of the "end of ideology" school while interpreta- tion of history as moral drama remains the basic assumption of the New Left.

tainly an adherent of the moral drama view of history. The philosophy of history of his mentor Hegel, with its emphasis on the gradual march of man toward freedom (as he understands that term), is basically concerned with history as a metaphysico-moral drama. During the latter forties, however, particularly after 1848, we find Marx gradually turning to the technico-economic sphere as the sphere in which the ultimate moving forces of history, "the forces of production," are to be found. He does so, however, without displacing the moral drama view of history. The forces of production are the ultimate moving forces, but they must be mediated through the relations of production. Relations of production are, however, indissolubly bound up with relations of property and relations of class, and class conflict embodies the whole moral conflict between the forces of social good and evil (although Marx would not, of course, admit such vocabulary in his more rigorously "scientific" moods). The ultimate dynamic is economic, but the mediating class struggle is just as important. Marx's concept of the industrial proletariat illustrates the uneasy marriage of the technico-economic and social-moral interpretations of history. The class owes its genesis and very nature to its role in the technico-economic process. On the other hand, the class is the social bearer of all those transcendental universal, redemptive qualities which will make possible the good society.

One of the most serious questions one can raise about Marx's suggestive synthesis is, of course, whether it created a successful fusion of these two views of history. In fact, it was to prove highly unstable among his followers. Turning to that follower who is the most important link between Marx and Mao, namely Lenin, we find that the young Lenin emerges from the milieu of the Russian intelligentsia in which the moral-revolutionary attitude toward history predominated. In explaining Lenin's turn from the Populists to Marx, one cannot help but feel that, on the one hand, a revulsion against the messianic hopes which had been lodged in the peasantry and, on the other, an attraction to the fresh expectations which Marx had lodged in the industrial proletariat played a leading role. He was still seeking the "bearer of revolution," but he wholeheartedly accepted Marx's emphasis on technico-economic development. Lenin's first Marxist writings (such as his tome on the *Development of Capitalism in Russia*) are heavily technico-economical and studded with statistics and learned references to obscure economic monographs. They are presumably coldly scientific, yet actually passionately polemical. They are designed to undermine the Populist faith in the socialist vocation of the peasantry by demonstrating that the peasantry itself was being brought squarely into the realm of capitalist class conflict. This attack on the Populists was, however, a negative reflection of a new positive faith in the revolutionary potential of the urban workers. Having fought and presumably won the battle against the Populist enemy, Lenin was, however, in very short order to find himself at loggerheads with his orthodox Marxist allies such as Struve and Plekhanov who were indeed prepared to accept all the implications of Marx's doctrine of technico-economic causation. Having been attracted to the proletariat in the first instance because of its potential as a revolutionary vanguard in Russia, as well as because of the promise of an imminent socialist revolution in the West, Lenin was hardly prepared to wait for the "forces of production" to perform their tasks. He was not prepared to wait because his faith in "spontaneous" economic forces was at bottom strictly limited and much of the remainder of his life was spent in whittling down and chafing against the stress of the primacy of "economic forces" in Marx's mature system. Lenin's obsession was with revolution, and the mystique of revolution belongs to history as a moral political drama, rather than to history as a strictly technico-economic process.

One of Lenin's first and most spectacular statements of doubt concerning the efficacy of spontaneous economic forces comes, of course, very early in his famous tract *What Is to Be Done?* Here, he already goes so far as to say that while the economic forces have created the proletariat, these forces will, if left to their own devices, lead the workers in precisely the wrong direction (to the embrace of "petty bourgeois trade unionism"). Only the vanguard of professional revolutionaries can by its moral-political leadership lead the proletariat to its destined goal. The vanguard, however, is radically and qualitatively different from the economic class which it presumably represents. It is theoretically a product of a conscious rigorous moral and political training. Its moral qualities and "professional" behavior are no longer merely the haphazard product of its economic condition. It has, of course, often been pointed out that this "Jacobinist" development in Lenin probably owes much more to the Narodnaya Volya than to anything in the writings of Marx. It must, however, immediately be pointed out that the outlook of the Narodnaya Volya and Tkachev owes everything to the Jacobinist tradition of the latter end of the French Revolution, to the tradition of Robespierre, Babeuf, and Buonarroti. Its genealogy is quite as Western as the Marxist element in Lenin.

There were other ways in which Lenin manhandled the technico-economic component in Marx. The relationship between stages of economic development and class relations becomes quite loose. The bourgeoisie proves incapable of making a bourgeois revolution, while the proletariat inherits the task of doing so. Yet it would be a simplification to say that Lenin ever completely abandoned the technico-economic component in Marxism, however much he may have struggled with it. He continued to the end to harbor some faith in the imminence of world revolution in the heartland of mature capitalism. He continued to believe that the proletarian vanguard ought to be in close touch with its economic class base. His retreat from "war communism" to the New Economic Policy in the early twenties was undoubtedly a practical response to a critical situation, but it was greatly supported by an appeal to the more orthodox Marxist view that one could not possibly hope to achieve full socialism in an isolated country as economically backward as Russia. Furthermore, while Lenin is perhaps much more the heir of the moral drama view than of the technico-economic view, we need not doubt that his view of the ultimate socialist-communist society of the future involved the wholehearted acceptance of the role of industrialization. He certainly no longer shared the Jacobin anti-economic bias. This attitude toward the future may have been due in part to Marx, but undoubtedly also reflected the "demonstration effect" of the whole industrial development which had already occurred in the West —a development which Robespierre and Babeuf could hardly have anticipated. Yet at the time of Lenin's death the whole question of the subsequent relationship between the moral drama of "class struggle" and economic development in the Soviet Union was left in an enormously murky state.

Turning to the subsequent Stalinist development, we find that its net effect on Marxism-Leninism as it existed at the time of Lenin's death was to constrict still further the dynamic role of technico-economic forces. Again, this was not because Stalin was a thinker anxious to elaborate new theory. He was essentially much less of a utopian than either Lenin before him or Mao Tse-tung after him (which does not mean that he did not believe in his messianic role). His response to the situations which faced him may have been motivated by personal and state power considerations, but his policies naturally led him to the espousal of the doctrine of "socialism in one country"; to the notion that the "proletariat" (CPSU) could "create" socialism (state ownership of the means of production) in a backward economy and use "socialist relations of production" to initiate industrial development. This is, of course, a direct inversion of the Marxist view that technico-economic development would create socialism. One of the new arguments for "socialism" used both by Stalin and Khrushchev—an argument that might have astonished Marx—is that "socialism" is valuable because it creates favorable conditions for the industrial development of underdeveloped countries. Here we find the precincts of the operation of the "conscious-voluntary" role of the "Party of the Proletariat" enormously extended. It is not only an instrument for achieving power. It is itself the Prime Mover of the forces of production.

As will be noted, Stalin's ground for asserting that socalism existed in the Soviet Union was the fact that private ownership of the means of production had been abolished. The organic tie which Marx saw between "production relations" and "property relations" had been sundered. It is also questionable whether Marx would have regarded the Soviet situation as socialism. Yet by a kind of doctrinal manipulation, one could derive out of Marx's writings the rationalization that with the abolition of private ownership of the means of production, the fundamental victory had been achieved in man's history as moral drama. Communism had not yet been achieved, but the objective institutional environment of "socialism" would itself produce those moral qualities in men which would lead without difficulty to the Communist man of the future. It was precisely because, according to this formula, the moral victory had been basically won, that Stalin could now turn his full attention to the technico-economic requirements of modernization without allowing abstract social ethical notions to interfere with the necessary prerequisites of his particular model of modernization.[5]

We have so far been dealing with matters seemingly far removed from China, but the assumption of our discussion is that it is still highly fruitful, meaningful, and even necessary to see Mao Tse-tung's emerging image of the world in terms of the evolution which we have so far been discussing, *as well as* in terms of the Chinese context. In a sense, what Mao has done in the whole course of his development from Yenan to the Cultural Revolution has been to carry forward—perhaps to its ultimate conclusion—a certain transformation which we have been following in the case of Lenin and Stalin. Again, he has not done this in a vacuum and one can never understand his treatment of Communist doctrine without reference to the concrete Chinese historical situations which he has confronted.

[5] What I have loosely called the "technico-economic" view has two quite disparate expressions. In one, the technico-economic forces are regarded as impersonal historic forces which determine the course of history. In the other "voluntaristic" version, technico-economic development is the conscious project of an enlightened elite of social engineers. Stalin's interpretation is of the latter type.

I would still tend to stress that during the Yenan period the Leninist concept of the "proletarian vanguard" becomes more decisively detached from its supposed economic class moorings in China than it had been in the case of Lenin or Stalin. The social bearer of the "proletarian virtue" is now definitely the Communist party in general, and the individual Communist party member in particular. While Mao Tse-tung had for a time participated in labor-union activities, surveying his life as a whole, one has a strong sense that he probably never deeply believed in the moral superiority of industrial workers in the flesh. What he seems to have appreciated in the concept of the "proletariat" was not its actual reference to tangible factory workers but the transcendental moral qualities which Marx assigns to the workers. "Proletarian nature" involves the transcendance of all particular, partial interests and the complete and happy subordination of the individual to the goals of the collectivity. It is plain that for the Mao of the Yenan period these qualities did not reside in the workers of remote Shanghai but were free-floating qualities which could be inculcated into prospective party members by the methods which have since come to be elaborated and described under rubrics such as "thought reform" and "transformation of souls." To the extent that they had a favorable social base, this base was to be sought in the fact of poverty in general rather than the particular poverty of industrial workers. It is precisely this total and decisive detachment of the proletarian ethos from its supposed class moorings and hence from its links to the technico-economic process which permits us to discern the filiation of Mao's concept of the "proletarian vanguard" with older Western ideas and experiences which lie behind Marx and Lenin and which filter through them. As the social bearer of the universal and general will, Mao's "vanguard" links up through Lenin and Marx with Hegel's "universal estate" and Robespierre's interpretation of Rousseau's "general will" as incarnate in such entities as the Committee of Public Safety and the Jacobin clubs[6] or, ultimately, in the leader himself.

Again, however, we must refrain from reading back all the modalities of the Great Proletarian Cultural Revolution to the Yenan period. A great deal of history has intervened between the two. In 1949, it was quite clear that the proletarian nature was incarnate in the proletarian

---

[6] In his *Origins of Totalitarian Democracy* (New York: Praeger, 1960), J. L. Talmon speaks of the "unceasing process of self-cleansing and purification entailing denunciations, confessions, excommunications and expulsions" characteristics of the Jacobin clubs under Robespierre's aegis.

vanguard, the Chinese Communist Party, and there was no hint whatsoever that doubts might some day be raised about the credentials of the party itself as the social bearer of Communist virtue. Similarly, while "thought reform" was now applied to the masses as a whole, there was as yet no clear notion of its relationship to all the tasks of modernization. There is certainly every reason to think that Mao himself, like Lenin and Stalin before him, was in 1949 committed to economic, bureaucratic, military, and educational "modernization," both for reasons of national power and for reasons of economic welfare. He was not a pre-industrial Jacobin. It was precisely in this area that he looked trustingly to the Soviet Union as teacher and guide. One has, to be sure, a certain sense of uneasiness and ambivalence. Mao's past great accomplishments had lain outside of this sphere. If he was a technician at all it was in the strategies of guerrilla warfare and in the kind of social and "cultural" mobilization which had not depended on the skills and technologies of modern urban society. However, as a fervent nationalist and student of Stalin (as well as of Yen Fu and Liang Ch'i-ch'ao), he undoubtedly saw the links between national power and industrial growth. A Robespierre living in the twentieth century might also have seen these links. Beyond this, one need not doubt that he appreciated the relevance of industrialization to the satisfaction of men's basic economic needs. One may nevertheless doubt whether he was ever deeply attracted to Western urban consumer society. Thus, Mao's orientation to "modernization" seems to have been all along in tension with a deep anti-technological, anti-economistic strain.

The Stalinist model, when viewed in retrospect, both facilitated and complicated matters. The doctrine that the achievement of "socialism" was by no means dependent on the stage of economic development had been fought through by Stalin. Thus the Chinese could carry out their "socialist transformation" at an even more primitive stage of industrial development than that of the Soviet Union in the late twenties. Nevertheless, the adoption of the model did involve a considerable concession to what the Maoists now call "economism," to differentiated material incentive, to technical know-how with the concomitant concessions to corruptible professionals and experts.

It was precisely in the Great Leap Forward of 1957–58 that Mao finally achieved his beatific vision. The sober, practical realization that Soviet methods might not, after all, be literally suited to Chinese realities links up paradoxically with Mao's "revolutionary romantic" perception that his own Yenan methods and maxims with their emphasis on moral-political force might, in China, be directly applied to the economic as well as other spheres of life. Precisely because China was "poor and blank," precisely because its masses lived a simple, austere life and were fundamentally loyal and amenable to the spiritual influence of their Communist leadership, they might achieve industrial development even while bypassing the corruptions of modern Western industrial civilization! The aim of Robespierre's dictatorship was to achieve the reign of virtue. To Mao the reign of virtue had become both an end and a means. It was an end in itself but it could also be used as a means of achieving an economic leap forward.

It was this perception which led to the apocalyptic announcement of the imminent arrival of Communism in China. If the guerrilla warriors and Communist cadres of the Yenan period had already been capable of Communistic selflessness and of sacrificing themselves to the general good in the primitive conditions of Yenan, if these virtues could in China play a major role in the very tasks of economic development, then the achievement of Communist virtue was totally independent of the stage of economic development. The Soviets, who viewed these "petty bourgeois" assertions with horror, had conveniently forgotten that Stalin's splitting of "socialism" from its supposed economic prerequisites provided the logical basis for this further extrapolation. However, the arrival of Communism is, after all, something different from the arrival of socialism. Even in Soviet doctrine (at least of the pre-Khrushchev era) Communism involves a kind of existential transformation of individual man not achieved by socialism while Mao, as we know, has simply identified Communism with the old Chinese concept of unselfishness (wu-ssu), which has now been transmuted to mean the absolute conquest of all individual and even group-segmental self-interest. The Soviet doctrine is, however, that socialism—the state ownership of the means of production—plus further affluence will provide the sufficient institutional and economic environment for the creation of Communist man. It is still the institutional fact which conditions people to the correct morality and in the institutional sphere the battle had been won. What has become increasingly explicit in Maoist doctrine, however, is that the Communist ethic is not the necessary outcome of either economic development or even the nationalization of property. The latter may be a necessary but is very, very far from being a sufficient condition for the achievement of a Communist disposition of soul. Furthermore, if Communism is primarily a disposition of soul, so is bourgeois selfishness. Soviet experience has glaringly demon-

strated that bourgeois selfishness is entirely compatible with the abolition of private ownership of the means of production, while the Chinese
Communist guerrillas of pre-socialist days were already exemplars of
Communist virtue. The good society can be achieved only by an unremitting and unrelieved stress on the transformation of souls. The
moral drama continues, and while it is still discussed in terms of the
Marxist rhetoric of class struggle, it is no longer entirely clear which
segments of society are the social bearers of human evil and which segments are the bearers of virtue. People of wrong class background are
still subject to discrimination, but the right background is no guarantee of virtue. The bourgeois disposition of soul can find its lodgement
in any established organization including the Communist party itself.
Indeed, one can only be sure of the leader himself.

In sum, then, I would suggest that the Marxist synthesis represented
in its concept of the "mode of production" has indeed disintegrated as
a synthesis within the evolution of Communism from Lenin to Mao.
The dynamic causative role of the technico-economic process has in
China shrunk to the vanishing point. Yet the whole interpretation of
history as a progressive moral political drama and the whole Jacobin
tradition have filtered through Marx and Lenin to Mao. One is indeed
struck by the affinity of the parts of the mystique of the Cultural Revolution to the mystique of the later Jacobin phase of the French Revolution. The enormous faith in the reign of virtue; in the readiness of the
masses to internalize the general will; on the other hand, the enormous
suspicion of the ever-present forces of selfishness which are likely to
emerge in any quarter; the wedding of the spirit of self-sacrifice to
messianic nationalism; the profound suspicion of the treacheries and
subtleties of intellectuals—all these elements are present in both cases.
It may, of course, be asserted that Mao knows little about the French
Revolution and its history. This is no bar to the transmission of this
cast of mind. Furthermore, we do find frequent references in current
mainland materials to the Paris Commune which, of course, occupies a
canonical place in Communist literature and which is understood largely in terms of the left Populist-Jacobinist interpretation.

I have thus far purposely stressed what might be called the Western
component of Mao Tse-tung's present vision of the world in the face of
growing tendencies to see the present developments as exotically
Chinese. These ideas can hardly be—so we are led to believe—the expression of a Western, pragmatic, sensible, rational outlook. What is involved in all this is an identification of the West with a particular

brand of technocratic and decidedly economistic liberalism now dominant in the American academy. We are invited to forget that phenomena such as Jacobinism and the Paris Commune are an integral part of our Western experience and that the view of history as moral drama grows directly out of the Western heritage.

What then, of Mao's relationship to his Chinese heritage? In actuality, as we know, there has never been a period in the history of Chinese Communism since 1949 when the *conscious* attitude of Mao and his group has been more negative toward the entire cultural heritage of the past. Nevertheless, this conscious attitude by no means precludes the possibility that unconscious or semiconscious predispositions derived from the past may continue to shape the outlook of the present. Indeed, it is quite possible to see many resonances between the ideology of the Cultural Revolution and certain traditional orientations and ideas.

Must we then choose between China and the West? If one accepts the kind of cultural holism which asserts that all the elements of a given culture are generically peculiar to that cultural monad and incomparable to anything in other cultures, then we must make this choice. If one is prepared to assert, however, that universally human tendencies, motifs, and ideas are likely to appear in somewhat modified form in many cultures, one need not be shocked by the possibility that there may be given orientations and predispositions of Chinese culture which coincide with and even reinforce certain orientations derived from the West. There has probably never been a motto more redolent of rich Chinese traditional associations than the current motto, *"p'o ssu li kung"* ("Smash selfishness, establish the public good"). The notion that the impulses of selfish individualism can be overcome by a proper spiritual training carried on by a spiritual elite; the negation of the desirability of a diversity of views and outlooks (*ssu-i*) and plurality of competing interests, and the stress on a kind of preestablished harmony are all present in this motto but are all also perfectly assimilable to the Populist-Jacobinist syndrome we have been describing.

In the particular case of Mao Tse-tung, one can point to other strains of the cultural heritage—perhaps minor strains—which probably form part of the background of his present outlook. The whole "knightly" (*yu-hsia*) ethos, which he derived from his early reading of Chinese epic novels with its stress on comradeship-in-arms and on the battle of the champions of the good against the forces of evil, can also feed into that enormous stress on combat and struggle which is such a central feature of his outlook. It also coincides very well with emphasis on conflict and struggle derived from the West.

None of this involves the assertion that Confucianism is the same as Jacobinism or that Rousseau is the same as Mencius. It rather involves the possibility that elements of Confucianism, elements of Mencius, and elements of Chinese popular culture may reinforce rather than negate particular Western orientations, even while being quite inimical to other Western orientations. Beyond this, one need not preclude the possibility of the assimilation of Western ideas which *by no means* coincide with traditional cultural predispositions, and which mark a sharp break with the past. The Populist-Jacobinist and pre-Marxist socialist notions which come through Marx and Lenin and from other sources also contain elements of radical novelty. History is not a repetitive moral drama but a progressive moral drama. It is true that in his Manichaean passion to see history as constant struggle between the forces of good and evil, Mao often implies that the struggle may go on ad infinitum, but there is the notion of a constantly growing triumph of the good over the evil within time. The Populist-Jacobin ideal also involves the constant, active, and total participation of the whole citizen body in the collective undertakings of the nation and not the passive "yielding" (*jang*) unselfishness of Chinese tradition. Furthermore, I would argue that the traditional (Confucian) ideal of unselfishness (*wu-ssu*) involved not so much the surrender of the "ego" to the overriding interests of an all-absorbing collective entity—the people-nation—as the abnegation of self in the interest of maintaining the "Tao," the normative social-moral order with its network of horizontal social relations. Finally, it would be a mistake, even now, to think that even Maoism at the ultimate has gone over completely to the anti-economism of either the Chinese past or of the early Jacobin tradition. Mao still seems genuinely to believe, or desire to believe, in the assumption of the Great Leap Forward that one can "boost production by grasping the revolution." This does not mean that the Cultural Revolution is simply a device "to get the economy going," but we need not doubt that Mao hopes that this will be one of its effects. He thus remains committed to the untraditional Promethean war on nature, but really seems to feel that he has found a new moral-political way of achieving this end.

This vision is, of course, terribly simple and extravagantly utopian (it matters little whether we find the utopia attractive or repugnant). Its more extreme features are not likely to survive. In explaining the background of this vision, however, we must keep in view the *two worlds* which have shaped the mental world of both Mao and his contemporaries. It may seem strange but it is not exclusively Chinese.

Comments by Stuart R. Schram

Professor Schwartz has raised so many issues in his very stimulating paper that in order to deal with all of them it would be necessary to write a comment of equal length. In my remarks I shall endeavor to focus on three points: the nature of the Western tradition of social thought, and especially of Marxism; the essential traits of Mao's thought; and some problems regarding the nature and limits of intercultural influence in general, and the interaction of Chinese and Western ideas in Mao's mind in particular.

History as "Technico-Economic Progress" and as "Moral Drama"

There is no doubt that Western culture does contain the two strands which Professor Schwartz designates by the expressions just cited, and that the intellectual history of the past two centuries can be viewed as the interaction of these tendencies. Personally, I should prefer to substitute for "moral drama" a more neutral term such as "the pursuit of moral values." Unquestionably, certain Western thinkers, especially in the socialist tradition, do view history, as Professor Schwartz puts it, as a moral drama in which "moral passion, indignation, and the hatred of social evil and injustice play a large part," and in which "the social good finally triumphs over social evil." But others are concerned rather with the moral perfectibility of the individual, which may be seen in terms of a slow and steady process of education, or as the result of a struggle against the corrupting influences of the growing wealth and complexity of society, rather than as the consequence of some cosmic battle between good and evil. (In fact, the passage from Buonarotti cited by Professor Schwartz fits rather into this category.)

It is, as Professor Schwartz rightly points out, one of the distinguishing characteristics of Marx's thought that in it these two strands are inextricably intermingled. Although in his earliest writings Marx does, as Professor Schwartz indicates, view history as moral drama, one should not overemphasize the rupture between the "young Marx" and the

Marx of the later years. Few works are animated with greater moral passion than the first volume of *Das Kapital*, with its descriptions of the sufferings and indignities inflicted on the workers in mid-nineteenth–century England. And it is precisely in the posthumous third volume of the same work that Marx has left us the classic definition of his own utopian goal, which deserves to be quoted at length, for it draws together in striking fashion both the concept of history as technico-economic progress and the stress on the moral and intellectual development of the individual:

> Thus the true wealth of society, and the possibility of a continual expansion of the process of its reproduction, does not depend on the duration of surplus labor, but on its productivity, and on the more or less fruitful conditions of production under which it is performed. The realm of freedom really begins only where work conditioned by necessity and external purpose ends; thus, by the very nature of things, it lies beyond the sphere of material production as such. Just as the savage must wrestle with nature in order to satisfy his needs, maintain his life and reproduce himself, so the civilized man must do, and he must do it in all forms of society and under every possible mode of production. With his development this realm of natural necessity expands, because his needs expand; but at the same time the productive forces which satisfy these needs are expanded. Freedom in this domain can only signify that socialized man, the associated producers, bring their interchange with nature under their collective control and organize it in a rational fashion, instead of being dominated by it as by a blind force; that they carry it out with the least expenditure of energy and in the conditions best adapted to and most worthy of their human nature. But all this remains a realm of necessity. Beyond it begins the manifestation of human powers taking itself as its own end, the true realm of freedom which, however, can flourish only upon that realm of necessity as its basis. The fundamental prerequisite of this is the shortening of the working day.[1]

This passage makes crystal clear that, if Marx measured progress in terms of the collective mastery of the forces of production, he regarded

[1] Karl Marx, *Das Kapital*, vol. 3 (Berlin, Dietz Verlag, 1956), pp. 873–74. The above translation is my own, revised after comparison with that of Ernest Untermann (Chicago: Charles H. Kerr & Co., 1909, pp. 954–55). The version recently published in Moscow (Foreign Languages Publishing House, 1959, pp. 799–800) is so bad as to be virtually useless.

such progress as a means to the broader aim of the transformation and the liberation of man. There is an unbridgeable gulf between this ideal vision in which the ultimate aim of the socialist economic organization of society is to reduce the working day and free men for that self-expression taken as an end in itself which constitutes the only true realm of freedom, and the Spartan ethos dominant in Peking today.

The Nature and Uses of Mao's Thought

As Professor Schwartz points out, there is a fundamental difference between Lenin and Mao as regards the relative importance they attribute to the technico-economic and moral strands in the Marxist heritage. At the same time, in this respect as in so many others, Lenin appears as a transitional figure between Marx and his Chinese disciples today.

On the one hand, as Professor Schwartz writes, Lenin's "view of the ultimate socialist-communist society of the future involved the whole-hearted acceptance of the role of industrialization." Indeed, Lenin's commitment to the redemptive mission of technical progress was perhaps even more profound than Professor Schwartz implies. His well-known formula, "Communism equals the soviets plus electrification," and his great admiration for the organizational achievements of German Social Democracy and for the technological drive of both German and American society point in this direction.

And yet there was a certain ambiguity in Lenin's attitude, a certain hesitation as to whether salvation would come from technology or from the moral values inherent in the oppressed classes and also in the oppressed peoples of the world. This ambiguity is directly related to Lenin's hesitation between Europe and Asia. Throughout his life, he detested the Slavophils and their cult of what he regarded as in large part the most backward traits in Russian society. He felt himself to be a European, and was passionately committed to the Europeanization of Russia, which he envisaged above all as the lifting of Russia to the same economic and technical level as the rest of Europe. (In this he was, of course, following the lead of Marx, who had explicitly stated that the future of Asia lay in Europeanization.) Nevertheless, toward the end of his life, bitterly disappointed by the failure of revolution in Europe and especially in Germany, Lenin began not only to attach greater weight to Asia in his vision of the world revolution as a whole, but to feel a certain kinship or solidarity with the peoples of Asia because they found themselves in a position similar to that of Russia. In his very last article, "Better Fewer, But Better," dictated in February 1923, a few weeks before another stroke put an end to his literary and intellectual activity, he wrote:

In the last analysis, the outcome of the struggle will be determined by the fact that Russia, India, China, etc., account for the overwhelming majority of the population of the globe. And during the past few years it is this majority that has been drawn into the struggle for emancipation with extraordinary rapidity, so that in this respect there cannot be the slightest doubt what the final outcome of the world struggle will be. In this sense, the complete victory of socialism is fully and absolutely assured.

. . . To ensure our existence until the next military conflict between the counter-revolutionary imperialist West and the revolutionary and nationalist East, between the most civilised countries of the world and the Orientally backward countries which, however, comprise the majority, this majority must become civilised. . . .[2]

"To become civilized" obviously meant for Lenin to assimilate the modern knowledge and scientific habits of thought of the West. Thus he vacillated between the conception of redemption as a "moral drama" —that is, as the struggle of the oppressed and exploited peoples against imperialism, and as the consequence of technical progress, attaching considerable weight to both these aspects. Mao, as Professor Schwartz indicates, also embraces both these ideas, but he places the accent far more heavily than Lenin on the human and moral side of progress as compared to the objective and technical side. To be sure, Mao's preoccupation with righteousness as he understands it has not implied, at least hitherto, a lack of interest in technical progress, still less hostility to economic development. As Professor Schwartz writes: "To Mao the reign of virtue had become both an end and a means. It was an end in itself but it could also be used as a means of achieving an economic leap forward." But at the same time, Mao has always nourished a certain uneasiness about the possible corrupting effects of economic development, to the extent that it might lead to a preoccupation with material welfare and selfish satisfaction. As Professor Schwartz observes, "Mao's orientation to 'modernization' seems to have been all along in tension with a deep anti-economist strain," which he defines as an antipathy to a Western-type consumer society.

A few years ago, I drew an analogy between Mao and Tseng Kuo-fan:

Just as Tseng regarded the values of the Chinese "way" as superior to any economic or political gain, and preferred to sacrifice such strengthening of the country as could only be bought at

[2] V. I. Lenin, *Collected Works*, Vol. 33 (Moscow: Progress Publishers, 1966), pp. 500–501.

the cost of inroads on what he regarded as its *raison d'être,* so Mao Tse-tung places the political criteria of doctrinal purity—which for him are also moral criteria—ahead of mere economic necessity. Like Tseng, he refuses to recognize that economics has its own logic, partly independent of any broader criteria; for him, as for Tseng, practical activity must be penetrated from beginning to end with moral values.[3]

This emphasis on "revolutionary" morality at the expense of economic efficiency is only too obvious in the patterns of the Great Proletarian Cultural Revolution, during which it has been found more important to send adolescents into the busses to read passages from *Quotations from Chairman Mao* than to continue their education. But, as Professor Schwartz very correctly emphasizes, the balance between the various strands in Mao's personality and thought, and in particular between technical efficiency and moral values, has not remained constant over the years.

As Professor Schwartz suggests, when Mao came to power in 1949 he "probably wholeheartedly accepted the notion that one must look to the Soviet Union as the model in . . . the 'modernization process.' " Beginning in the middle 1950's, Mao lost faith in the validity of the Soviet example for China, and sought inspiration in his own past experience, especially during the Yenan period. But the Yenan heritage itself is, as Professor Schwartz shows very well, an ambiguous one. It had, as he says, its "soft" as well as its "hard" side. It also involved, alongside of the guerrilla ethos which has been glorified in recent years, a respect for technical competence and administrative experience which contrasts strangely with the "rebel" ideology of the Great Proletarian Cultural Revolution. Thus, in 1939 Mao saw revolutionary potentialities in the sons of landlord families who had received a "scientific education." Regarding the government functionaries and white-collar workers of industry and commerce (*chih-yüan*), he went even farther, declaring: "Economic, governmental, and cultural construction cannot be carried out without them."[4]

The great divide in Mao's evolution can be located, as Professor Schwartz points out, in late 1957 and early 1958, when he adopted radical policies inspired by his "revolutionary romantic" faith in the infinite capacities of the masses to transform the world through their

---

[3] *The Political Thought of Mao Tse-tung* (New York: Praeger, 1963), p. 84.

[4] *Chung-kuo ko-ming yü Chung-kuo Kung-ch'an-tang* [The Chinese Revolution and the Chinese Communist Party] (Yenan: Chieh-fang she, n.d.), pp. 21, 25. (These passages have been eliminated from the current edition of the *Selected Works.*)

action. Mao's thought and action have, of course, been characterized from the beginning by an extreme voluntarist tendency. Thus, in January, 1930, he criticized Lin Piao for "overestimating objective forces and underestimating subjective forces."[5] But, beginning with the Great Leap Forward, this tendency was carried a step farther than either Mao or anyone else had done before. For example, in an article of 1958 expounding Mao's thought, we find the statement: "There are only poor systems for cultivating the land; there is no such thing as poor land."[6]

One of Mao's most remarkable statements to the effect that the transformation of man is the key both to the transformation of society and to economic progress is to be found in the article which he contributed to the first issue of *Hung-ch'i* in the spring of 1958. I am referring to his famous claim that the Chinese people can progress with exceptional speed because they are "poor" and "blank." Poverty as one of the roots of revolution is, of course, a Marxist notion, though for Marx the redemptive mission of the proletariat does not depend merely on the fact of exploitation, but also on the fact that in playing their role in the productive process they carry the whole of society on their backs. But the notion of blankness as a positive factor in economic development has assuredly nothing to do with Marxism. Moreover, as Professor Schwartz shows very well, in Mao's eyes China's poverty was not only a stimulus to revolution, but a source of virtue. Thus, while in 1958–59 Mao was still intensely concerned with rapid economic development (it will be recalled that one of the slogans of the Great Leap Forward was "Overtake England within fifteen years"), it was only a step from the emphasis on virtue as the key to material accomplishment to the exaltation of virtue even at the expense of economic necessity.

This step Mao has now taken, in fact if not in words. It is claimed, of course, that the study of Mao Tse-tung's thought makes the Chinese capable of solving all manner of scientific and technical problems and of multiplying production in both industry and agriculture, but it is hard to believe that even Mao is altogether convinced of this. What seems to have happened is that certain paired values or aims which have coexisted in Mao's thought and action throughout his career have been replaced by one-sided conceptions in which, systematically, the utopian and voluntarist components have won out over the realistic

[5] *Hsüan chi* [Selected Works] (Chin-Ch'a-Chi Hsin-hua shu-tien, 1947 ed., supplement), p. 99.

[6] *Hsüeh-hsi Mao Tse-tung ti szu-hsiang fang-fa ho kung-tso fang-fa* [Study Mao Tse-tung's Methods of Thought and Methods of Work] (Peking: Chung-kuo ch'ing-nien ch'u-pan-she, 1958), p. 73.

and pragmatic components. Thus Mao's hatred of bureaucracy has largely obscured his hitherto striking grasp of the importance of organization, his fear of the corrupting effects of ease and affluence has led him to have second thoughts about the goal of "wealth and power" for China which he has pursued for half a century, and an overwhelming emphasis on conformity has left little place for that spontaneity and "conscious action" which have always been essential ingredients of his formula for ideological indoctrination and thought reform.

Professor Schwartz finds that in the "Cultural Revolution" Mao's *furor ideologicus* "burns more fiercely than ever." In a sense this is true; but it must be added that the influence of ideology in China has changed not merely in degree, but in nature. In a word, what we are witnessing is the transformation of what is still called Marxism-Leninism ("the thought of Mao Tse-tung" being, of course, the highest form of Marxism-Leninism in our era) from an instrument of analysis to a kind of revolutionary litany.

This process began with the preparation of the current edition of Mao's *Selected Works* in the years immediately after 1949, when texts dating from widely different periods were rewritten to give the impression that Mao's ideas and behavior had been more consistent than in fact they were. Nevertheless, this edition consisted of relatively long and complete texts presented in chronological order. In the *Quotations from Chairman Mao,* which were first published by the Political Department of the Army in May, 1964, and became widely known in 1966 as the bible of the Red Guards, all historical perspective has disappeared. These short extracts of a few lines each are chosen in such a manner that they appear, not as fragments of analysis of concrete historical situations, but as universally valid precepts to be learned by heart. To be sure, the Red Guards and others who read these texts are supposed to "apply" them. But what is to be applied is not a Marxist method of analysis, but Mao's conclusions, which amount essentially to the affirmation of the omnipotence of the human will and the exhortation to struggle relentlessly and accept no compromise whatsoever, either with "U.S. imperialism" and "Soviet revisionism," or with the objective difficulties encountered in the path of economic development.

Chinese and Western Influences in Mao's Thought

The recent change in the uses of Mao's thought is directly related to the problem of the balance between Chinese and Western components in his vision of the world to which Professor Schwartz devotes a large part of his paper. The reading in unison of passages from the Chairman's writings is reminiscent of Christian liturgical services, but the sacred character attributed not merely to Mao's words but to the little red book containing them recalls rather the Koran, and the title (*Mao Chu-hsi yü-lu*) is characteristic of the Buddhist scriptures.

The same issue of Chinese versus Western influences is raised by the fact, emphasized by Professor Schwartz at the beginning of his paper, that Mao sees in his "thought" something which "is not incarnate in any organization but rather transcends and breaks through the limits of all organizations." It is an axiom of Marxism-Leninism that the Communist party is the ultimate repository of authority and of ideological orthodoxy. There have, of course, been instances in which Communist political systems were dominated by the personal tyranny of one individual, but none of these dictators, including Stalin, has ever placed himself explicitly above the party. On the contrary, even as he established and consolidated his own absolute power, Stalin claimed to be merely the mandatary of the party, the instrument of the party's will as vested in the Central Committee. Mao today openly presents himself as the sole source of truth, not by virtue of his position in the party, but as one of the attributes inherent in his role as leader of the Chinese people. To some extent, Mao's right to lead is justified by the fact that he has supposedly always been right in the past. But basically his unique position remains as mysterious and unexplained as that of any divine-right monarch or of any of the other popularly-acclaimed "leaders" in the recent past. There is here a mixture of Communism, Fascism, and a Chinese emperor mediating between his people and its historical destiny which will probably go down as one of the most singular instances of intercultural borrowing.

As a reaction against the currently fashionable tendency to see the Great Proletarian Cultural Revolution as something essentially oriental and exotic, Professor Schwartz has stressed in his paper the analogies with Western thought and Western history. In particular, he has developed a most interesting parallel between the climate in China today and the climate in the late Jacobin phase of the French Revolution. Many of the resemblances he points out are striking: "the enormous faith in the reign of virtue"; "the enormous suspicion of the ever-present forces of selfishness"; "the wedding of the spirit of self-sacrifice to messianic nationalism." On the other hand, whatever may have been the "profound suspicion of the treacheries and subtleties of intellectuals" during the French Revolution, it is hard to imagine that irrationalism can have reached such levels then as in China today. But in any case, Professor Schwartz is quite right to remind us that "Western" is not necessarily a synonym for "pragmatic, sensible, and rational," and that the passionate pursuit of utopian goals is quite as much an integral part of our own tradition.

Professor Schwartz refers to the "transmission" to Mao of the cast of mind characteristic of the later phases of the French Revolution. There seems to be, however, a certain ambiguity in his paper regarding the mechanism by which this transmission has taken place. Mao has undoubtedly been exposed to certain authors and ideas of the French Revolution both directly, through the reading of Chinese translations of books or extracts from this period, and indirectly through the discussions of these questions in Marx, Lenin, and other Marxist writers. At the same time, if Mao has adopted certain aspects of the Jacobin mystique, this is not merely because he has happened to encounter these ideas at some point in his career. It must also imply that the problems and needs of Chinese society at its present stage of development, as seen by Mao, make the heritage of the French Revolution appear relevant. As Professor Schwartz states, Mao is not "the mere embodiment of transcendental forces." His ideas are not simply the reflection of an objective situation. But they *are* one possible response to a situation— a response affected both by all the ideas, Chinese and Western, by which Mao has been influenced in the course of his life, and by his own personality and political aims. Thus, if the parallel between the mystique of the Cultural Revolution and that of the Jacobins is as close as Professor Schwartz suggests (and he makes a very strong case), one would have to seek the explanation both in Mao's "romantic" personality, and in the fact that China is now passing through a "romantic" age.

Thus, one approach to the evaluation of Mao's thought and its role in China today would endeavor to relate Chinese tradition, Western influences, and the needs of the objective situation as they intersect in and are mediated through the personality of the individual Mao. But Mao's mind and intellectual itinerary can also be considered as one illustration of the transformation of Chinese culture under the impact of the West.

Mao's own view regarding learning from the West, put forward in 1940 in *On New Democracy,* is one of "selective absorption." "We must," he wrote, "treat these foreign materials as we do our food, which should be chewed in the mouth, submitted to the workings of the stomach and intestines, mixed with saliva, gastric juice and intestinal secretions, and then separated into essence to be absorbed and waste matter to be discarded." In fact, the process is certainly neither so conscious nor so simple. Professor Schwartz in his paper evokes the possibility that "elements of Confucianism . . . may reinforce rather than negate particular Western orientations, even while being quite inimical to other Western orientations." He also suggests that other ideas may be assimilated which "mark a sharp break with the past." One could, perhaps, envisage an even wider range of possibilities in the encounter between Chinese and foreign elements:

1. The reaffirmation of traditional values or ideas as still valid today in their own terms, as Mao and Liu Shao-ch'i frequently did in the late 1930's.
2. The use of traditional ideas or concepts as an envelope or camouflage for new ideas of foreign origin to make them more acceptable.
3. The reemergence of traditional ideas in Westernized guise.
4. The acceptance of new foreign ideas which have no counterpart in traditional culture, because they relate to completely new domains of activity, and therefore encounter no resistance from tradition.
5. A frontal attack on traditional ideas and values, where these come into head-on conflict with the values of Western origin required by a modernizing society.

Though one can find instances of all five of these situations throughout Mao's career, there is no doubt that, ostensibly at least, he has in recent years downgraded (2) in favor of (5). But, as suggested above, the inspiration of Mao's current policies is not so exclusively Marxist and Western as the term Great Proletarian Cultural Revolution would lead one to believe, and in fact (3) undoubtedly plays a considerable role in China today.

Comments by Donald J. Munro

Throughout much of the thought of Mao Tse-tung runs the theme that the key to the good society lies in the transformation of souls into selfless parts of the whole. Selflessness ("the absolute conquest of all individual and even group-segmental self-interest") is both a means and an end. In a fascinating study Professor Schwartz shows that the roots of this position may be traced back not simply to the Confucian ideal of unselfishness (*wu-ssu*),[1] but also to the gradually unfolding "contest" in the West between the "moral drama" view of history and the alternate thesis that in the technico-economic sphere lie the ultimate moving forces of history. The thought of Mao Tse-tung carries on the attachment to the moral drama thesis which became progressively more evident in the writings of the early Marx, Lenin, and Stalin.

Professor Schwartz was certainly right to emphasize the importance of the transformation of souls into selfless parts of the whole in the thought of Mao Tse-tung. My remarks on his paper will be in the form of a supplement, not in the form of a contradiction to that emphasis.

I feel that it is important to regard Maoism as a mixed bag and that it is very easy to overlook the place of technico-economic progress in that bag. There are perhaps two reasons why that aspect is easily neglected. First, this is due to the difficulty in defining exactly what is the thought of Mao Tse-tung. It may be necessary to distinguish between the ideas of Mao himself and their actual implementation in China, but this is complicated. It is hard to measure how much of themselves the implementors inject into the Chairman's ideas. I would suggest, however, that "Maoism" in operation must be considered if one is speaking about the thought of Mao Tse-tung. One sector where Maoism can be found in operation is in political education (and in some aspects of educational policy in general). If one does look for its meaning in that education he will discover some interesting things about the importance of the technico-economic process in Maoist thought. Secondly, the place of the technico-economic process can easily be overlooked because Western economists may (rightly) view as ineffective the Maoism which is concerned with spurring development in that sphere. But this does not mean it is not in the mixed bag. Chinese economists and officials who favor quasi-Soviet or Yugoslav economic policies which seem sound to Western analysts have been attacked and purged. Mindful of this fact, one would still be misinformed if he viewed Maoism as unqualified revolutionary romanticism. My remarks should be taken simply as the qualification.

A not insignificant portion of Mao's thought has been concerned with breaking down customs and habits in the Chinese people which he feels impede modernization. He is not the first Chinese in the twentieth century to focus on this as a key to progress. Even many of the habits which he has singled out for correction were identified long ago as

---

[1] *"Wu-ssu"* was an ideal of Taoists and Buddhists, too, I might add.

impediments to economic modernization by such predecessors as Lu Hsün (in *The True Story of Ah Q*) and Hu Shih. In the following remarks I will indicate how thoughts of Mao (including Marxist maxims contained in his writings) have been put to work to eliminate those customs and habits. One crucial thing to remember is that political education among workers and peasants is often qualitatively different from that received by intellectuals. Among the former it is frequently concerned with breaking down these old habits and also with such matters as hygiene and sanitation. The "romanticism" of Maoism may be more present in the political education absorbed by intellectuals. But some of the "habits" to be broken cut across the population board, and Maoism is also addressed to these.

The essence of the Marxist epistemological doctrine is pinpointed in the phrase "the unity of theory and practice." "Theory" was defined by Stalin as ". . . the experience of the working-class movement in all countries taken in its general aspect."[2] Practice is said to be involvement in the concrete process of material production, class struggle, and scientific experimentation. Practice is the only criterion of truth. There are no innate truths discoverable by the intellect alone. The doctrine has been incorporated into the thought of Mao Tse-tung through the vehicle of the Chairman's essay *On Practice*. A number of ideas in this essay have been used to justify changes in the educational system in China. The purpose of these changes is to terminate the kind of rote learning which has hitherto taken place in the Chinese classroom. Teachers are to foster not the capacity to parrot a book or lecture but the ability to apply knowledge and to think creatively. A number of specific changes have been called for. Teachers have been told to do less lecturing and to involve students actively in the learning process by having them present their own solutions to problems. Closer ties have been ordered between the classroom and the laboratory, workshop, and fieldwork. Open-book examinations have been given trials, in part as a means of reorienting the students' approach to learning from memorization to problem-solving. All of this has been justified in the name of "combining theory and practice." Its ultimate aim is to create students who can *apply* knowledge to the "production and science struggles," rather than students who can only parrot the text.[3]

[2] From *Foundations of Leninism* (1924), quoted in Gustav A. Wetter, *Dialectical Materialism* (New York: Praeger, 1963), p. 259.

[3] Tuan Li-p'ei, "Yao shih hsüeh-sheng tsai te chih t'i fang-mien sheng-tung huo-p'o ti chu-tung ti te-tao fa-chan" [Having Students Receive a Lively and Active Development in the Realms of Morality, Knowledge, and Physical Fit-

This same principle, coupled with that of the "mass line," was consistently used during a campaign which Mao initiated in November, 1964, and which lasted into 1966. The campaign's aim was to revolutionize designing in China.[4] There were many aspects to the campaign, and a number (such as the blatant anti-foreignism) were hardly necessary. But one of the aims was to adapt designs on all products to the local needs and to draw on the knowledge of those who use the products in improving them. In other words, Western designs of machines, bridges, trains, and so forth, were to be adapted to Chinese requirements. Furthermore, Chinese designers were forced to involve themselves on the scene where their products were being used. Once again, the principle of combining theory and practice was invoked to justify such measures.

Ideas from *On Contradiction* are called upon to justify breaking down other habits deemed negative by the Chinese Communists. One of these habits has been called the "Ah Q Spirit" by a leading Chinese Communist philosopher.[5] In general terms this means a Chinese tendency to rationalize problems away rather than to face them squarely. The "problems" arise either in the "contradictions between the people and their enemies" or between the people and nature (as in attempting to build an airport or dam). This tendency is often linked up with another which has many roots. One of these roots is traditional authoritarian instructional practices in which the person in the learning role was expected obediently to imitate the methods and practices of the party in the "teaching" role (be he a real teacher, or father, or grandfather, or employer). The "habit" to be eradicated involves the failure to examine a new problem objectively, coupled with a tendency to "give up" in the absence of precedent (that is, where father's or grandfather's teachings provide no answer). The demon created by these associated habits is "passivity."[6] In political education in China today

---

ness], *Chung-kuo ch'ing-nien* [China Youth], no. 7, 1964, pp. 19–21. See also *Jen-min jih-pao* [People's Daily], April 3, 1964, and September 10, 1964.

[4] An example of one of the hundreds of articles on the revolution in designing is "The Revolutionizing of Designing Work," *Kung-lu* [Highway], no. 7 (1965); trans. in *Joint Publications Research Service*, no. 32 (U.S. Department of Commerce), p. 433.

[5] Kuan Feng, "Chuang-tzu che-hsüeh p'i-p'an" [Critique of Chuang-tzu's Philosophy], *Chuang-tzu che-hsüeh t'ao-lun chi* [Collected Discussions on the Philosophy of Chuang-tzu] (Peking: Chung-hua shu-chü, 1962), pp. 4–5.

[6] For an attack on "Passivism," see *Kuang-ming jih-pao*, July 16, 1965.

a number of quotations from *On Contradiction* are used in the attempt to overcome these habits. Discussions of the "dialectical world outlook," for example, stress how problems are to be solved "dialectically." In actual fact, in political education among peasants and workers, "to solve a problem dialectically" (to look for the contradictions involved in it) means to look at the *objective* situation and try to figure out what the variables are and what is required for solution, rather than to give up trying to solve it in the absence of precedent.

One final use has been made in political education among workers and peasants of ideas in *On Contradiction*. This is to foster a willingness to be critical and frank with one's co-workers on matters of both on-the-job performance and personal conduct. In the name of "the struggle between opposites," workers have been exhorted to replace a traditional reticence with a willingness to be frank when frankness is required. This means that if the person on the lathe next to you is doing something wrong, you do not hesitate to tell him so. "Dividing one into two"[7] would require that a person look for both the good and bad features in any situation.

Mao Tse-tung is obviously a man with "visions" of the future, to use an expression of Professor Schwartz, and many of his "thoughts" speak of the nature of the Chinese millennium. However, such "thoughts" must be regarded from two points of view. On the one hand, they can be understood as statements of goals to be achieved, and they influence major national policies in this connection. On the other hand, they can be seen in terms of the role they actually play in political education among factory workers and peasants today. Two examples will be illustrative.

First, Mao's crystal ball reveals China as a place where the distinction between mental and manual laborers will be totally eliminated. Like the all-around man in Marx's *German Ideology*, the Chinese of the future will be capable of both "animal husbandry" and "criticism." However, in political education today these thoughts of Mao have very immediate applications. They are used to cope with the problem of what the Chinese Communists call "mental aristocrats." The term "mental aristocrats" refers, among other things, to people with a modicum of education (including among others many intellectuals and cadres) who are unwilling to do manual labor at their place of employment or to involve themselves where actual productive labor is

[7] Mao's interpretation of dialectics, which of late has been juxtaposed to the "two combine into one" doctrine of Yang Hsien-chen (former head of the Higher Party School in Peking), which stresses compromise and harmony.

done for which they are responsible. For example, the "thoughts" about eliminating the distinction between mental and manual labor are used to "educate" clerks and accountants to help with the harvest when the work team is short of manpower, and they are used to "insure" close liaison between front-office factory directors and the production process itself.

There is a related practical problem to which the ideal of eliminating the difference between the two kinds of labor is addressed in political education. This is the occupational placement of the enormous numbers of middle-school graduates who enter the job market every year. There simply are not enough urban and white collar positions for them. Students with the kind of education which formerly would have insured them a non-manual job are being "educated" to volunteer for the farm and factory on the grounds that they are pioneers in breaking the barrier between "those who work with their minds and rule and those who work with their hands and are ruled" (Mencius).[8]

Second, the crystal ball reveals a nation of "selfless" members of the collective. The Maoist idea of "selflessness" includes both the recognition by the individual that he is part of a whole and the intention to act unselfishly or with the whole in mind. Maoist tracts on this theme are endless. For the past few years one of the most widely distributed is *In the Service of the People* (*Wei jen-min fu-wu*), which teaches that the ultimate in unselfishness (giving one's life for the people) means that one's death will be "heavier than Mount T'ai" and not "lighter than a feather." However, in political education today, the theme of "unselfishness" is often used to deal with a very real Chinese problem. This is the need to extend the sense of responsibility beyond the family or small group to which in certain matters it was often restricted. One of the major concerns has been to cultivate a responsibility for the care of machines and tools now owned by the "impersonal" state. In other words, "unselfishness" in the pages of *Kuang-ming jih-pao* may refer to something rather excessively romantic and visionary. In the factory or farm it often means: do not abuse or neglect the machine just because it does not belong to you or your village.

While on the subject of "unselfishness" I would like to make one further point; Professor Schwartz holds that for Mao it is both an end and a means. Unselfishness is a state of mind in people during Communism. It is also a means for achieving miracles now, such as the

[8] I am indebted to Professor Michel Oksenberg of Stanford University for bringing the population statistics on the matter to my attention.

Great Leap Forward. I think that one needs to go beyond the concept of "unselfishness" to find the really operative assumption at work in the Great Leap romanticism. I mention it because it definitely has very deep roots in Chinese tradition. This assumption can be isolated from the virtue of "unselfishness," although they are closely related. It is that if people have the knowledge of what is right and the attitude that right takes precedence over all other considerations, then success in very concrete forms is assured. For Mao, "unselfishness" merely suggests the terms in which "what is right" will be defined. At certain other times in China's past the terms defining "right" may have been different. But the belief in a necessary connection between knowledge of the right (plus the attitude that it takes precedence over all other considerations) and practical success was consistently held. One can see it in the *Great Learning* discussion of the progression from having sincere thoughts and a rectified mind (*ch'eng i, cheng hsin*), to achieving order in the state and peace in the world. This essay also informs us that virtue is the root, wealth the branches. The former is crucial, but the latter follows from it. The same theme pervades the thought of Wang Yang-ming (1472–1529), who held that "Knowledge is the beginning of action; action is the completion of knowledge." "True knowledge" of what is right will necessarily have consequences in practice. It is no accident that Wang Yang-ming is the favorite philosopher of Chiang Kai-shek at the same time when one can discover "Maoist idealism" (as Chalmers Johnson calls it) behind some of the policies of Mao Tse-tung.[9] I am not claiming that Mao is a new Wang Yang-ming, for the differences between the "knowledge" and "action" each of the two has in mind are too obvious to need spelling out. But I think that if one is speaking of Mao's romanticism it is important to remember the strength of this legacy from the past.

The theme of the relationship between Western philosophy and Mao-ism is an important one in Professor Schwartz's paper. I would like to conclude with a few remarks about the role of Western philosophy in the aspects of the thought of Mao Tse-tung which I have been discussing. First, certain statements which derive from the Western philosophical tradition provide the sanction of Marxist orthodoxy for the solution of purely Chinese problems of modernization. Of course this is not the only function served by these ideas from the West, but it is one

[9] See Chalmers Johnson, "Chinese Communist Leadership and Mass Response: The Yenan Period and the Socialist Education Campaign Period," in this volume, pp. 397–437.

that should not be forgotten. Second, Western philosophical ideas unwittingly serve as targets for much of the abuse which the Chinese also level at their own Chinese legacy. For example, the bourgeois philosophy of education is said to treat only book knowledge as knowledge and to denigrate practical experience as a source of knowledge. Some Chinese read into the West the faults which they discover in their own traditional practices.

Finally, Professor Schwartz has stressed one unconscious debt to Western philosophy in Maoism. I might conclude by suggesting the possibility of another. It may be that there is an unacknowledged debt to the teachings of John Dewey in the particular application of the "union of theory and practice" doctrine to the educational system. Dewey left his legacy after the 1919–20 lectures in China. The faith was proselytized by Hu Shih, Chiang Mon-lin, and by many American-trained Chinese educators. The idol of pragmatism and its priests were smashed by the Communists. But the memory of (Dewey's) arguments in favor of "combining learning and doing" may have helped insure that the Marxist epistemological doctrine which speaks of the "union of theory and practice" would play the role which it has played. Of course this could not have occurred if the objective situation in education in China had not urgently called for such changes, and there probably is a certain amount of overlap of the current Chinese style of teaching with the objective situation in American teaching practices at the time when Dewey and Thorndike helped carry out their "revolution."

None of what I have said should be understood as denying that Mao is on the irrational side of a split over economic policy in China. It is simply intended to round out the picture of what is in the mixed bag called "Maoism" and to suggest that in attempting to eradicate the "four olds" the Chairman demonstrates his concern with the technico-economic process.

Chalmers Johnson

6

Chinese Communist Leadership and Mass Response: The Yenan Period and the Socialist Education Campaign Period

The function of social science theory when applied to Chinese Communist reality is to generate hypotheses about the nature of the Chinese social system.[1] Such hypotheses, if sustained by available evidence and actual events, can enhance our understanding of Chinese society through the use of universal social systems variables; these hypotheses permit us to make comparisons with other social systems, and they open up the possibility of utilizing knowledge gained from the study of many social systems in analyzing the purposes and consequences of particular Chinese Communist policies. Even if such hypotheses are overturned, our perception of and insight into the variables that were imperfectly weighed may nevertheless be advanced. As Roberta Wohlstetter concludes from her devastating critique of an earlier attempt at "Asia watching" by Westerners, "To discriminate significant sounds against [a] background of noise, one has to be listening for something or for one of several things. In short, one needs not only an ear, but a variety of hypotheses that guide observation."[2]

In this paper I shall explore one such hypothesis—namely, that in two different periods of Chinese Communist leadership, periods in which the policies of the Communist party were based on roughly the same fundamental strategy of organization and goal attainment, the

[1] Research for this paper was carried out partly in Hong Kong under a grant from the Joint Committee on Contemporary China, Social Science Research Council.

[2] *Pearl Harbor, Warning and Decision* (Stanford, Calif.: Stanford University Press, 1962), p. 56.

population under the effective control of the party responded positively in the first instance and tended to remain aloof and even to subvert the policies in the second. The two time spans to be considered are the Yenan period, 1936 to 1947, and the period between the Tenth and Eleventh Plena (September, 1962, to August, 1966) of the Eighth Central Committee—that is, the era of the Socialist Education Campaign and the beginning of the Great Proletarian Cultural Revolution.

It will be suggested that the policies adopted by the party in Yenan elicited an overwhelmingly favorable response from the people within the base areas (and to a lesser extent in certain areas outside the bases) and that, as a consequence, the Communist forces won the Chinese civil war. This is in line with General Chassin's observation that, "Victory in a civil war is almost always won by the side which knows how to gain the support of the people."[3] At the same time it would seem that policies very similar in theory and often explicitly justified in terms of those implemented in the Yenan period, when they were applied between 1962 and 1966, have elicited precisely the opposite result. As a consequence, the authority of the Chinese Communist Party (CCP) to rule without relying primarily on coercion and terrorism of the Stalinist variety appears to have been significantly attenuated. This is a hypothesis, and I am the first to acknowledge that it is impossible to make statements about mass support in China based on the direct observation of behavior or on attitudes and other types of orientations that may be discovered through the use of social science field research. This does not mean, however, that we can ignore the subject. It is understandable that scholars of China in the West, sensitive to the dangers of blind anti-Communism, have tended to discount stories of mass discontent in China, but it would be embarrassing indeed if the Chinese people themselves were to prove the "China watchers" wrong.

It is problematical whether or not political authority in the strict sense of the term has existed in China, at least on a centralized basis, for the past fifty years. Relationships of authority—that is, relationships in which certain role players may issue commands backed by the legitimacy of their office and in which certain other role players obey these commands partly because they recognize them to be legitimate (morally acceptable) and partly because they know them to be enforceable through means that are collectively supported—have been approached

[3] Lionel Max Chassin, *The Communist Conquest of China, A History of the Civil War 1945–49* (London: Weidenfeld and Nicolson, 1966), p. 249.

in China, but the alternate means of eliciting obedience, coercion and persuasion, have been equally important. Hannah Arendt draws the distinctions between authority, coercion, and persuasion most clearly:

> Since authority always demands obedience, it is commonly mistaken for some form of power or violence. Yet, authority precludes the use of external means of coercion; where force is used, authority itself has failed. Authority, on the other hand, is incompatible with persuasion, which presupposes equality and works through a process of argumentation. Where arguments are used, authority is left in abeyance. Against the egalitarian order of persuasion stands the authoritarian order which is always hierarchical. . . . The authoritarian relation between the one who commands and the one who obeys rests neither on common reason nor on the power of the one who commands; what they have in common is the hierarchy itself, whose rightness and legitimacy both recognize and where both have their predetermined stable place.[4]

In the sense in which stable values held by the great majority of socialized, non-deviant actors in a social system make possible true relationships of authority, Chinese leaders in the Nationalist and Communist periods have not ruled through authority. In a looser sense, the Communist victory of the Yenan period laid the foundations of party authority; and the party, at least until recent times, has been able to rely appreciably on its war-won authority to cause the population to work in accordance with its policies. However, by far the most common form of CCP leadership has been the use of a special form of persuasion— namely, the organizing of the population to work for specially articulated goals which the party and the population agree upon at least temporarily. And, as Hannah Arendt has explained, in order to persuade a people of something or in order to organize them to do something, processes of argumentation must be employed.[5]

[4] "What Was Authority?" in C. J. Friedrich (ed.), *Authority* (Cambridge: Harvard University Press, 1958), p. 82.

[5] The fundamental variables, authority, persuasion, and coercion, can all themselves be broken down further into types. Forms of persuasion include organization (in the sense in which "organizing" is both the act of agreeing upon concrete goals and the explicit division of labor in order to achieve these goals), material remuneration (or "inducement"), and direct invocation of the values of a social system (or "appeals to conscience"). The use of influence is a variety of authority. Threats, fining, deterrence through the maintenance of forces in readiness, and the use of force are types of coercion. The literature

From the point of view of an elite leadership group, the difficulty involved in persuading or organizing a person is that neither action can be carried out against the person's will; the persuader and organizer must meet the individual whose compliance they are trying to elicit on the basis of formal equality, and they must convince him of the desirability of acting in a prescribed manner—usually on the basis of self-interest or some form of collective interest. In short, the intentions of the organizer and the interests of the organized must coincide to some degree. Even though the organizer may at some point trick the organized through propaganda or some other artifice, this act generates a process of learning (or "feedback") that greatly impairs the ability of the organizer to repeat his success.

When these pure, or persuasive, forms of organization fail—that is, when the person subjected to the activity is unpersuaded or feels that he has been tricked—the organizer must resort to coercion or else abandon his effort. Midway between persuasion and coercion stands a hybrid form, which might be called "coercive organization," that the Chinese Communists have developed to a high art. This hybrid form involves atomizing the population by applying coercion capriciously (for example, reform through labor, Red Guards' activity), by using terms of argumentation that are vague and therefore treacherous ("reds and experts," "bad elements," "bourgeois survivals," "modern revisionists," and, most recently, *niu-kuei she-shen,* or "freaks and monsters"), and by using spies and informers to prevent counter-organization. These devices so threaten a person's security and ability to orient his own behavior to that of others that he comes to accept the organizers' proposals as a means of escape (for example, the Chinese Communist organizational technique called "thought reform"). However, this hybrid form of organization involves diminishing returns. Since the interests of organizer and organized do not coincide, increasingly greater amounts of coercion must be applied until the entire façade of persuasion is subverted. True organization, on the other hand, is a form of social cooperation; it rests on persuasion—on a common denominator of goals that are mutually agreed to by organizer and organized.

These elements of organizational activity are very familiar to the Chinese Communists. Mao Tse-tung's famous principle of the "mass line" (*ch'ün-chung lu-hsien*) is nothing less than a statement of them in

---

on this subject is large, but one of the most seminal recent works is Talcott Parsons, "Some Reflections on the Place of Force in Social Process," in Harry Eckstein (ed.), *Internal War* (New York: The Free Press of Glencoe, 1964), pp. 33–70.

Chinese Communist language.[6] By "mass line" the Chinese Communists mean that in order to organize a people for any purpose, the Communist party must perform two functions. First, it must discover what social issues or problems are of most immediate concern to the mass of the population, what the best rallying cry is for the party's use in organizing the masses. The Chinese Communists call this function either "mobilization" (*tung-yüan*) or "from the masses" (*ts'ung ch'ün-chung chung lai*). Second, having discovered what program has the greatest potential for eliciting a favorable response from the masses, the party must organize and lead the people on the basis of this program. This function Chinese theorists call either "organization" (*tsu-chih*) or "to the masses" (*tao ch'ün-chung chung ch'ü*). Soong Ch'ing-ling has described the mass line as follows:

> "From the masses; back to the masses." Herein lies the role of the Communist Party and its members: to go among the people so as to learn from them; to analyze in Marxist-Leninist terms their demands and insights, crystallizing and systematizing these ideas and elevating them to a theoretical level; on the basis of this, to project the right policies and methods of work; to take these back to the masses, explain and popularize them, and arouse the masses to support these policies so they will act on them as their own.[7]

As a Communist party spokesman wrote in 1965, "The mass line is the party's fundamental political and organizational line."[8]

The basic sociological insight of the mass line is that in order for any

[6] On the need to take Chinese Communist jargon seriously—in a sociological sense—see Franz Schurmann: "Despite the volume of available material, the impression is still widespread in the West that little is known about Communist China. Though the reason usually given for this impression is false, the fact of the impression is true. Communist documents cannot be read as if they were written in conventional language. . . . The Chinese Communists have developed a rich vocabulary which has in many ways changed the Chinese language. Ideas and terms have come into popular usage that never existed before. . . . One of the major contributions of the practical ideology of the Chinese Communists has been the generation of these many new and useful categories and language. It has also given the Chinese a new manner of thinking" (*Ideology and Organization in Communist China* [Berkeley and Los Angeles: University of California Press, 1966], pp. 61–62).

[7] Soong Ching-ling, "Sixteen Years of Liberation," *China Reconstructs*, 15, no. 1 (January, 1966), p. 5.

[8] Yü Hsin-yen, *Ch'ün-chung lu-hsien shih-t'i* [Ten Topics on the Mass Line] (Peking: Chung-kuo ch'ing-nien ch'u-pan-she, 1965), p. 3.

organizational campaign to succeed, the goals of the organizers must encompass some irreducible nucleus of the aspirations of the organized. As we shall see, the mass line lies at the heart of Yenan Communism, and a major reason why the Communist party was so tremendously successful during that period was that the party acted more or less in accordance with mass line dictates. Similarly, the party's deviation from the mass line, while it continued to implement policies predicated on the functioning of the mass line (for example, guerrilla-type campaigns), helps to explain why its imperfectly founded authority began to totter during the Socialist Education Campaign.

Yenan Communism and the Mass Line

Yenan is a time, a place, and a symbol; it is also, and above all, the name of a revolutionary strategy which uses the mass line to serve a revolutionary purpose. Yenan Communism is to a large extent synonymous with the strategy of "people's war," and it is this aspect of the Yenan experience that has had the most tenacious hold over a segment of the Chinese Communist leadership. These facts have not been well understood outside of China. An earlier generation of Western students of Chinese revolutionary history tended to overlook the "people's war" component of the thought of Mao Tse-tung. Fifteen years ago, of course, Stalin was still alive and passing judgment on any Communist in the world who challenged his monopoly over Marxist-Leninist theory; the obvious questions then concerned whether or not Mao Tse-tung was a good Communist, an innovative Communist, or a heretical Communist. Scholarly attention was drawn not to Mao's strategical thinking but to his reliance on the peasantry as the class—in the Marxist sense—that would wage the revolution in China, and to his insistence that the Communist party—in the Leninist sense—should organize and lead this class.

As Benjamin Schwartz wrote in 1951:

> Essentially, the Maoist strategy involves the imposition of a political party organized in accordance with Leninist principles and animated by faith in certain basic tenets of Marxism-Leninism onto a purely peasant mass base. . . . These peasant masses are to be won by a program of land reform designed to satisfy the basic grievances of the bulk of the peasantry within the areas under Communist control.[9]

[9] *Chinese Communism and the Rise of Mao,* 2nd ed. (Cambridge: Harvard University Press, 1958), p. 189.

Schwartz concludes that this approach of Mao's to the problem of revolution in China is a Marxist heresy and that "Marxism has in its movement eastward—into situations for which its original premises made little provision—undergone a slow but steady process of decomposition."[10]

There is no disputing this analysis on its own terms; after ten years of critical scrutiny of the Marxist record in China, several other students have come to the same conclusion.[11] Nevertheless, Schwartz opened his book with the caveat: "It is *not* [this study's] primary purpose to consider the [Chinese Communist revolutionary] movement in terms of the 'objective' social and political conditions which have encouraged its growth, or in terms of its effect on the masses."[12] As a strategist of the revolutionary seizure of power, however, Mao Tse-tung was interested in nothing else but "its effect on the masses."

During the nineteen-twenties and early thirties, Mao discovered the revolutionary advantages that might be obtained from exploiting the agrarian question. But there was another concern of Mao's, one as old or older than his concern for peasant problems and one of much greater historical continuity. This was Mao's concern with revolutionary war. Among the various streams of theoretical interest to be found in the "thought of Mao Tse-tung," it is the one of revolutionary war that certain Chinese Communist leaders—all of them apparent winners in the 1966 inner-party struggle for leadership—tend to regard as the essence of Mao's contribution to Communist theory.

Lin Piao, for example, argues:

> Comrade Mao Tse-tung's theory of and policies for people's war have creatively enriched and developed Marxism-Leninism. The Chinese people's victory in the Anti-Japanese War was a victory for people's war, for Marxism-Leninism and the thought of Mao Tse-tung. . . . The special feature of the Chinese revolution was armed revolution against armed counter-revolution. The main form of struggle was war and the main form of organization was the army which was under the absolute leadership of the Chinese

[10] *Ibid.*, p. 4.

[11] See e.g., Stuart Schram, *Mao Tse-tung* (Harmondsworth, England: Penguin Books, 1966); Donald M. Lowe, *The Function of "China" in Marx, Lenin, and Mao* (Berkeley and Los Angeles: University of California Press, 1966); and John E. Rue, *Mao Tse-tung in Opposition, 1927–1935* (Stanford, Calif.: Stanford University Press, 1966).

[12] Schwartz, *Chinese Communism*, p. 1.

Communist Party, while all the other forms of organization and struggle led by our Party were co-ordinated, directly or indirectly, with the war.[13]

Yeh Chien-ying echoes, "Military affairs form the most brilliant facet in the life of Chairman Mao. We are all his students."[14] Even Ch'en Po-ta, the most anxious of Chinese writers on Maoism to maintain Mao's Stalinist orthodoxy, writes, "The establishment of revolutionary bases by armed force was the starting point of the road along which Mao Tse-tung guided the revolution to nation-wide victory."[15] In a different essay on Mao's thought, Ch'en adds, "The mass line is the key to activating all kinds of work; it is also the means with which Comrade Mao Tse-tung has correctly led the Chinese revolution."[16]

What is the relationship between Mao's theory of the mass line and his strategy of people's war? The answer to this question is complex, but it is the heart of Mao Tse-tung's thought during the Yenan period and again today; without it, the issues that divided the Chinese Communist leadership during the Socialist Education Campaign cannot be understood. From the time of Mao's flight with the survivors of the Autumn Harvest Uprising into Chingkangshan, he sought to find a way around Trotsky's old warning that a revolutionary party can succeed without the army, but it cannot succeed against it.[17] Mao believed that, given correct policies and leadership, an armed revolution could be made to succeed against the professional armies of the Nationalists and local rulers.

Mao began his approach to this problem by admitting the military inferiority, absolutely and in detail, of his small band of mutineers and peasant rebels vis-à-vis the enemy's forces. His grand strategy, in its most fundamental military sense, was to obtain a decisive intelligence advantage over his otherwise invincible foes. If he could obtain near-perfect intelligence concerning his enemies' strength and movements—

13 *Long Live the Victory of People's War* (Peking: Foreign Languages Press, 1965), pp. 3, 26.

14 People's Liberation Army, General Political Department, *Kung-tso t'ung-hsün* [Bulletin of Activities], no. 26 (July 13, 1961).

15 *Mao Tse-tung on the Chinese Revolution* (Peking: Foreign Languages Press, 1963), p. 29. (Originally written in 1951.)

16 *Notes on Ten Years of Civil War (1927–1936)* (Peking: Foreign Languages Press, 1954), p. 97. (Originally written in 1944.)

17 Leon Trotsky, *The Russian Revolution*, abridged ed. (New York: Double-day Anchor Books, 1959), p. 318.

and at the same time deny such intelligence to the enemy—he could begin to correct the material and professional imbalance between the two antagonists. With intelligence, he could set ambushes, concentrate superior numbers in any battle, choose his time and place of fighting, avoid all evenly-matched or unfavorable engagements, escape mopping-up campaigns, and demoralize the enemy's rank and file.

Thirty-five years after the fact, Nationalist leaders were able to describe exactly where Mao Tse-tung had been superior when they fought him during the first Anti-Communist Encirclement Campaign (December, 1930–January, 1931):

> The intelligence collection capability of the Kiangsi Soviet in late 1930 was already a tribute to [a] year of Communist totalitarianism. Small boys, members of the Youth Corps, sitting beside a hundred dusty trails scattered from one end of the Soviet to the other; old men and women, staying behind when fresh government troops entered an otherwise deserted village; cooperative young women, entering government bivouacs to entertain the lonely Hunanese peasants [government forces in the first campaign were drawn chiefly from Hunan and Kwangtung]; Communist "defectors," infiltrating government units [that were] suffering from rising losses and failing morale; old men offering themselves as "guides"; all were members of a finely-spun web of information that, in its total effect, gave the Communist military leaders almost perfect vision, down to the tactical level. The government troops, on the other hand, thanks to the counter-intelligence efforts of the Communists, moved into a vacuum of information as they plunged deeper into the Soviet.[18]

With this type of intelligence organization, Mao Tse-tung enjoyed a tactical advantage despite his overall strategic inferiority; and by committing himself to a long struggle of attrition, so long as the government was unable to break his intelligence organization, he ultimately achieved strategic equality and, finally, strategic superiority as well.

The fundamental dynamic problem of this strategy is how to create the web of intelligence upon which it is based. Mao's solution of this

---

[18] Lt. Col. William W. Whitson, U.S. Army, and Lt. Gen. Liu Chi-ming, Republic of China Army, ret., *A Strategy for Counter-Insurgency* (Taipei: privately distributed, 1966), p. 5. For a thorough study of the military aspects of Chinese Communist strategy, see H. L. Boorman and S. A. Boorman, "Chinese Communist Insurgent Warfare, 1935–49," *Political Science Quarterly*, 81 (1966): 171–95.

problem is contained in the organizational techniques of the mass line. By arousing the mass of the population and organizing them into a common united front, the party obtains decisive advantages over its opponent in intelligence, recruitment, mobility, morale, and capacity for superior concentration in any pitched battle. Without the mass line, there could be no "people's war" as the Chinese Communist Party conceives it.

According to the mass line, the party must meet the people on the basis of formal equality and it must engineer an ad hoc community of interests with them. The problem of equality extends also to the rank and file of the Communist army, since it must be recruited and systematically enlarged from among the people. Mao is one of the most inventive of guerrilla leaders in devising principles and rules in order to project an image of the Communist army as the equal—indeed, as the servant— of the population rather than as the weapon of a revolutionary elite. He created the so-called "three-eight style" to ensure that the army avoided actions that might damage its relations with the population, and his party camouflaged its own pervasive control over the army by establishing "political officers," in all cases party members, within the military hierarchy itself.[19]

Probably the most famous of Mao's egalitarian devices was that of "internal army democracy," an organizational technique that Mao and Lin Piao reintroduced throughout the People's Liberation Army (PLA) in 1965. As the New China News Agency wrote on June 7, 1965, "The practice of political democracy, economic democracy, and military democracy in the PLA, a concrete embodiment of the mass line of the Chinese Communist Party and the theory of Chairman Mao Tse-tung on army building, has strengthened the political unity of the officers and men and of the higher and lower levels." On June 8, 1965, *Jen-min jih-pao* (People's Daily) interpreted internal army democracy as one of the key elements of the strategy of people's war:

> At the very earliest stages of the building of our army, Comrade Mao Tse-tung made it clear that a revolutionary army must practice democracy under centralized guidance. . . . During the Anti-Japanese War and the War of Liberation, the People's Liberation

[19] On the "three-eight style" and the organization of party political work in the army, see Ho Lung, *Democratic Traditions of the Chinese People's Liberation Army* (Peking: Foreign Languages Press, 1965), pp. 12–15; Chalmers Johnson, *Peasant Nationalism and Communist Power* (Stanford, Calif.: Stanford University Press, 1962), pp. 76–84; and Johnson, "Lin Piao's Army and Its Role in Chinese Society," *Current Scene*, 4, nos. 13 and 14 (1966).

Army took over the Red Army's democratic tradition and greatly enhanced the class consciousness of the commanders and fighters and the combat effectiveness of the armed forces by applying democracy in the political, economic, and military spheres. That is why, united as one man, the army equipped with inferior equipment was able to defeat the superior enemy.

Although the Communist army's so-called "Chu-ke Liang Meetings" may occasionally have enhanced combat effectiveness through rank-and-file criticism of inept leadership or by eliciting basic intelligence information from locally-based soldiers, there is scarcely any evidence to support such a claim. Army democracy was, instead, a technique for evoking commitment through a façade of self-determination; it was not predicated on a positive valuation of political freedom. As *Kung-jen jih-pao* (Worker's Daily) explained:

> Of course, the democracy we are to promote is democracy under centralized guidance, not the extreme democracy in a state of anarchy. For democracy and centralization are two facets of a unity contradictory to each other, and neither can be dispensed with. What we practice is centralization on the democratic basis and democracy under centralized guidance; such is democratic centralism. The purpose of freely promoting democracy is, in the final analysis, to arouse fully the enthusiasm and initiative of the masses, to guarantee smooth progress of the socialist revolution and socialist construction.[20]

Through such devices as the "three-eight style," political work, and internal army democracy, Mao's armies were able to meet the people as equals, sometimes even as partners. This in itself was a revolutionary accomplishment in China, but it alone would not have gotten the strategy of people's war underway. The heart of the matter was always the popular united front: could the revolutionary directorate discover some issue salient among the masses which the party might champion, thereby giving it access to the masses and allowing the party to organize them for guerrilla warfare?

As a revolutionary strategist, with his own basic values and goals thoroughly compartmentalized, Mao Tse-tung recognized the need to exploit opportunistically *any* political issue that might bring about the desired level of mass organization. Tactical flexibility with regard to matters of Marxist ideology is the most fundamental attribute of Mao's

[20] *Kung-jen jih-pao* [Worker's Daily] (editorial), January 30, 1965.

theory of people's war. Moreover, the entire record of inner-party struggle during the Kiangsi and Yenan periods concerns Mao's efforts to get his idea of the flexible use of united front accepted by his party colleagues. Only Mao, the master tactician, was able to support a variety of different positions without confusing them with his own Marxist commitments or forgetting that his fundamental objective was a Communist party victory. During the revolution he always based his operations on the mass line: in order to find out what kind of political program the masses will support, he argued, go among them and ask them. Mao's approach may have been bad Marxism, but it was superb guerrilla-war technique.

Following his personal "Report of an Investigation into the Peasant Movement in Hunan" (1927), Mao concluded that the peasants—which is to say, in China, the great majority of the population—were ready to revolt because of landlord exploitation; and he proposed offering to confiscate and redistribute landlords' and rich peasants' land if the mass of the peasantry would support his army in return. His proposals were not at variance with official Communist party policy, as Jerome Ch'en has shown.[21] Where he did differ from party directives was in his freedom from Marxist dogmatism in carrying out the policy and in his insight into the relationship between agrarian reform and revolutionary army building. As Ch'en argues:

> Since survival and expansion were the foremost tasks at the [Chingkangshan] base, the land policy had to be adapted to the accomplishment of such tasks. Here Mao's attention was concentrated on the "middle class," the rich peasants and small landowners who should not be unwisely alienated by harsh and excessively radical measures. While at the Chingkangshan base, Mao carried out the Party's policy of indiscriminate confiscation of all land, but later, in April 1929, he introduced a milder land policy at Hsingkuo by confiscating only the land belonging to the local government and landlords.[22]

In fact, Mao tinkered with land-reform policies throughout the Kiangsi period, particularly at times when he was not constrained by the ideologically rigid leaders of the party. His criterion of an effective land policy was always whether it promoted or detracted from the building of his army.

21 *Mao and the Chinese Revolution* (London: Oxford University Press, 1965), p. 111.
22 *Ibid.*, p. 162.

The real evidence of Mao's tactical flexibility in implementing the mass line appears in his analysis of the various "contradictions" that existed within Chinese society. As early as 1930, he had identified the following issues as potentially exploitable bases for the mass line: (1) the contradictions between imperialism and the Chinese nation, and among imperialists themselves; (2) the contradictions within the counter-revolutionary ruling cliques; (3) the contradictions between rulers and the broad masses of the ruled; (4) the contradictions between the landlords and the peasantry; (5) the contradictions between the bourgeoisie and the working class; (6) the contradictions between warlords and their troops; and (7) the contradictions between the counter-revolutionary regime and the intellectuals and students.[23] At the outset of his guerrilla revolution, Mao chose number four—the contradictions inherent in the agrarian situation—as the most promising immediate basis for the mass line, and he experimented with several different formulations of Red Army land policy in trying to exploit this issue. But he never forgot the other contradictions and always stood ready to shift his efforts to one of them in light of changing political realities. It was the inflexibility of his Moscow-trained colleagues—for example, their failure to exploit the 1933 rebellion of Ts'ai T'ing-k'ai in Fukien (an instance of contradictions numbers one and two)—that Mao later denounced as "left deviationism," although it remains questionable whether or not Mao himself advocated supporting Ts'ai in 1933.

The political situation actually did begin to change significantly in 1931, and Mao Tse-tung began to adjust his strategy along with it. As Ch'en Po-ta recalls:

> In 1931, as a result of the occupation of Northeast China by Japanese imperialists certain changes took place in the political relations of classes in China, but there was still no change in the views of the "Left" opportunists. This "Leftist" mistake constituted the main danger at that time because it hindered the Party from linking itself with the broad masses and from taking full advantage of the various contradictions to facilitate the revolution.[24]

The error of all deviationists in the thirties and forties was to take party pronouncements too seriously in an ideological sense. After Mao shifted the mass line to a nationalistic, anti-Japanese united front, the

[23] "A Single Spark Can Start a Prairie Fire," (January 1930), *Selected Works*, vol. 1 (New York: International Publishers, 1954), pp. 119–21; and Ch'en Po-ta, *Ten Years of Civil War*, pp. 29–30.

[24] *Mao Tse-tung on the Chinese Revolution*, p. 41.

same "leftist" deviationists of the Kiangsi Period now committed right-wing errors: they mistakenly believed that the long-range objective of the anti-Japanese united front was to defeat Japan and preserve China from foreign conquest. Ch'en continues:

> But after the anti-Japanese national front was formed in 1937, some comrades represented by Ch'en Shao-yü [Wang Ming], who had committed "Leftist" mistakes, then committed [a] Rightist mistake. The Rightist mistake constituted the main danger at that time because it hindered the Party from struggling against the reactionaries and the reactionary trends in the united front and exposed the proletariat to the danger of losing its independence.[25]

As we shall see, Mao was always arguing with comrades who did not understand the requirements of people's war; Mao gained leadership over the party in 1935, but the thought of Mao Tse-tung did not win its final victory until after the *cheng-feng* movement of 1942–44.

When, in January, 1935, Mao became chairman of the Central Committee's Political Bureau, one of his first acts was to put forward the slogan *"pei-shang k'ang-Jih"* ("go north to fight the Japanese") in order to bolster the deteriorating morale of his harried Long March soldiers.[26] Mao had probably decided to shift to this new mass-line policy some time earlier, and in his Seventh Party Congress address, Chu Teh tried to explain the entire Long March in terms of "a great strategic transfer" of the First Front Army "to put itself in a position to fight Japanese aggression in North China."[27] The logic of Mao's shift in mass-line tactics was pure "people's war," and no one ever expressed this logic with greater candor than one of Mao's Kiangsi rivals, Po Ku. On June 20, 1937, in an interview with Nym Wales, Po Ku (Ch'in Pang-hsien) explained, "For nine years we have struggled under the Soviet slogan and have had no success in the whole of China. The petty bourgeois masses and others did not support the Soviet slogan but they can support the nationalist and democratic slogan."[28]

From the point of view of Mao's theory, the earlier attempts to exploit the agrarian question had not been ill-advised; it was, rather, that

---

[25] *Ibid.*

[26] Jerome Ch'en, *Mao and the Chinese Revolution*, p. 189.

[27] *The Battle Front of the Liberated Areas* (Peking: Foreign Languages Press, 1955), p. 16, n. 1. (Originally written in April 1945 as a report for the Seventh Congress.)

[28] Nym Wales, "My Yenan Notebooks" (mimeographed; Madison, Conn.: 1961), p. 121.

new events opened up much more promising opportunities. Moreover, the agrarian strategy had not worked well enough. In 1934 the party enjoyed the support of from seven to nine million people in the central China soviets, but that was not enough to prevent Chiang Kai-shek from encircling and destroying the Communist enclaves. In 1936, after the Long March, the Communists held only north Shensi, with a population of from 500,000 to 900,000, and their army was down to 80,000–90,000 men. Nym Wales summarized Mao's answer to this problem very simply: "In 1934 all provinces cooperated against the Reds, so they had to decide to get new allies on the basis of resisting Japan."[29]

Mao Tse-tung faced two major difficulties in shifting the tactical basis of people's war to an anti-Japanese line. The first was that, prior to the Japanese invasion—the exact timing of which he was unable to foresee even though he did predict Japanese aggression against China—Mao was open to severe attack from rigid Marxist dogmatists—so-called "Trotskyites" in the Chinese Communist parlance of the time—for selling out the domestic social revolution. The second was that, after the Lukouch'iao Incident, the new tactic worked so well his party was in danger of being inundated with newly-recruited patriots, and his personal rivals in the party now tried to use the Kuomintang-Communist united front against him.

Mao dealt with the first problem by moving very slowly. In 1936 the party experimented with the new anti-Japanese line in its invasion of Shansi. Ho Ch'ang-kung described the results. "When we reached Shansi we still had the land redistribution program, but the main slogan was against traitors. But we formed no Soviets, only [National] Salvation Associations. Even the landlords welcomed us and sent contributions for the anti-Japanese struggle."[30] The party's full implementation of the anti-Japanese strategy led to a drastic modification in its land policy and dictated the stand taken by Chou En-lai during the Sian Incident of December, 1936.

Possibly the most crucial period in the entire history of the Chinese Communist revolution occurred between the Sian Incident, December 12, 1936, and the outbreak of war with Japan on July 7, 1937. Nym Wales, who was in Yenan at that time, indicates the issues at stake:

> Mao Tse-tung . . . was one of the few persons who thought a war between China and Japan was imminent in 1937. As early as August, 1935, he began reorganizing his party line to meet this war situation. It was not an easy task to bring all the Communists

---

[29] *Ibid.*, p. 84.   [30] *Ibid.*, p. 39.

into line, and there was some trouble about deciding to give up the Soviets in the beginning. Even when I was in the Soviet districts in the summer of 1937, there was a big campaign against potential Leftists and Trotskyists, who did not want to cooperate with the Kuomintang. But Mao succeeded without causing a split in his Party. . . . July 7, the day of the Lukouch'iao Incident, was a day of great victory for Mao, vindicating his political omniscience and right to leadership of the Chinese revolution.[31]

Differing from virtually all other political groups in China, Mao was ready for the Japanese invasion. "The very day after the Lukouch'iao Incident," Chu Teh recalls, "the Central Committee of our Party and all officers and men of the people's army issued an appeal for the people's army to be sent to the front to fight the Japanese."[32]

Mao's wartime mass line consisted of two complementary policies. The first was the organizing of the rear-area population, which had been mobilized by the brutality of the Japanese invasion and occupation, through an appeal to its nationalist and patriotic interests; the second was the double-faceted policy known as *chien-tsu chien-hsi* ("reduce rent and reduce interest") and *chiao-tsu chiao-hsi* ("pay rent and pay interest").[33] These policies proved to be fantastically successful. According to details and maps published in *Jen-min jih-pao* on the twentieth anniversary of the defeat of Japan, by 1945 the Communists controlled six rear-area guerrilla bases in North China, ten in Central China, and two in South China. Adding in Shen-Kan-Ning, which was not invaded by the Japanese, there were 19 Communist enclaves with a total population of 160,000,000.[34] This was approximately an eighteenfold increase in the party's mass following over that of the Kiangsi Period.

Mao differed from many foreign and domestic observers of his revolution in believing that the peasants were potential patriots, not solely tillers of the soil and payers of land rent. He had long recognized that

[31] *Ibid.*, p. 211.

[32] *Battle Front*, p. 17.

[33] Hu Hua (ed.), *Chung-kuo ko-ming shih chiang-i* [Lectures on the History of the Chinese Revolution] (Peking: Chung-kuo jen-min ta-hsüeh ch'u-pan-she, 1962), p. 420.

[34] *Jen-min jih-pao*, August 27, 1965, p. 5. See also *K'ang-Jih chan-cheng shih-ch'i chieh-fang-ch'ü kai-k'uang* [A General View of the Liberated Areas during the War of Resistance against Japan] (Peking: Jen-min ch'u-pan-she, 1953); and Johnson, *Peasant Nationalism and Communist Power*.

the peasants were politically isolated and lacked organization,[35] but he also recognized that the Sino-Japanese War was ending their isolation and creating new demands among them for organization. As Mao wrote in *On Protracted War* (1938):

> Such a gigantic national revolutionary war as ours cannot succeed without universal and thoroughgoing political mobilization. China was greatly remiss in failing to undertake anti-Japanese political mobilization before the war of resistance. By this, she lost a move to the enemy. Even after the war of resistance began, political mobilization had been far from universal, let alone thoroughgoing. News about the war reached the great majority of the people through the enemy's shelling and air bombing. That also constituted a kind of mobilization, but it was done by the enemy, not by ourselves. People in remote regions who cannot hear the guns lead a tranquil life even now. This situation must be changed, otherwise there can be no victory for our life-and-death struggle.[36]

Mao's political workers, attached to every level of the Communist armies then infiltrating behind the Japanese lines, did their best to change this situation. The result was that peasants of all strata, landlords who had not fled in the face of the invasion, students and middle-class refugees from the cities, all responded to the party's call for armed resistance in a way that they had never done before in answer to a Communist party program.

Mao's success in creating a genuine mass line itself created problems. One was the tendency of several regional party leaders to become so absorbed in fighting Japan that they neglected the party's long-term interests. As a recent party history reveals:

> After the outbreak of the Anti-Japanese War in 1937, the main danger in the party was rightwing capitulationism, a view held by

[35] Mao's chronicler, Ch'en Po-ta, writes: "There is no doubt that since China is primarily an agricultural country, the Chinese proletariat and its political party cannot succeed in the revolution if it does not keep contact and unite with the peasant masses, if it does not organize a solid alliance of the workers and peasants. At the same time, as the peasant masses are politically and organizationally weak, they cannot liberate themselves until they clearly see their political objective and organize themselves under the leadership of the proletariat and its political party" (*Ten Years of Civil War*, p. 40).

[36] As translated in Stuart Schram, *The Political Thought of Mao Tse-tung* (New York: Praeger, 1963), pp. 208–9.

persons who, in the name of the united front, wanted to compromise with the Kuomintang. . . . Wang Ming personified this capitulationism, which he implemented within the Yangtze Bureau [Ch'ang-chiang Chü] in December, 1937. He praised all of those who fought against Japan as his friends and lauded the Kuomintang. He stressed agreement with the Kuomintang in the anti-Japanese united front, and he distorted the position of the anti-Japanese war in the Chinese revolution. He did not recognize that it was a part of the development of a new democracy, and he believed that after the war Chiang Kai-shek would rule China. He advocated a liberalization of party discipline, and he published his erroneous views without respect to the policy of the Central Committee of the CCP.[37]

Mao counterattacked against Wang and the remnants of the "Returned Bolsheviks" faction with a barrage of pamphlets and articles stressing the correctness of his policies of guerrilla warfare, criticizing Kuomintang leadership of the resistance (Mao argued his own concept of "protracted war" as opposed to what he called Chiang's concept of "rapid victory"), and assuring the people of eventual victory—so long as they learned and followed his strategy. (It is significant that of the 158 articles in the four volumes of the *Selected Works of Mao Tse-tung*, 93 were written in Yenan.)[38] On November 6, 1938, Mao convened in Yenan the Enlarged Sixth Plenary Session of the Central Committee, the first plenum held since 1934, in order to strengthen party guidance over the ever-expanding resistance movement. At this plenum, Mao issued instructions for the organization of party committees at every level of the rear-area hierarchy, created party inspection committees at various levels, and demanded adherence to the principle of democratic centralism.[39]

Also at the Sixth Plenum, Mao returned to an old theme. He stressed that the war was promoting a Communist victory in the Chinese revolution, not because it made possible the second Kuomintang-Communist

[37] Hu Hua (ed.), *Chung-kuo ko-ming shih*, pp. 379–81.

[38] "Mao Tse-tung's Thought Is the Common Treasure of the World's Revolutionary People: An Account of the Visits of Foreign Friends to Yenan," *Peking Review*, September 30, 1966, p. 18.

[39] Wang Chien-min, *Chung-kuo Kung-ch'an-tang shih-kao* [A Draft History of the Chinese Communist Party], vol. 3 (Taipei: published by author, 1965), p. 286; Hu Hua (ed.), *Chung-kuo ko-ming shih*, p. 387.

united front and thereby gave a few Communists voices in the Chungking government, but because it offered ideal conditions for enlarging the Communist army. According to historian Hu Hua:

> In his criticism of rightwing trends, Mao contended that rightwing elements did not recognize the importance of armed struggle in the Chinese revolution. Without armed struggle, revolutionary tasks could not be achieved: the main form of struggle in China was war and the main instrument was the army. Rightwing elements in the Party, failing to recognize the significance of armed force, relied instead on legal movements, such as those afforded by the united front in Wuhan.[40]

Mao never saw the second united front in Leninist terms—that is, as a vehicle for positioning the CCP in order to attempt a coup d'état.[41] Instead, Mao consistently conceived of the Chinese revolution as a revolutionary war, and with that in mind, he supported the united front only so long as it helped to advance his military preparedness. Mao was quite willing to see the collapse of the united front rather than have his armies absorbed into the Kuomintang forces.

Mao's policies naturally elicited a strong anti-Communist response from factions within the Kuomintang (KMT). Nationalist armies reestablished the blockade of Shen-Kan-Ning that they had lifted in 1937, and in January, 1941, KMT forces wiped out or captured some 8,000 Communist regulars, whom the KMT accused of spreading Communism under the guise of resisting Japan, in the so-called South Anhwei, or New Fourth Army, Incident. The effects of these actions on the Communists were severe, but Mao Tse-tung adroitly turned them into long-term advantages. The blockade, combined with Japanese pressures, gave rise to the so-called Great Production Movement (1940–45) in the border areas; and as we shall see, this movement produced organizational forms and concrete results that have influenced the Communist movement down to the present time.

The South Anhwei Incident actually advanced Mao's mass line. After the disaster Mao denounced the KMT for its treachery and successfully characterized it in his propaganda as little better than the Japanese puppets. He also put forth a twelve-point demand for democratic gov-

[40] *Chung-kuo ko-ming shih,* p. 384.

[41] For an analysis of the differences between Lenin's and Mao's strategies of revolution, see Johnson, *Revolutionary Change* (Boston: Little, Brown, 1966), chap. 8.

ernment in China, a demand that was and remained very embarrassing to the KMT internationally. In March, 1941, the KMT attempted to recover its advantage by convening the first session of the Second People's Political Council, but the CCP refused to attend so long as the KMT insisted on a unitary political and military command within the united front. The net result of the South Anhwei Incident was a perceptible shift in loyalties among middle-of-the-road factions to the Communist side.

Also in March, 1941, largely as a reaction to the South Anhwei Incident, a federation of liberal democratic groups opposed to the Nationalists' single-party dictatorship formed the Democratic League. The League's platform called for the granting of a constitution, protection of civil rights, and the peaceful resolution of disputes between the Communists and the Nationalists. On September 18, 1941, the tenth anniversary of the Manchurian Incident, the League began publishing its influential *Kuang-ming jih-pao* in Hong Kong. Throughout the resistance and civil wars the League helped to legitimatize the Communist party through its "liberal democratic" propaganda against the Kuomintang. The final irony came in the anti-rightist campaign of 1957, when the League itself was thoroughly purged of all its "bourgeois rightist liberals."

Another of Mao's problems connected with the success of his mass line, one closely related to that of right-wing capitulationism among party leaders, was the very rapid growth of the party itself. According to Communist sources, there were 40,000 party members in 1937 (the same number as in 1928 but 260,000 below the high of 300,000 reached in 1933); by 1940 this figure had grown to 800,000, and by 1945, to 1,211,128.[42] Party historians themselves describe these new members as being 90 per cent petty bourgeois in origin.[43] Something had to be done, particularly under the heavy Japanese pressure that began in 1940, to counteract the wavering, defeatism, and criticism of party leadership among them. Most of these new party members had joined the party from patriotic motives; and they had to be educated in Mao's version of Communist ideology without at the same time losing their fundamentally nationalistic commitment.

According to a Communist study of the Chin-Chi-Lu-Yü (Shansi-Hopei-Shantung-Honan) base, Mao began his "rectification" of the

[42] See the statistical chart compiled by John W. Lewis, *Leadership in Communist China* (Ithaca: Cornell University Press, 1963), p. 110.

[43] Hu Hua (ed.), *Chung-kuo ko-ming shih,* p. 422.

party in 1940 with a purge. The leadership was purified on the basis of members' class backgrounds, the leadership's proletarian nucleus was strengthened, and opportunists in the party were weeded out.[44] Then, in March, 1942, the educational campaign got under way in Yenan and spread, in April, to the guerrilla areas. In July, 1943, the rectification movement was carried to the *hsien* level and into the armed forces. Most of the basic study materials used in the campaign were Mao's works, including *On Protracted War, On Contradiction, Reform Our Study, Rectify the Party's Style in Work,* and *Oppose the Party's "Eight-Legged Essay"*; and Mao gave a special series of lectures to the reformees in Yenan, the most famous being his "Talks at the Yenan Forum on Art and Literature."

The essence of Mao's message to the neophytes, according to Hu Hua, concerned the dangers of "subjectivism." This evil manifested itself in the party in two ways—either as dogmatism or as empiricism. In attacking dogmatism, Mao reinforced the nationalistic commitment of his listeners. Dogmatism, he said, was blind to the revolutionary situation in China; it ignored Chinese history and the problem of creatively applying Marxism-Leninism in China. Dogmatists engaged in theorizing for its own sake, and they underestimated the contributions of the workers and peasants. Mao traced the origins of dogmatism back to Confucian scholarship, which he said ignored practice. Empiricism, on the other hand, Mao traced to the characteristic way of thought of the petty bourgeois class. It hindered party unity, but it could be overcome if new party members would adhere rigidly to the principle of democratic centralism. Mao then directed that party members purge themselves of subjectivism, dogmatism, and empiricism through the methods of criticism and self-criticism.

The result of the *cheng-feng* campaign, according to the Communists, was to eliminate the deviationist tendencies that had existed in the party line since 1931; from the point of view of the external observer, the *cheng-feng* established the thought of Mao Tse-tung as the official ideology of the Chinese Communist Party. This first inner-party rectification movement laid the ideological foundation for the Seventh Party Congress of 1945 and created degrees of unity and control within the

[44] Ch'i Wu (ed.), *I-ko ko-ming ken-chü-ti ti ch'eng-chang: K'ang-Jih chan-cheng ho chieh-fang chan-cheng shih-ch'i ti Chin-Chi-Lu-Yü pien-ch'ü kai-k'uang* [The Establishment and Growth of a Revolutionary Base: A General Account of the Shansi-Hopei-Shantung-Honan Border Region during the Anti-Japanese War and the War of Liberation] (Peking: Jen-min ch'u-pan-she, 1958), p. 205.

party that did not call forth further purges or rectification until the civil war was well under way.[45]

In addition to appealing to the nationalism generated by the invasion, Mao's wartime mass line also made an appeal to the economic interests of the peasants through the "reduce rent, reduce interest" campaign. The policy itself was initiated in 1937, before the war broke out, as part of the price Mao had to pay in order to obtain a united front from the KMT; Chiang required that the Communists abandon their earlier policy of forcibly confiscating and redistributing the property of landlords and rich peasants. As we have seen, Mao himself had already come to the conclusion that the contradictions within imperialism offered him a better mass-line platform than the contradictions surrounding the agrarian situation; therefore he was willing to end the old program. But, as a revolutionary tactician, he did not rely solely on the appeal to nationalism. His reduced-rent program helped to solidify a good deal of his rear-area peasant support, which he won initially on the basis of resistance to the invaders.

The most complete policy statement of the economic mass line during the war is the Central Committee's "Decision Concerning the Land Policy of the Anti-Japanese Resistance Bases" of January 28, 1942, published in *Chieh-fang jih-pao* (Liberation Daily), February 6, 1942. This decision set down three basic principles of land policy to be adhered to throughout the period of the resistance war:

(1) Peasants (including sharecroppers) are the basic strength for sustaining the war effort and production. Therefore, the land policy must help the peasants, must reduce feudal exploitation, must bring about reduced rent and interest, and must assure the peasants of their personal, political, and property rights. This policy is intended to improve peasant livelihood and heighten peasant enthusiasm for production and the war effort.

(2) It is conceded that the majority of landlords want to resist Japanese aggression and that many enlightened gentry are for democratic reforms. Therefore, the land policy is only to go so far as to help the peasants and lessen their burden of feudal exploitation; it is not to wipe out once and for all the system of feudal exploitation in the present stage of development. If it did, the support of the enlightened gentry might be alienated. Radical

[45] Hu Hua (ed.), *Chung-kuo ko-ming shih,* pp. 421–29. The next *cheng-feng* came in 1948 to correct excesses in the carrying out of the land-reform movement in the old liberated areas.

land confiscation without compensation is to be used only in dealing with Chinese traitors to the war of resistance.

(3) It is conceded that the capitalistic mode of production is still an advanced form of production for China at this stage of development. The [support of the] petty bourgeois and national bourgeois classes in particular is indispensable to production and to the war of resistance.[46]

The party vigorously pushed this campaign on at least three different occasions: in April, 1940, in May, 1942, and in a "follow-up" campaign during the winter of 1944/45. We can only speculate about what the peasants thought of the campaign, but we do know that the numbers of middle peasants during this period increased appreciably, at the expense of both rich and poor peasants. Table 1 presents data collected from 15 "representative villages" located in 12 different *hsien* in the T'ai Hang district of the Chin-Chi-Lu-Yü Border Region on the results of the *chien-tsu chien-hsi* policy.

The figures in table 1 reveal a marked growth in the number of middle peasant households, a change brought about chiefly by raising the level of land ownership among former poor peasants. The land made available to the poor peasants came primarily from the sale of surpluses formerly held by absentee landlords. The data on average size of farm per household serve as a check, since they show that the farm size for middle peasants did not change as the stratum increased in numbers, although average farm sizes for landlords and rich peasants declined sharply. The figures also reveal the anomalous fact that the percentage of land owned by rich peasants increased between May, 1942, and the winter of 1944. The government explains this development by arguing that during 1943 it encouraged a rich peasant economy in order to increase production and that, for the same reason, many landlords were redesignated rich peasants.[47] The important point about these figures and about the entire rent reduction scheme is that it was not a radical program. Far from constituting an "agricultural revolution," it in fact tended to recreate the traditional patterns of rural land use on a more equitable, and therefore more stable, basis.

It is true that *chien-tsu chien-hsi* was not the party's sole wartime economic measure directed toward the peasantry. There was a co-opera-

[46] Ch'i Wu (ed.), *I-ko ko-ming ken-chü-ti*, pp. 119–20. See also Chao Kuo-chun, *Agrarian Policy of the Chinese Communist Party* (Bombay: Asia Publishing House, 1960), pp. 41–47.

[47] Ch'i Wu (ed.), *I-ko Ko-ming ken-chü-ti*, p. 128.

TABLE 1

EFFECTS OF RENT REDUCTION CAMPAIGN, 1940–1945*

Social Stratum	1940–42	May, 1942	1944–45
	Percentages of Households per Social Stratum		
Landlords	2.75	2.02	1.65
Entrepreneurial landlords (*ching-ying ti-chu*)	.50	.41	.33
Rich peasants	7.25	6.90	5.99
Middle peasants	37.80	46.79	55.20
Poor peasants	48.95	42.12	33.33
Sharecroppers	1.88	.95	.49
Totals	99.13	99.19	96.99
	Percentages of Farmland per Social Stratum		
Landlords	23.04	8.79	3.64
Entrepreneurial landlords (*ching-ying ti-chu*)	1.59	.91	.58
Rich peasants	18.68	14.53	17.18
Middle peasants	37.02	54.87	60.85
Poor peasants	18.98	20.05	17.01
Sharecroppers	.25	.39	.18
Totals	99.56	99.54	99.44
	Average Farm Size per Household (In *mou*)		
Landlords	98.64	42.28	
Entrepreneurial landlords (*ching-ying ti-chu*)	37.32	21.82	
Rich peasants	30.37	20.74	
Middle peasants	11.56	11.54	
Poor peasants	4.57	4.69	
Sharecroppers	1.57	4.26	

* Derived from Ch'i Wu (ed.), *I-ko ko-ming ken-chü-ti ti ch'eng-chang: K'ang-Jih chan-cheng ho chieh-fang chan-cheng shih-ch'i ti Chin-Chi-Lu-Yü pien-ch'ü kai-k'uang* [The Establishment and Growth of a Revolutionary Base: A General Account of the Shansi-Hopei-Shantung-Honan Border Region during the Anti-Japanese War and the War of Liberation] (Peking: Jen-min ch'u-pan-she, 1958), p. 127. Percentages do not total 100 because the editor has dropped the stratum "Other," usually less than 1 per cent, from the original survey data. Names of the surveyed villages are given in the source.

tive movement in Chin-Chi-Lu-Yü, beginning in 1943, but it was a modest effort. Figures from 19 *hsien* in the old liberated area of T'ai Hang show 418 co-ops (91,929 members) in June 1943; 1,177 co-ops (250,507 members) on December 31, 1944; and 4,166 strictly village co-ops (740,000 members) on December 31, 1946.[48] Moreover, Chin-Chi-Lu-Yü, being an old liberated area, carried out land reform—that is, the destruction of the landlord class and the redistribution of land on an equal basis—between July, 1946, and August, 1948. However, even this campaign, radical as it was, did not destroy the traditional rural socioeconomic structure in the way that collectivization and communization attempted to do a decade later. All of the wartime campaigns reinforced the old patterns that had existed before landlord exploitation became extreme; in this sense, the wartime campaigns were more like the spontaneous land reform of the Russian peasants in 1917 than like Stalin's collectivization measures.

Without doubt, *chien-tsu chien-hsi* and land reform helped to win peasant support for the CCP and encouraged peasants to trust the Communists and to work harder for the resistance and for the revolution. The two facets of Mao's mass line—appeals to nationalism and mild reform of agriculture—thus reinforced each other. However, it does not follow that Mao's wartime agrarian policy was either in accordance with his Communist vision of how agriculture ultimately should be organized or that the peasantry welcomed this ultimate vision because they welcomed his wartime policies. The peasants supported an agrarian policy designed to further the war effort and, with the exception of landlords and rich peasants, they profited from it. However, when a radically socialist conception of rural organization was presented to them in 1958 and after, they did not necessarily see merit in or support it.

One measure of the organizational success of Mao's Yenan mass line is to be found in the accomplishments of the so-called Great Production Movement of the later years of the resistance war. This movement, although little studied outside of China, has great relevance to the second and third five-year plan periods because it provided more economic precedents for later years than any other specific campaign of the revolutionary era.

The winter of 1942/43 was a very difficult one for the Chinese Communists. In addition to the tight blockade maintained against them by 300,000 of Chiang Kai-shek's troops, the Japanese army had just mounted and was continuing to pursue the most severe counter-guer-

[48] *Ibid.*, p. 192.

rilla measures. This was the period of Japan's "drain the water tactics" (*t'ao-shui chan-shu*), General Okamura's answer to the Eighth Route Army's swimming as fish in the sea of North China peasants.[49] The Japanese, who were also blockading the Communists,

> took further steps to strengthen [their] encirclement and blockade of the [Chin-Chi-Lu-Yü] border region base. In Southern Hopei, by the end of 1939, there were about 50 enemy strongpoints; by the end of 1940 this figure had jumped to 246, by March 1941 to 329, and by May of the same year to 369. Following the very large and savage "mopping up" operation which began on April 29, 1942, the enemy increased his strong points to about 800 and shortly thereafter to about 1,100. . . . By the end of 1940 the length of highways, both repaired and newly constructed, totalled about 4,000 *li*. This figure grew rapidly to 5,000 *li* by the spring of 1941, and it reached 9,000 *li* after the April 29, 1942 "mopping up" campaign. In the same period the length of the blockade walls and trenches was increased to about 3,200 *li*.[50]

Differing from later guerrilla movements, the Chinese Communists did not possess a "privileged sanctuary" or foreign sources of supplies; the party had to live out the Japanese-KMT blockade or go under.

Mao's answer was the Great Production Movement. Chiang Chen-yün, writing in 1965, recalls that as early as 1939,

> confronted by the blockade of the Kuomintang reactionaries, Comrade Mao Tse-tung asked the following question at a cadres meeting: "Are we going to starve to death or disband ourselves? Or are we going to do it ourselves?" He said: "Since no one wants to starve or disband, to do it ourselves is the answer." He said: "We are convinced that we can solve the economic difficulties. Our answer to all problems in this connection is to do it ourselves."[51]

The basic problem of border-area production was that there were very few skilled engineers, technicians, or craftsmen. The party had to rely on makeshift methods, discovered and taught to each other by the

[49] *K'ang-Jih chan-cheng shih-ch'i chieh-fang-ch'ü kai-k'uang*, p. 34.

[50] Ch'i Wu (ed.), *I-ko ko-ming ken-chü-ti*, p. 62.

[51] "On Self-Reliance—Notes on the Study of Chairman Mao's Works," *Ching-chi yen-chiu* [Economic Research], no. 1 (1965); trans. U.S. Consulate General, Hong Kong, in *Survey of China Mainland Magazines* 460, hereafter cited as *SCMM*. See also *Peking Review*, September 30, 1966, p. 19.

people themselves, and it had to motivate the population to undertake experiments and try new techniques. Many organizational devices were employed, including work-study schools, rewarding labor heroes, giving multiple defense and production functions to individual units, using masses of manpower in place of machinery, and employing the army to do production and land reclamation work. In a phrase suggestive of the later communes, a contemporary Communist account says:

> Government personnel, troops, and students hoe the land, grow vegetables, cut firewood, spin wool, make clothing, go into trade, and destroy the boundary between mental and physical labor. [The tasks of a] worker, peasant, tradesman, student, and soldier are all assembled into a single body (*kung-nung-shang-hsüeh-ping chü chih yü i-shen*).[52]

Possibly the most famous of the Yenan production projects was the land reclamation at Nanniwan. It is significant that, under the slogan of *"Nanniwan ching-shen"* ("The Nanniwan spirit"), the party revived the memory of Nanniwan as a model to be emulated during the Socialist Education Campaign. In 1940 Nanniwan was a desolate area about 60 *li* from Yenan, overgrown with wild grass and depopulated from the time of the Moslem uprisings about a century earlier. During the winter of 1939/40, Mao pulled the 359th Brigade of the 120th Division of the Eighth Route Army out of the Chin-Ch'a-Chi battle zone and sent it to Nanniwan to reclaim the area and cultivate it. The leaders of the 359th were Commander Wang Chen, Political Commissar Wang Shou-tao, and Deputy Political Commissar Wang En-mao. Interestingly enough, both Wang Chen and Wang En-mao have continued to work in the field of land reclamation—Wang Chen as Minister of State Farms and Land Reclamation and Wang En-mao as First Secretary of the CCP Sinkiang Uighur Autonomous Region Committee and concurrently Commander and Political Commissar of the Sinkiang Military Region. In addition to reclaiming Nanniwan, the 359th Brigade had to maintain its military readiness as the main defense force in the Yenan area, and after 1944 the 359th saw continuous combat duty until the end of the civil war.[53]

In early 1940, the three Wangs established their brigade headquar-

[52] Quoted by Wang Chien-min, *Chung-kuo Kung-ch'an-tang shih-kao*, III, p. 260.

[53] For Wang Chen's sortie from Yenan to South China beginning in November 1944, see Ma Han-ping, *Wang Chen nan-cheng chi* [Record of Wang Chen's Southern Expedition] (Hankow: Chung-kuo ch'u-pan-she, 1947).

ters at Chinp'anwan. The task before them appeared impossible: there
were no houses or tools, and they had to melt down a temple bell to
make their first implements. Four years later, in mid-1944, Wang Chen
described to Gunther Stein the procedures he had followed:

> There were many . . . difficulties to overcome. One of them was
> that I knew too little of production myself. But we solved this,
> like all our problems, in a democratic way. I asked each and
> every one in my brigade to offer us his knowledge and experi-
> ence, to criticize the plans I made for them, and to suggest
> changes. We discussed everything together, just as we did all
> the work together.[54]

When Stein visited Nanniwan as a member of the "Northwest Press
Party" (which left Chungking May 17, 1944), there were 35,000 acres
under cultivation, and Wang Chen estimated that Nanniwan could
support 200,000 people after liberation.

Nanniwan may have been the enterprise that inspired Mao Tse-
tung's initial conception of the people's communes. When Mao paid
it an inspection visit in May, 1943, Nanniwan was producing millet,
rice, wheat, corn, vegetables, cotton, hemp, and tobacco. The soldiers
were raising cows, goats, pigs, chickens, ducks, and rabbits; and they
lived in dormitory caves with communal dining rooms and social clubs.
The Takuang textile mill was located in the brigade area; and Nanniwan itself had workshops engaged in uniform making, blacksmith
work, printing, and the manufacture of paper, soap, and alcohol. There
were also a locally built hospital and sanitarium. In addition to production, military training was stressed. According to Wang Chen:

> Even during the months of work in the fields there is not a day
> when they [the brigade's soldiers] don't practice hand-grenade
> throwing, bayonet tactics, and all sorts of other techniques in
> their rest periods. You have seen them take their rifles with them
> to the fields. They are always ready for action.[55]

[54] *The Challenge of Red China* (New York: McGraw-Hill, 1945), p. 68. See
also Chao Ch'ao kou, *Enan hito tsuki* [One Month in Yenan] (Kyoto: Chūgoku Bunka Sha, 1946, pp. 63–66; and *Chieh-fang jih-pao* (Yenan: October 16
and December 12, 1942; and February 3, 1943). I would like to thank Mark
Selden for bringing these *Chieh-fang jih-pao* articles on the activities of the
359th Brigade to my attention.

[55] Stein, *The Challenge of Red China*, p. 72.

In all of this, including anti-Japanese political education, officers allegedly worked with their men, and all engaged in criticism and self-criticism sessions.[56] The similarities between Nanniwan and the ideal of the communes are striking.

Nanniwan was of course only one of the Great Production Movement's programs. Another was the mass campaign to return to hand-spinning of locally grown cotton in order to meet the need for cloth under the blockade. Still another was co-operativization: by 1944 there were some 200,000 households organized into 400 co-ops in the Shen-Kan-Ning border area. Extensive use was also made of labor heroes and labor emulation; one of the best-known Yenan figures was a peasant, Wu Men-yu, who had contributed greatly to the expansion of agricultural production. And, of course, all students in the various Communist educational and indoctrination institutions in the border area took part in productive labor, a fact that is suggestive of the later "half-work, half-study" schools that began to be founded on the mainland in 1958.[57]

The people of Yenan and of all the rear-area guerrilla bases worked very hard, fought very hard, and made great sacrifices during the climactic Yenan period of the Chinese Communist revolution. As far as can be judged from available Chinese, Japanese, and contemporary journalistic sources, Mao obtained this labor from the people because he had developed a genuine mass line—one based on policies the people wanted to support: Chinese nationalism and economic improvement. Mao and his party in turn profited greatly from these policies; the masses joined his armies and, in 1949, helped him to win a revolutionary victory.

The Socialist Education Campaign and the Mass Line

Although Mao created the mass-line strategy and guided it to victory, he seems to have amazed himself by the size and thoroughness of his own accomplishment. After 1949, he appears to argue to himself and his associates that what was a demonstrably effective revolutionary strategy may also be good Marxist-Leninist philosophy. For example,

[56] Tung T'ing-heng, "Chairman Mao's Inspection of Nanniwan," *Jen-min jih-pao,* August 22, 1965.

[57] See U.S. Department of Health, Education, and Welfare; Office of Education (Robert D. Barendsen), *Half-Work Half-Study Schools in Communist China* (Washington: Government Printing Office, 1964).

in reflecting on his own revolutionary achievement, Mao discovered the brand-new Marxist-Leninist concept of the "people." In *On the Correct Handling of Contradictions Among the People* (1957), he asserted:

> The term "the people" has different meanings in different countries and in different periods in each country. Take our country, for example. During the War of Resistance to Japanese Aggression, all those classes, strata, and social groups which opposed aggression belonged to the category of the people, while the Japanese imperialists, Chinese traitors, and the pro-Japanese elements belonged to the category of enemies of the people. During the War of Liberation, the United States imperialists and their henchmen—the bureaucrat-capitalists and landlord class—and the Kuomintang reactionaries, who represented these two classes, were the enemies of the people, while all other classes, strata, and social groups which opposed these enemies belonged to the category of the people. At this stage of building socialism, all classes, strata, and social groups which approve, support, and work for the cause of socialist construction belong to the category of the people, while those social forces and groups which resist the socialist revolution, and are hostile to and try to wreck socialist construction, are enemies of the people.[58]

As we shall see, Mao's isolation of the categories "people" and "enemies of the people" had already moved him some distance away from the basic sociological validity of his mass-line concept and into the Communist quagmire of "ideological definition"—that is, into the realm of dogmatism which he had so often warned against. And Mao's position in 1957 was only the beginning; he moved much further away from the spirit of the mass line during the Socialist Education Campaign.

One consistent element in Chinese Communist analyses of their own revolutionary past concerns the functions of the "will power," or "spirit," of the people. This concern was present in the Yenan period, but it was always expressed then in conjunction with the theory of people's war. Mao and his associates often argued that the people did not know their own strength, that if the people were mobilized and organized *and* if their energies were put to work to serve a coherent guerrilla strategy, they could triumph over the Japanese invaders. But this line of argumentation was used to overcome the people's natural anxieties

[58] Text in Harvard University, East Asian Research Center, *Communist China 1955–1959* (Cambridge: Harvard University Press, 1962), pp. 275–76.

that, in launching guerrilla warfare, they were only inviting certain destruction as the targets of a Japanese mopping-up campaign.[59] Communist propagandists sought to show that if the people had the will to resist, the party would show them how to co-ordinate their collective energies in order to survive and achieve victory. During the Yenan period, the CCP never forgot that the sources of the spirit that led people into guerrilla battles or risky production undertakings were hatred of the invader and a belief in the possibility of economic improvement. The people's will power and spirit were stimulated, so to speak, by the conditions of the times; the Communist party's achievement was to recognize the existence and nature of this spirit, and its task was to convince the people, through the party's actions and programs, that the Communists could harness this spirit for the common good.

A decade after the end of the Yenan period, the party seemed to forget where the heightened spirit of the war-mobilized population had come from. It began instead to speak of will power and spirit in isolation, as independent variables affecting the outcome of any kind of activity that the party chose to define as a "revolution" or a "struggle." This new party interest in the "miracles" achieved during the Yenan period by will power and spirit alone has given rise to an openly idealist tendency in recent Chinese Communist thought.

Idealism, according to an encyclopedia definition, "is the name of a group of distinct but allied philosophical theories all of which agree (1) in denying that mind has originated from or may be reduced to matter and (2) in affirming that mind is a more fundamental feature of the universe than matter is." Contemporary Chinese Communist theory has attempted to avoid the idealist label by paying lip service to the doctrine that all mind is a reflection of social class. Even here, however, the recent debate over "natural redness" (tzu-jan hung)—that is, over the potentiality of members of the ideologically progressive classes to hold enemy-of-the-people views—has seriously undermined this position. It seems as though mind may actually be superior to social class, since "naturally red" sons and daughters of workers or guerrilla veterans may go astray and "naturally bourgeois" sons and daughters of Shanghai shopkeepers may become revolutionaries by working in the Sinkiang Production and Construction Corps of the PLA.[60]

[59] See, e.g., Johnson, *Peasant Nationalism and Communist Power*, pp. 147–49.

[60] See Sun Yi-ch'ing, "Lay Down the Load, Advance with Light Equipment," *Chung-kuo ch'ing-nien pao* [China Youth News], November 17, 1964; trans. U.S. Consulate General, Hong Kong in *Survey of China Mainland Press* 3349, hereafter cited as *SCMP;* and "*Chieh-fang-chün pao* Conducts Discussion on

In its concrete, daily application, Maoism has taken a frankly idealist direction and no longer worries overly much about keeping its philosophical anchor lines to Marxism orderly or untangled. For example, we may read the archetypal idealist aphorism, "Where there's a will, there's a way," in recent issues of *Jen-min jih-pao*—"*t'ien-hsia wu nan-shih, chih-p'a yu hsin jen*"—or, in a slightly different form, in Wang Chieh's diary—"*shih-shang wu nan-shih, chih-p'a yu hsin jen.*"[61] This kind of remark has led some observers, such as David McClelland, to conclude that materialism has become only an "ideology" in Maoism. Contrasting Chinese Communist and American thought, McClelland observes:

> The Communists are ideologically materialists: they believe that economic or materialistic forces shape the course of history. Yet in actual fact much of their effort goes into changing people's *ideas.* . . . The Western democracies on the other hand, and particularly the United States, are philosophical idealists yet practical materialists.[62]

There are without doubt many sources of this Chinese Communist idealistic orientation; but one of them, as we shall try to show, is the experiences of the Yenan period.

How extensive is this idealistic tendency? Does it penetrate deeply into Chinese Communist thought or it is merely propaganda? In order to analyze the mass-line problems of the Socialist Education Campaign, it is necessary first to present a range of evidence on the type, or quality, of thinking that has underlain it. One type of evidence is the number of persons who have been attacked in China in recent years precisely because they too had noted a growing idealistic tendency and had criticized it. For example, Sun Yeh-fang, former director of the Institute of Economics of the Chinese Academy of Sciences, seems to have drawn blood in some of his comments. The critics of Sun write:

'How Young Soldiers May Revolutionize Themselves,' 'Can One Be Naturally Red by Having Good Family Background?' " *Jen-min jih-pao,* November 26, 1964 (*SCMP* 3356).

[61] "Learning the Revolutionary, Tough-boned Spirit of the PLA," *Jen-min jih-pao* (editorial), March 10, 1964, p. 1; and Wang Chieh, *I-hsin wei ko-ming* [Wholeheartedly for Revolution] (Peking: Chung-kuo ch'ing-nien ch'u-pan-she, 1965), p. 79.

[62] David C. McClelland, "Motivational Patterns in Southeast Asia with Special Reference to the Chinese Case," *Journal of Social Issues* 19 (1963): 17.

Chairman Mao teaches us that politics is the commander, the soul. Political work is the lifeblood of all economic work. Sun Yeh-fang regards putting politics in command as grit in his eye. He venomously attacked it as "talking politics divorced from economics, replacing objective economic laws with the mass line and the putting of politics in command, and replacing [an] economic with [a] political approach, which is not only an idealistic view but can also be called lazy man's thinking in economics."[63]

Sun was a victim of the early months of the Great Cultural Revolution.

An even earlier critic, Feng Ting, formerly deputy chairman of Peking University's Philosophy Department, had the misfortune to write a book entitled *Kung-ch'an chu-i jen-sheng-kuan* ("The Communist View of Life" [1956]), in which, among other things, he characterized heroic acts of self-sacrifice as acts of "impulse."[64] During the Socialist Education Campaign, the People's Liberation Army convened various soldiers' forums to criticize Feng Ting's views on heroism. Both *Chieh-fang-chün pao,* and *Kuang-ming jih-pao* reported these forums favorably:

> A revolutionary soldier's body can be destroyed, but his will cannot be destroyed. . . . Every revolutionary soldier and every revolutionary civilian should acquire the spirit of self-sacrifice, which is needed not only in time of war but also in time of peace. It was needed not only in the past but is also needed today and will be needed in the future. Without thousands upon thousands of revolutionary martyrs who displayed the self-sacrificial spirit, there would not have been a new China. . . . In short, without the spirit of self-sacrifice, we would have nothing.[65]

An idealist theory must show that spirit is an independent variable within a particular human environment, and it must show that spirit influences its environment in a fashion at least comparable to the influence that an environment may have on spirit. These characteristics are precisely the ones that contemporary Chinese Communist theory seeks to demonstrate with regard to "revolutionary spirit." Although it

[63] Men Kuei and Hsiao Lin, "On Sun Yeh-fang's Reactionary Political Stand and Economic Programme," *Peking Review,* October 21, 1966, p. 23.

[64] On Feng Ting's trials generally, see Adam Oliver [pseud.], "Perspectives on the Intellectual in Communist China: Rectification of Mainland China Intellectuals, 1964–65," *Asian Survey,* 5 (1965): 483–86.

[65] *Kuang-ming jih-pao,* November 7, 1964 (*SCMP* 3341).

is a very dangerous subject for Marxists, there can be no doubt as to
where the Chinese Communists come down on the question of spirit as
an independent variable: "We do not reject objective conditions favorable to revolutionization, but subjective efforts must be added before these objectively favorable conditions can be made to function."[66]
This conclusion should be compared with Mao's denunciation of "subjectivism" during the Yenan *cheng-feng* to see how far the Chinese
have come.

No less a figure than Yeh Chien-ying clearly regards spirit as an
independent variable in talking about the need for ideological education in schools and colleges. He writes:

> Whether political-ideological work is well done or not is the prin-
> cipal standard by which to examine the work of our colleges and
> schools. . . . Why is that? The question deserves some thought.
> Take for example agricultural production. In the same *hsien* and
> the same commune, some places have increased their output while
> others have reduced theirs although soil, irrigation, and climatic
> conditions are the same. Why? The principal reason is that there
> is a difference in them with regard to the thinking of the people,
> their spiritual state, and their attitude toward labor. In other
> words, if the work on man and political-ideological work is well
> done, the people's consciousness raised, and their activism mobil-
> ized, it will be possible to increase output.[67]

The principle that spirit influences environment, that "spiritual
force can turn into material force," is firmly established today in Chinese Communist theory. The press speaks continually of "spiritual
atomic bombs" (*ching-shen yüan-tzu-tan*); of "miracles wrought by
rifles, hand-grenades, and even such primitive weapons as bows and
arrows and knives in the hands of the revolutionary people" (Lo Jui-
ch'ing); of "the [PLA's] 'three-eight working style,' a gigantic spiritual
force which, when transformed into a self-conscious act of the masses,
will become a powerful material force"; of the idea that "you must
have a gun in your heart before you can hold your gun firmly in your
hands"; and, with regard to public health tasks, of "the small size of
the hospital is nothing to be afraid of; what needs to be feared is a

---

[66] Sun Yi-ch'ing, "Lay Down the Load."

[67] "Hold High the Great Red Banner of the Thought of Mao Tse-tung and
Run Our Colleges and Schools in a Highly Proletarian and Fighting Way,"
Kuang-ming jih-pao, March 16, 1965; reprinted from *Chieh-fang-chün pao*
(*SCMP* 3431).

weak will. The bad conditions are nothing to be afraid of; what needs to be feared is poor working enthusiasm."[68]

The concrete operating principle of the Chinese Communists during the Socialist Education Campaign was, "Political work takes first place relative to economic work. Comrade Mao Tse-tung has always emphasized that politics is the concentrated expression of economics. Politics must take command of economics, and not vice versa. The view that 'to be good economically means to be good politically,' and 'to be good in production means to be good politically,' is wrong."[69] And what is political work? "Political work is the task of mobilizing the masses, organizing the masses, and arousing their enthusiasm."[70] Even Chou En-lai, speaking before the first session of the Third National People's Congress, argued, "We believe that following the victorious development of this Socialist Education Campaign, there will be not only a new high tide in socialist revolution, but also a new high tide in socialist construction."[71]

This idealistic quality of the Communists' contemporary thought is evidence primarily of the persistence of their "guerrilla mentality"— that is, of the abstract organizational ideas that they distilled from their guerrilla experience. Many foreign observers in China have testified to the fact that Chinese idealism derives from a particular interpretation of Yenan Communism. Sven Lindqvist, for example, who was studying in China during 1961–62, writes that in the Great Leap Forward, "Mao tried to translate his knowledge of the farmers' revolutionary potential from military and political to economic strategy. The people's commune was the result, a kind of decentralized revolutionary base in the struggle against poverty. The parallel with the revolutionary struggle

[68] Bombs: *Ts'ung Lei Feng tao Wang Chieh* [From Lei Feng to Wang Chieh] (Hong Kong: San-lien shu-tien, 1965), p. 4; Miracles: Lo Jui-ch'ing, *Commemorate the Victory Over German Fascism! Carry the Struggle Against U.S. Imperialism Through to the End!* (Peking: Foreign Languages Press, 1965), p. 37; Three-eight style: *Jen-min jih-pao* (editorial), February 1, 1964; Gun in heart: "Hsin-li ti ch'iang ho shou-li ti ch'iang," *Jen-min jih-pao,* July 18, 1964; Hospital: *Jen-min jih-pao,* April 5, 1964 (*SCMP* 3204).

[69] "Politics, the Supreme Commander, the Very Soul of Our Work," *Hung-ch'i* [Red Flag] no. 1, 1966: 1–2.

[70] Peking *Ta-kung pao* (editorial), August 1, 1965.

[71] *Shih-shih shou-ts'e,* no. 4 (February 1965) (*SCMM* 461). For a thorough treatment of the Socialist Education Campaign and the history of inner-party policy disputes prior to the emergence of the Great Cultural Revolution, see Nakajima Mineo, *Chūgoku bunka taikakumei* [The Chinese Great Cultural Revolution] (Tokyo: Kōbundō, 1966).

explains why plans for future projects are often couched in military terms."[72] Another observer, the Tokyo *Mainichi*'s veteran China correspondent, Takata Fusao, who last traveled to the mainland in 1964 with the third Matsumura Mission, describes the era of the Socialist Education Campaign as China's "second Yenan period."[73]

What do the Chinese Communists themselves say? One of the most highly praised examples of what can be accomplished through spiritual force in China is the Tach'ing oilfield and refinery. According to *Jen-min jih-pao,*

> Army generals [prior to the abolition of ranks on May 22, 1965] who have seen action in hundreds of battles praise the people of Tach'ing as a "Liberation Army wearing blue uniforms," while old comrades who spent many of the revolutionary years in Yenan said with joy: "When we came to Tach'ing, we seemed to have returned to Yenan. Here, as we can see, the revolutionary spirit of Yenan is given the fullest expression."[74]

To take a different example, Wang Cho, writing in a January, 1965, issue of *Kung-jen jih-pao* addresses himself to "The Philosophical Basis of the 'Four Firsts.'" These are the principles which Lin Piao first introduced into the PLA in 1960 in order to reform its training along lines that had recently been approved by Mao Tse-tung. Wang asks:

> Why do men take precedence over material in their relations? What is its philosophical basis? . . . Have there not been such questions as: Can ideological work increase the grain, coal, and iron and steel output? Does the principle of the "four firsts" conflict with the materialist principle of the material first and the spiritual secondary?

His answer to these questions is a proof drawn from the Chinese Communists' revolutionary history:

> In war, man is the determining element. This principle has been proved by the fact of China's revolutionary victory. The revolutionary masses relied on millet and rifles to defeat several million U.S.-equipped reactionary Kuomintang troops. The

[72] *China in Crisis* (London: Faber, 1965), p. 87.

[73] *Taiyō o iru Chūgoku* [China Shoots for the Sun] (Tokyo: Kōbundō, 1965), pp. 23–33.

[74] *Jen-min jih-pao,* April 20, 1964.

principle of man being the determining element expounded by Comrade Mao Tse-tung is also applicable to the struggle between man and nature.[75]

It was this type of thinking that led directly to the Socialist Education Campaign. Following the disaster of Mao's first attempt to advance the economy through mass-line techniques—that is, the Great Leap Forward of 1958—and the food crises of 1959–61, the party was forced to retreat and to sanction an economy based in important respects on material incentives in order to restore production.[76] However, Mao and some of his associates did not renounce the mass-line strategy upon which the Great Leap Forward had been based. They stuck stubbornly to Mao's 1957 *definition* of the "people" and their alleged interests during the era of socialist construction. Since by definition the people "approve, support, and work for the cause of socialist construction," something had gone wrong during the Great Leap Forward. There were far too many "non-people" who had balked at the Great Leap Forward and who were delighted by the restoration of private plots and market days. Before a new and successful Great Leap Forward could be launched, these "enemies of the people" would have to be reeducated to think as Mao's people should. When the people were "revolutionized," then the mass line would once again produce its miracles, just as it had in Yenan.

This was the overarching theory of the Socialist Education Campaign. Contained within it were many concrete campaigns, such as those to counter the growth of "modern revisionism," to train "revolutionary heirs," to force cadres to perform physical labor, and to expose corruption, that might have been undertaken even without the general theory. However, when these specific campaigns are seen as elements in the overall movement, it becomes clear that the Socialist Education Campaign was inspired by more than the need for routine self-maintenance of the system. The Socialist Education Campaign's main themes were to learn from the PLA, from Tach'ing, and from Tachai; to conceive of socialist construction as a new "revolution"; to "revolutionize" (*ko-ming-hua*) all thinking; and, above all, to learn from the thought of Mao Tse-tung. According to *Ching-chi yen-chiu,* "In 1962, after the Tenth Plenum of the Eighth CCP Central Committee, the Socialist Edu-

[75] *Kung-jen jih-pao,* January 2, 1965.

[76] See Johnson, "Building a Communist Nation in China," in R. A. Scalapino (ed.), *The Communist Revolution in Asia* (Englewood Cliffs, N.J.: Prentice-Hall, 1965), pp. 47–81.

cation Campaign was methodically launched."[77] It lasted down until mid-1966, when it was superseded by the so-called Great Proletarian Cultural Revolution.

One of the most interesting facets of the Socialist Education Campaign was the revival of the "Spirit of Nanniwan" in connection with the campaign to learn from the PLA. One unit of the PLA which was held up as a model was the Sinkiang Production and Construction Corps, a body that the Chinese press claims was directly descended from the 359th Brigade in Yenan and that was operated in accordance with the "Nanniwan revolutionary traditions." "The overwhelming majority of the first group of veteran backbone elements of this corps were soldiers of the Red Army or the old Eighth Route Army who had participated in the Great Production Movement in Nanniwan."[78] During the Socialist Education Campaign, however, the army veterans in the corps were largely replaced by the sons and daughters of Shanghai bourgeois families or by young people whose parents lived in Hong Kong. These youths allegedly chose the "revolutionary road" by volunteering to do land reclamation and farming work in Sinkiang.[79]

There were two lessons that the people as a whole were to learn from the Nanniwan spirit and its contemporary application in Sinkiang. The first was the spirit itself:

> The revolutionary spirit of self-reliance and hard struggle displayed by the inhabitants of Nanniwan in the Great Production Movement during the period of the War of Resistance against Japan is still of vital, realistic significance to state farms in the socialist era. . . . It was so during the war period; it is also so in the period of national construction. The Nanniwan spirit is applicable in industry and agriculture, in the collective economy as well as in enterprises adopting the system of ownership by the whole people.[80]

[77] Chung Huang, "Revolutionization and Modernization of Socialist Industrial Enterprises," *Ching-chi yen-chiu*, no. 12 (1964): 21–29.

[78] China News Service, Urumchi, March 13, 1966 (*SCMP* 3660).

[79] Yü Shan-ling, "I Chose the Revolutionary Road," *Kung-jen jih-pao*, June 30, 1965 (*SCMP* 3503); and "Visit of Chou En-lai and Ch'en Yi to Shihhotzu Reclamation Area of the Production and Construction Corps of Sinkiang," *Chung-kuo ch'ing-nien pao*, August 10, 1965 (*SCMP* 3523).

[80] "Promote the Nanniwan Revolutionary Spirit," *Jen-min jih-pao*, July 11, 1965.

The second lesson was to learn the organizational style and spirit of the PLA, since Nanniwan and Sinkiang were both manifestations of the army's superior methods.

> The building of state farms in our country began with army land reclamation. Many farm workers are officers and men transferred from the PLA. The state farms run by the Sinkiang Production and Construction Corps and the Northeast China General Bureau of State Farms and Land Reclamation have all along preserved the PLA's organizational forms and traditions of political work.[81]

Therefore, these state farms were to be studied and emulated throughout China.

The results of the Socialist Education Campaign were ambiguous. The economy continued to improve, foreign trade with Japan expanded, agriculture reached approximately 1957 levels, and certain specially favored endeavors—such as the nuclear weapons and petroleum industries—made notable achievements. However, these successes could be accounted for in terms of the post-crisis policies of economic rationalism and the favoring of high-priority programs. Nothing was accomplished through the use of mass-line methods that was commensurate with the rhetoric of the period. At the same time, the party revealed that serious internal disputes over "guerrillaism" versus "professionalism" existed in the army, and it showed its faltering faith by refusing to tamper with the post-crisis organization of agricultural decision-making arrangements, which had to a large extent reinstated China's traditional "marketing areas" and procedures.[82] The end result of the Socialist Education Campaign was not a second Yenan-type victory but the most serious inner-party struggle since the establishment of the People's Republic—that is, the snarling attacks of 1966 on "bourgeois royalists," "freaks and monsters," and "power holders who have wormed their way into the party," combined with raids by Red Guards on local party organs and the people themselves. Clearly, there were important groups within China that had grown disenchanted with the latest manifestation of the mass line.

[81] New China News Agency, March 13, 1964; *Jen-min jih-pao,* March 14, 1964 (*SCMP* 3194).

[82] See G. William Skinner, "Marketing and Social Structure in Rural China, Part III," *The Journal of Asian Studies,* 24 (1965): 363–99.

The Masses and the Mass Line

Why did the strategy of poverty—the organizing of the people and the use of their combined energies to overcome objectively unassailable foes—succeed in the Yenan period and appear to fail in the Socialist Education Campaign period? First, it must be said that success in this context means only the actual receipt and use of a mandate from the masses. It would be unfounded to suggest that the defeat of Japan or of the KMT ought to be understood solely, or even primarily, in terms of the theory of people's war. However, it would be equally un-founded not to acknowledge that the CCP succeeded in gaining mass support for itself and its policies in the Yenan period, and that fifteen years after Yenan, the CCP no longer continued to enjoy mass support anywhere approaching its popularity at the time of nation-wide victory or during the land-reform movement.

The reasons for this discrepancy are varied. Nature is not necessarily to be conceived analogously to an enemy in a guerrilla struggle, and the methods that work in a civil war do not necessarily work in civil engineering. The international situation differs markedly between the two periods: in one the party could not compromise with its block-aders; in the other the party seemed to be blockading itself. Moreover, it is not at all clear to some Chinese Communist leaders that the inter-nal situation demands a strategy of poverty; the first five-year plan, after all, was not exactly a failure.

One particular reason for the discrepancy in results appears to be a difference in the CCP's understanding of the interests of the masses. This is not a factor upon which the foreign observer can obtain any but the most tenuous evidence. However, Mao Tse-tung himself has pro-vided Chinese and external observers alike with the tools for analyzing the dynamics of the problem—namely, with the concept of the mass line as a principle of organization. According to the mass line, the party must make investigations and find out what are the interests and aspirations of the masses; then, on the basis of these findings, it is to project back to the masses organizational initiatives designed to achieve the people's aspirations.

In the Yenan period, Mao accurately discerned that Chinese national-ism was the foremost concern of all Chinese citizens, particularly those in the path of the Japanese armies' advance, and that a desire for alle-viation of landlord exploitation and for peasant proprietorship was widespread among the rural population. He constructed his policies accordingly, and he was richly rewarded for his insight and actions.

In the Socialist Education Campaign period, Mao did not investigate the interests and aspirations of the people; he defined them—the "building of socialism." In so doing he appears to have violated the main working principle of his own mass line. Furthermore, the evidence of popular performance in the Socialist Education Campaign period suggests that such an investigation, had it been made, would not have sustained the policy of "building socialism" as a proper platform for mass line organizational efforts. What it would sustain is hard to know, but the popularity of China's nuclear and technological achievements among overseas Chinese and the economic recovery achieved by the post–Great Leap Forward reforms suggest that contemporary mass aspirations may be similar to those of the Yenan period—that is, Chinese nationalism and economic development. If this is the case then Mao's attempts to achieve a "Communist" China *via the mass line* are doomed to failure. Organizational theory indicates that, in this situation, Mao must either replace the mass line with policies of coercion or abandon his Communist vision in favor of some form of "modern revisionism."

Comments by S. Y. Teng

"The basic sociological insight of the mass line," Professor Chalmers Johnson suggests in his methodologically and theoretically sophisticated analysis, "is that in order for any organizational campaign to succeed, the goals of the organizers must encompass some irreducible nucleus of the aspirations of the organized." After a careful comparison of the Yenan period and the Socialist Educational Campaign period, he concludes that the Chinese Communist Party (CCP) gained popular support during the former period because it acted more or less in accordance with the mass line and that its imperfectly founded authority began to totter during the latter period because it in effect deviated from the mass line.

Professor Johnson's description of the early success and recent failure in gaining popular support reminds me of three aspects of the political tradition of China. These are the concept of "the mandate of heaven" (*T'ien-ming*), the dynastic cycle, and the notion that the destiny of a government is determined more by internal factors than by external forces. Let us take the most obvious point first. In political science terms as I understand them, *T'ien-ming* may simply mean popular support. To receive the mandate of heaven is to receive popular support; to lose the mandate of heaven is to be deprived of popular support. *T'ien* or heaven, in many classical usages, may be treated as an equivalent of *min*, people. As Mencius said, "Heaven sees according to my people see; Heaven hears according to my people hear."[1] Here Heaven is almost a symbol of the people. Heaven does not speak; it merely presents a person, as Yao presented Shun, to the people and "the people accepted him." Thus, to receive the mandate from Heaven (*shou-ming yü T'ien*) actually means to receive popular support from the people. Mencius said: "There is a way to get the kingdom—get the people and the kingdom is got."[2] He further stated: "They who accord with Heaven are preserved, and they who rebel against Heaven, perish."[3] These statements may be taken to mean that those who work in accordance with the need of the people will prosper, whereas those who act against the wish of the people will perish. Thus, mandate of heaven, popular support, and the mass line are closely related.

Dynastic cycle is not unique to Chinese history. The same phenomenon can be found in the history of other nations—Korea, Japan, the Ottoman empire—in which the top positions of the hierarchy were hereditary, not elective. The dynastic cycle is intertwined with a process of personal psychological degeneration. This process operates even within revolutionary movements. After the conquest of power through a revolutionary war, the leaders and the followers have a tendency to dislike hard work and to prefer an easy life. Unless there are frequent purges, corruption, personal rivalry, and inefficiency are unavoidable. The leaders of the Taiping Rebellion in the 1850's and some Kuomintang (KMT) members in the early 1930's and 1940's are cases in point. Can the CCP avoid the same fate?

In Chinese history, the destiny of a government has generally been decided by internal factors rather than external forces. The fall of the

[1] *The Work of Mencius*, trans. James Legge, *The Chinese Classics*, II (Hong Kong, 1960 reprint), p. 355.

[2] *Ibid.*, p. 300.   [3] *Ibid.*, p. 296.

Yüan dynasty was caused more by its internal weakness than by the strength of its external enemy. The collapse of the Ming dynasty was due largely to its internal decay giving rise to the rebellion led by Li Tzu-ch'eng, who took Peking, rather than the result of the military might of the Manchus who were invited to China proper by the Chinese themselves. The inept leadership under the unbelievably corrupt and ignorant Empress Dowager Tz'u-hsi and other Manchu elite was a more important factor in the demise of the Manchu dynasty than the 1911 revolution under the remote directorship of Dr. Sun Yat-sen.[4] The KMT's debacle on the mainland was not due to lack of military power or foreign aid but to the low morale of its soldiers and the loss of popular support. If this historical generalization is correct, only the Chinese Communists themselves, rather than any foreign power, can determine the fate of Communist China.

Turning our attention to a more recent period of history, I should like to note the origin of the mass line in the early phases of the Chinese Communist movement, so as to supplement Professor Johnson's account of the Yenan period. From the very beginning, the Chinese Communists tried to organize the masses. They played a part in instigating the seamen's strike in Hong Kong in 1922 and the Peking-Hankow railway workers' strike in 1923. In order to gain access to the masses, they joined the KMT, used Canton as a revolutionary base, and propagated the slogans, "down with warlords" and "down with imperialism," singling out the two most hated enemies of the Chinese people according to their analyses. These clever slogans were so carefully chosen that it seems as though they "came from the masses." The Chinese Communists used these attractive catchwords to mobilize and organize the masses into action, following almost the same process of the mass line as Professor Johnson described in his paper.[5] The Communist leader, P'eng P'ai, and others organized a peasant movement in the Hailufeng districts in Kwangtung in May, 1922, and this is the first instance of Communist exploitation of peasant discontent in China. They formed peasant unions, labor unions, and peasant self-defense corps. When the First Peasant Congress of Kwangtung province met in May, 1925, it represented a membership of some 210,000 in twenty-two *hsien*. After the split with the KMT, the Chinese Communists estab-

[4] S. Y. Teng, "Dr. Sun Yat-sen and the Chinese Secret Societies," *Studies in Asia*, 1963, pp. 81–99.

[5] Chalmers A. Johnson, "Chinese Communist Leadership and Mass Response: The Yenan Period and the Socialist Education Campaign Period," in this volume, pp. 397–437.

lished in 1927 and 1928 the Hailufeng Soviet Government which lasted for several months. At the time of its liquidation, they claimed 134,000 members in their peasant association.[6]

The May 30th incident (1925) was a mass movement directed at first against Japanese imperialism and then against British imperialism. Huge strikes soon spread from Shanghai to Canton, Hong Kong, and then to Shashih and Wanhsien in Szechuan, Kiukiang in Kiangsi and other localities in the Yangtze Valley. Adroitly exploiting the upsurge of nationalist and revolutionary sentiments, the Foreign Minister, Eugene Ch'en, was able to induce the British to return the British settlements at Hankow and Kiukiang to the Wuhan government in 1927.[7]

The Communist leaders, Ts'ai Ho-sheng, Teng Chung-hsia, and Liu Shao-ch'i, took advantage of the May 30th incident to organize the Shanghai General Federation of Labor. In March, 1927, the organized workers were so strong that they could pave the way for the occupation of Shanghai by KMT forces. The Communist membership also increased from 900 to 20,000 after the May 30th movement.[8]

In 1925, Mao Tse-tung started organizing a peasant movement in Hunan. In early 1927, he reported that there were more than 2,000,000 members in the peasant associations in his native province. A few months later, he led the Autumn Harvest Uprising in the same area and adopted a platform which included the confiscation of the properties of landlords and the establishment of a Soviet army and government. After the failure of the uprising, he continued the peasant mass line in the Juichin period. An effective intelligence network was set up; every child playing in a field and every old man sitting by the roadside might report Chiang Kai-shek's troop movements to the Soviet government. In the mountainous areas the Communists did not have many opportunities to fight imperialism; instead they concentrated their en-

[6] P'eng P'ai, "Hai-feng nung-min yün-tung" [Peasant movement in Haifeng], in *Ti-i-tz'u kuo-nei ko-ming chan-cheng shih-ch'i ti nung-min yüntung* [The Peasant Movement during the First Period of the National Revolutionary War] (Peking: K'o-hsüeh ch'u-pan she, 1953), p. 98; Shinkichi Eto, "Hai-lu-feng: The First Chinese Soviet Government," *China Quarterly*, October–December, 1961, pp. 161–69 and January–March, 1962, p. 152.

[7] William Ayers, "The Hong Kong Strikes," *Papers on China*, 4 (1950): 94–130; William Ayers, "Shanghai Labor and the May 30th Movement," *ibid.*, 5 (1951): 1–38; Hu Hua, *Chung-kuo hsin min-chu chu-i ko-ming shih* [History of the New Democratic Revolution of China] (Shanghai: Hsin-hua shu-tien, 1950), p. 56.

[8] Ho Kan-chih, *A History of the Modern Chinese Revolution* (Peking: Foreign Languges Press, 1959), chap. 3.

ergy on battling feudalistic landlords. Rents and taxes were reduced. The land of landlords and religious monasteries were confiscated. The central leadership also appealed to the masses to unfold all-out guerrilla warfare in October, 1934.[9] The current minister of foreign affairs in Peking, Ch'en Yi, wrote a verse:

> We must rely on the people,
> And never forget their support.
> They are second parents to us.
> We, their good sons in the fight,
> Gaining strength in the revolution.[10]

Thus the mass line already lay at the heart of the Kiangsi Communism.

The CCP also tried to exploit the rising nationalism to gain popular support. In February, 1932, when the Nineteenth Route Army fought the Japanese in Shanghai, the Chinese Soviet Republic declared war on Japan and called on all groups and classes in China to resist Japanese aggression. This heralded a united front policy against Japanese imperialism. The CCP repeatedly issued manifestoes on the anti-Japanese united front on January 15, March 4, and April 15, 1933.[11] During and after the Long March, it made important shifts in policy toward the KMT in order to stop the civil war. Partly as a response to the united front policy of the CCP, massive student movements developed, especially in Peiping, Nanking, and Shanghai where hundreds of thousands of students marched in demonstrations in opposition to the civil war and in support of a policy of resisting Japanese invasion. No doubt many Communists were working among the students. This is another example of the mass line in operation.

The Socialist Education Movement, which started in 1962 and later developed into the Cultural Revolution, deserves a careful examination. What is socialist education? According to Chang P'ing-hua, the first party secretary of Hunan province:

> The [aim of the] socialist education campaign is to prevent revisionism. The thoughts of Mao Tse-tung are entirely revolu-

[9] Hsiao Tso-liang, *Power Relations within the Chinese Communist Movement* (Seattle: University of Washington Press, 1961), p. 311.

[10] Quoted in Yang Shang-kuei, *The Red Kiangsi-Kwangtung Border Region* (Peking: Foreign Languages Press, 1961), p. 44.

[11] Conrad Brandt, Benjamin I. Schwartz, and John F. Fairbank, *A Documentary History of Chinese Communism* (Cambridge: Harvard University Press, 1952), p. 37.

tionary, leading [carrying the?] revolution [through?] to the end. To prevent revisionism in China, the cadres take part in manual labour; and we have two systems of education, one is the half-study, half-work education.[12]

It seems to me that revisionism does not necessarily mean Khrushchevism or right-wing thought. The attack on revisionism seems to be an attack on bourgeois thinking and living, the desire for an easy-going life, corruption, extravagance, and capitalistic tendencies. The Socialist Education Movement can be seen as an attempt to arrest the "dynastic cycle." Various Japanese visitors in mainland China have observed that the purpose of the Socialist Education Campaign is to arouse the people's spirit which for several years has been showing signs of relaxation due to the economic improvement.[13]

Another purpose of the campaign is to compete with Soviet Russia in the race to reach the stage of communism first. To achieve this goal, Lu Ting-yi, the former Vice Premier and propaganda director, said that "all the people" would have to heighten their political consciousness, and universal education for "the entire population" must become a reality.[14] Providing universal education for the huge population in China is no easy task; moreover, China needs workers and peasants to work in factories and farms. To meet the two practical needs, education and work, the policy that "education must be combined with productive labor" was adopted. These "half-work and half-study" schools and spare-time education for workers in Communist China have come into existence since 1958 or 1959.[15] Actually, the Chinese Communist Administration Council had issued the "Directives on Developing Spare-Time Education for Workers and Staff Members" in June, 1950, but the plan was not vigorously implemented for many years.

Now let us take a look at the Chinese leadership. No doubt Chairman Mao Tse-tung is, in the eyes of many Chinese Communists, the

[12] *China News Analysis,* no. 608 (1966), p. 4.

[13] "Oya Group's Report on Communist China," pt. 8, *Sunday Mainichi,* Translation Service Branch, American Embassy, Tokyo, November 14, 1966, pp. 45–47.

[14] Lu Ting-yi to the editor of *Kuang-ming jih-pao,* December 26, 1959.

[15] Munemitsu Abe, "Spare-Time Education in Communist China," *China Quarterly,* October–December, 1961, pp. 149–59; Robert D. Barendsen, *Half-Work, Half-Study Schools in Communist China,* pp. 4–5; Paul Harper, *Spare-Time Education for Workers in China.* The last two are pamphlets published lished by the Office of Education, Washington, D.C., in 1964.

greatest and most valiant leader of the Communist world. His constant wish is to be "second to none." He has been a ceaseless revolutionary fighter since childhood. He successfully fought his conservative father. He struggled against Li Li-shan in 1930. He was elected chairman of the Chinese Soviet Republic at Juichin in November, 1931. After the Tsun-i Conference in Kweichow (January, 1935) he assumed party leadership; after reaching Yenan, he controlled the whole military power of the Red Army. After the Seventh Congress of the Comintern held in Moscow in the summer of 1935, he gained unchallenged power over party affairs.[16] Through the *Cheng-fêng* Movement in 1942–43 he tried to correct erroneous tendencies of the Communists in all spheres of work. He launched an "Increase Production" Movement. He put forward "Ten Proposals"—fight the enemy, improve the army and administration, love the people, reduce rent and interest rates, educate the masses about current affairs, and so on.[17] This important movement strengthened the Chinese Communist forces and enhanced the morale of the people.

Chairman Mao has never lost his fighting spirit. Under him, China participated in the Korean War. He liquidated Kao Kang and Jao Shu-shih in 1955. According to T. F. Tsiang, Kao Kang allegedly allied himself with Soviet Russia to achieve autonomy in Manchuria.[18] P'eng Te-hua and Huang K'e-ch'en were purged in 1959.

The ebullient Chairman Mao is very anxious to make China rich, strong, and able to achieve socialism as soon as possible. After the Great

[16] See Chang Kuo-t'ao's answer to inquiries in Wang Chien-min, *Chung-kuo kung-chan tang shih-kao* [A Draft History of the Chinese Communist Party], vol. 3 (Taipei: Cheng-chung shu-chu, 1965): 724–27; Howard L. Boorman, "Mao Tse-tung: The Lacquered Image," *China Quarterly*, October–December, 1963, pp. 20, 24.

[17] Chieh-fang she (comp.), *Cheng-feng wen-hsien* [Documents on the Rectification of the Styles of Work] (Hsin-hua shu-tien, 1949), pp. 1–44, 91–145.

[18] Address by Dr. Tingfu F. Tsiang, the late Chinese Ambassador to the United States, before the Institute of Sino-Soviet Studies, George Washington University, Washington, D.C., May 6, 1964. Mimeographed copy distributed by the Chinese Embassy. Tsiang said: "Manchuria under the local boss, Kao Kang, became almost autonomous. Kao Kang, a protégé of the Soviet Union, did not allow Mao's currency to be circulated in Manchurian domain. Kao Kang concluded commercial agreements with the Soviet Union without reference to Mao. . . . Mao was not free to send units of his army into Manchuria. It was only as a part of the Korean war that Mao managed to send a large number of his armed forces into Manchuria. . . . After the Korean adventure was ended, Mao liquidated Kao Kang" (p. 3).

Leap Forward Movement, Chairman Mao, still acting as if in his prime, seems to have taken endless pleasure in his struggle against heaven, earth, and man.[19] He fought bad weather conditions continually for two or three years; he wrestled with nature by building huge water reservoirs and by controlling the floods in the Yellow and Huai rivers. He overcame Chinese scientific backwardness and pushed forward the development of nuclear weapons.

Chairman Mao believes in the materialism of Marxism and Leninism but he also shows respect for idealism; that is, will power. Strong will is more important than machine power. According to him, manpower still counts as a great asset even in modern warfare. "Walking on two legs" may be more dependable than using machines alone to reach a destination. The masses can do anything.[20] Unhappily for Chairman Mao, after so many struggles and living so long a Spartan life, many comrades, especially the middle-aged or the old revolutionaries and even cadres who have undergone strict training, cannot keep pace with him.[21] The result is the revival of the so-called "bourgeois capitalist forces," which, to Chairman Mao, is the basic danger to the socialist revolution and the Chinese Communist government. He is obliged to take the political steps to prevent the "bourgeois revisionist" influence from becoming stronger.[22]

At the Tenth Plenum of the Central Committee of the CCP held in September, 1962, it was proclaimed that to combat the attempted comeback by "unregenerate landlord and bourgeois elements," a prolonged, acute struggle would be necessary. The *hsia-fang* movement ("to go to the lower levels," or "to go to the countryside") was intensified. Some bourgeois members were sent to work with rural peasants for a short period, but many assignments were on a permanent basis. Many physicians and nurses were compelled to leave modern, large cities for the rural areas so that they could serve the people.[23] The reassignment

[19] Hsiao San, *Mao Tse-tung t'ung-chih ch'ing-hsiao nien shih-tai* [The Childhood and Boyhood of Comrade Mao Tse-tung] (Peking, 1950), pp. 13, 27–28.

[20] Stuart R. Schram, *The Political Thought of Mao Tse-tung* (New York: Praeger, 1963), pp. 253–54.

[21] For cadres' training, see John W. Lewis, *Leadership in Communist China* (Ithaca, N.Y.: Cornell University Press, 1963), pp. 176–203.

[22] This idea comes from a Japanese on-the-spot observer, Tadao Ishikawa, Professor of Modern History at Keio University. See his "Chinese Communist Party's Mass Mobilization Formula," *Chuo Koron,* November, 1966, pp. 196–203 (trans. Political Section of the American Embassy, Tokyo).

[23] *Jen-min jih-pao,* July 21, 1962.

of cadres throughout the nation, especially to frontier areas, does not seem to have been very effective because cadres had become the elite class.

Chairman Mao, in the summer of 1964, stressed the theme of "bringing up millions of successors to prevent China from changing color," that is, from becoming fascist or revisionist. He urged China to learn from the People's Liberation Army. Peking operas on modern themes should be staged. Literature and art should serve the people. Waging struggle against bourgeois tendencies, building up models of revolutionary heroes, appealing to young people to become shock troops, abolishing military ranks, urging the cadres to learn from the people, and attacking tradition, etc.—all came to the fore in 1965.[24] A re-examination of popular movies, operas, and plays uncovered many masterpieces written by Communist leaders, such as T'ien Han's *Hsieh Yao-huan*, Hsia Yen's *Lin's Shop*, Wu Han's *Dismissal of Hai Jui*, as works propagating feudalistic, reactionary, and revisionist ideas. These writers were sharply criticized and they lost their high positions.[25] The total repudiation of tradition in all its forms would appear to be related above all to Chairman Mao's desire to appeal to the very young as the only generation uncorrupted by bourgeois ideas and thus fit to carry on his revolutionary mission after he is gone. His former method of peaceful "transition to socialism" proves to be too slow. The older he grows, the more impatient and short-tempered he seems to become.[26]

Suddenly, in August, 1966, the Red Guards emerged. Chairman Mao shook hands with them or smiled at them as would a benevolent father or sage god. This revolution may have started in May, 1963, when Mao named the goblins, intellectuals, and anti-revolutionary "royalists" as the three targets of struggle.[27] It was accelerated with the case of Yang Hsien-chen, whose theory of combining two into one was regarded as a philosophical justification for "peaceful coexistence," "peaceful tran-

[24] *The Globe and Mail,* October 17, 1966.

[25] For more information, see Donald J. Munro, "Dissent in Communist China: The Current Anti-intellectual Campaign in Perspective," *Current Scene,* June 1, 1966.

[26] Arthur A. Cohen, *The Communism of Mao Tse-tung* (Chicago: University of Chicago Press, 1964), pp. 115–35, 202–6.

[27] Ando Hickotarō, Professor of Modern Chinese Economy, Waseda University, "My Observation in China," Translation Service Bureau, American Embassy, August 23, 1966, pp. 15–16.

sition," and compromise with the bourgeoisie.[28] The purge of Lo Jui-ch'ing, chief of staff of PLA, followed. Thus the seeds of the Great Proletarian Cultural Revolution were sown years ago, and its immediate predecessor may be the Socialist Education Campaign. These two movements overlapped each other and it is hard to find the line of demarcation between them. The Cultural Revolution is actually the culmination of the revolution under the direction of Chairman Mao since the mid-1930's. His slogans and tempo may change from time to time, but his leadership tolerates no challenge.[29]

The last point for a brief discussion concerns the future stability of the Communist regime. Professor Johnson points to "mass discontent in China," and he concludes that "Mao's attempts to achieve a 'Communist' China *via the mass line* are doomed to failure." As a student of history, I find it premature to commit myself definitely to this view. From history I have learned that many Chinese problems are solved from within, not from without, or from both within and without. If the Communist leaders kill each other wantonly, this would certainly be a sign of collapse.[30] The new regime, however, may survive as in the case of the Han and Ming dynasties. So long as the chief leader, whether he is called emperor, dictator, autocrat, or president, retains the mandate of heaven or popular support, he may still maintain his rule.

Mao Tse-tung undoubtedly has many enemies including the capitalist class and the intelligentsia, but both are minorities in comparison with Chinese peasants and other impoverished people who used to have little to eat and whose children could never have had the good fortune of being able to go to college or of holding political and social positions without the CCP. These once downtrodden and hopeless Chinese have been given a status higher than that of their former oppressors in a

[28] Wen-djang Chu, "A Theoretical Debate among the Chinese Communists after Their Break with the Soviet Revisionism, *Yi-fen-wei-er* vs. *He-er-er-yi*," *Contemporary China* (Pittsburgh: University of Pittsburgh Press, 1966), pp. 1–9.

[29] Many key documents in *Communist China, 1955–1959*, with a foreword by Robert R. Bowie and John Fairbank (Cambridge: Harvard University Press, 1962), show the continued movement. See, for example, Document No. 4, "Mao's Preface to the Book, *Socialist Upsurge in China's Countryside*" (1955); Document No. 13, "On the Dictatorship of the Proletariat" (1956); Document No. 27, "Ch'en Po-ta's New Society, New People" (1958); and *passim.*

[30] "Introduction" and "Conclusion," *The Nien Army and Their Guerrilla Warfare* (The Hague: Mouton, 1961).

process called *Fanshen*.[31] The children of the *Fanshen* families, in Mao's estimation, are grateful to him, admiring and worshiping him as a living deity. At first I could not understand why Chairman Mao made use of the Red Guards and bypassed the CCP organizations. Now it is clear that the party apparatus is largely under the control of Liu Shao-ch'i and Teng Hsiao-p'ing. Chairman Mao has to rely on the Red Guards who are quietly protected by Lin Piao's armed forces. If a majority of the armed forces and the young generation are supporting Mao, it is hard to say that his days are numbered.

The Red Guard movement seems to have three aims: One is to re-train the young boys and girls through the actual experience of revolution so as to foster worthy successors in the next generation; second, the movement seems to be aimed at toppling the power structure of the state leadership; third, the Red Guards are used to curb corruption or capitalistic tendencies.

This new movement is also aimed at elimination of the three great antitheses: first, the antithesis between physical and mental work; second, the antithesis between urban and rural life; and third, the antithesis between workers and farmers.[32] In other words, the purpose of the Great Proletarian Cultural Revolution is to destroy the old culture, habits, customs, and thoughts and create new ones for the benefit of the masses at the cost of the former intelligentsia or gentry class, once so very powerful in Chinese history.

This is undoubtedly an unprecedented task. Contradictions will mount. Let us wait and see whether Chairman Mao *"yu pan-fa"* ("has a way to handle it") or not. As the *New York Times* well phrased it: "Mao's crisis is his own doing."[33] To many young Chinese on the mainland, Mao Tse-tung *is* Communist China, and Communist China is Mao Tse-tung. Whether he succeeds or fails, his fate will affect millions of people for decades.

[31] William Hinton, *Fanshen: A Documentary of Revolution in a Chinese Village* (New York: Monthly Review Press, 1967).

[32] Tsutomu Suzuki, Japanese Socialist Party Member of the House of Representatives, "My Visit to China under Great Cultural Revolution" (Translation Service Branch, American Embassy, Tokyo, November 14, 1966).

[33] *New York Times,* January 15, 1967, p. 3.